Rag Rug by Jo

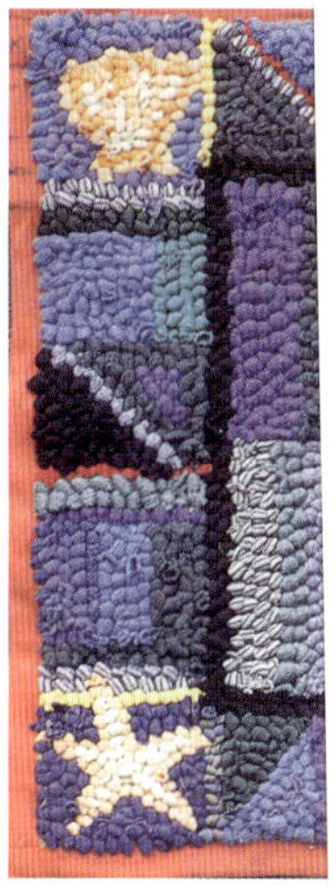

Signboard for C

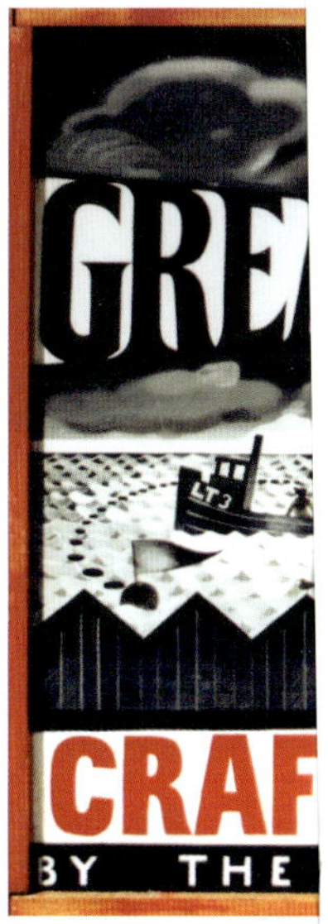

Shell Fish with P

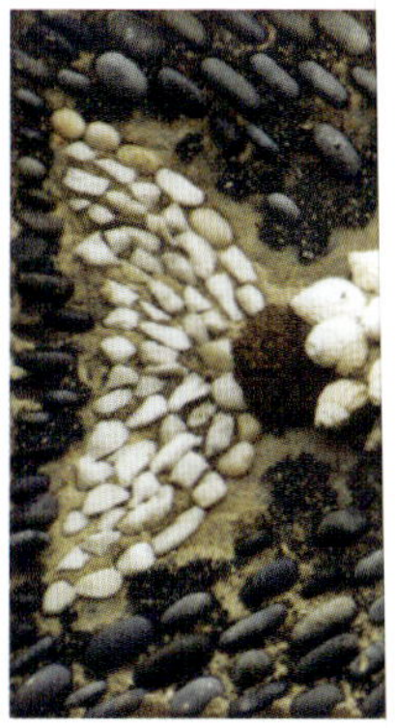

This book is for

Joachim Jacobs

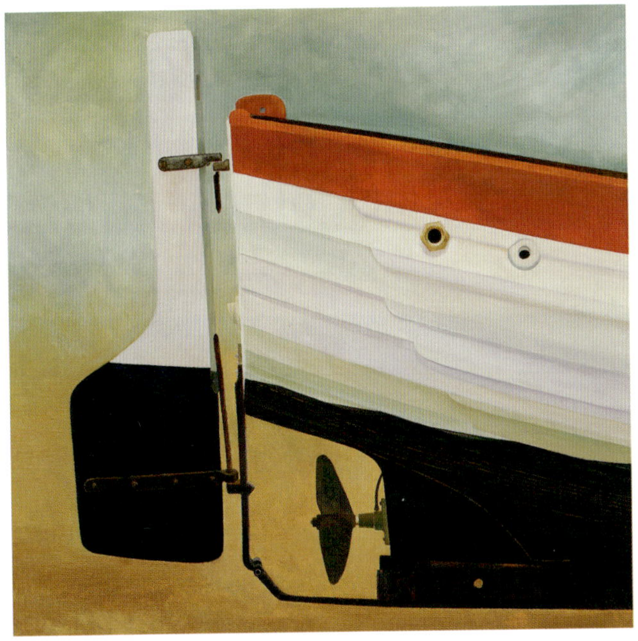

*Stern*, James Dodds, oil on canvas (above).
*Towards Southwold*, EMILY WHALLEY (born Canada 1953, moved to Southwold 1983), oil on canvas (previous page).

Published in 2005 by Black Dog Books,
104 Trinity Street, Norwich, NR2 2BJ



ISBN 0-9549286-1-X



Printed by Print Wright Ltd, Ipswich, IP1 5BN

Typeset in Times New Roman and Trade Gothic Light

# Introduction

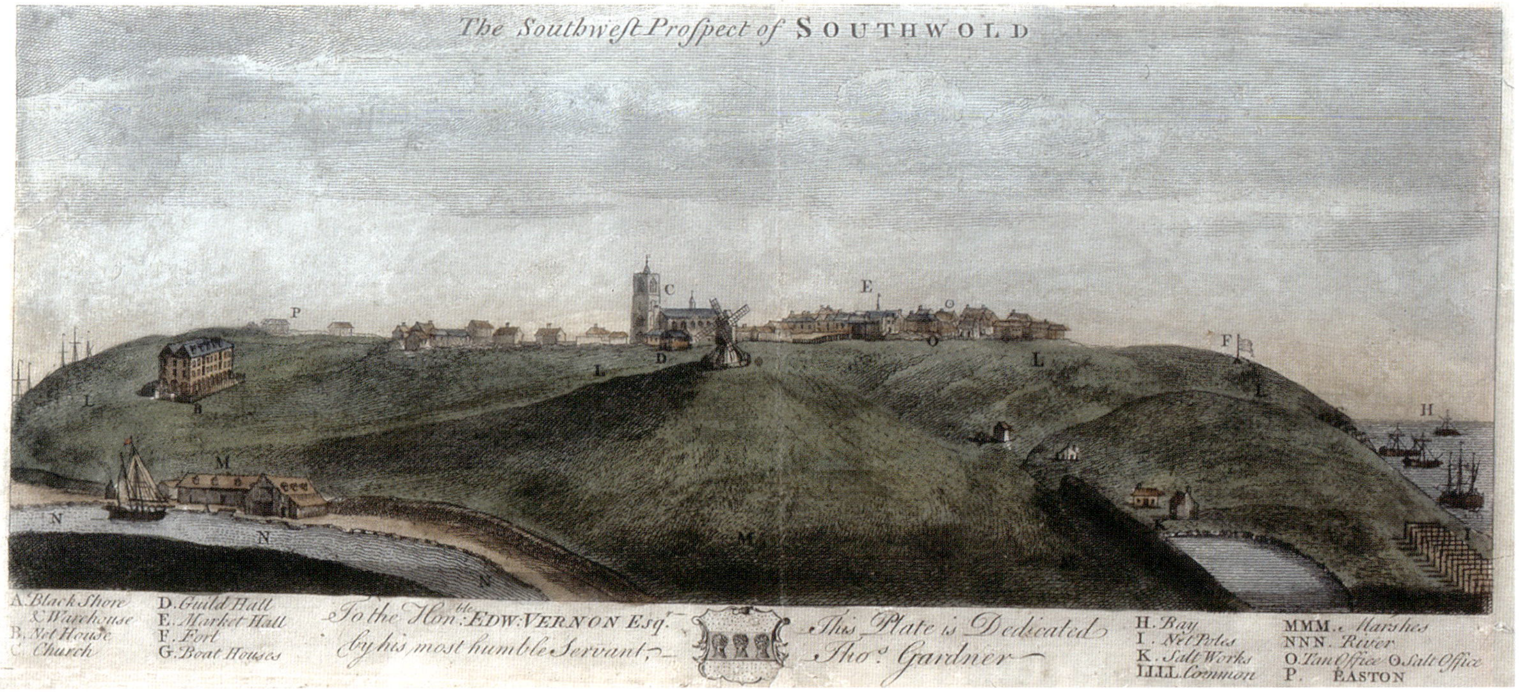


In 1754 antiquary and salt officer Thomas Gardner produced this topographical study for his catchily-titled tome *A Historical Account of Dunwich, Anciently a City, now a Borough, Blythburgh, Formerly a Town of Note, now a Village, Southwold, once a village now a Town Corporate, with Remarks on Some Places Contiguous Thereto*. Two hundred and fifty years later *Making Waves* takes a similar focus.

Marked on Gardner's Southwest Prospect of Southwold we see St Edmund's Church, the Guild Hall and Market Hall, Net House (headquarters of the British Free Fisheries) and net poles, Tan Office and Salt Office, warehouses and boathouses, windmill, fort and salt works and open spaces of both later settlement and lasting conservation.

Almost a century after a ruinous fire, the Town Corporate was in a period of brief prosperity before later revival as a sublime seaside resort. This snapshot sets the scene and charts the changes.

Gardner's house still survives in Park Lane, now complete with a plaque in his memory. His gravestone, asserting that the historian lies between his wives Honour (aka Rachel) and Virtue (Mary), leans against a wall of the church he loved.

**Ian Collins**, Southwold, October 2005

# Foreword

What would we now see if the artist had not seen Southwold? Or St Ives? What would an English village tell us if John Clare had not existed? Some places contain a single vision which enlightens us, others a burst of interpretation by many painters. These latter have been called schools – the Newlyn School – but Southwold and Walberswick have escaped this collective honour. For more than 120 years all kinds of artists have been drawn to this particular water's edge, have met but not affiliated, have at times been somewhat on top of each other, though without touching. What lured them was the lowlying-ness of this little town with its flat commons, tall skies and huge wall of sea. Quite how it has retained its distinctive levels and heights is a mystery, but it is clear that these possess an endless attraction for painters who find them energising, bright in all weathers and unlike anything they have found anywhere else.

*Southwold Harbour*, Peggy Somerville (1918-1975), oil on canvas.

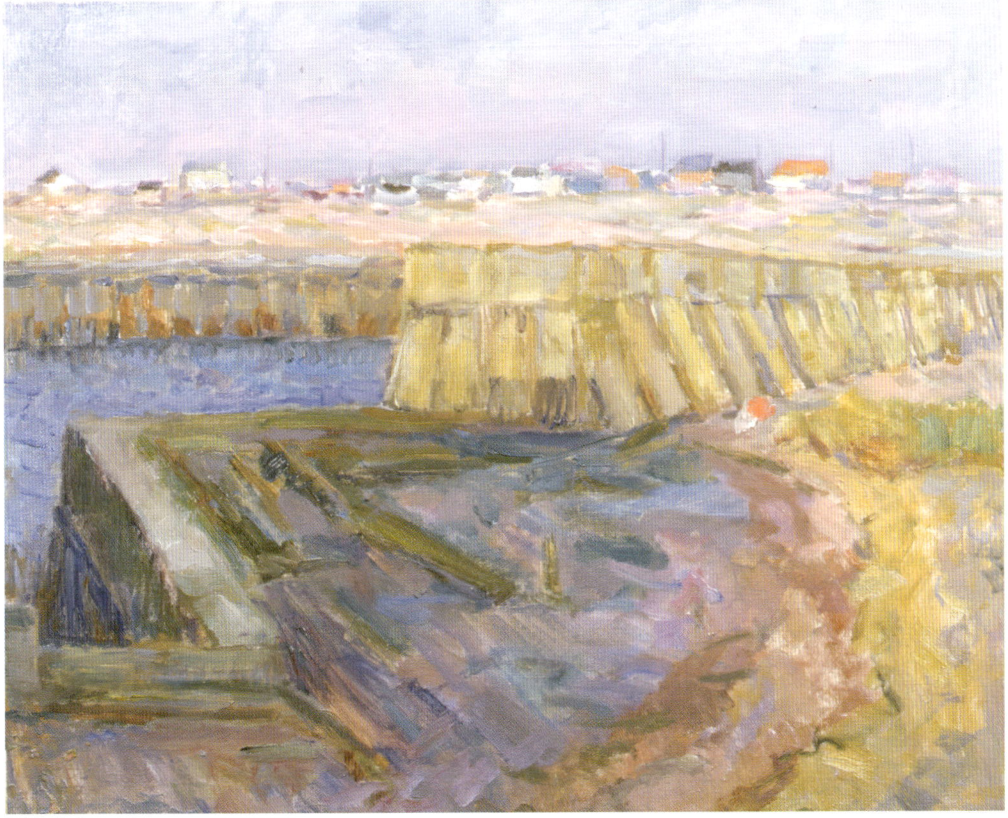

Ian Collins's gallery of them is startling. It doesn't add up to an instantly recognisable Southwold group, but it does show how artists themselves 'write' on canvas and in sketchbooks a marvellous architectural, marine and social history of a seaside borough, as well as creating many personal accounts of its quiet collective beauty. The author's approach to them is entirely original, avoiding formal art history on the one hand and art criticism on the other. What we have is a delightful introduction to all the celebrated and unknown people who have come especially to Southwold to draw and paint since the 1880s. Brought together like this, they are quite a shock. We are able to observe them as they observe our familiar shore, the greens, the lighthouse, the spectacular church and shadowed streets, the generations, the special feel which brought them to Suffolk. No one reading Ian Collins's Southwold through artists' eyes will ever view it as they did previously. He is great on colour, a writer with his own palette, as it were, native when it comes to boats, careful with facts and the best apologist imaginable for East Anglia. The writing is fresh and eager – 'coastal' one might call it – and is full of his love for artists past and present.

I used to come to Southwold long ago with Juliet Laden and **PEGGY SOMERVILLE**, when the latter was living first at Westleton and then at Middleton. They would sit on the beach and do pastels while I roamed about searching for plants and gazing at old houses. It was Juliet's home town. Her mother and her uncles Martin and Geoffrey Shaw had lived there before the First World War, and it was to remain sacred ground to them all. Joined occasionally by Gordon Craig and James Pryde, their ambition was to modernise the English theatre, not to paint seascapes. Music came in and out with the tides, and Martin Shaw's setting of Gerard Manley Hopkins's *God's Grandeur* would be performed at the first Aldeburgh Festival in 1948.

Juliet Laden's father, the artist Christopher Perkins, who had studied at the Slade with Paul Nash, Carrington and Stanley Spencer, bought a cottage at the foot of South Green (now called the Bolt Hole). It was fully furnished with deckchairs, towels, an easel and a kettle, and there we talked – Bonnard. And there we shivered until ordered to take a brisk walk. Juliet would fetch Peggy Somerville and myself in her three-wheeler car, through the broken floor of which we could watch the tarmac speed by. We would hurry to the sea, and the girls, Bonnard-ish in their billowing Horrocks dresses, would set out their pastels. Both were enchanting colourists. I was sent off to explore Southwold and Walberswick, search for flowers, stare at birds, observe other walkers, splash in the sea, then to return to help carry home the pictures, and sometimes their 'finds' – a strange bit of sea-wrack, shells, something still useful though thrown overboard.

This was the time when I met **MARY FEDDEN**. She and her husband Julian Trevelyan were friends of Lance and Maisie Sieveking and we all stayed at the White House, Snape. Maisie and Mary had shared digs in Bristol and London, and now they faced the airy rigours of Suffolk. It was thrilling to be in their company. More recently, Mary has painted oil and watercolour images recalling visits to Dunwich. Naturally, the artist who comes to an area sees what the local artist has not seen, and vice versa. East Anglia is one of the most celebrated examples of this dual vision, John Constable's and J.M.W. Turner's. In St Ives an old fisherman-artist would actually challenge an entire art movement. Magaret Mellis brought with her some of the spirit of St Ives when she came to live in Southwold and her driftwood patterns form a blue link of the Atlantic with the North Sea. She, Mary Fedden and **MARY NEWCOMB**, all seem to me to possess what I can only describe as 'joy', a mysterious happiness. In Mary Newcomb's case it can have a sinister side, or rather it moves into a kind of pictorial poetry which is both disturbing and lyrical. Ian Collins says that 'Each of her locally inspired images has a particularly powerful root. The drawing (pictured here) of motorcycle and sidecar hurtling between two banks of bindweed records a scene glimpsed for a split second on the road from Southwold to the Hen Reedbeds'. Alas, she missed seeing Juliet Laden's three-wheeler by decades.

This might be the moment to say how hard-up most of us were, writers and artists, and how this fact created a certain simplicity and even purity in our work. So many of the pictures reproduced in this book are touched with the kind of intimacy which entices the viewer to enter a private dimension, even if, as it so often is, the sensation being conveyed is one of swimming in a cold sea.

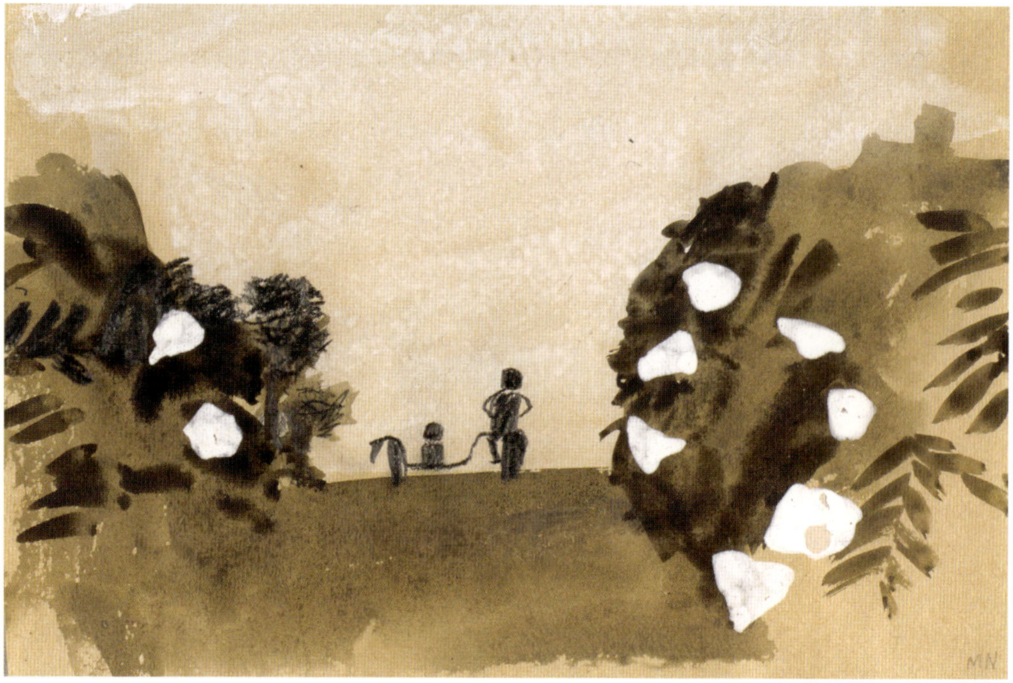


*Man on a motorcycle,* Mary Newcomb, mixed media.

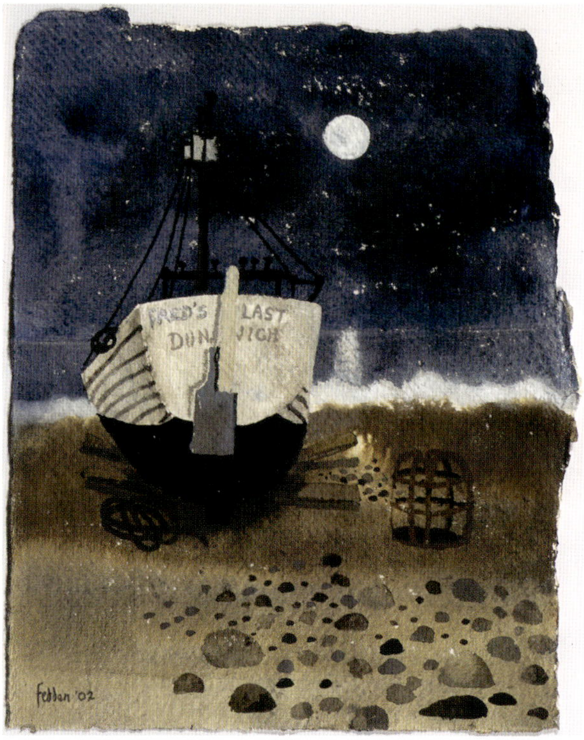


*Fred's Last, Dunwich,* Mary Fedden (b 1915), watercolour (left).

Photography came to the fishing communities much about the same time as they became resorts, picturesque and healthy places in which to retire or have a holiday. And with photography came the truly great art of the picture postcard. A collection of these will often tell one more about a small town than a shelf of social history. For the first hundred years of the camera most people were more likely to have been photographed at the seaside than anywhere else. Thus Ian Collins's witty inclusion of the photograph. And in Southwold it would have its most controversial genius, P.H. Emerson, the man who saw things as they were, and not as material for a new kind of genre art. He arrived in the town in 1884 – 'the most significant year in Southwold's artistic history' says Ian Collins – and his pictures of the coast, and of the Broads in particular, would revolutionise the conventional attitudes to the watery Eastern landscape and its hardy people. A quarreller, an exotic, a photographer in the Julia Margaret Cameron league, he deserves his place in *Making Waves*

While Southwold bred the local artist to a respectable degree, it has since the days of Philip Wilson Steer become, like its lighthouse, a beacon, especially for the watercolourist, and for a kind of artist-quietist whose introspective pictures work magic on the eye. Only a few of these migrant talents have taken up residence over the years, thus their studies contain appreciations, discoveries and pleasures which possess both a newness and a feeling of impending departure. Whereas in a city or the capital itself the brief stay of a famous name would have little significance, the coming to Southwold of any artist, well-known or not, is of real consequence, and it is his realising this which makes Ian Collins's book an important as well as an entertaining work. Whether we are reading about Henry Davy or Charles Keene or Walter Sickert or Damien Hirst, or an entire host of known and forgotten artists, they have all contributed to the picture of Southwold and the surrounded scene as we now comprehend it.

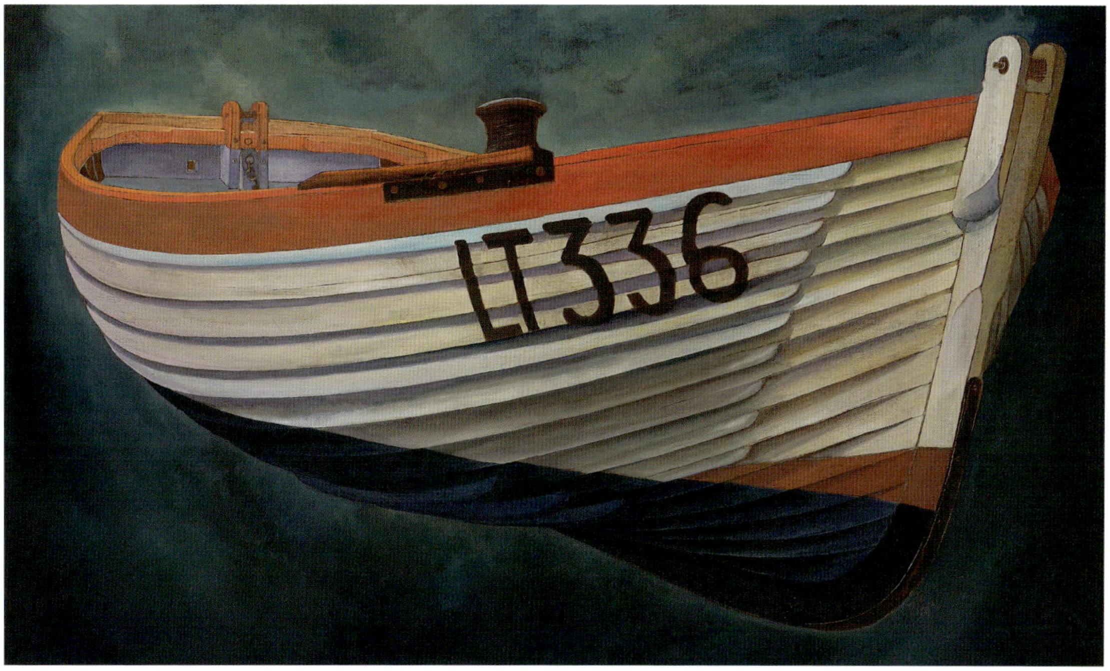


*Boat II*, James Dodds, oil on canvas.

To bring them together like this, and so knowledgeably, makes this book more than a tribute. It is the necessary story of the soul of the 'seaside' itself as it exists in one remarkable spot. It is also about privacy and relationships, modesty and hard work. The latter is reflected in the magnificent boat paintings of **JAMES DODDS**, shipwright turned artist, whose hand-built craft might have sailed or been rowed from Sutton Hoo. Ian Collins, too, is a coastal man; an easy authority with all things, and all art in particular, coastal is natural to him. Where painting itself is concerned, his deep understanding of it derives from his friendships with artists. They are his universe.

*The Burning of HMS Royal James at the Battle of Sole Bay, 28th May 1672*, Willem van de Velde the Younger, oil on canvas.

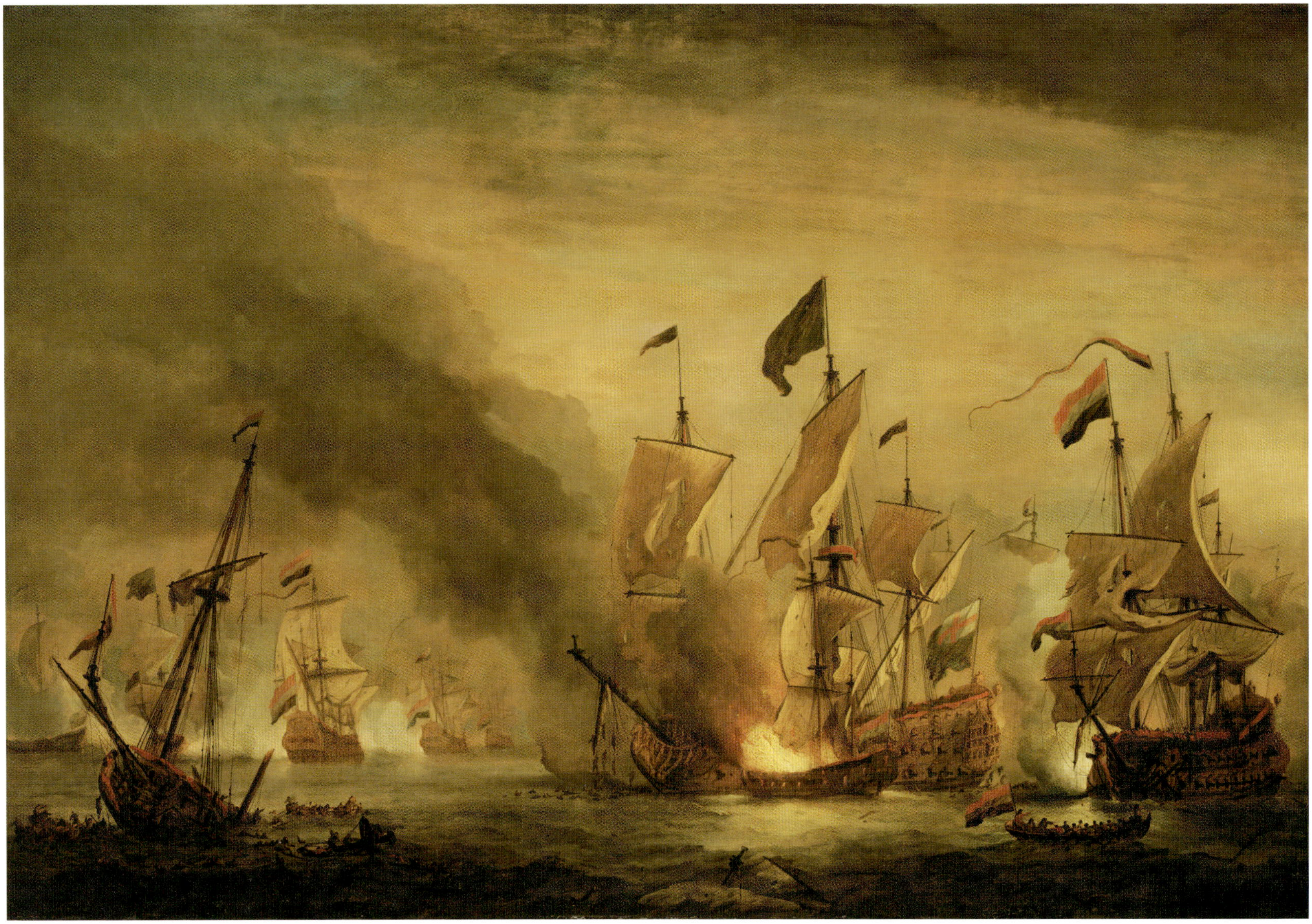

Chapter One

# Disaster Zone

Southwold, in the 17th century, was a place of recurring calamity: fire, disease and war wrought havoc among a population which, struggling to make a living from land and sea, tested the art of survival at the best of times.

In 1659 the little port town gained the dubious distinction of being declared Britain's first official disaster zone, after hundreds of properties – including the town hall, market house, jail, granaries, fish, malt, brew and tackle houses and 238 dwellings – were lost in a devastating blaze. The historian Thomas Gardner reports that appeals for aid were read from every church pulpit across England, even though, with thatched and timbered buildings burning so readily, much of England went up in flames in that strife-torn century. Blythburgh blazed in 1676, for instance, and Walberswick in 1633 and 1683.

The popular belief that Southwold's splendid network of open spaces began as fire-break greens may be fanciful at least in part – for a fair was held on St Bartholomew's Green in the Middle Ages. But there were definite compensations for many burned-out citizens: the town hall was razed along with all the records in it; and so, as Southwold lacked a lord of the manor, copyholders were effectively turned into freeholders overnight.

Fire has continued as a sporadic hazard, of course – in parched summers in this driest part of England there have been regular conflagrations on tinder-box heaths and commons. And, when gutted in 1949, The Bell pub in Walberswick lost its thatched roof together with artists' drawings on the walls and ceilings dating from the 1880s.

As a port, Southwold would have seemed a likely point of entry for the waves of Black Death or Bubonic Plague which, spreading from the fleas carried by black rats, and speeding from China along trade routes, wiped out a third of Europe's population in the middle of the 14th century and was still ravaging Restoration England more than 300 years later. But there is no known record of a major epidemic, and the 'pest house' built in 1774 on the site of a former workhouse was for smallpox victims. Still, the last British plague case occurred just after the First World War, just south of Lowestoft.

It was ironic that post-fire Southwold was rebuilt along faintly Dutch lines – an influence still to be seen in Church Street cottages and the gable of the marvellous museum in Victoria Street – because this style could have been construed as saluting the enemy. For the community was to be hit hard when three Anglo-Dutch wars raged in the third quarter of the 17th century over the latter's mastery of the seas and resulting riches from lucrative trading links. Crucially for our story, such might and wealth and patronage had allowed the arts to flourish. In each conflict, Sole Bay – a

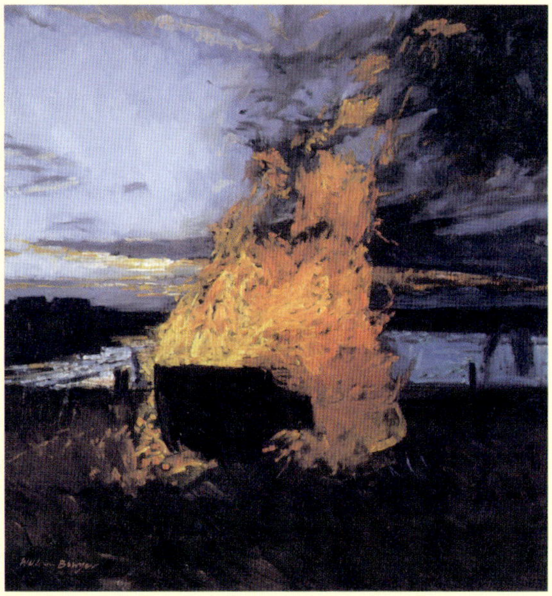

This William Bowyer painting of a burning boat, on the slipway for the old steam ferry at Walberswick, recalls an instant-ancient tradition he himself helped to hatch one 1980s evening in The Bell pub. The fiery spectacle flared for several summers as a fund-raising venture until extinguished on health and safety grounds.

sheltered haven between Easton Ness and Dunwich, both a mile or more out to sea than they are today – was the main east coast anchorage for the English fleet. Our beleaguered town became the chief base of the naval operation, and so was raided by press gangs and landed with hungry troops, casualties and prisoners.

With the Dutch came an official war artist, **WILLEM VAN DE VELDE THE ELDER** (1611-1693). Born in Leiden, this shipmaster's son had gone to sea as a boy and ever afterwards depicted the marine world in his pictures. The earliest painter to accompany a fleet into action as an official recorder, he sketched ships and their engagements in brilliant detail – also being one of the pioneers of *grisaille* pen-painting which created an almost sculptural relief from ink. A namesake son based in Amsterdam, **WILLEM VAN DE VELDE THE YOUNGER** (1633-1707) then used the battle drawings as notes for bravura pictures in oil much favoured by men in power.

At the start of the second war, in 1665, the elder Willem had been given a sailing ship by the Dutch authorities to record what became the Battle of Lowestoft – although no painting was commissioned on that occasion as the continental forces were routed (an outcome prompting a royal order for portraits of 13 victorious English commanders, known as the *Flagmen of Lowestoft*, from Dutch emigré artist Sir Peter Lely). The Dutch certainly got their revenge two years later when they sailed up the Medway and burned the English fleet at anchor.

When hostilities erupted again, in 1672, after a shady deal between London and Paris signed in the secret Treaty of Dover, the Duke of York and second-in-command Earl of Sandwich were based in Sutherland House in Southwold's High Street.

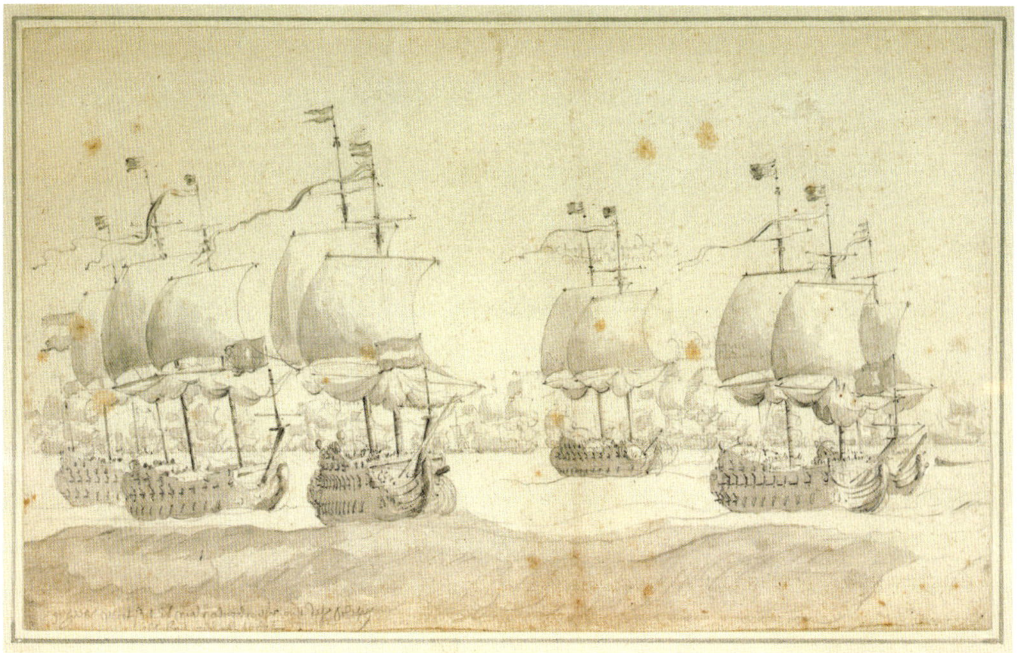

*The day after the battle of Sole Bay, 28th May - 8th June 1672,* Willem van de Velde the Elder, graphite and grey wash.

Opposite: part of the sequence of Sole Bay battle tapestries, now in Hampton Court palace.

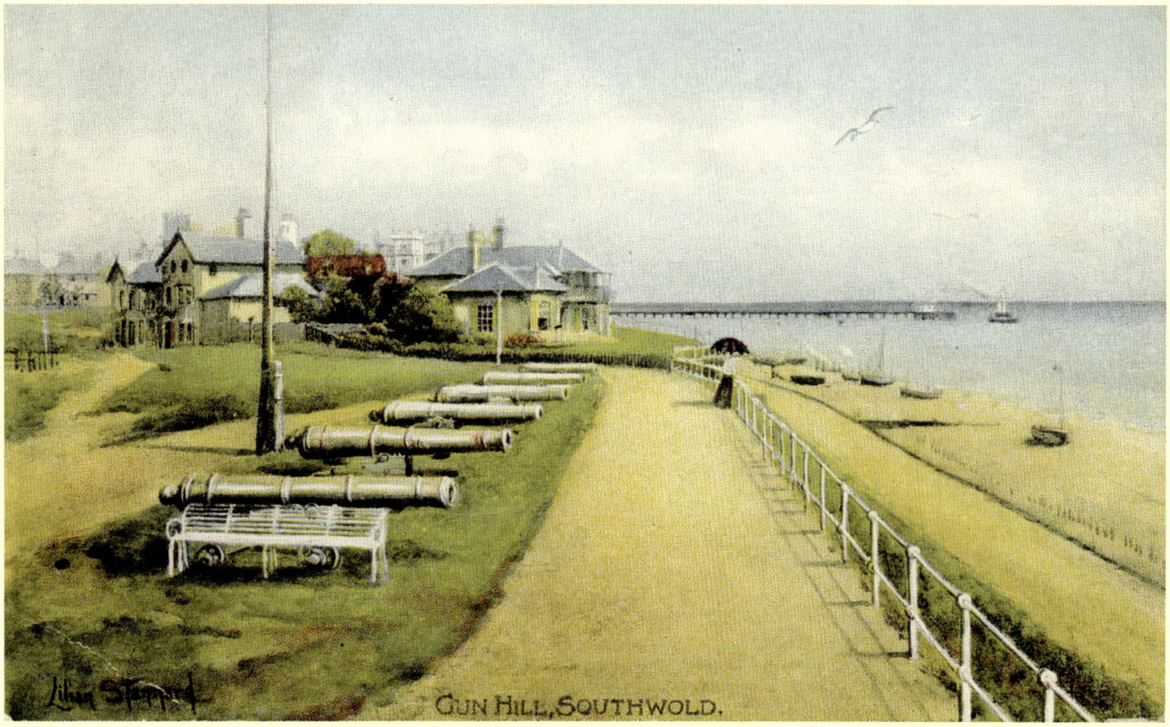


Edwardian postcard of Gun Hill from a watercolour by Lilian Stannard.

The six Elizabethan cannons which give Gun Hill its name – some cast with the Tudor rose and crown – are said to have been captured at the Battle of Culloden in 1746 by the Duke of Cumberland and presented to Southwold on the voyage back to London. They were to provide a fateful focal point, one unwary Victorian being killed when they were last fired in celebration. And as their presence led to Southwold being shelled in the First World War as a fortified town, the cannons were hurriedly buried in 1939.

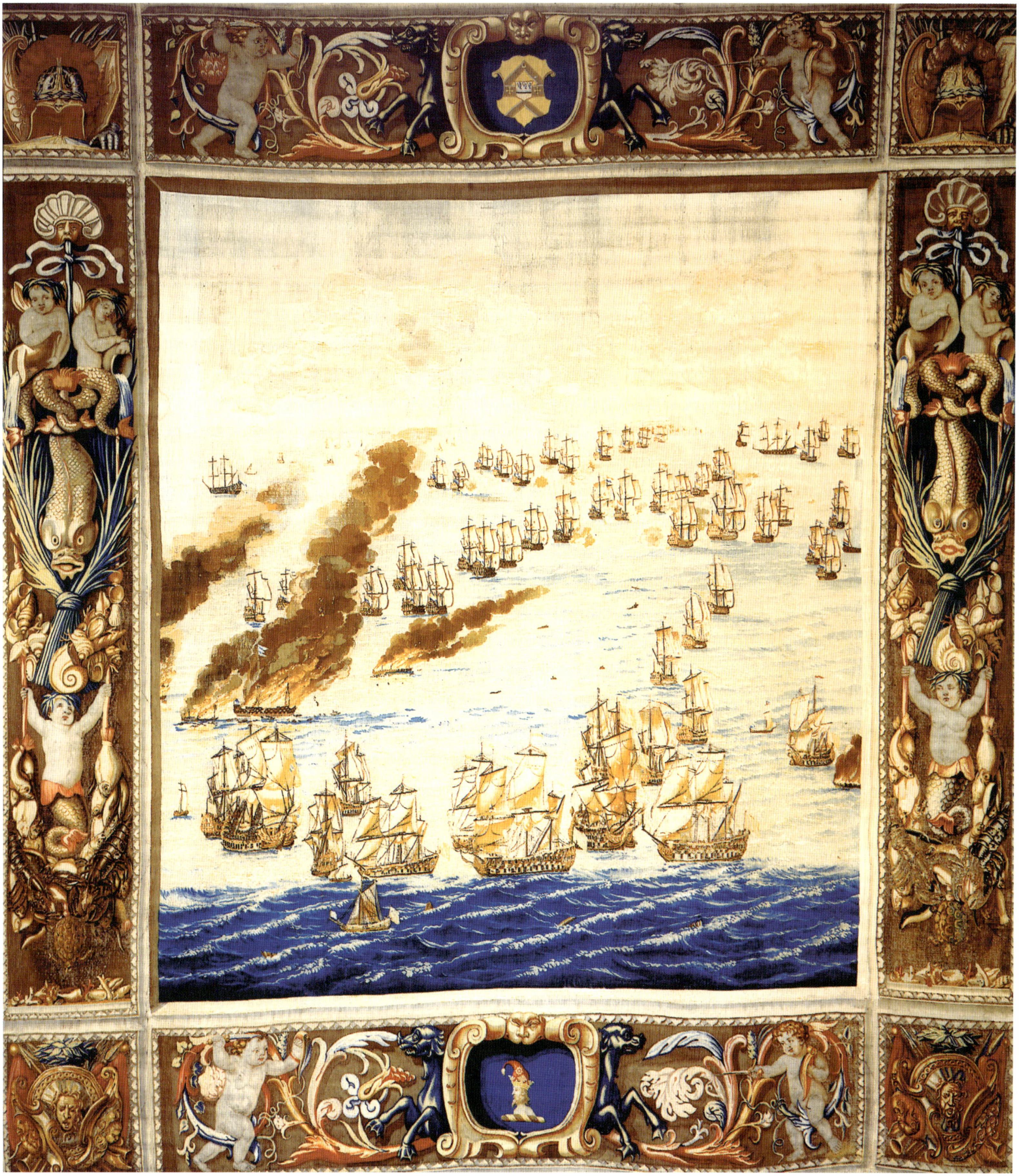

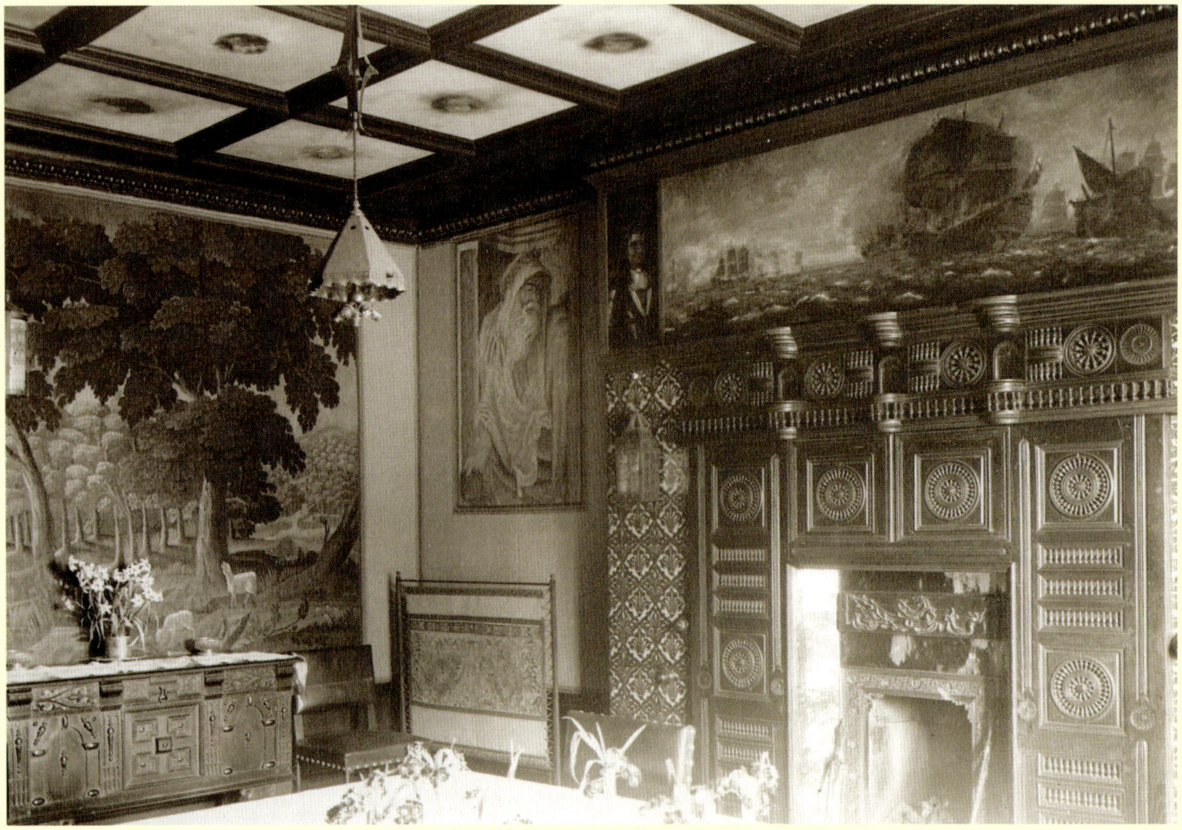

A South Green dining room photographed in 1910. The Sole Bay battle panorama above the fireplace, by LAWRENCE CARRINGTON GRUBBE, sixth son of veteran Victorian mayor John Eustace Grubbe, is now in Sutherland House. The ceiling panels, depicting the angelic heads of Edwardian children set against clouds, are attributed to REGINALD GRENVILLE EVES RA (1876-1941) – friend of John Singer Sargent and portraitist of Southwold visitor Thomas Hardy.

Sandwich, the wily officer who had risen under the Commonwealth but whose defection in the chaos after Cromwell's death had been decisive to the Restoration, was fatally overruled. James insisted that the arrival of Dutch forces was not imminent, but an advancing fleet was indeed sighted early in the morning of May 28. So he had little time to prepare for the Battle of Sole Bay – allegedly being detained further by a dalliance with a maid, whose ghost is said to wait for him to this day. Many of his men were diverted by the brew for which Southwold remains famous.

But the ever-industrious van de Velde had made meticulous plans, creating 70 drawings with amazing speed and accuracy in the run-up to the engagement. More followed in the thick and wake of the fighting. Waged against 61 Dutch warships were 71 in the Anglo-French force. Due to muddled orders, rather than to the rumoured treachery, French forces sailed south and largely out of the action pursued by 20 ships from Admiral de Ruyter's fleet. Sandwich, only too visible in his flagship Royal James, was the first to engage the Dutch and he was soon surrounded as a 17th century naval tussle turned typically gory. Port-holes and ships' interiors of the period were painted red for a very good reason: to hide the sea of blood.

Guns firing solid cannon balls could only demast and disable vessels – killing and maiming in the process. But they were unable to hole below the water-line, so the final blow came from fireships directed at each stricken hull. Once Royal James was ablaze, Sandwich died on board or drowned while trying to transfer to another ship. His battered body was found 12 days later in the sea off Harwich, identified by tattered finery including the Star of the Garter.

The Duke of York had to switch ships twice before the battle ended in a bloody stalemate - a change of weather eventually forcing a Dutch retreat. In an engagement probably involving more than 50,000 men, 4000 lives were to be lost. With the fighting between nine and 12 miles out to sea, those watching from the shore had seen chiefly smoke clouds and heard the boom of cannons. Later, 800 wounded would arrive in Southwold, while for weeks afterwards debris, corpses and body parts came ashore with every tide (local people, who had been drilled to defend their town in the event of a Dutch victory, received a shilling for every retrieved body).

A ship's figurehead traditionally linked to the Battle of Sole Bay, now adorning the Red Lion pub at Martlesham.

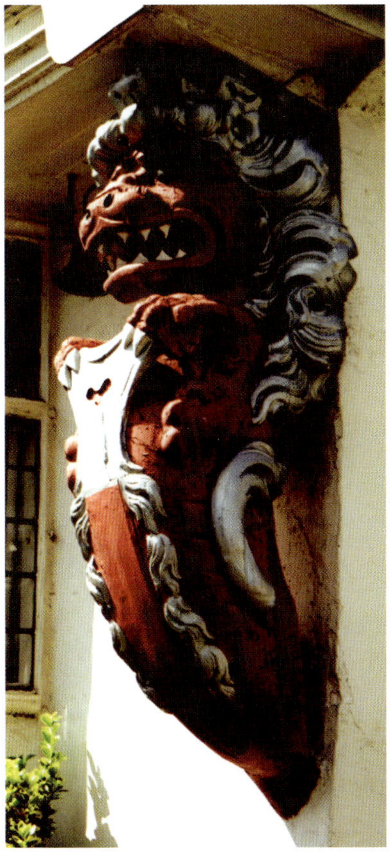

And with the Dutch states in dire straits – the French were in Utrecht and Amsterdam was saved only by a tactical flooding of the land – Charles II then invited craftsmen and artists to move to England. A packet service continued to ply between Briel and Harwich and, at some point in the winter of 1672-3, the van de Veldes were on it.

By February 1674 Charles was arranging with the Treasurer of the Navy to pay the elder £100 a year for making his quickfire battle-charting drawings, with a similar sum to the younger for putting them 'into colours'. That summer, the elder was in an English yacht recording the two battles of Schooneveld before the king banned him from attending the Battle of Texel for fear he might be killed.

The artists, glittering prizes in a propaganda war, were fêted with a commission to design a series of vast tapestries depicting the Battle of Sole Bay which were to be woven at Mortlake and hung in Hampton Court. Six were completed, three later to bear the arms of Robert Walpole, the Norfolk squire, long-serving Prime Minister and art collector who died with a fabulous collection of Old Masters and a dazzling debt (his grandson solved the latter problem by selling most of the pictures to Catherine the Great of Russia: had they remained in Norfolk's Houghton Hall most would have been consumed in a subsequent fire). One tapestry, showing the English fleet in formation as the Dutch advance, and set within an imposing border of tritons, dolphins, amorini and shells, can now be seen in the restored Queen's Private Bedchamber of the Thames-side palace – though to modern eyes and minds it seems a remarkably unrestful choice for a room in which royal couples were at their most intimate.

The van de Veldes were given a studio in Queen's House, overlooking Greenwich Park. The Palladian gem, England's first purely classical building, had been commissioned in 1616 by Anne of Denmark, wife of James I, and now comprised grace and favour apartments. Here the artists and their apprentices – soon to be joined by Willem the Younger's son, Cornelis – worked on major commissions, including a view of Charles II visiting the fleet in the Thames

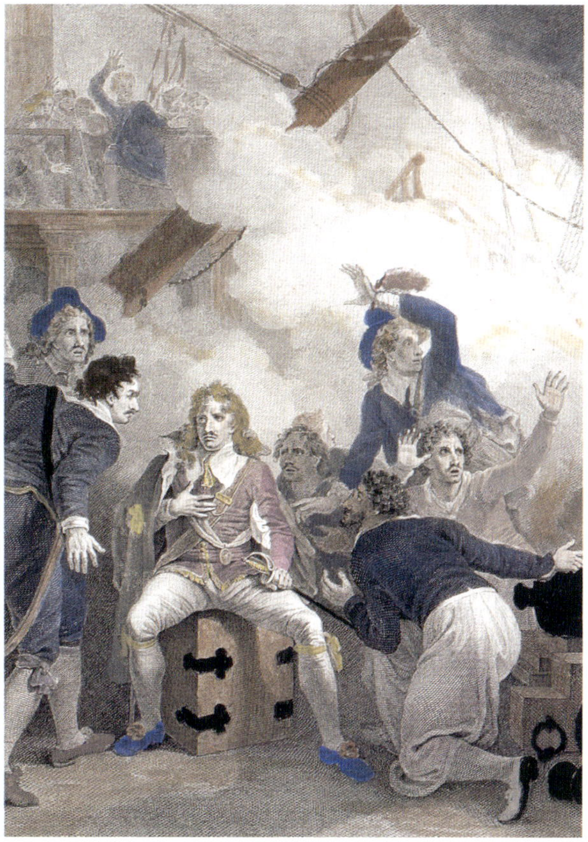

Hand-coloured engraving of 1798 by W. Byrne, entitled *Earl Sandwich refusing to leave his ship while on fire in the battle of Sole Bay*, from an oil painting by Robert Smirke RA (1753-1845). In reality the naval hero weighed almost 24 stone.

estuary after the Battle of Sole Bay. But, when the admiralty wanted the work cut in two, the younger Willem refused to sell it. The pristine picture now has pride of place among van de Velde paintings displayed in their former studio.

When Willem van de Velde the younger died, in 1707, he was buried with his father in the artists' church of St James's Piccadilly. The Queen's House collection shows that these two men founded what we now view as the English tradition of marine painting. In an upstairs room they had also laid out tapestry designs up to 24 feet in length. A second set was ordered by James II – the former Duke of York – in 1688, but he was in flight before its completion. Ironically, the Catholic convert was ousted by his daughter Mary and her husband … the Dutch William of Orange.

Ben Lowsey's oil painting of *Right Hon W.E. Gladstone passing by Southwold Sept 15th 1883*.

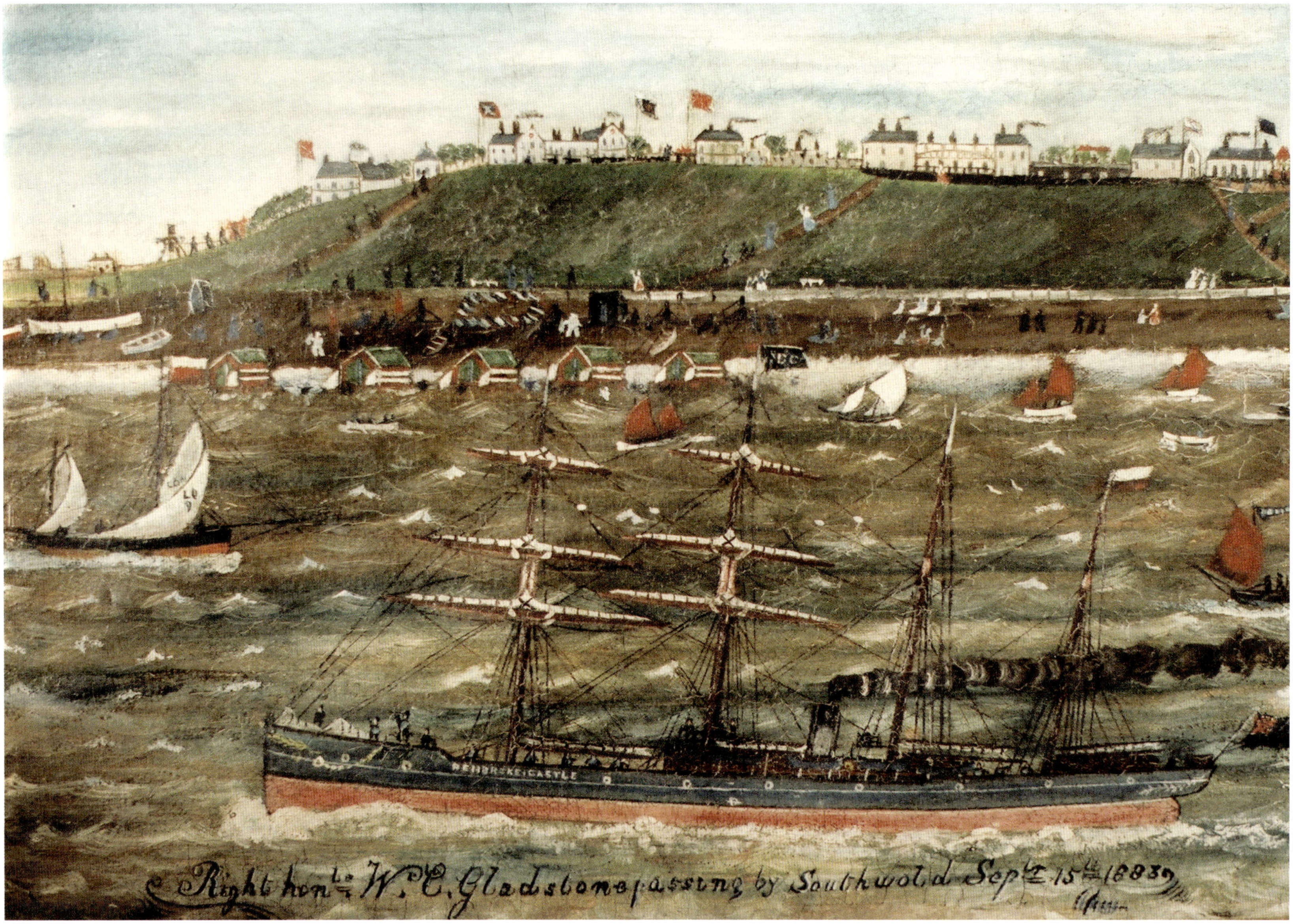

Chapter Two

# Port and Harbour

Viewed in hindsight, as if through the wrong end of a telescope, the story of Southwold appears compacted into one elemental conflict – an epic struggle with the sea (and with fellow sea-faring folk) for livelihood and life. Before the Norman Conquest what was then the hamlet of Reydon supplied the monks of Bury with 20,000 herrings annually, a toll rising to 25,000 fish in the Domesday Book year of 1086. Fortunes could ebb and flow with every tide, but the general rise of Southwold was linked to the fall of Dunwich from medieval might to submerged rubble. Heading seawards from Blythburgh, and then turning to run parallel with the coast, the River Blyth provided Dunwich with a magnificent harbour until the great gale of 1328 opened a new mouth two miles closer to Southwold. Four more mouths were to be cut, until the men of Southwold and Walberswick settled the issue in 1590 by digging out a course very similar to that of today. On the way there had been lobbying, bribing and bullying, mayhem and murder.

An 1818 engraving of Henham Hall by J.C. Varrall, from a sketch by T. Higham.

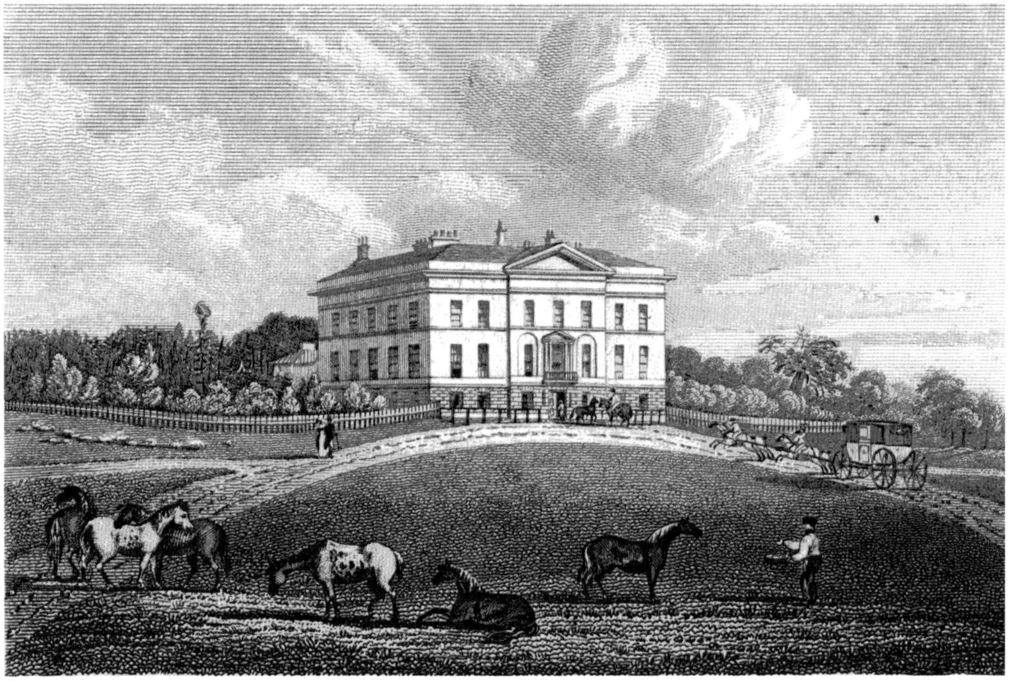

By Tudor times catches of herring and sprats were joined by cod and ling from perilous voyages to Iceland. More than a fifth of England's cod fleet in 1528 came from Southwold, Easton Bavents and Covehithe, with blubber pans and tackle houses arrayed along a quay at Wood's End Creek (later Buss Creek). The little town was dotted with curing sheds, and although the end of fasting with the Reformation harmed a fish-based economy, Southwold still weathered the decline.

The 17th century brought periodic bouts of war as well as attacks from pirates and the marauding mariners of Dunkirk. All this as the tides conspired to silt up the precious harbour and fishing families toiled to keep it open. By 1688 the Port of Southwold ran from Covehithe to Thorpeness, with Blackshore assigned as the legal quay from which goods could be exported or imported. But it was a constant struggle for an isolated community dependent on the sea.

There was a brief burst of prosperity in the mid 18th century when an oak pier was built along the Southwold bank of the harbour in 1749, to be followed three years later by another on the Walberswick side. The Blyth port then became the base of the Free British Fishery, with warehouses along Blackshore, a net-house on the Common and square-rigged fishing busses berthed in what was now known as Buss Creek. From the 1760s the river was navigable for black-sailed wherries, the juggernauts of the era, as far as Halesworth. But when, around 1795, an anonymous artist produced the pen and ink panorama illustrated overleaf, the harbour was in trouble once more. The free fishery had foundered after successive poor seasons and the effort and expense of maintaining the wooden piers remained immense. In 1796 war with France saw fishermen lost to the navy and two volunteer corps set up in the town. Human conflict was not the only challenge: during the Napoleonic era, which ran until 1815, the silting

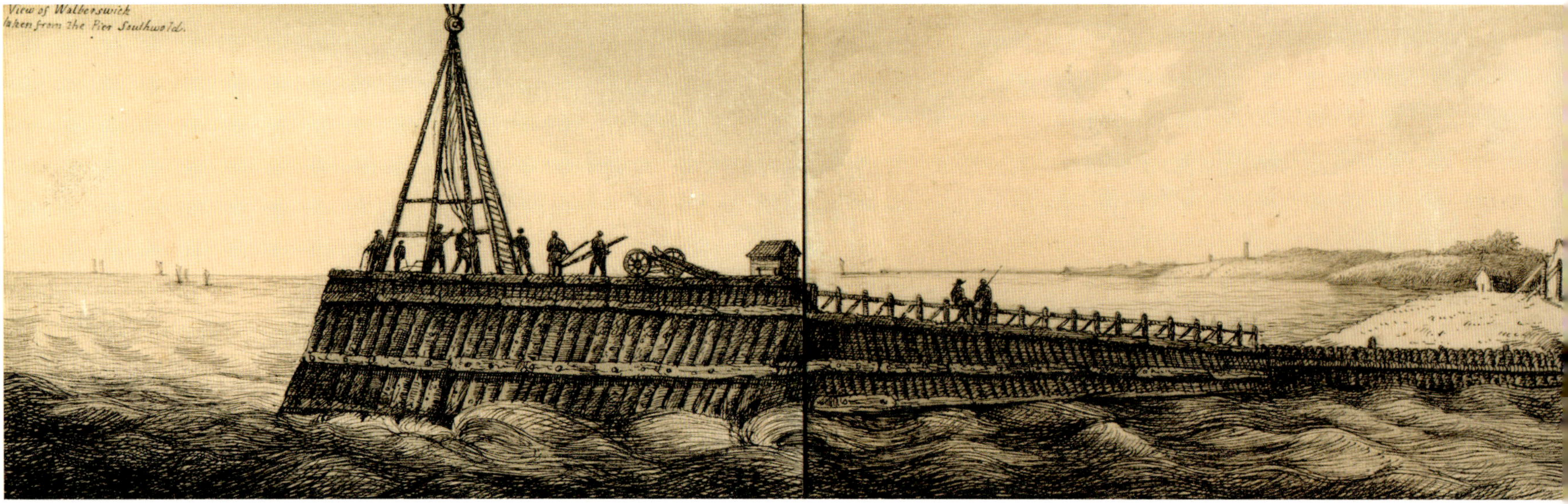


harbour had to be dug out 13 times. Still, the artist who completed the view of Walberswick from Southwold, across four sheets of paper, was engaged in a subtle celebration. For looming above the river inland, thanks to a stroke of artistic licence, can be seen the newly-completed Henham Hall – James Wyatt's stately seat for the Rous clan, descendants of William the Conqueror who produced the feuding earls of Stradbroke and probably commissioned this peaceful picture. With the mansion's demolition in 1953, the fine stone coat of arms from above the main door was moved to the Stradbroke Arms pub in Darsham and now lies propped against the rebuilt Victorian tower of

Pen and ink panorama of the Walberswick pier of Southwold Harbour, probably 1790s.

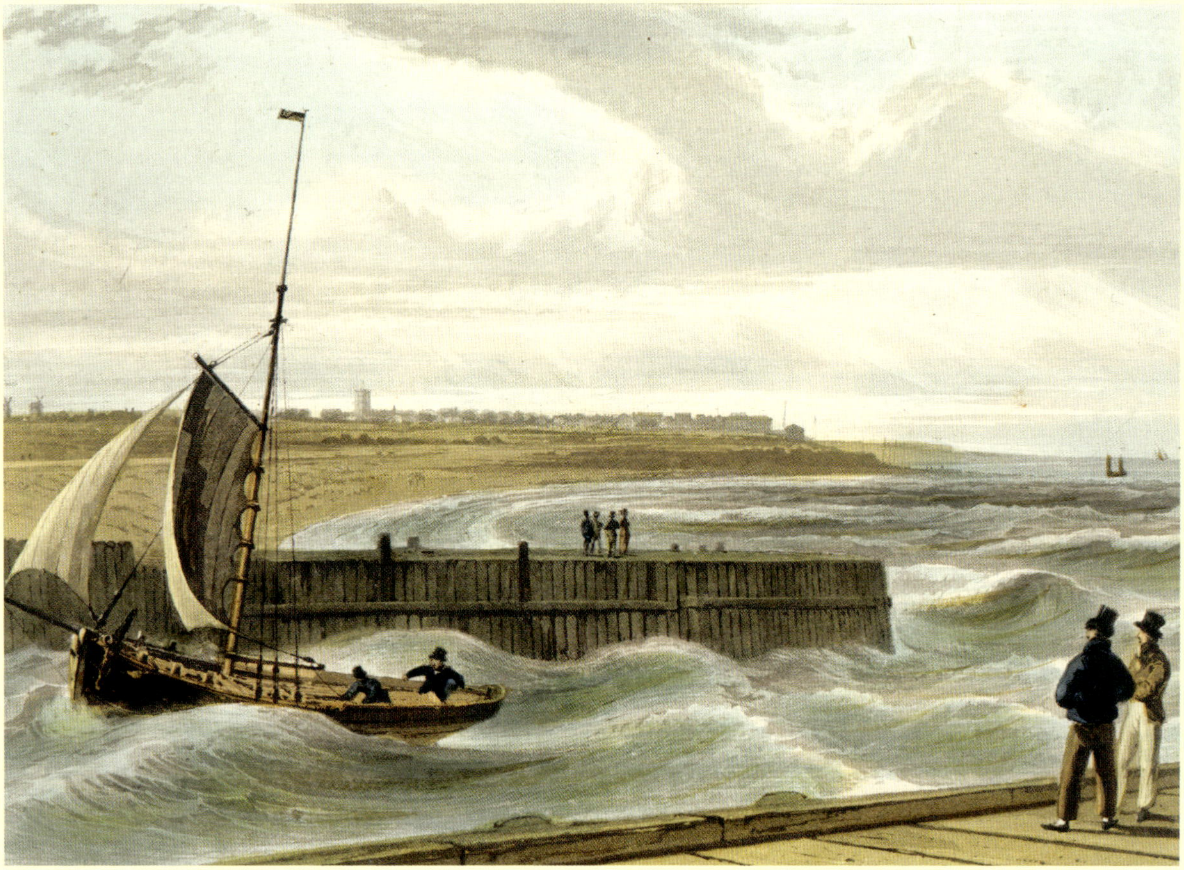

When WILLIAM DANIELL (1769-1837) visited Southwold near to the end of his decade-long *Voyage Round Great Britain* – an enterprise recorded in eight volumes of aquatints – he caught the drama of a small boat riding the swell into the harbour as local citizens congregated on the piers. This was in 1822, the year Daniell was elected a Royal Academician, when Southwold seemed a small village in the distance, dominated by its church and two windmills on the Common, and with boat masts just visible on the beach.

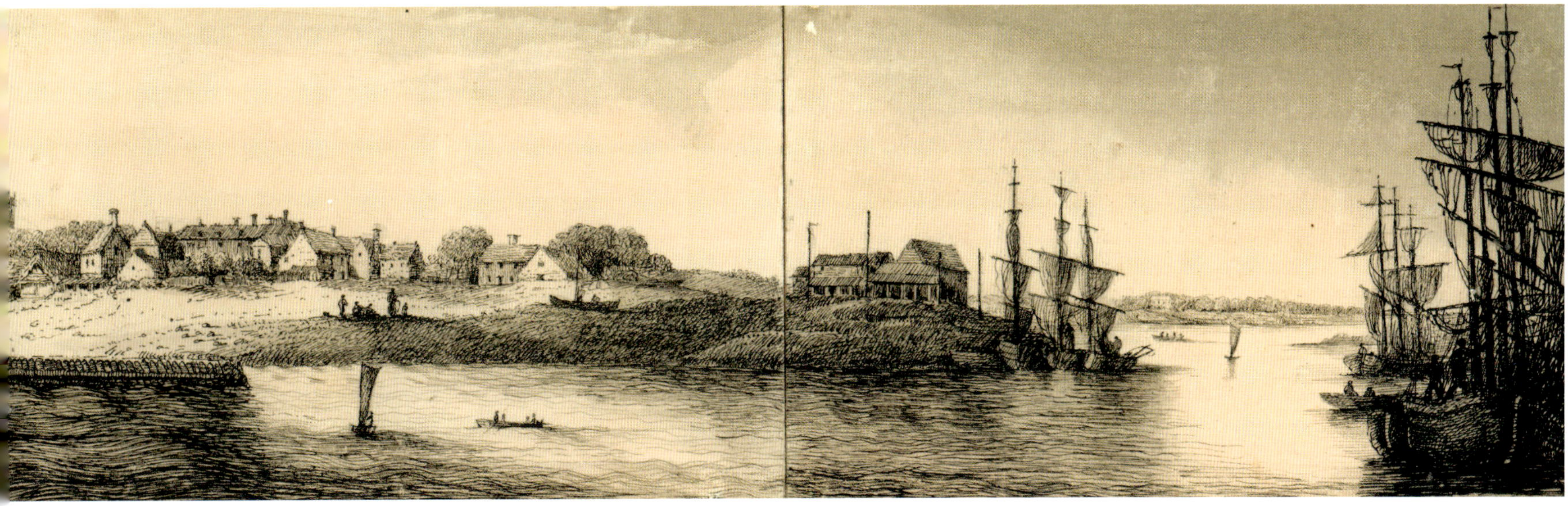

Wangford church. It bears the 1100-year Rous motto *I Live in Hope*, changed by the 6th earl, an Australian sheep and cattle farmer with a flock of children named after nearby Suffolk villages, to *We Fight Like Lions And Breed Like Rabbits.*

In August of 1822 **JOSEPH MALLORD WILLIAM TURNER** (1775-1851) was sailing up the east coast en route to Edinburgh. With sketchbooks, pencils, watercolour paints and brushes always in his pockets, he whiled away the journey by drawing. One resulting image shows the cliff-front profile of Southwold. Possibly intrigued by such a glimpse, this most tireless of roving recorders was touring coastal

*Dunwich, Suffolk*, J.M.W. Turner, watercolour.

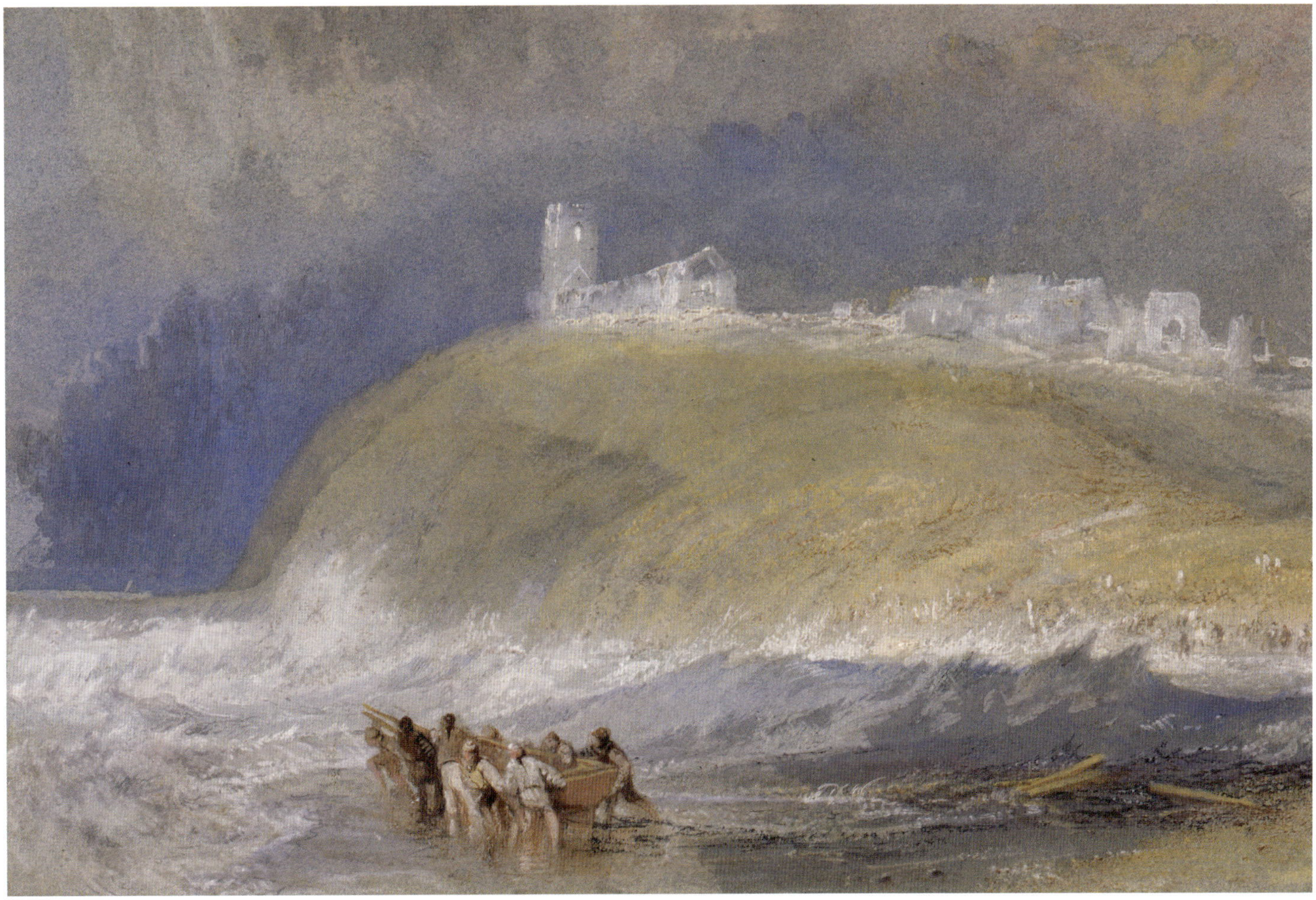

East Anglia two years later to sketch out a series of engravings to be called *The East Coast of England* (masterly prints of Orford, Lowestoft and Yarmouth would ultimately ensue). Naturally a romantic artist so fascinated by lost cities and civilisations paused at Dunwich – plotting this wild watercolour in which fishermen launch their fragile vessel into a stormy sea against a backdrop of ghostly church ruins also poised to plunge into the waves.

Turner was heading north to Lowestoft and we now know that he simply walked along the beach, probably savouring a sunrise over the watery horizon as he went. Arguably the greatest artist England ever produced, this much-travelled Londoner certainly left an unrivalled volume of work from a 60-year career: almost 550 oil paintings, 1600 finished watercolours and 20,000 drawings in sketchbooks or on single sheets of paper. Although a scandal that 136 years elapsed before his bequest to the nation was displayed in a purpose-built gallery as his will directed, it's less surprising that the full catalogue of works is still being completed. In 2003 Geoffrey Munn looked at a sketchbook in the Tate archive containing a labelled sketch of Walberswick and was able to pinpoint several pictures, each previously described as *Scene on the East Coast*, to Southwold. Clues lay in the distinctive cannons on Gun Hill and the tower of St Edmund's church.

If Turner was a passing visitation, other giants cast more long-lasting shadows over Southwold. John Crome and John Sell Cotman, pioneers of the Norwich School, which exhibited from 1805, founded creative clans of relatives and pupils. Crome's distant kinsman **JOHN BERNEY LADBROOKE** (1803-1879) published a famous print recalling the *Wreck of Princess Augusta* of London on October 28 1838, the vessel being stranded on Southwold beach on the homeward voyage from St Petersburg when laden with hemp and linseed. The lithograph by Belgian print-maker **LOUIS HAGHE** was taken from a painting by **CAPT. HENRY ALEXANDER**, reputedly produced on the spot. A drawing of Southwold from the sea by another Norwich School stalwart, Crome's most talented son **JOHN BERNEY CROME** (1794-1842), was turned into an etching by G. Hawkins junior for Dr Robert Wake's history of the town in 1839. Five years earlier J.B.Crome had been shipwrecked by bankruptcy.

A very different image was captured from a similar vantage point when a local naïve painter

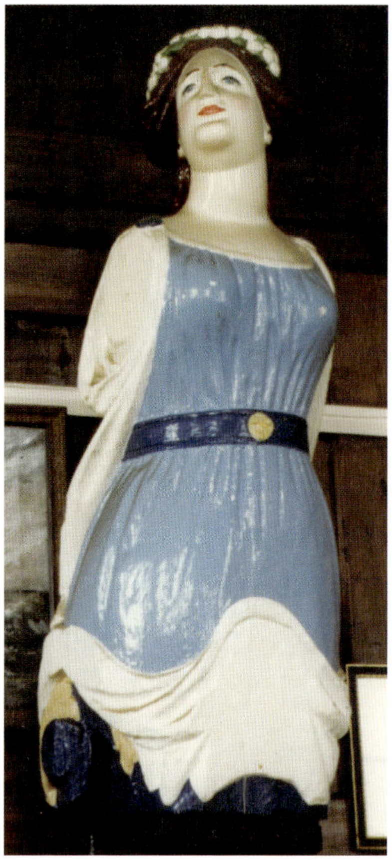

Victorian ship's figurehead in the Sailors' Reading Room.

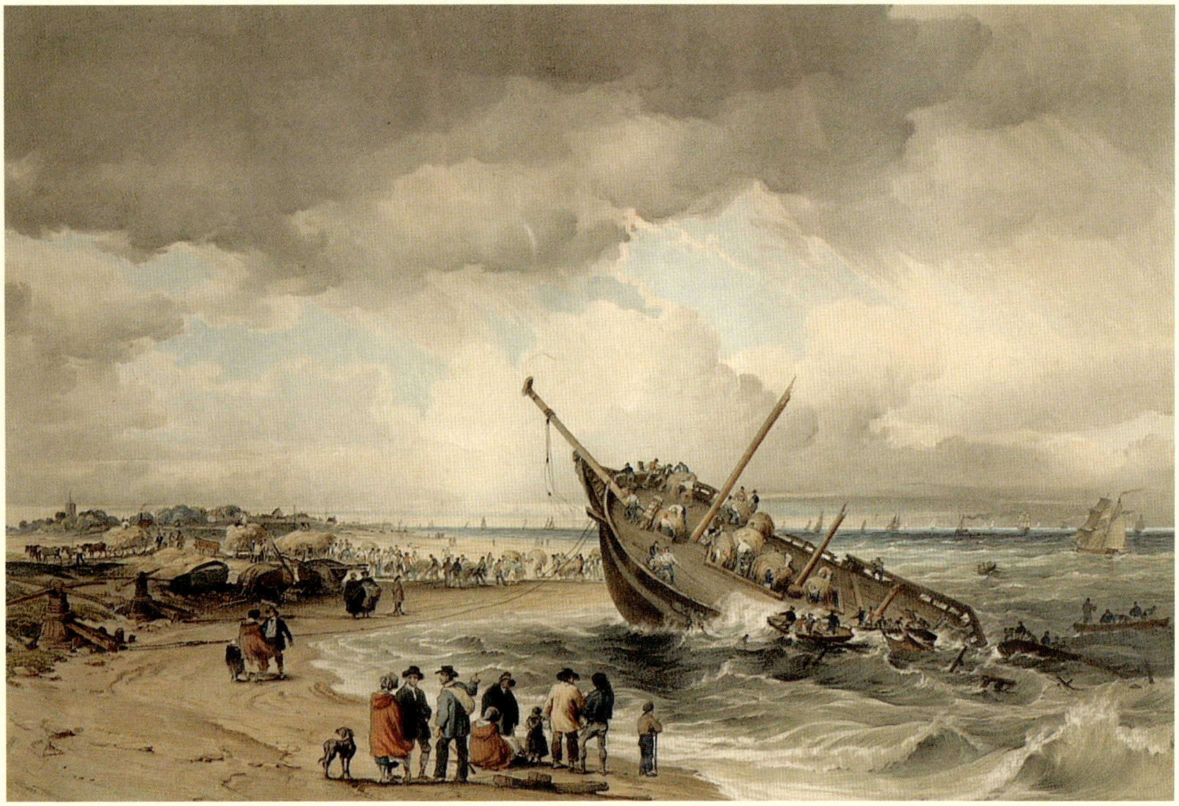

When John Berney Ladbrooke published this lithograph of the 1838 *Wreck of the Princess Augusta* on Southwold beach, he was recording an ancient local industry of salvage or plunder in a county whose storms and shifting sandbanks have wrecked an average of 20 ships per mile of coast. As well as windfall profits there were turf (or sand) wars between the men of Southwold, Walberswick and Dunwich. As Bella Bathurst wrote in her 2005 book *The Wreckers*: 'For a fully-laden general cargo vessel to run aground in an accessible position is more or less like having Selfridges crash-land in your back garden ... a Selfridges with all the prices removed.'

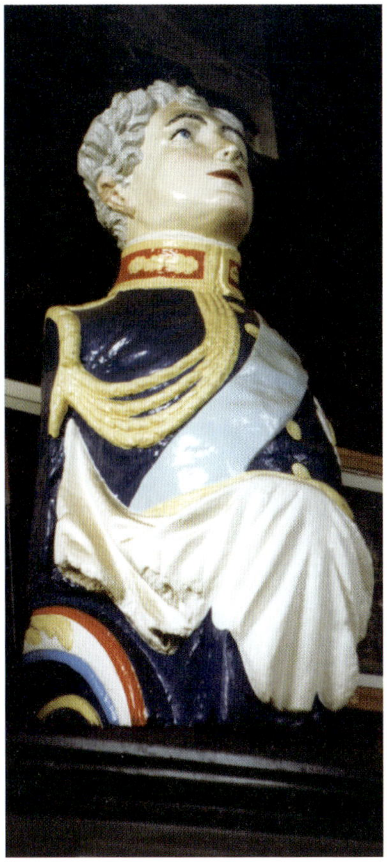

The Sailor King - 1820s ship's figurehead of William IV.

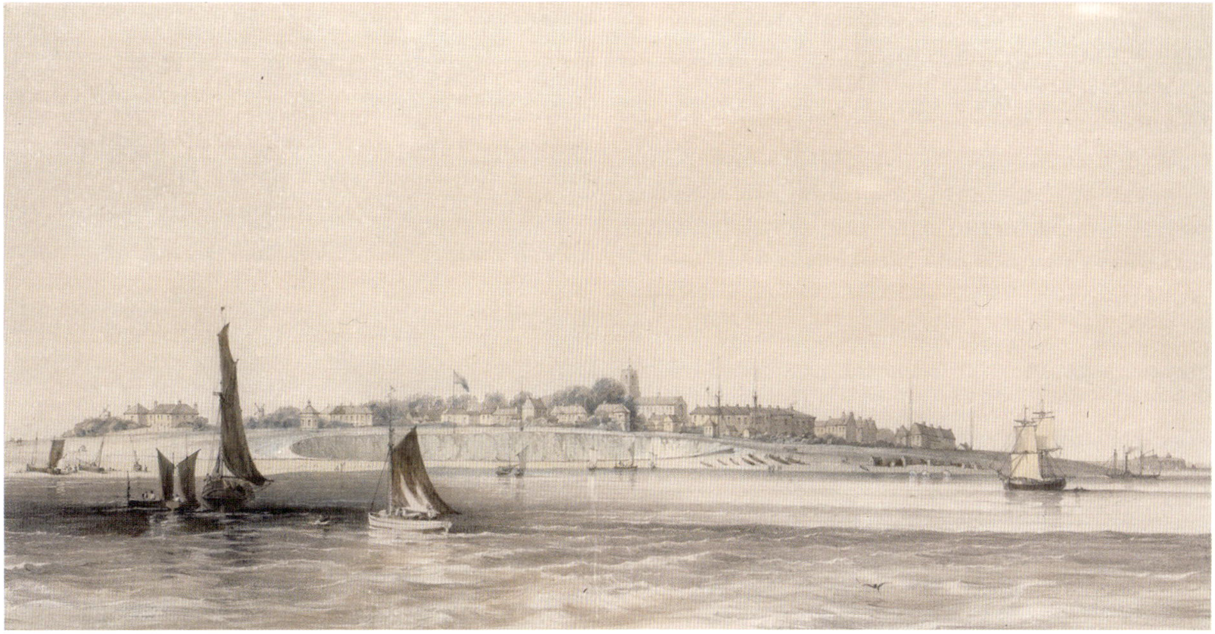

*South East View of Southwold.* On stone by G. Hawkins Jnr from a drawing by John Berney Crome. Taken from the sea expressly for Mr Wake's *History of Southwold and its vicinity.* Day & Haghe, lithographers to the Queen, 1839.

provided a vivid record of William Ewart Gladstone's passing by aboard the steamship Pembroke Castle on September 15 1883. It is one of many relics in Southwold Sailors' Reading Room – an 1864 gift from the widow of Captain Charles Rayley, who sought to prevent sailors going to sea on the Sabbath and to the pub on any day of the week – which show the vibrant creativity of the local fishing community. They whittled name plates and model-boats – and, from 1892 until the First World War, their woodcarving skills were honed during winter classes in the much-prized School of Industrial Art, founded by Arthur Flower and housed in an Arts and Crafts building in Park Lane (in 1926 former pupil William Bennett carved the mayor's chair and desk from an ancient trunk of bog oak beached at Benacre). In the pubs they sang folk songs and told ghost stories in a rich vernacular language. When Bob Jellicoe interviewed the last of the Victorian-born fishermen in the

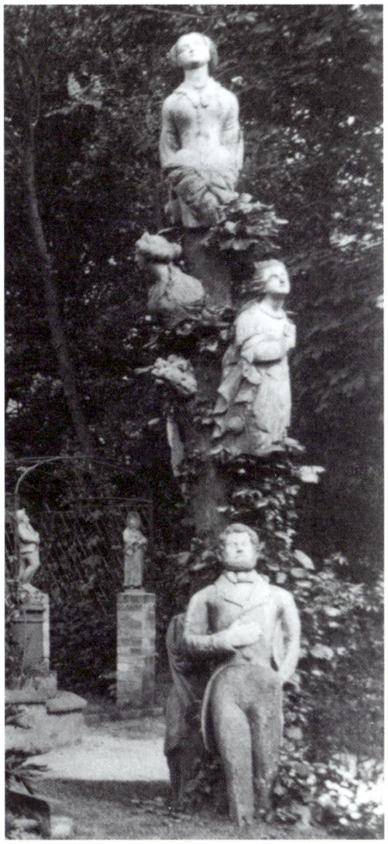

This totem pole, made from salvaged ships' figure-heads, stood in a Southwold garden in 1910. Others hung like trophies above the doors of fishermen's huts along the beach and harbour. In the 1950s Olive Cook found the wreckers' booty still leaning from certain doorsteps and her husband, Edwin Smith captured another in his East Green photograph (see p141). Today there is a figure-head on Douglas House in Stradbroke Road, while others are in the museum and sailors' reading room.

Southwold School of Industrial Art.

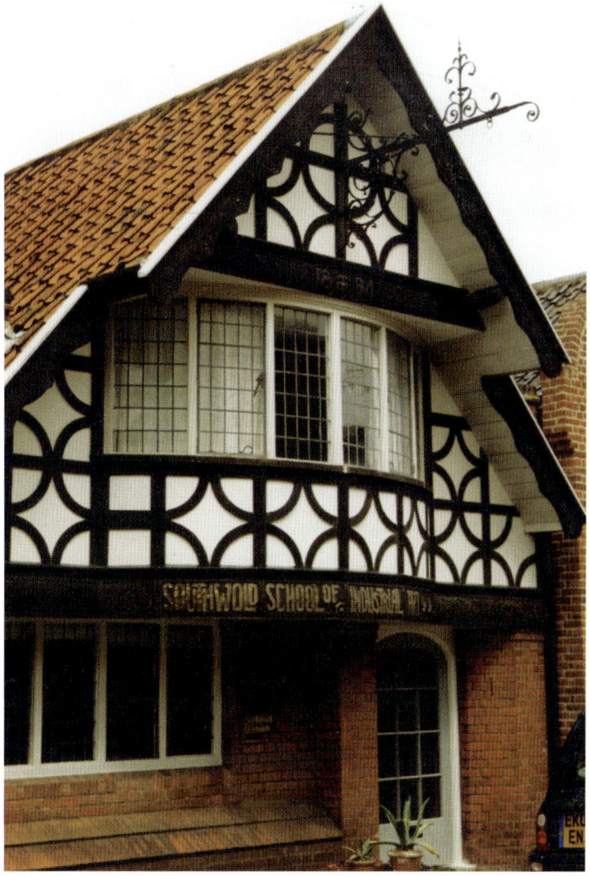

1970s, their memories were related in vivid dialect and with words such as ‘barmskin’ (for an oily apron worn by fish-gutters) which Chaucer used in *The Miller’s Tale*.

In the early years of the 20th century Ralph Vaughan Williams made almost annual searches of East Anglia for the folk songs which he wove into his own music and also published in separate collections. In October 1910 he and George Butterworth (the composer of *Banks of Green Willow*, soon to be killed in the First World War) came by train to Southwold. They visited Charles Newby, formerly publican of the White Horse in the High Street, and now one of the first residents of the Arts and Crafts almshouses in Reydon. But their main source was the Hurr family who lived in the fishermen’s cottages in and around Victoria Street and in newer terraces to the north of the town. Three of the brothers, erstwhile lifeboatmen William, Robert and Benjamin Lowsey Hurr, were unable to work their

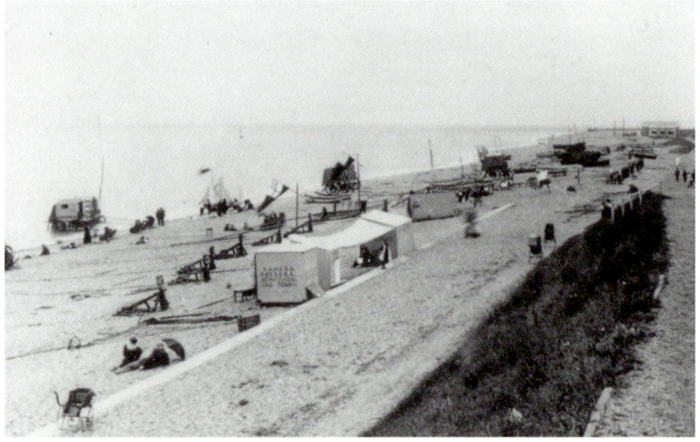

*Camera Obscura operated by Ben Lowsey, (left).*

longshore luggers (beach-berthed vessels trawling within a couple of miles of the coast for cod, sole, herring, sprat, shrimp and mackerel in season) due to a bout of bad weather – so they were free to serve up 11 songs for the recorder-composers, almost certainly in a pub.

The contribution of Ben Lowsey Hurr (1860-1934) included *The Cobbler*, a bawdy affair of a cuckold dating back 600 years, and *Jones’s Ale* which was known to have been sung in the 1590s. The Sailors’ Reading Room painting of the Pembroke Castle bears the initials B.L. on a bobbing barrel. Two nearby and similarly striking seascapes which depict the *Loss of the Martina Maria,* off Southwold on January 18 1881, in great swirls of white paint are signed B. Lowsey. The three-masted bark from North Shields sank in front of Centre Cliff with only three of her

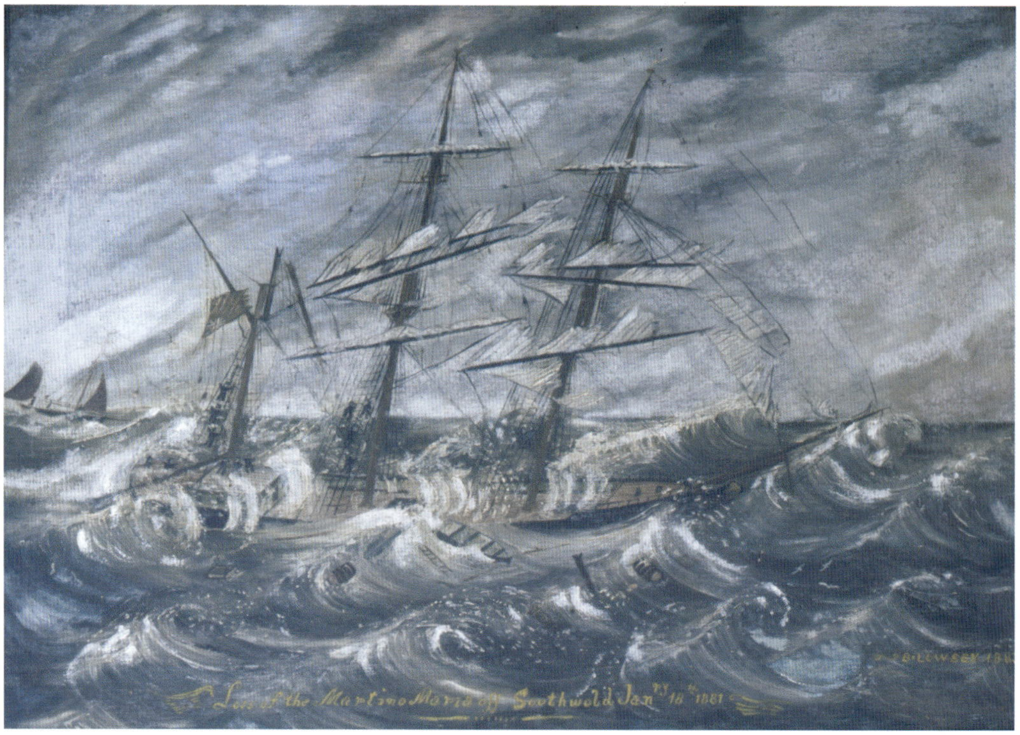

*Loss of the Martina Maria,* oil by Ben Lowsey.

crew surviving. Ben Hurr would himself be left bereaved by shipwreck, with his brothers Tom and Sam being lost in their father’s fishing punt, Susannah, in 1893.

With forenames passed down generations of Southwold’s fishing families, men were known by nicknames to avoid confusion. Ben Lowsey Hurr’s middle name probably honoured a more distant family name (another common practice) – so the folk singer was linked to a line of Benjamin Lowseys and a kindred creative spirit. The **BEN LONGLEY LOWSEY** (1837-1901) who operated

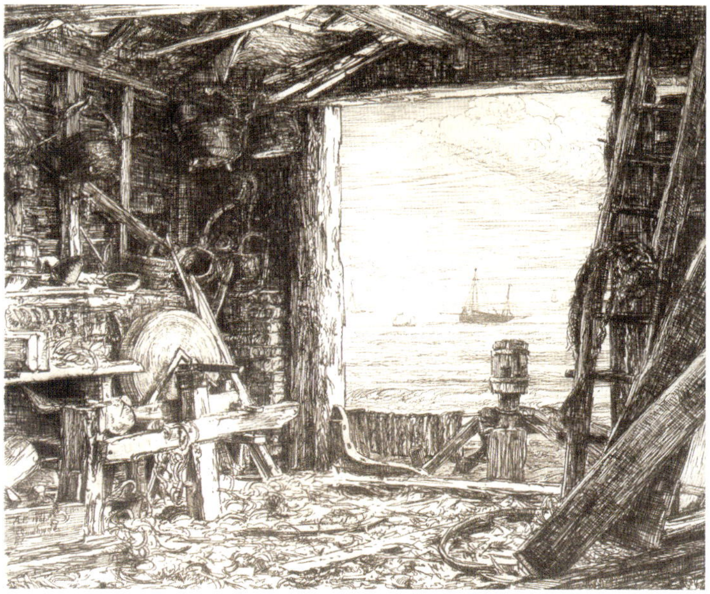

*Critten’s Boatbuilding Shop,* etching by Arthur Evershed.

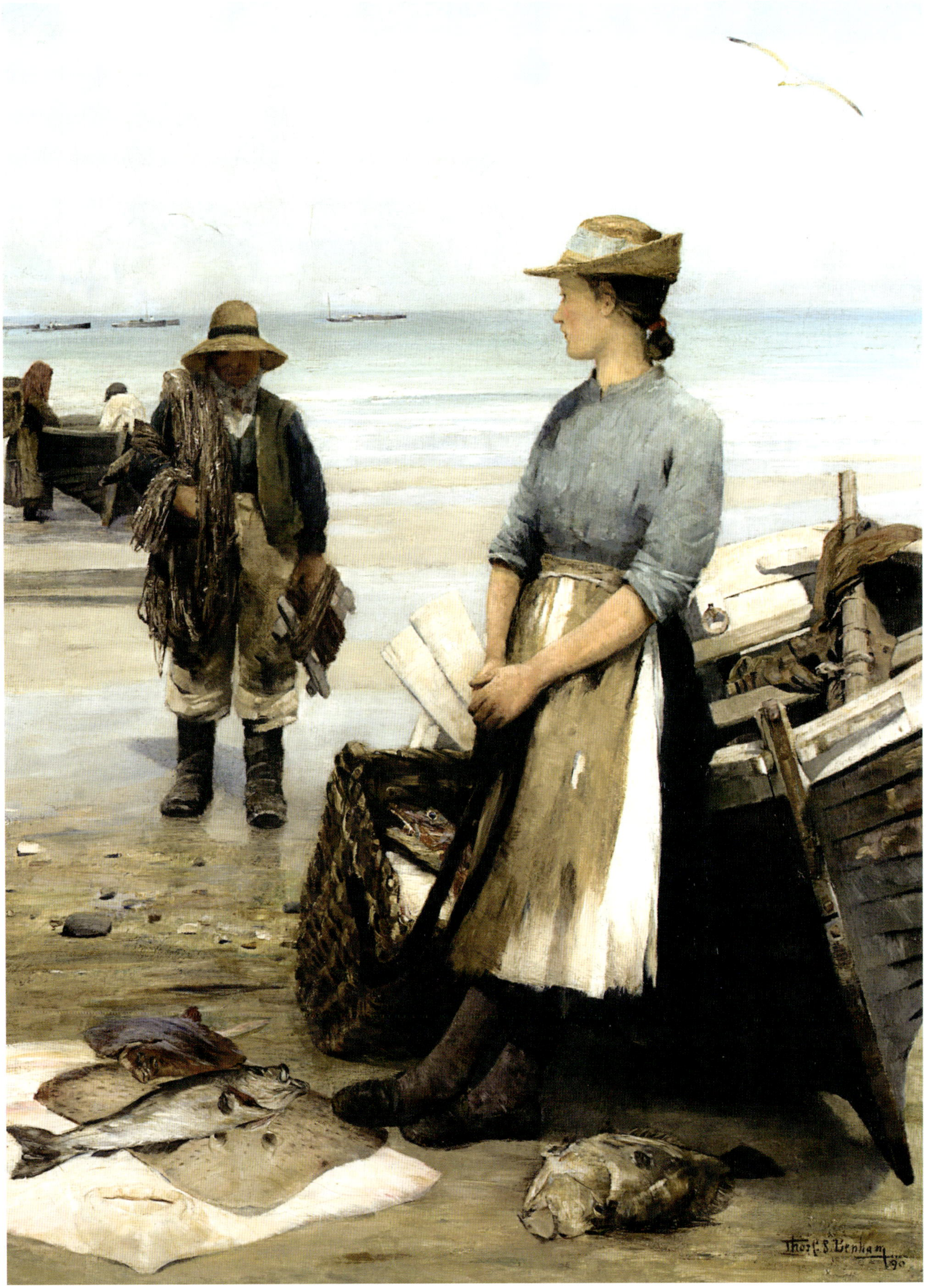

*The Day's Catch*, Thomas C.S. Benham, oil on canvas, 1890.

the camera obscura, a Victorian sea-front attraction in which surrounding scenery was reflected on to a table by means of a lens and mirror, also painted pictures. Sadly, like many former fishermen, he died in the Bulcamp workhouse.

The beach was busier than the harbour for the 19th century fishing industry. Longshore men's black-tarred huts were lined above the high-water mark in front of the town beside a beach village housing 16 families in the mid-Victorian era – the latter was lost in 1862 and the huts by the 1920s. Artists recording this vanished world included Charles Keene and **ARTHUR EVERSHED** (1836-1919), the Hampstead doctor of Kate Greenaway and the Du Mauriers, who became a professional painter, print-maker and illustrator and produced a series of evocative etchings of workaday scenes in the 1880s. One 1881 image, on view in Southwold Museum, shows the celebrated Critten's Boatbuilding Shop below Kilcock Cliff – recalling a family which prospered after moving from Aldeburgh to Southwold around 1780, whose base shifted from tiny Adelaide Cottage on St James's Green to the Manor House on the High Street and whose story was told in the 1933 novel *Bredon and Sons* by clan member Neil Bell (later Stephen Southwold). Another visiting Londoner, barrister **JOHN ROBERT KEITLEY DUFF** (1862-1938), was a prolific exhibitor in oils, watercolours,

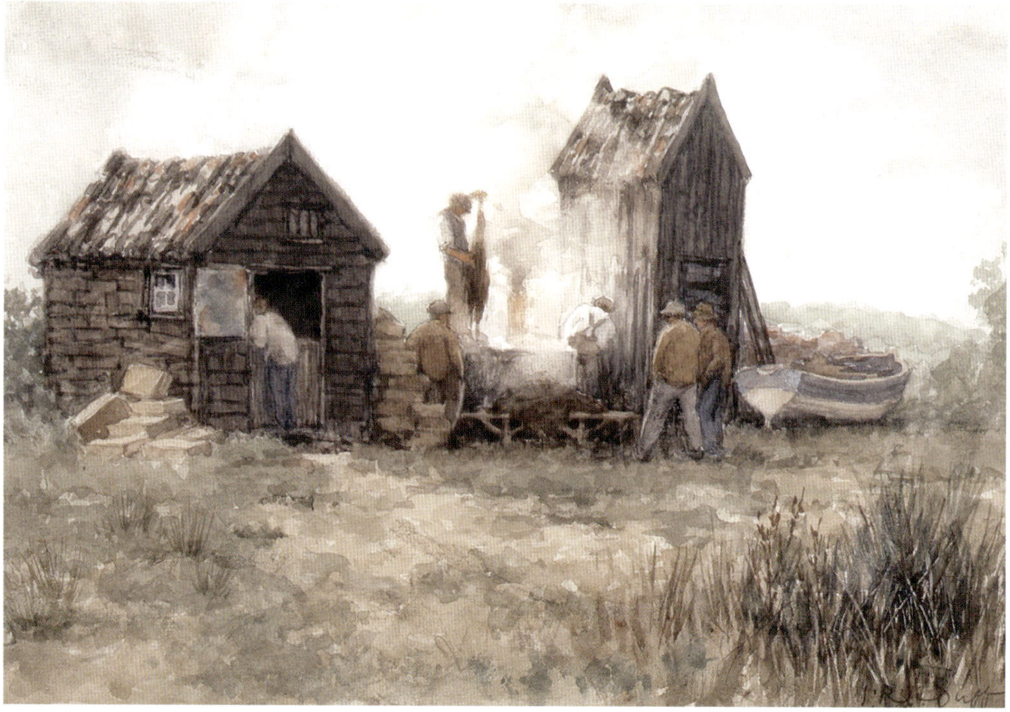

*Dipping the Nets,* J.K. Duff, watercolour.

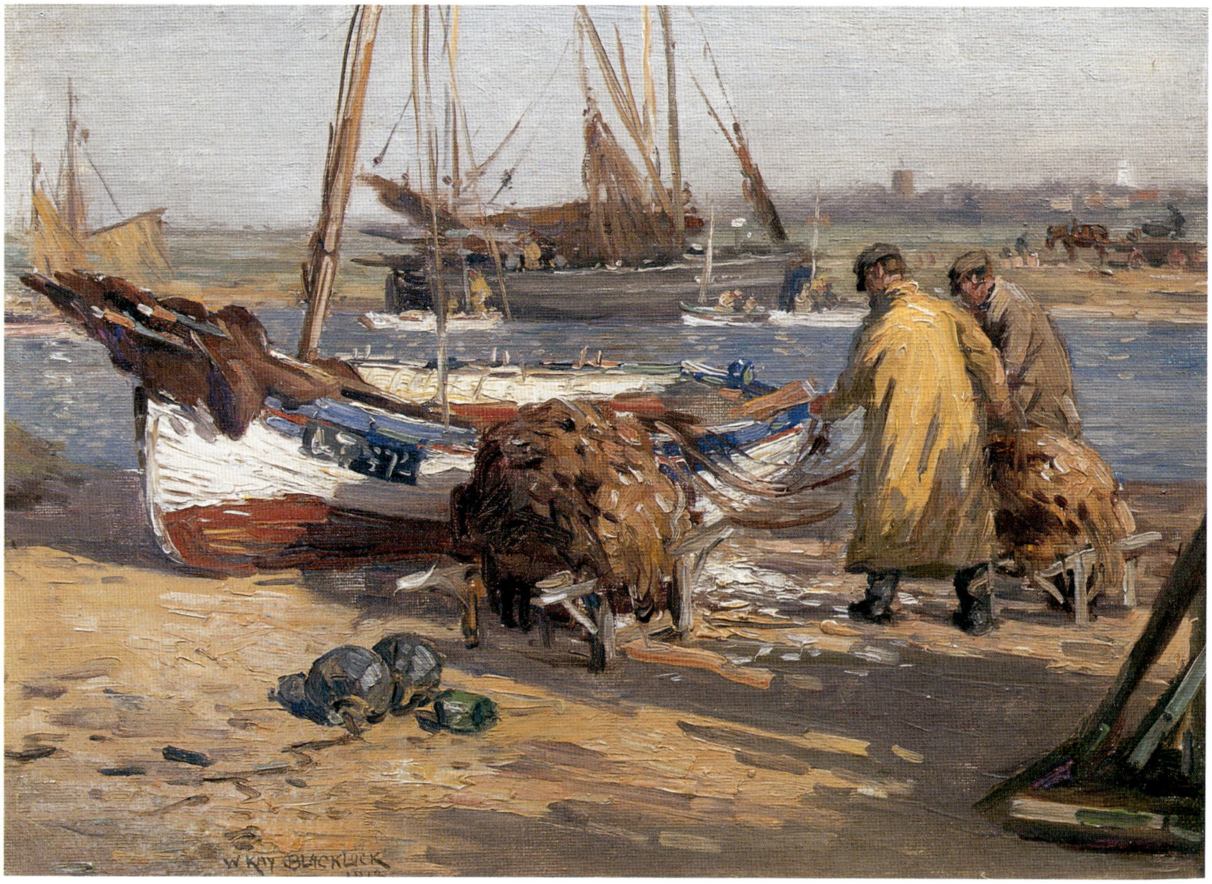


*Landing the Catch,* William Kay Blacklock, oil on canvas, 1913.

pastels, etchings and enamels – 1890s watercolours donated to Southwold Museum shortly before his death include studies of net dipping, the salt mill and an old brick well exposed by erosion below Centre Cliff. Meanwhile, the fortunes of Southwold's port and harbour ebbed and flowed: river navigation closed in 1884 and piers and wharves fell into disrepair, to be rescued by an Edwardian regeneration scheme which prompted a surge of Scottish fishing vessels. Two painters who evoked a sense of life and livelihood in heaving catches of fish were **WILLIAM KAY BLACKLOCK** (1872-1922) and **THOMAS BENHAM** (1856-1922), both of whom were based in Walberswick by 1908. And if those pictures seemed, at least in retrospect, to belong to a golden age before the First World War, Prunella Clough's semi-cubist harbour scenes from the late 1940s suggested a paradise of peace regained – even if the focus on food belonged to an ongoing era of rationing.

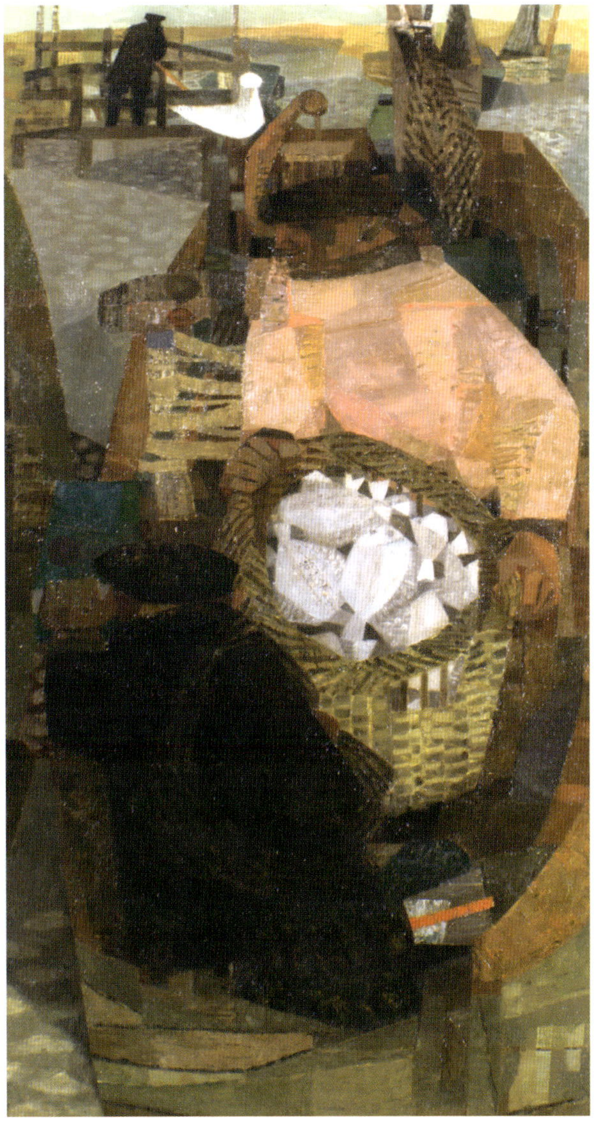

*Seagull*, Prunella Clough, oil on canvas, late 1940s.

Painter and print-maker MOSS FULLER (b1937), who lives at Laxfield, produced this screenprint card in a Southwold Houses series to mark the floating of Cromer Lifeboat Shed to a new site at the harbour in 1997. Now a museum holding the Alfred Corry – the Southwold lifeboat built for £800 in 1893 and in service until 1918, which was sold off and twice renamed before being rediscovered in Maldon in the 1970s. The antique building provides a harbour-side echo of the Fish Market erected in 1906 and blown down in the early 1920s.

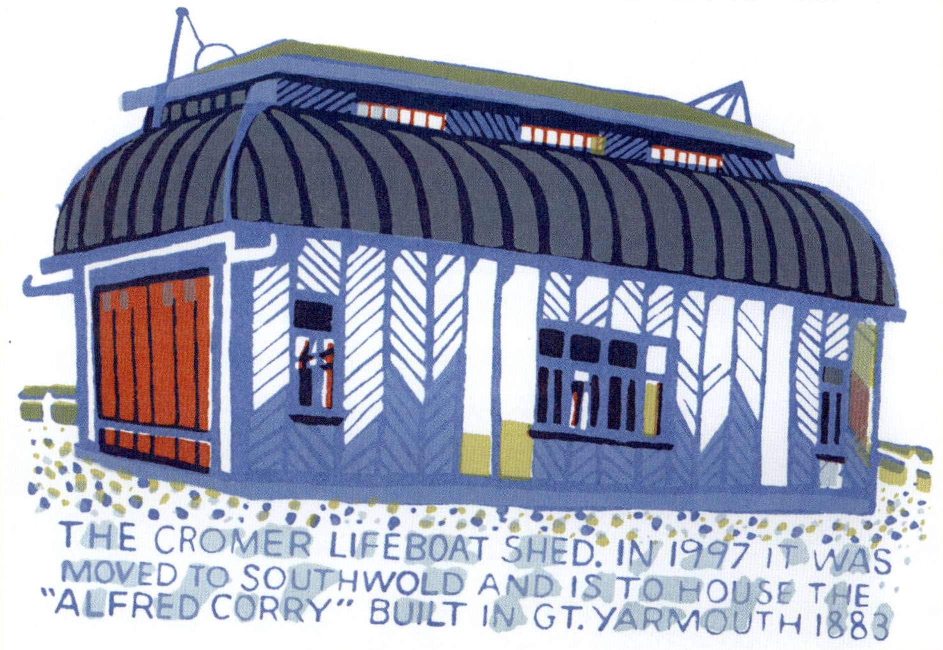


In recent decades Southwold has provided a growing haven for leisure boats, though a 1980s plan for a marina, with smart houses on stilts for Dutch yachting families in place of ramshackle tarred huts and workshops, was crushed by a floodtide of protest, as was a millennial proposal for a boat museum. At heart the harbour remains a place of work, with inshore fishing boats like that captured by painter and print-maker and shipwright James Dodds in several images of 2004 (see pp ii and vii) being built or repaired or painted along the bustling Blackshore between the sailing club and fresh fish stalls. And amid the fishing and boating folk artists continue to open their sketchbooks and set out their easels.

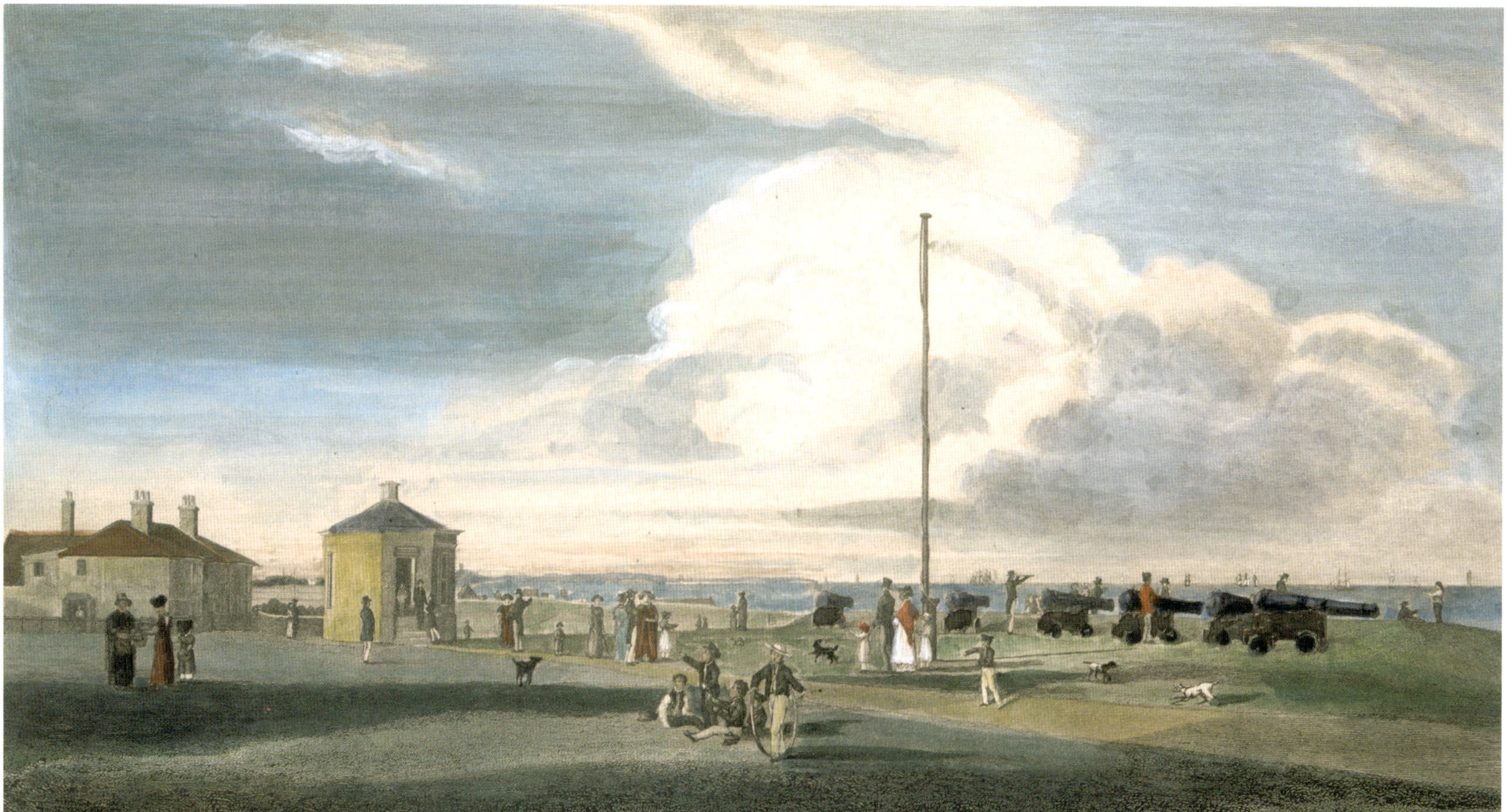

*Gun Hill*, Henry Davy, 1829.

Chapter Three

# Greens and Cliffs

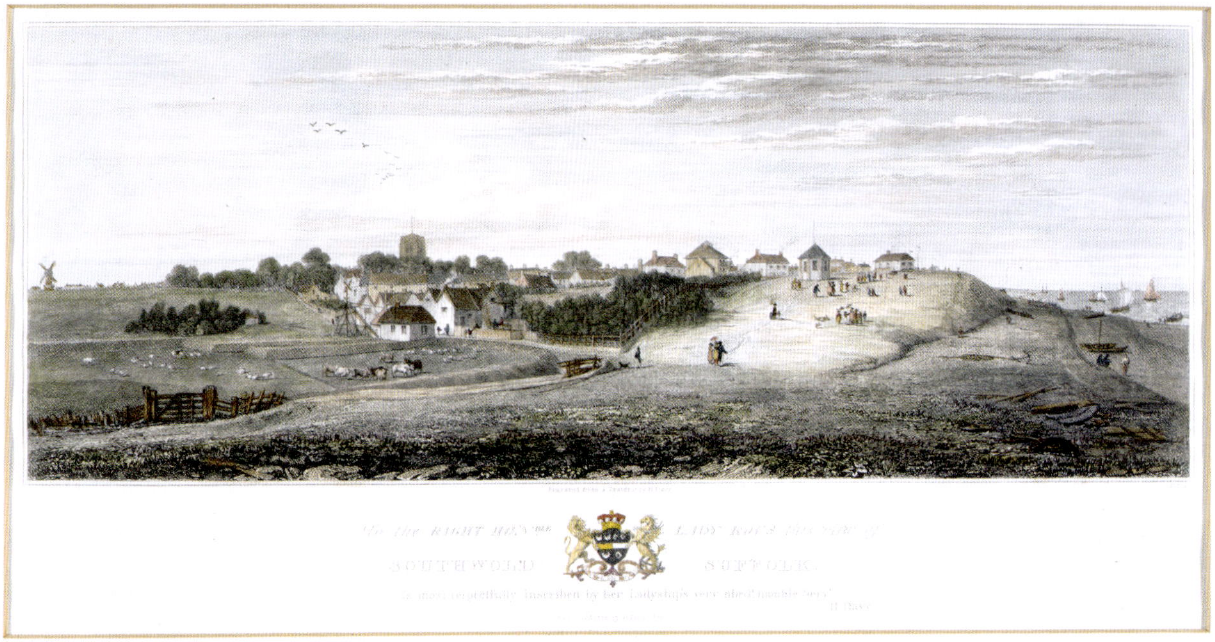

Henry Davy's 1820 view of Southwold from the harbour.

All of eight pages are afforded to Southwold in White's 1844 *History, Gazetteer and Directory of Suffolk* – with dozens of traders listed, as well as nine lodging houses, two breweries, two maltings and two chapels. The guide reveals a local population doubling in four decades, with a rise from 1054 in 1801 to 2186 in 1841. The true increase was higher still, for an estimated 200 sailors were discounted from the census while away at sea. A settlement previously clustered around church, high street and marketplace, beach and harbour was becoming altogether broader and also rather grander – though still occupying only the southern half of the present site – and the changing face of the town would be recorded by two near-contemporaries in words and in pictures.

James Maggs (1797-1890) was raised in Walberswick, where his father ran the Blue Anchor inn, and he taught briefly in Dedham (where Constable was an old boy) and Westminster before marrying in his native village and opening a school in Southwold in 1818. For more than 50 years, 'Limping Jem' was the eyes and ears of the town – serving variously as schoolmaster, auctioneer, assistant overseer of the poor, clerk to James Jermyn (thrice-appointed, twice-dismissed recorder of Southwold), surveyor of highways, secretary of friendly societies, census enumerator and coroner. In 1842 he produced a *Handbook to the Port and Shipping of Southwold* complete with beautiful drawings of coastal craft, but his main claim to fame lay in a private journal, kept from 1818 to 1871, charting the (mis)deeds and (mis)fortunes of his neighbours as scattered between the great events of birth, marriage and death. Here he coolly recorded epidemics of debt and drowning, petty crimes and punitive punishments and confinements in Melton Asylum and Bulcamp House (the workhouse). He had a taste for the unusual – a whale washed up on the beach, a cow struck by lightning - and the telling detail. For instance, after noting the 'Large New Iron Gates' supplied to the church by Messrs Child & Son in December 1838, he added: 'The Model of those Gates were (sic) made by Mr Jas Boyce – who assisted in fixing & erecting them – and was the

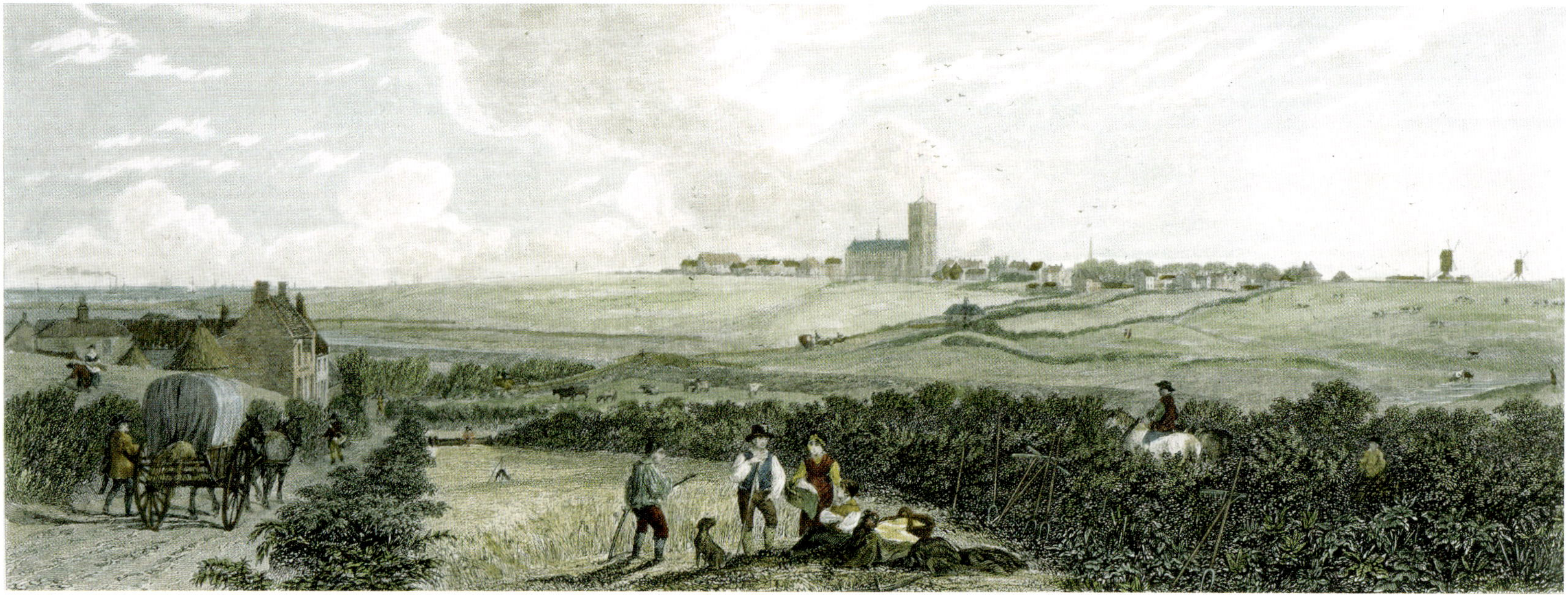

Henry Davy's view of Southwold from Reydon.

first Corpse carried thro' these Gates – Mr B died Jany 19th 1839 aged 36.' Moving house frequently, Maggs spent his final years at 20 Park Lane, where there is a plaque in his memory.

The town portrayed by Maggs was a place of small traders and fisherfolk and a large amount of poverty, but it had been growing as a watering hole for the gentry from Regency times. Indeed, the man with a finger in so many Southwold pies also kept a lodging house on South Green in the 1830s, and was typically meticulous in noting down the names of all his boarders. At nearby Tamarisk Villa (now May Place), the lofty Dr Robert Wake deigned to enlighten a band of subscribers with his 1839 volume *Southwold and its Vicinity* – one being James Maggs, who also aided the project on a visit to London by obtaining from Wyld's in Charing Cross a map of the Blything Union. For a depiction of this sedate side of Southwold we need to look to the engravings and watercolours of **HENRY DAVY** (1793-1865). His father was a Westhall farmer and his maternal grandfather a Wangford surgeon, William Gibson. He himself was destined for the army, until turning to art and studying under **JOHN SELL COTMAN** (1782-1842), greatest master of the Norwich School. Like his tutor, Davy travelled to Yorkshire – staying in Hornby Castle, where his brother was agent to the Duke of Leeds and a lasting lesson in the need for aristocratic patronage. It is tempting to picture pupil and mentor touring the coast and countryside around Southwold in search of subjects, but no proof survives. When Cotman began a large drawing of church ruins in 1804, while holidaying at a farmhouse in Covehithe with the family of his patron, Yarmouth banker Dawson Turner, Davy was only 11 years old.

In 1824 Davy married Sarah, daughter of Southwold master mariner James Bardwell. He lived in the town for the following six years – with two of his children born here, and the two Cotman-influenced volumes *A Series of Etchings Illustrative of the Architectural Antiquities of Suffolk* and *Views of the Seats of the Noblemen and Gentlemen in Suffolk* printed here in 1827. He published from the stationer's in the marketplace (now the dress shop), in the first year of the

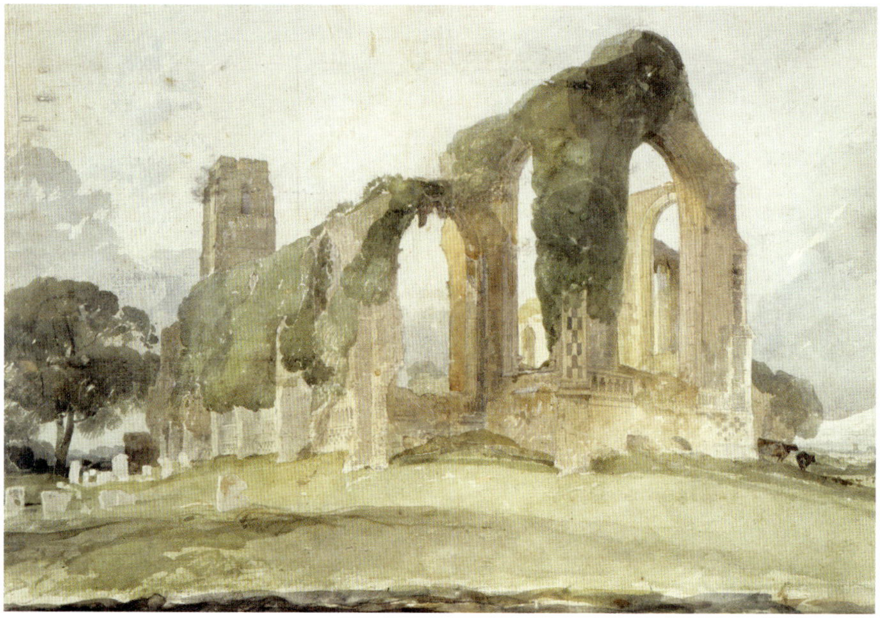

*Covehithe Church*, John Sell Cotman, pencil and watercolour.

*South Green* and *East Cliff Villas* (right) from the Rock series.

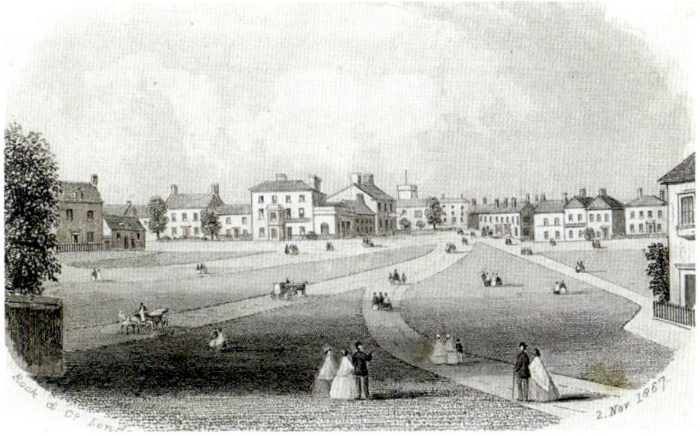

tenancy of Mrs Bardwell – his mother-in-law. In the guide *Discovering Southwold* Alan Bottomley and John Hutchinson add: 'Her own son, William Bardwell, became a successful, if hardly

Hand-coloured engraving of *Centre Cliff* from the 1867 Rock series.

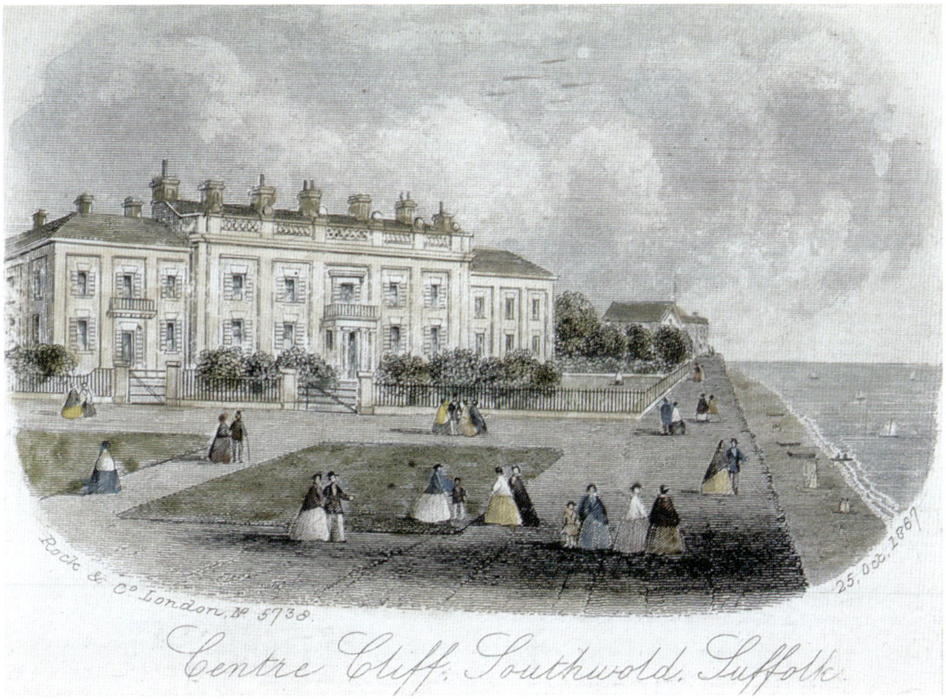


distinguished, architect. His elephantine family tomb in the churchyard is the only example of his work in his native town, which was spared his Town Hall intended to stand next to his mother's shop only by the state of the borough finances and

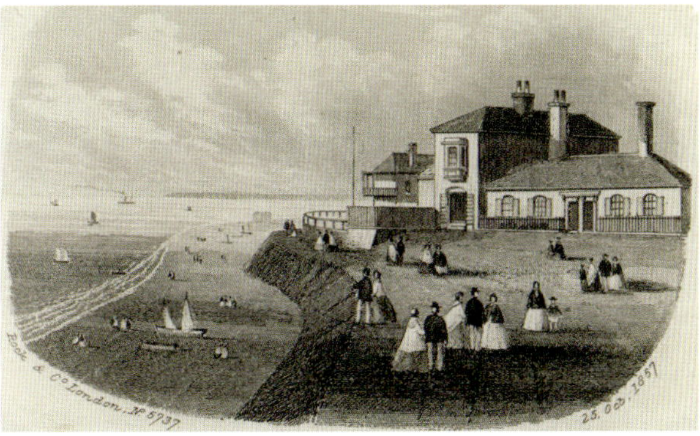

*South Cliff* and *The Beach* (right) from the Rock series.

the intervention of the Treasury. The nation was similarly saved from his Houses of Parliament, designed to illustrate the history of English architecture.'

Henry Davy produced drawings and watercolours of marine activities at the beach and harbour and prospects of the town which were turned into popular etchings. The prolific artist

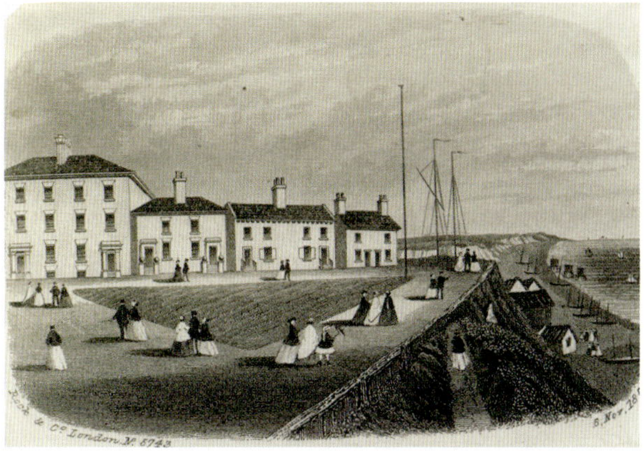

moved to Ipswich in 1830, where he published 136 etchings of Suffolk churches between 1837 and 1849, and where he died in 1865. Of his 16 children, most of whom died in infancy, one became a portrait painter and another an art master. After his death his copper etching plates were sent to Birmingham to be auctioned – but a cache of surviving pictures is now lodged in the British Library. The example, if not the actual hand, of

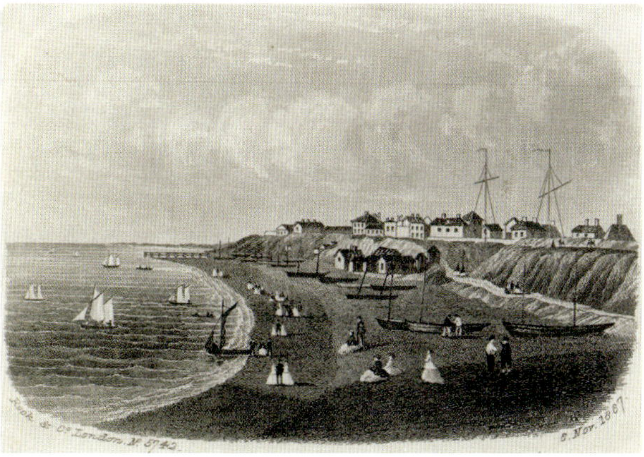

Davy can also be detected in a charming sequence of black-and-white Southwold prints – of Centre or Middle Cliff, South Cliff, East Cliff Villas, of South Green, Gun Hill and The Beach - published by Rock & Co of London in the 1860s and subsequently hand-tinted. Here a habit of seaside holidays, started elsewhere by royalty and taken up by the nobility, had produced a town apparently awash in a tide of mid-Victorian gentrification.

Davy shared rather more than a death date with **THOMAS CHURCHYARD** (1798-1865). This son of a Melton butcher and grazier fell under the spell of the Norwich School's second great master, John Crome, whose paintings he copied and collected with a life-long passion. Most of all, however, he was in awe of John Constable, in whose wake he had followed as a pupil at Dedham Grammar School and in whose work he found the perfect model of artistry. For four years from 1816 Churchyard was articled to a Halesworth solicitor, before a final year of legal training in London. After that, he set up as a lawyer in Woodbridge, where he would remain for the rest of his life. He and poet friends Edward FitzGerald and Bernard Barton were dubbed 'the Three Wits of Woodbridge' and it was chiefly the local landscapes of the Deben Valley that Churchyard came to celebrate in hundreds of animated little watercolours and oils. But, most probably from his early days in Halesworth, he was also familiar with the more northerly Suffolk coastline and three delicate wash drawings of Victorian Southwold, pages from a broken-up sketchbook, have lately come to light. Usually unsigned and undated, his pictures were still massed in his possession as money problems burdened his final years – each image to be inscribed on the back with the name of one of his seven daughters, as the best he could provide by way of a legacy. Harriet, his eldest child, would be especially tireless in promoting his memory. Even so, Thomas Churchyard was to be long forgotten, with his reputation restored only after an exhibition to mark the centenary of his death. His many supporters in East Anglia now claim him as a key link between Constable and British Impressionism.

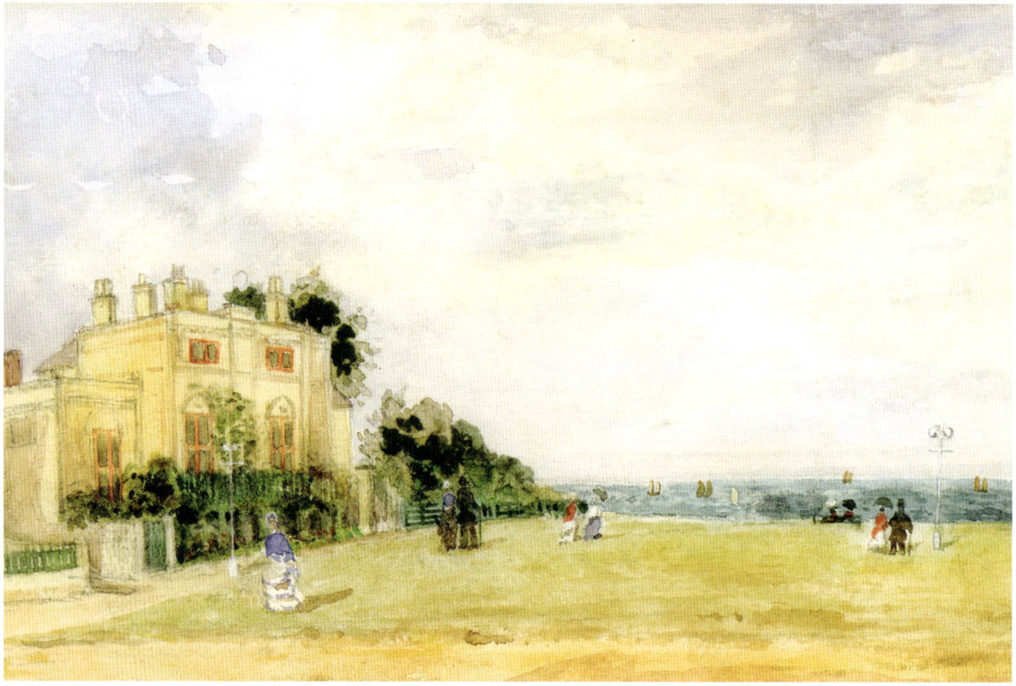

*South Green,*
Thomas Churchyard, watercolour.

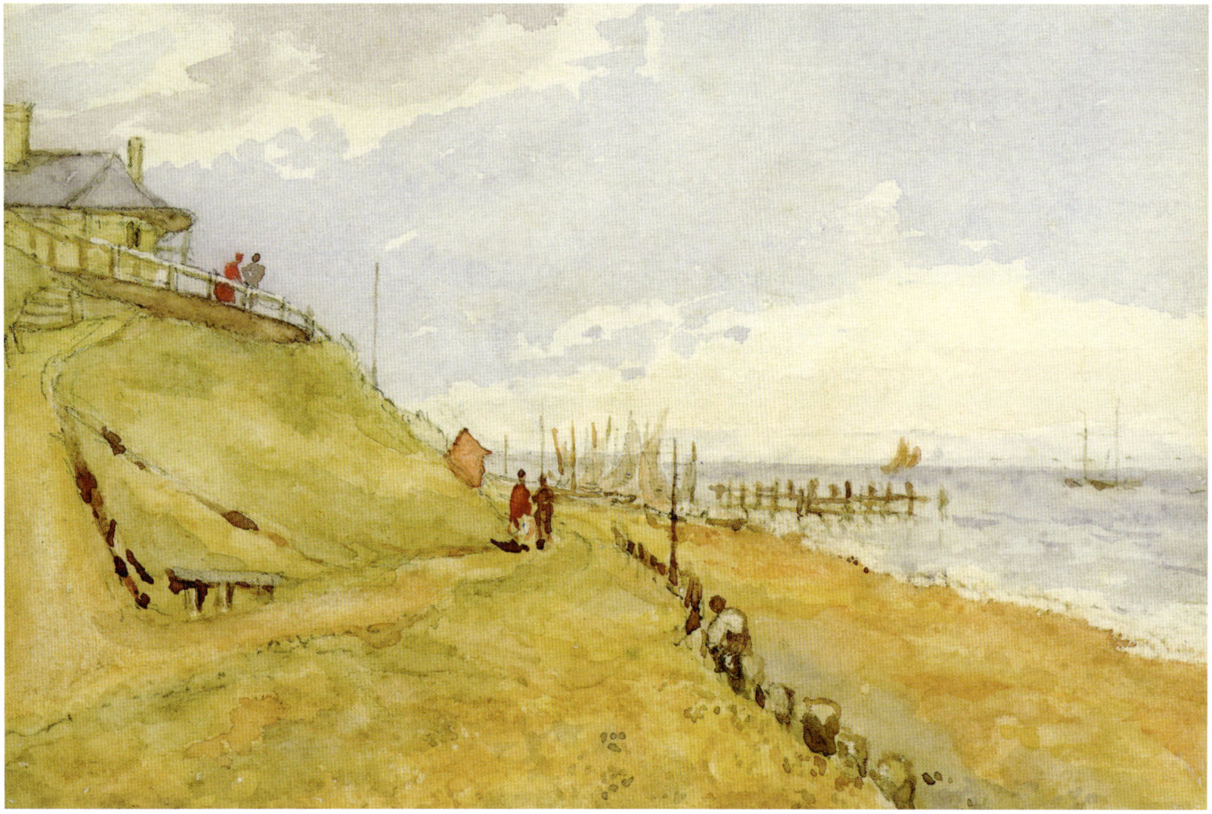

*Southwold Beach,*
Thomas Churchyard, watercolour.

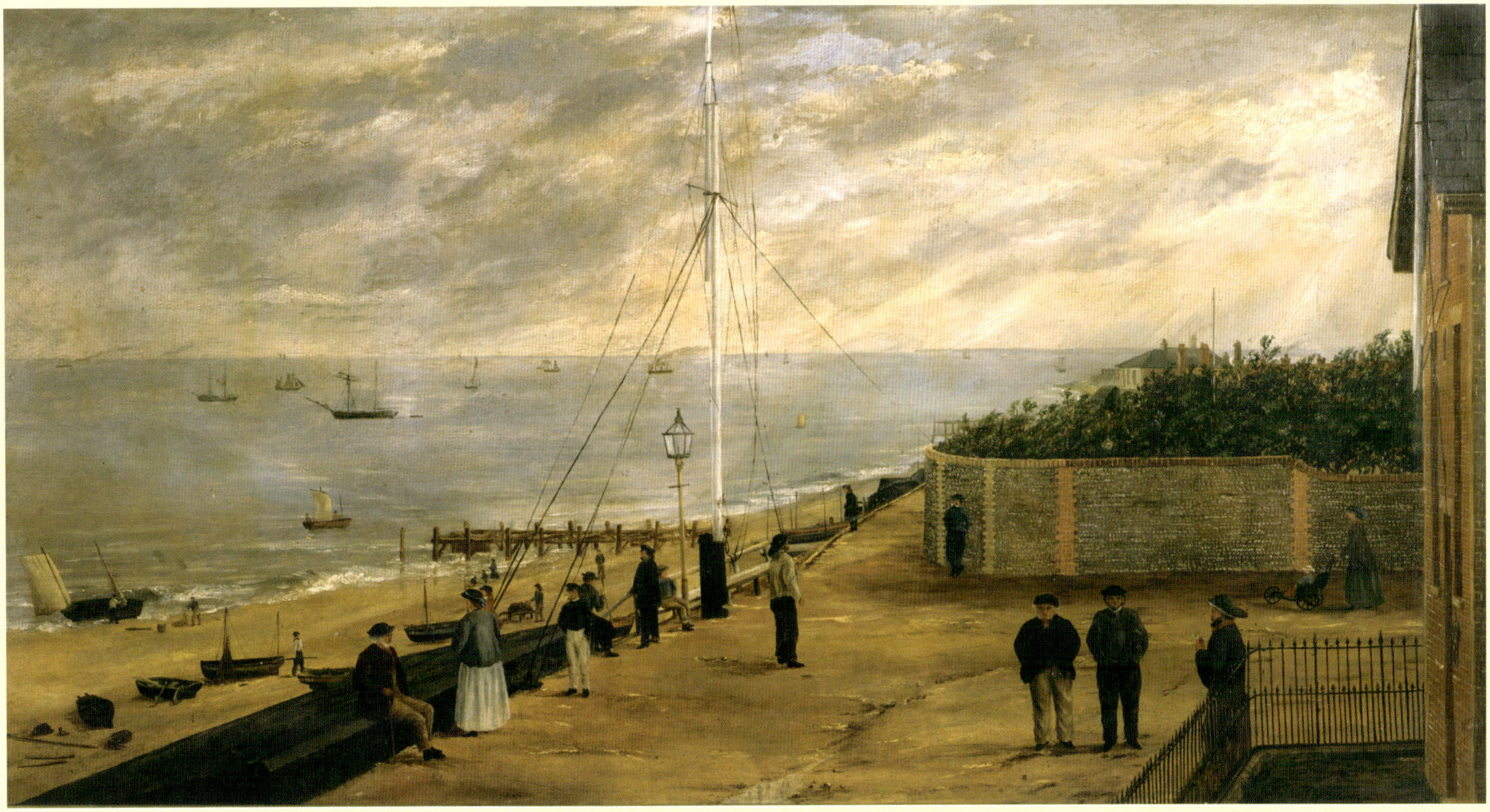

This image by EDWARD RALPH BLACKETT, now hanging in Southwold Town Hall, shows Long Island Cliff and the Sailors' Reading Room. It was painted in 1868 – the year William Morris holidayed in Southwold. Blackett, a local doctor, took as his vantage point the town's new social centre, looking over a cliff whose name denotes a historic bond with America (the settlement of Southold, on Long Island, having been founded by natives of Southwold).

Meanwhile, William Morris (1834-1896) – pioneering artist, poet, novelist, conservationist, socialist, activist, translator, romantic dreamer, commune-maker and designer and manufacturer of furniture, fabrics, wallpaper, stained glass, tapestries and books – had architecture as his first and last love. He found much of interest in the Blyth Valley. But in Southwold he suffered a lovelorn holiday, suspecting that passionate letters were being exchanged between his wife Janey and the poet and painter Dante Gabriel Rossetti, their close friend back in London. The architect of a rural utopia would remember this particular rural landscape as 'a mournful place'.

Morris was probably drawn to Southwold and still more to Blythburgh following recent visits by fellow artist George Wardle, with whom he later founded the Society for the Protection of Ancient Buildings. Wardle left exquisite pencil, ink and watercolour drawings of church features and treasures. Some are now in the Victoria and Albert Museum together with a photograph by 'J. Court Photographic Artist, Southwold' showing St Edmund's church interior and a woman believed to be Mrs Madeleine Wardle. Before her marriage, Madeleine Smith had been tried in Scotland on a charge of murdering her lover with poison. The case was found Not Proven.

By coincidence, one of Churchyard's chosen subjects for his Southwold sketches was later copied by roving Suffolk artist **THOMAS SMYTHE** (1825-1906), in an oil study of the beach wrongly linked to Dunwich in subsequent decades (illustrated p.22). He exhibited Southwold pictures with the Ipswich Art Club on three occasions from 1879. His favourite views seen from the harbour suggest an unchanging town, but major shifts were signalled with the arrival of the railway, not least in the imminent decline of the port and the end of river navigation. All this Smythe would have noted in his visits during the 1880s. Fifteen years younger than his more celebrated painter brother, Edward Robert (1810-1899), Thomas

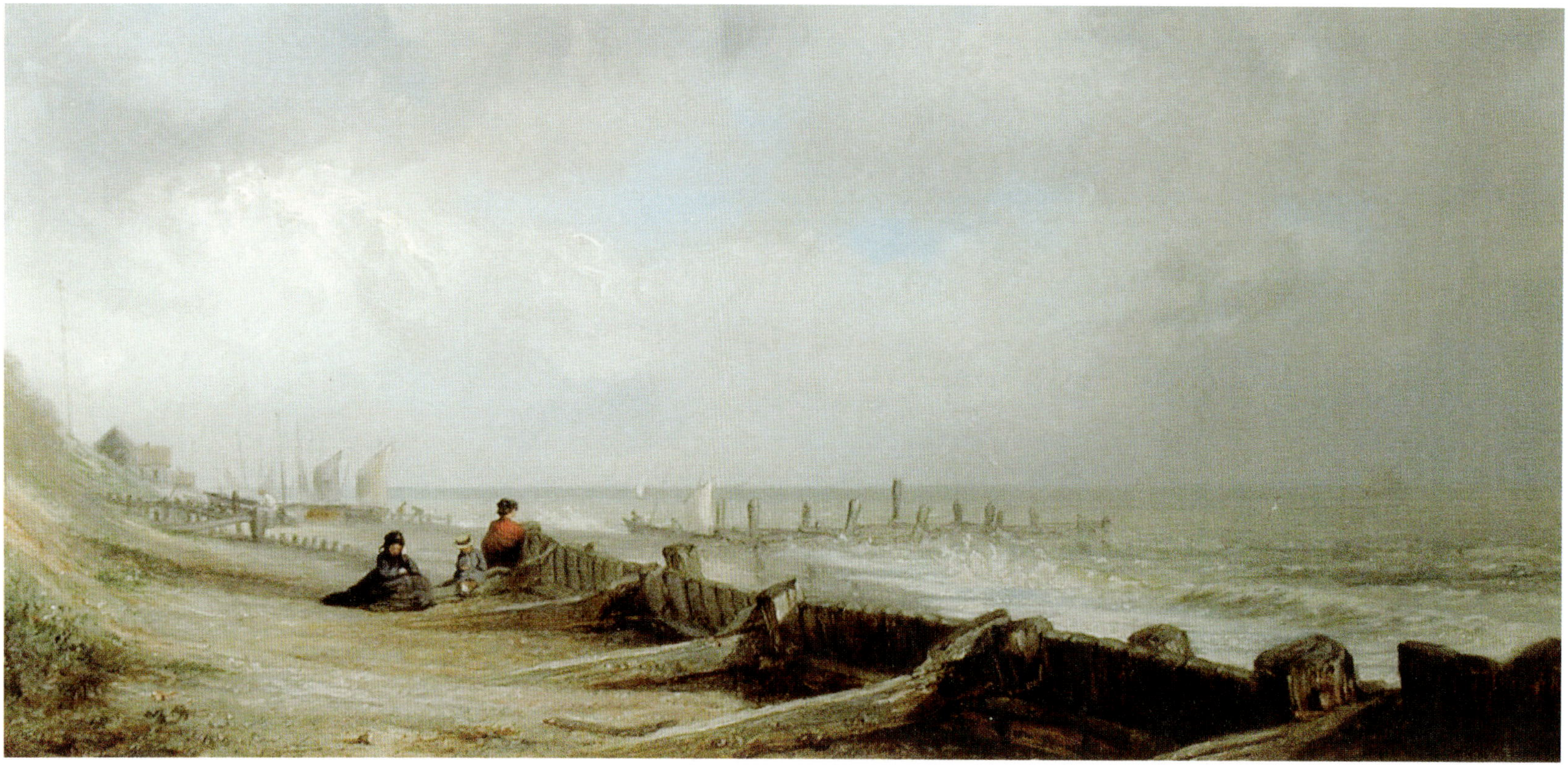

had five children – the eldest of whom, also called Thomas, displayed promise as an artist before his death in a bicycling accident at the age of 19. Ernest, the second son, became a book illustrator in London, where Thomas senior would spend his last seven years.

After being invalided out of the last world war and being given only a few years to live, as will be outlined in a later chapter, artist-architect Clifford Russell spent several decades admiring the buildings of the Blyth Valley. This 1949 watercolour of Southwold High Street from the marketplace shows that the heart of the town has been almost unchanged over six decades save for the recent invasion of traffic. The cast iron waterpump-lampstand of 1873 in the foreground, by George Child, stands on the site of the Charles II covered Market Cross which was dismantled in 1809 – James Maggs numbering the weathervane among his salvaged souvenirs.

**HUGH FULLER** (b1933) has a particular eye to appreciate the vernacular architecture of Southwold, having been the fourth generation in a family building business in the capital now run by his son - a firm founded by a carpenter forebear who moved from Woodbridge to London in the 1870s. He has completed numerous commissions on listed buildings, for

*Southwold Beach,* Thomas Smythe, oil on canvas.

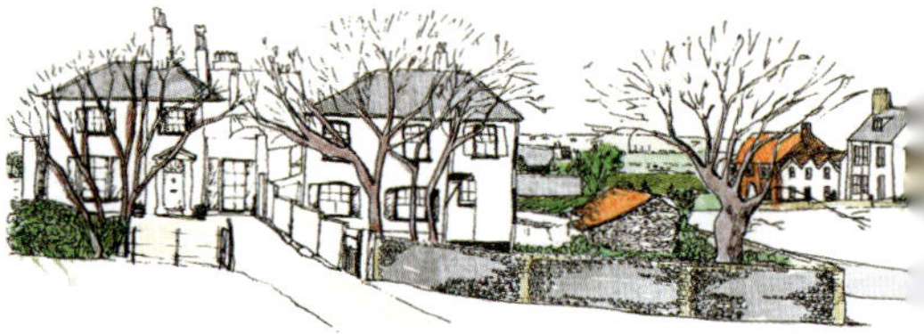

*Southwold High Street from the Marketplace,* Clifford Russell, watercolour.

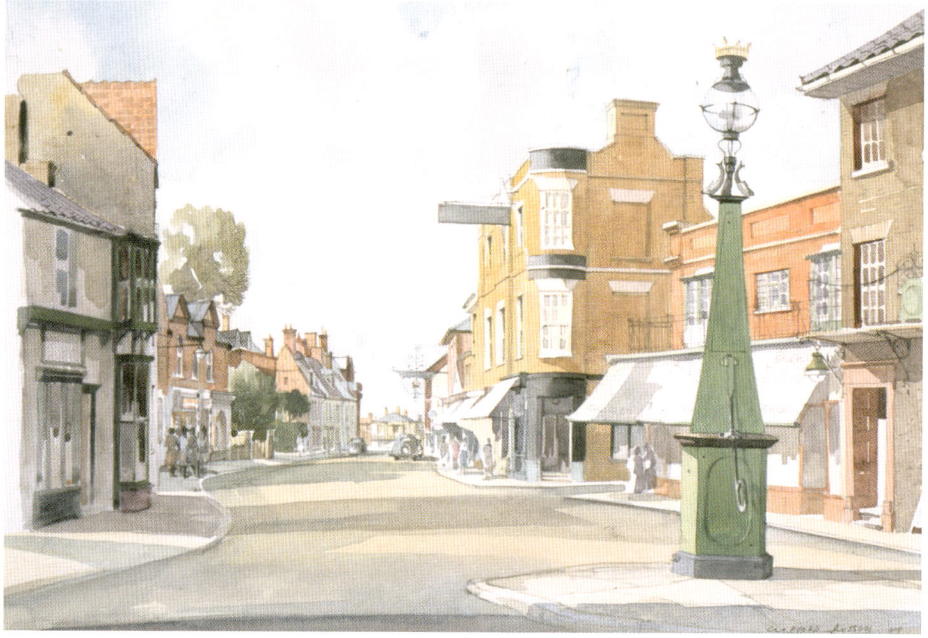

instance replacing an Inigo Jones gateway to St Paul's Covent Garden and working on Wren churches from All Hallows London Wall to St Giles Cripplegate. His wife Ann ran Ann Fuller Designs, starting with peg dolls for Liberty's and ending with 60 outworkers producing her novelty gifts.

The Fullers moved to Southwold in 1997, beautifully restoring Ginger's Cottage on South Green. Each year they produce an ingenious hand-made Christmas card – with pop-up model of Southwold's church or railway, a snowman flying a kite on the Common or the front of their house with lit Christmas trees wired to a star. Their 2003 card was Hugh's montage of historic and idiosyncratic Southwold houses, shown here. It has been printed on to a fund-raising mug for the town museum in Victoria Street, whose Dutch gable is among the featured facades.

Another creator of splendid Christmas cards is Woodbridge-born **SALLY KIBBLE** (b1955), who, along with her husband David, has also brilliantly restored a house on South Green. She makes panoramic watercolour drawings of topographical views from the Common or the lighthouse, and this charming rollcall of her South Green and Constitution Hill neighbours, a print of which is now in the Southwold Museum collection. The Kibbles have run the Suffolk-based company Plastic for Games since winning the UK concession in the 1980s for the wheels and wedges of a new board-game called Trivial Pursuit. Now each year they export millions of dice all over the world. Sally has published a comic novel entitled *Sowl Searching*, featuring a Southwold ghost-buster called Jessie Precious, a reincarnation of devil dog Black Shuck and Satan himself. She has also written a historical saga based on the life of Thomas Churchyard.

*South Green*, Sally Kibble.

*Southwold Houses*, Hugh Fuller (bottom).

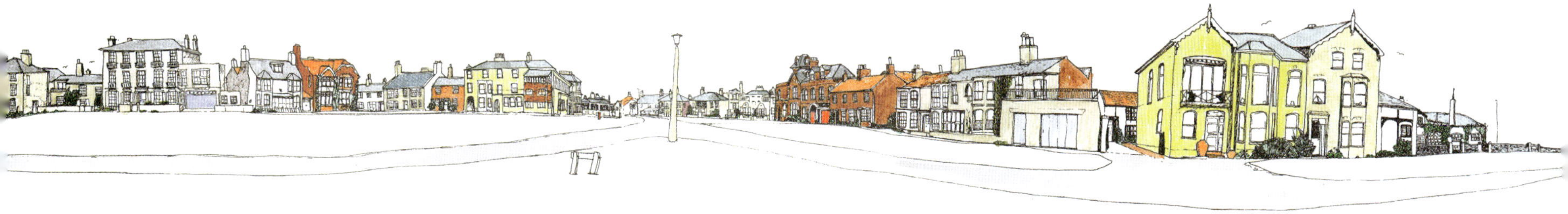

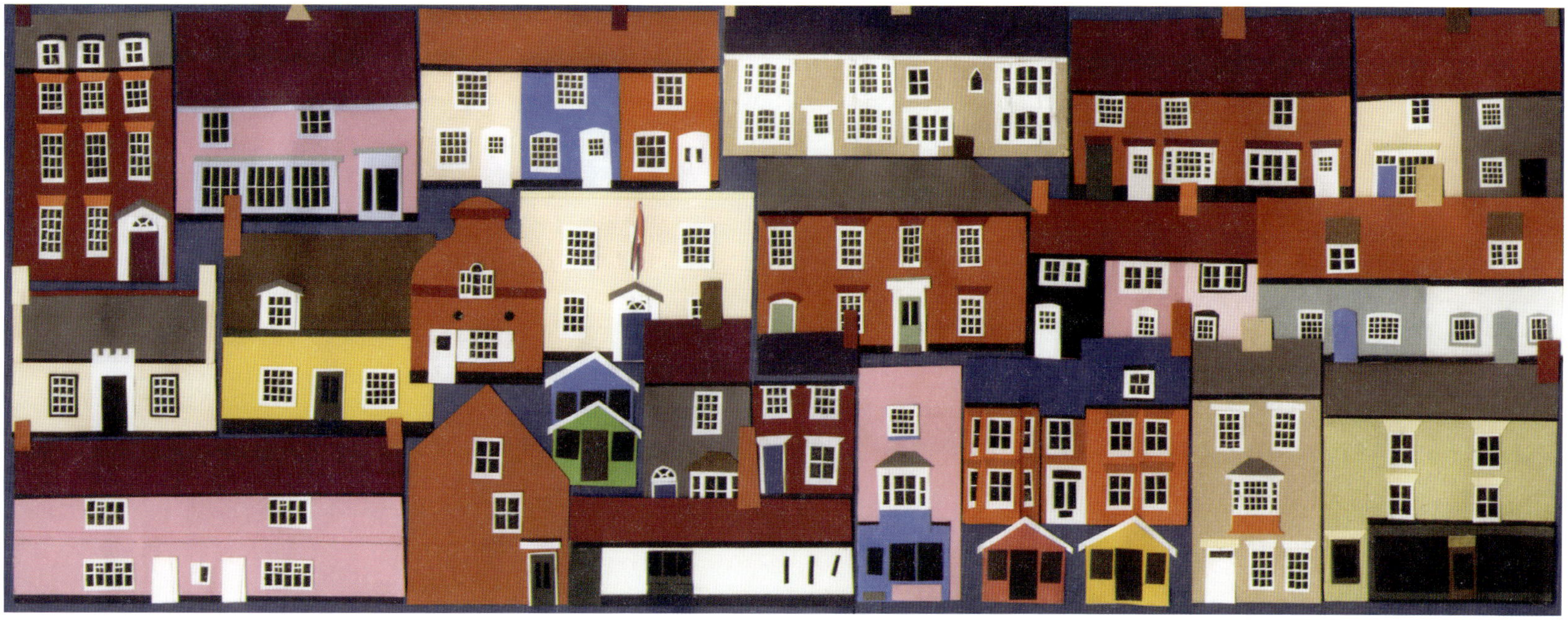

*Southwold II*, John Piper,
watercolour and gouache, 1965.

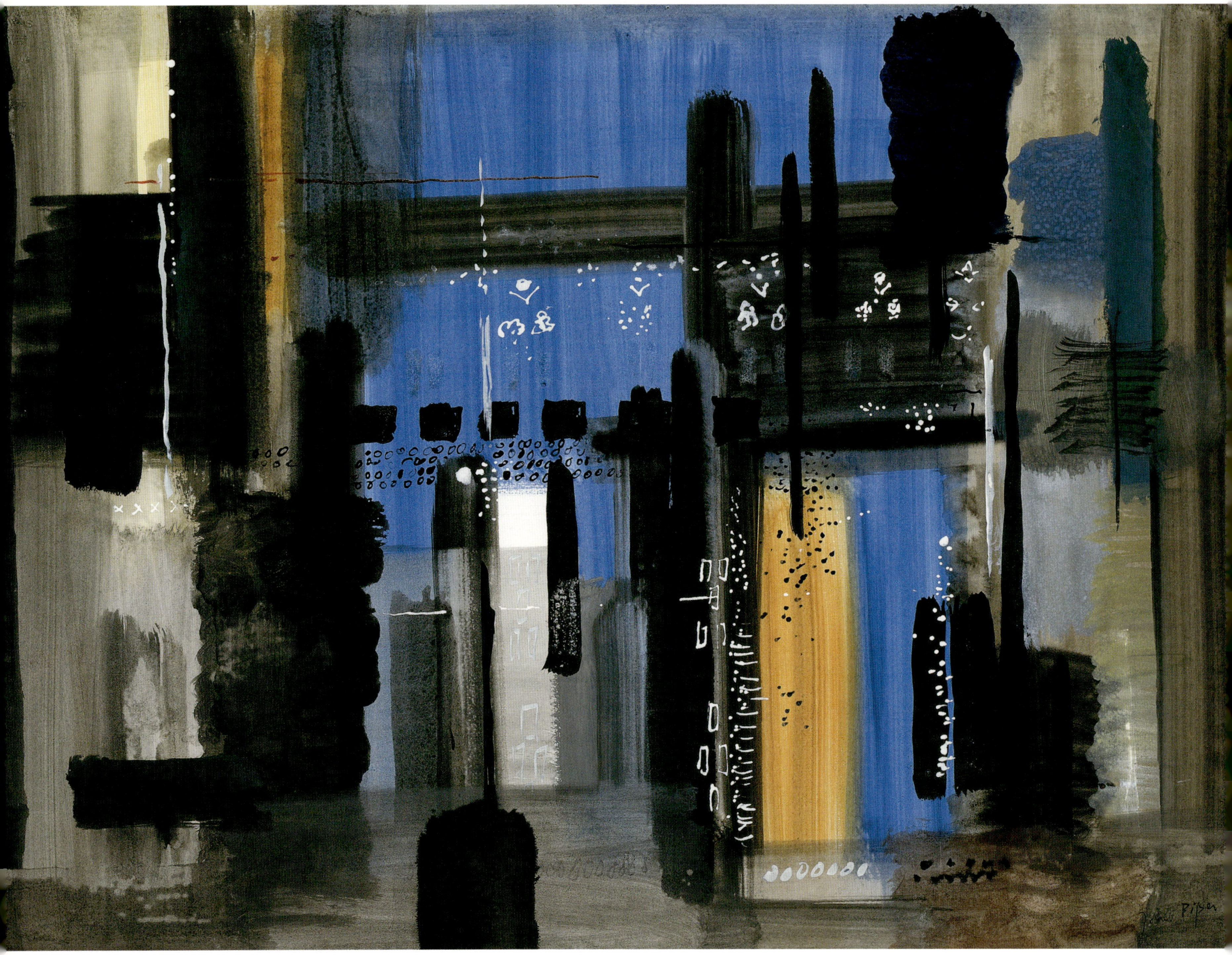

Chapter Four

# Brilliant Beacons

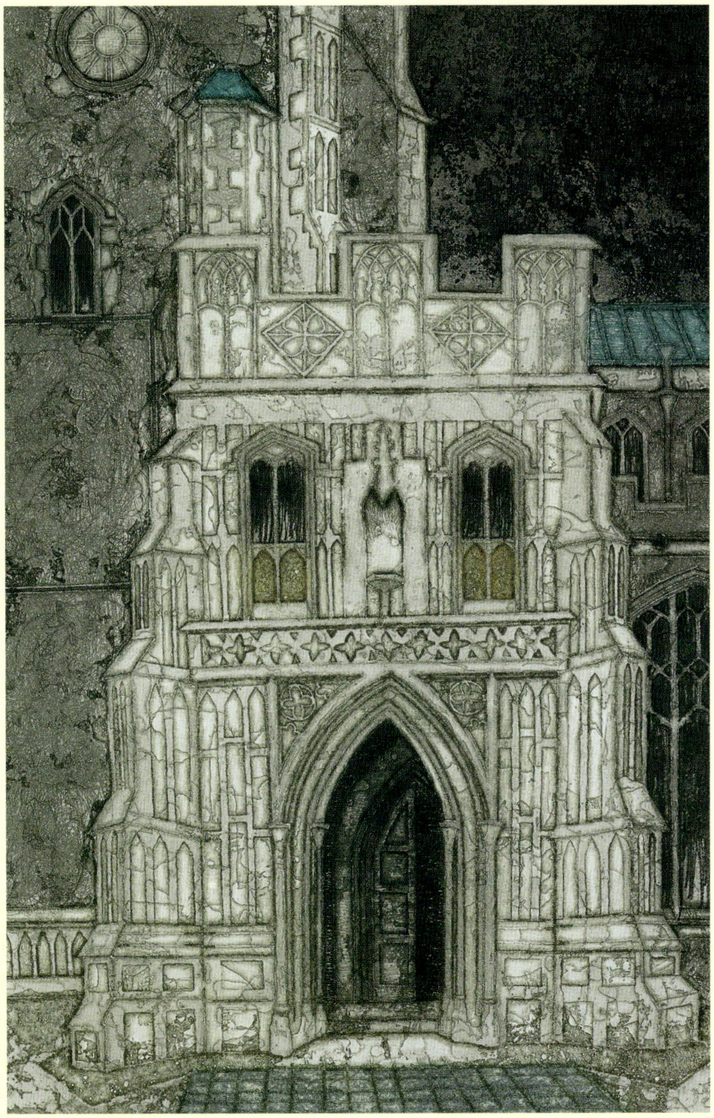

London-born painter and print-maker VALERIE THORNTON (1931-1991), who lived latterly at Chelsworth near Hadleigh, produced a series of etchings of East Anglian churches from the 1970s, among which was this striking etching and aquatint of the porch at Southwold. Afterwards she found inspiration in Romanesque religious buildings in France, Spain and Italy. An artist of great precision, she was fascinated by the effects of weathering and erosion on ancient stone.

Fifteenth-century Suffolk saw a frenzy of church construction, with new and remodelled buildings soaring straight towards Heaven in the Perpendicular style. Coastal towers also served as beacons for shipping while interiors were universally rife with kaleidoscopic colour – the faithful being guided by cautionary and celebratory tales recounted in wall paintings, stained glass and carved and decorated wood. Endowed with what has been described as 'post mortem fire insurance', parish churches became spectacular galleries of folk and fine art. Southwold's great church to St Edmund had arisen within barely a generation and was then most splendidly adorned. With the passing of the centuries it is hard to imagine the sensation of stepping into this late medieval miracle when gleamingly new. But perhaps **JOHN PIPER** (1903-1992) gives a glimpse into history in the picture shown here. In the late 1930s a fear that Britain's architectural treasures were about to be blitzed returned an abstract artist to the fragile real world. For the rest of his long life he toured the country, focusing on buildings which had withstood human and elemental wreckers – but, as few of these subjects were entirely unscathed, an elegiac note still crept into most of his prints and paintings. Piper loved to depict Suffolk churches, having a deep affection for Covehithe and Blythburgh and also providing the memorial stained glass window at Aldeburgh to his friend Benjamin Britten.

Although our patch of north-eastern Suffolk produced many nameless artists and craftsmen who spent their working lives on religious commissions, it also nurtured a notorious Civil War iconoclast. William Dowsing, yeoman farmer from Laxfield, was driven by puritan piety to remove 'superstitious' imagery from churches across and beyond East Anglia. In a week-long trawl, lasting April 3-9 1644, he and his deputies visited Kenton, Bedingfield, Tannington,

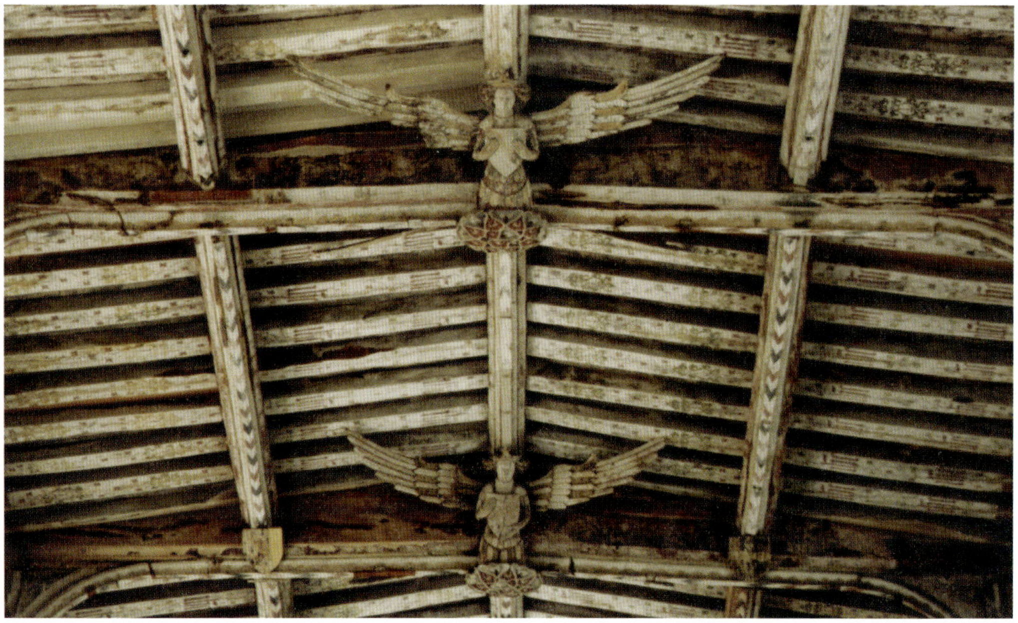

Angel roof, Blythburgh – medieval carvings which flew beyond the grasp of puritan vandals.

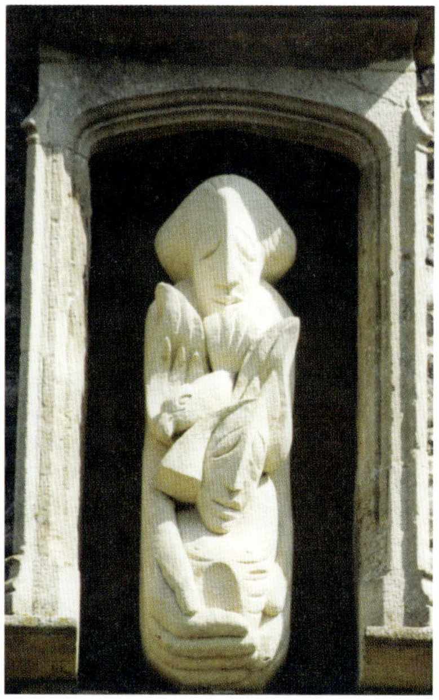

Blythburgh's church porch holds this Holy Trinity sculpture by NICHOLAS MYNHEER (b1958).

Brundish, Wilby, Stradbroke, Linstead Parva, Linstead Magna, Chediston, Halesworth, Great Redisham, Ringsfield, Beccles, Ellough, Sotterley, Benacre, Covehithe, Rushmere, Mutford, Frostenden, South Cove, Reydon, Southwold, Walberswick, Blyford, Blythburgh, Dunwich (St Peter's and All Saints'), Bramfield and Heveningham. The destruction of thousands of pictures, sculptures and inscriptions in these 30 churches – on the spot or outlined in orders to parishioners to be completed within days – was meticulously recorded in the journals Dowsing regarded as a report to God. Presumably the church at Easton Bavents was spared because it was already slipping into the sea. Certainly the cost of puritanical cleansing helped to spur the people of Covehithe and Walberswick into demolishing their grand structures later in the 17th century, and raising smaller churches within the ruins.

It is astonishing to think that the clear light and plain beauty now so admired in Blythburgh's 'Cathedral of the Marshes' was achieved by smashing and burning. The attack on adornment continued, though more unwittingly, when 18th century jackdaw-clearance peppered the faces of surviving ceiling angels (too high for Dowsing to topple) with shot. With a ravaging sea, and a rising nonconformist tide which filled barns and cottages with worshippers, empty Anglican churches fell into dereliction. But romantic ruins attract artists. And dwindling Dunwich, keeping two MPs but few constituents, fascinated lovers of gothic melancholy. Scores of Georgian and

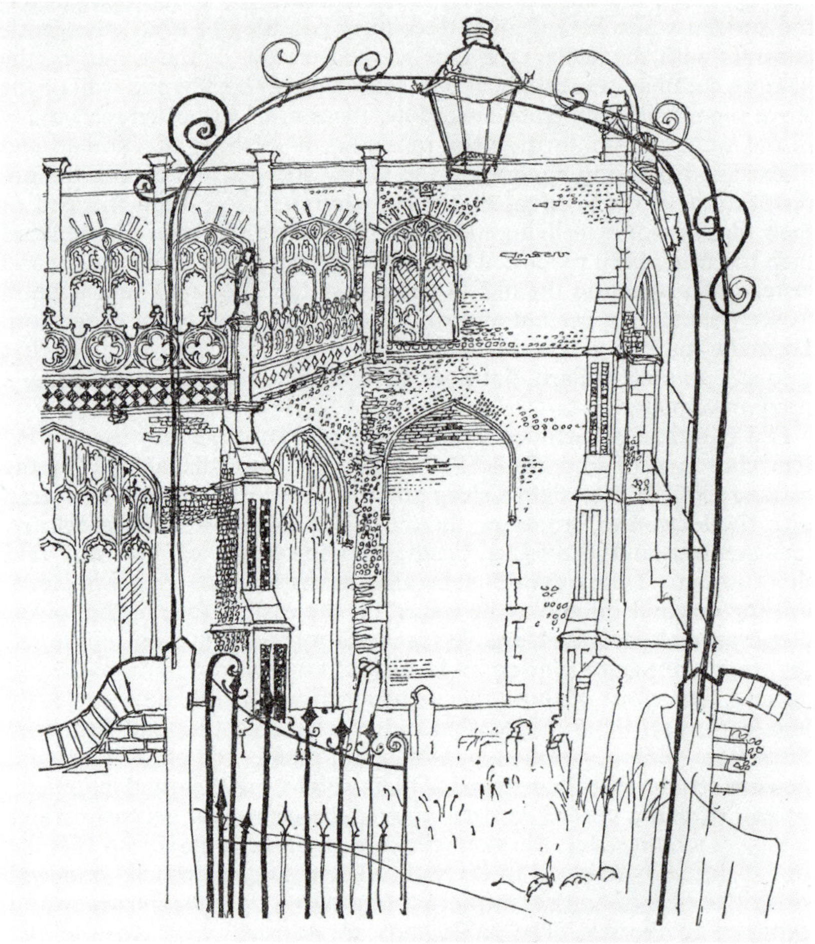

*Blythburgh Church*, John Piper, ink drawing for John Betjeman's *English Parish Churches*, (1958).

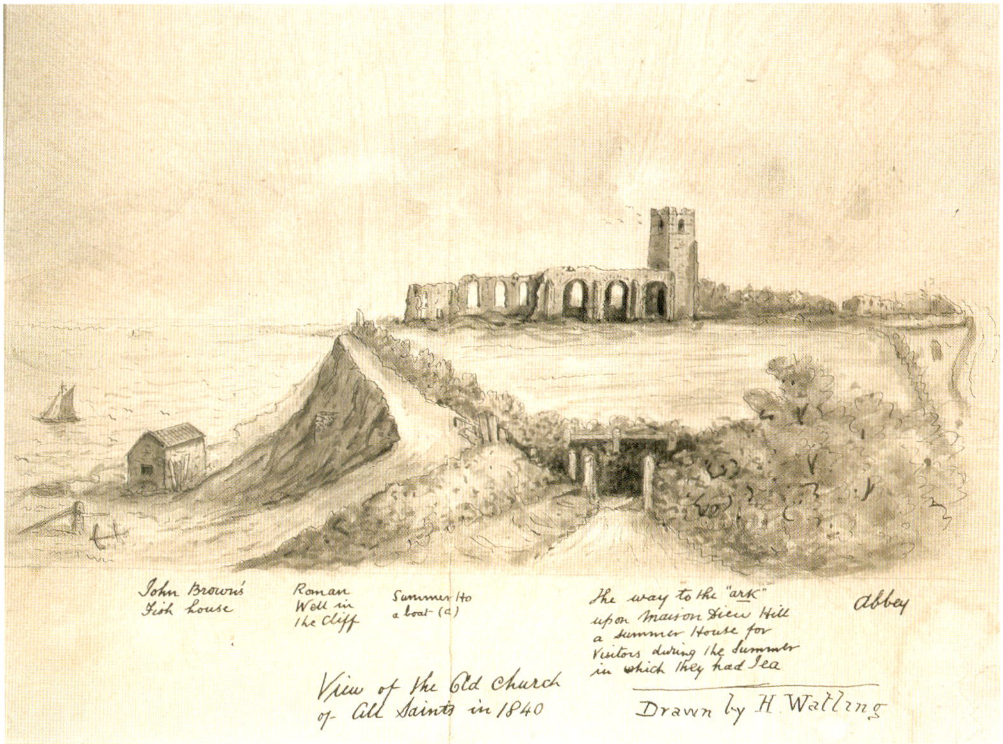


*View of All Saints', Dunwich,* Hamlet Watling, drawing.

Victorian artists depicted All Saints' – the last great medieval church of Dunwich – as the building came step by step to the cliff edge and then, in the early years of the 20th century, toppled arch by arch over it. These recorders ranged from Henry Bright (1814-1873), a clockmaker's son from Saxmundham who moved to Norwich as an apprentice chemist but changed course after art lessons from John Sell Cotman and others, to Charles Keene (star of a later chapter) and Nelson Dawson (1859-1941).

The battered wealth of Suffolk churches in the 19th century was recorded by antiquarian artist **HAMLET WATLING** (1818-1908) in many hundreds of drawings and watercolours. This teacher's son from Kelsale started his own school in Wangford, also living in Dunwich for six years before taking another teaching post in Earl Stonham and finally retiring to Ipswich. He began by cataloguing Southwold's church treasures, and later made copies of these drawings for sale at local charity bazaars. He also had an abiding interest in Blythburgh. His precise records are now invaluable documents – also being cited in the preservation versus restoration argument which raged among Victorians as crumbling churches all over the country were done up or done in.

In 1874, amid much muttering, Southwold called in portrait painter George Richmond (1809-1896) to revive the rood screen installed 400 years earlier and whose fine quality suggests the genius of the Ranworth screen-painting school. Scratches to the faces of angels, apostles and prophets were believed to have been caused less by Puritan vandals than by Victorians who propped umbrellas against the painted panels. Though untrained as a

ANDREW DODDS (1927-2004), whose drawings and watercolours appeared in many books and magazines, and in the *Eastern Daily Press* each week for almost 50 years, often sketched in Southwold. This churchyard study from 2003 features a carved stone memorial to David May – great-uncle of lifeboat coxswain Sam May – who was slain by pirates in the Gulf of Florida, aboard the Indiaman Ann West, in 1819. Only he and the captain resisted the attack and their bodies were never recovered, though the killers were later captured and hanged. The epitaph 'inscribed by his Widow as the last Melancholy tribute of Affection' reads:

Not yet have ceas'd to flow a Widow's tears
O'er scenes remembered amidst the lapse of years
On foreign Seas he fell, but not by storm
When boist'rous winds the heaving waves deform
Nor by the Rock beneath the tide conceal'd
Nor by the Sword which warring nations wield
But by the foe receiv'd in Friendship's guise
By hand of treach'rous Pirates Lo he dies
Thou, too, art mortal hast'ning to the grave

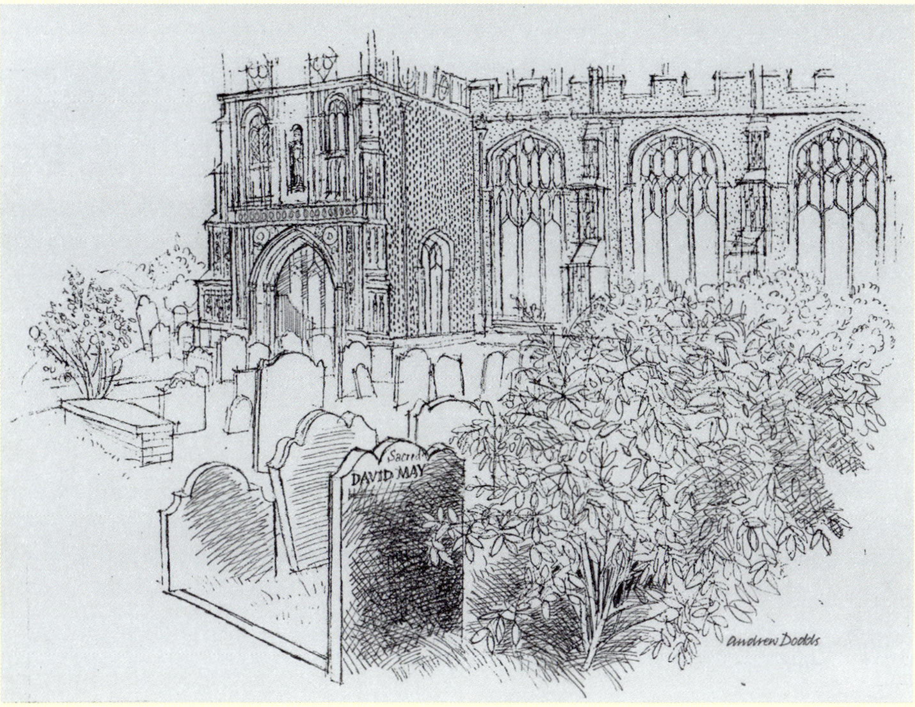

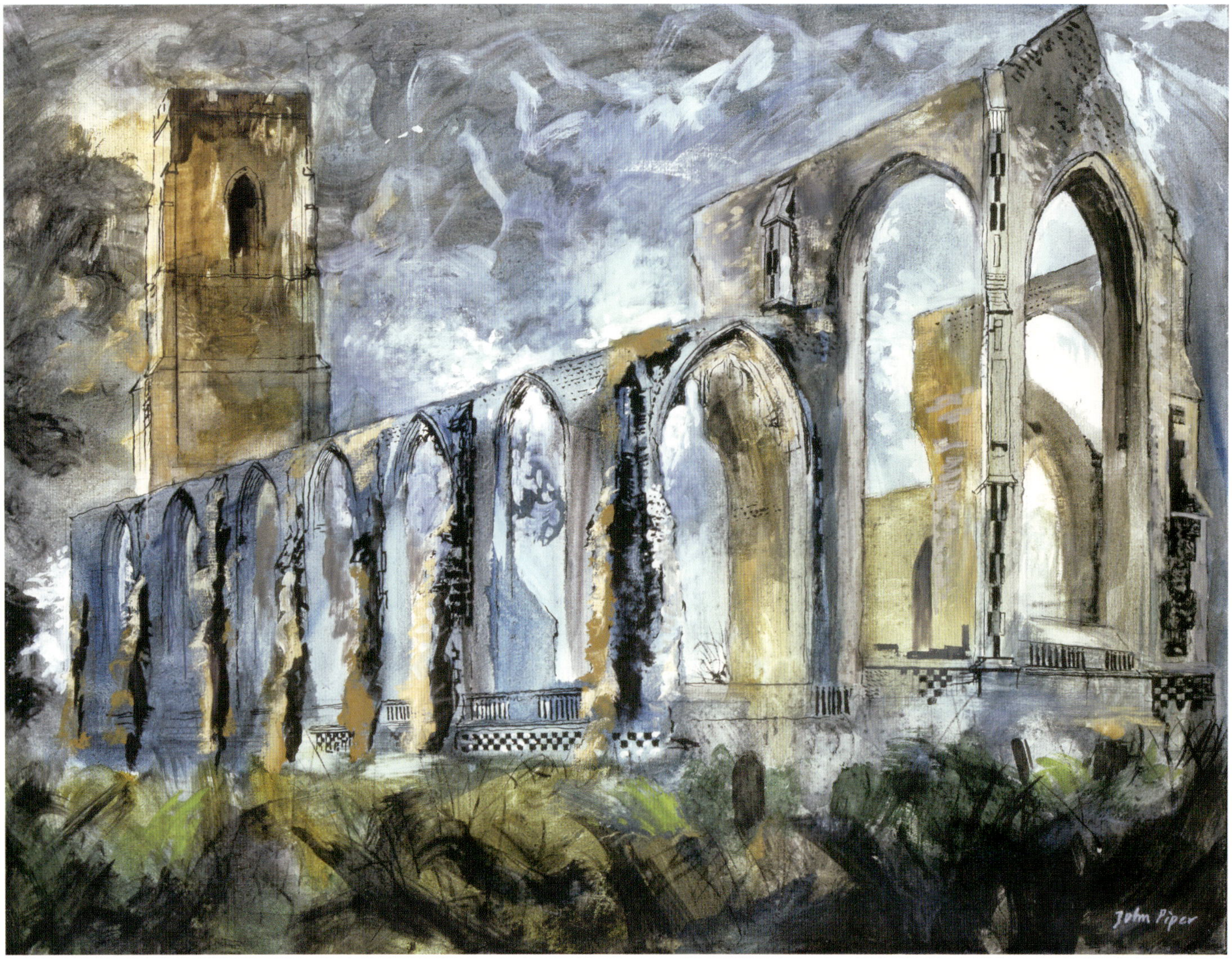


*Covehithe Church*, John Piper, watercolour.

GERARD STAMP (b1955) a past master in the art of advertising, snapped some rather golden chains to work as a Cotman-influenced watercolourist and draughtsman in rural North Norfolk. His first solo show, a sellout success at the Norwich Grapevine Gallery in 2005, comprised lyrical views of East Anglian churches and landscapes - including this study of Covehithe. Steeped in the work of the East Anglian greats, he opens his website with a famous quote from John Constable: 'Painting is but another word for feeling.' Agony is another word for feeling, too. In the run-up to that debut exhibition there were several frustrating years when Stamp drew and painted largely for the bonfire, before he slowly began to make a mark as he wished. The artist's brother is the architectural historian Gavin Stamp.

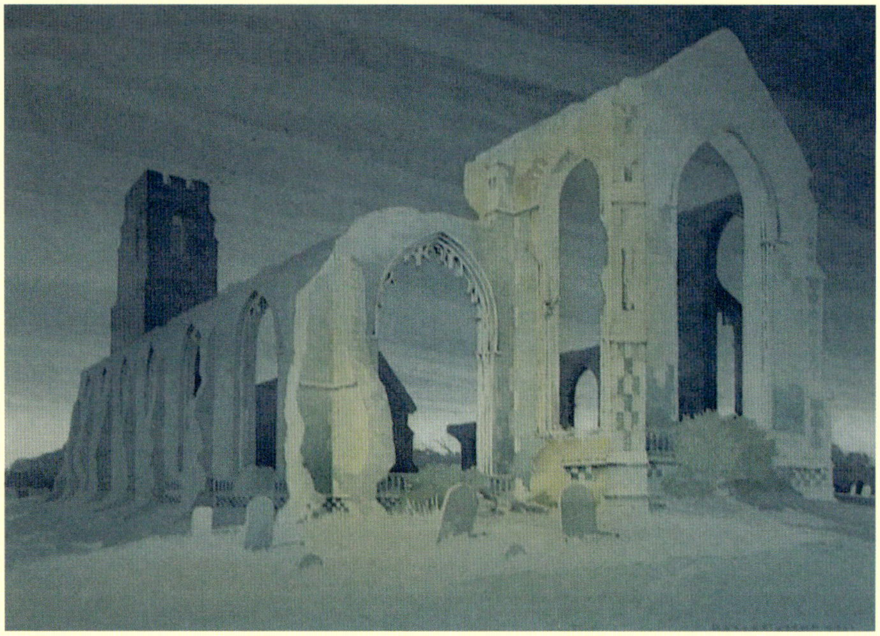

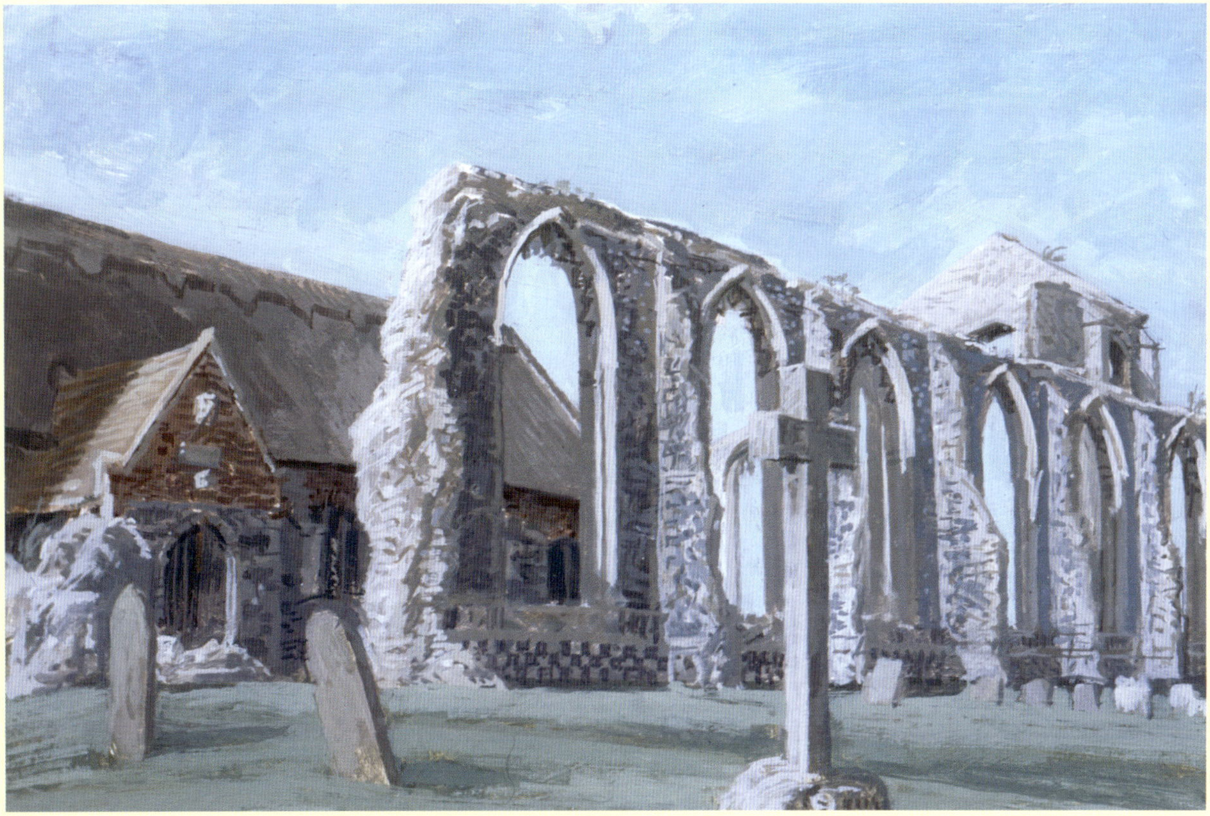

Covehithe's church continues to fascinate artists as the cliff edge moves closer year by year. In these contrasting oils of 2002 architectural painter and muralist ALAN DODD (b1942), who lives near Beccles, concentrates on the thatched chapel within the ruins. CAROLINE McADAM CLARK (b1947), drawn to wild landscape from Orkney to Suffolk, steps back to depict the church like a child's sandcastle about to be engulfed by the sea.

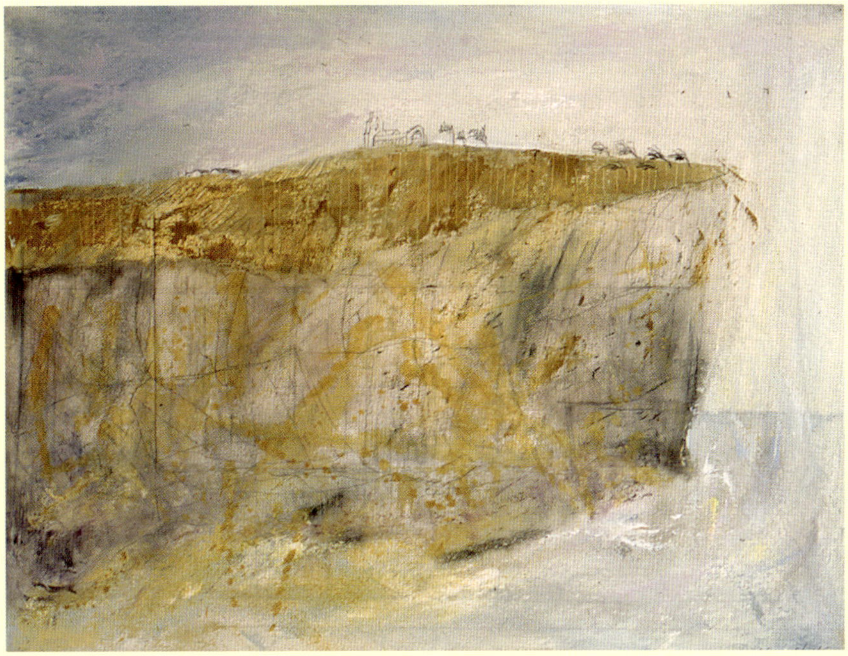

conservator, the Royal Academician employed a sympathetic touch – with occasional quirky flourishes (St Jude came to resemble the incumbent rector). His skills were handed down to his son Sir William Blake Richmond, who rented Southwold's Centre Cliff House and also the Worlingham estate near Beccles and who decorated the dome of St Paul's Cathedral.

The worsening condition of Holy Trinity Blythburgh during the 19th century culminated in its closure in 1881 for three years after warnings that the roof could collapse. The Society for the Protection of Ancient Buildings had been founded by William Morris, George Wardle and Philip Webb in 1877, to resist the rebuilding of medieval relics with inappropriate styles, methods and materials, and the Suffolk church became a test case. A 25-year struggle ensued. When Morris visited the church in the summer of 1895 he did at least ensure that the south porch was repaired rather than restored. But in 1906 when a local committee held fast to restoration plans drawn up by father and son architects George Edmund and Arthur Street – despite appeals from influential supporters of Morris such as Queen Victoria's sculptor daughter, Princess Louise - SPAB withdrew from the

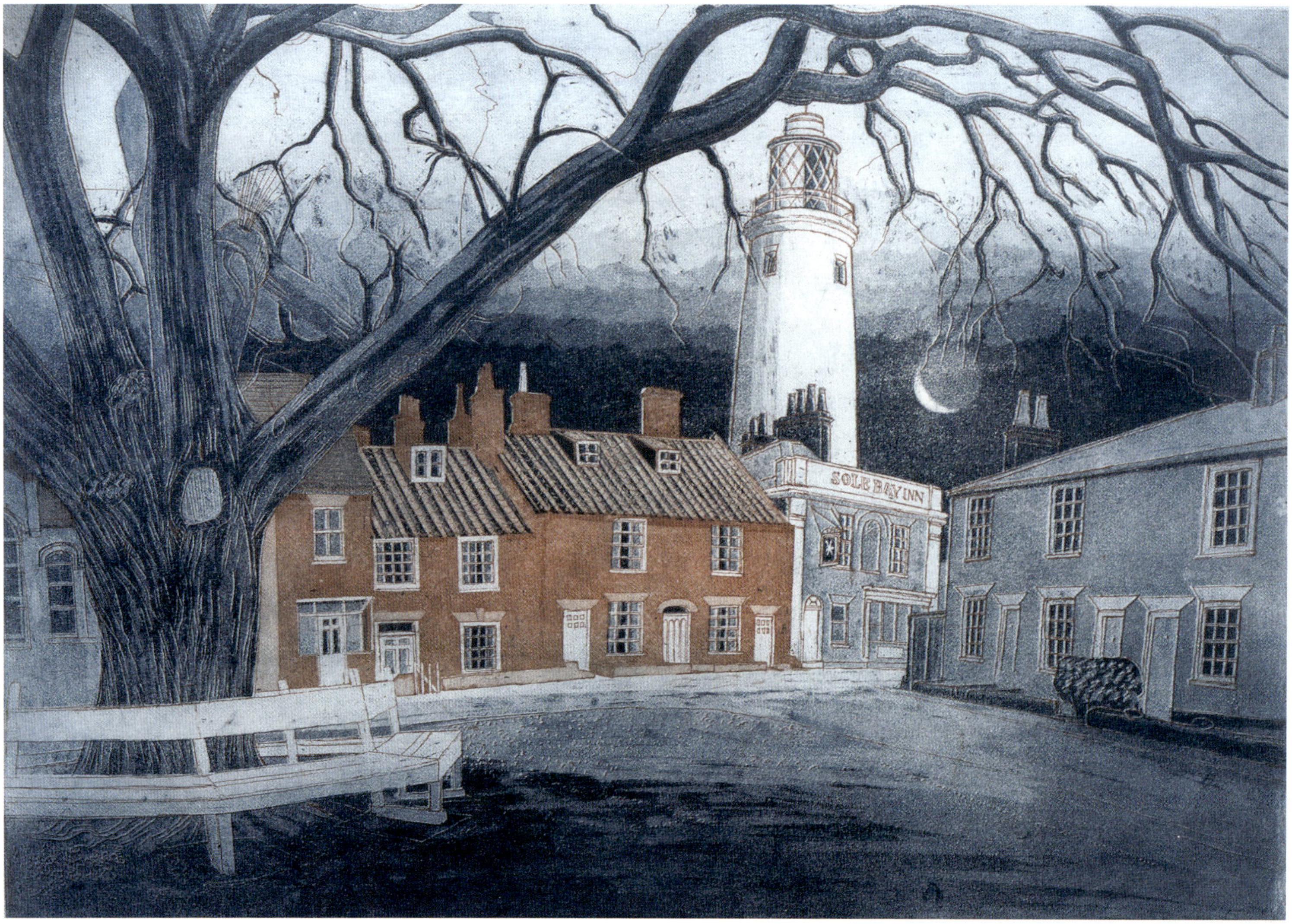


*East Green*, Richard Bawden, aquatint (top).
*Southwold*, Edward Bawden (right).

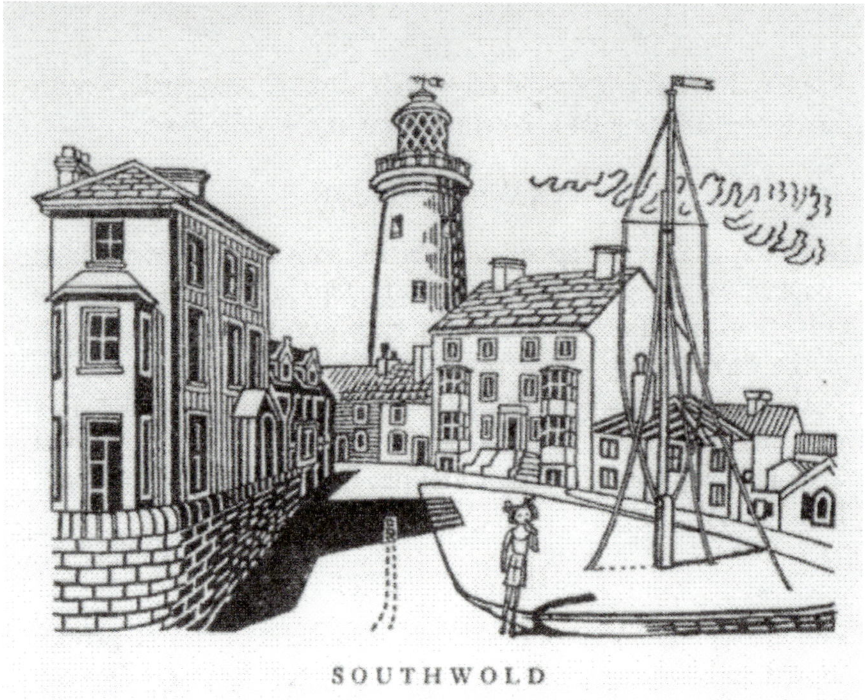


project in apparent defeat. But the Arts and Crafts pioneer had ensured at least a partial victory – because no one cared or dared to fund a scheme opposed by so great an arbiter of taste as William Morris. Over the centuries a lack of cash has saved a lot of ancient architecture.

Ironically, amid all the furore and deadlock over Holy Trinity, two Royal Academicians radically remodelled ancient buildings in the shadow of the church. Military artist Ernest Crofts (1847-1911) and Sir John Seymour Lucas (1849-1923) – purveyor of Victorian scenes, stage designs and book illustrations – rebuilt The Green and The Priory in the late Edwardian era to mimic model medieval survivals. Mr Crofts, however, met a very modern fate – being killed in a car accident near his Blythburgh home. He was the RA's Keeper at the time and his students provided a wall tablet in the church in his memory.

In recent decades art has returned to local churches, with new sculptures above the porches at Southwold and Blythburgh. The 1954 east window in Southwold's church was the last work of Ninian Comper and the marvellous engraved figure of St Edmund, the young warrior king, in a memorial window to the Tennyson family was completed by New Zealand-born John Hutton (1906-1978) at the last minute. Shortly before the dedication service, the self-taught craftsman-artist best known for a screen in Coventry Cathedral ascended a step ladder with his power tool and added finishing touches to the saint's face in a master stroke of skill and nerve. Churchyards are also being renewed as sacred sculpture parks thanks to sterling work from the Suffolk-based Memorials by Artists group.

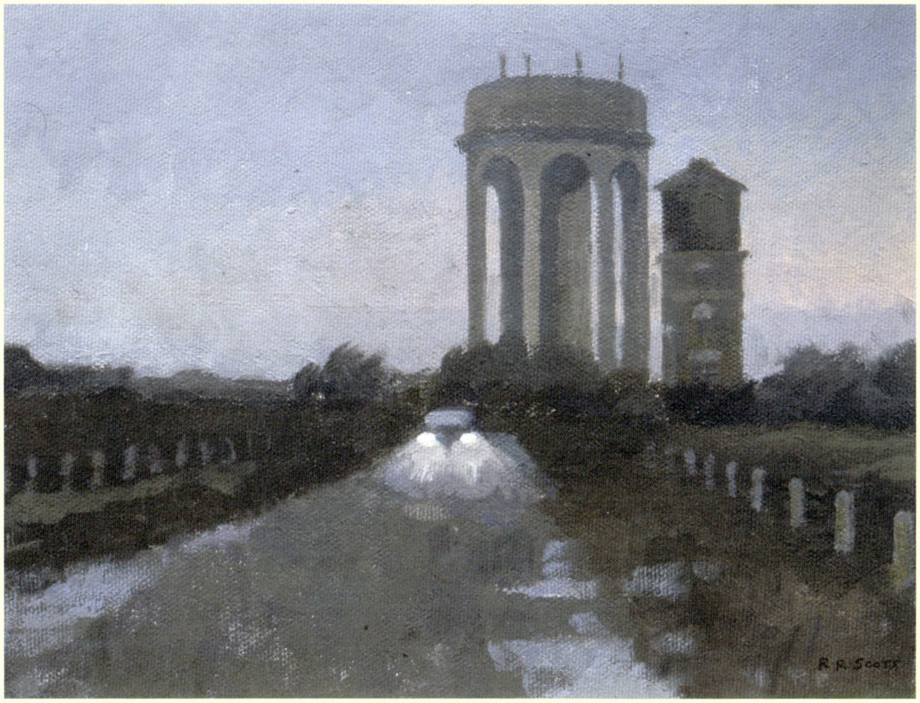

RICHARD SCOTT (b1938) is the historian of artists in Walberswick and a faithful recorder of miniaturist local scenes enlivened by major effects of light. Richard's painter father Eric bought a house behind the dunes at Walberswick in 1950. Richard has lived and worked there since 1965, using an attic studio with a view clear to Sizewell nuclear power station, whose globular and rectangular silhouette has appeared in his eerily-lit pictures. In this image a car illuminates the Southwold harbour road beside the old lighthouse-like water tower of 1886 and the great concrete jellyfish of its 1937 replacement which so offended architectural historian Nikolaus Pevsner.

Originally sail-powered, the Victorian tower is said to be haunted by the ghost of George Neller who, on Valentine's Day 1899, was found mangled between the cogwheels of the pumping house after his coat got caught in the machinery.

But since 1890 the dominance of the church tower in Southwold's profile has been challenged by a brilliant beacon – a 101ft tall white tower with a flashing lantern. A lighthouse was established at Orford Ness in 1637, with a light on the beach and another out to sea from 1720. When the beach light was knocked out for the ninth time, in an exceptional storm of 1887, Trinity House opted for a site further up the coast, more readily visible to shipping approaching from the north. Southwold, on a slope of land nearly four miles east of Orford Ness, was the obvious choice. While the new tower was being built – the materials transported by rail (including the eight-ton lantern in two sections) – a temporary beacon was installed on the denes of California Sands. The new light, originally provided by Argand oil burners, was electrified and unmanned from 1938. The present 1500 watt lamp, flashing red and white every 20 seconds, can be seen at a range of 18 sea miles (33.3km). Various artists have assessed the way in which the warning tower looms large over the little town. Both Carel Weight and Mary Newcomb produced pictures partly drawn from their immense imaginations.

In 1954 Edward Bawden provided a characteristically witty drawing of the view of St James's Green from the sea to help promote *East Anglian Holiday*, a British Transport Films venture. The right-hand corner shows part of the old coastguard station, which had been staffed by retired Royal Navy men (living at 13-29 Victoria Street and walking nightly as far as outpost stations at Covehithe and Minsmere) from at least the 1890s until a 1923 shift to the Casino on Gun Hill. Three decades later Edward's son **RICHARD BAWDEN** (b1936), whose creativity ranges across painting, print-making and illustration, and who has designed everything from garden seats to church windows, came to Southwold. He left with the idea for one of his most powerful images. In this aquatint, from May 1984, moon and lighthouse wink above the Sole Bay pub and an East Green looking all the more ghostly for the natural beacon of the spreading wych elm it later lost.

Benjamin Britten was born in 1913, at 21 Kirkley Cliff Road, a double-fronted, semi-detached villa overlooking the sea at the southern end of Lowestoft. His father, Robert Victor Britten, ran a dental surgery in downstairs rooms. But *Kelly's Directory* for 1904 lists an R.V. Britten operating as a dentist at 13 Market Place Southwold. So the sound of the waves lulling the future composer through childhood might so easily have been heard further down the coast.

As it was, our native musical genius appeared to have leap-frogged over Southwold when, together with Peter Pears and Eric Crozier, he founded a festival at Aldeburgh in 1948. True, Southwold church – like that of Blythburgh – was to host occasional festival concerts. And when Britten's *Peter Grimes* premiered at Sadler's Wells theatre in London in 1945, the saga of a fisherman who had a careless way with apprentices, displayed many authentic Suffolk notes. Based on a George Crabbe poem, and composed largely at Snape, the opera boasted the glorious (North) *Sea Interludes* and a backdrop recognisably Aldeburgh save for one towering detail: looming above the Boar Inn was Southwold lighthouse.

Set and costume designer **KENNETH GREEN** (1905-1986), at that time art master at Wellington College in Berkshire, had wanted to salute his home town – he had lived at Westholme, near The Common, until the late 1920s. The commission came about because his wife and son had been evacuated to Long Island, where they had a chance meeting with Britten and Pears. On returning to England in 1942 the partners contacted Green with family news and learned that he had been a patient of R.V. Britten. The rapport from these coincidences led to an illuminating double portrait – the singer supporting and shadowing the composer – now in the National Portrait Gallery, and a likeness of Britten now in the Britten-Pears Library at Aldeburgh. But the artist's greatest reward, the design of sets and costumes for *Peter Grimes*, went largely unsung as he was eclipsed as Britten's stage designer of choice by John Piper. Although Kenneth Green would paint and draw many tributes to Southwold, illustrate books, produce further theatrical designs and hold a 1971 retrospective show at Kettle's Yard in Cambridge, his career never hit such starry heights again. *Peter Grimes* would not be staged at Aldeburgh until the year 2000.

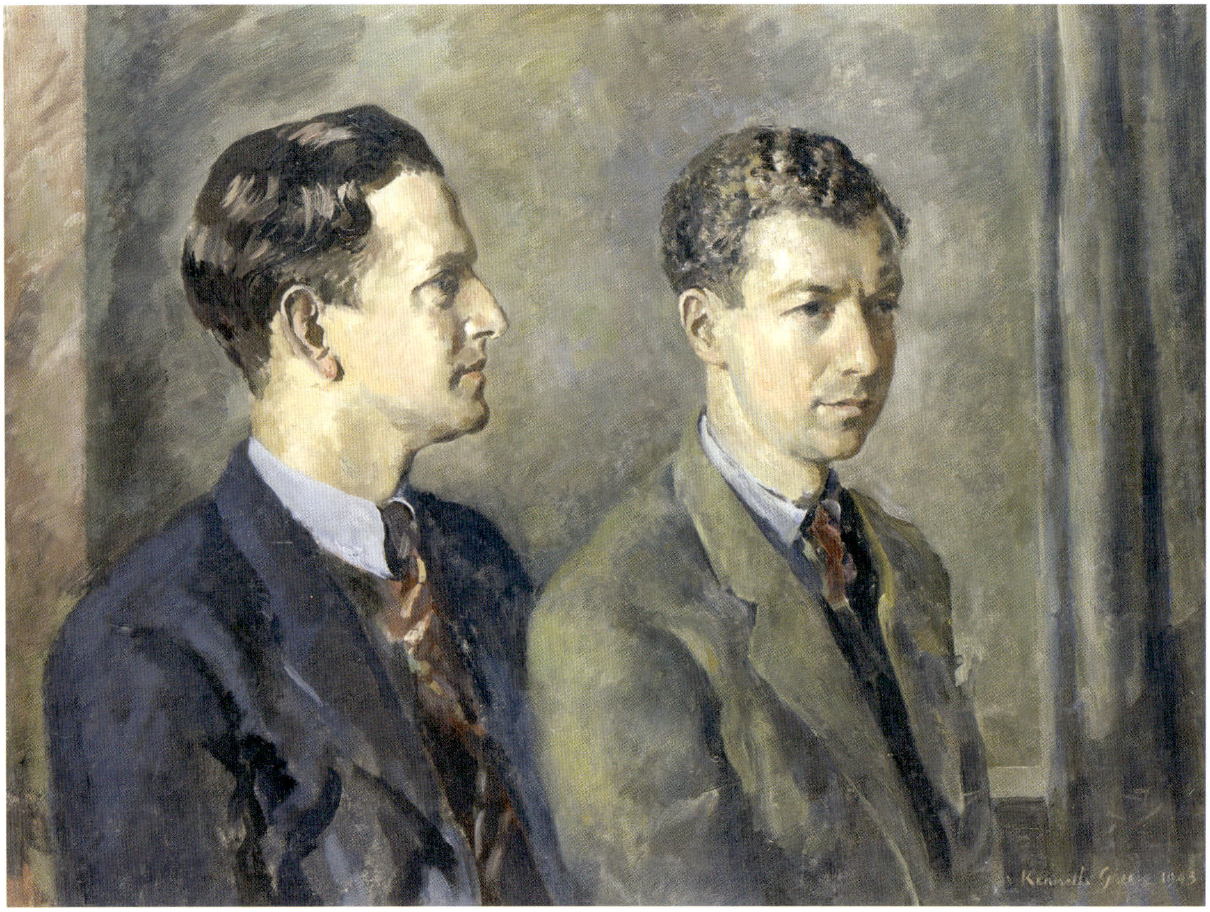


*Peter Pears and Benjamin Britten*, Kenneth Green, oil on canvas, 1943.

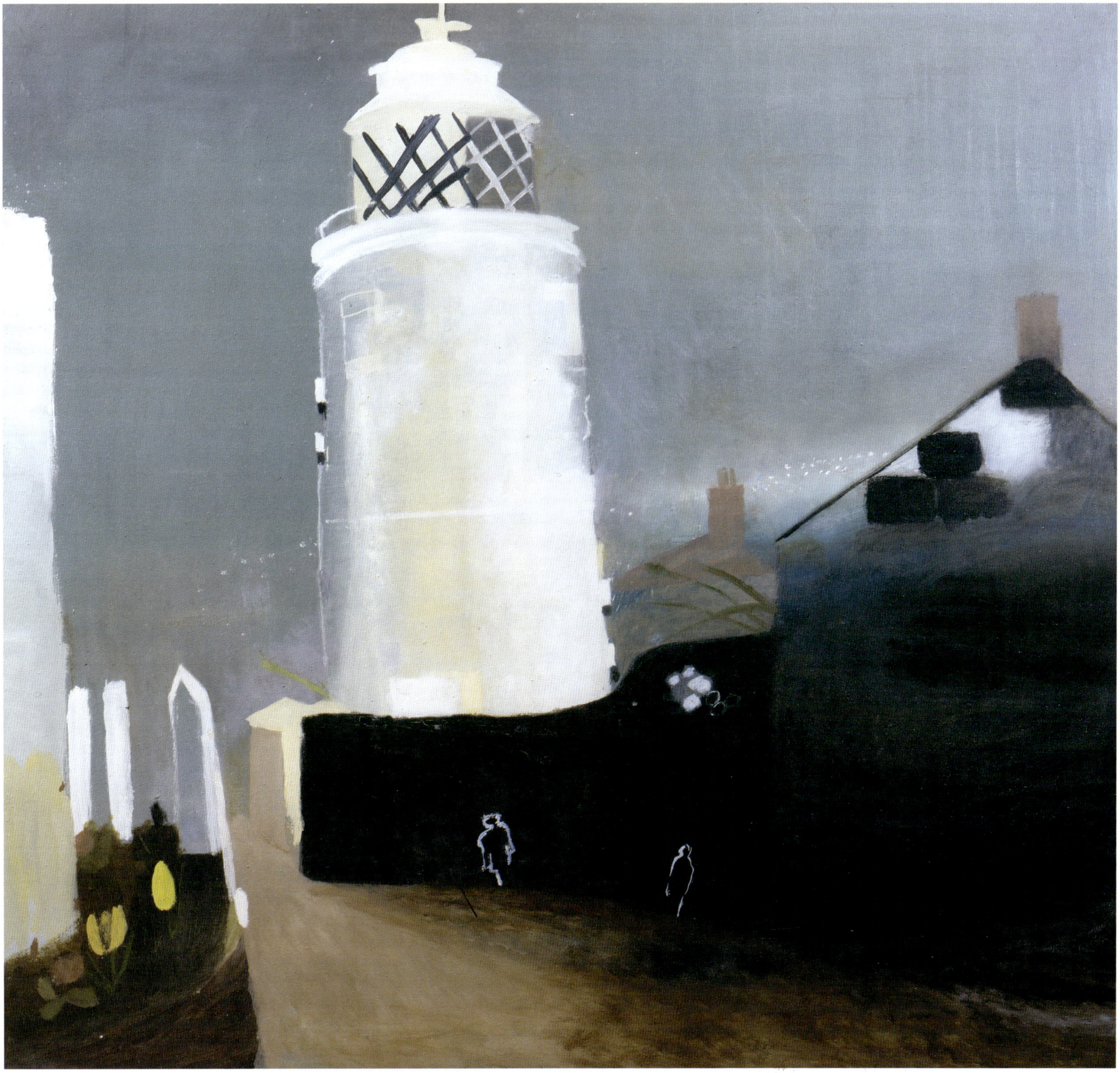

*The Little Lighthouse Town*, Mary Newcomb, oil on canvas, 1982.
Of this picture the artist wrote: 'The lighthouse stands as a guardian and a guide for us all, and lights us home.'

*Walberswick Ferry*, J.T. Hamilton
Macallum, oil on canvas.

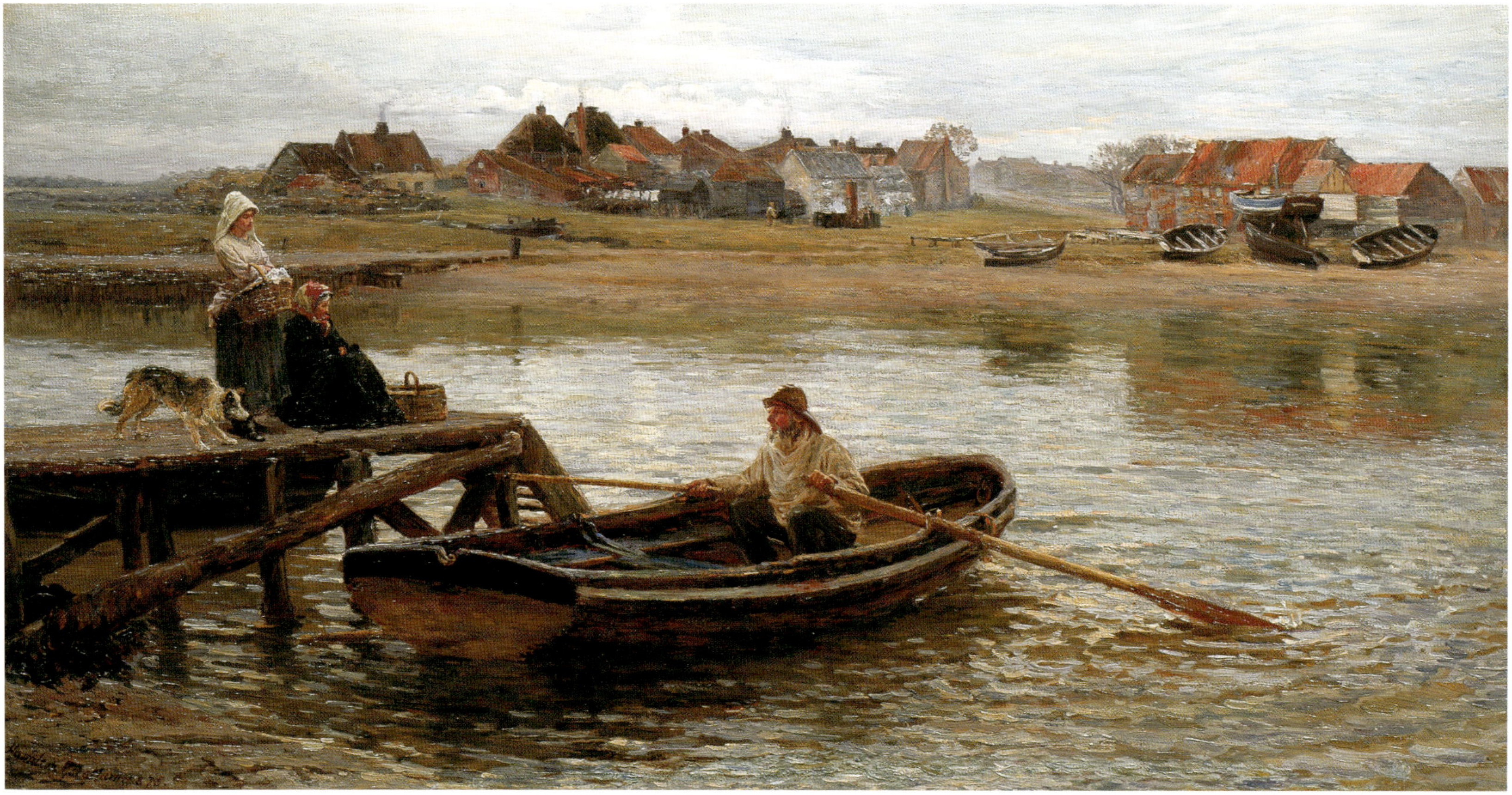

Chapter Five

# Spectral Shadows

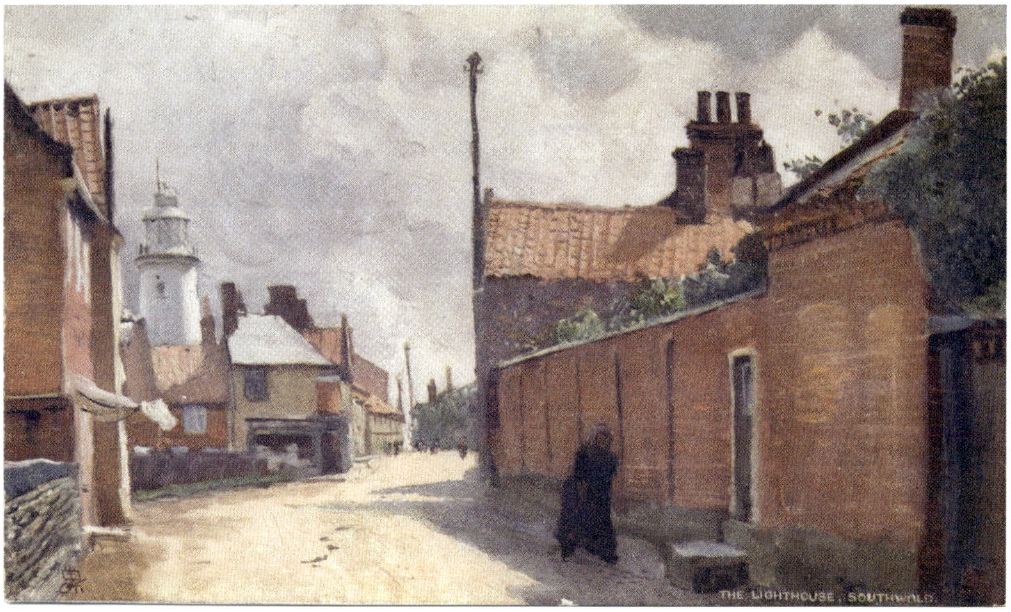


*The Lighthouse*, Edwardian postcard from an original painting by Frank Emanuel.

*Henry James* by his niece Ellen Emmet, oil on canvas, 1900.

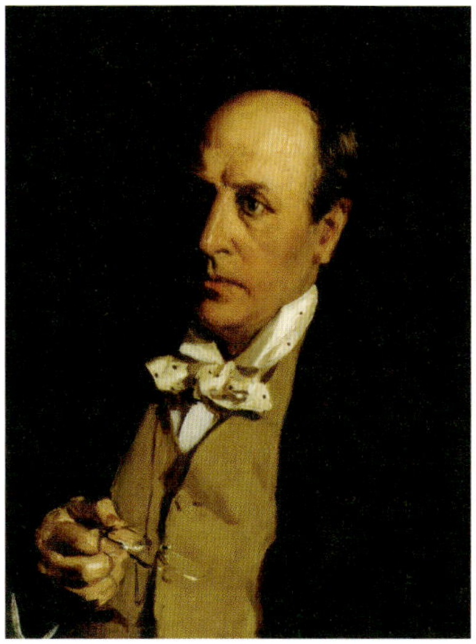

Suffolk is saturated with ghosts, and nowhere more so than the drowned city of Dunwich, above which a bell is said still to toll on stormy nights at sea. American expatriate Henry James walked along the receding shore in 1897 and felt oddly uplifted. 'I defy any one, at desolate, exquisite Dunwich to be disappointed in anything,' he wrote. 'The minor key is struck here with a felicity that leaves no sigh to be breathed, no loss to be suffered; a month of the place is a real education to the patient, the inner vision.'

A year before writing *The Turn of The Screw* the visiting author came companioned by a ghost – that of his brilliant cousin Minny Temple, who had died young after an unheeded plea to join James in Europe. Minny was now with him wherever he went, and she – or the person she might have become – would appear throughout his stories (for instance in the lately-completed *What Maisie Knew* and as the heroine of *The Awkward Age*, whose saga ends in Beccles). In Suffolk she must have seemed all the more present because James was here at the request of her sister, who was staying in Southwold for the summer. And he was further propelled by some remarkable coincidences: the letter of invitation, postmarked Saxmundham, had arrived soon after James had been intrigued by the name of the town while reading the letters of Suffolk's Edward FitzGerald. Later that same day, walking on the beach at Bournemouth, he had met a boatman who was the brother of FitzGerald's sailor friend Joseph 'Posh' Fletcher. And the Dunwich lodgings found for him by his kinswoman turned out to be in the cottage taken by the translator-poet in the 1870s.

Minny's sister was accompanied by her children, one of whom, **ELLEN EMMET** (1875-1941), known in the family as Bay, was already creating a stir as an artist while studying with the American sculptor and painter Frederick MacMonnies in Paris. Ellen had also met John Singer Sargent in London the previous November, who had written to James that she possessed 'more talent than any man or woman of her age' he had ever seen. And the writer was to find himself similarly impressed, informing his brother: 'Bay has brought back from Paris the most marked evidence of her really very great talent.' Such gifts were rather taken for granted among an Emmet generation which was to produce five noted women painters – one being Ellen's cousin Jane, who lived in Chelsea after marrying the artist Wilfrid de Glehn, Singer Sargent's close associate. Ellen depicted Henry James at Rye in 1900, while he was writing *The Ambassadors*. Returning to America she found immediate success portraying New York society – her career climaxing in 1933 when, long using her married name of Ellen Emmet Rand, she was commissioned to paint the White House portrait of Franklin D. Roosevelt.

This part of the Suffolk coast has inspired tellers of terrifying tales from M.R. James to P.D. James – the former, an antiquarian and director of Cambridge's Fitzwilliam Museum, used the Dunwich legend of the three crowns in his story *A Warning to the Curious*. Moreover: a wild man

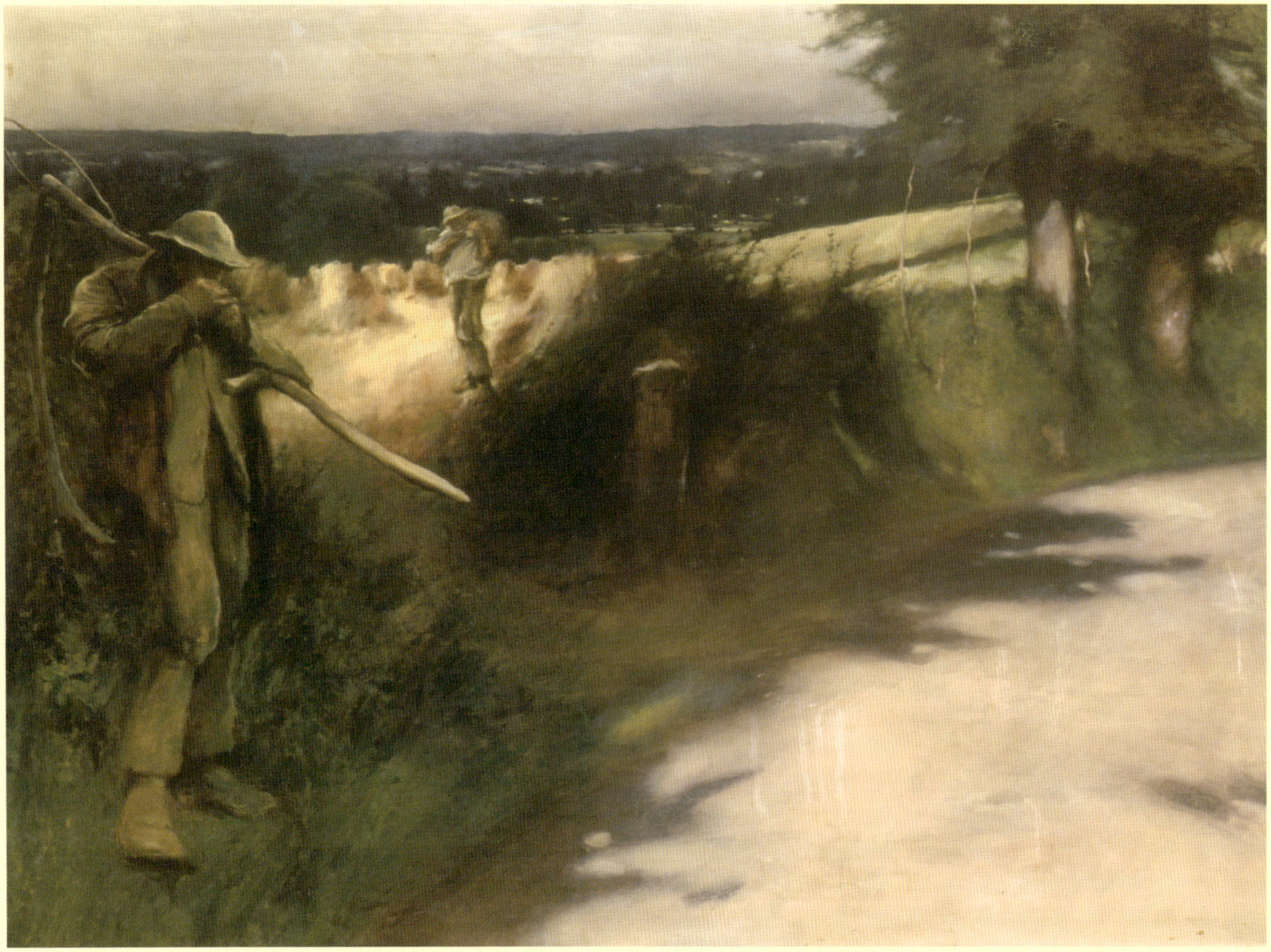

Two ghostly farm workers light up smokes as they leave a Blyth Valley harvest scene in this haunting image by HARRY BECKER (1865-1928). Born in Colchester, the doctor's son had trained in Antwerp, Paris and Bushey – in the latter meeting his future wife, Georgina Waddington, in the former narrowly missing Van Gogh. When migrating to Suffolk in 1913, he was in retreat from snubs delivered in the harsh spotlight of artistic life in London.

For the next 15 years, living first in Wenhaston and then in Hinton, Becker toiled in the fields behind Southwold to capture the stoical skills of horsemen, ploughmen and labourers in a severely recessed agricultural landscape. In his frenzy of work, it was almost as if he had seen a vision that this hard life – where sons of clay seemed part of the very soil – was about to be mechanised out of existence.

Stacks of oils, drawings, watercolours and lithographs would remain unsold (and largely unseen) on Becker's death, after which his widow and daughter moved to the Old Vicarage in Wangford. Gradually revealed in ensuing decades – Georgina dividing her legacy between the Loftus family and Becker's former pupil Kenneth Green – was a unique portrait of vanished rural labour.

Becker's pictures appealed to Adrian Bell, a fellow refugee from London, who chose them to illustrate an edition of his best-selling trilogy (*Corduroy, Silver Ley, The Cherry Tree*) about life on an old Suffolk farm.

But they mirrored the bleak memories set down in Ronald Blythe's 1969 classic *Akenfield*, based on the village of Charsfield. One farm worker, Leonard Thompson, had seen a marquee filled with dead bodies on joining the Dardanelles campaign in World War One. 'I thought of Suffolk and it seemed a happy place for the first time,' he said. In the ensuing film – scripted by the author and directed by Bury St Edmunds-raised Peter Hall – the only respite from hard labour for those pre-1914 farm workers was an annual outing to Southwold.

Small wonder if native ghosts stalk the shadows of our landscape. But Harry (né Henry Otto) Becker had also imported some of his own – being anxious in a xenophobic climate to hide his once wealthy German origins. His family had fled from Bismarck's policies shortly before he was born.

was allegedly netted off medieval Orford, wilder dogs have padded across the myths of East Anglia – Arthur Conan Doyle hearing the story that would prompt *The Hound of the Baskervilles* on the golf links at Cromer. On August 14 1577 a service in Blythburgh church was halted when the spire was struck by lightning. Amid debris crashing to the floor, smashing the font and killing two people, there appeared a fiendish dog with flame-red eyes and fiery breath. Howling and battering to get out, beast and storm then took off towards Bungay. Clawmarks remaining in the north door were widely regarded as a sign of the devil.

Nearby Dead Man's Corner is believed to be haunted by the spirits of women hanged amid Civil War chaos when maniacal Matthew Hopkins rode roughshod over East Anglia as a self-appointed Witchfinder General. His two-year rampage resulted in the deaths of up to 68 people in Suffolk alone (mostly elderly widows or spinsters with pets) before he himself was denounced and reputedly executed for witchcraft – though, in truth, he died in his Manningtree bed. The hills and hollows of the old quarries at Toby's Walks are said to be patrolled by the shade of black drummer Tobias Gill, who came to Blythburgh in 1750 with a regiment commanded by Sir Robert Rich. A strong man with a weakness for drink, he was often confined to camp for alcohol-fuelled violence and could be a model soldier for as long as he was sober. Then the trouble would begin again with his release. Returning one night from the ale houses of Walberswick – by this time Blythburgh shunned him – Tobias met Ann Blakemore walking across the common. The next morning he was found, still in a drunken stupor, beside her corpse and was arrested for rape and murder. Tried and sentenced to death, 'Black Toby' pleaded in vain to be dragged behind the mail coach. He was hanged and his body placed in a gibbet on the exact spot of his crime, where it was picked clean by crows. The gibbet stood for 50 years until it fell to pieces, at which point the nails were claimed for a thatching comb.

The oldest and most ghost-laden part of Southwold is the ferry, which has probably operated on the Blyth for a thousand years, almost always as a rowing boat. Ferryman David Church

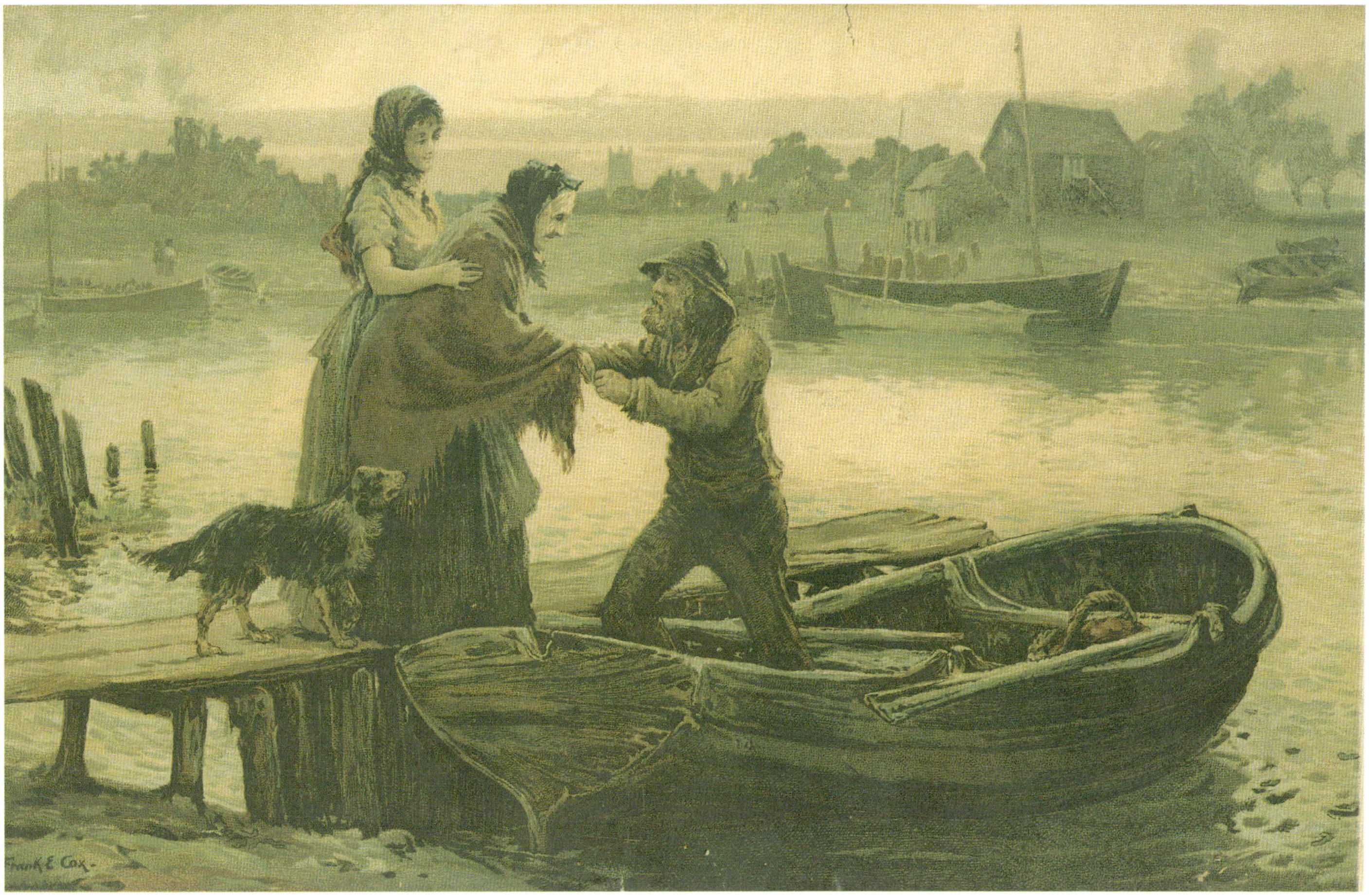


*The Ferry*, a lost painting by Frank E. Cox. This ghostly image is taken from the framed reproduction hanging in The Lord Nelson inn.

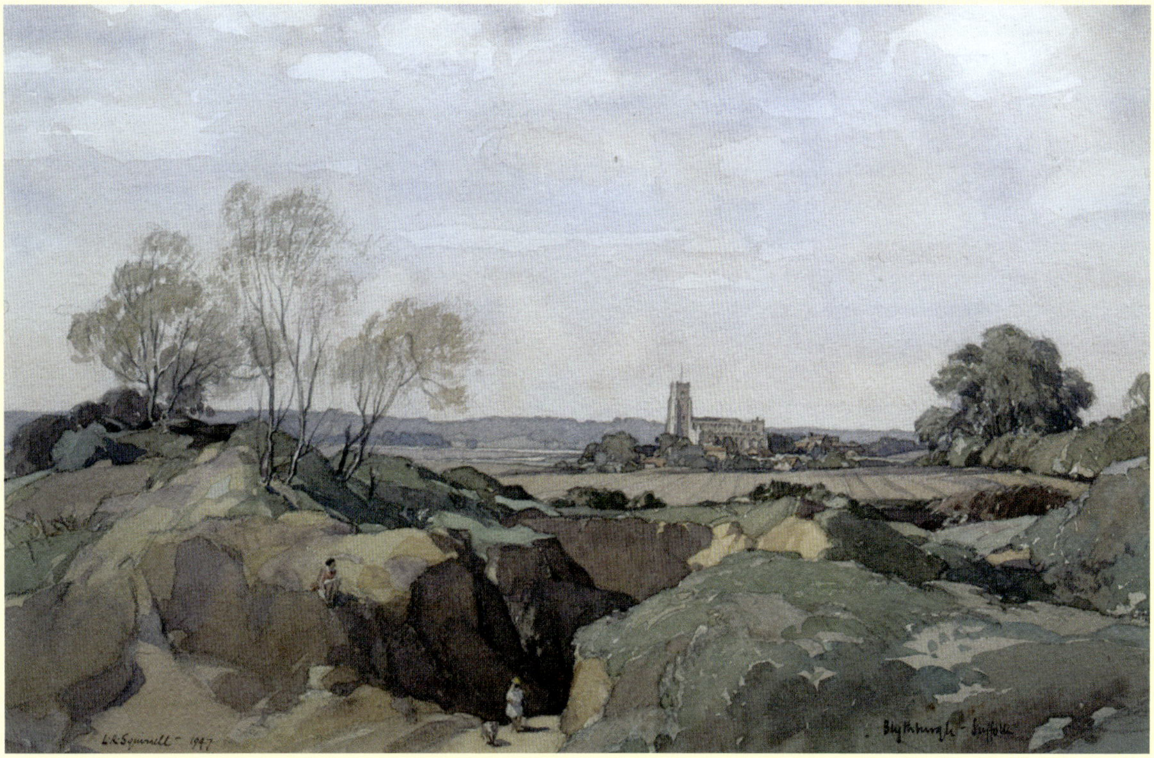


Moved by the spirit of Norwich School painter John Sell Cotman, Ipswich-born LEONARD SQUIRRELL (1893-1979) charted the distinctive landscapes and architectural views of Suffolk in masterly etchings and watercolours after training in his native town and at the Slade School in London. He depicted the incongruous contours of Toby's Walks in this picture of 1947 during one of his regular visits to the Blyth Valley. Long used for building materials, sand and gravel was quarried here for Second World War airfields and, until the 1950s, for road repairs.

received an obituary in the *Times* in 2001 for his 47-year service, having assisted his grandfather and uncle from the age of 12; he was then succeeded by his daughter, Dani. There have been many studies of this picturesque transport service in the last two centuries, some of an eerie and melancholy nature. But none has been more haunting than those of Londoner **FRANK E. COX** whose work was widely exhibited between 1880 and 1895, with 16 showings in the Royal Academy alone. He was fascinated by Old Todd the ferryman who featured in a ghost story related by locals and visitors alike. One, en route to the rowing-boat ferry, overtook an elderly man leading a child by the hand. Thinking that Todd might fail to spot them, he suggested a moment's pause so they could catch up. Then, looking back, he found that the two figures had vanished. 'We never waits for them,' said the ferryman. A woman who saw the same apparitions while living in Walberswick and also alerted the oarsman was told in a whisper: 'They never cross!'

Our local ghostly assembly ranges from monks at Blythburgh and cruel squires at Westwood Lodge to the servant girl who walks the corridors of Sutherland House still waiting for the Earl of Sandwich and whose presence was likened by

Old Todd rowing a party across the Blyth in the 1880s.

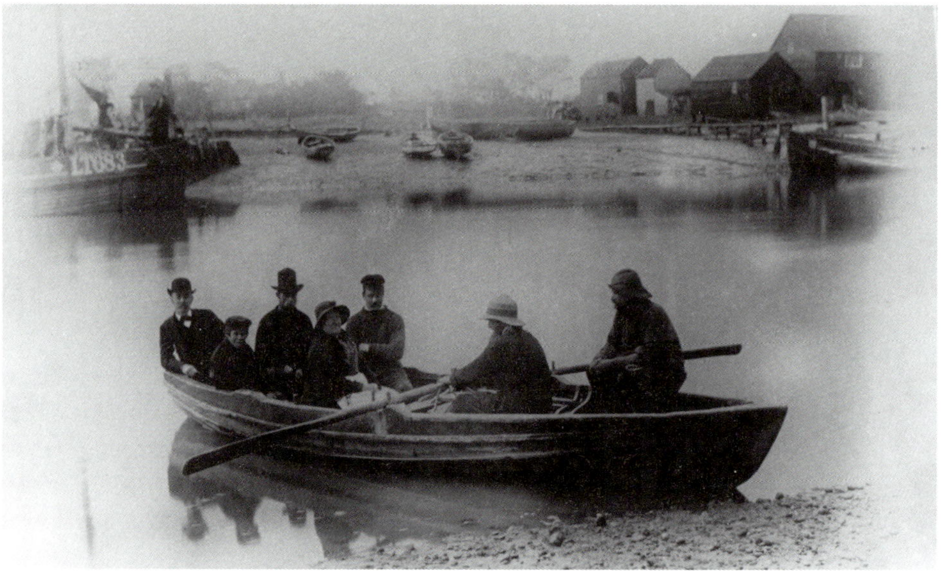

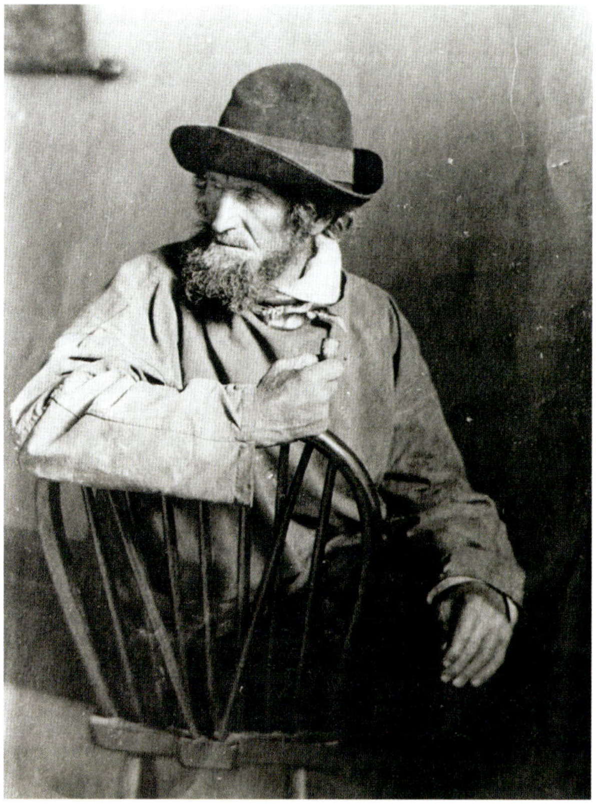

George Todd, ferryman and model for Royal Academy paintings. This fine 1880s portrait photograph suggests the hand of P.H. Emerson.

one former resident to walking through cobwebs. Motley 'elementals' throng a Southwold lane near the Saltings and a mysterious shawl-covered woman wafts over Gun Hill close to an all-too-identifiable decapitated man (the spectre of a spectator who rashly peered into a gun barrel when the cannons were last fired). William Hurr – whose sons gave folk songs to Ralph Vaughan Williams – used to relate how he met a stranger near Field Stile, north of the town, who introduced himself as the King of the World and invited the fisherman to follow him. Luckily Mr Hurr noticed that the tempter had cloven hooves instead of boots, declaring: 'No I shall not go with you. By the help of God I have got this far, and by the help of God I hope to get home.' At the mention of the Almighty the fiend vanished forever in a puff of brimstone. But more persistent cases have included a coach driven by headless horses and presaging death when seen careering past Reydon Hall and a spectral pedestrian on a bend of the A1095 beside the Hen Reedbeds. Doubtless the fog of sea frets, poor eyesight and alcohol has clouded such stirring stories with added atmosphere.

But Eric Arthur Blair – who became George Orwell, and who lived intermittently with his parents at their successive homes in 40 Stradbroke Road, 2 Queen Street and finally Montague House in the High Street from 1921 to the late 1930s – was convinced he had seen the ghost of a man dressed in monkish brown in Walberswick churchyard, where he so enjoyed reading the stories of M.R. James. On another occasion he felt like an M.R. Jamesian character when discovering a cloth-lined box arranged with tiny furniture during a walk on Walberswick Common. In Southwold, which he found too staid and stuffy, he had been driven into disturbing the peace by posting a rat to the town clerk – a practical joke which got him expelled from the Craighurst crammer on North Parade (he had anyway just qualified for a posting with the Burma police). Here he wrote part of *Down and Out in Paris and London* and *Keep the Aspidistra Flying* and all of *The Clergyman's Daughter* – the latter's Knype Hill being a loose satire of Southwold. Then rife with retired colonial civil servants, the town had a rigidly stratified society to whose upper reaches – golf course, Blyth Club, bridge circle – his parents clung for dear life. But Ida Blair also took art lessons from Madame Tabois, the town's resident French artist who had a studio on Ferry Road. Eric himself often worked with watercolours on the beach, and during one such episode, in 1930, he met the holidaying Hampstead socialist Mabel Feirz, who

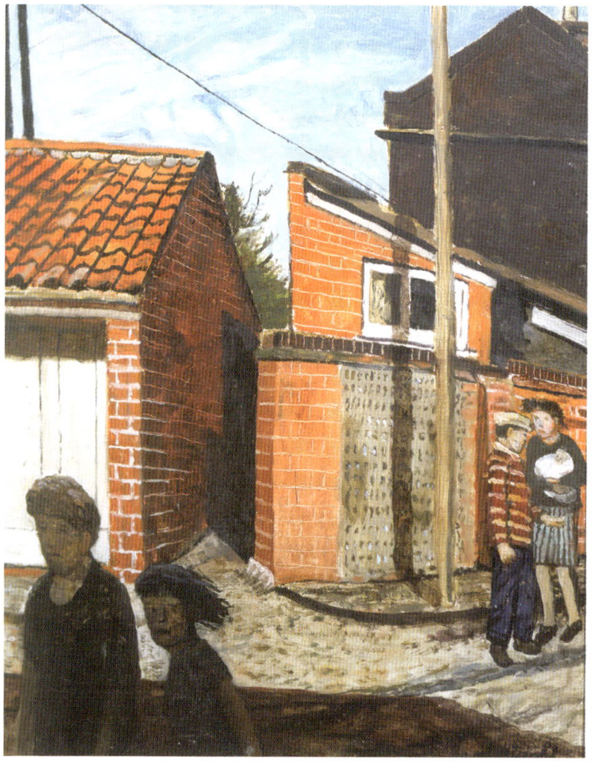

*Disturbed Children*, Carel Weight, oil on canvas (right).

urged his move to London and put him in touch with a literary agent who in turn secured a publishing deal. His last recorded trip to Southwold, in June 1939, was for his father's funeral. As D.J. Taylor, Orwell's Southwold-devoted biographer, has noted, he left with the memory of Manor Farm Close, a culvert off the High Street close to Montague House. Soon the name would re-emerge in the satire on Stalinism, *Animal Farm.*

**CAREL WEIGHT** (1908-1997) was a painter who detected fantastic menace in mundane things – but during several long-weekend visits to Southwold in the early 1990s he found himself stuck for a subject. He brought with him a background of dramatic peculiarity – his grandfather was Edward VII's chiropodist, his socialite mother also attended to the hands and feet of stage stars – and Anglo-German dislocation. Born into a wealthy family in London, he had been farmed out during the week to poor foster parents and had run wild in the mean streets and alleys of Hammersmith, Fulham and Battersea. Like his painted figures he was chased thereafter by the magnified monsters of memory. His sense that something nasty might happen at any minute was secured forever when his Shepherds Bush studio was lost in the Blitz.

While influenced by the Surrealists, Pre-Raphaelites, Goya, Munch and Stanley Spencer – and being for decades an acclaimed tutor at the Royal College of Art – Weight's art, and to a lesser extent his life, was positioned on the lonely edge of everything where phantoms wandered. In his unique and vividly-painted vision, witches, angels and ghosts took flight in the most ordinary suburbs, where women and children also ran in terror after fires, fairground tragedies, zoo maulings, muggings and murders. Southwold was to test his imagination to the full.

In his final decade he was brought to the town by his friend Jeff Horwood to stay on Centre Cliff, in a fine property with a commanding view over the sea. 'He complained that he couldn't find anything to paint,' Mr Horwood recalls. 'But, after he had walked around a lot to eye up the place, he finally set out with paints, brushes, canvas and easel to capture two pictures on the spot.' One is ostensibly a view of the lighthouse, but as seen from a characteristically perverse angle – a cul-de-sac off East Green, beside a rickety fence and ramshackle wall. A telegraph pole with a spider's web of wires frames a fictitious foreground figure, with a passing resemblance to Barbara Hepworth, whose facial expression suggests that Southwold is the last resort.

Jeff Horwood pursued his guest on a second painting sortie, and was surprised to find that, with the wealth of picturesque locations to choose from via the beach, harbour, town and common, he had got no further than a corner of the garages behind Centre Cliff. 'I couldn't understand why he had chosen such a nondescript spot – but then I saw how all the curious elements of the scene, so typical of Carel's art, came together in the resulting picture,' he says. The sun shines overhead but imaginary figures hug the shadows, looking at the artist accusingly as if they have been disturbed in some dubious plot.

Southwold had been recommended to the painter of macabre magic by his life-long

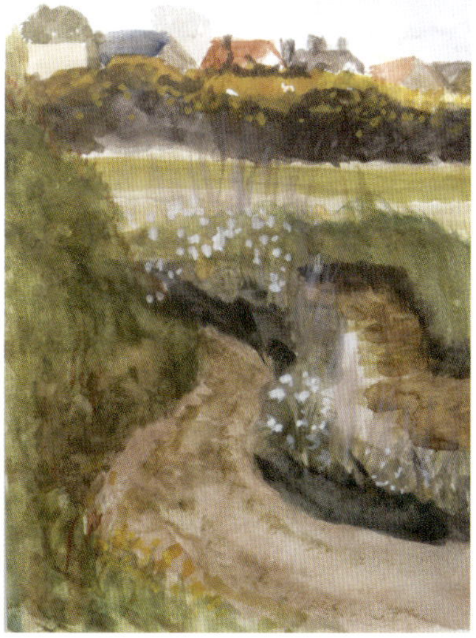

*Butterfly Walk*, HELEN ROEDER, (1909-1999), watercolour.

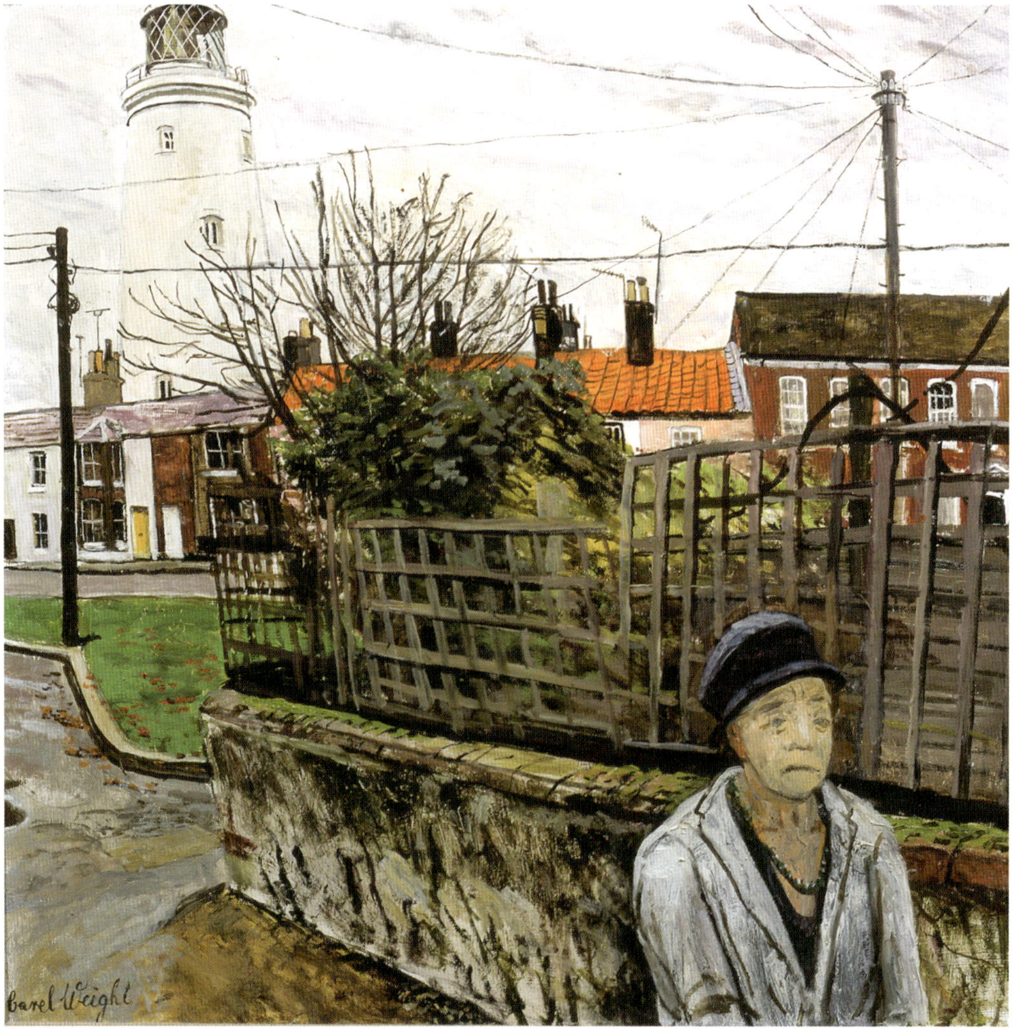


*Mad Woman*, Carel Weight, oil on canvas.

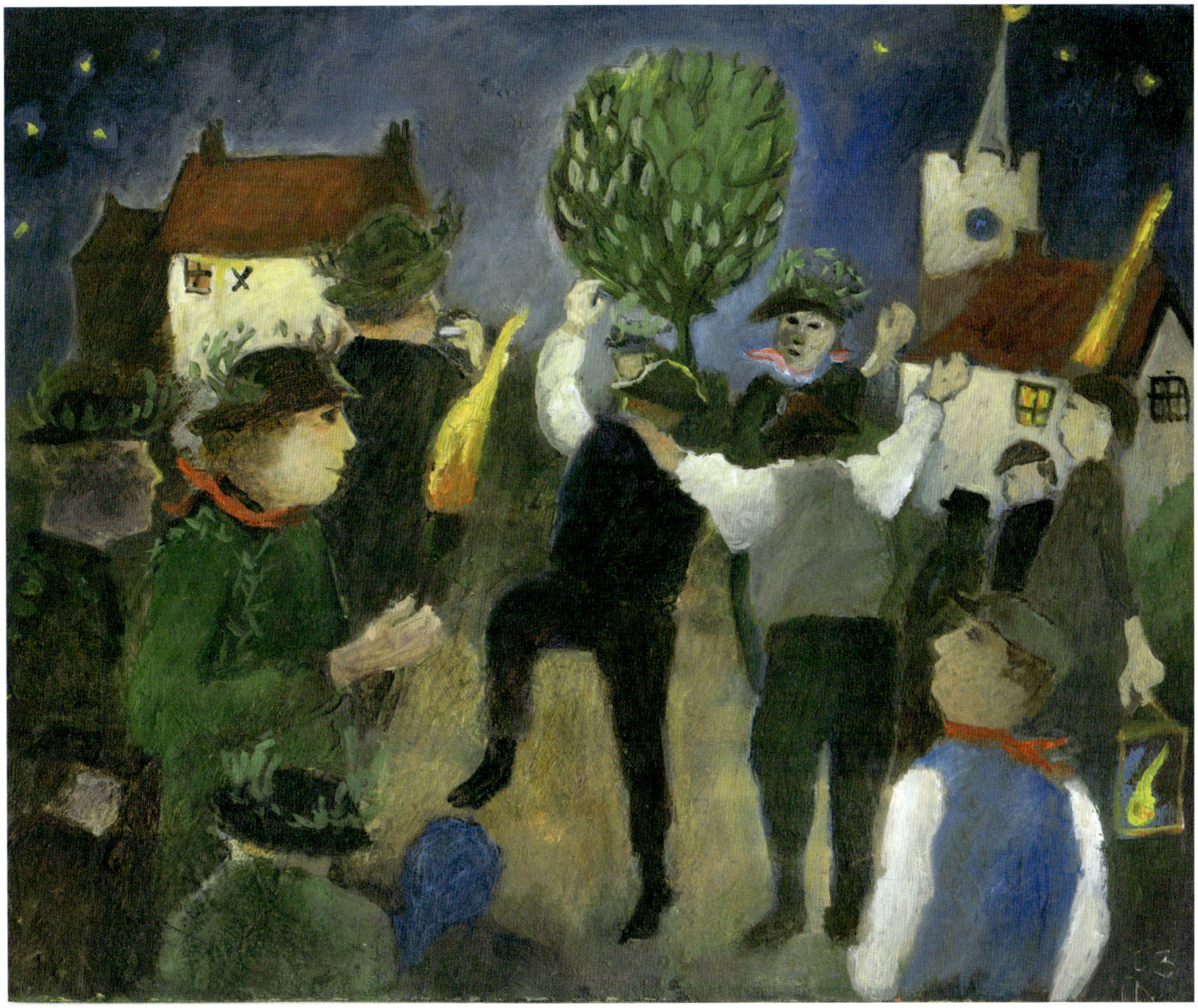

*Molly Dancers*, Tessa Newcomb, oil on board.

companion **HELEN ROEDER**, whom he met at Goldsmiths' College School of Art in the early 1930s. She served on the Artists' Refugee Committee during the war and worked as a secretary in the Industrial Design Partnership. Retirement gave her more time for her art, and then she and her friend Connie Winn often took the bus from Victoria Station to Southwold, to paint while staying on Centre Cliff. Carel Weight and Helen Roeder finally married in 1990.

Meanwhile, in recent Decembers, old ghosts seem to have returned to Southwold backstreets and to other former haunts throughout the Blyth Valley – most of all, on the Feast of St Stephen, to Middleton. Here the Molly Dancers have revived a tradition so secret that nobody knows its original patterns. At Middleton the disguised troupe re-enacts the hunting of a wren, an emblem of darkness which must be banished at the winter solstice to appease the pagan gods and allow light to return to the world. An evening of torch-lit drinking and dancing by male mollies, to musical accompaniment from women, ends with the pretend slaughter of the tiny bird whose 'corpse' is then paraded through the village in a cage of holly, ivy and coloured ribbons like a lantern on a pole. With blackened faces and wearing wreathes of ivy, the mollies appear in 19th century costume – probably recalling the efforts of partying farm labourers to disguise their identities from puritanical employers who viewed dancing, let alone pagan ritual, as the work of the devil. **TESSA NEWCOMB** (b1955) watched the festivities for the first time in 2003 and then, returning home to nearby Wenhaston, stayed up all night painting three oil studies which exude the vivid vigour of the renewed ritual to drive the dark away. The daughter of Mary Newcomb, who was raised on farms in the Waveney Valley, and attended art schools in Norwich, Bath and Wimbledon, is now a prolific producer of quirky and eerie art which illuminates the world between Dunwich and Southwold.

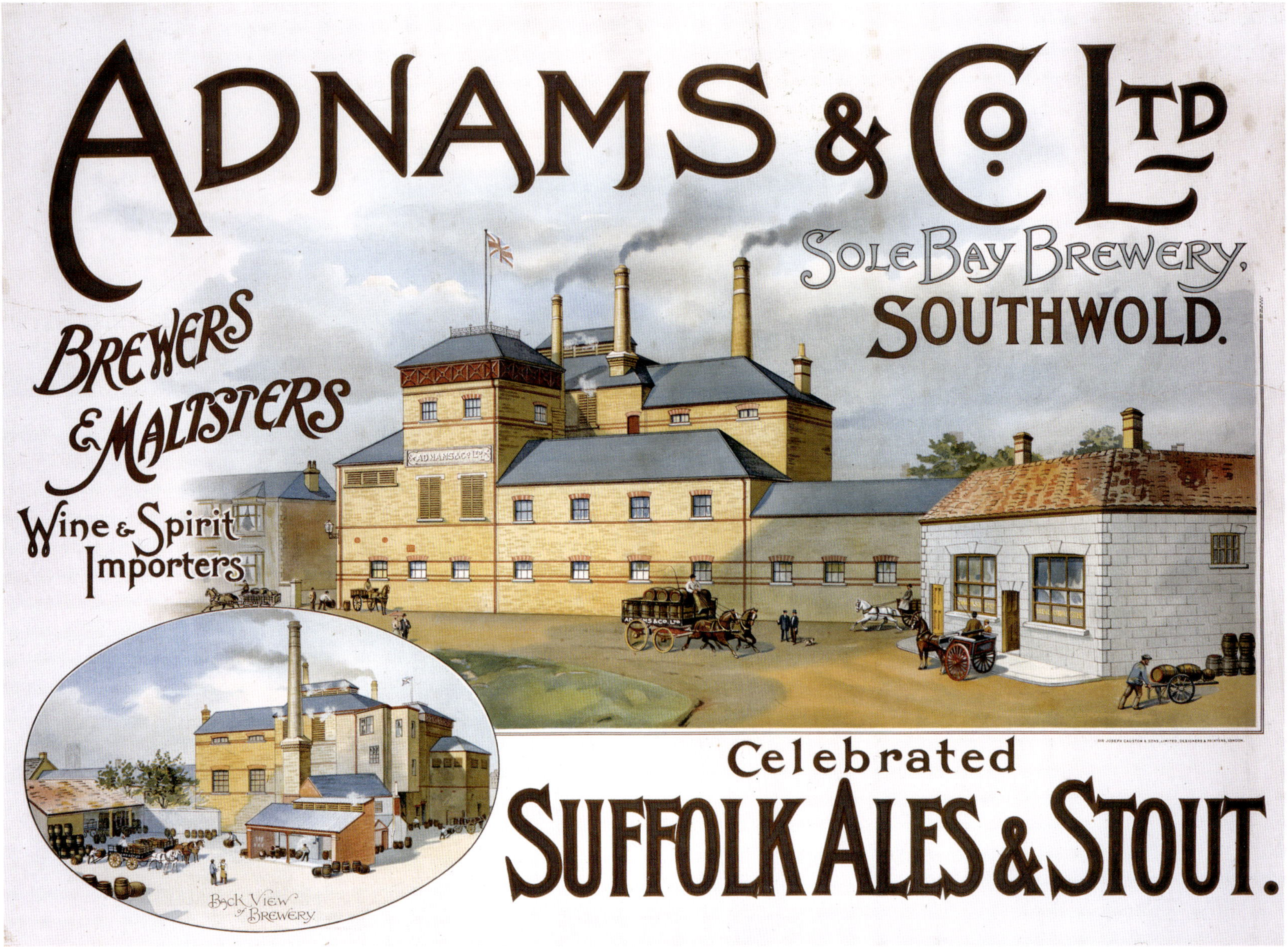


This widely-circulated poster shows the Adnams brewery as enlarged and rebuilt to the designs of Inskipp and Mackenzie in 1896 and with production at the new plant in full swing.

Chapter Six

# Toast of the Town

So often the words 'sedate' and 'genteel' are attached to descriptions of Southwold, but the town has always had a working core – with brewing long a dominant, and latterly a defining, industry. Sole Bay Brewery, with roots going back to 1345, can claim to be one of the oldest in Britain. Originally part of the Swan Hotel, it was probably owned by ale wife Johanna de Corby who made regular court appearances in the mid-14th century for selling an inferior product at inflated prices and also for breaches of the peace. The present site dates from the great fire of 1659

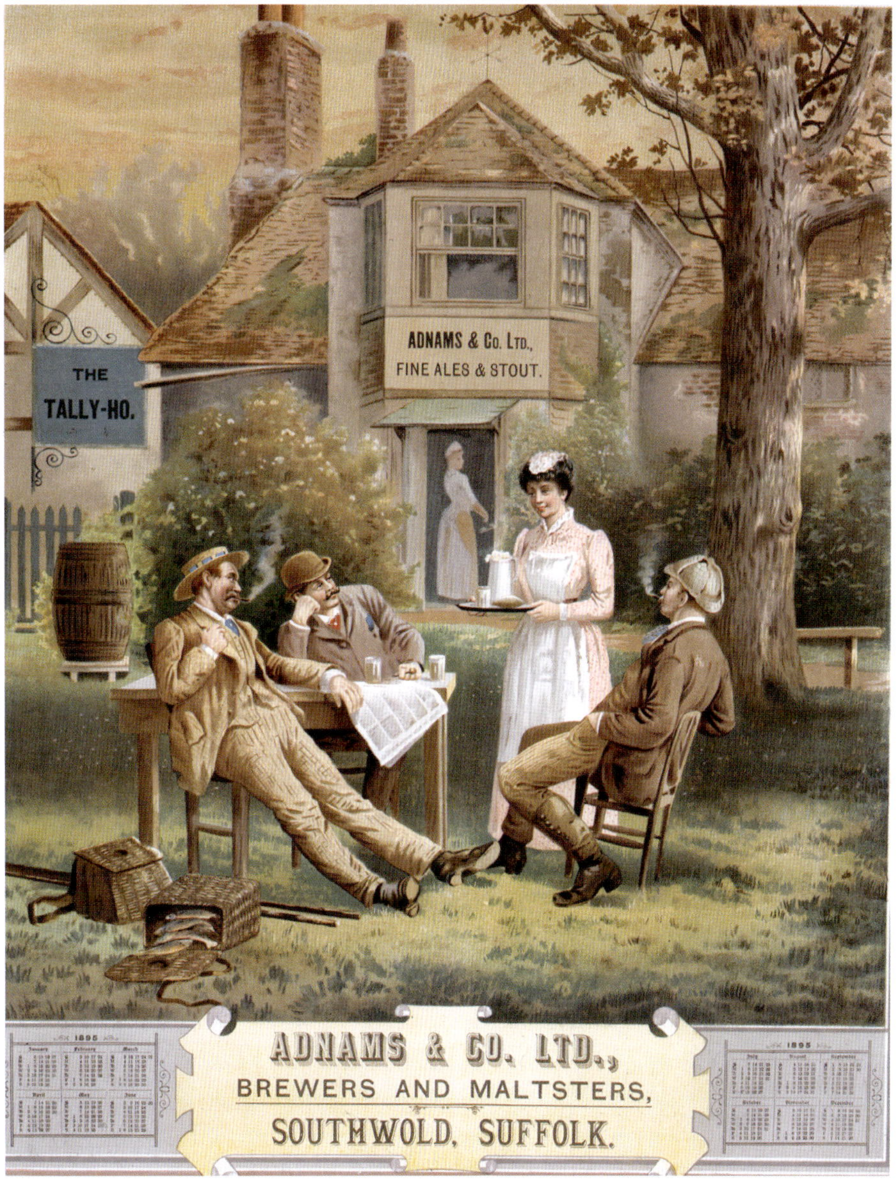


By 1890 Ernest Adnams had developed a pool of 20 pubs and was brewing 5000 barrels a year including his famous Tally Ho, plus mild, stout and pale ale. This poster captures the flavour of the period.

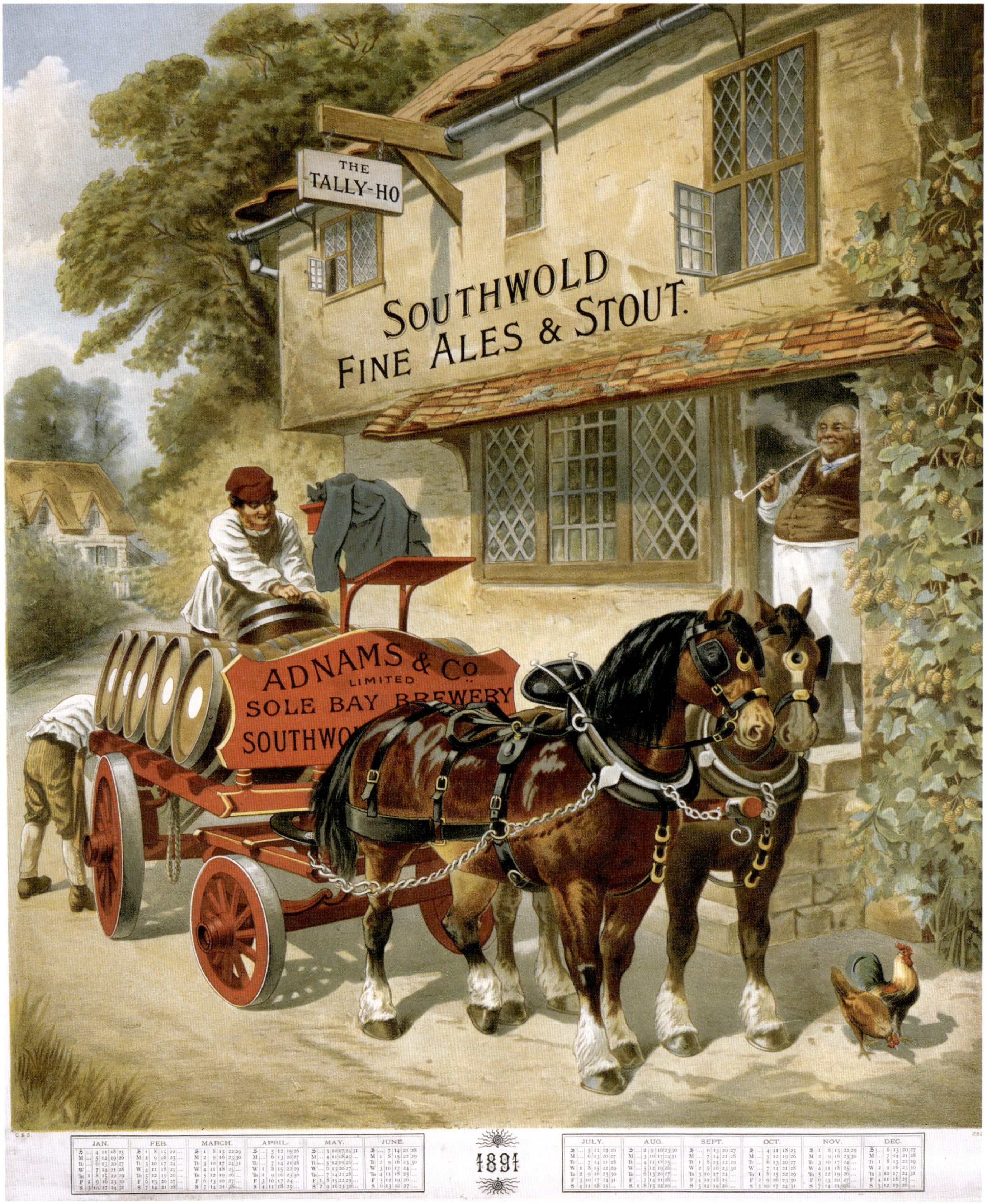


In recent years Adnams of Southwold has become one of the last British breweries to continue delivering beer barrels to local pubs by horse and dray. This poster shows that traditional transport had been a proud boast of the company for many decades.

L.S. Lowry may have visited Southwold while staying with the artists David and Barbara Carr at Starston Hall near Harleston from the 1940s. He certainly painted at Aldeburgh and Lowestoft and his spirit hangs over this spirited drawing from 1930 in the Lowryesque central figure. A note on the reverse says that the artist, JOHN WALTER GEORGES, then at St Martin's School of Art in London, and living in Battersea Rise, was recalling the bar of the Harbour Inn in the summer of 1911. The remembered figures, left to right, are landlord Charles James Prior, fisherman John Cannell of 3 Town Farm Cottages, North Road, Southwold (83 in 1930), ex-basketmaker W.M. Rogers (the blind son of 'Old Dog' Rogers), the late fisherman Henry Ladd and the artist himself.

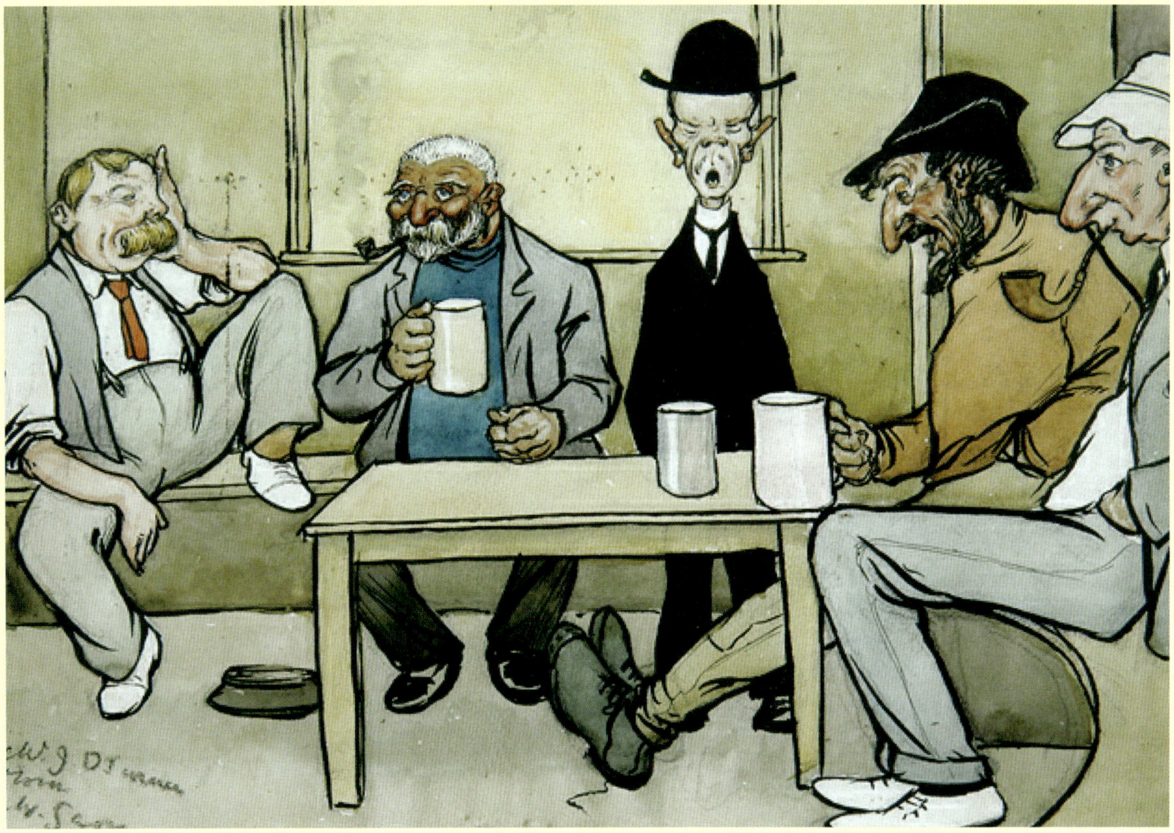

*Blackshore Quay* – an Edwardian postcard showing the old smugglers' haunt of the Harbour Inn. From an original watercolour by Sylvester Stannard.

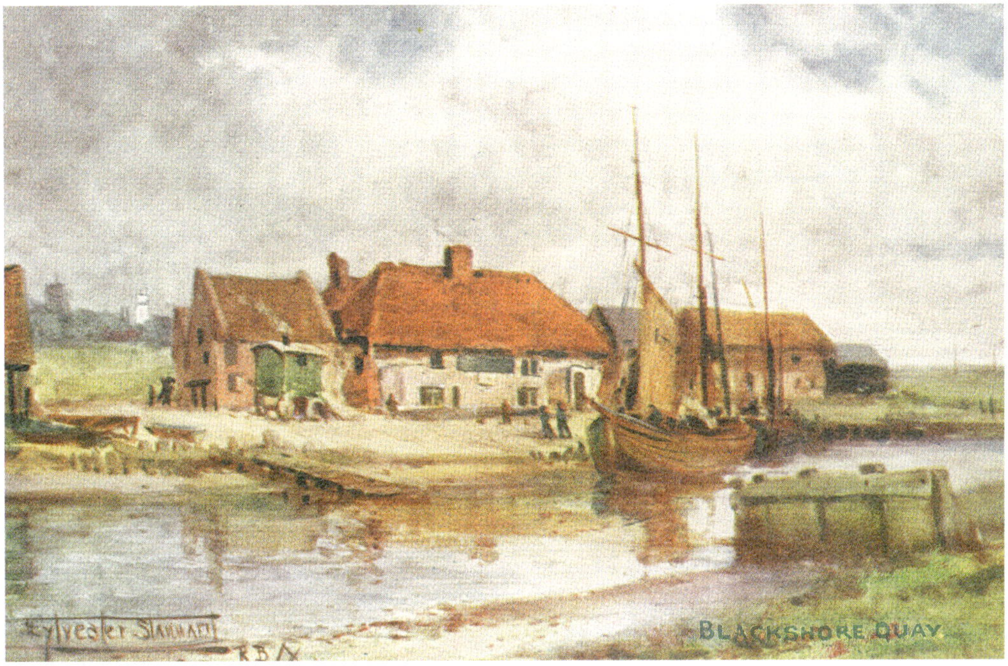


and for a prolonged period the operation was in rivalry with a brewery and maltings linked to the White Lion inn in Victoria Street and the Home Maltings in the High Street (in what is now Barclays Bank) as well as several pub-based producers. But in Georgian times the major challenger for alcoholic supplies to local pubs came from the smuggling trade – with contraband wine and spirits often landed at the harbour and on local beaches at dead of night, where there were more than occasional skirmishes with armed excise officers. The Blythburgh gravestone with the inscription 'Here I lies, Kill'd by the XIS' is not unique.

In 1872 Sole Bay Brewery, having already consumed the White Lion and Home Maltings enterprises, was taken over by George and Ernest Adnams. The former subsequently left for Africa where he faced a sobering fate - being eaten by a crocodile in the Zambezi. When Ernest joined forces with Pierse Loftus, having been under-brewer at the Natal Brewery, one of the largest in South Africa, and later became an MP for Lowestoft, a century of expansion was begun. There were 7000 brewers in Britain at the end of the Victorian era, and Adnams proceeded to swallow as many as it could, acquiring C.J. Fisher & Co of Eye in 1905, E. Rope & Sons of Orford in 1922 and Flintham & Hall of Aldeburgh in 1924. It also extended its range of beers and pubs, and produced attractive advertising posters such as those illustrated here. Helped in the 1960s by the increasing popularity of Real Ale, Adnams came into its own so that Southwold's finest brews can now be bought across the country and on the continent. Although these days beer is ferried for long distances in lorries sporting profiles of Southwold on their sides, Adnams entered the new millennium as one of the few breweries in Britain still to deliver beer to local pubs by dray horses. The expanding brewery, with an associated wine-importing business, a string of pubs and a pair of flagship hotels in the Crown and Swan would amaze Johanna de Corby with its proof that a reputation for quality really pays.

So many pictures of Southwold incorporate

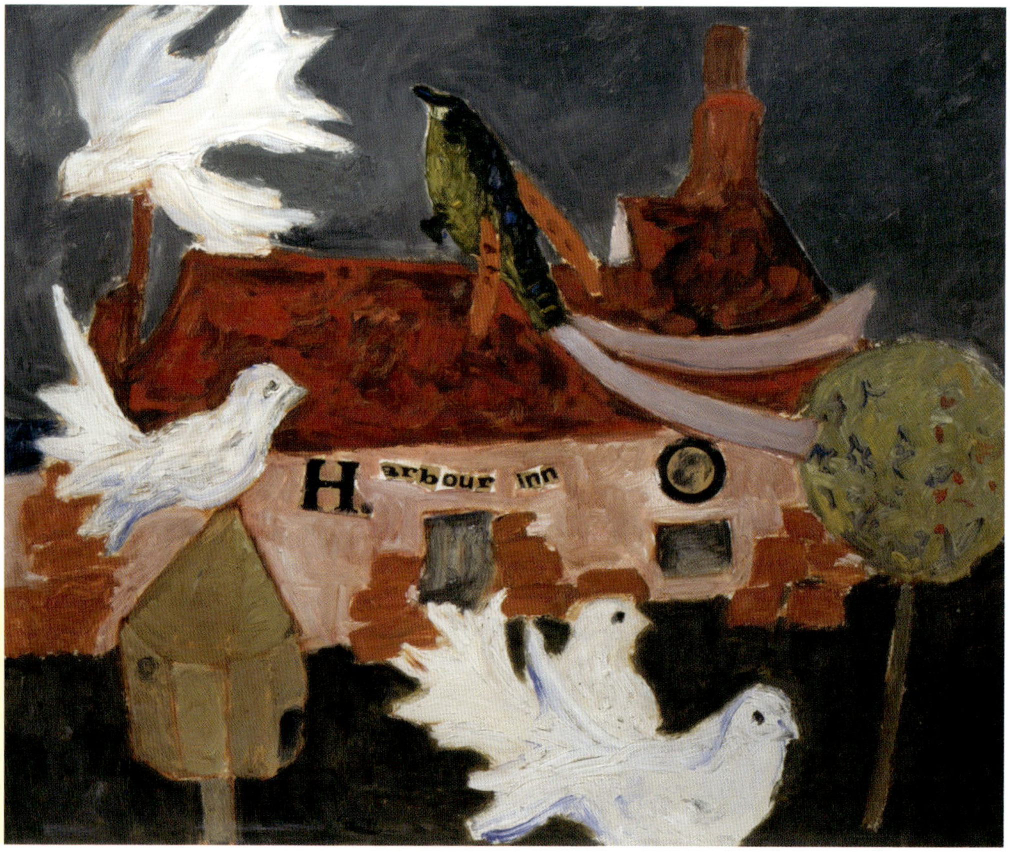


Olive Cook's painting and collage of the Harbour Inn, produced during one of her Blackshore holidays with her painter-photographer husband Edwin Smith, veers into surrealism with the wild touches of a dovecot formerly in the pub's back garden and an Indian toy belonging to the artist.

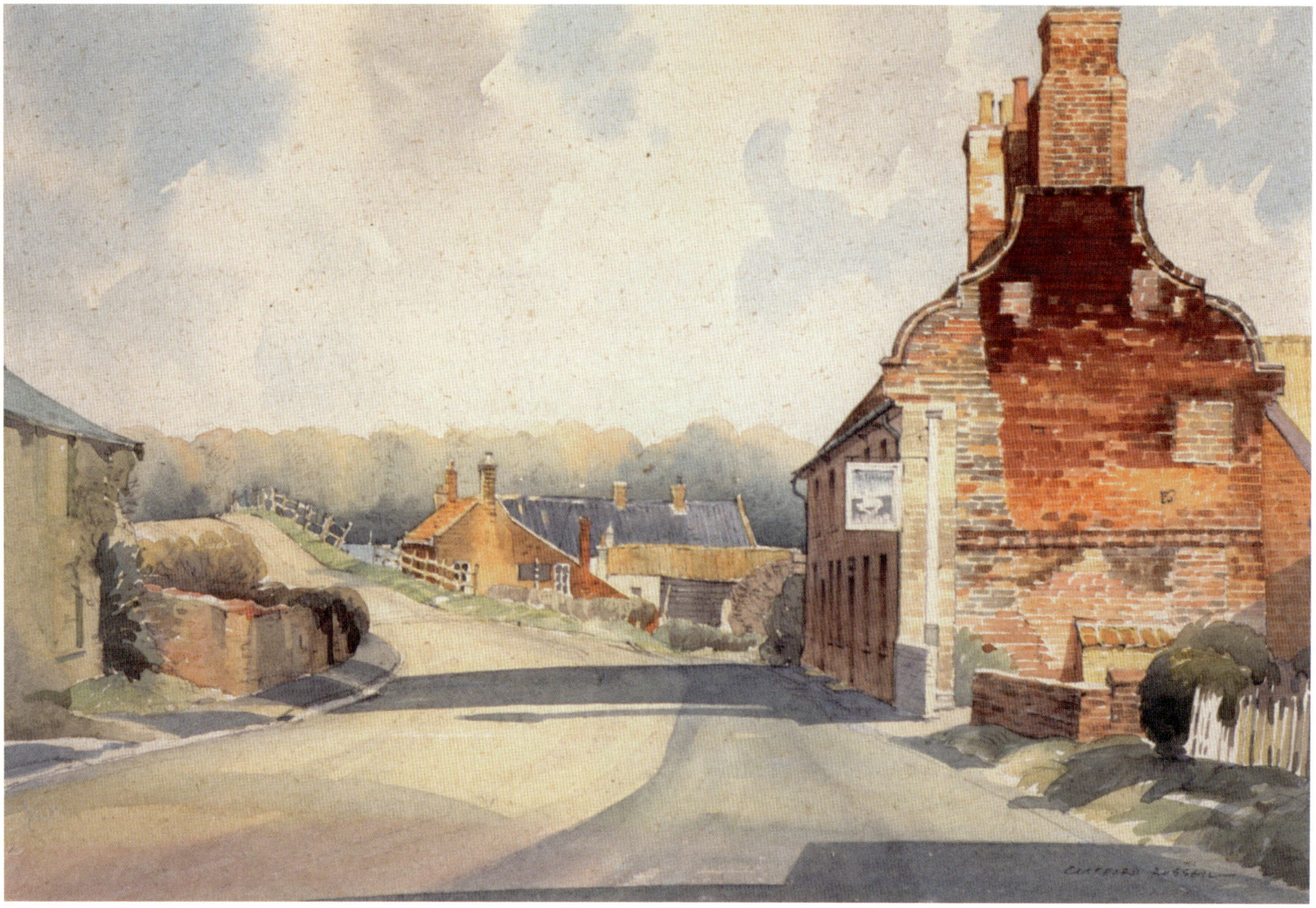

Clifford Russell's 1940s watercolour view of the White Hart inn at Blythburgh shows an almost-unrecognisable stretch of the A12. The old railway bridge pictured here was lost in a road-widening scheme of 1961.

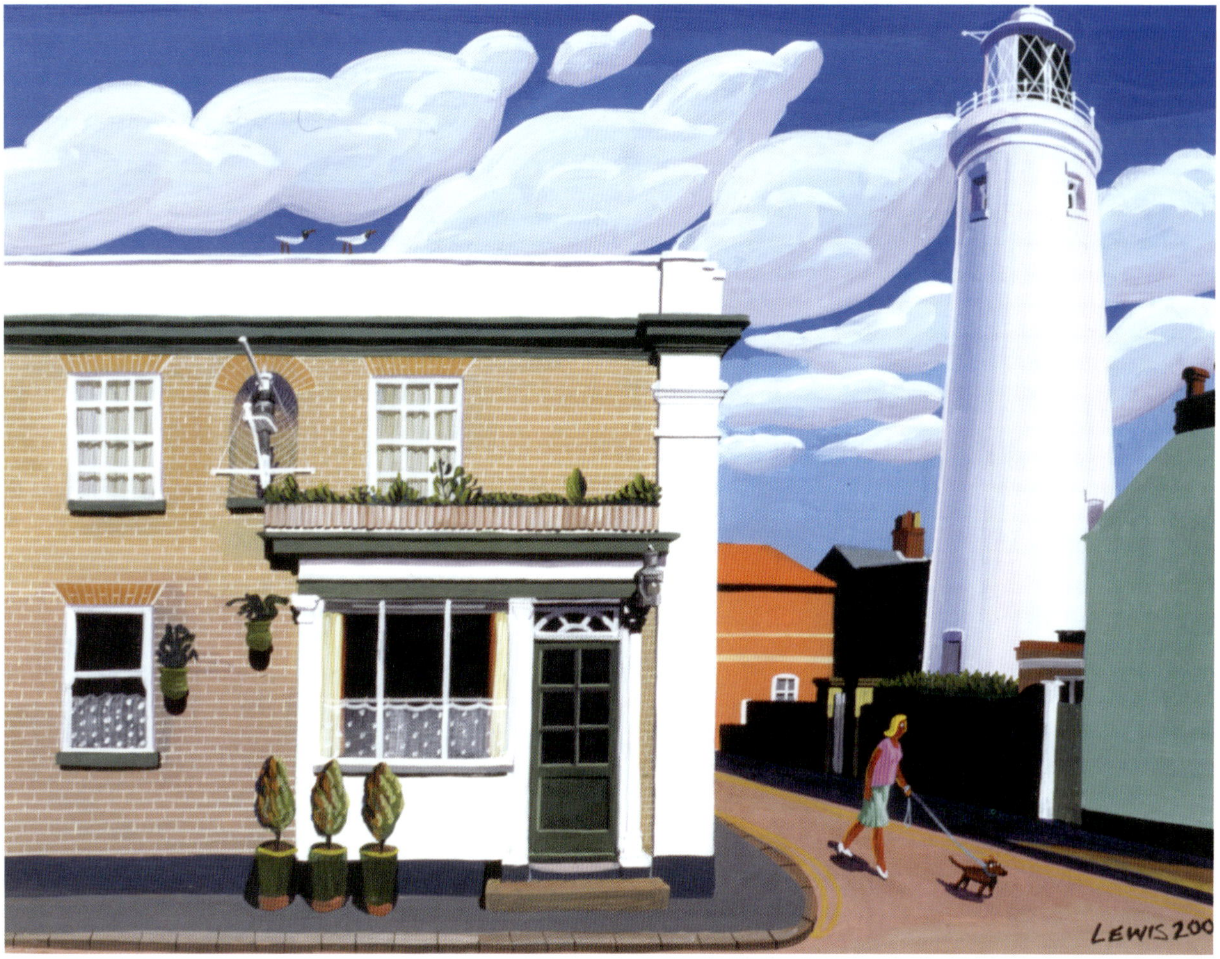


This jaunty Brian Lewis painting, *Lighthouse IV*, polymer on gesso board, shows the Sole Bay Inn and lighthouse from East Green. It also pays tribute to a town which at times appears to have as many dogs as people.

pubs, whose locations – and, still more, whose names – have shifted over time. The celebrated haunt of smugglers on Blackshore, dating from the early 1700s, was known variously as the Nag's Head and Fishing Buss before being relaunched as the Harbour Inn in 1874. The Nag's Head sign was to be trailed over the town, being associated with what is now the Crown Hotel and what was once the Victoria Inn (premises also called the Star and Pilot Boat before their current incarnation as a winebar and restaurant). The Crown was also the New Swan when its illustrious neighbour was the Old Swan. The Red Lion on South Green began as the Queen's Head. The Southwold Arms, a High Street hostelry closed in the 1990s, was formerly the Joiners Arms and the Green Man. It joined a long list of earlier losses – the Tom and Jerry on Constitution Hill, the Bear Inn at Bridge Foot in Reydon, the Two Brewers on the corner of Church Street and the High Street, the White Horse at 19 High Street opposite the Marquis of Lorne (previously the Wagon and Horses). Small wonder that the muddled pub-crawlers of mid-Victorian Southwold coined the verse:

*The Lion bit the Bear*
*And made the Old Swan fly*
*Turned the Pilot Boat upside down*
*And drank the Lord Nelson dry.*

Amid all these changes there emerged three stalwart survivors: the Lord Nelson opened in East Street in time to honour the Norfolk-raised naval hero killed at the Battle of Trafalgar in 1805; the Sole Bay Inn – which would become the most-depicted pub in Southwold after the Harbour Inn, thanks to its handsome frontage and position on East Green almost below the lighthouse – was in active service from the 1860s; and the 17th century property beside Barnaby Green sold by Southwold historian Thomas Gardner in 1799, and later the home of diarist, teacher and auctioneer James Maggs, was first licensed as the King's Head in 1836.

The Swan used to send a carriage to meet trains at Darsham, and then for 50 years from 1879 the hotel carrier met arrivals at Southwold station. Many artists completed the last leg of their

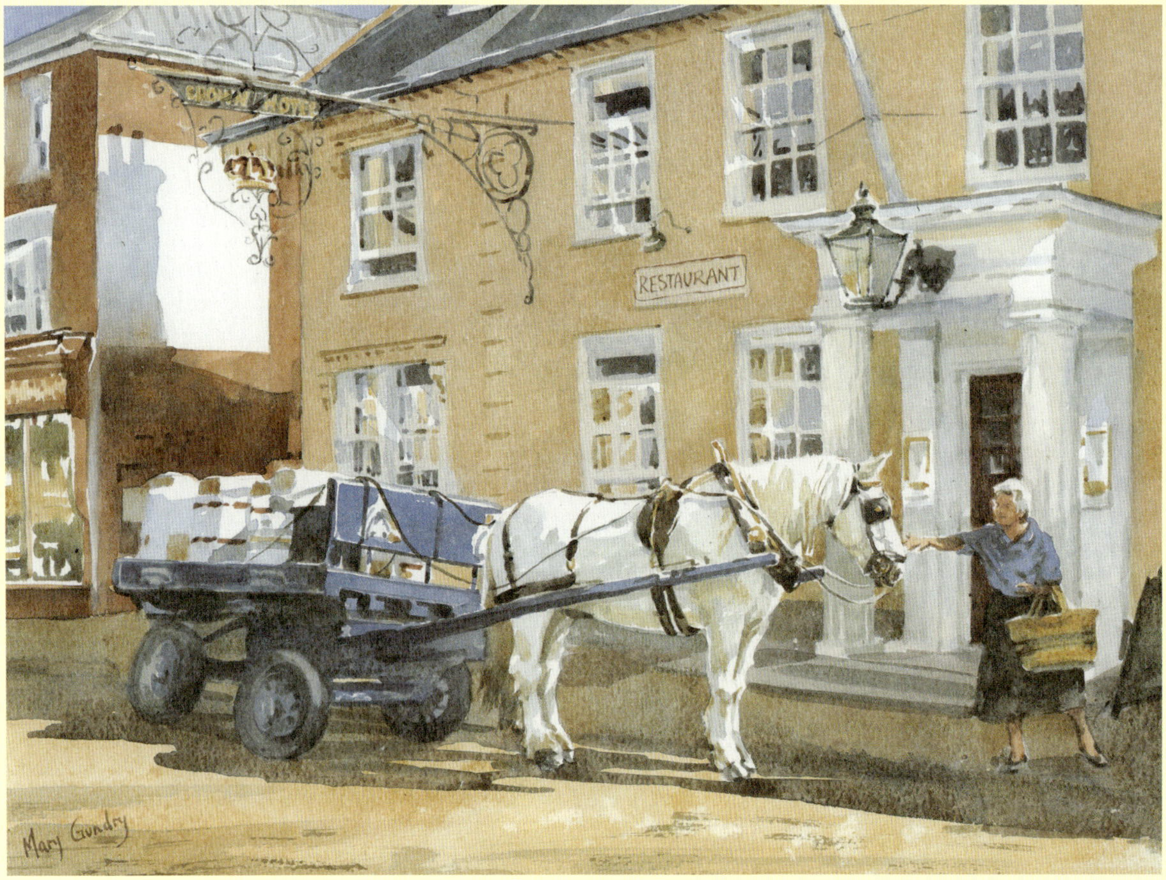


Timeless images of Southwold's streets and pubs – the Nelson, Sole Bay and Crown – as well as summer beach scenes are among best-selling watercolours, prints and greetings cards by MARY GUNDRY (b1951). The Hunstanton-raised artist left Anglia Television in Norwich, in 1989, to concentrate on Southwold-centred painting. Until 2005 she owned the Garden Gallery in the High Street – featuring her own work alongside that of local landscape and marine painters such as Matthew Garrard, Tony Garner and current owner Karen Keable. The artist and former gallery owner now lives and paints in Blythburgh.

journey by such means. The branch line also prompted Adnams to develop two new hotels to similarly grand villa designs – the Station Hotel (now the Pier Avenue Hotel) and the Randolph in Reydon, lately returned to its original title, honouring Sir Randolph Churchill, after a stint as the Cricketers.

But the great brewery also saw off one upstart rival operating in its shadow. The Brickmakers Arms in Church Street brewed its own beer from the 1880s. A century later the humble beer house, having been closed in 1958, was rebuilt as part of a fake terrace frontage to hold and hide part of the expanding Adnams production plant.

In past eras many artists began their careers as sign-painters – and East Anglian talents from John Constable to Cedric Morris to Southwold's Clifford Russell gladly accepted

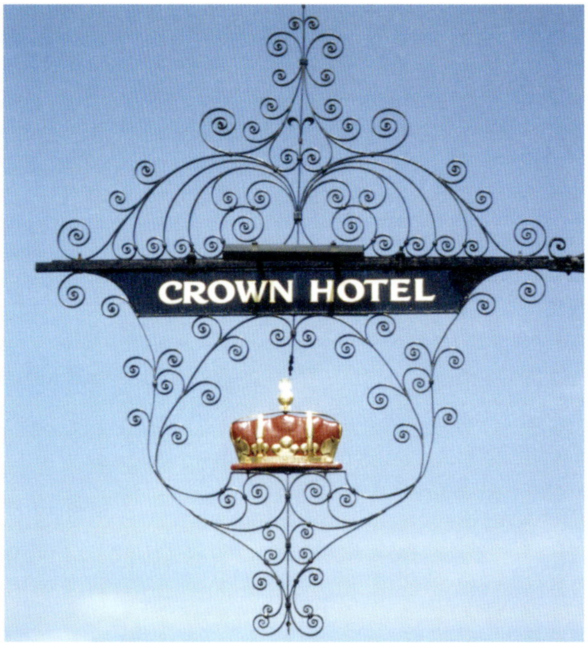


The Crown Hotel's sign in the High Street – one of the best remaining works by Southwold ironfounders Edmund and George Child. It inspired a drawing by Charles Rennie Mackintosh in 1897.

Advertising poster from the 1980s.

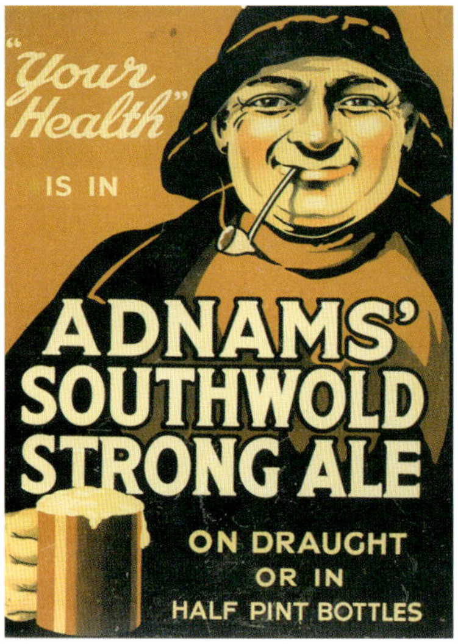

Based in London, the artist CHRISTOPHER WORMELL (b1955) has had his heart in the countryside and on the coast since his first childhood holiday - in Walberswick. Spearheading an Adnams advertising campaign from 2003, he was delighted to renew some cherished links.

He says: ‘My father, John, taught at Hornsey School of Art. He had nine children, so holidays were out of the question - until, in 1965, the painter David Tindle told us about Francesca Wilson who let artistic waifs and strays stay in a former pottery she owned beside the harbour. That's how we all came to catch the train from Liverpool Street, and to cram into the only two taxis from Darsham. We were taken to East Point, a heavenly place on stilts, for the most magical summer I can remember.’

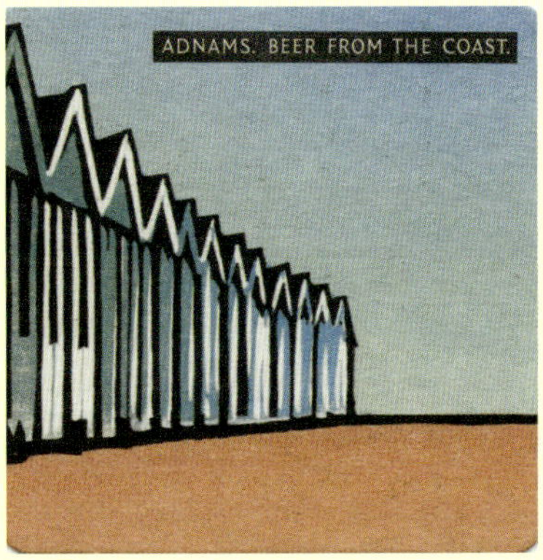


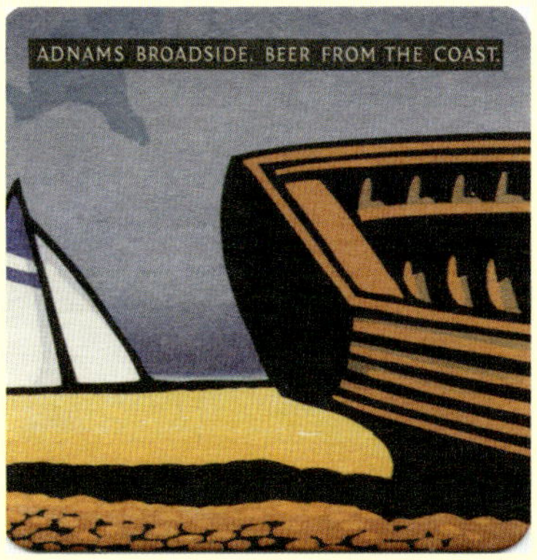


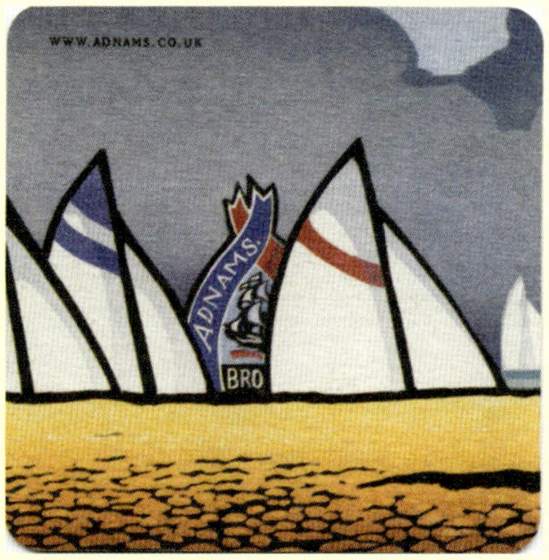


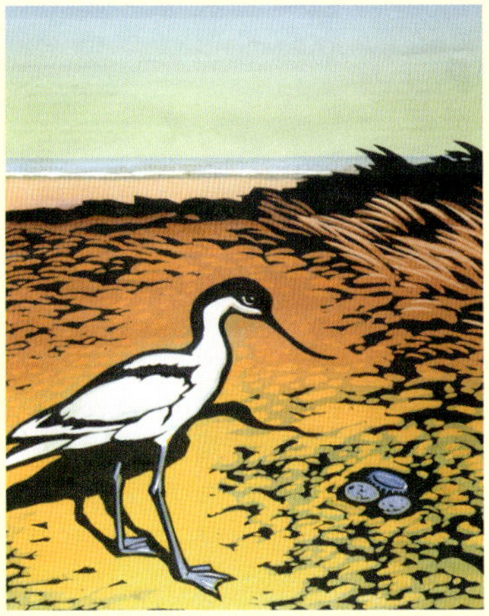

The redoubtable Miss Wilson, a writer and traveller mostly on the move between Walberswick and Hampstead, had also taken in refugees from the Spanish Civil War. Cash-strapped artists for whom she provided a coastal refuge included Frank Beanland and future Royal Academicians Bernard Dunstan and Diana Armfield.

The ten-year-old Christopher Wormell was keen on linocuts - a medium to which he would return as an adult artist, after graduating through the rigours of wood engraving. A devotion to William Nicholson was then added to a love of Thomas Bewick, as he also developed a new way of cutting into the linoleum block to create a dark and dramatic edge.

This dual sense of harking back and pitching forward, now seen in many Wormell prints, book illustrations and Rare Breeds postage stamps, suits Southwold and Adnams and admirers of both. Beer mats spirited from Adnams pubs are now regularly posted to the artist for signing.

commissions to produce pub signs. But when Charles Rennie Mackintosh paid his first visit to Southwold in 1897 his sketches included the decorative metalwork still to be seen surrounding the Crown Hotel’s sign. The town’s best-known iron founders were father and son Edmund and George Child whose beautifully-formed works ranged from the church gates and pump-lamp in the middle of the marketplace to apparatus for the Southwold Gas Company. Here Mackintosh appeared to turn a Victorian flourish into a prototype for one of his own Art Nouveau designs.

By 2005 Adnams had commissioned a new range of graphic art in witty beer mat design from empty bottles awaiting collection outside beach huts to bottle tops glinting in the shingle. Print-maker Christopher Wormell has also produced a fanciful panorama from the beach to decorate the sides of delivery lorries (see below).

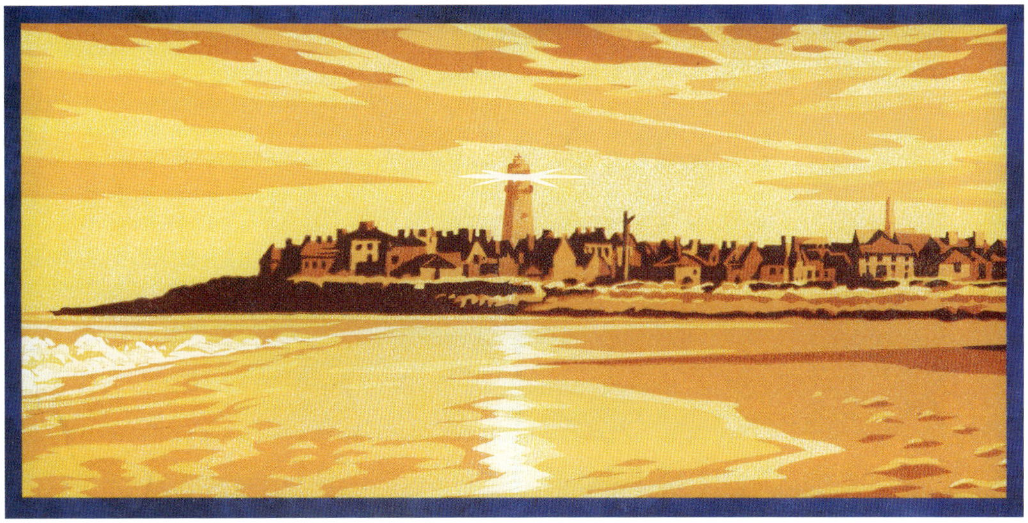

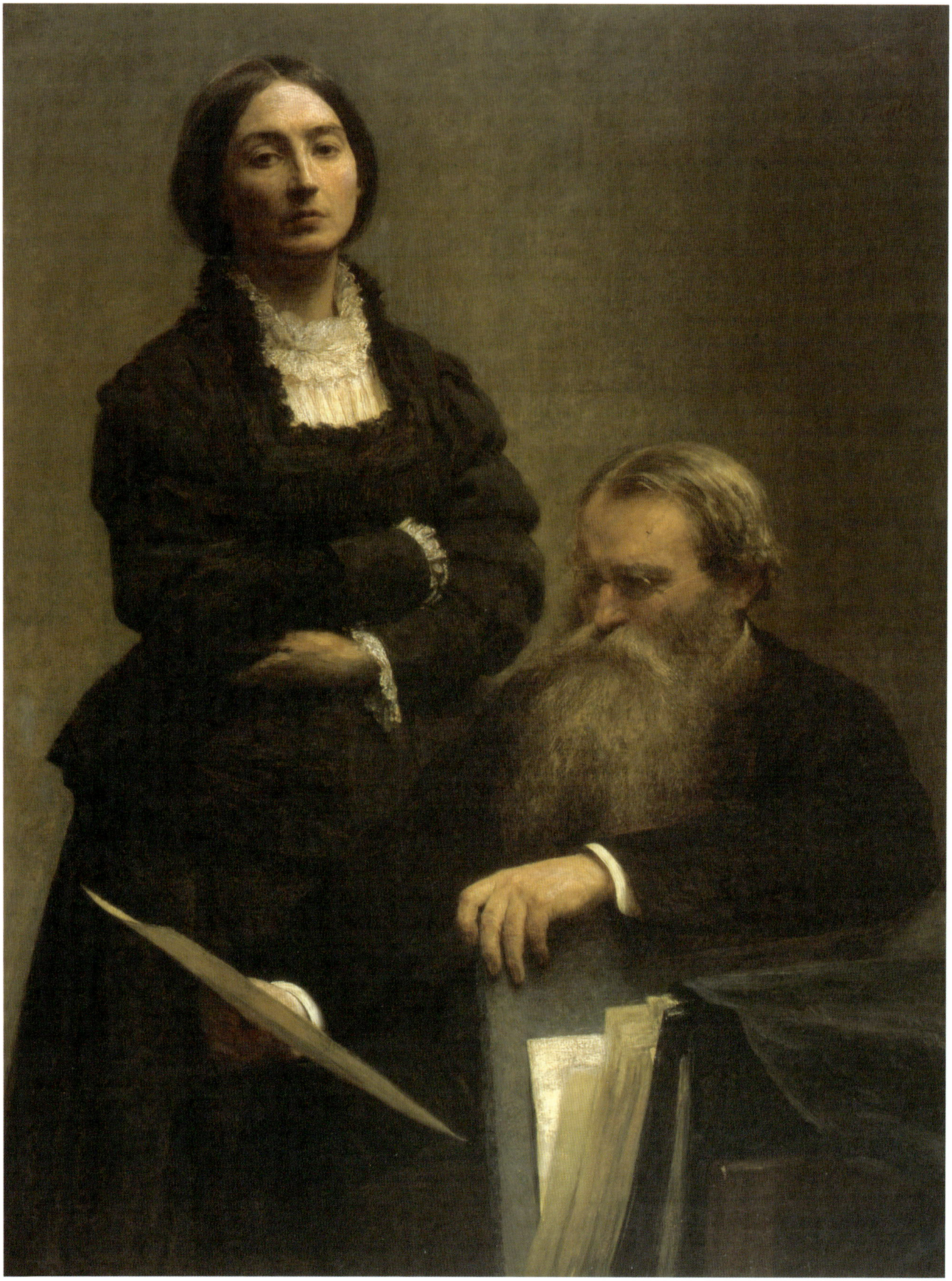

*Mr and Mrs Edwin Edwards*, Henri Fantin-Latour, oil on canvas.

Chapter Seven

# Portrait of Mr and Mrs Edwards

In the National Gallery's rooms of Impressionism there is a remarkable double portrait of Mr and Mrs Edwin Edwards by **HENRI FANTIN-LATOUR** (1836-1904). Painted in 1875, such a marriage of French and English art is clearly a depiction of deep devotion. Fantin was honouring a friend and fellow artist, and also the stalwart wife who stood over him like a 'guardian angel'. But on closer study the picture becomes more puzzling: the imposing Mrs Edwards gazes wistfully at the painter and at us; her spouse, lost in reflection on one of his etchings, possibly of Southwold, looks defeated and decrepit – a vast beard adding to an impression of immense age in a man barely fifty.

**EDWIN EDWARDS** (1823-1879) was born in Framlingham into a well-to-do family of bankers, merchants and lawyers noted in several memorial tablets in the parish church. One of four sons of Charles Edwards, whose seat was at Bridgham Hall in Norfolk, he was schooled in Dedham – the Stour Valley village lately celebrated by John Constable, who grew up in neighbouring East Bergholt. Then Edwin was sent to study in Paris so that, with added trips to Germany, he could acquire a cosmopolitan education. Multi-lingual,

*Southwold,* Edwin Edwards, etching, 1867.

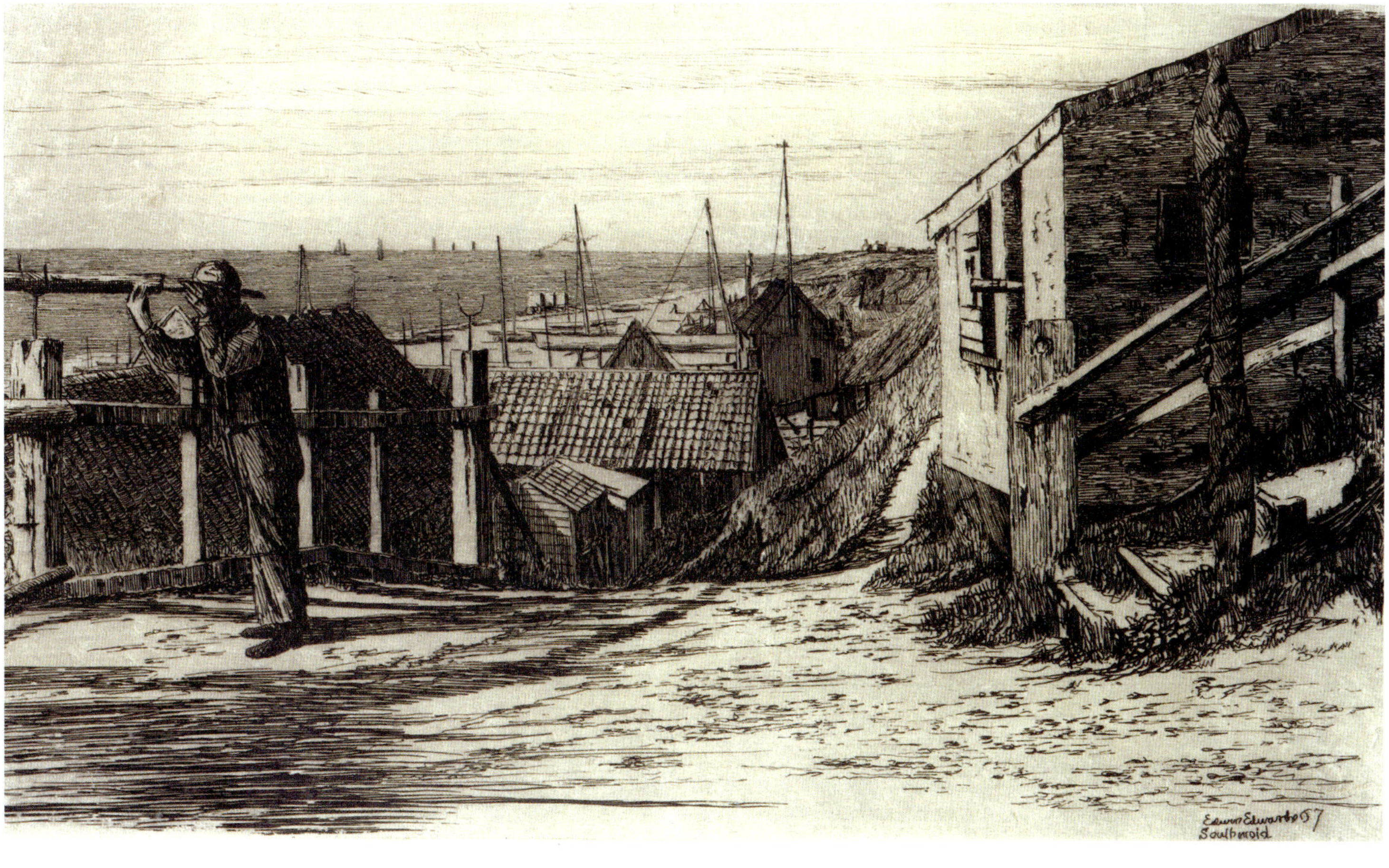

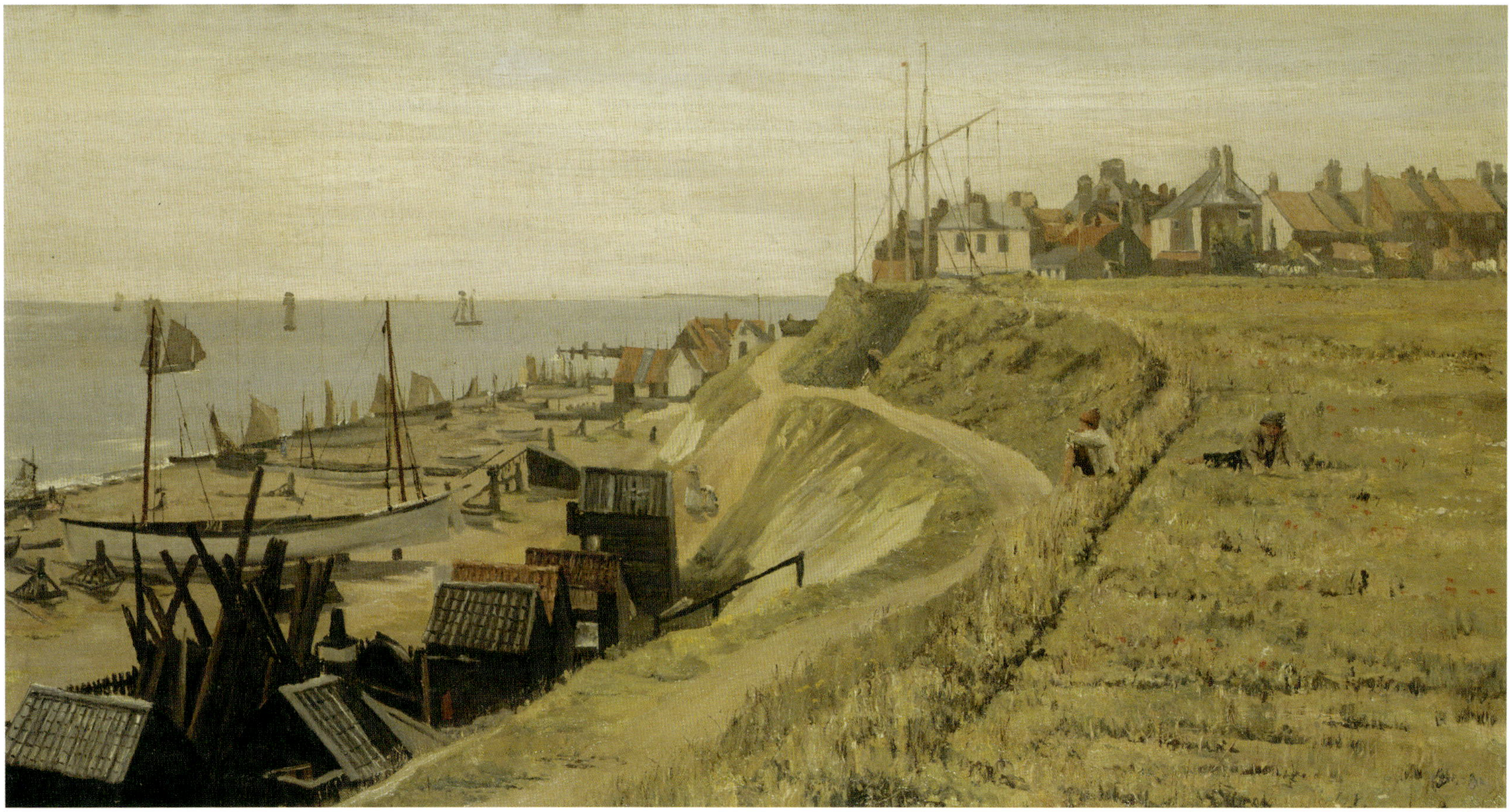

musical, an amateur artist and writer, and soon a dedicated collector of pictures and of people, he decided to follow his brother Charles in seeking his fortune as a London lawyer. And he succeeded brilliantly, practising in the Admiralty courts and penning a number of textbooks. After marriage to (Elizabeth) Ruth Escombe, at Hendon in 1852, a bright professional future, cosseted in culture and comfort, seemed assured.

Ruth, whose father was a senior figure in the Indian Civil Service, had steely elegance, intelligence and a genius for organisation. She shared her husband's ardour for art and persuaded him, after a revelatory 1859 visit to the Tyrol, to abandon law for landscape painting. Friends who warned that he had left so momentous a move too late – perhaps sensing the limit to his talent – went unheeded. So Edwin headed for Paris to immerse himself in art and there, in 1861, met Henri Fantin-Latour and other leading French artists of the day. Turning from watercolour to oil, he exhibited at the Royal Academy and alongside works by his beloved Constable, Cotman and Crome in Ipswich. He would also follow Constable in depicting Gainsborough's Lane, Ipswich, a canvas which drew one reviewer to comment: 'The painting by Mr Edwin Edwards would have shown to better advantage had it not been hung next to a Millais.' There lay the story of his life.

At their riverside house in Sunbury-on-Thames Mr and Mrs Edwards established an artistic salon, involving at various times Edouard Manet, Fantin-Latour, **CHARLES SAMUEL KEENE** (1823-1891) and, when fresh from Paris, James Abbott McNeill Whistler and Alphonse Legros. With an etching revival already underway, Legros scratched images on to copper plates with fluent expertise. The future Professor of Etching at the Royal College of Art enthused his host so much that Edwin then dashed to London to buy all the necessary equipment for a new passion. A black and white medium of painstaking precision suited the former compiler of detailed legalistic briefs rather better than the vital vivacity of paint. At last he could make his mark.

Touring the country from Cornwall to Kent, and rising at 3am to catch scenery in its dawn freshness, Edwin worked with frantic fervour. He also roamed abroad, touring Holland with Fantin and amazing friends in Paris by wandering into the city very shortly after the lifting of the Prussian siege in 1871. In all he would complete

This painting by Edwin Edwards neatly illustrates the northern limits of Southwold in the 1860s. The mid-Victorian town gave way to farmland at St James's Green. In contrast, the beach was far busier than it is today – with fishermen's sheds, workshops and cottages (soon to be lost to storms), as well as boats being built or berthed.

some 370 etchings before his death, possibly from over-work, at the age of 56. When Edwin sketched in a boat, Ruth steadied the oars; when he used a portable glass hut in order to work on winter landscapes on the spot, she wiped away the condensation blurring his view. And once the etching plates were engraved, Ruth printed them. Eventually she earned an accolade as the best printer of the age next to Auguste Delatre in Paris. This devoted helper courted curators, dealers and critics, and sorted frames, transport and exhibition hangs to project the name of Edwin Edwards. She was tireless in tiring him out.

Mr and Mrs Edwards frequently visited the Suffolk coast that Edwin had known from childhood and whose enduring charms were pressed by Charles Keene. They took summer leases on The Ferns – a cottage opposite what was then The Barne Arms (now The Ship Inn) at Dunwich, with a fine view from the back over marshes and along the sweep of Sole Bay to Southwold. And in August 1867 a Southwold landlady wrote to Keene ('Sir, I receaved your kind noat this morning…'), probably giving us the date when he first arranged for his friends and himself to stay together in the town. Cliff Cottage became a favourite base, and it was while lodging here that Edwin devised the engraving reproduced on page 51 and the oil painting on page 52, each providing a fascinating portrait of mid-Victorian Southwold.

Given the wide artistic circle of Mr and Mrs Edwards, and their habit of hosting a salon, it is tempting to speculate on the star painters (Fantin, Manet,Whistler) who might have visited them in East Anglia. Stellar art certainly came in their wake: after being hailed at the Paris Salon by the likes of Emil Zola, Fantin's *A Portrait of Mr and Mrs Edwin Edwards* was exhibited at the Victoria Hall in Norwich in 1878. But the journey from London to the Suffolk coast remained arduous, with coaches meeting the train at Darsham (the branch line from Halesworth to Southwold was opened only in the year Edwin Edwards died). Sunbury was far more accessible, and doubtless more comfortable too. The couple would have met up with Edwards relations who remained in the Framlingham area, plus Suffolk-linked artists of their acquaintance. Woodbridge poet Edward FitzGerald, who had introduced an element of exotica into Victorian England with his translation of *The Rubaiyat of Omar Khayyam*, was one regular visitor. And Keene was almost a fixture – Edwin and Ruth's love of music notwithstanding, this eccentric guest was encouraged to play his Northumbrian pipes in solitude on the beach.

Ruth Edwards ensured that her husband's etchings were in the Louvre, and when widowed spread his work among public collections in Britain and abroad. She presented the Fantin double portrait to the Tate in 1904 (which passed it on long-term loan to the National Gallery in 1997). But how had Keene, an illustrator principally for *Punch*, who declined to exhibit his work, hating publicity and praise (and even handshakes!), become so lionised as a draughtsman in France? Monet and Pissarro admired him, Degas collected him. He gave his drawings away, and worked at etchings and wood engravings only to make his hand more certain. But Ruth insisted on printing them and then, it seems, on quietly distributing the resulting images among eminent contacts on both sides of the Channel. She was a faithful friend and formidable champion.

The same age as Edwin Edwards, Keene had been born and largely raised in London but his mother hailed from the Sparrow family of Ipswich and looked homeward in times of trouble. When her lawyer husband ailed and died she moved with

*Westleton Common,* Edwin Edwards, oil on canvas.

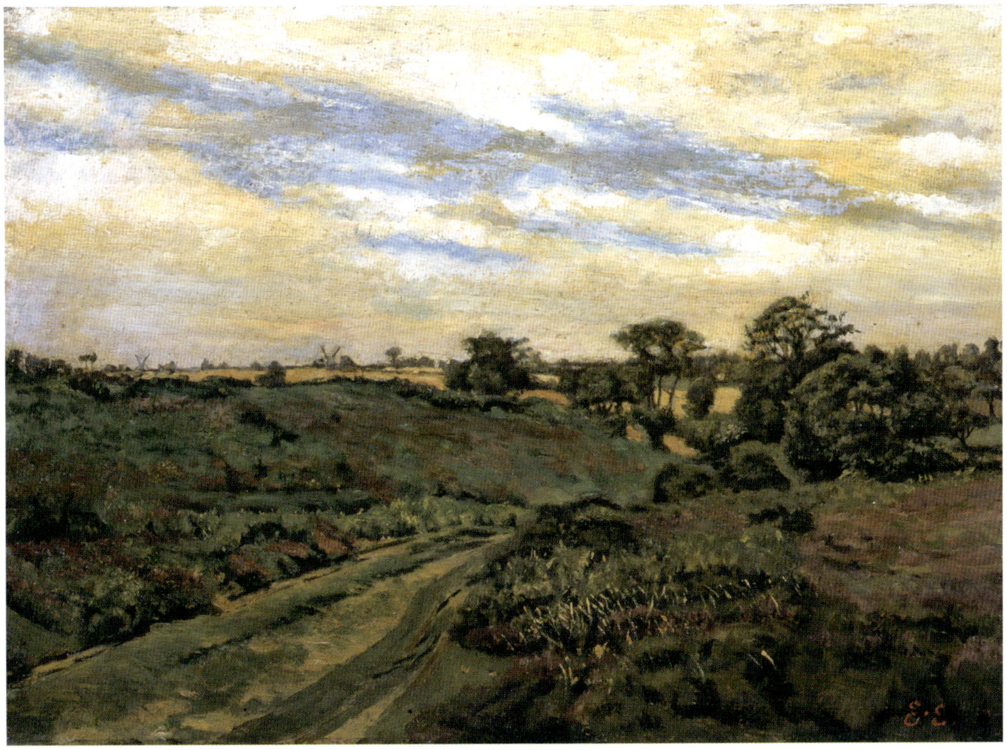

her children – two boys and three girls – to a clan base in the Butter Market. Later the Ancient House bookshop, its surviving pargetted façade includes the arms of Charles II who was reputed to have hidden there during the English Civil War. Charles attended Ipswich School before Mrs Keene decided on a return to London. But for a budding artist, with a bent towards history and romance, Suffolk was established as a place of wonder.

Moreover, the acutely reserved Charles Keene was to feel at ease with Suffolk people – learning the dialect, collecting books about the county, cherishing local characters and folklore. He leapt at the chance of a five-year apprenticeship with Messrs Whympers book-illustrators, in part because the brothers were Ipswich men. With support from family and friends, he established and sustained himself as an artist-illustrator – working first with the *Illustrated London News* and then, for 40 years, with *Punch.* Drawing images for jokes often provided by others, he came to demonstrate serious talent through the economy and honesty of each depiction and through a lively line in light and shadow. Based on intense observation, his evolving style avoided a retreat into caricature. 'I never could do any work without a foundation from nature,' this taciturn man once confessed.

A confirmed bohemian bachelor, he lived for his art and for antiquarian researches in a succession of crammed London studios – where a strict regimen of peculiar meals eaten alone, plus lethal preparations of tobacco puffed from salvaged clay pipes, played havoc with his health. In the street he was spotted looking like a cross between a gamekeeper and an army volunteer, with an added colonial dash and a knapsack slung over his shoulder as if in readiness for any adventure.

Keene hiked, camped, and explored the East Coast in a fishing boat with his painter friend Henry Stacy Marks. He loved the eerie emptiness of Dunwich, which he recorded in a stark etching and described in a letter to fellow artist and antiquarian Joseph Crawhall: 'All along at the base of the sandy cliff (striped with layers of rolled pebbles) you come upon human bones that have dropped from the shallow alluvial soil at the top. The land is sinking all along this coast, and a great city that flourished in Saxon times and was decaying at the Norman Conquest lies miles under the sea. There is one ruined church left just at the edge of the cliff. I

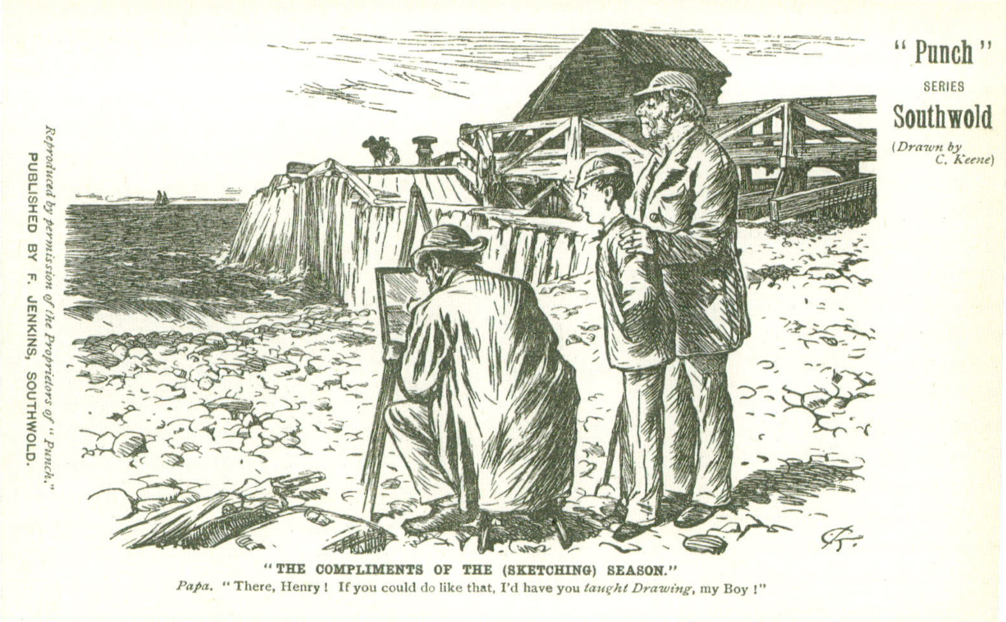


believe "the oldest inhabitant" can just remember when it was used for service, but its only congregation now is the owls and bats!'

He enjoyed spooky Dunwich all the more thanks to the warm hospitality of Mr and Mrs Edwards, whom he dubbed 'The Master' and 'The Mistress'. While in their care the wood engraver Horace Harral was also observed digging out human bones from the cliffs, disinterring enough to make several skeletons 'if only the bones had fitted'. In such a quiet-as-the-grave setting Keene said they looked on a trip to Southwold as a 'roistering' event. Sketching

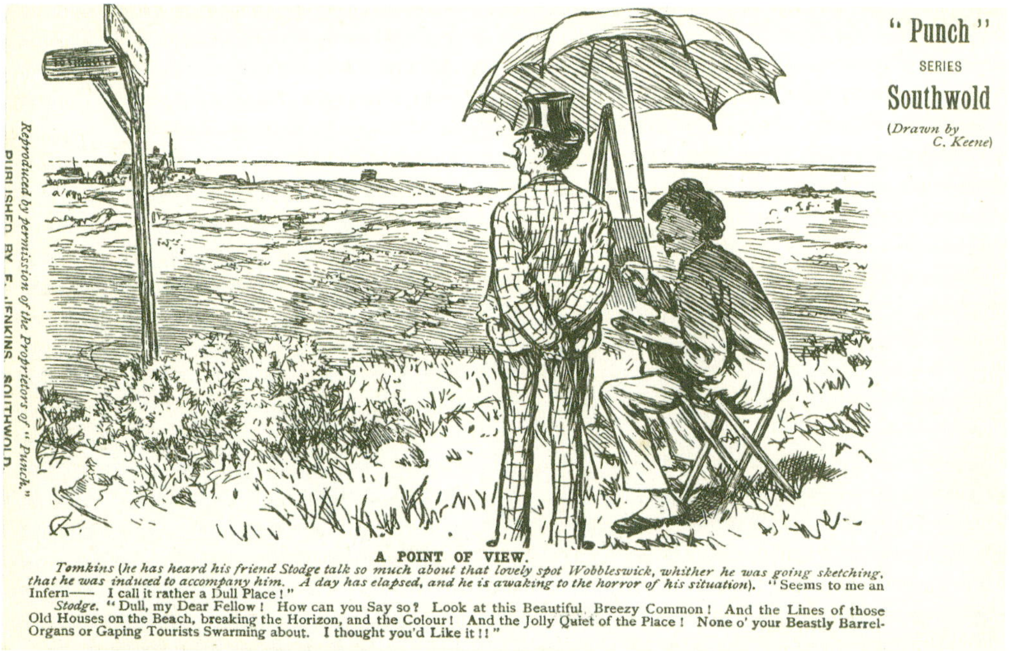


Southwold cartoons for *Punch*, drawn by Charles Keene and later reproduced as postcards by Frederick Jenkins.

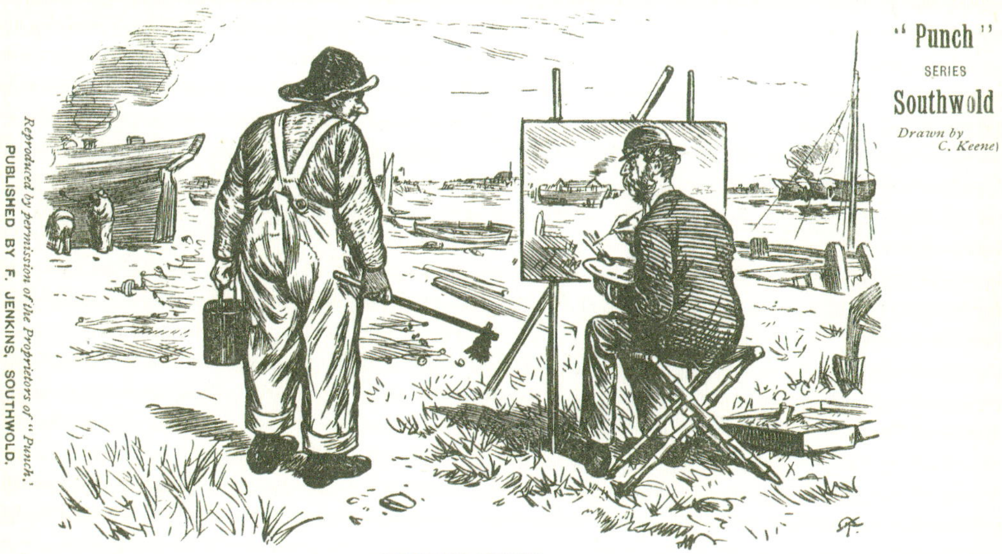


"BROTHER BRUSH."
*Ship-Painter.* "Nice Dryin' Weather for our Business, ain't it, Sir?"
*Amateur (disconcerted).* "Ya-a-s!"— [*Takes a dislike to the place.*

along the beach and harbour – capturing the scene for the only etching to be published in his lifetime – Keene drew huts and boats and fisherfolk for a *Southwold* series in *Punch*, or else for scattered images of *Wobbleswick*, some of which were later produced as postcards. The best show comic encounters between old tars and visiting artists in which the locals are the less mocked. *Punch* artists who followed in his wake were possibly more free with their ridicule. The Scottish artist Cecile Walton remembered from Edwardian visits the likes of Frank Reynolds, Lewis Baumer and W.W. Jacobs who had offended fishermen by

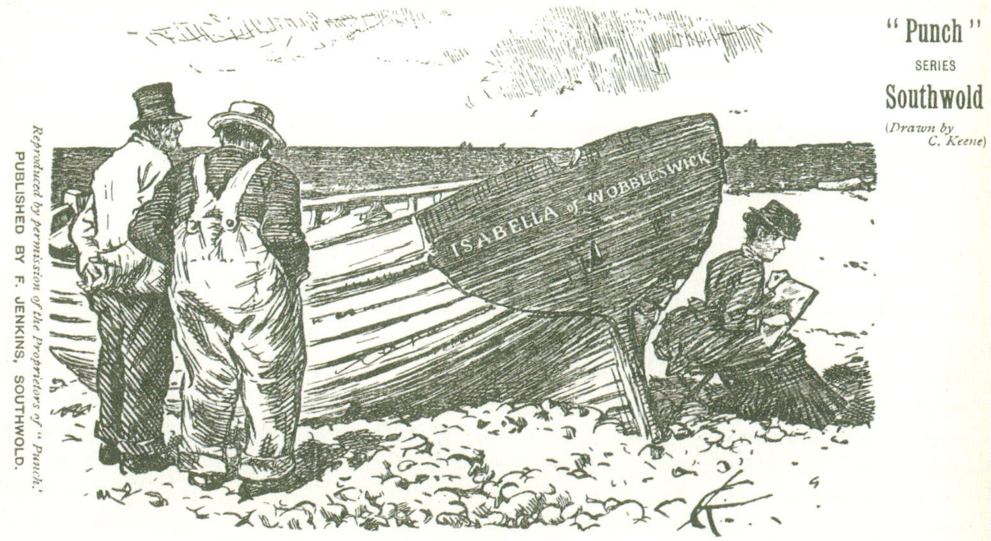


PERIL!
*Gruff Voice (behind her—she thought she heard her own Name).* "She's a gettin' old, Bill, and she sartain'y ain't no Beauty! But you and I'll smarten her up! Give her a good Tarrin' up to the Waist, and a Streak o' Paint, and they 'ont know her again when the Folks come down a' Whitsun'. Come along, and let's ketch 'old of her, and shove her into the Water fust of all!!"
*Miss Isabella.* "Oh! the horrid Wretches! No Policeman in sight! Nothing for it but Flight!" [*Is off like a bird!*

plying them with beer, listening to their stories and then 'making fun of them in the magazines'. If Dunwich was all chill to Keene, Southwold was all cheer. After one holiday stay with Mr and Mrs Edwards, he wrote to Ruth: 'The face of Nature seemed to fall yesterday directly I had left Southwold; the horses toiled along as if they were dragging something very heavy, and the sky loured and the rain fell all in accord with my spirits as we crawled into Darsham.'

Keene was pathologically frugal – mending his lamps with the gummed strips around postage stamps – but also generous to friends and acquaintances. He and other artists secretly provided funds so that 'Old Todd' the former Blyth ferryman, whose weathered figure had featured in many Royal Academy exhibitions, could end his days in a Walberswick cottage rather than the much-feared Bulcamp workhouse (where hundreds of inmates had rioted after the harsh conditions imposed by the New Poor Law of 1834, including the separation of husbands from wives and parents from children, and where bleak resignation now reigned). Through his thrift, and still more his industry, Keene left a fortune of almost £30,000. Ruth Edwards attended him to the last, cutting a lock of his hair as a keepsake, helping to settle his estate, selling his pictures from her base in London's Golden Square and probably arranging a memorial show at the Fine Art Society. There has been speculation about the full extent of their bond, though scores of letters now in Cambridge's Fitzwilliam Museum invariably begin 'Dear Mrs Edwards'.

But a romantic spirit flowed through work which caused the egomaniacal Whistler – for once an enduring friend – to judge the *Punch* illustrator 'the best artist since Hogarth'. Walter Sickert added: 'Keene…for a three-penny weekly made drawings that are on a level with the finest in the world. Keene was the first of the moderns. He saw things never seen before. He observed the reflected lights in shadows and expressed them in lines drawn in diluted ink. The Impressionist painters were great admirers and students of his work. The painting of trees in sunlight by Monet and Sisley is based on his drawings. Keene's influence on these painters was stronger than Constable's.' Tellingly for this study, another painter who revered Charles Keene was Philip Wilson Steer.

*Southwold at Last*: looming largest among all the true-to-life names and figures is Reg Carter himself. Original ink drawing for a postcard in the first *Sorrows of Southwold* series.

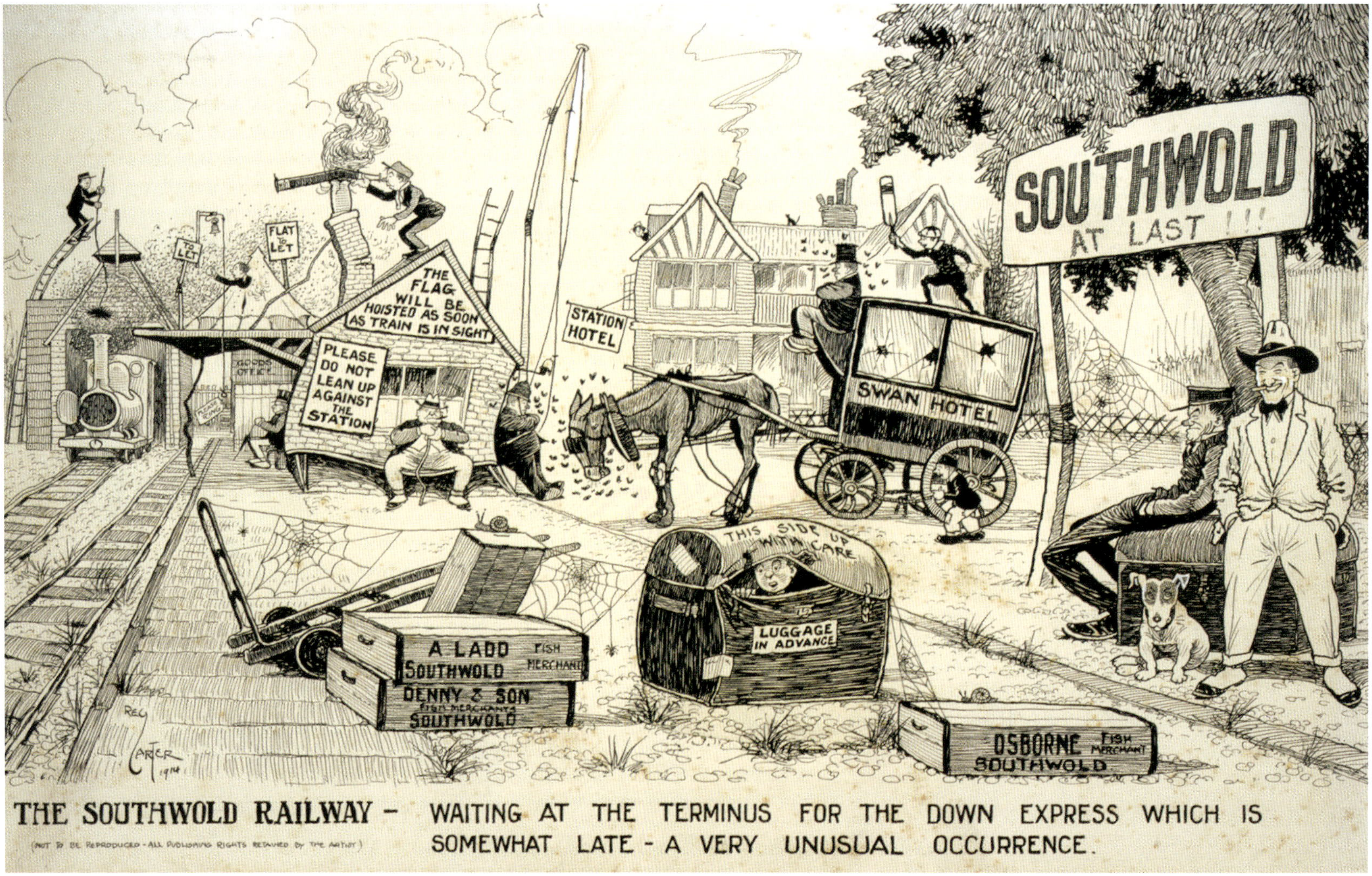

Chapter Eight

# Twig Line

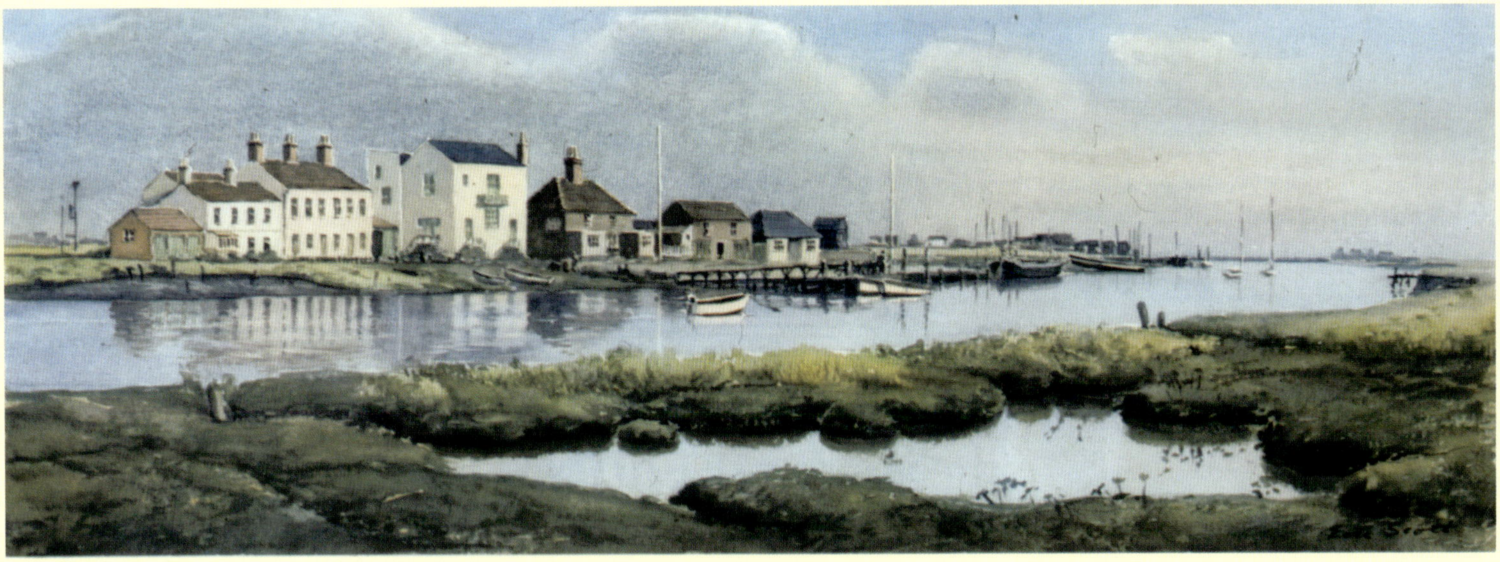

Between the late 1930s and the mid-1960s hundreds of coloured prints of British land, sea and townscapes were produced for display in train carriages. The eastern region, served by the London & North Eastern Railway, pioneered and added prolifically to this subtle exercise in advertising – promoting many watercolour artists in the process.

Friends Frederick William Baldwin and Leonard Squirrell produced 16 images apiece – the former including a view of Southwold. Around 1950 ERIC RONALD SCOTT (1904-1960) executed a pair of pictures: *Blythburgh* and *The River Blyth at Southwold* illustrated above.

Eric Scott had been raised in India, his father being an English professor in Madras and his mother hailing from a Bangalore family with Dutch origins. In England from 1925, he trained as an electrical engineer. But his passion was always for painting and he was much encouraged by the acceptance of two pictures in the Royal Academy Summer Exhibition of 1935.

Bombed-out and shattered by war-time duties, he became a full-time artist in 1950 – a year after Noel Carrington recommended a painting trip to Walberswick. Soon he had moved to a house behind the beach which was ultimately inherited by his artist, writer and teacher son, Richard.

When future cartoonist **REGINALD ARTHUR LAY CARTER (1886-1949)** was born in Southwold on the eve of Queen Victoria's Golden Jubilee, the town's miniature railway line from Halesworth was raising a modest head of steam. All three village stations and one mill halt en route were finally up and running. A moveable bridge, thrown across the River Blyth from Walberswick, was in full swing.

This tiniest of lines – more twig than branch – followed in the wake of a mid 19th century genius for engineering and enthusiasm for rail travel. It came late to the construction party, by which time there was not always the most sober assessment of underlying business plans. In 1854 Halesworth had become the terminus of a line from Haddiscoe via Beccles, and by the end of the decade the town would have good links to the national rail network via Norwich and Ipswich. Although Mrs Jane Catton, proprietress of the Swan Hotel, provided a horse-drawn yellow omnibus to meet trains at the nearest station – Darsham, nine miles away –

Southwold felt left out and let down. Over a 25-year period there were to be several abortive schemes to provide trains or trams, before sufficient investors were found, an Act of Parliament secured and a unique 3ft narrow gauge railway opened across an 8.75-mile stretch of the Blyth Valley. Rather optimistically as it turned out, the entire journey was scheduled to take 37 minutes – with Rule 92 of the new company's regulations threatening any engine driver who exceeded the statutory 16-miles-per-hour speed limit with a two-year jail term.

But even on the grand opening day, September 24 1879, the Southwold Railway proved ripe for lampooning. Building work had begun despite the resignation of the board amid worries over finance, but it had not been concluded. Of the intermediate village stations, only Wenhaston was complete. Blythburgh and Walberswick would have to be finished later. Southwold dignitaries led by town mayor John Eustace Grubbe waited at a terminus bright with flags and bunting for passengers who never arrived. The first scheduled train came in empty, having failed to reach a crowd of trippers at Halesworth because a flood had washed away part of the track at Wenhaston. Celebratory sporting events continued on the common as planned, however, where another disaster was only narrowly averted. An entrant in a horse race nearly broke his neck, as organisers had forgotten that it was necessary at the end of the course to allow space for a steed to stop.

Rolling stock began with three locomotives – No 1 Southwold; No 2 Halesworth; No 3 Blyth – six carriages with tram-style benches on either side and six freight trucks, but as revenue remained too low to service interest payments locomotive No 1 was returned to its Manchester makers as early as 1883. And so the original Southwold engine was regauged and sold five years later to the Santa Marta Railway in Colombia, where it remained in service until 1932 – longer than it would have managed if remaining in Suffolk. Happily, as more people took to the little rural railway – among them many visiting artists – the tenth anniversary of the departure of No 1 Southwold was marked by the arrival of its namesake replacement. By 1902 grandiose proposals were even afoot to convert the line to standard gauge, and extend to Kessingland, via Reydon, South Cove (with a siding for the brickworks) Wrentham and Henstead; however, they hit the buffers through lack of cash. But during the Edwardian era the twig line flourished, with harbour reconstruction from 1906 adding the hope of fresh profits and the reality of a fierce battle over who should fund a rail extension along Blackshore. The dispute was finally resolved, a No 4 Wenhaston locomotive ordered and track laid. Alas, the year was 1914. Not for the first time Southwold Railway experienced a tragi-comic problem of timing – a daily fact mocked in that fateful year

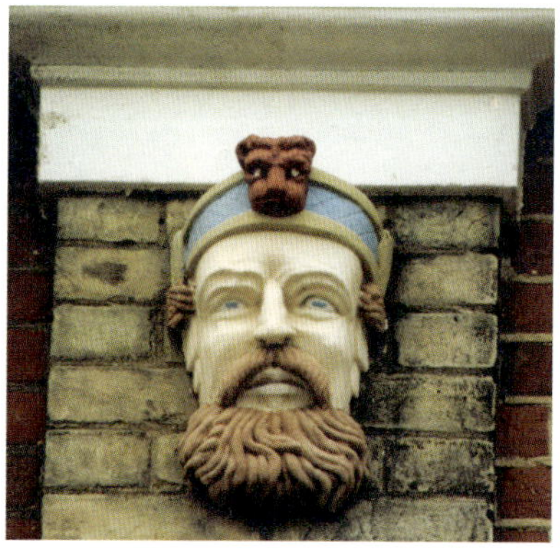

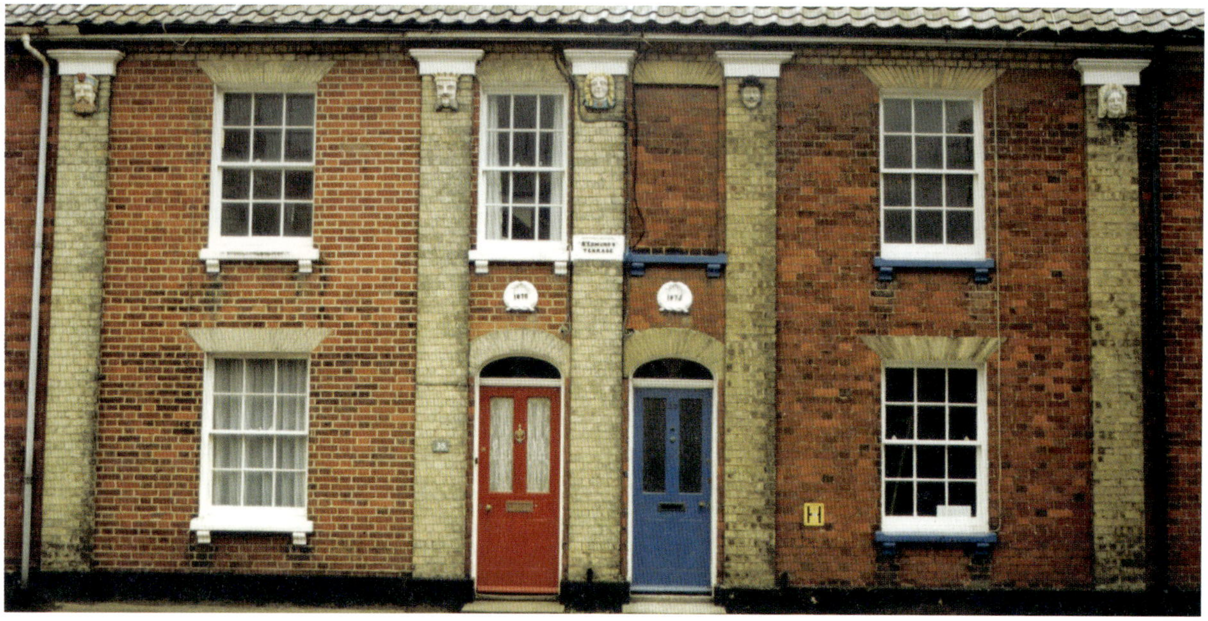

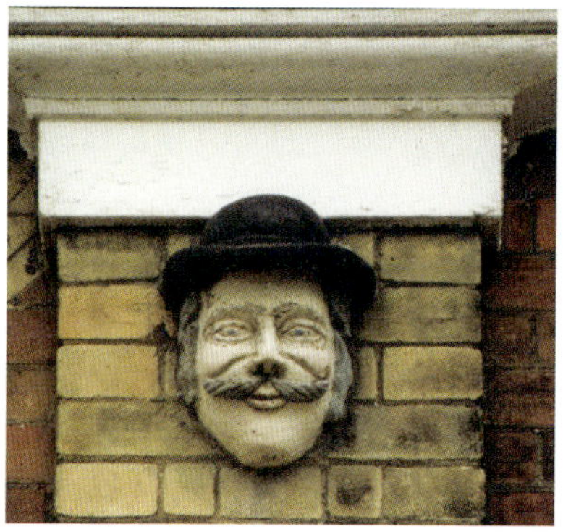

St Edmund's Terrace, Victoria Street, with corbel stones by Henry Carter.

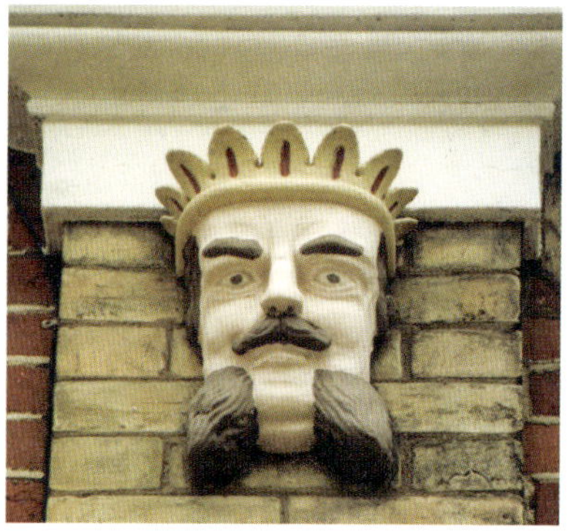

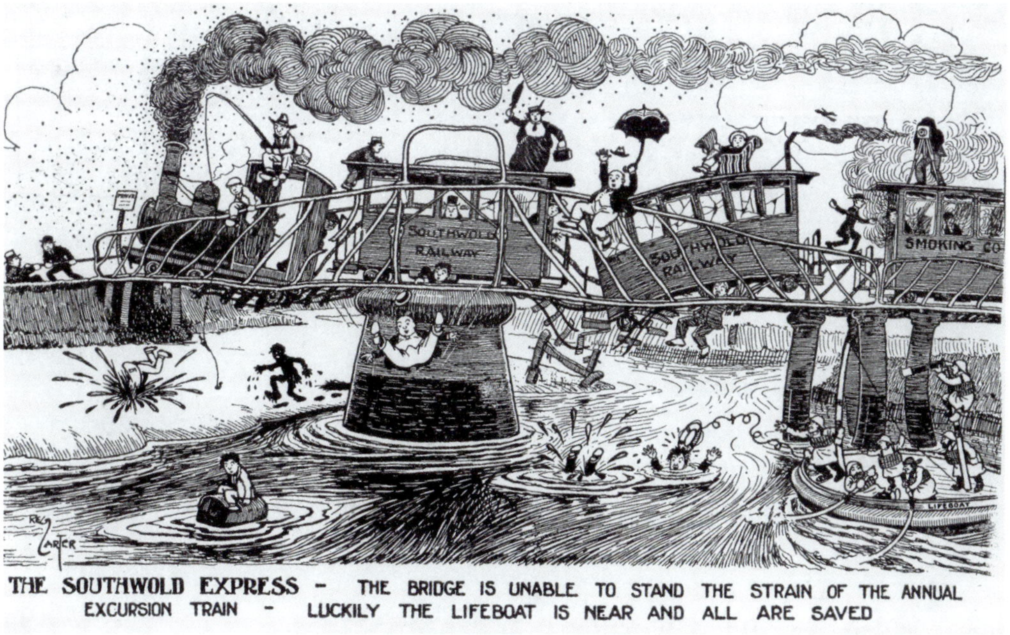


Reg Carter's postcard pictures Southwold Express trippers leaving Halesworth by train and arriving in Southwold by lifeboat.

in Reg Carter's first set of satirical postcards.

Growing up in Granville House, on Southwold's High Street, Reg was a bricklayer's son who showed such a gift for art that he was soon provided with a studio at the bottom of the garden abutting Bank Alley. Classmate Bert Girling, later to be Southwold's last stationmaster, recalled: 'Reg was about my age. He always had the desk-lid up, sketching something. You should have seen his maps. He could draw beautiful maps.' And clearly a talent for caricature ran in the family. His builder grandfather Benjamin Howard Carter constructed St Edmund's Terrace in Victoria Street, to which his uncle Henry added amusing corbel stone portraits ranging from royalty to local workmen. The initials B.H.C. and the date 1861 can be seen carved into the corner of a building opposite, which was a Carter family grocery store until converted into houses in 2003.

Reg Carter left school at 14 to work as a junior clerk in a Southwold solicitor's office. He didn't stay long: some of the picture postcards he was designing in his spare time helped to launch the publishing company of Adolph Ernst Wildt and Henry Joseph Kray in 1904. At 17 he was a successful commercial artist and would remain so for the rest of his life, contributing 1500 ink or watercolour images to at least 32 postcard printers, illustrating sports books and children's annuals (the latter written by the local author who changed his name from Neil Bell to Stephen Southwold), and cartoon strips for comics including the cover of *The Beano* for its first decade from 1938. On his death, in 1949, he left the equivalent of £300,000. Not bad for a bricklayer's son who had lived entirely on his wit.

While colourful Carter postcards covered every possible seaside topic, plus romance, sport,

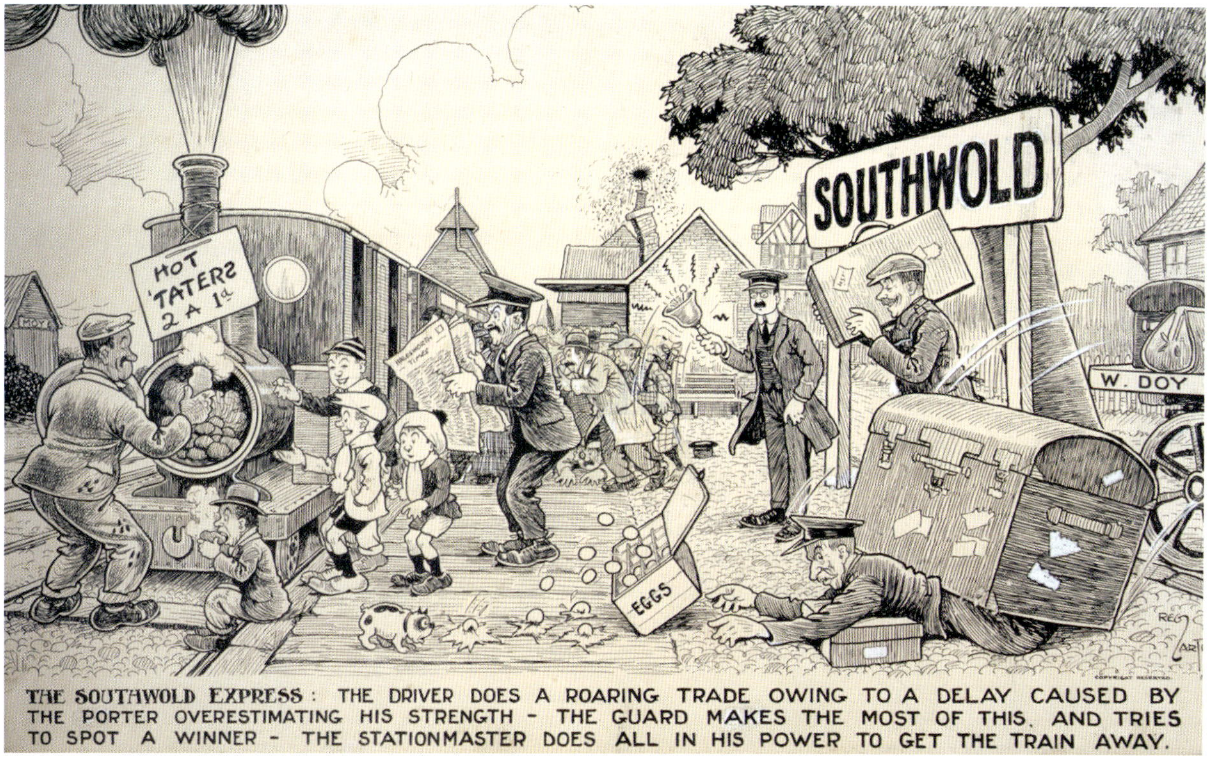


Carter the cartoonist shows us, in this original ink drawing, the eggshells on which he is unafraid to walk.

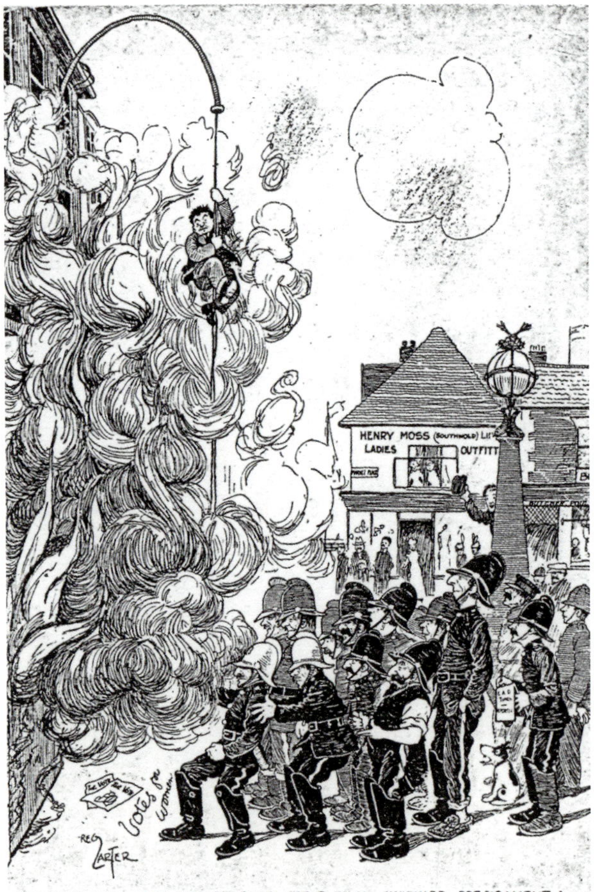


THE SOUTHWOLD FIRE BRIGADE FINDS ITSELF IN AN AWKWARD PREDICAMENT! SUFFRAGETTES FIRE THE TOWN HALL MAKING IT IMPOSSIBLE TO GET AT THE FIRE ENGINE. LUCKILY THE SURVEYOR ESCAPES FROM A TOP WINDOW via THE FLAG-STAFF HALYARDS

transport, fashion and politics, he remains best known for his wicked black and white skits on the Southwold Railway – though the inspiration was at times more subtly shaded. Some early cards, for instance, showed a Chinese influence. Local historian Hilary Huckstep has traced this theme to Southwold Railway locomotive foreman William George Jackson, who had been a driver for the Woosung & Shanghai Tramway until it was closed down by the Mandarins. In Shanghai Cottage in Station Road (demolished when Crick Court was built) Mr and Mrs Jackson held many social gatherings – the highlight being their pantomime appearance in full Chinese costume. Moreover, in the 1948 book *Story of Southwold*, which she also edited, artist Harry Becker's daughter M. Janet Becker wrote a chapter on the myth-rife railway. She noted: 'A persistent legend said that at first this train ran through the Suffolk marshland painted yellow with green dragons, because it was said to be one of a pair ordered by the Emperor of China and not delivered, as his courtiers believed the Devil to be in the first one! The Emperor is said to have had a light railway constructed about this time, but whether the sombre brown and red paint of the Southwold railway carriages ever hid such decorations will never now be known. Anyhow, the man who was first guard on the train indignantly denied the story in 1932.' Sixty years after that angry denial the story would be picked up and polished by W.G. Sebald during the long walk through coastal East Anglia which led to his acclaimed book *The Rings of Saturn.*

Reg Carter's *Six New & Original Postcards of the Southwold Railway* of 1914, produced by the Southwold Press in a buff-coloured envelope for 9d (4p), were a hilarious shot across the bows of a gallant but eccentric enterprise. The accompanying message 'with apologies to all' was all the more necessary because so many of the figures were drawn from life. The artist placed himself beaming impishly beneath a station sign reading 'SOUTHWOLD AT LAST!!!'. Other notices en route read 'The company do not guarantee arrival at the terminus' and 'Passengers are asked to sit perfectly still so as not to spoil the springs in the seats'. Each scene featured a delayed or defunct locomotive, and the man who also saw humour in a Belle steamer crashing into the pier now showed the swing bridge unable to bear the strain of the annual excursion train ('luckily the lifeboat is near and all are saved'). Most controversially, a suffragette was depicted in a track-side tree shouting 'Votes for Women!' and lobbing a bomb. The artist had already produced a postcard depicting Mrs Pankhurst's followers setting fire to Southwold Town Hall. But now it was a joke too far. With the franchise granted to married women over 30 in 1918, the bomber was removed for later editions.

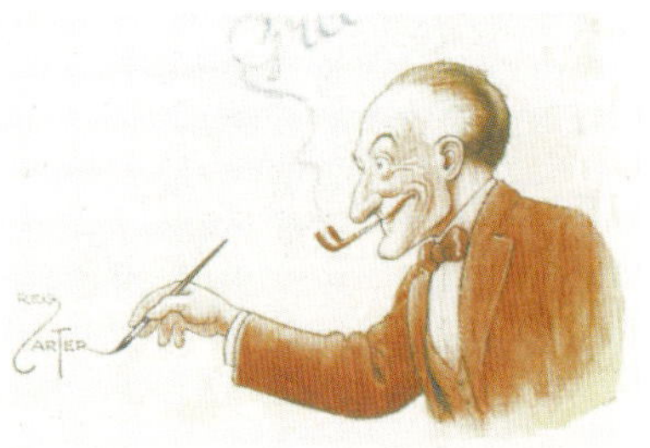

Reg Carter self-portrait & (left), Southwold fire brigade to the rescue as, in Carter's imagination, suffragettes set the town hall ablaze.

A joke that went too far: the bomb-lobbing suffragette was erased for a later edition of this Carter card.

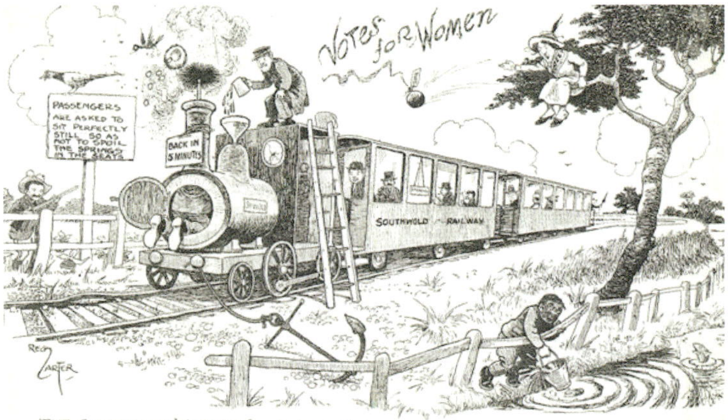


THE SOUTHWOLD 'EXPRESS' A SLIGHT ENGINE TROUBLE CAUSES A DELAY – BUT IS SOON REMEDIED.

In 1921 a second set of railway postcards appeared, which was just as funny as the first. One was captioned: 'The first class passenger supported by all the third class shew great annoyance at an unexpected stop – to learn from the guard that "The driver seeing a choice crop of groundsel – is gathering it for his canary".' Another quipped: 'The guard as a profitable sideline puts the dinners of the cottagers along the route on the up train – these being done to perfection by the return journey – the process of curing the renowned Southwold bloaters is shewn.' The steam train's boiler was also viewed as a handy oven for roasting chestnuts and baking potatoes, though it might be blocked by birds' nests and fuelled by dead cats.

In between the two series of light-hearted railway sorrows, Reg Carter had been swept into the true tragedy of the First World War. Alas, he had even issued patriotic cards – one urging young men to enlist because soldiers in their smart uniforms got the girls. But when the artist served as a gunner his attitudes changed. Cards ridiculing army procedure are said to have earned him a charge for subversion.

Perhaps Southwold's smile at the constant gibes of its comic son was also wearing thin. After the war Reg still lived with his widowed mother in Granville House, but following the publication of his second railway card series he had a house built in Haywards Heath. In 1923 – the year an LNER offer to purchase the little line was fatefully rebuffed – he married a local girl and moved permanently to Sussex. Links to business contacts in London were made easier, but maybe distance from his home town was also a good idea.

In 1920 the Arts and Crafts metalworker Philip Alexander (1864-1954), who had moved his family to Walberswick in 1904 – commissioning Frank Jennings to build Far End in Millfield Road – persuaded Professor Henry Tonks to accept

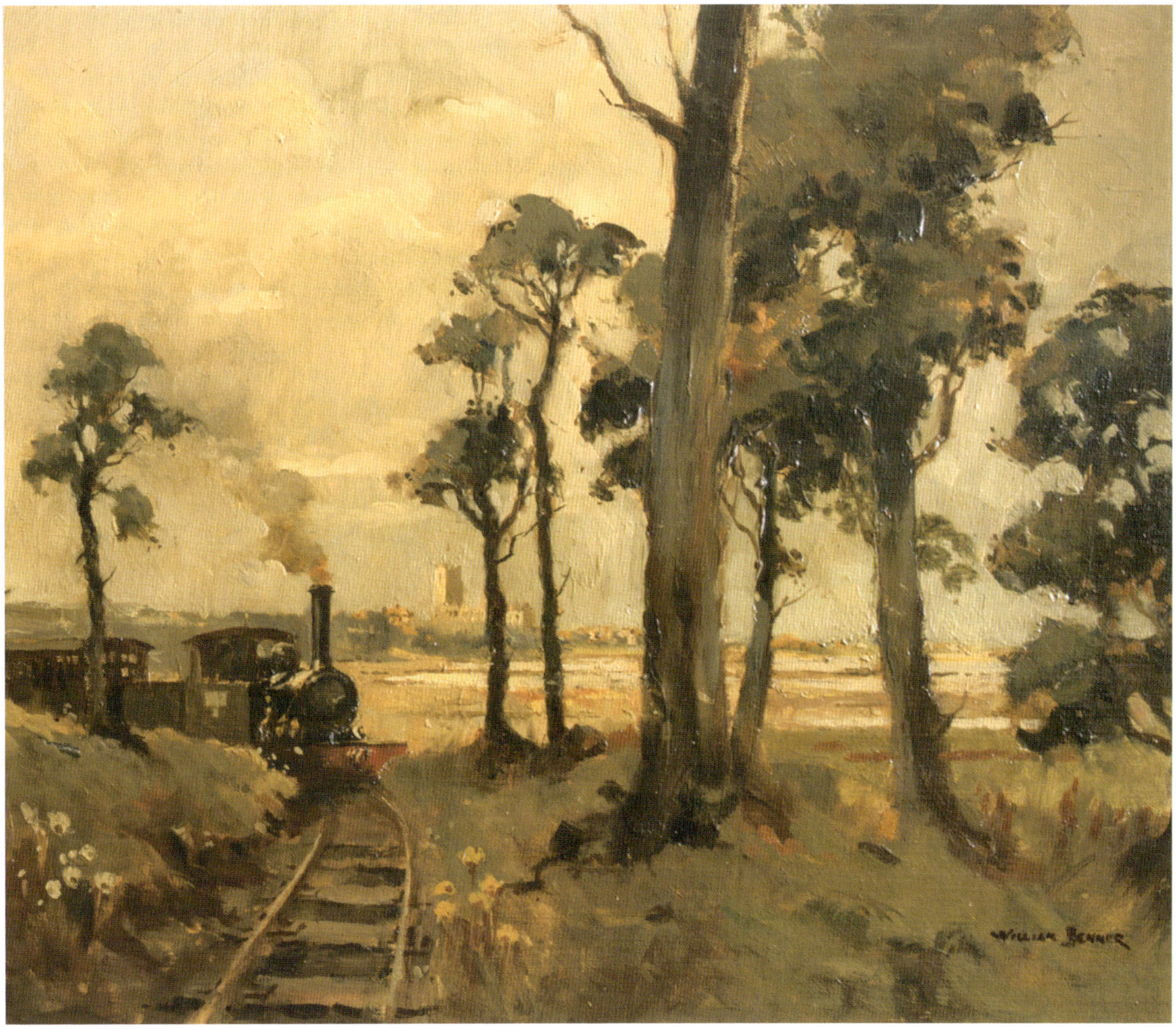


*Train at Blythburgh*,
William Benner, oil on canvas.

daughters Margaret and Catharine into the Slade School. In an unpublished memoir written in 1989, Catharine – who married Noel, brother of Bloomsbury artist (Dora) Carrington, and was the mother of painter Joanna Carrington – recalled: 'On our holidays from the Slade Art School in London we used to arrive on the little train in the dark, with a lantern swinging from the ceiling and a lamp in the carriages, rattling along over the common and the heronry at about 10 miles per hour – all very exciting!' That was how many people remembered the lost railway. But cars, vans and lorries took trade from the trains during the 1920s and when, in 1928, Southwold Borough Council allowed a bus company to pick up passengers within its boundaries, the death knell sounded for the twig line. When the service was summarily closed, on April 11 1929, with the loss of 30 jobs, large crowds attended a rather festive funeral.

Nostalgia grew and grew for the Southwold Railway, lopped almost four decades before Dr Beeching took an axe to Britain's rural rail network. Popular memory turned into a painting by **WILLIAM BENNER** (1884-1964) who moved to Blythburgh in the 1950s and began producing oils and watercolours of the railway steaming through marshes and bluebell woods in its imagined heyday. Born, trained and living most of his life in Nottingham, he had haunted local railway stations during breaks from an art-teaching career. After visiting relatives in Wenhaston, and while on the coach journey home, Mr and Mrs Benner had spotted a pair of condemned cottages for sale – with a former dame school in the garden that, they saw in a flash, would make an ideal studio. Soon the deal was done. The resourceful Mrs Benner restored the cottages and sold one, while her unworldly husband sold paintings from the studio door to passing motorists and served as church organist. Living beside the old railway track, and having a vast knowledge of rolling stock, he conjured up an era he had never actually seen. He also painted pleasing local landscapes – putting his old firewatcher's duffel coat over his pyjamas and cycling off after dawn. His grand-daughter remembers that he was so absorbed in his art that he might wash out his brush in his tea mug and drink from his water jar.

The charm of William Benner's train pictures hardened the conjecture of cruel distortion in Carter cartoons. But back in 1950 reminiscences at a railway reunion dinner at the Blythburgh White Hart – landlord: former Southwold stationmaster Bert Girling - confirmed that Reg was a realistic recorder. One veteran recalled an occasion when a Cash On Delivery item was a live lion. No cash being forthcoming on delivery in Southwold, staff had to beg meat from a local butcher until a visiting circus raised the necessary funds. Blythburgh's ex-stationmaster remembered wild-fowling in the intervals between trains; platelayers had set rabbit traps along the line. A former driver recollected suddenly noticing that his engine was no longer trailing any trucks – he had left them several miles down the track. But all agreed that the enterprise had displayed uncommon courtesy. When the last (7.30pm) train was due out of Southwold the guard would look up Station Road to see if anyone was coming – and signal to any figure rounding the bend not to rush. And on one occasion a passenger, approaching the 12.50pm train at Halesworth, shouted to the guard: 'Is there time?' To which the thirsty employee replied: 'There'll have to be. I'll have one with you.' Both then entered the Station Hotel. Host Bert Girling also knew, however, that the twig line went beyond

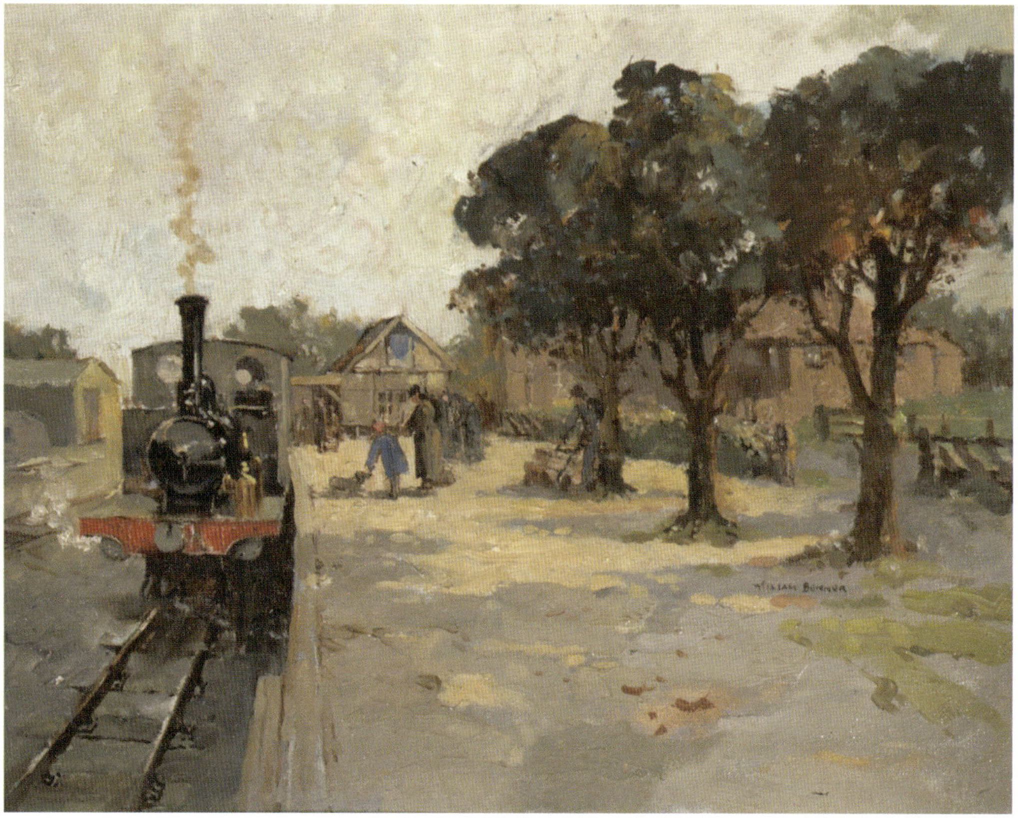

*Southwold Station,*
William Benner, oil on canvas.

a joke: on Christmas Eve 1927 his brother, a father of seven, had been killed by a train while serving as stationmaster at Wenhaston.

Essayist Adrian Bell pondered the distinctive spirit of Southwold in 1956. Writing about the former rail terminus in his long-running *Countryman's Notebook* column in the *Eastern Daily Press*, he concluded: 'I think they rather like to be cut off, in their pretty painted town. There was once a railway which linked it to the world. But they mocked it: a series of comic postcards caricatured it. Now it is closed, the lines torn up. The severing of the rail link was symbolic. It is not that they are exclusive, it is just that their own place preoccupies them. The sea is always pounding away, and trying to infiltrate into the marshes and take them in the rear. For a garrison of distinguished veterans in a state of perpetual siege, they are really very friendly. And yet – homeward bound, I turned to look back on the town in the early dusk, and asked myself once again, "What is it that makes them such a Peculiar People?" The lighthouse winked, and left me in the dark.'

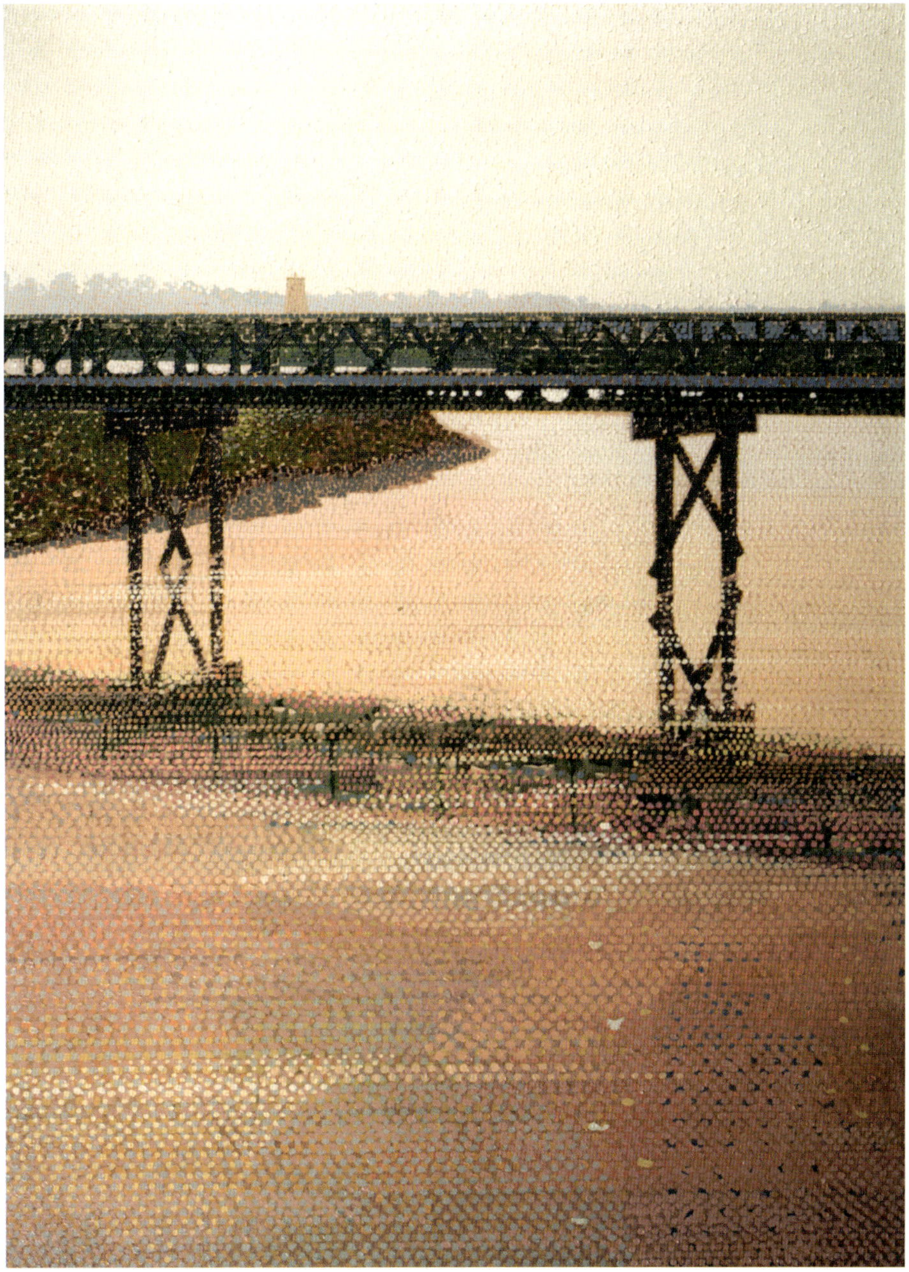

*The Old Railway Bridge over the Blyth*, Lionel Bulmer, oil on canvas.

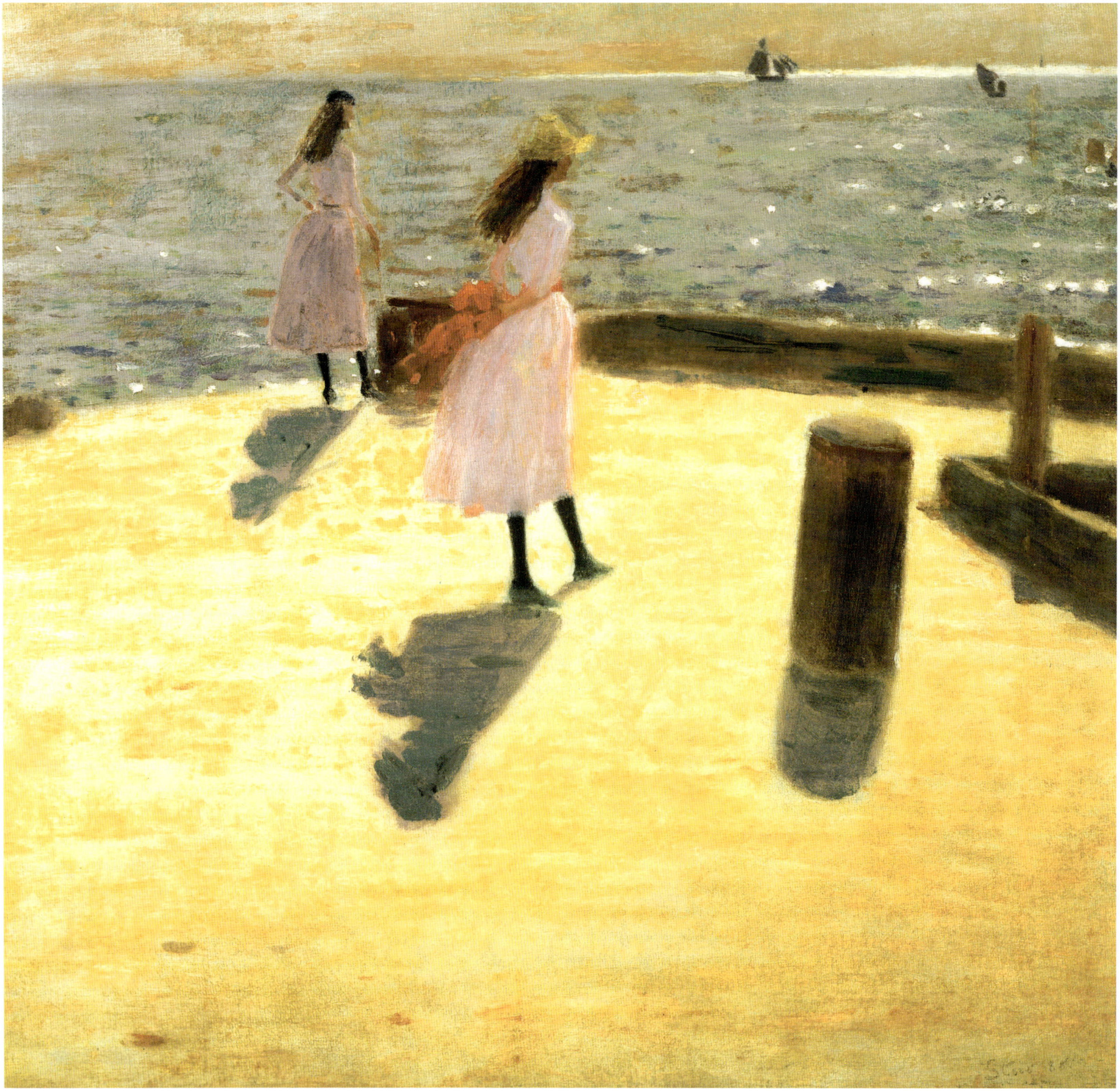

*Two Girls on a Pierhead, Walberswick,* Philip Wilson Steer, oil on canvas, 1887-88.
'I have never seen a canvas which is more like sun and wind,' wrote Sickert of this picture. 'The pink cotton frocks cling and flutter around the little figures. The figures stand up to the wind. You feel their weight, and that they are alive to their fingertips. You feel that sunshine and wind and youth are glorious things, and that life, if it be only a reprieve, renewed from day to day, is a gift to be grateful for.'

Chapter Nine

# Making Waves

Rarely has an obituary proved more premature than the notice printed in an 1881 edition of *The Etcher*. Alongside what appeared to be valedictory views of Southwold harbour by Charles Keene and Theodore Dalgliesh, a deathly commentary declared that the silting of the River Blyth and arrival of the railway had finished off this easterly outpost as a fertile sketching ground. Such a black and white verdict then went on to mourn a lack of colour along the Walberswick bank due to the tarred roofs of fishermen's shacks. All the fun of the funeral.

But what a wake! Barely three years later Southwold was making waves as a major haven for artists, and during subsequent summer months the village of Walberswick was being all but engulfed. Once lodging in either venue, most creative visitors then crossed the Blyth by train or ferry, thus drawing inspiration from both places. The mid and late 1880s would mark the heyday of the closely-linked coastal communities as attractive bases for painters – though the appeal, now so firmly established, would never be lost. The annual invasion began in 1884 with the arrival of radical young painters who, returning from studies in Paris or Antwerp, wanted to build on their liberating discoveries by working directly in front of nature (two years later they would join forces in the New English Art Club). St Ives and Newlyn in the far west of Cornwall were rival magnets – especially for those who had spent recent summers with artist colonies on the kindred coast of Brittany. But the eastward charge was led by a shy, twentysomething painter named **PHILIP WILSON STEER** (1860-1942), for whom Walberswick and Southwold would have such an incendiary effect that the rest of his long career carried a faint taste of dust and ashes.

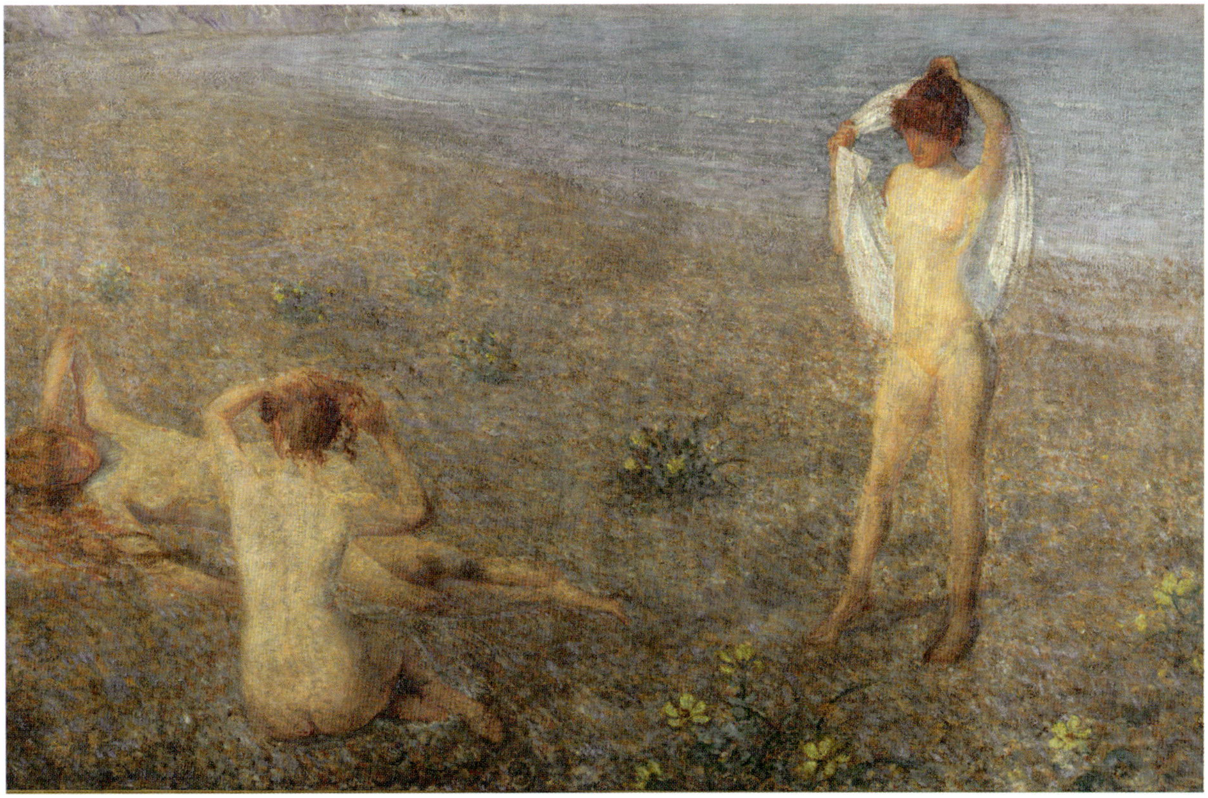

*A Summer's Evening*, Philip Wilson Steer, oil on canvas, 1887-88. One critic of this vast (146 x 228.5cms) painting, at the New English Art Club show of 1888, wrote: 'This is a picture you could warm your hands at, or boil eggs over, and it should be looked at – just once.'

Born in Birkenhead, the son of a conventional portraitist and landscape artist, Steer descended from Devonshire farmers and shipbuilders. He was soon returned to rural roots when his family moved to idyllic countryside near Ross-on-Wye. At 18, having already visited Paris, he began his art training in Gloucester, then briefly attended the South Kensington Drawing Schools before being rejected by the Royal Academy Schools. That failure propelled him to Paris, to study under conservative teachers Bouguereau and Cabanel and then to rebel completely. But besides a revelatory introduction to the work of Manet in the French capital, the withdrawn art student may have been smitten by the daring ideas of Impressionism during holiday tours of London galleries.

Wherever and however Steer had found his focus, when he returned from France in 1884 he appears to have headed straight for Walberswick. And there, making lengthy and almost annual visits until 1891, he translated the language of the revolutionary French artists, and reworked references to Whistler, to create a painterly vocabulary of his own. Ironically, another great influence was the Suffolk-raised John Constable who had died in 1837 with his achievement only dimly noted in Britain – but his work went on to light up successive movements in French art culminating in the sunburst dazzle of Impressionism.

Steer may have been accompanied on his first working visit to Walberswick by several young artists of like mind. Rochdale-born **EDWARD STOTT** (1859-1918), a fellow student of Cabanel, was certainly present that summer. An 1884 painting by Stott of two children playing on a gate in a marshy landscape beside the Blyth suggests that the most inspirational figure at that moment was the French rustic realist Jules Bastien-Lepage. Elsewhere similarly stark pictures were being created by Henry Herbert La Thangue (who moved to remotest north Norfolk in 1884) and George Clausen (then living in rural Berkshire but relocating to north Essex in 1891). Together they were rendering scenes from Thomas Hardy sagas in paint. But it would still be three years before Steer's experiments on the Suffolk coast arrived at a native English Impressionism.

How and why everything suddenly came together for Philip Wilson Steer in Walberswick in 1887 – and then fell apart only a few years later – remains a mystery. Taking the enigmatic painting *The Bridge* as a guide and as a title, Maggie Hemingway's 1984 novel imagined the life-long bachelor appearing for his annual painting visit to find one Isobel Heatherington and her three young daughters already in residence for the summer. The book, filmed in 1992 by Sydney Macartney, then had Philip painting Isobel's portrait and the couple falling in love before jealousy and tragedy took a melodramatic toll. Artistically at least, the real Steer would have been infinitely more interested in those daughters.

For Steer, the broken brushstrokes and the pure, vivid colours of Impressionism best expressed the

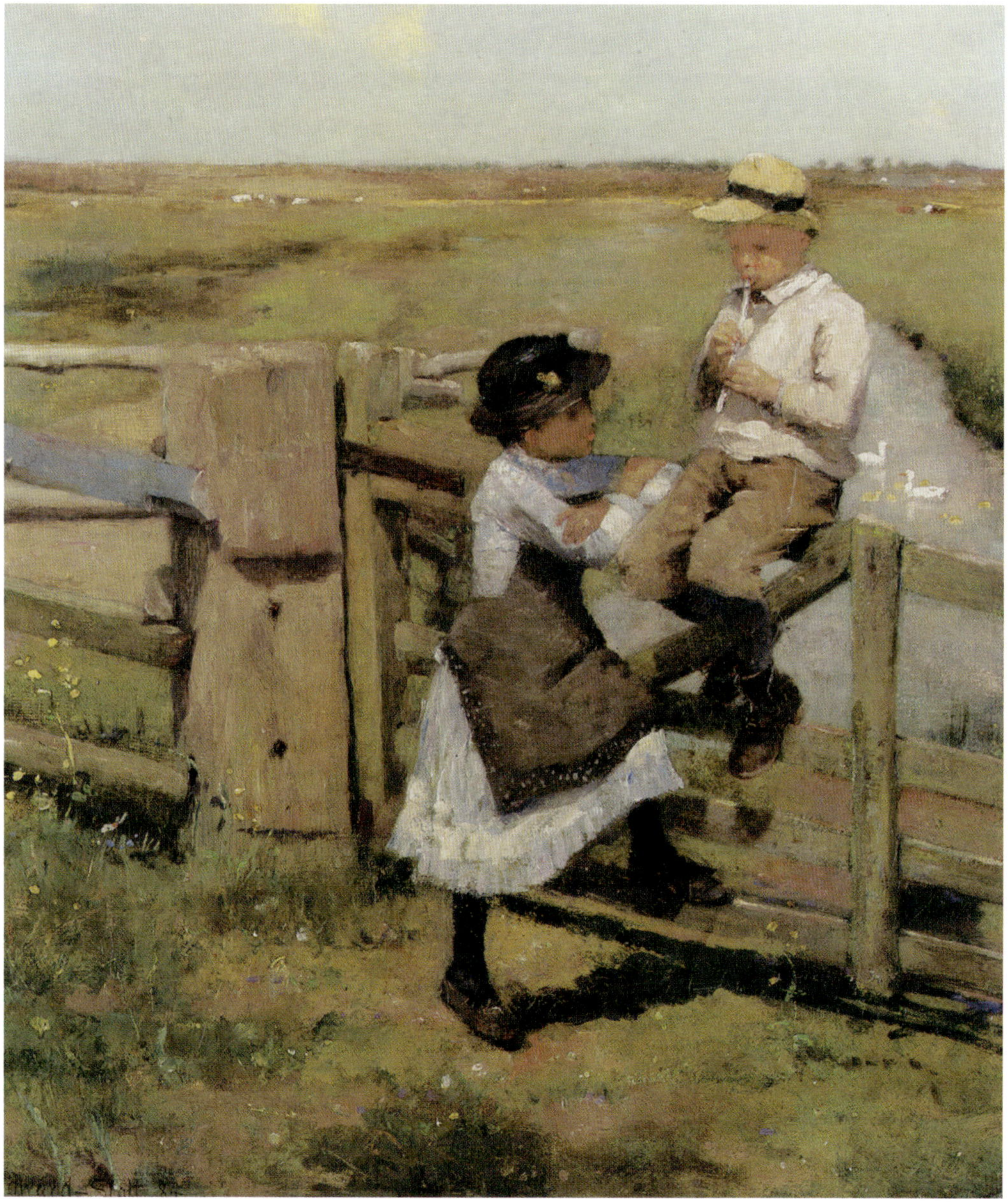

*Children by a Gate,* Edward Stott, oil on canvas, 1884.

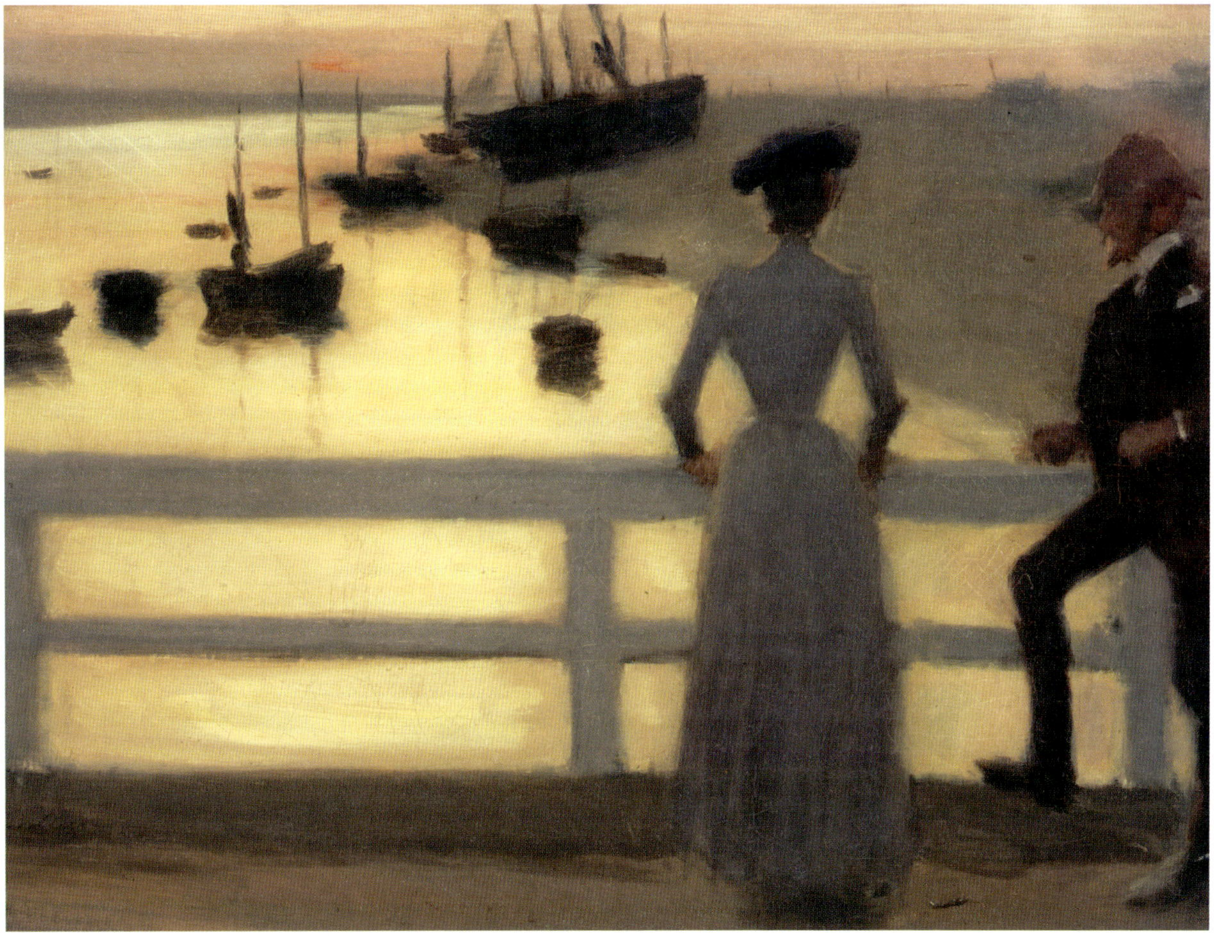

*The Bridge*, Philip Wilson Steer, oil on canvas, 1887.

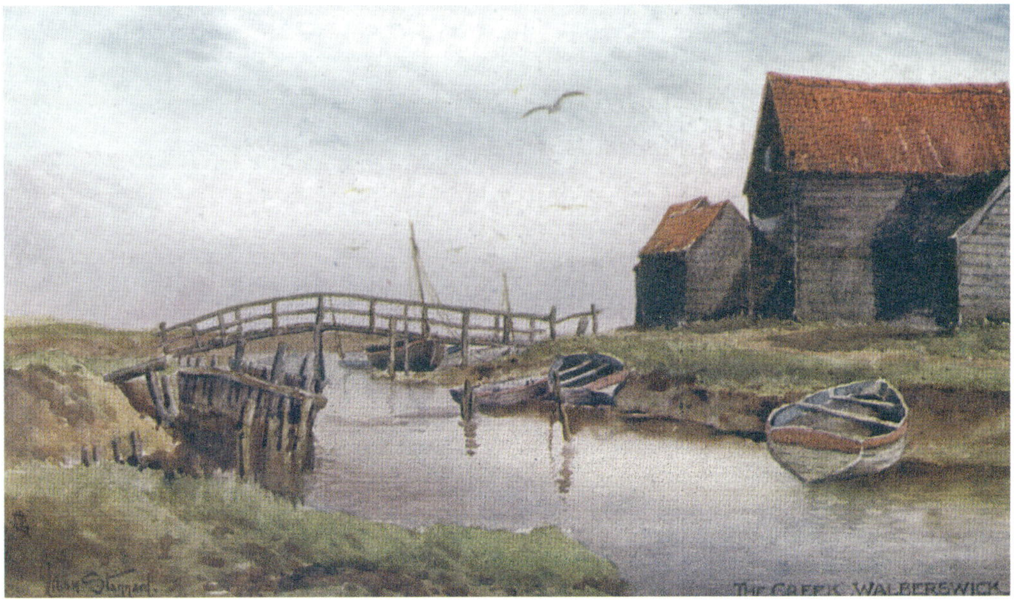


*The Creek, Walberswick* – an Edwardian postcard of Sylvester Stannard's watercolour.
A memory of the 'kissing bridge' may have fed into Steer's most enigmatic painting (above).

brilliance and brevity of a seaside summer and the image of fleeting youth. In a parade of bright paintings, lithe young girls with long flailing hair paddled, played, ran, lazed or gazed enigmatically out to sea. Although pictures of vitality, these models were never quite so lively as the quicksilver light glancing, glittering and dancing all around them (and whose myriad effects on water are recorded in several unpeopled paintings). But however idealised they may seem in such presentations, these were portraits of real people. The Gilbert and Grace children featured in *Knucklebones* – in which Steer evolved something close to the pointillist technique of Seurat to depict a pebbly beach – and Dolly Brown skipped across several canvases in a pink or white dress, black stockings and a scarlet sash. She later married portrait painter Frank Morley Fletcher and helped him to run an art school in California. Her sister Emma, another child model, wed Steer's artist friend Walter Cadby.

Steer's paintings of Walberswick and Southwold exude immediacy but emerged after intense and sometimes marathon struggles. He wandered around the area making lightning notes in pencil and black crayon – Edward Stott preferring chalks – and adding swift oil sketches on small panels for further detail. By these means he compiled a catalogue of colour and composition for the final oil paintings, which were

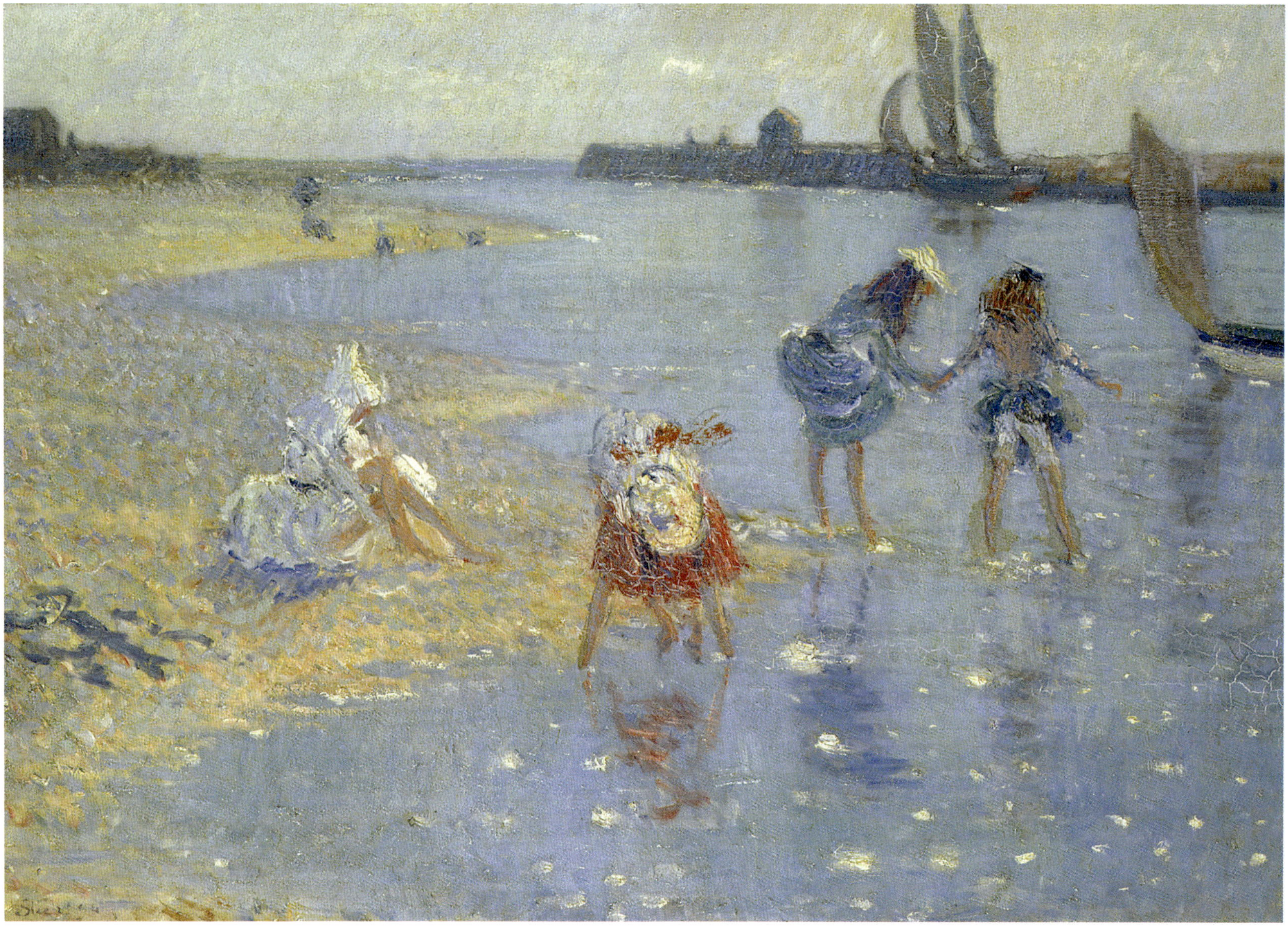

most likely to be winter productions in a Chelsea studio. For, in practice, nature came next to art for this artist. Distanced by time and place, and sometimes worked and reworked over several winters, these pictures acquired an ethereal magic which masked the agonies of their creation. In *Girls Running, Walberswick*, the paint surface has been pitted and pummelled by sustained attention. And *pentimenti* – where later layers of paint have become transparent with age – show that the two girls were originally holding hands (as their shadows still do). Favourite motifs and colour combinations were taken to new heights of harmony in *Children Paddling, Walberswick*, but the foremost figure was a latecomer to the party: cracks in the red paint of her skirt now reveal beach colours underneath. Even the title is rather detached from reality, for the setting is actually Southwold.

By 1890 these scintillating pictures had earned their creator a reputation as the most 'ultra' painter of his day. This was not meant as a compliment. Critics branded the works 'crudely horrid' and an 'aggressive affectation' and almost nobody wanted to buy them. Visiting the artist in London at this time, William Rothenstein found a studio filled with unsold pictures of 'yachts and the sea, and of girls with long legs like Sheraton tables'. Lucien Pissarro wrote to his father, Camille: 'Here is a real artist! However, he has had doubts because the others laugh at him and no one understands him.' No wonder Steer's confidence faltered and his focus shifted. Following a final 1891 visit to the Blyth Valley, he continued to work for a while on

*Children Paddling, Walberswick*, Steer's last fling with Suffolk finished in 1894, reveals a lapse of artistic memory. The figures are paddling in Southwold.

his iconographic imagery of seaside sylphs. Then he fell back on to the classic British landscape tradition, with pictures too obviously indebted to Constable and Turner. He roamed widely, visiting Harwich in 1914 and 1929, and Framlingham in 1928, while – apart from one brief visit, in 1906 – forever steering clear of Southwold and Walberswick where he had basked in a vivid vision before the sun went down.

*Young Woman on the Pier*, Philip Wilson Steer, oil on canvas, 1887-88.

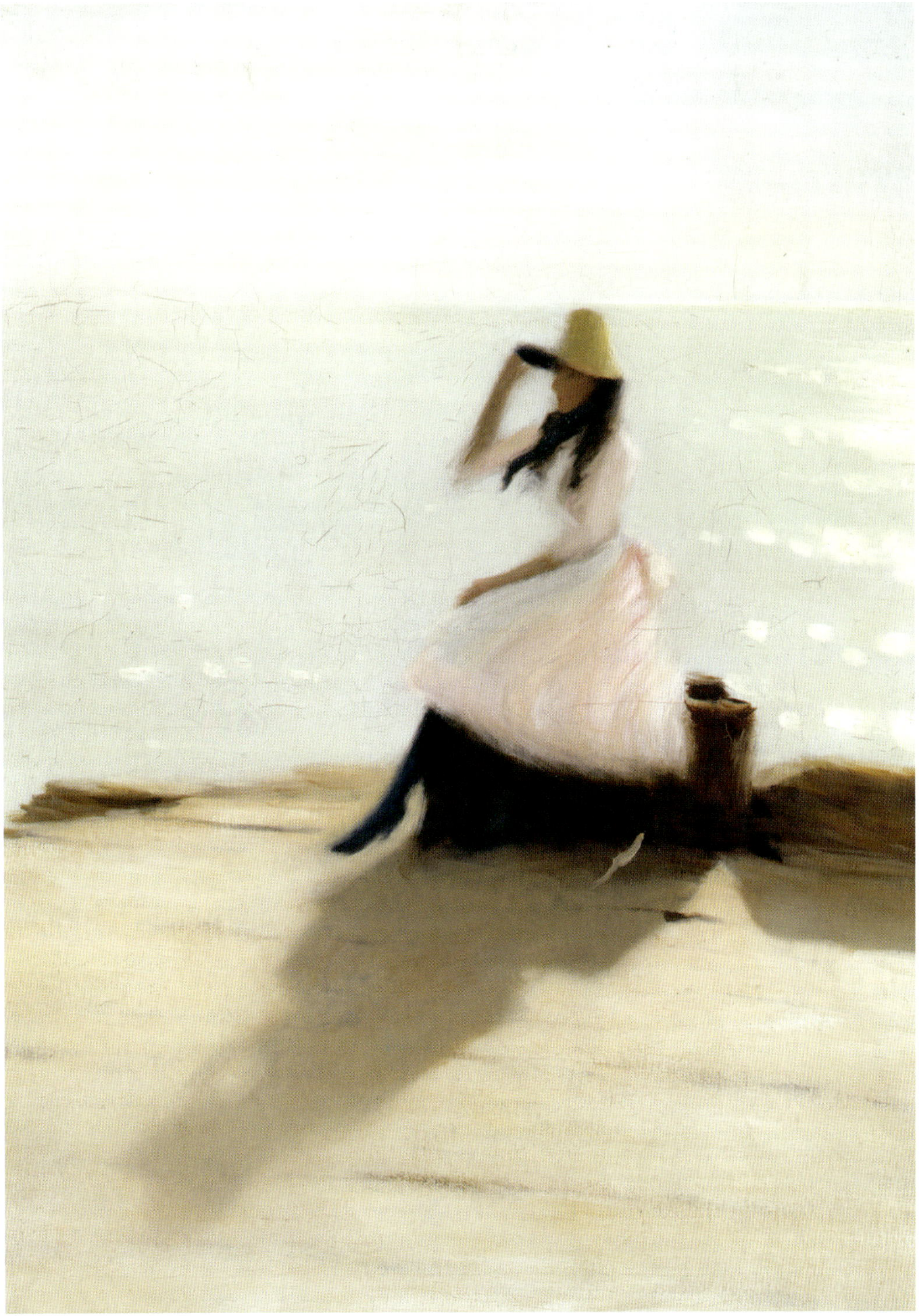

In that halcyon summer of 1884 Philip Wilson Steer had met the Irish artist **WALTER FREDERICK OSBORNE** (1859-1903) in Walberswick – which the latter was visiting in the company of his friend and former teacher Augustus Nicholas Burke (1838-1891), who had visited the area the previous year. They were soon to be joined by another fellow Irishman Nathaniel Hill (1861-1934) and William Blandford Fletcher (1858-1936). Osborne, Hill and Blandford Fletcher had all studied at the Antwerp Academy, as had Fred Hall (1860-1948) who was also painting in and around Southwold at this time. How these artists had got to hear about the appeal of the Blyth Valley is still unclear. Richard Scott has traced a possible line of recommendation from the landscape painter Edwin Hayes, via fellow Royal Hibernian Academicians Burke and Osborne, to Edward Stott and finally to Steer. Alternatively, they might all have followed the cue of Charles Keene, a major influence on many artists in the 1880s. Other Irish painters to reach the Blyth Valley in Burke and Osborne's wake included Sarah Purser, Nathaniel Hone, Norman Garstin, Joseph Malachy Kavanagh and Aloysius O'Kelly.

Once at the Suffolk coast, Osborne, always alert to the appeal of a child-centred subject, promptly painted *Boy on a Beach* – with the solitary figure set against the old river wall at Walberswick. That same misty sunshine – sometimes threatening murkier sea fret on the North Sea coast – would recur in his picture *An October Morning*, a study of children, fishermen and fish on the Southwold side of the harbour wall. The intense stillness of each picture is quite uncanny – Osborne was a dab hand at capturing mood and atmosphere. The landscape and genre painter William Blandford Fletcher, later to follow his friend Stanhope Forbes to Newlyn, concentrated on leisurely movement. He produced one of the last scenes showing Todd's rowing-boat ferry – by the following summer the old man who had featured so often in pictures displayed at the Royal Academy had been replaced by a pontoon ferry. And Augustus Burke plotted an atmospheric and unpeopled picture – *Twilight, Walberswick* – looking inland along the Blyth estuary at a popular vantage point for visiting artists known as the Skate's Nose.

For W.F. Osborne 1884 marked a further

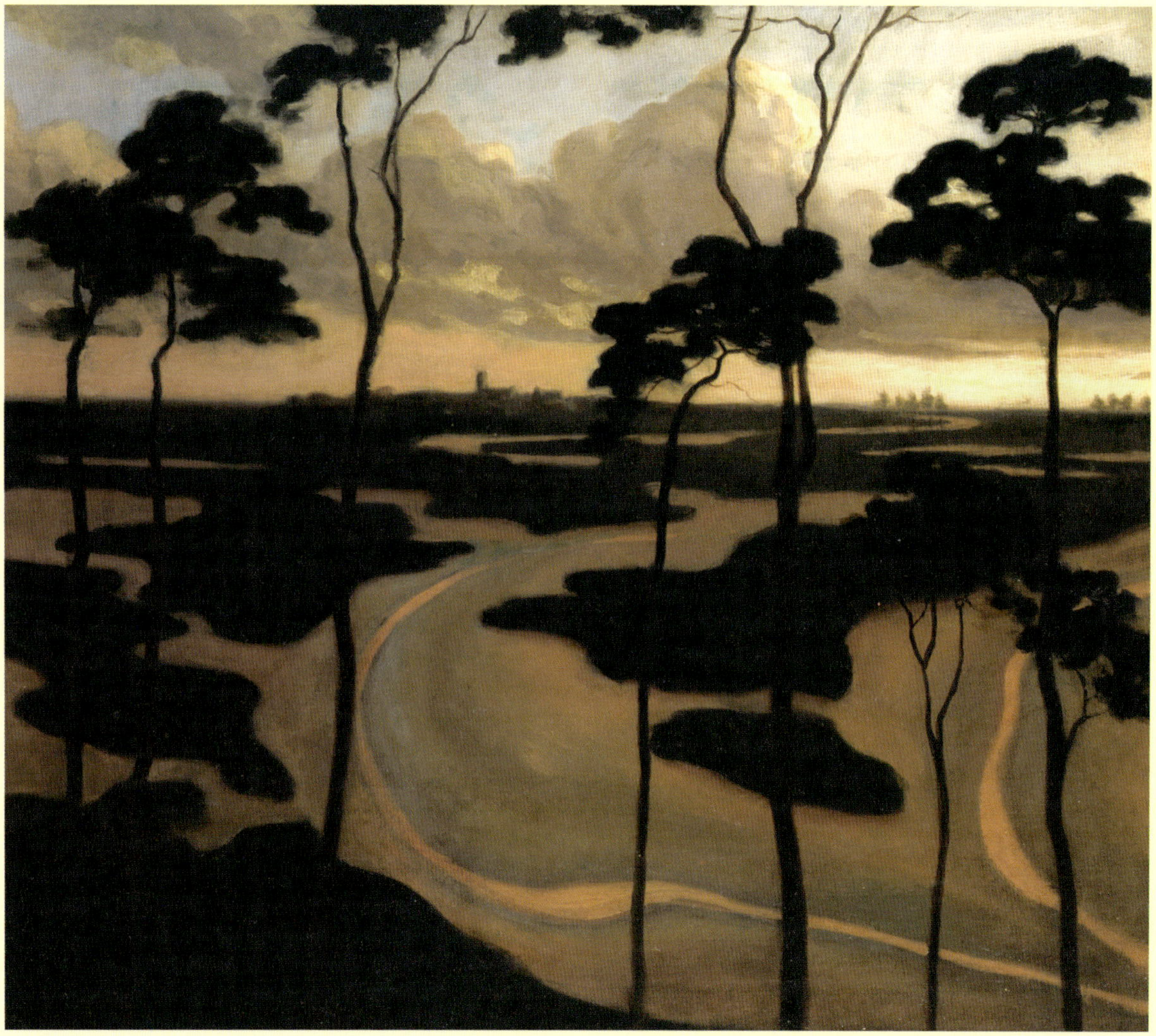

ROGER FRY (1866-1934) alighted on this Blythburgh view during a holiday in 1893 – the year of his election to the New English Art Club – and his painting was reworked as a rare exercise in Symbolism. He wrote to his father: 'I am repainting most of my Suffolk pictures as I found they were too detailed and literal and that for the final effect I must get away from nature.' As a critic and curator he was to be best known for staging ground-breaking Post-Impressionist exhibitions in London, but he was also a central figure in the Bloomsbury Group and founder of the associated Omega Workshops for art, craft and interior design.

The Bloomsberries had mixed views on the Blyth Valley. In 1912 Leonard Woolf and Virginia Stephen stayed at The Bell during their engagement. Three years later Mrs Woolf was waspish in a note of thanks to Margaret Llewellyn Davies for a gift of embroidery. 'How did it come to Walberswick?' she asked. 'Don't tell me that it is the produce of one of those little artistic cottages which used to annoy us so – I don't want to credit the artists of Walberswick with any decent feelings.'

But in 1916, war-time conscription sent artist Duncan Grant and writer David Garnett to attempt to work a smallholding at Wissett Lodge near Halesworth, which had been owned by Grant's lately-deceased aunt. Painter Vanessa Bell soon followed with her two sons, a nursemaid and a cook. Only Bell had much time to paint, though the house was decorated with a riot of figures and forms which had to be whitewashed over when it was time to leave. Even Virginia Woolf was charmed by the sense of wellbeing that her sister Vanessa managed to create in her domestic environment, and began drafting *Night and Day*, with the central figure based on her sibling, after a visit to Wissett.

The idyll ended when Grant and Garnett were called before the Blything Tribunal and threatened with prison despite a speech by Maynard Keynes in their defence. They won an appeal in Ipswich to continue with land work but were barred from self-employment. So the household shifted to Charleston in Sussex, where Grant and Bell would be based for the rest of their lives.

turning point. It was the last year in which he signed himself Frederick Osborne (a practice established to avoid confusion with his painter father, William). From 1885 his pictures bore the name Walter F. Osborne. But having been raised in, and later returning to, Dublin, he found less and less occasion to travel to scenic locations in Britain in pursuit of his increasingly acclaimed art. His keen concerntration on the figure in any picture expanded until, by the 1890s, he had turned almost exclusively to portraiture.

Sadly a man always noted for his vigour died in 1903 from a sudden bout of pneumonia: he was 43 and in his painterly prime. There was a memorial exhibition and artistic friends and admirers clubbed together to buy his Southwold gem *An October Morning* for the City of London's Guildhall Gallery. Contributors enlisted by Albert Chevallier Tayler included Edward Stott, Henry Herbert La Thangue, Stanhope

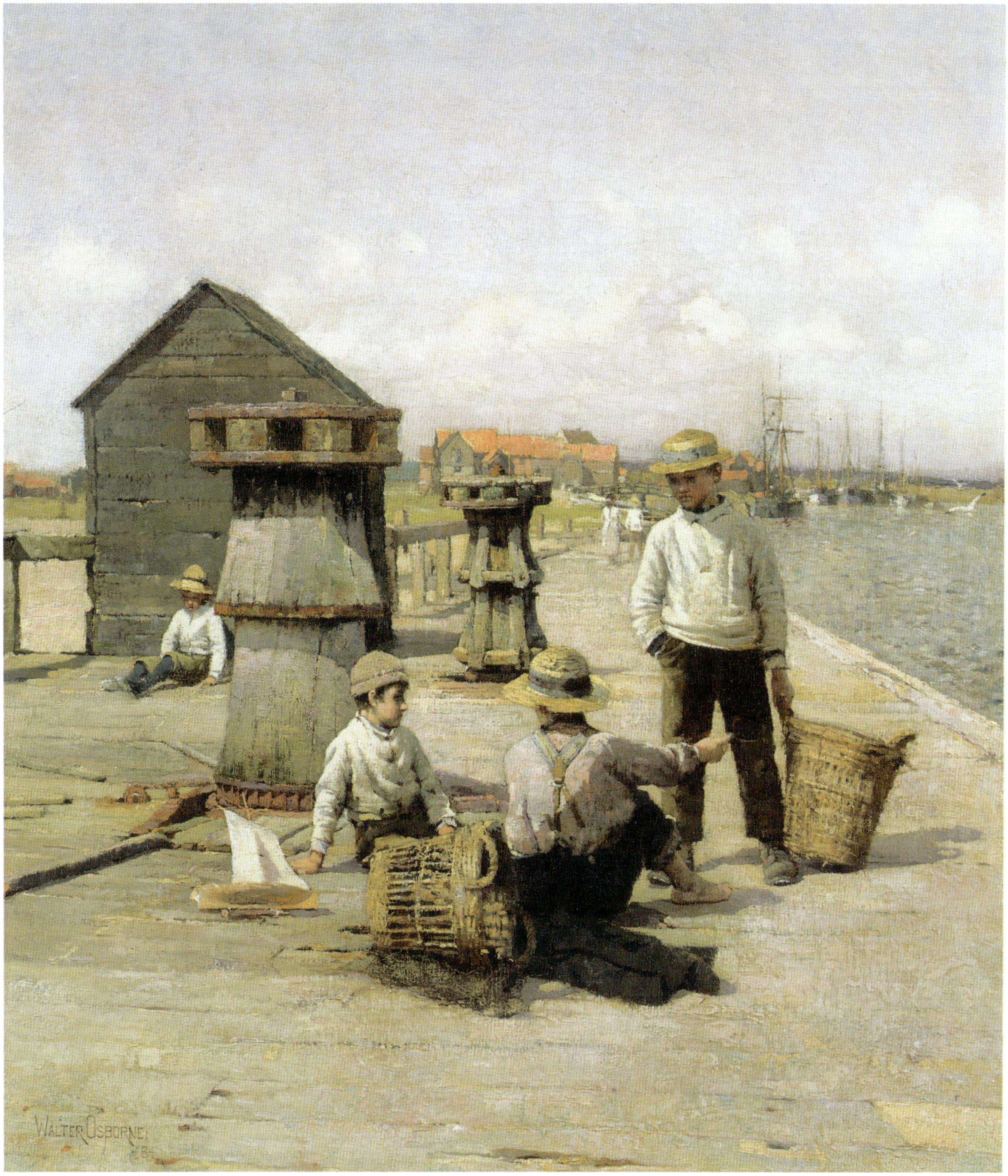


*A Tale of the Sea*, Walter Osborne, oil on canvas, 1884.

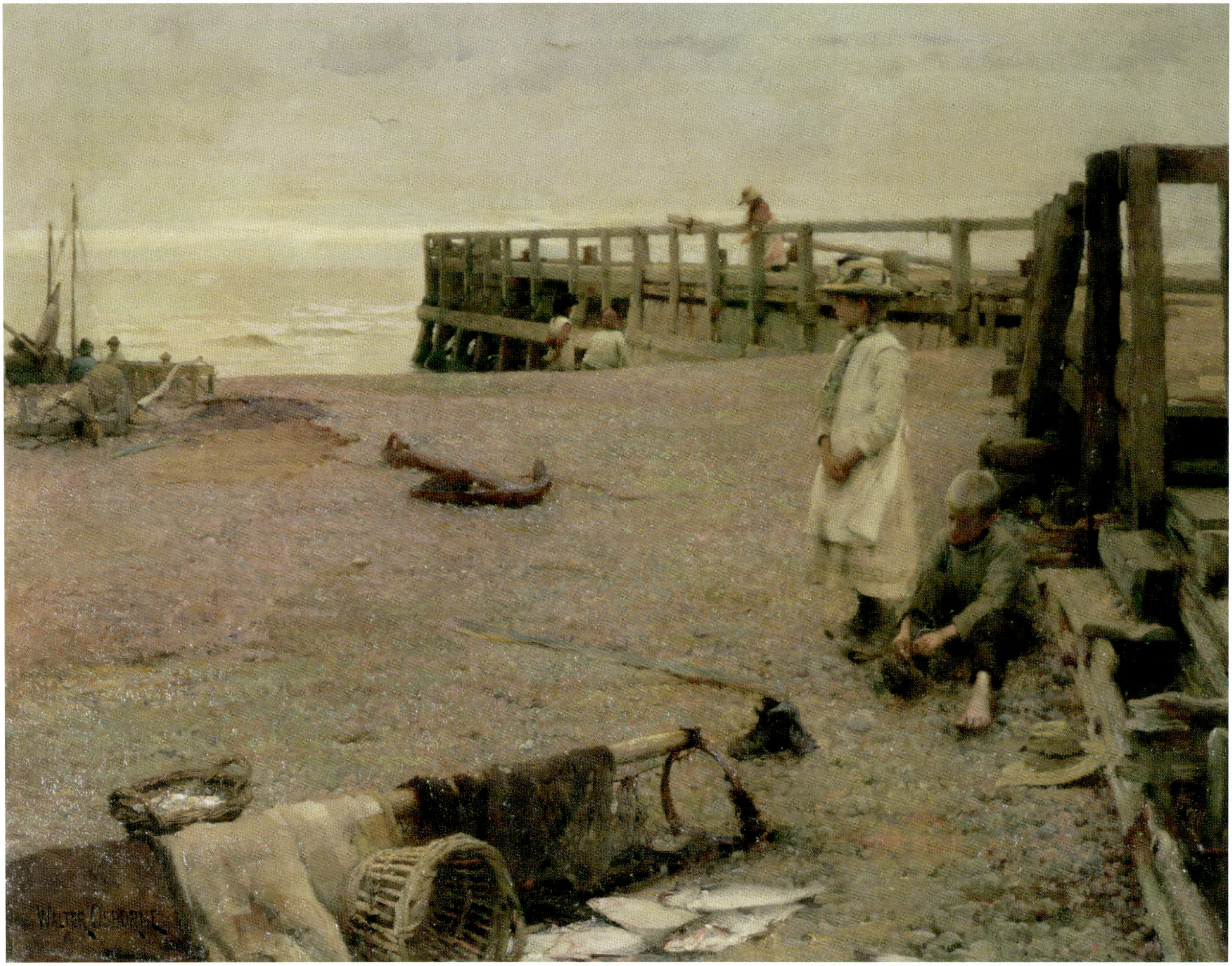


*An October Morning*, Walter Osborne, oil on canvas, 1885.

Forbes, Fred Hall, Henry Scott Tuke, Arnesby Brown and Sir Lawrence Alma-Tadema. But despite such enthusiasm, Osborne's reputation steadily declined outside Ireland until his art was dismissed and then virtually forgotten. Rediscovered in recent decades, and lately hailed as the work of an Irish master, his pictures now sell for huge sums.

In 1888 and 1889 Steer visited Southwold and Walberswick in the company of **FREDERICK BROWN** (1851-1941), a Chelmsford-born, Paris-trained Westminster School of Art tutor who had helped to found the progressive New English Art Club in 1886 and who had immediately nominated his friend for membership. Later, after being appointed Slade Professor of Fine Art in 1892, he gave Steer a permanent teaching position at the school. But, especially at this time, his work was in thrall to that of the younger man and it seems that his character was no less impressionable. Sickert sneered: 'Brown was caught up in our movement as by a cowcatcher on a train.'

Most important of all Steer's associates is, **WALTER RICHARD SICKERT** (1860-1942) and, in this regard at least, also the most elusive. These exact contemporaries were polar opposites in personality terms but their artistic aims were

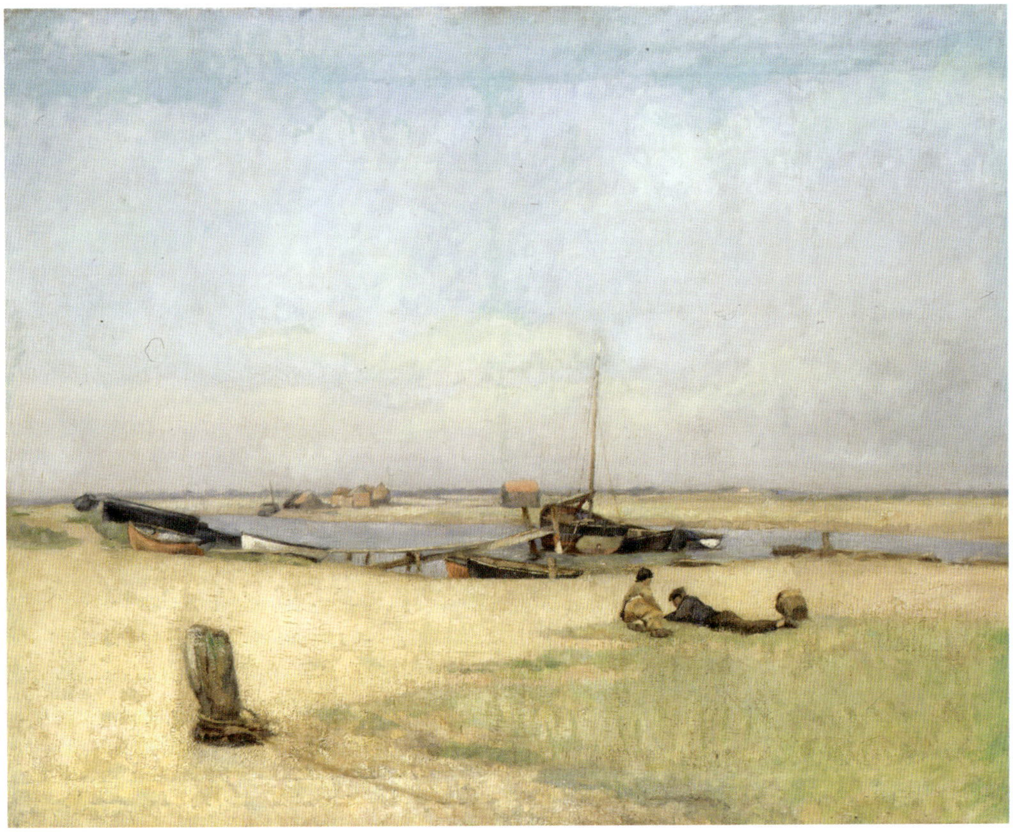

closely linked during the former's sojourns in Suffolk. Sickert bought *The Bridge,* championed his friend's scintillating seascapes in print and even produced a fine 1889 etching of *Knucklebones*, which was published in Herbert Vivian's weekly magazine *Whirlwind.* But theirs was essentially a London friendship, and how far their paths crossed in Suffolk is tantalisingly unclear. In a 1959 letter to Margaret Thomas, Clare Atwood recalled visits to Walberswick while at the Slade, probably with fellow student Ethel Walker. 'Steer and Sickert were there, and we worshipped their work,' she wrote. 'Steer was a particularly kind man and Sickert most inspiring and rather wonderful in an odd way.' On a trip to St Felix School in the 1920s – a hilarious episode recounted in a later chapter – Sickert remembered visiting Southwold in the 1890s with James McNeill Whistler, and, given this information, it is tempting to see several of the latter's seascapes of the period in a Sole Bay light. Although they had nearby Chelsea studios, there is no record that Whistler and Steer ever met. But that altogether enigmatic painting

*Estuary at Walberswick*, Walter Osborne, oil on canvas. c.1884-84.

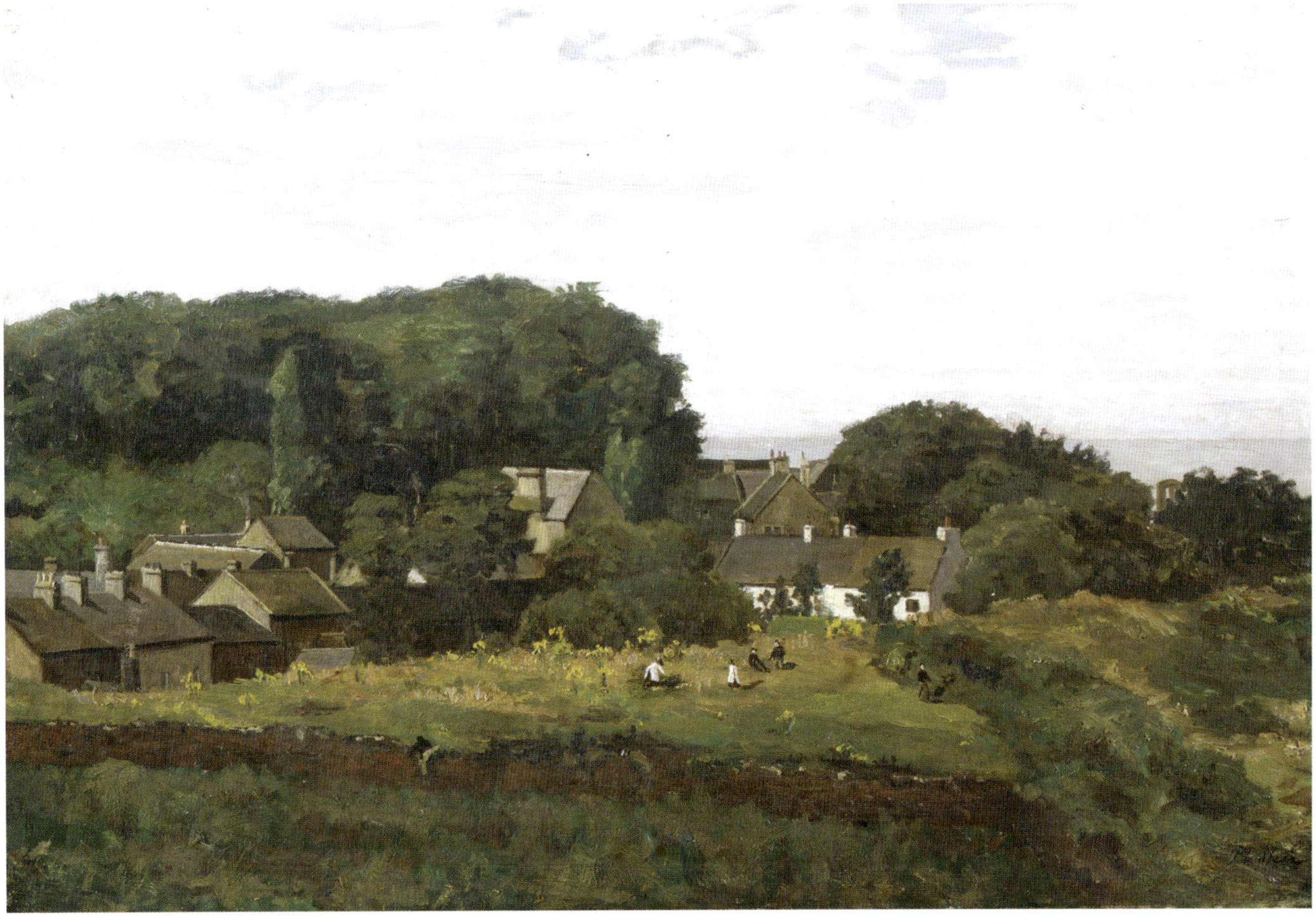

*Whin Hill, Southwold*, attributed to Frederick Brown, oil on panel, c1888. This puzzling picture may be mistitled.

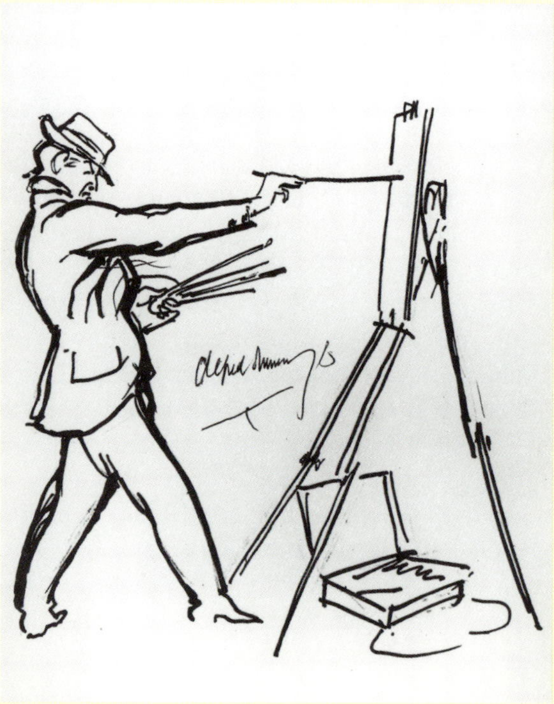

One native East Anglian artist who, early on at least, caught that exhilarating breeze from France as it created impressions across Suffolk, was ALFRED JAMES MUNNINGS (1878-1959).

A miller's son – like John Constable – Munnings was born at Mendham and roamed the Waveney Valley from early childhood amid the subjects of future paintings. At 14 he was training as a poster designer in Norwich, studying at the local art school each evening. By 20 he had lost an eye and had the first of 289 pictures hung in the Royal Academy – an institution he would ultimately embarrass as an ultra-reactionary president.

Munnings later lived at Swainsthorpe, near Norwich and then in Constable Country at Dedham, but this restless spirit seemed always on the move. Criss-crossing East Anglia for horse-rife scenes – loving army and gypsy camps, circuses, fairs, sales, studs, races, hunts, and pubs thereafter; admiring heavy Suffolk Punches still working on farms and sleek thoroughbreds working out around Newmarket – the dapper painter often came to Southwold. But he was likely to be in a Rolls-Royce, and bearing gifts of eggs, on a visit to his tailor. His suit measurements remain preserved in Denny of Southwold's prized order books near to those of Eric Blair (aka George Orwell), Peter Pears and Benjamin Britten. Founded in 1851, this esteemed clothes shop in the Market Place once employed 25 tailors and fielded its own football team.

The artist and his second wife, Violet, had an animal attraction. When he first saw her out riding, he promptly fell for the horse. Lady Munnings, in turn, adored her dog, Black Knight. She held the amazingly ageless pet wherever she went, including the coronation. The Denny children, on stroking the pooch, discovered to their horror that it had been stuffed.

*The Bridge* – a dreamy affair probably based on the old footbridge over Dunwich Creek at Walberswick – hints at a meeting of minds. It is Steer's most Whistlerian nocturne.

The year 1884 – the most significant in Southwold's artistic history – also saw a human whirlwind moving into town. **PETER HENRY EMERSON** (1856-1936) who 'knew all the Chelsea artists' swept through Wellesley House, dumping wife Edith, young son Leonard and new daughter Sylvia. He had first spied the Blyth port the previous August, taking 'several photographs that were destined to revolutionise photography and make my name in photographic circles'. Ditching a medical career, if not a more recent desire to become an explorer, he had then decided to rove with his camera in watery East Anglia – to capture images of rustic naturalism and to elevate photography into art. He wandered along the beach and paused long enough at the family's new home to admire the view of the Common and note: 'The river is flowing high in the middle distance...but who shall describe what none can paint? – the unsurpassed splendour of the golden gorse.' Then he was off again, hiring a yacht to tour the Broads with his brother, the wonderfully-named Just William.

Peter Henry (né Pedro Enriques) had been born in Cuba, on a slave-worked sugar

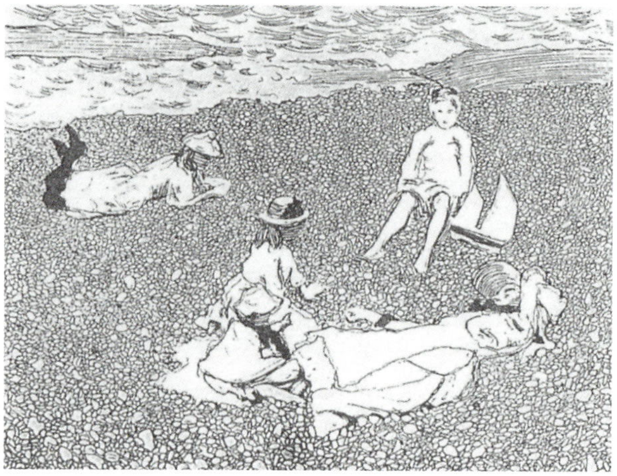

*Knucklebones*, Walter Sickert, etching after Steer, 1889.

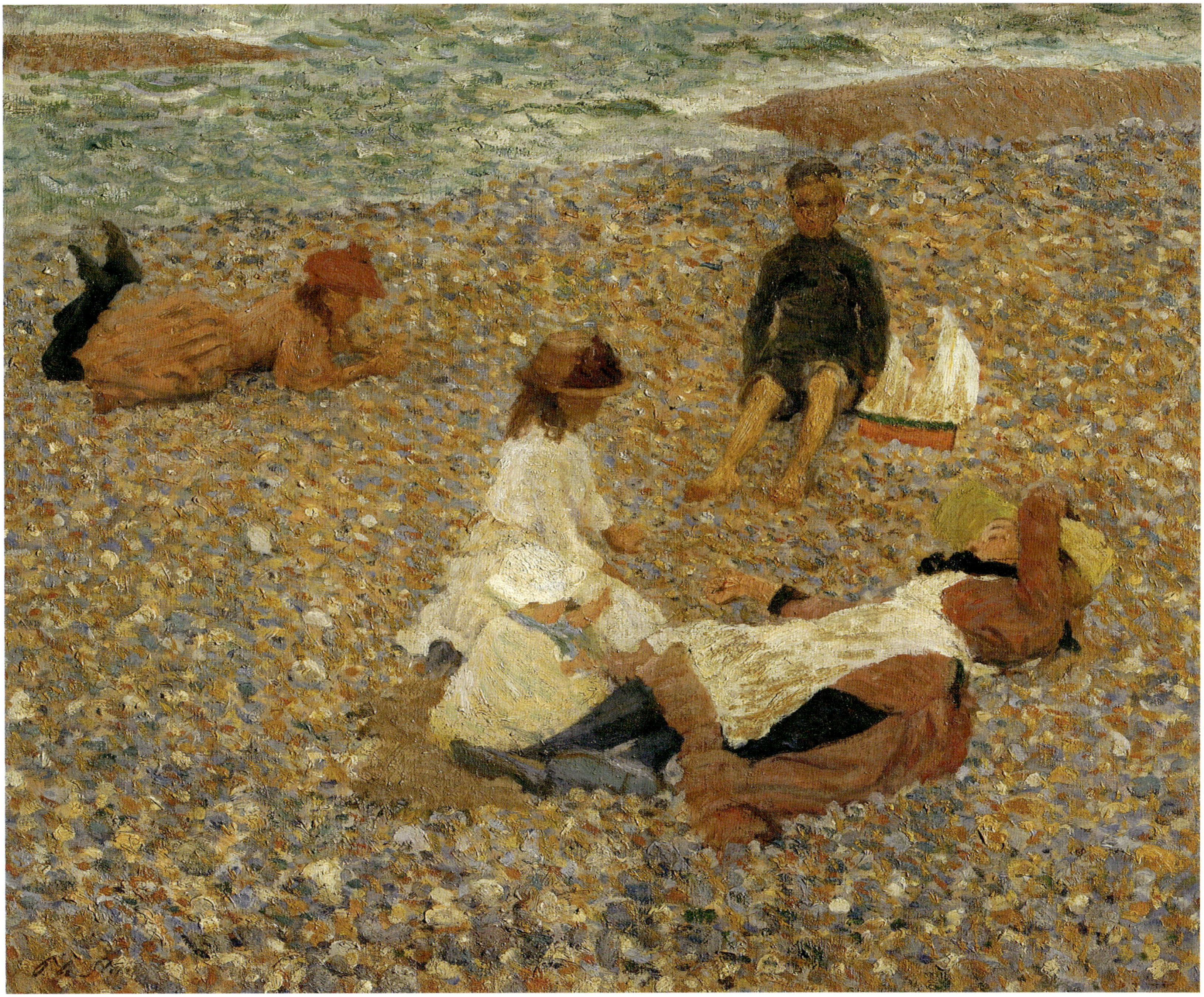

*Knuckblebones, Walberswick,* Philip Wilson Steer, oil on canvas, 1888-89. The girls in brown dresses are the daughters of James Grace (1851-1908), who worked in Walberswick from the mid-1870s.

plantation, to an American father and English mother. His childhood was marked by dramatic scenes from the American Civil War and Cuba's revolt against Spanish rule as well as, he claimed, storms at sea with sailors drunk, diseased or mutinous. After his father died from dysentery, and his sister from typhoid, he and his brother were taken to the safety of England. At school, by his own admission, he saw, did and won everything – also discovering that no one likes an all-round genius. All his life his relations with other (inferior) people would be a series of battles and betrayals. Just William was abandoned when Peter Henry moved in with painter Thomas Frederick Goodall (1857-1944), friend of La Thangue and fellow fan of Southwold, on his houseboat on South Walsham Broad. Photographer and painter then amassed material for what became *Life and Landscape on the Norfolk Broads*. Emerson, finding the subjects for remaining pictures in the lanes around Southwold via a pony and trap, hogged the resulting credit – though the most famous image, *Gathering Water-Lilies*, was surely taken

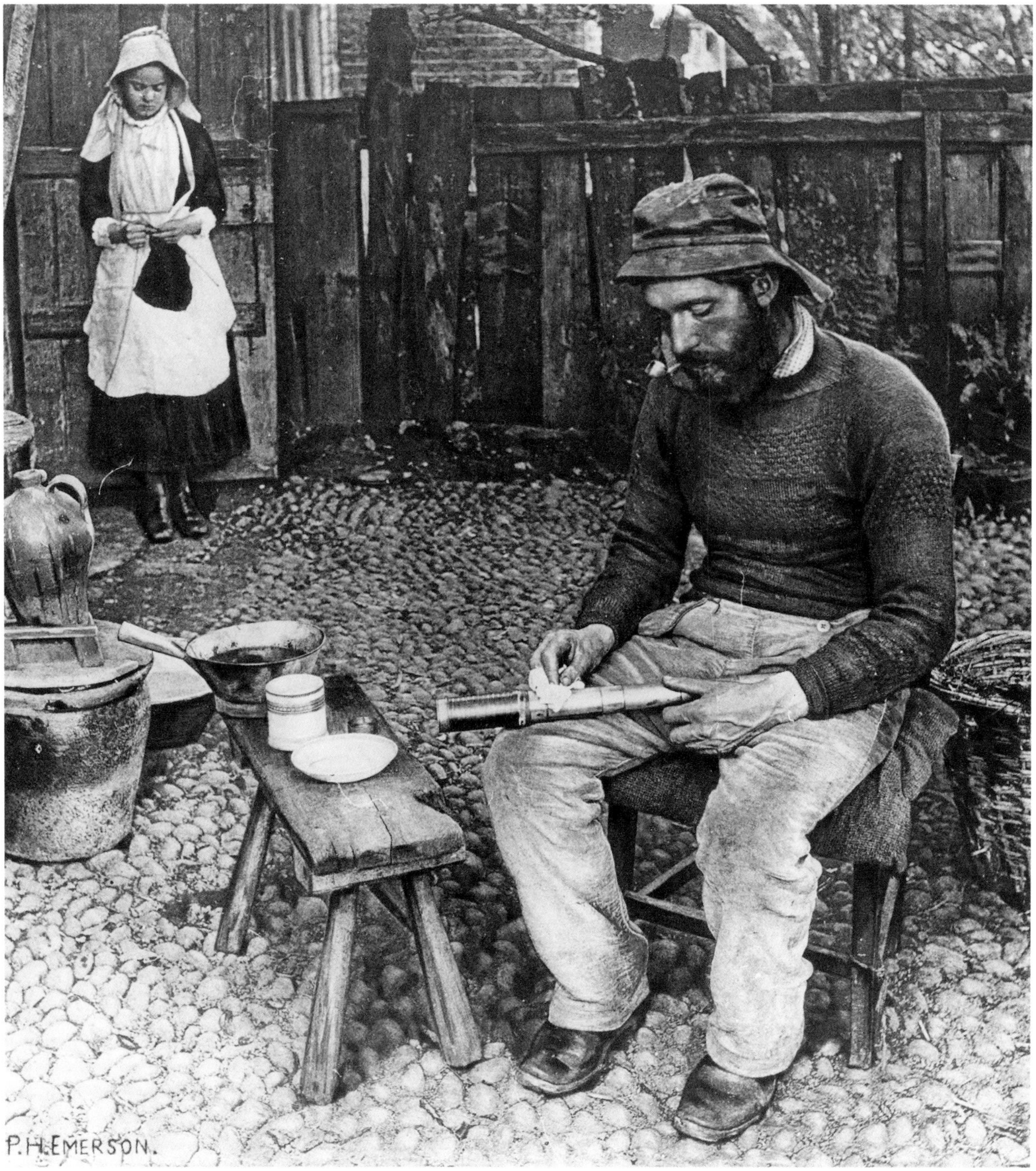


*A Fisherman at Home,*
P H Emerson,
(Plate XX in *Life in Field and Fen*).

by Goodall. Most of the 20 photogravures in a sequel volume, *Pictures from Life in Field and Fen,* showed scenes near Southwold. But in June 1886, with baby Gladys added to his brood, Emerson shifted his family to London: the rail journey to the capital was slow, and fame was beckoning urgently. Edith Emerson, less wife and more nurse and nanny, now left the little green outside Wellesley House known to Southwold folk as Nursemaid's Park.

In 1887 Emerson joined Goodall in his new houseboat on Breydon Water to collaborate on *Wild Life on a Tidal Water*. When that book appeared, in 1890, he was vowing to spend a year aboard his own wherry but ended up living in Anglesey, returning to Lowestoft in 1895 by way of Ramsgate and Broadstairs. The next year he was near Goodall and his family in Oulton Broad, though their friendship was to be abruptly broken. Whatever caused the breach, the trauma for a sensitive painter was calamitous – only a handful of his pictures survive, including one haunting work in Norwich Castle Museum.

*On Southwold Marshes*,
P.H. Emerson,
(Plate VIII in *Life in Field and Fen*).

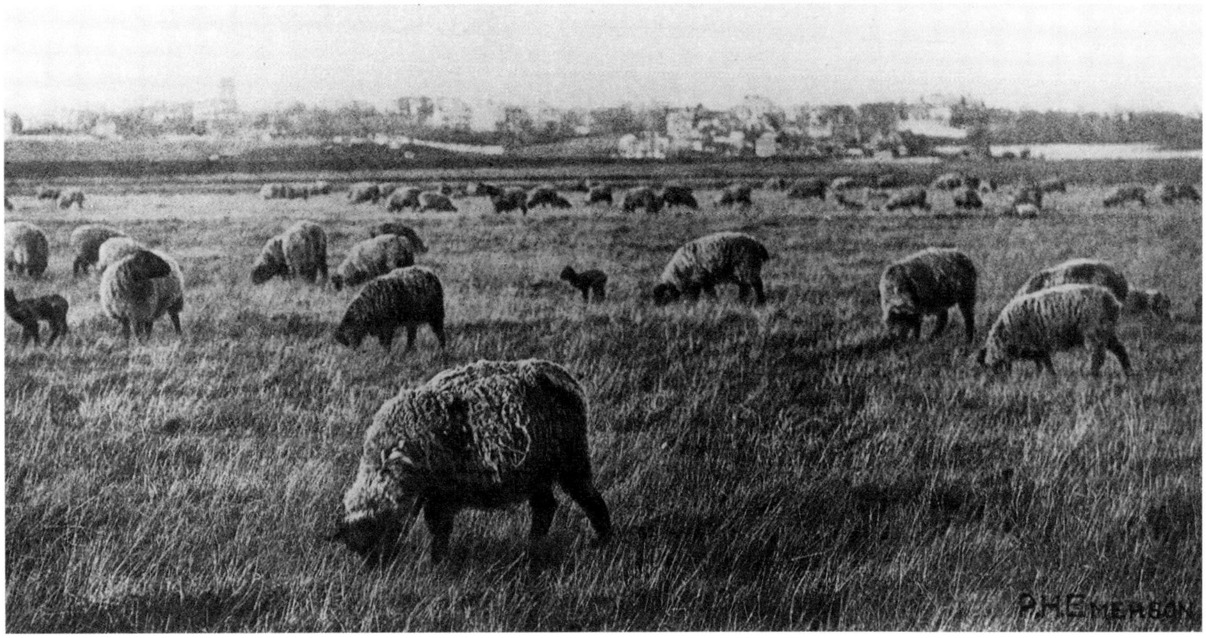


*Sunrise at Sea*, P. H. Emerson,
(Plate XII in *Life in Field and Fen*).

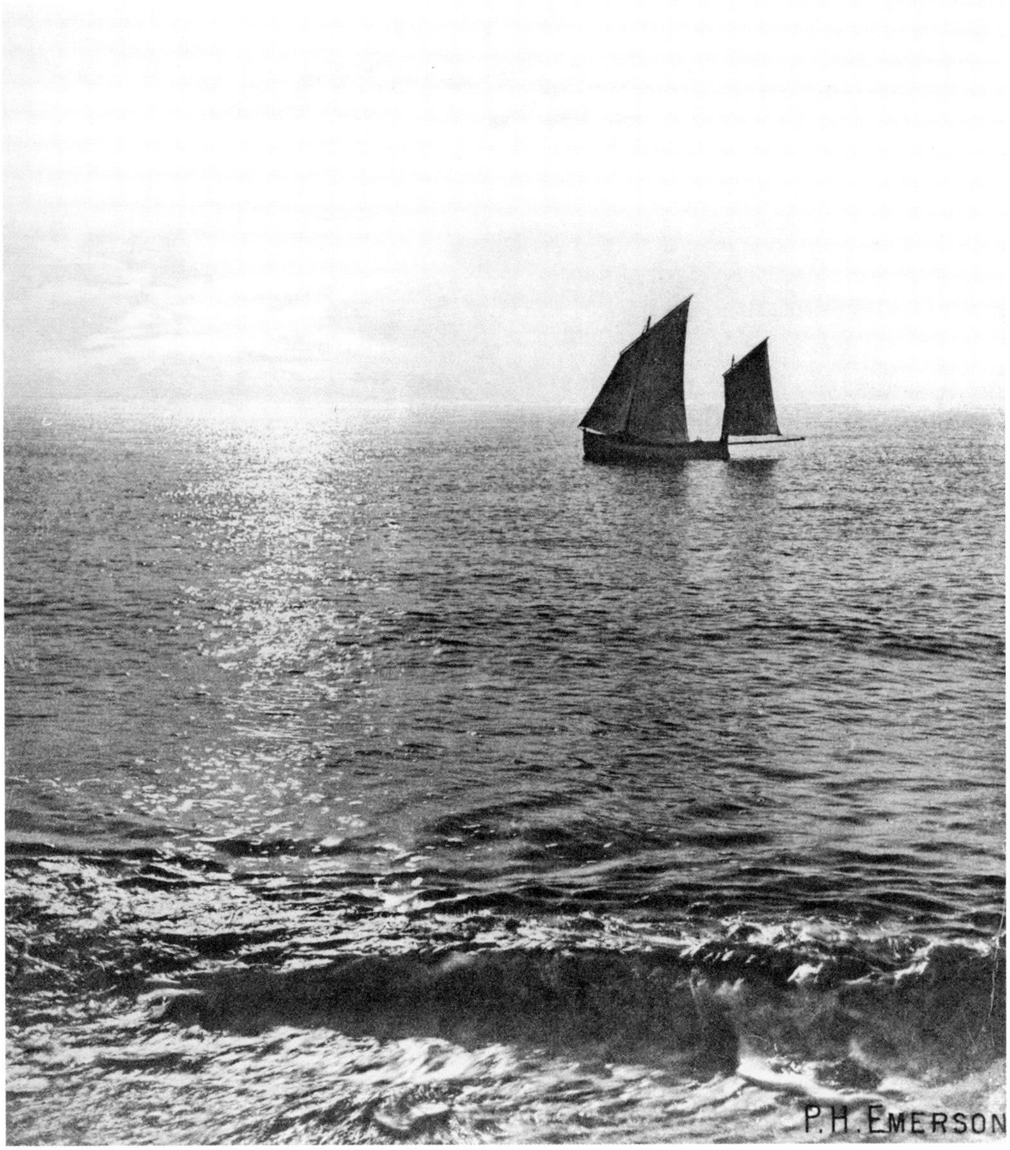


Writing (family history, essays, crime fiction) and raging, Emerson later lived outside Bournemouth, then in London, Lancashire and Eastbourne. He returned briefly to Suffolk – to Somerleyton – before breathing his last in Falmouth. The whirlwind was spent. As far back as 1900 a retrospective show at the Royal Photographic Society had been diminished because Emerson had taken to destroying every plate he could find. Having long sent leading artists unsolicited examples of his work, plus scrawled cover notes, he had finally agreed with George Clausen that photography could never equal art. Ruskin's reply – 'If you condescend yourself to learn to write beautifully, and engrave clearly, you will soon cease to interest yourself in the arts of idleness' – had been less persuasive.

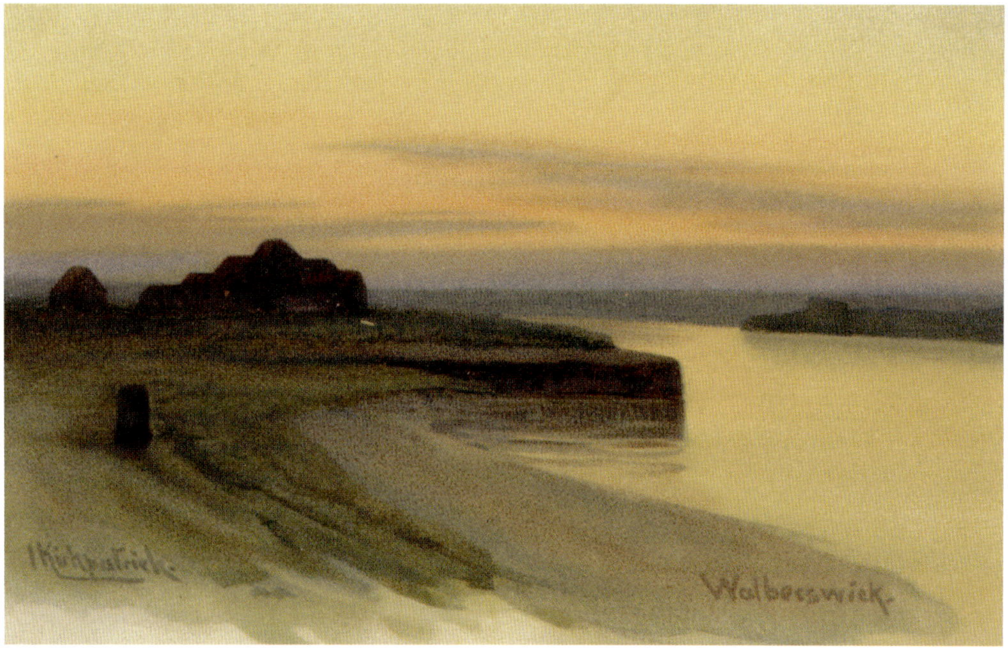


*Walberswick,*
Ida Kirkpatrick (left).

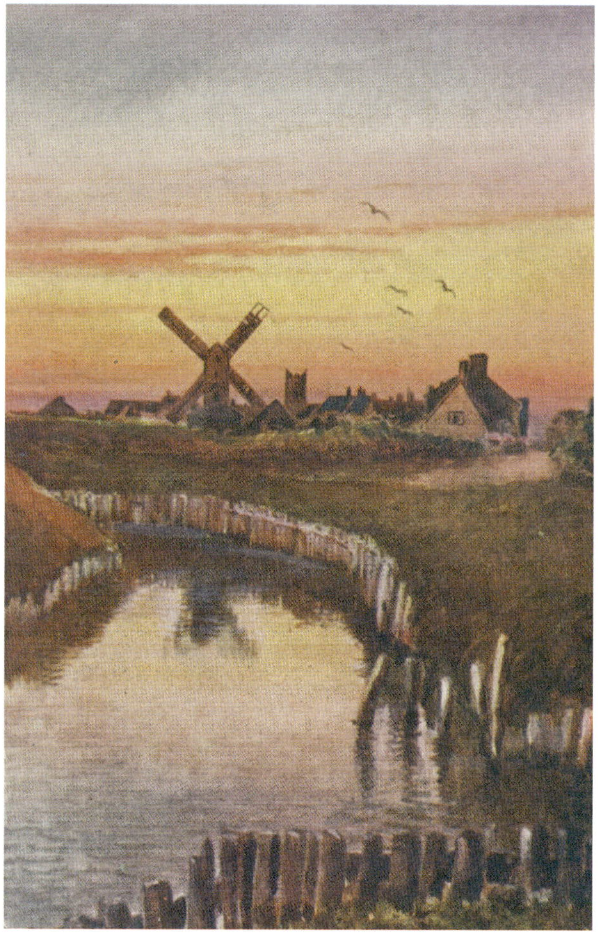

*Walberswick,* Lilian Stannard.

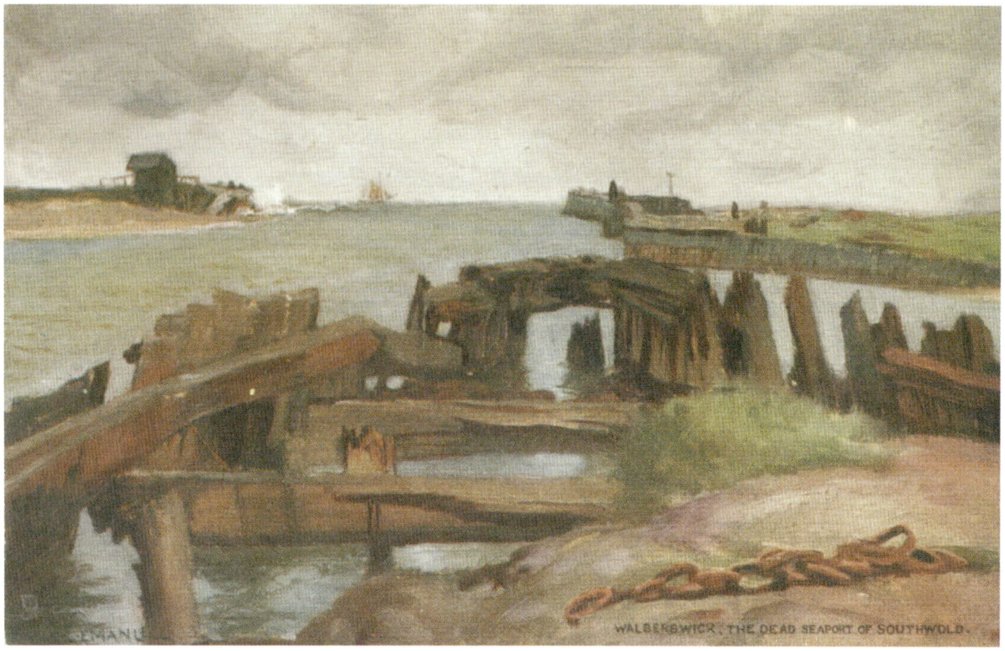


*Walberswick, The Dead Seaport of Southwold*, Frank Emanuel.

Chapter Ten

# Postcards from the Edge

Before the epoch of universal telephones – let alone our present world of emails, mobiles and text messages - the most popular means of communication was pen and paper. From 1902, when Britain became the first country to permit senders of postcards to write on the same side as the address, there was a wonderful means of broadcasting the bliss of seaside holidays. The pictures were cheap and cheery and the accompanying messages could be blessedly brief.

Tens of millions of postcards were produced throughout the 20th century, to be sent or saved as souvenirs, but their heyday was in the dozen years leading up to the First World War. During the Edwardian era companies across Europe began to publish high-quality cards in full colour illustrating the work of popular artists of the period – the firms Raphael Tuck & Sons ('Art Publishers to Their Majesties the King and Queen') and C.W. Faulkner & Co led the field in Britain, both creating several fine cards which reproduced paintings of the Southwold area.

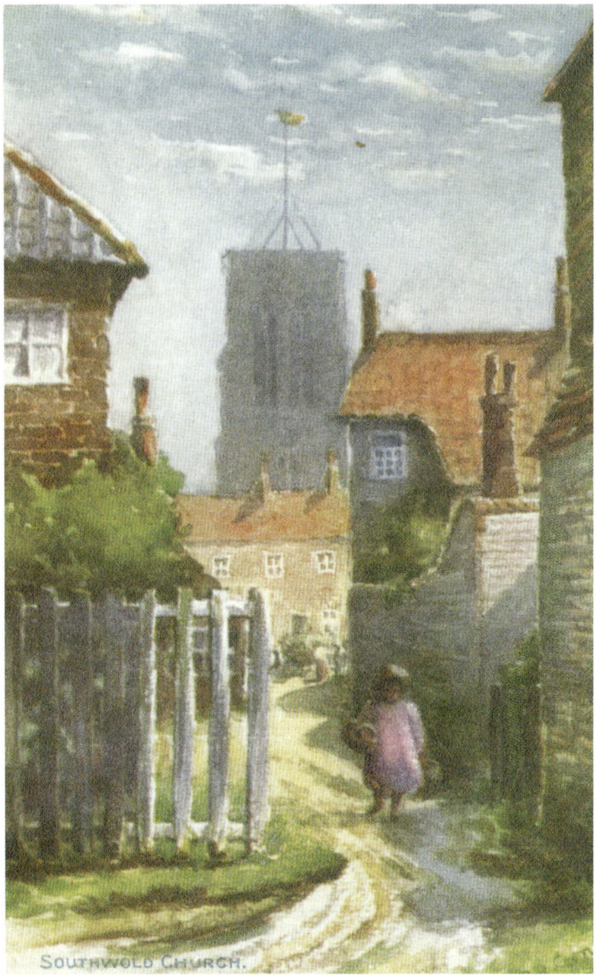


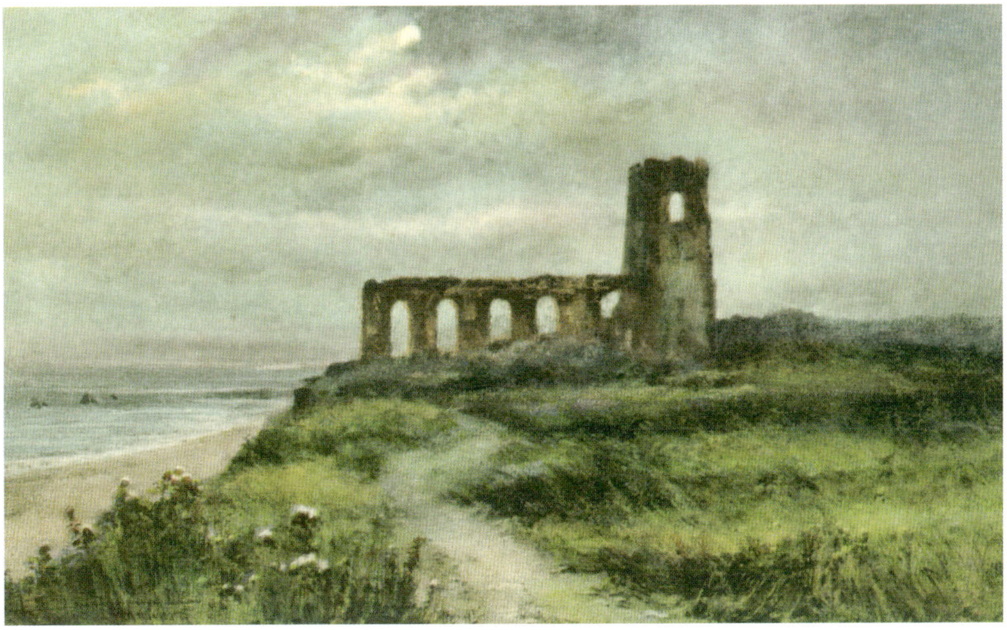

*All Saints' Church, Dunwich*, Lilian Stannard, and (right), *Southwold Church*, Susan Ruth Canton.

In 1900 the photographer and publisher Frederick Jenkins arrived in the Suffolk resort and set up a camera shop at 92 and 94 High Street (opposite Barclays Bank). For the next half-century he snapped every memorable episode of Southwold life, and every vernacular view, and speedily turned the resulting pictures into cards which were sold in his store from tuppence a time or up to ten for sixpence. An early advert asked: 'Is it wise to buy Postcards from a man who can only show you an assortment of 18 or 20 different views, when by going to F. Jenkins you can have over 200 different Local Postcards to select from?' This man was also skilled in the art of marketing.

Soon the Jenkins miniature picture empire extended over Southwold cartoons culled from Charles Keene caricatures in *Punch* and 'Oilette' cards replicating local paintings. In 1906 or 1907 he chanced upon watercolour artist and teacher **HENRY JOHN SYLVESTER STANNARD** (1870-1951) whose annual English Counties Sketching Tour brought a band of amateurs – and a few budding professionals – to Southwold for two successive Augusts. A very fruitful collaboration followed.

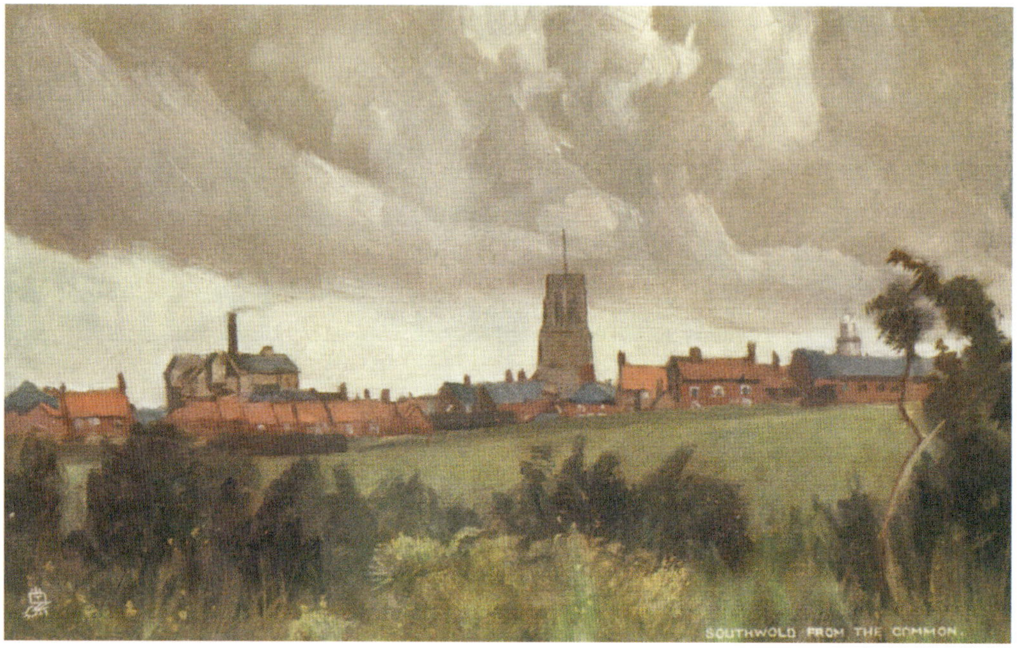


*Southwold from the Common,*
Frank Emanuel.

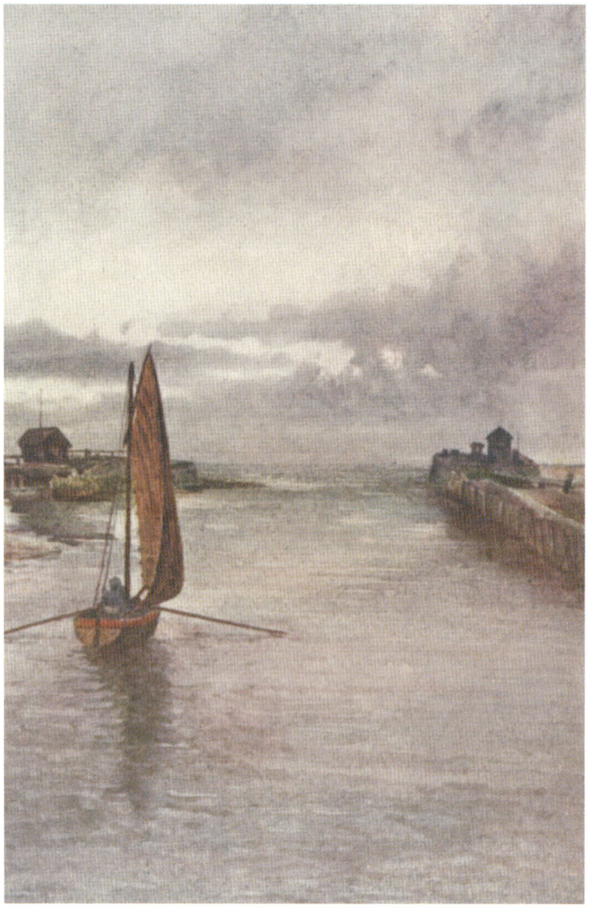

*The Harbour, Southwold,*
Lilian Stannard (left).

Sylvester Stannard was the most notable talent in a family of Bedfordshire-based artists which included his grandfather, father, three sisters, brother, daughter and two nieces. The clan claimed distant kinship with the far more famous Norwich Stannards, and several members painted and exhibited in Norfolk possibly to press the point. In 1905 Sylvester sought and obtained permission to work at Sandringham and over ensuing years he depicted landscapes and sporting scenes on the royal estate which earned him a certain celebrity. Queens Alexandra and Mary bought several of his pictures, but they were later presented to recipients as diverse as the Queen of Norway and the Port of Hull Society Orphanage Bazaar. Today only a watercolour of Sandringham Lake the size of a 10p piece remains in the Royal Collection. It hangs in the Queen's Dolls House.

At least a dozen Sylvester Stannard scenes of the Blyth Valley were reproduced by Frederick Jenkins. The painter, who had qualified as an art

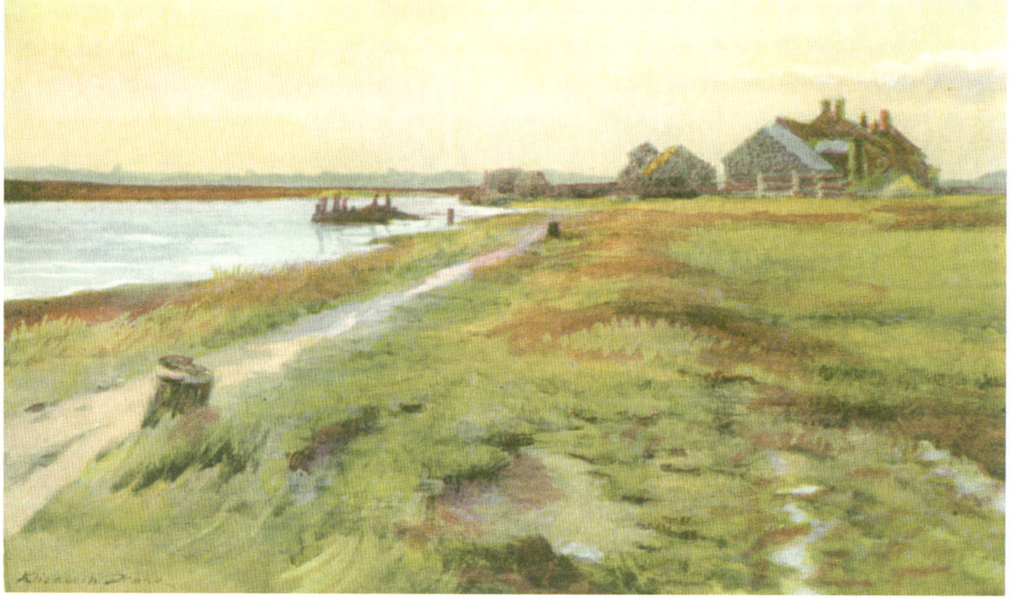

*Blackshore, Southwold,*
Elizabeth Drake.

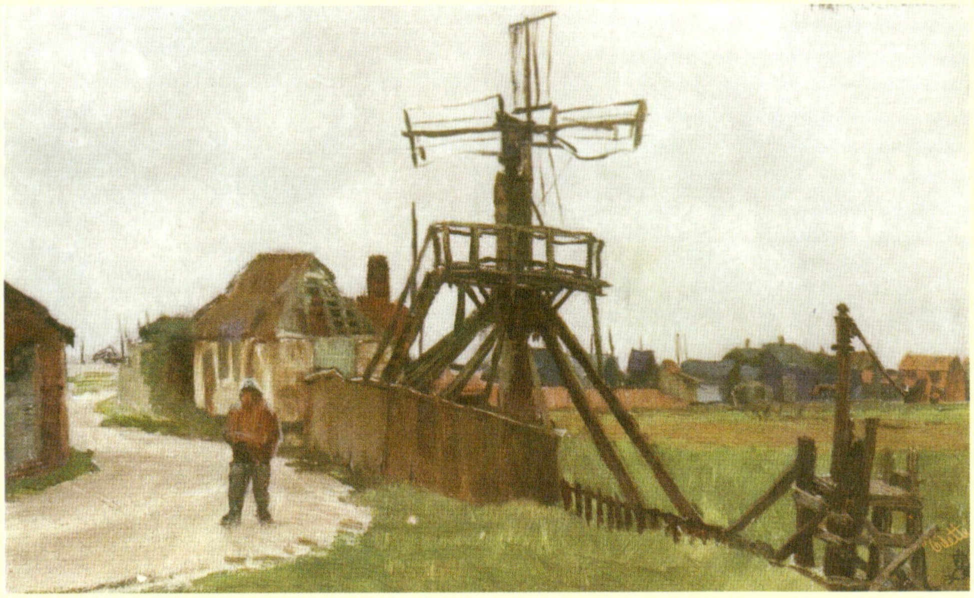

*Old Salt Works, Southwold.* Frank Emanuel's early Edwardian Tuck postcard salutes an enterprise operating from 1660 until 1894 at the 'Towns End' turning of South Green into Ferry Road. Seawater from the harbour was let into Salt Works Creek at high tide where it flowed to a well at the head. After a pause to allow unwanted solids to settle, the briny solution was pumped over Ferry Road to a building holding saltpans via a windmill or back-up handpump (both can be seen in this picture).

The brine was strengthened with dissolved rock salt mined in Cheshire and then boiled up, with different degrees of heat for coarse salt and refined table salt. The works flourished from 1750, when large harvests of herrings required tons of preservative. A fall in fortunes was plugged by early Victorian times through the opening of a Hot Salt Water Bath House – with a huge chimney alongside – in what is now a public lavatory block. This also features in Emanuel's image.

teacher when aged 16, and whose first picture (of 35) to be accepted by the Royal Academy was entitled *Dusk*, gave a master class in capturing atmospheric effects – concentrating on the glowering and the gloomy. Most of these images might have seemed calculated to keep tourists at bay, as storms lashed a beach crowded with berthed boats, a sinister figure speared eels on the marsh at Walberswick and the Harbour Inn appeared a haven for press gangs and smugglers. Besides *Moonlight on Dunwich Ruins* and *Sunset on the Heronry near Blythburgh* perhaps his greatest tour de force was *East Green by Moonlight*, with glinting sea and ghostly lighthouse beacon. Flocks of sheep populate the postcards entitled *Southwold from its Harbour* and *Waiting for Walberswick Ferry,* while two unusually jolly scenes, *Sunny Southwold* and *Walberswick Bridge*, demonstrate Stannard's debt to Myles Birket Foster (1825-1899), a popular Surrey-based watercolourist who toured the South Coast for charm-laden subjects but also found inspiration in the Blyth Valley. Jenkins often provided pithy caption commentaries on his cards, and for *Walberswick Bridge* he wrote rather tartly: 'The picture shows where the Creek, draining the saltings or marshes, forms the river Blyth, and is spanned by a rustic bridge which bears the entirely unnecessary legend "This bridge is dangerous." The Harbour mouth and open sea are seen in the distance.'

*East Green by Moonlight,* Sylvester Stannard.

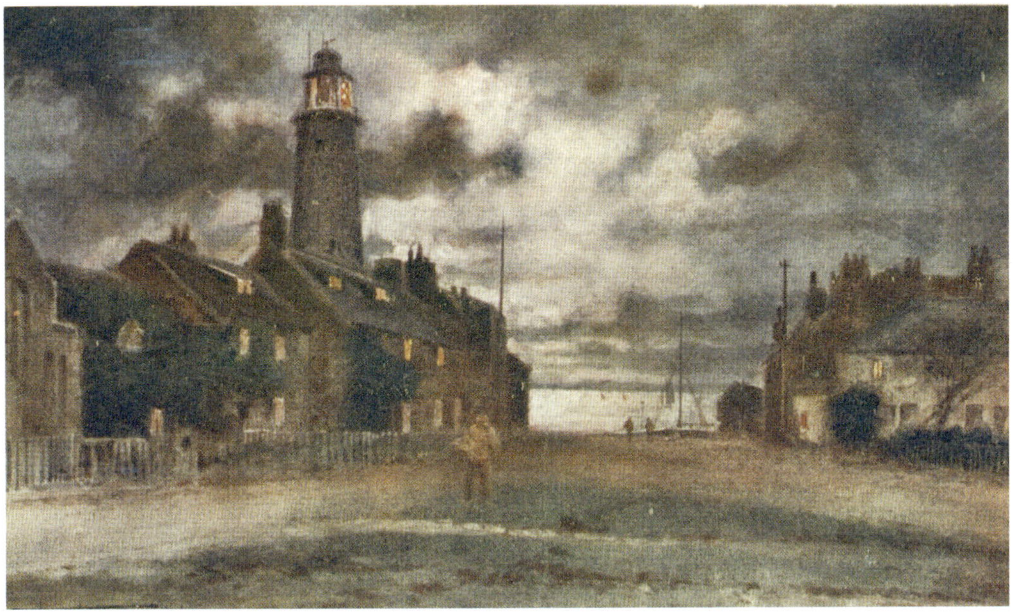

Sylvester Stannard was probably accompanied on at least one of his sketching tours to Southwold by his sister **LILIAN STANNARD** (1877-1944), who began her career painting butterflies and made her name depicting luxuriant gardens. She certainly produced similar images to those of her brother while working in this corner of Suffolk. Her view of *The Creek, Walberswick* is a perfect partner for his *Walberswick Bridge*. Lilian contributed at least seven images to the Jenkins 'Studio Series' and the Tuck 'Oilette' sequence – with one Dunwich view of sheep about to ford the stream which at that time ran across the village street, and another of gulls winging over Walberswick windmill. She produced a pair of River Blyth studies and an upright composition of a yacht about to leave the harbour at dawn (p.80). Best of all was a highly topographical view from Gun Hill leading the eye along Cumberland's historic cannons in the foreground to the lately-completed pier almost stretching across the horizon. It's illustrated in the first chapter of this book.

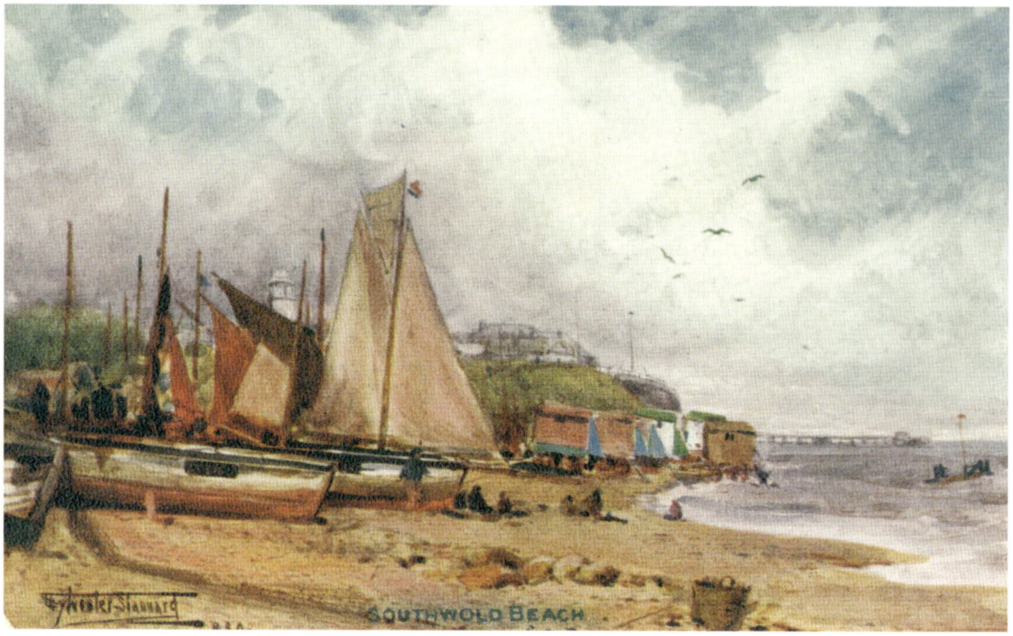


*Southwold Beach*, Sylvester Stannard.

**SUSAN RUTH CANTON** (exh.1880-1920), whose competent work was widely displayed at the Royal Academy and elsewhere in the opening years of the 20th century, proved adept at finding innovative vantage points for views prompting up to a dozen Jenkins postcards. She depicted lovers walking arm in arm over the Haven Marshes, the lighthouse looming above cottage roofs and gardens and (in an image dated 1910) *A Corner of Southwold Common* – where a panorama takes in fishermen's huts arrayed along California Beach in front of Ferry Road, against the sweep of Sole Bay and the silhouette of Dunwich ruins in the background.

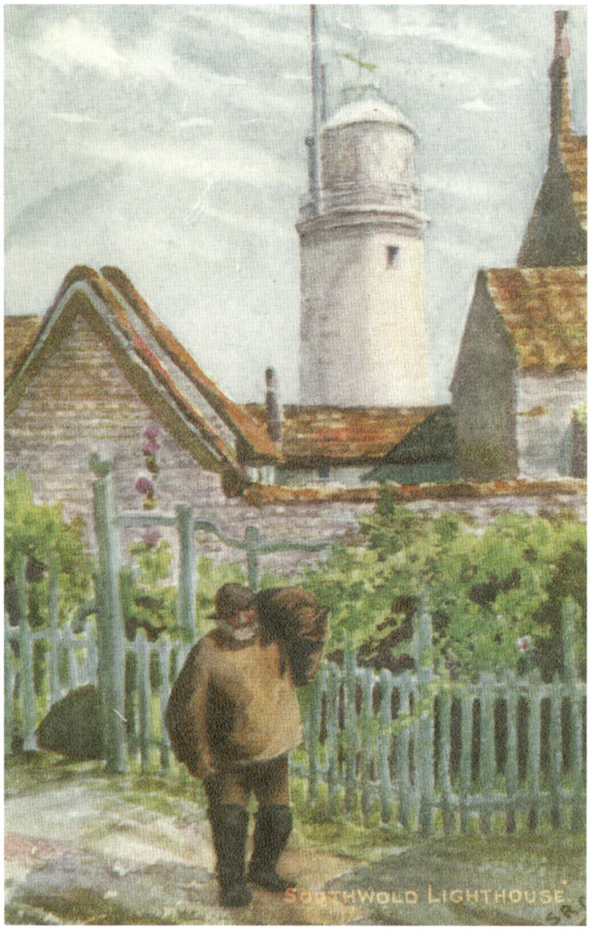


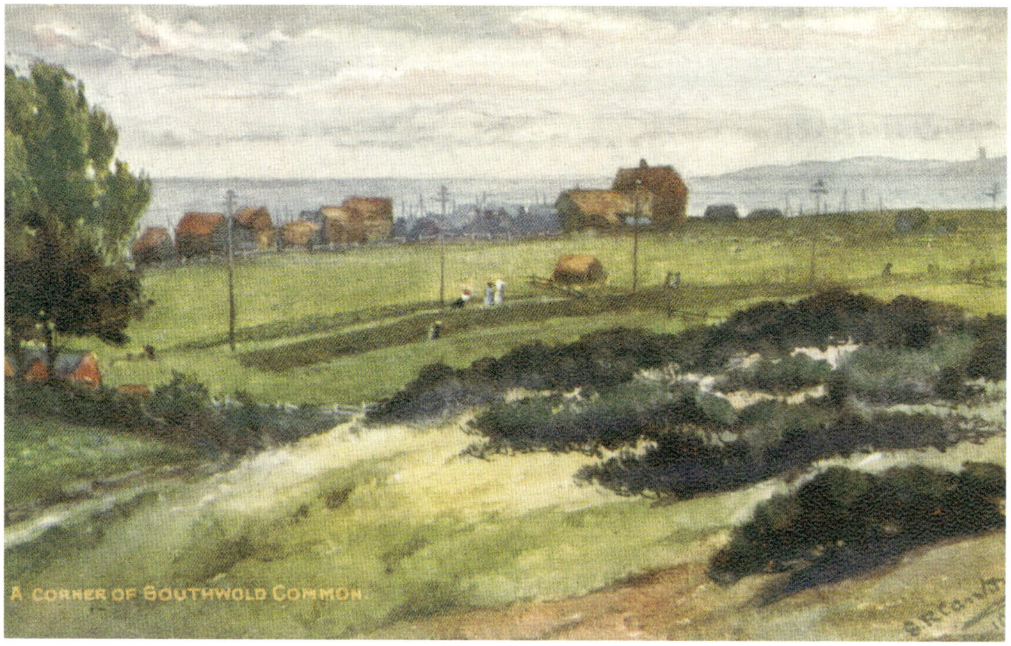


*A Corner of Southwold Common*, and *Southwold Lighthouse* (left), Susan Ruth Canton.

A Jenkins postcard of *Blackshore, Southwold* (p.80) reproduced a 1907 picture by the much-travelled painter, miniaturist, lithographer and teacher **ELIZABETH DRAKE** (1866-1954). She in turn possibly crossed paths with **IDA KIRKPATRICK** (1866-1950) and Ethel Kirkpatrick (1869-1966) who, based in Harrow on the Hill but enjoying sketching tours in Britain and abroad, paid summer visits to Walberswick over a 20-year period from 1902. Probably drawn to Suffolk by their kinswoman Jessie Newbery, the sisters proved prolific recorders of local scenes – with Ida's evocative Blyth Valley sunsets prompting a series of Faulkner picture postcards in full colour as early as 1903 (p.78).

Sturdy, almost swashbuckling, scenes by **FRANK LEWIS EMANUEL** (1865-1948) – several appearing in the 'Quaint Corners' series of Tuck 'Oilette' cards – reflect the restless spirit and boundless energy of a painter, etcher, illustrator, teacher and writer who was a roving artist for the *Manchester Guardian* for many years. His images include *Old Salt Works* (p.81) and *Southwold from the Common* (p.80)– with steam from Adnams brewery chimney dwarfed by towering clouds. And works such as *Walberswick, The Dead Sea Port of Southwold* (p.78) and *Her Last Haven: Walberswick*, doom-laden depictions of wrecked piers and beached hulks, suggest that the artist's visits preceded harbour redevelopment from 1906.

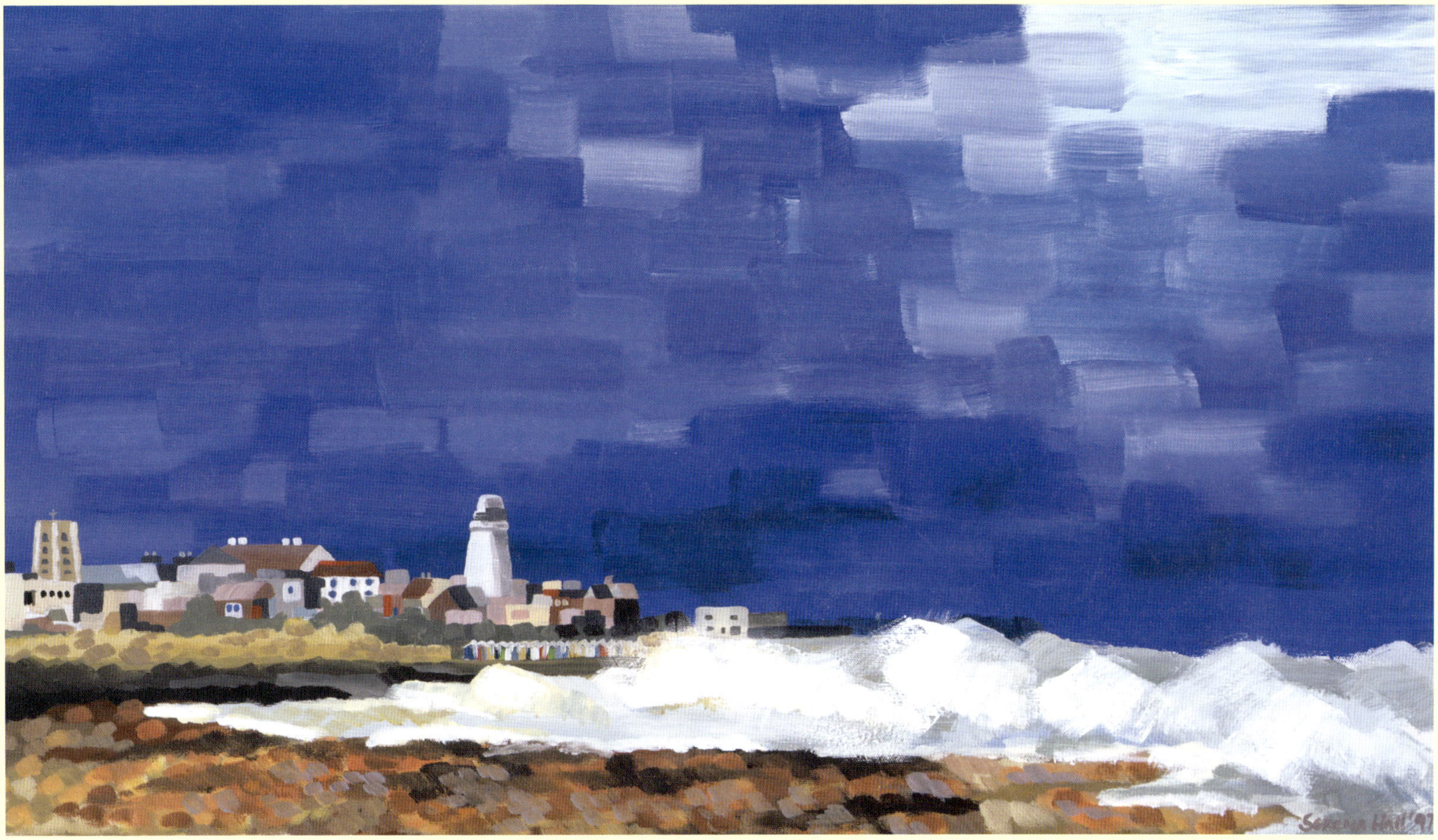


Many visitors to Southwold become aware of the area's artistic heritage through postcards of the Orwell Press, which began in 1985 when writer and academic Richard Webster and his then wife opened a High Street bookshop. First they sold existing postcards, then they reprinted a Lionel Bulmer scene and acquired three Margaret Green cards published in Germany by Te Neues but never distributed in England. In the summer of 1989 the Orwell Bookshop took delivery of 80,000 postcards – 5000-strong editions of 16 different images. When the shop was sold Richard kept the Orwell Press and continued to publish fine art cards and prints of the Suffolk coast as he divided his time between a new home in Oxford and a cottage in Westleton. The publication list now includes works by Turner, Steer, Charles Rennie Mackintosh, Stanley Spencer, Mary Potter, William Bowyer and Mary Fedden.

The best-selling Orwell Press card to date is the vibrant view by painter, ceramicist and designer SERENA HALL (b1973) pictured here. She moved to Southwold at the age of 12, when her parents Derek and Val (he a noted journalist and children's author, she a potter) bought The Inch on Ferry Road. From Reydon High School Serena trained at Lowestoft College and Cumbria School of Art before specialising in printed textiles at Edinburgh School of Art. In her Southwold gallery, initially beneath John's Wet Fish Shop in East Street, and in Queen Street since 2000, she displays her multifarious work alongside that of 50 other artists and craftspeople. Her paintings are characterised by broad brushstrokes and bold, joyful colour.

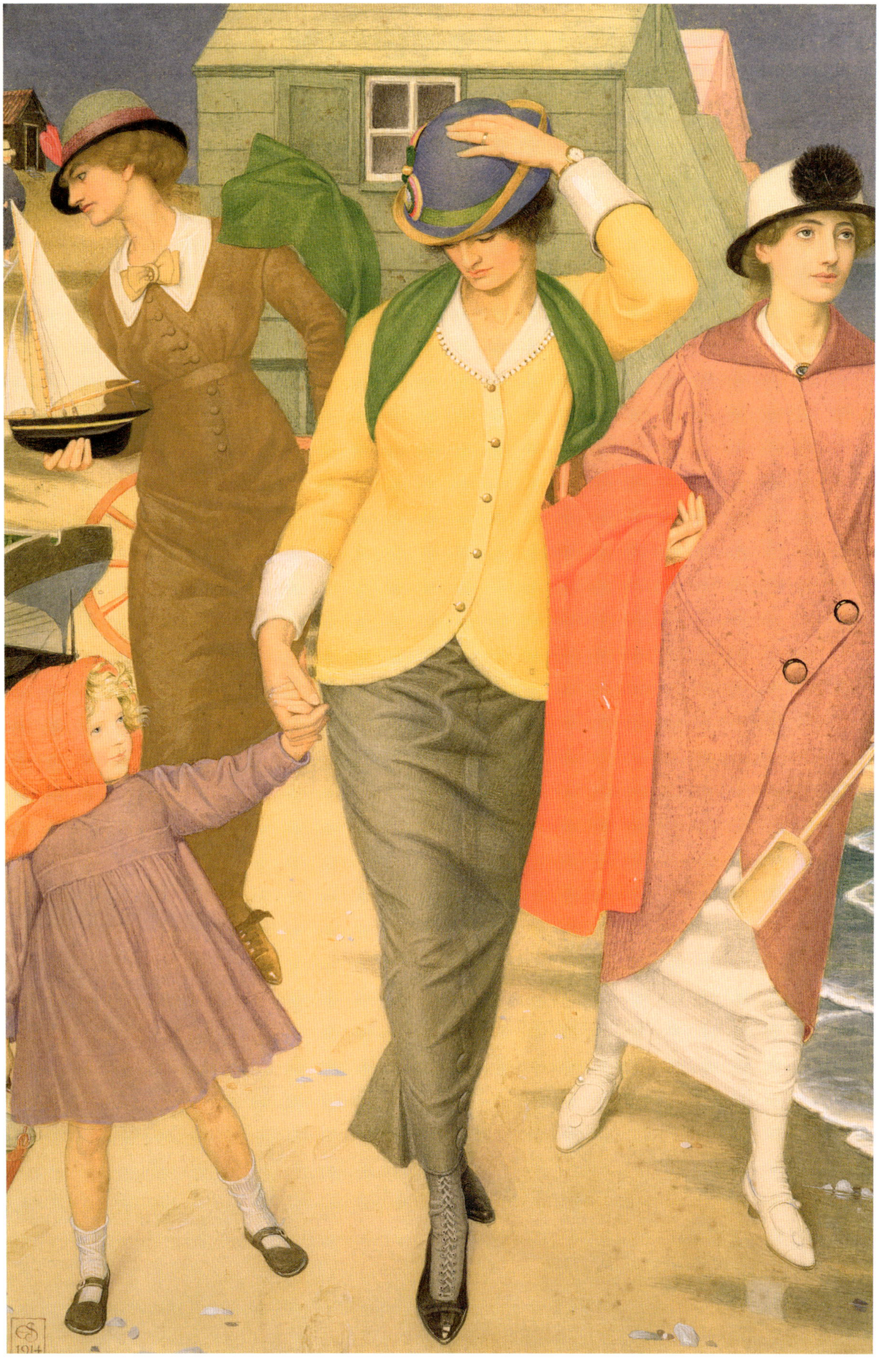

*Along The Shore*,
Joseph Southall,
tempera on silk, 1914.

Chapter Eleven

# Golden Holidays

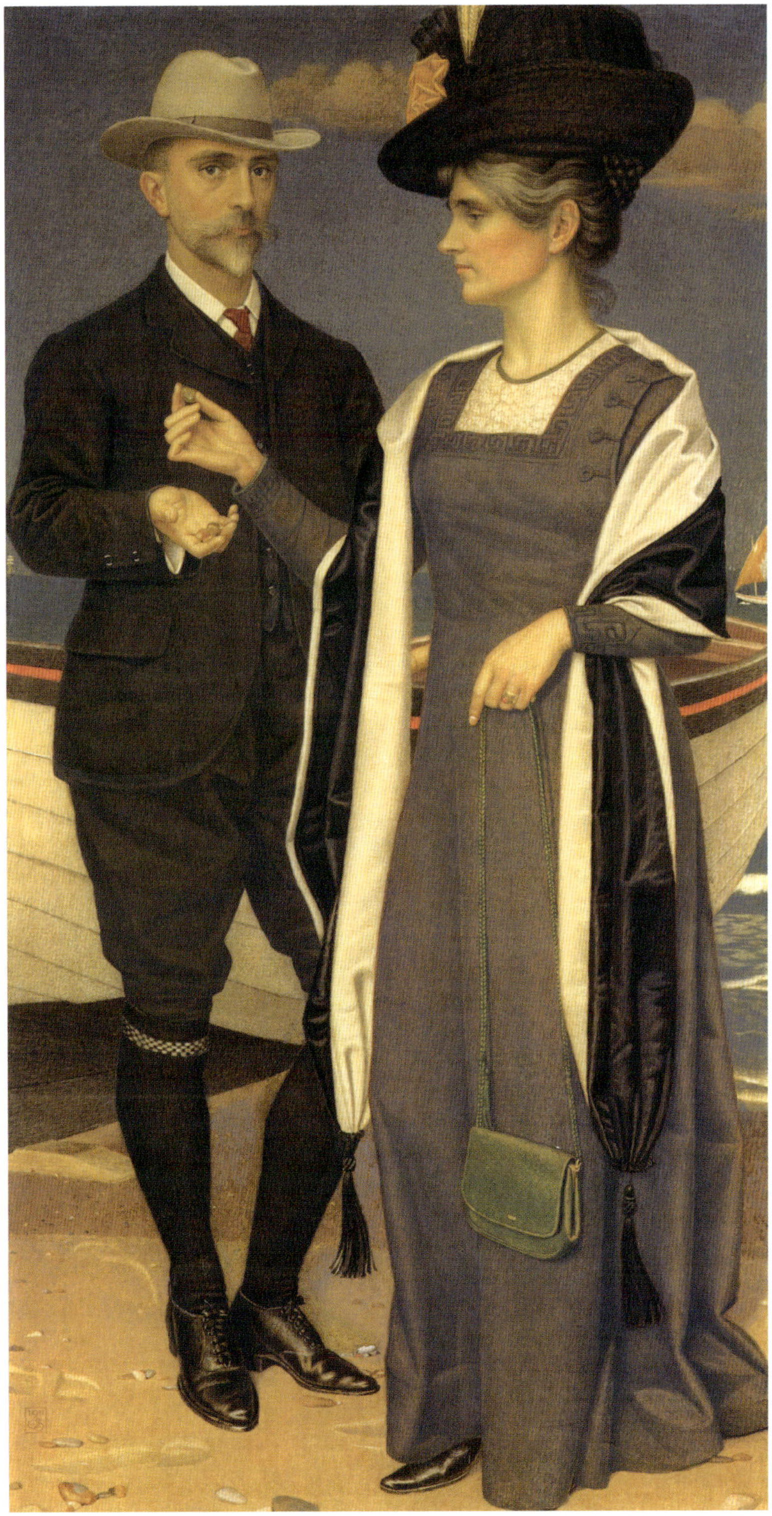

On the face of it an unlikely revolutionary, **JOSEPH EDWARD SOUTHALL** (1861-1944) abandoned architecture for art and later launched a revival of tempera painting almost 400 years after it fell from fashion. He was otherwise constant in all things – and most especially in his love of Southwold.

Southall was born in Nottingham but moved early on to his maternal family in Birmingham following the death of his father. He hailed from Quaker stock on both sides, so an inherent radicalism – pacifism, socialism, individualistic creativity – lay deep within his seemingly conservative nature. He pitied 'clever (so clever too) chappies who really don't seem to have any principles to keep them from going all to pieces'. Articled to an architect for four years from 1878, he developed an exquisite skill in draughtsmanship but gave up his studies when a planned commission for mentor John Ruskin was still-born. Already with a small independent income, the young man then inherited an uncle's house in Edgbaston where he would live for the rest of his life.

Believing that 'living architecture' had been created by capable craftsmen, who could carve statues or paint frescoes, and not by plan-plotters sitting at office desks, he set out on the path of art and craft. With medieval art his first love, Southall came under the spell of the pre-Raphaelites – and under the wing of Birmingham-born Sir Edward Coley Burne-Jones in the latter's final years. After the first of many visits to Florence and Venice, he opted to revive the tricky but brilliantly precise and vivid medium of the early Italian painters: egg tempera.

This 1911 double portrait of the finely-dressed Southalls searching on Southwold beach for semi-precious stones is called *The Agate*. Now on long-term loan to the National Portrait Gallery, it formerly lodged in the ladies' lavatory of a Birmingham department store – latterly hidden behind a mirror after complaints from customers.

This 1923 pen and ink portrait by WILLIAM FLETCHER THOMAS in Southwold Museum is a memorial tribute to Samuel Charles May, who was born in the town in 1860 and became a local hero. After a boyhood spent among the boats on the beach he worked as a longshoreman. In 1891 he was appointed second coxswain of Southwold's two lifeboats, Quiver II and Coal Exchange (formerly Harriet), being elected coxswain in 1898. In 27 years he never failed to get the rescue boat afloat from the beach, receiving a French government medal for saving four men from the rigging of the Joseph et Yvonne in 1905 and a special medal from the Queen of Holland for rescuing a crew of four and the captain's wife from the Dutch schooner Voorwaarts on January 12 1912 (the five survivors having the dubious fortune in our brewery town of being accommodated in the Temperance Hotel in East Street, now a charity shop). On that same night the Norwegian three-masted bark Idun was driven ashore off St James's Green, the crew being rescued by breeches buoy and the scene being recorded in a dramatic painting by Reg Carter. In 25 years the *A*lfred Corry lifeboat never put to sea without Sam May, and when he retired with a pension in 1918 he continued to hire out beach huts until his death five years later. A plaque beside his seat in church is inscribed 'Samuel Charles May, Coxswain of the Lifeboat, Town Councillor, benefactor of the Church, 1923'. But a cartoon artist spoke for Southwold when

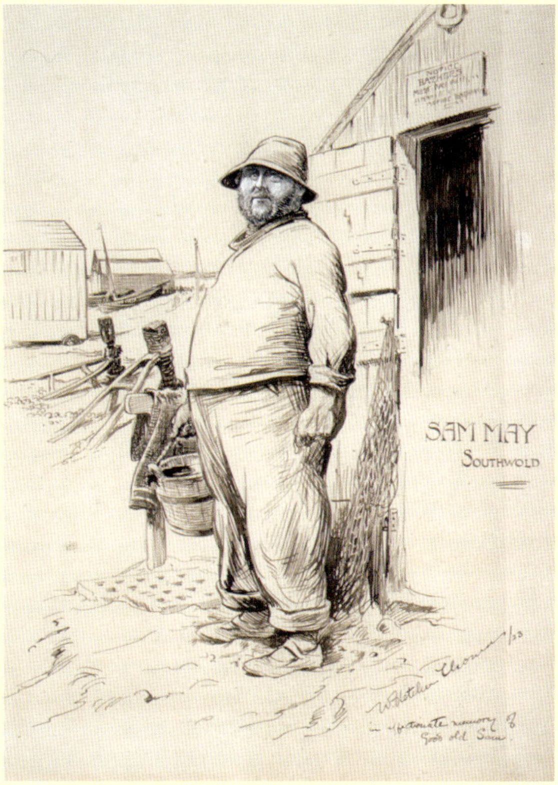


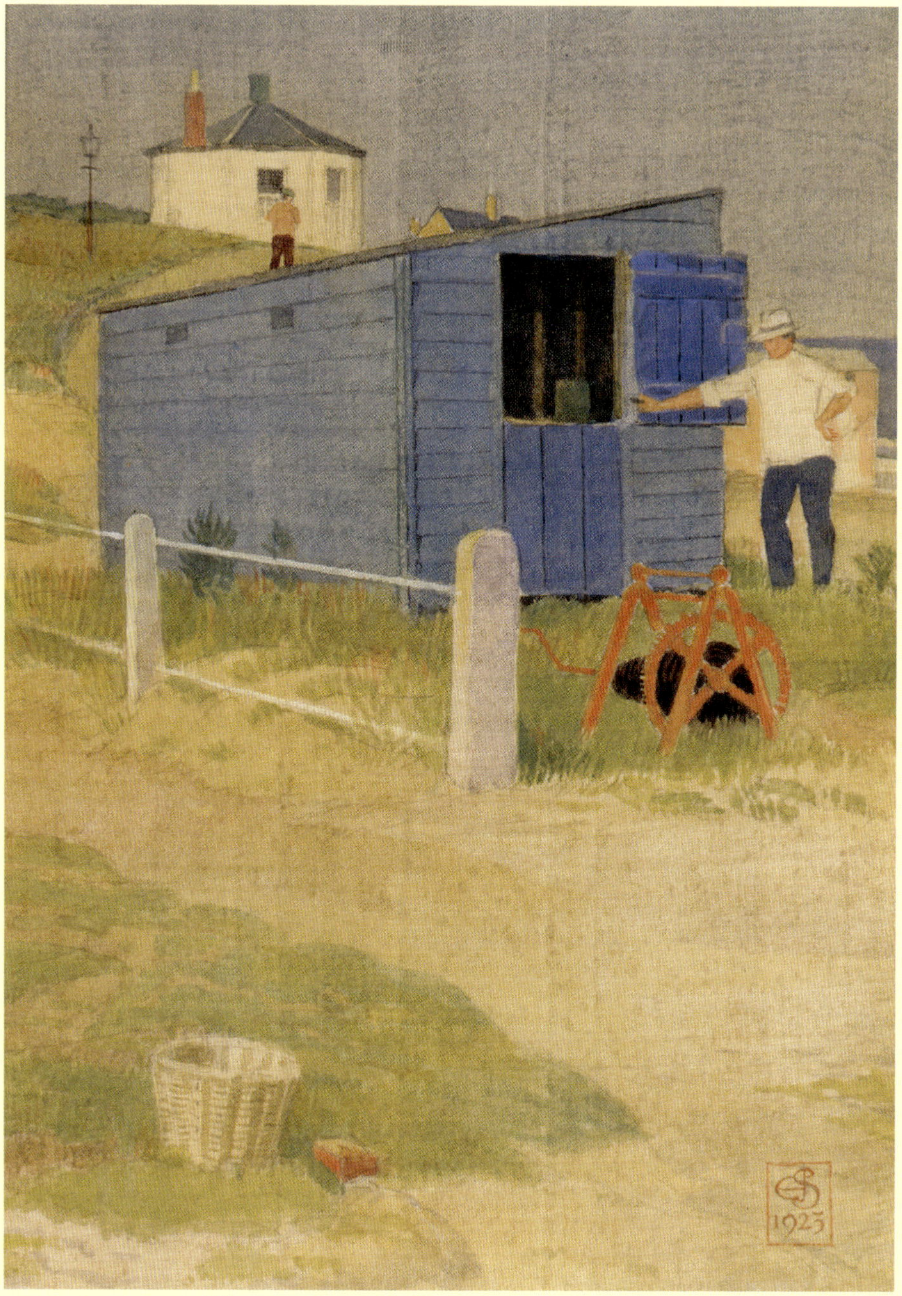

he annotated his portrait 'In affectionate memory of good old Sam May'.

William Fletcher Thomas lived at Lydstep House on Constitution Hill, from which address he produced Southwold-centred prints and sent his sole exhibit to the Royal Academy in 1901. But his gift for caricature was deployed from 1888 on weekly drawings relating the inept antics of Ally Sloper, the world's first comic strip character when launched in *Judy* magazine 21 years earlier. The character was killed off in 1916, but not before the Army Service Corps had been nicknamed Ally Sloper's Cavalry.

*Sam May's Hut*, Joseph Southall, tempera on linen.

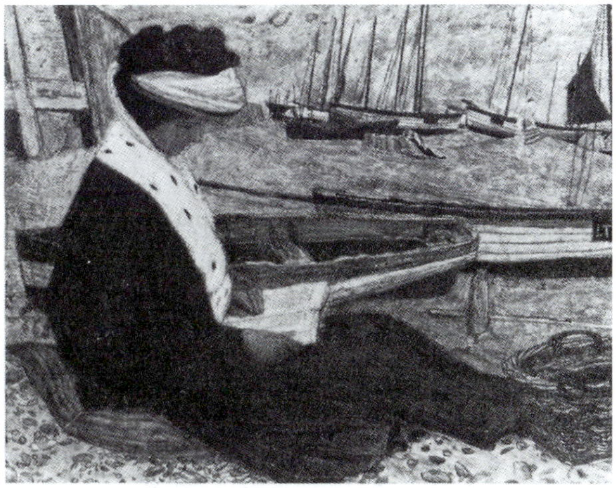

*Southwold Beach* (portrait of Georgie Gaskin), Arthur Gaskin, oil on panel, 1904.

This was soon taken up by his closest friend, **ARTHUR GASKIN** (1862-1928) and then by disciples from Maxwell Armfield to Southwold visitor Eliot Hodgkin. Armfield dedicated his 1930 tome *A Manual of Tempera-Painting* 'to J.E.S. and all pioneers' – though 16 years later admiration had cooled into this tepid posthumous tribute: 'Dowered with little imaginative power and no rhythmic vitality he (Southall) has gained recognition for the presentation of a glory of colour, which, if not universal throughout his work is at least an individual contribution to the characteristic of tempera painting.' A love of colour did indeed light up his entire career.

In June 1903 the artist married his first cousin, Anna Elizabeth ('Bessie') Baker – given the closeness of their family link the happy couple had long delayed their wedding and resolved to remain childless. They honeymooned in Southwold. Southall had painted on the north Norfolk coast, at Cromer and Overstrand, in 1900 and may have come across the Suffolk port resort by chance or possibly recalled a recommendation by one of his tutors, the painter William Blake Richmond. A sketchbook from that blazing summer, now in the British Museum, set the pattern for dozens of future visits. There were vigils by the beach, promenade and harbour to capture a parade of fleeting scenes with notepad, pencil and pocket paints.

*Up from the Sea*, Southall's tribute to three generations of a Southwold fishing family, tempera on silk, 1920.

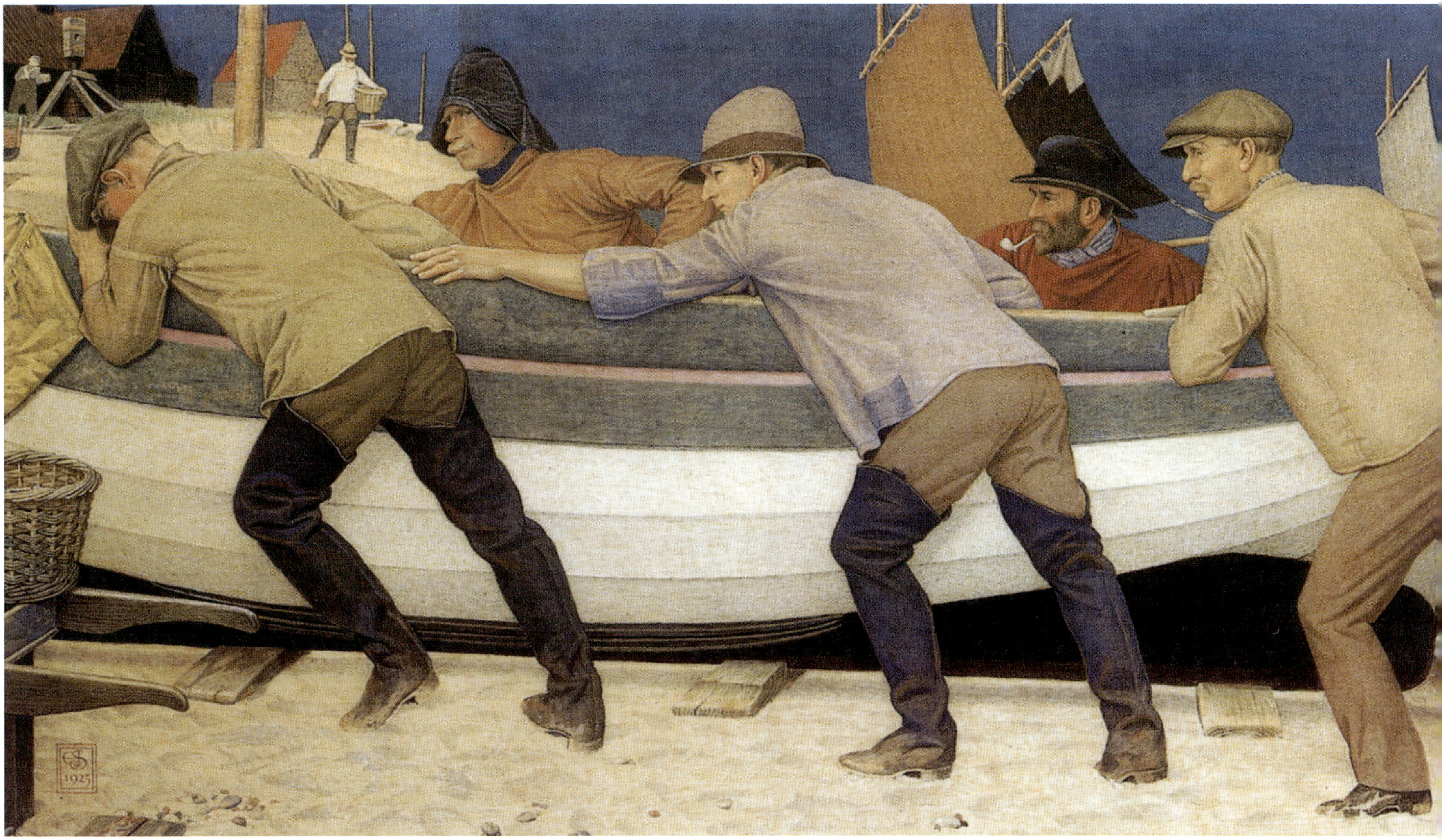

Southall and Gaskin – 'Joe' and 'Artie' – exchanged lively letters in which both men displayed their gifts for comedy and caricature. One of the wittiest, penned by Southall from Southwold in July 1905, notes: 'There are endless pictures to be done here.' Alas, Arthur Gaskin was not to create endless pictures anywhere. An artist's son from Birmingham he, like Southall, had first set his sights on architecture before settling on painting. The young friends had shared plans and travels, visiting William Morris and Burne-Jones together. But their initial explorations of medievalist and mythological themes had come at a time when critics were turning against pre-Raphaelite obsessions, and scorn was poured on Gaskin's beautiful pictures in particular. Lacking Southall's independent income, he needed to earn a living – and all the more so after marriage to Georgie Evelyn Cave France in 1893 and the eventual birth of two daughters (in 1910 Southall would make his name on the continent with a Paris exhibition from which Gaskin had withdrawn in fear of costly failure). Inevitably, he concentrated on teaching. Herself a brilliant designer, Georgie Gaskin (1866-1934) ran the household and much of her husband's career. The Gaskins collaborated on book illustration, metal-working and jewellery – especially after Arthur's appointment as head of the Birmingham School of Jewellery and Silversmithing in 1903. Marvellous enamels emerged from his execution of her designs. But the paintings were mostly for private pleasure. Georgie was often portrayed with long, flaming red hair – a wig of her own locks which had fallen out early in life due to illness. In an oil panel from 1904, Mrs Gaskin is shown reading on Southwold beach beneath an extravagant Edwardian hat. The couple, who retired to the Cotswolds in the 1920s, used their periodic visits to the Suffolk coast to collect cornelians which were then incorporated into jewellery.

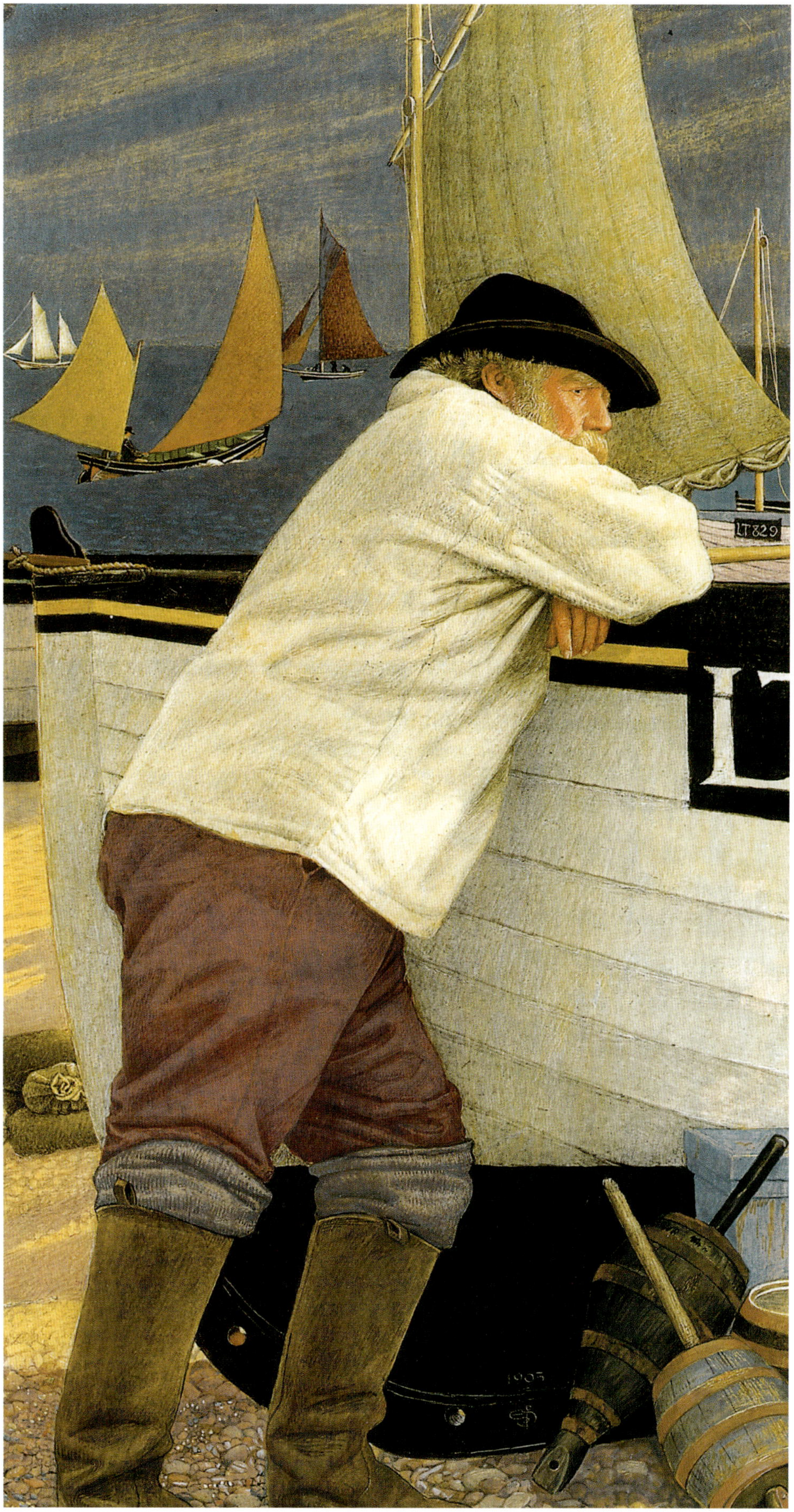


*The Old Fisherman*, 1903. Southall's receipt, dated January 9 1909, reads: 'Received of Arthur J Gaskin the sum of twenty pounds in payment for a Tempera picture called "The Old Fisherman" which I believe to be honestly worth about seven and sixpence (but the frame is a gold one) and which I painted during my honeymoon June & July 1903.' A drawing above the text shows an enthroned Gaskin handing a bag of money to the supplicant artist.

Joseph and Bessie Southall also worked in close partnership. Occasionally the artist painted on panel or silk, but mostly on handwoven linen which his wife tacked and sewed to a wedged frame. She then applied up to eight coats of gesso, smoothed to an ivory finish and sealed with two washes of size (obtained from prolonged boiling of parchment clippings). Once a picture was complete – with no varnishing allowed to gloss or cloud the pure pigment – she would help to carve the generally ornate frame and to add the gilding. With that stress on capable craftsmanship, Southall preferred to grind his own paints and mix his own colours by straining egg yolk through muslin, adding water and preservative, and blending with the powdered pigment on a ground glass slab. Such painstaking preparation followed lengthy experiments in handling tempera – he ended with hatched brushstrokes of thinly-applied paint in transparent, watercolour-like glazes. Given his intense study of the Italian Primitives, he sought to achieve a similarly golden glow to his own work with an initial layer of raw siena. Ironically, as picture restorer Jill Dunkerton has pointed out, part of this effect in the pictures he loved was due to accumulated dirt and yellowed varnishing. Still, no matter how inauthentic its artistic origins, such an immaculate bathed-in-gold viewpoint made for an image of heavenly seaside holidays.

For most of the 34 summers following their wedding, the Southalls came to Southwold religiously. Although they made repeated trips to the continent, chiefly to France and Italy, the little Cornish port of Fowey was the only other choice for working holidays in England. All these stays resulted in a comprehensive portrait of the

*Parasols*, Joseph Southall, watercolour, 1929.

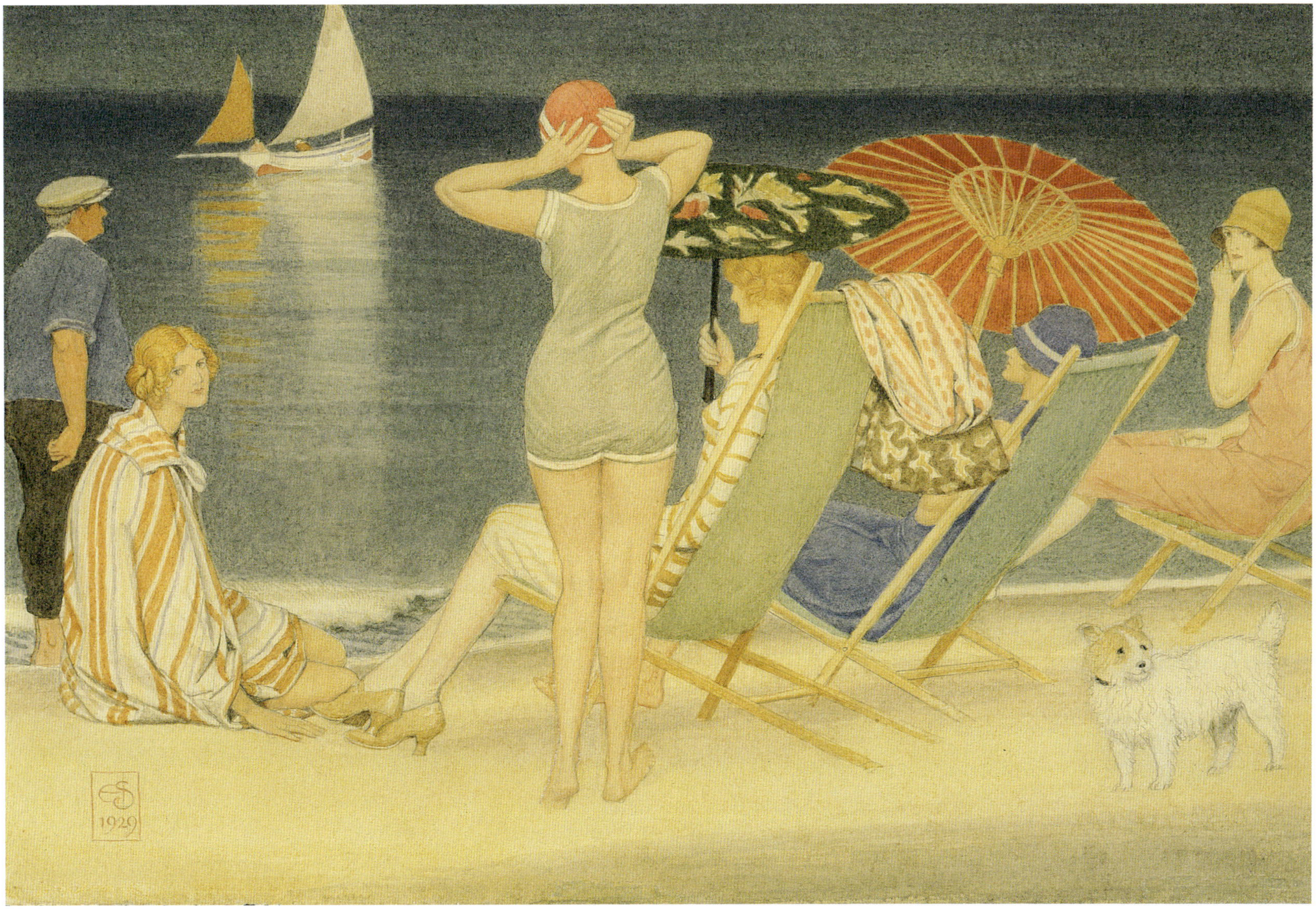

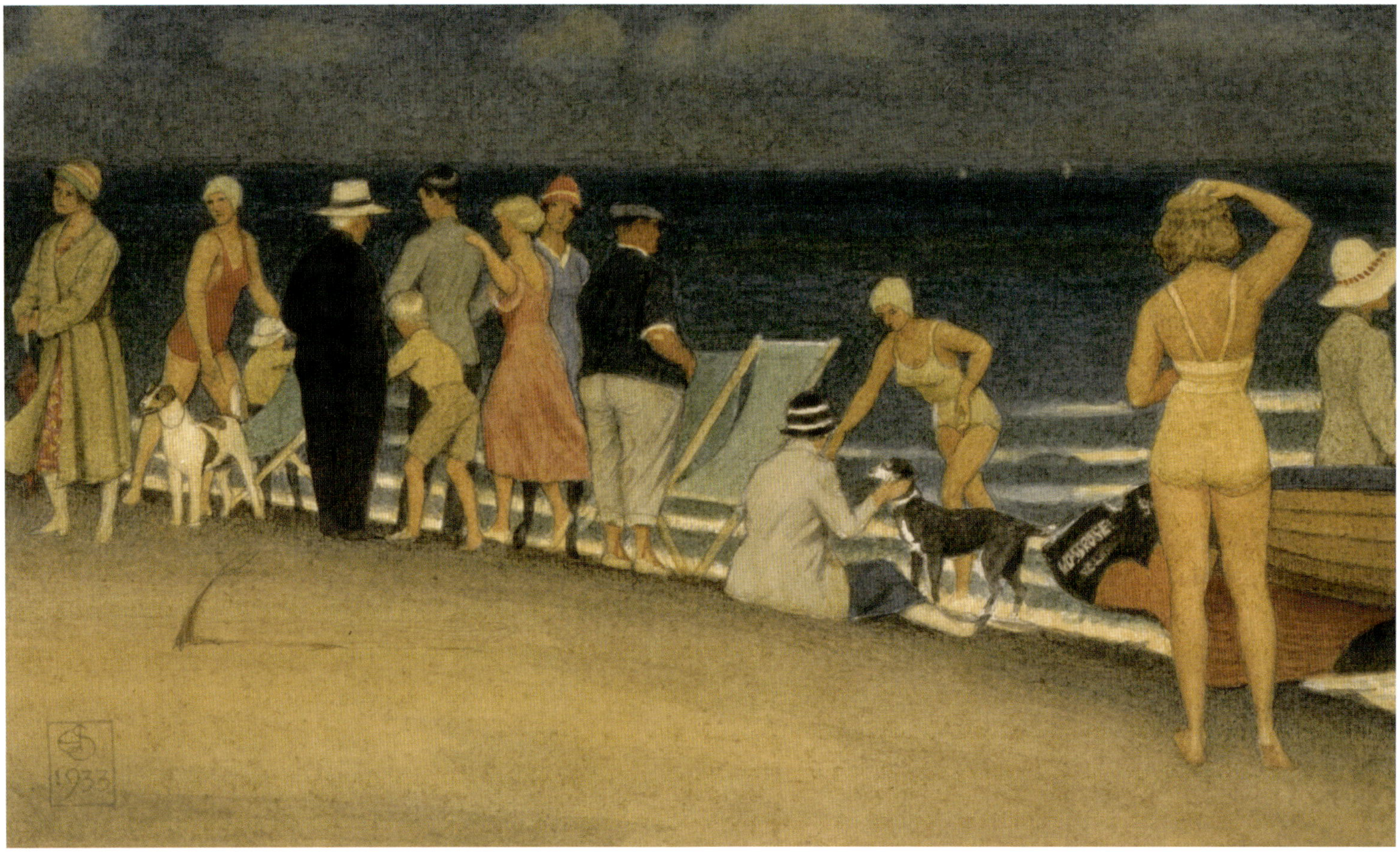

*The Trippers,* Joseph Southall, pencil and watercolour, 1933.

Suffolk town – where legend wrongly insists that nothing ever changes – as it was transformed from a sedate Victorian watering hole into a modern seaside resort. This seachange was made still more vivid by Southall's love of fabulous fabrics. Burne-Jones had exhorted him to 'draw constantly…draw drapery' but he needed little urging. In *The Agate*, the artist's bold 1911 portrait of himself and his wife on the beach at Southwold (see p.85), an air of theatricality in the clothing suggests that the figures have walked out of Southall's earlier mythological pictures with a few added nods to contemporary fashion. A note in a pocketbook of around 1900 mentions the 'Artists' Costume Supply Association 195 High St. Kensington' and the artist sketched decorative textile details in the Victoria & Albert Museum. Most poignantly, one lot in the 1948 auction following Mrs Southall's death was a 'box containing quantity of fancy clothing for studio posing purposes'.

Colour was always the key. Whereas the arrangement of pigment in 14th and 15th century Italian painting was constrained by iconographic tradition, Southall was free to work as he wished. In a 1922 letter to Maxwell Armfield he confessed that his favourite combinations were 'plum colour against crimson – crushed strawberry against scarlet – ultramarine ash against vermilion, sea green beside ultramarine' all harmonised by that underlying golden hue. He had already proved this in his paintings, of course, in which elegant young women – 'goddesses' in his letters – flitted like birds-of-paradise across the sand, swathed from head to toe in silken finery. In *Along the Shore*, the most surreal of these scintillating images (p.84), the three graces plus child approach the water's edge as if it is a shop window in London's Bond Street. They appear amazingly out of their element. But according to sketches and colour notes, Southall was painting the 1914 scene almost exactly as he saw it. By the 1930s, however, the bevy of observed beauties has changed into bathing belles who sport skimpy swimming costumes and bare their limbs to the cult of the sun. One resort, two generations: worlds apart.

As a dedicated political activist over difficult decades of war and peace, Southall hated cruelty, poverty and inequality. But he was altogether lulled in Southwold, finding here an ideal community. For instance the three generations of a fishing family watched by a young holidaymaker as they push their boat up the beach in the 1920 picture *Up From The Sea* (p.87) are not borne down by their labour. They are ennobled by it. They are firmly united. And they will remain in Southwold when trippers have to go home.

If there was a failure to connect between locals and visitors, then it had comic implications. A portly figure akin to Sam May – the celebrated lifeboat coxswain who operated a bathing hut concession and was depicted by Southall outside his HQ below Gun Hill (*Sam May's Hut*, p.86) – reappears in other pictures amid the lithe ladies of fashion, either ignoring or ogling them and with amusing implications in each case. And so a witty idea sketched out by Charles Keene in the Victorian era was developed for a new century.

Joseph Southall was sincere and steadfast to the last. As a Quaker he refused to pay that portion of his rates which would go to teach children the doctrines of the established church. So every six months he gave his testimony in court and suffered distraint on his goods – always forfeiting the same two antique silver spoons, which he then repurchased. Ill-health would be borne with similar fortitude. In 1937 the artist had a major operation after which, according to his wife, he needed 'a little attention from his surgeon, under an anaesthetic, every 2 or 3 months, sometimes oftener'. Travelling was curtailed, but painting continued until his death in 1944.

Well before the end, with his love of sailing ships and goddesses and permanently golden afternoons, Southall's talent might have seemed to some antiquated and nostalgic however marked the changes in featured female costumes. But in 1950 Sir Osbert Sitwell recalled a late 1920s visit by Picasso to Violet Gordon Woodhouse. Fellow guests were astonished as he kept returning to a little room to admire pictures 'bought from an old gentleman' and eventually offered to buy them. They were a 'portrayal, in pure, bright, almost encaustic tones of paint, of sailing ships in full rig against a flat sea'. The artist was Joseph Edward Southall.

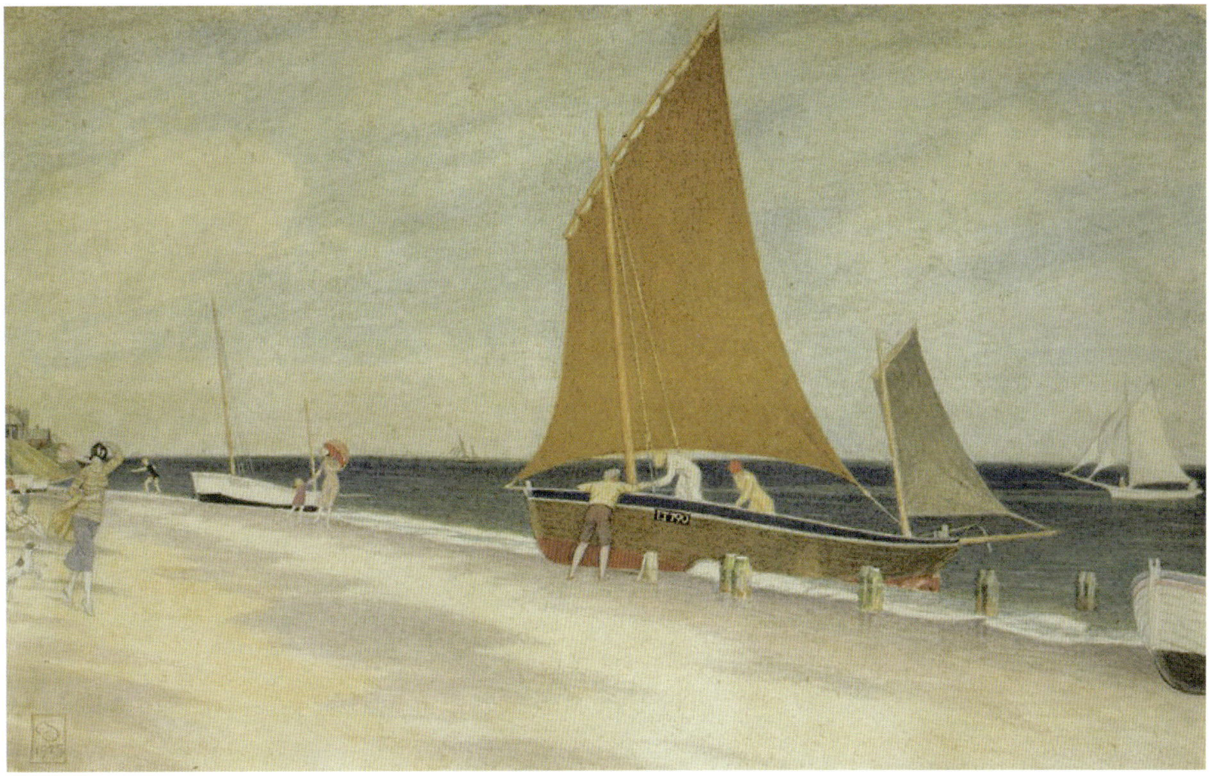

*Pleasures of the Seaside*, Joseph Southall, watercolour, 1925.

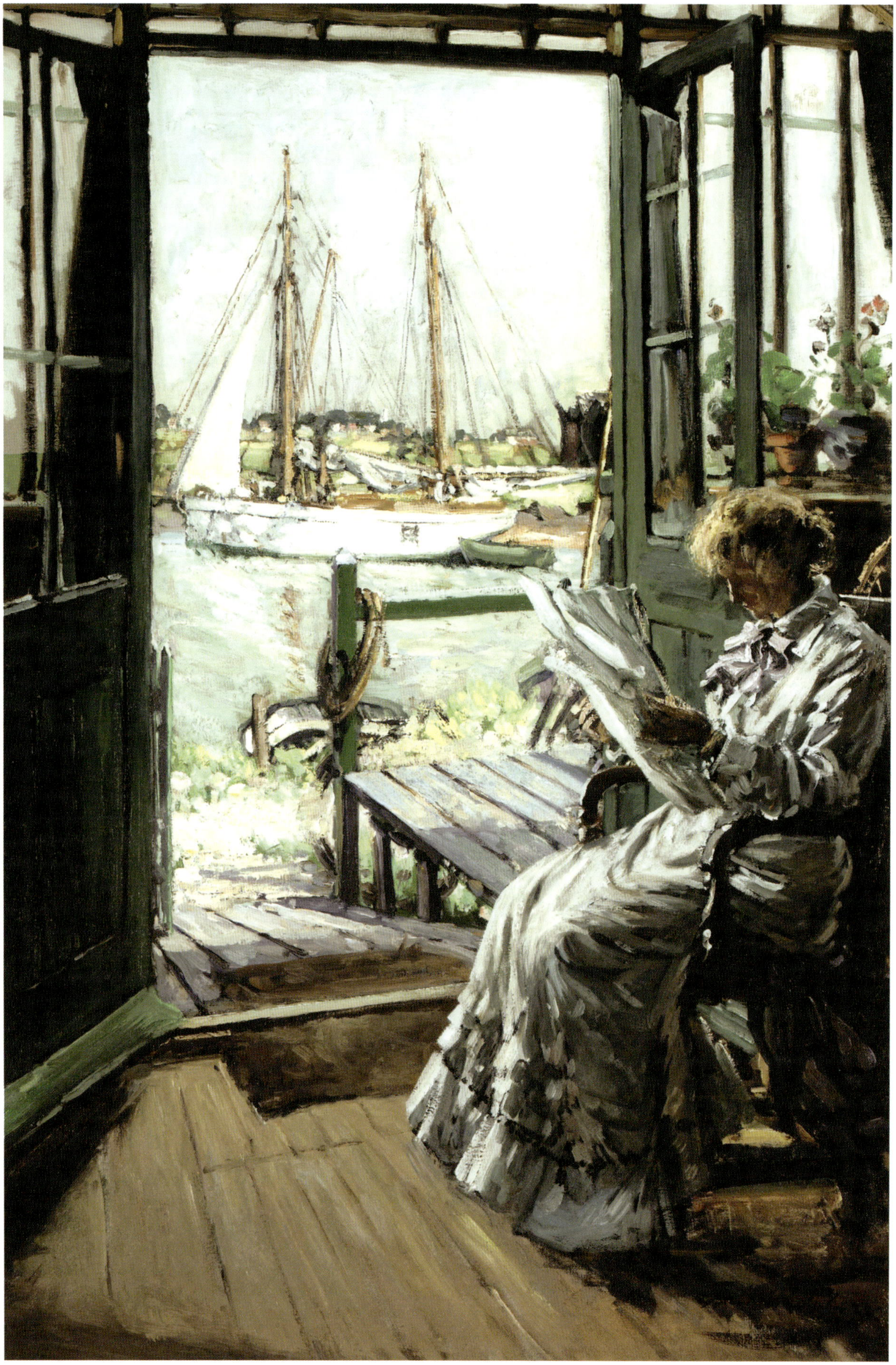

*Summer's Day*, Francis Newbery, oil on canvas, c1912. The view is towards Southwold from the artist's harbour-side studio, with his wife, Jessie, in the foreground.

Chapter Twelve

# Flower of Scotland

*'Art is the flower – life is the green leaf. Let every artist strive to make his flower a beautiful living thing – something that will convince the world that there may be – there are – things more precious – more beautiful – more lasting than life.'*

(Charles Rennie Mackintosh 'Seemliness', 1902.)

Coastal communities link up through their floating populations, and for centuries fishing boats from Scotland were familiar sights in Southwold harbour. Scottish accents and Gaelic speech were more familiar still when women followed teeming herring as they migrated down the coast – gutting catches of what the Scottish poet and Suffolk marine biologist James Burns Singer called 'living silver' on convenient docksides, then salting and packing the fish in barrels for transport to London or export to the continent. Large numbers of 'herring girls' reached Southwold, the most southerly point of their journey, late each September from 1907 and were last seen in Suffolk in the 1950s. They were noted for taking up their knitting needles as soon as they had laid down their gutting knives.

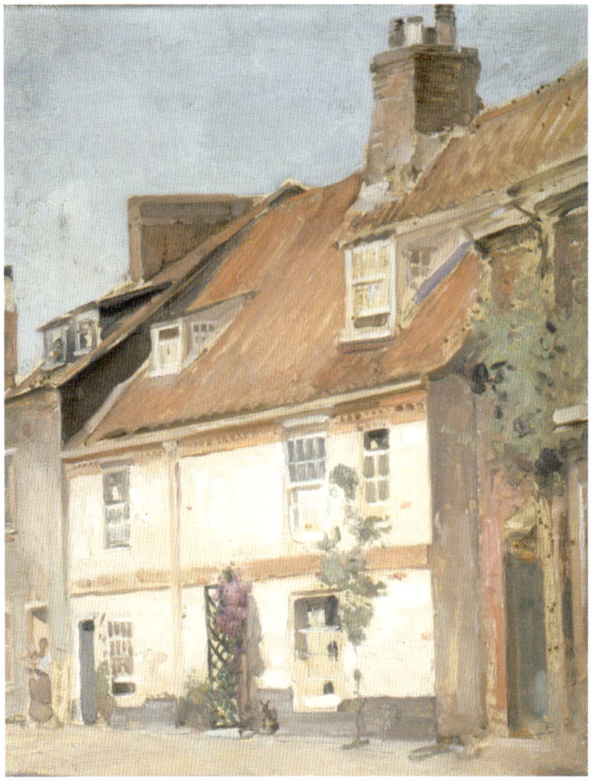

E.A. Walton's 1908 oil of a house in Park Lane, (right).

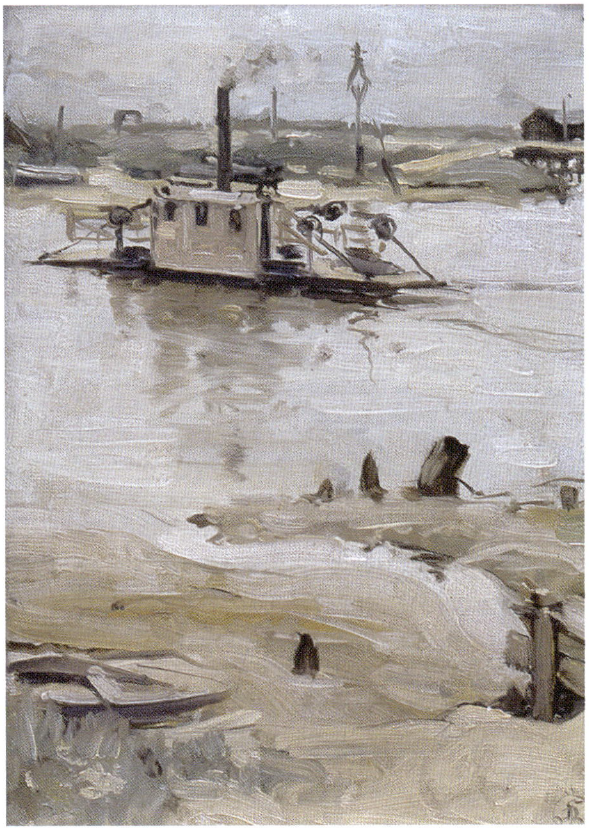

*The Ferry on the Blyth*, Francis Newbery, oil on canvas, c1900.

With agriculture in decline from the 1870s, as homegrown harvests failed through heavy rains and the American Mid-West began to yield vast supplies of cheap wheat, part of the fertile East Anglian landscape was left to run wild in peacetime. Farms became ramshackle, cottages fell into ruin. And in the global depression of the inter-war years, sturdy emigrants from rural Scotland rented derelict farms and turned round the faltering fields of Suffolk through sweat and skill.

There was also to be a strong Scottish voice in the artistic life of Southwold and the surrounding area, thanks to two pioneers in particular – **E.A. WALTON** (1860-1922) and **FRANCIS NEWBERY** (1855-1946) – who alighted on the Suffolk scene at roughly the same point. Edward Arthur Walton was born in Renfrewshire into a large and creative family. With Joseph Crawhall Jnr, James Guthrie, John Lavery and James Paterson, he formed a mainstay of what became known as The Glasgow Boys thanks to links of friendship and to an early shared enthusiasm for the plein-air naturalism of Jules Bastien-Lepage. In 1893 he moved to London and soon afterwards to Cheyne Walk where neighbours included Lavery, Steer and, most significantly, Whistler, whose subjective and seductive approach to art prompted a break with rigid realism. His circle also comprised the ex-pat Scots Alexander Mann (1853-1908) and Arthur Melville (1855-1904), inveterate travellers who had first visited Southwold and Walberswick in 1890. While living in Chelsea Walton enjoyed two Walberswick holidays before taking a long-term lease on the Old Vicarage at Wenhaston, where successive summers were spent working on pastoral landscapes in oil and watercolour. Walton was also a sensitive portraitist, executing *The Briony Wreath* at his Suffolk retreat, with a local gamekeeper's daughter serving as model. He continued to enjoy seasonal stays in the Blyth Valley village – which had a station on the branch railway line from Halesworth to Southwold – after quitting London for Scotland in 1904. In September 1908 there was a commission from historian and biographer John Bury for an oil of his house in Southwold's Park Lane. It was a present for his wife, whose portrait was also to be painted.

Devon-born Francis ('Fra') Newbery trained at Bridport Art School and London's Royal College of Art. Appointed director of the Glasgow School of Art in 1885, he transformed a provincial centre with a modest schedule of evening classes into a leading centre of creativity – with acclaimed teaching and a dazzlingly distinctive line in art, craft and design which became known as the Glasgow Style. After marriage to the embroidery expert Jessie Rowat in 1889, he found the perfect partner for putting his arts and crafts theories into practice, assisted by talented (and very often female) former students and by exchanges with similar centres of artistic innovation across Europe, notably Munich, Vienna and Turin.

Engrossed in this great project, Newbery

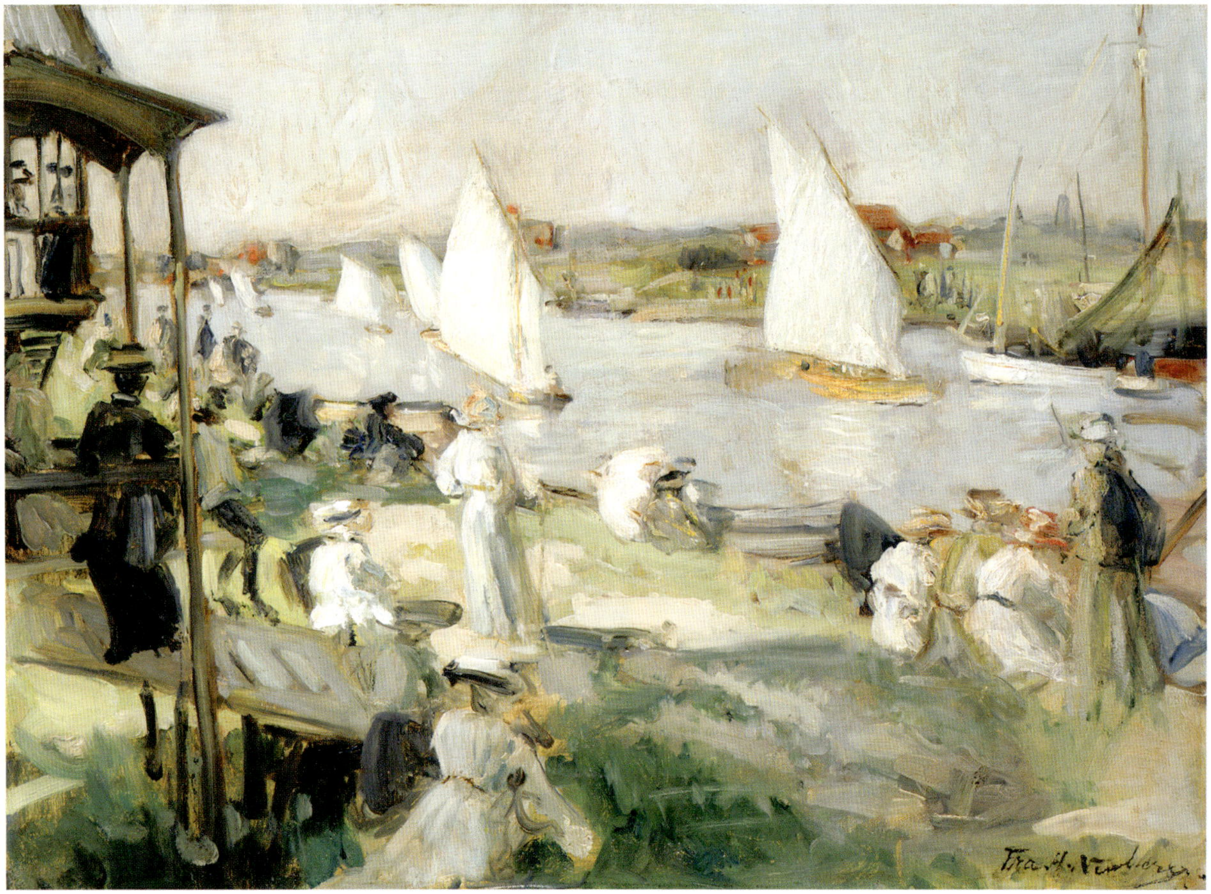

*A Regatta*, Francis Newbery, oil on canvas.

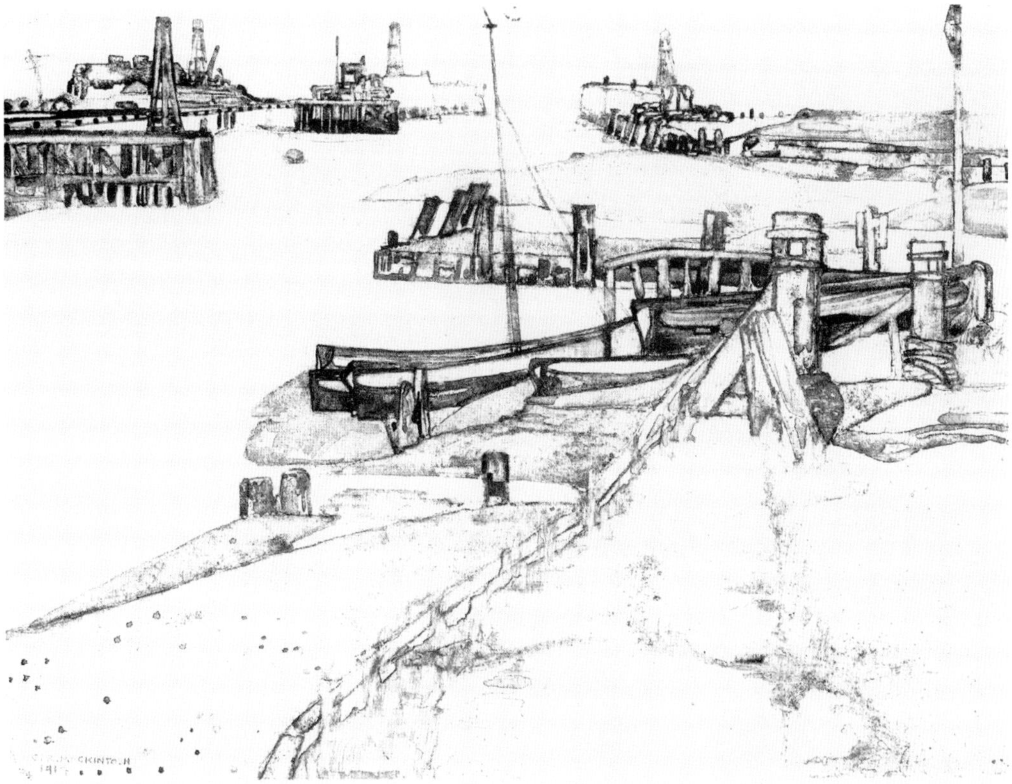

*Walberswick,* Charles Rennie Mackintosh, watercolour, 1915.

painted in rather limited spare time, a luxury he secured chiefly in Suffolk until his retirement to Corfe Castle in 1918. Possibly introduced to Walberswick by Steer in the 1880s, by the late 1890s he had taken a long-term tenancy of a house named Rooftree, also renting a fishing-hut studio beside the harbour. Here he produced some glorious oil paintings – with foreground figures of his wife reading (p.92) or a girl looking into the water from a veranda, while beyond busy configurations of yachts, drifters and steamers lay a view across the marshes to Southwold. Each lively scene was further invigorated by a semi-impressionistic handling of pigment.

Inevitably the Newbery household became a magnet for visiting artists, and there was much mingling with the Walton clan in particular. The painters' daughters Mary Newbery Sturrock (1892-1985) and Cecile Walton (1891-1956) were close friends, the latter looking back on idyllic youthful summers in Walberswick – with 'long weeks of hot sunshine, sandy lanes, hedges powdered white with dust; and cottage gardens a riot of vegetable-marrows, sunflowers, Madonna-lilies, opium-poppies and larkspur' – in an unpublished memoir entitled *More Lives Than One,* Cecile also recalled scorning 'townified children who were not allowed to risk getting soaked to the skin when, on stormy days of high wind, the breakers came roaring over the Pier-head; and who were not allowed to go alone to the Windmill in the marshes and climb the rusty spars up to the clanking wheel'. And she concluded: 'There is an expanding luxury of the body that only free and healthy children know. A wind-blown-ness, a sun-soaked-ness, a voluptuous caress of deep waters and the salty taste of the sea on the lips and strands of hair.'

But it was also at Rooftree that Cecile met the Scottish artist Eric Harald Macbeth Robertson. In 1914, following a fitful courtship, and much against her parents' wishes, they were wed. The marriage failed within nine years but during its stormy passage both partners produced Symbolist pictures of a high standard unmatched after their separation (when Robertson, ostracised by his former wife's wide circle, retreated to Liverpool). A small but wonderfully misty and moody oil of Southwold harbour survives, stamped with the entwined initials C and W. Fra Newbery is now best known as the patron of architect, painter and designer **CHARLES RENNIE MACKINTOSH** (1868-1928), whose brilliantly inventive work built a bridge between Symbolism and Art Nouveau – and still more between art, craft and design – in the most elegant epitome of Glasgow Style. In 1892 Newbery had introduced Mackintosh to Glasgow School of Art student **MARGARET MACDONALD** (1865-1933) and the pair had worked together on numerous creative projects before marrying in 1900. That was also the year in which, most fatefully for this story, the rising architectural star had exhibited with the Vienna Secession and formed links with the likes of Josef Hoffmann, Koloman Moser and Hermann Muthesius.

Mackintosh enjoyed prolonged sketching tours of distant regions during summer holidays and in 1897 – when his prized commission to design a new Glasgow School of Art was underway – he came to Southwold while wandering through Norfolk and Suffolk. Noting down vernacular details in exquisite drawings, and focusing on churches in particular, he also visited Reydon, South Cove, Blythburgh, Bramfield and Halesworth. He and Margaret were back in East Anglia in 1905, and possibly in 1911 when they may have visited the Newberys in Walberswick. What is certain is that as their troubles mounted

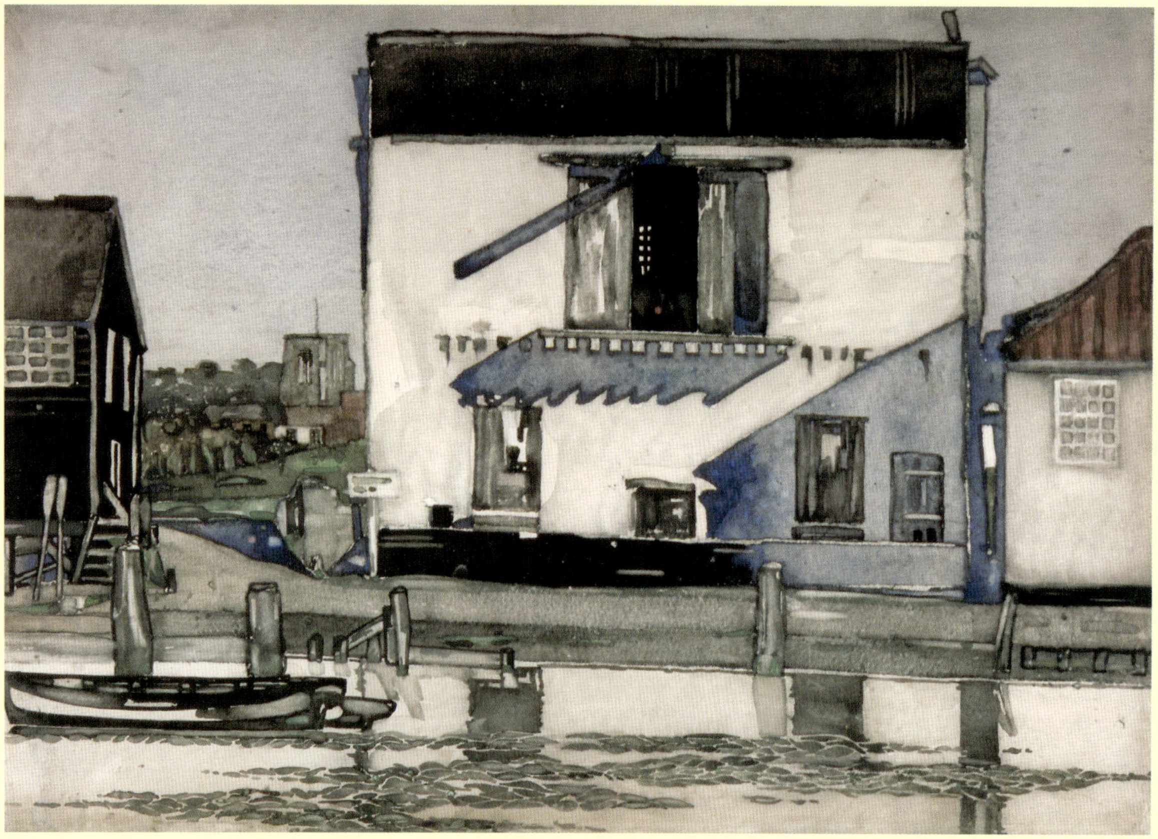

*Venetian Palace, Blackshore on the Blyth*, Charles Rennie Mackintosh. In this 1914 watercolour the artist has twisted perspective to incorporate Southwold's emergent Roman Catholic church, where a first mass was held in June 1916. Blackshore House, the 'Venetian Palace', was in reality a flimsy netstore. It collapsed in the 1960s after temporarily housing writer Penelope Fitzgerald, whose novel *The Bookshop* is set in Southwold. Her father was *Punch* editor E.V. Knox and her maternal grandfather Ernest Shepherd, original illustrator of *The Wind in the Willows* and *Winnie the Pooh*.

in Glasgow, with Mackintosh resigning his architectural partnership in 1913 after charges of arrogance and drunken indolence, and even an absurd allegation that he was no longer able to draw, refuge was sought on the Suffolk coast.

The couple arrived in Walberwick in July 1914, taking lodgings at Millside next door to the Newbery base in the main street and also renting a fishing hut near that used by their stalwart patron. When war erupted in early August, visiting artists scattered. But 'Toshie' and Margaret decided to stay on – after all, everyone said the conflict would be over by Christmas and they would just sit things out in the meantime. As Margaret later explained in a letter to her friend Anna Geddes: '(we intended) coming just for a holiday & then war broke out & I induced Toshie to just stop on & get the real rest-cure that he so badly needed for quite two years – it struck me as the right thing to do – there will be nothing really doing till the war is over for one thing & for another it is too dangerous to go on – when a man is over-worked he must rest or something serious will happen – so it was all arranged and I went back to Glasgow & let the house furnished for a year…and we are going to have a real Wanderjahr already Toshie is quite a different being & evidently at the turn of the year will be quite fit again & by that time we hope the war will be over & then perhaps he can have a hand in rebuilding the beautiful cities which are lost to us.'

While at Walberswick Mackintosh turned out several topographical watercolours, one showing harbour reconstruction in progress since 1907, another a huge and now lost harbourside shed. A third depicted the *Venetian Palace*, a strangely exotic structure on the Blackshore beside the Harbour Inn which fell to pieces in the 1960s and

*Gorse, Walberswick,* Charles Rennie and Margaret Macdonald Mackintosh, pencil and watercolour, 1915. The heaths are home to both common and rare Western gorse which blooms in autumn. Gorse was once cut as a fuel for cottage ovens and the bushes pegged drying washing – laundry absorbing the aroma of coconut.

whose site is now occupied by a white hacienda. The artist also peered in gardens and traipsed across dunes, woods and marshes in search of cultivated and wild flowers, shrub sprigs and tree twigs to add to a putative album. For he had a commission from Germany for a book and possibly an exhibition of coloured botanical drawings.

At least 40 resulting pencil and watercolour images, stylised into an almost Japanese purity of line and colour, are recorded in a body of work latterly rated among Mackintosh's finest achievements. They include larkspur, petunia, polyanthus, aubretia, arbutus, anemone and pasque, stagthorn, winter stock (twice), moth mullein, pine, pine cone and needles, lupin, lavender, ivy seed, field pea, bean flower, daisy, berberis, chionodoxa, kingcups, fritilleria, leycesteria, grape hyacinth, honeysuckle, veronica (twice), rosemary, jasmine, cactus flower, green hellebore, gorse, willow catkins and Japanese witch hazel. Although all these cited images are clearly stamped with a cartouche box containing date, location and the initials CRM and MMM, Margaret Macdonald Mackintosh has never been properly credited for her contribution to the colouring. Pages signed with the letters CRM alone (sorrel, borage, chicory, gaillardia) appear oddly incomplete. Then again, in their lifetimes the collaboration was wholly ignored, for the book, cancelled during the war, was forgotten when peace finally prevailed.

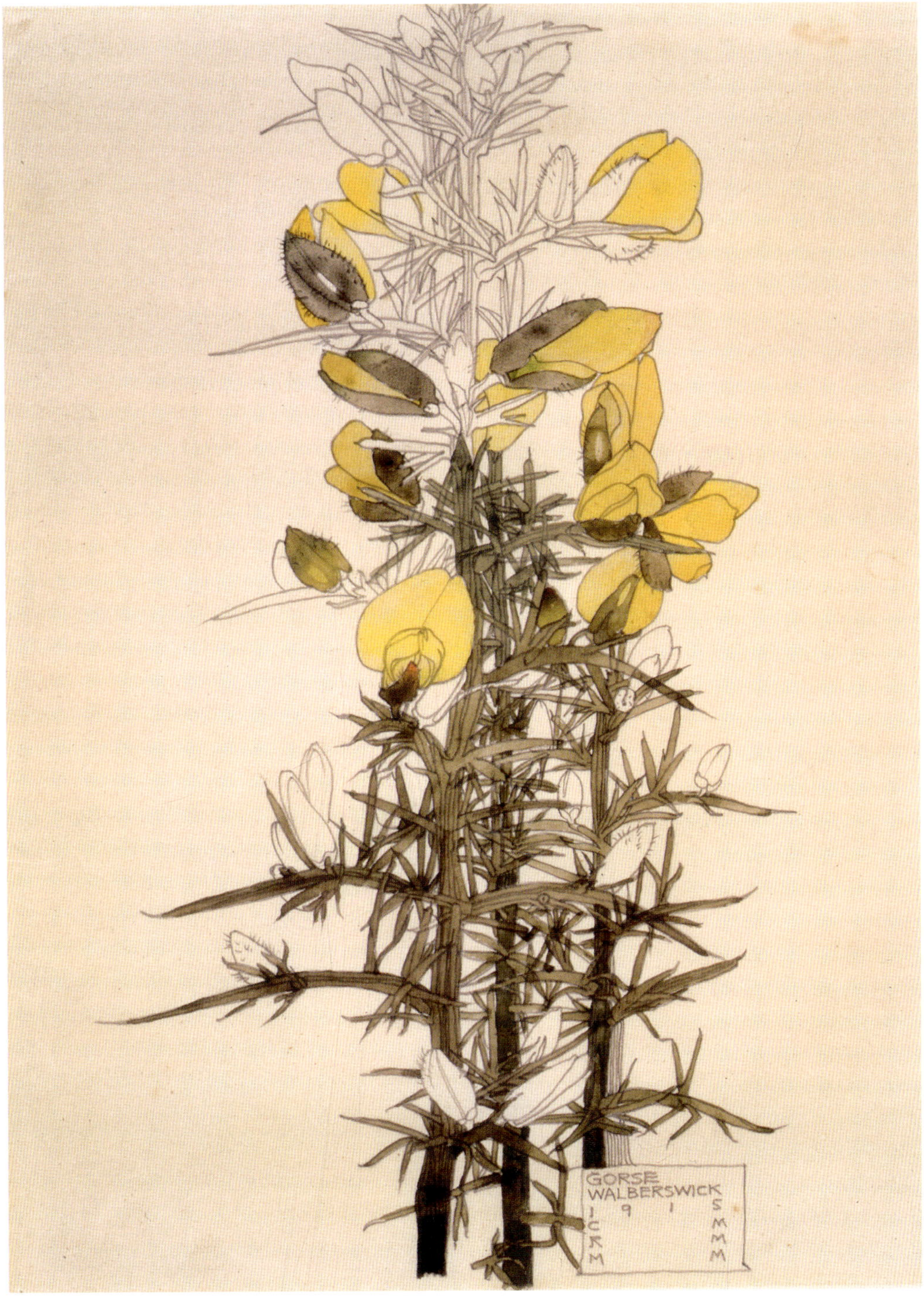


But as the fields of Flanders clogged with mud and blood during the early months of 1915, and fears of invasion gathered along the North Sea coast, local suspicions hardened over the peculiar outsider who should have left long ago and who was now so busy taking mysterious notes. However engrossed in his own world, the artist should have been warned by the case of Wangford schoolteacher William Smith, who had travelled to Germany before the war and received German visitors in return. Wild gossip turned into a witch hunt in the first weeks of conflict, which ended with a banishment order from the eastern counties under the emergency powers of the Defence of the Realm Act. The hounded man went no further than the hayshed behind his house, where he cut his throat. Later his distraught widow also killed herself.

In an unpublished memoir written in 1989 Catharine Carrington, daughter of the Walberswick-based Arts and Crafts metalworker Philip Alexander, recalled a conflict which had begun when she was barely ten: 'We were thrilled when in the middle of one night a German Zeppelin flew over from the sea. Our parents woke us and we all went out in the garden. My father felt it was not very safe for our family to be right on the East Coast.

'One of our friends staying in the village then

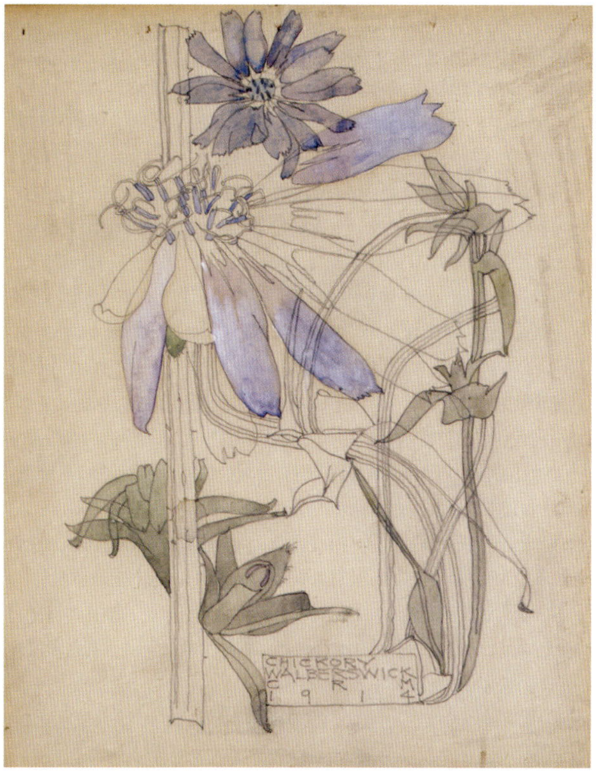


*Chickory, Walberswick*, Charles Rennie Mackintosh, watercolour and pencil, 1914.

*Anemone and Pasque, Walberswick*, Charles Rennie and Margaret Macdonald Mackintosh, watercolour and pencil, 1915.

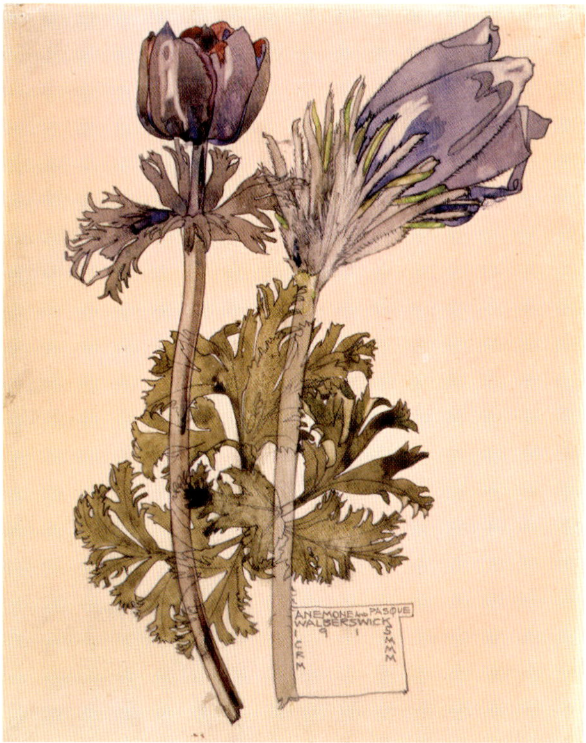


was Charles Rennie Mackintosh, dressed in a black cape and a large black hat making him look a somewhat unusual and sinister figure, and to make him more suspicious he used to wander around the country, the marshes and the village carrying a camera and also doing a lot of sketching. He was of course suspected of being a spy, especially as he never managed his blackout of windows properly. So the police arrested him, and my father had the job of going to court to get him released.'

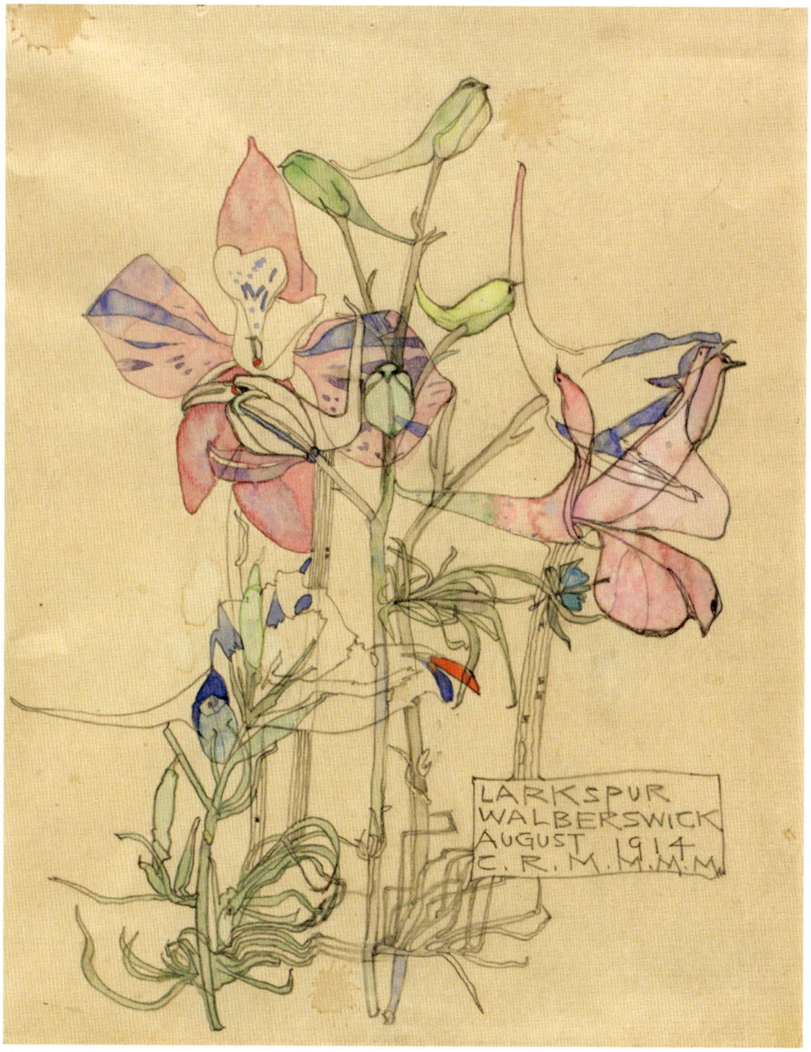


*Larkspur, Walberswick*, watercolour and pencil drawing by Charles Rennie and Margaret Macdonald Mackintosh, August 1914.

Rumours escalated with jingoistic paranoia and panic. It was said that Mackintosh had been seen waving a lantern in an upstairs room at Westwood Cottage where the painter Arthur Dacres Rendall had his studio – obviously signalling to ships at sea. But the final blow came with the report that the black-clad figure had received highly subversive letters. When police raided his rooms they duly discovered correspondence from German and Austrians linked to something called the Vienna Secession – not just enemy aliens but revolutionaries too.

And so almost a year after arriving in Walberswick, Mackintosh faced a potentially dire fate. Despite the intervention of well-connected allies such as Alexander, the artist was still expelled from Suffolk, Norfolk and Cambridgeshire. He and his wife fled to London and then, from 1923, to the South of France, where he proceeded to develop, before cancer advanced, the extraordinary watercolour landscapes and floral studies that no one wanted to see. After leaving England, in what was to be her last decade, Margaret ceased painting altogether. She survived the greatest artist Scotland ever produced by five years, in which time a sense of their shared failure must have seemed overwhelming.

Back in the spring of 1914 *The Studio* magazine had reproduced a watercolour entitled *The White Boat, Walberswick* in a lengthy tribute to **JAMES McBEY** (1883-1959), whose life was an astonishing story of triumph over adversity. He was born into lonely poverty on the north-east coast of Scotland and, after many adventures, died in Tangier an acclaimed artist, an American citizen and a man of means. He told the first part of his tale in *The Early Life of James McBey*, a small classic of Scottish literature unpublished until 1977. It outlined a granite resolve to escape from bleak beginnings – leaving a blind and embittered mother who eventually hanged herself in the cellar and a potential life sentence as a bank employee in Aberdeen – through self-taught art. Amazingly, he trained himself to etch and finally broke loose in 1911, when his first London exhibition was an outstanding success. The month before *The Studio* profile he had taken the lease on William Rothenstein's old studio in Hampstead.

*The White Boat, Walberswick* featured the billowing funnel of the steam ferry poised to cross the Blyth to Southwold. A similar view had been etched by David Muirhead Bone (1867-1953) after a visit the previous year. This Glasgow-born and trained talent had also moved to London and, like McBey, would soon be appointed an Official War Artist. Both were masterly draughtsmen and – along with David Young Cameron – prospered as Scotland's leading etchers until the hugely profitable market crashed with the Great Depression, never to recover. All three prolific artists continued to flourish however – McBey turning to oils and watercolours with all the crisp economy of his early study beside the Blyth. Muirhead Bone and D.Y. Cameron were latterly knighted as McBey's horizons spread ever wider between North America and North Africa. The cold North Sea became as remote to him as the North Pole.

*The White Boat, Walberswick*, James McBey, watercolour, illustrated in *The Studio* magazine March 14th 1914.

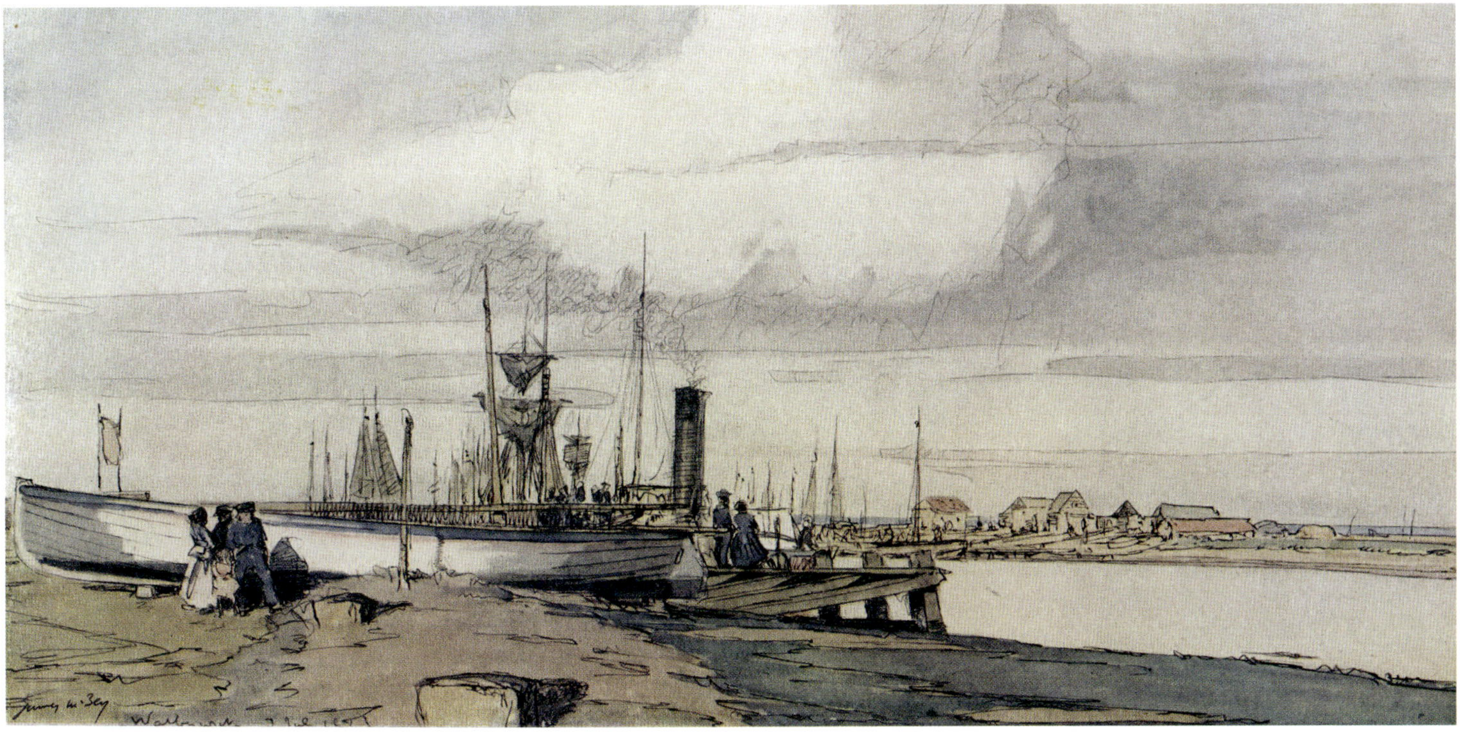

*The Saltings, Southwold*, Arnesby Brown, oil sketch on panel.

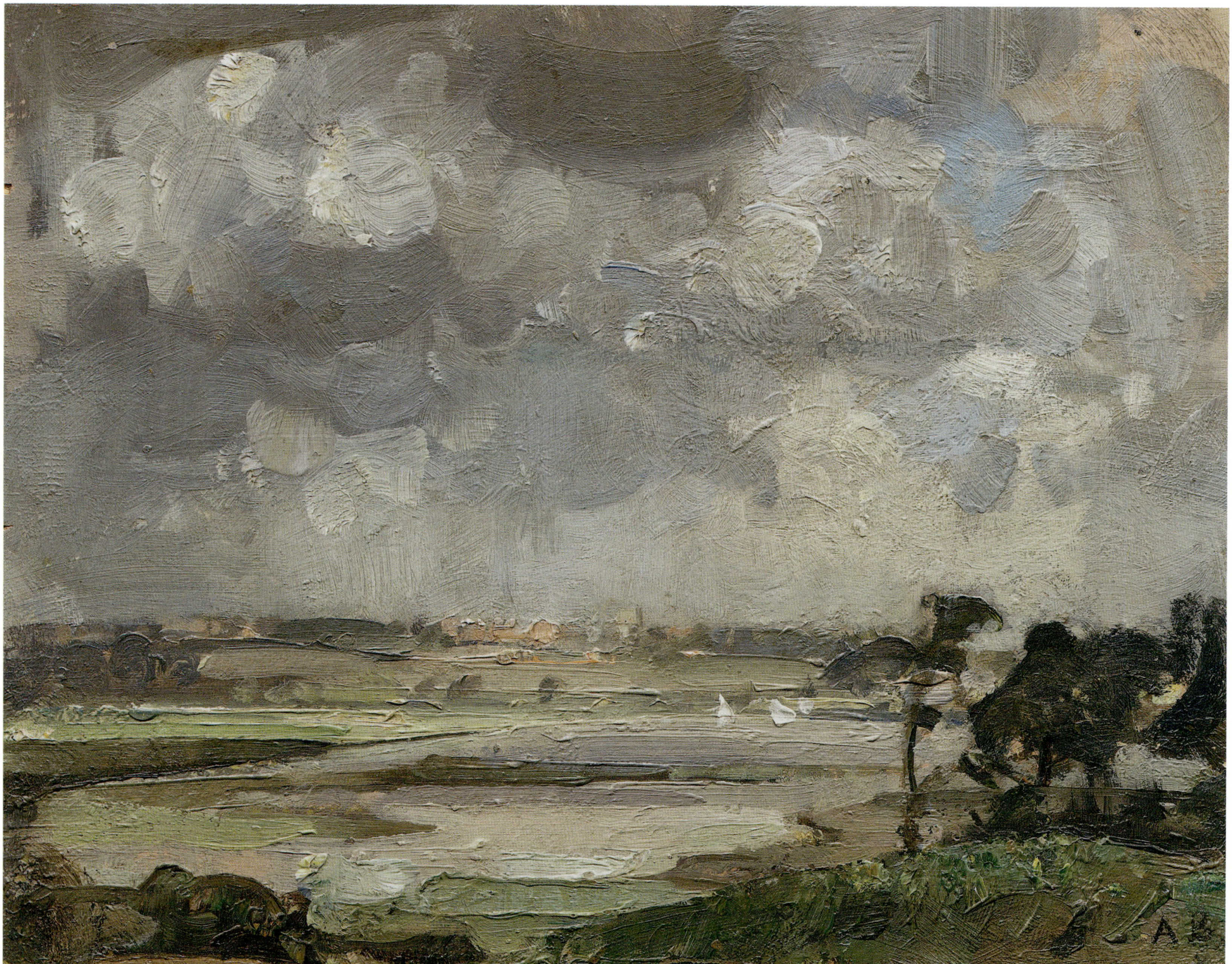

Chapter Thirteen

# School for Sensible Creatures

Southwold wouldn't be Southwold without St Felix School, though Margaret Gardiner's dream of a centre 'where girls are treated like sensible creatures' opened in Aldeburgh in 1897 and relocated to purpose-built premises in Reydon from 1902. A century later the school which had helped to pioneer the emancipation of women turned co-educational.

St Felix school, central bay of the Gardiner Hall.

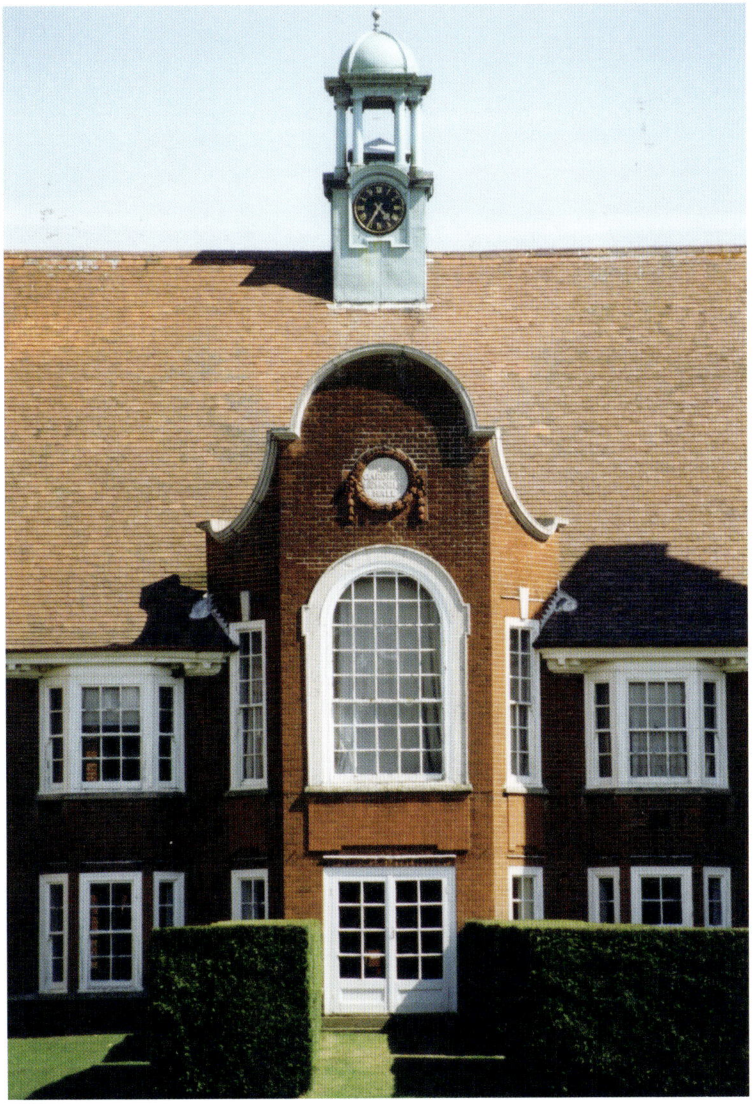

Miss Gardiner's efforts on behalf of sensible creatures involved an interim period in which, from 1898, large houses around South Green and Gun Hill and along the seafront were taken over for classrooms, dormitories and staff accommodation – with the ballroom of the Centre Cliff Hotel borrowed for dancing lessons and social functions. Then, when the founder's titanic task was all but complete, she sank into nervous collapse. Retreating into a 36-year retirement in Sussex, she occasionally returned to tour the school grounds secretly in the moonlight. Several girls would leave school convinced they had seen a ghost.

Enter the formidable Lucy Mary Silcox, who had a grand and noble vision but couldn't bear to lose at bridge. She promoted self-discipline within a regime of cold baths each morning followed by winter scrubs with towels frozen stiff in the dormitories overnight. Sure that teaching could succeed only in beautiful surroundings, the Cambridge scholar sought to feed eyes, minds and spirits with the sensual delight of lovely things. Instead of dowdy tweeds she sported 'Chinese embroidered jackets and brilliant peasant homespuns'. An inscription in a book presented by Old Felicians to the school in her memory added: 'She spoke often of beauty, of the beauty of Nature and of Art, of intellectual beauty, and the beauty of belief, and she set a standard for thinking and for living which was perhaps the most precious thing that those at school in her day carried away with them.' Miss Silcox was, in short, an inspiration and an eccentric.

The headmistress of St Felix School from 1909 had friends in highly-cultured places, from Bloomsbury hostess Lady Ottoline Morrell to the philosopher Bertrand Russell and future Poet Laureate John Masefield. Books with hand-penned dedications lined her study alongside

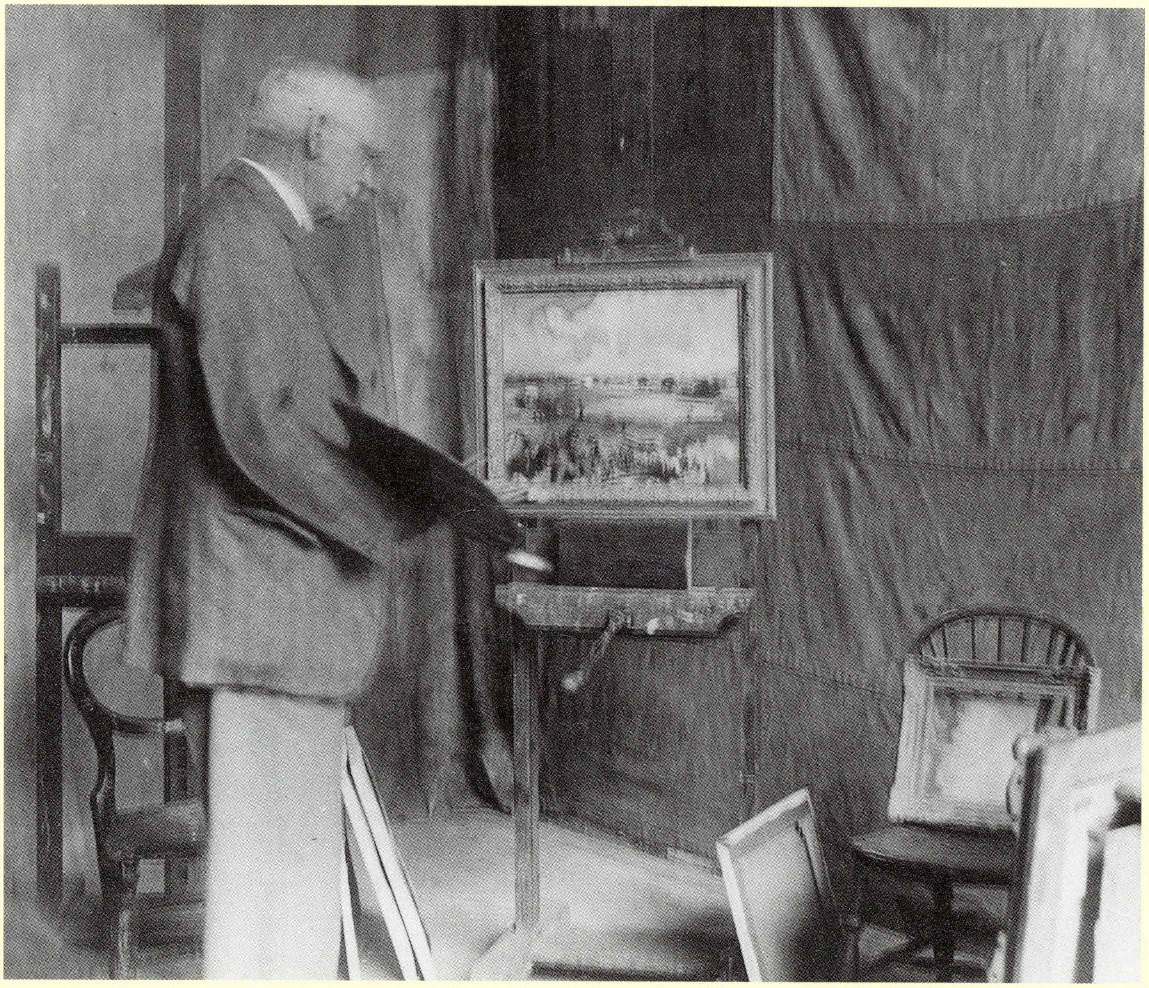

Nottingham-raised SIR JOHN ALFRED ARNESBY BROWN RA (1866-1955) studied under Sir Hubert von Herkomer at Bushey, but gravitated to the wide skies and marshy landscapes of East Anglia. He settled at Haddiscoe, in a house with a commanding view over wetlands from Acle to Beccles. Sketching trips were taken into surrounding scenes, sometimes with his Gorleston-based pupil Campbell Mellon (see p.149). And one summer day Arnesby Brown spotted a majestic view across the Blyth, with St Felix School and Southwold glinting in the distance. A resulting painting – the oil sketch for which is reproduced on p.100 – hung at the Royal Academy in 1934. The sketch was owned by Nancy Blott (1890-1983), Slade-trained art teacher at St Felix, who took this photograph of the artist with the RA picture in his studio.

In 1933 Arnesby Brown featured in the most remarkable exhibition Southwold has ever seen. The Sole Bay Group – comprising Tom van Oss, Margaret Delisle Burns, F. Burgess, Hester Cleminson, George Jackson, Cecil Lay, Dorothy Loftus and George Mostyn – had been lately founded by Walter Francis Crittall, a painter, draughtsman and etcher who introduced artists and his family's metal-framed windows to Walberswick after buying Old Farm. With his main base near Braintree, Crittall was a friend of Sir George Clausen, who now joined a distinguished list of guest exhibitors at the Stella Peskett Memorial Hall along with Amy K. Browning, Hilda and Richard Carline, T.C. Dugdale, Ronald Ossory Dunlop, Sir William Russell Flint, Bertram Priestman, Gilbert and Stanley Spencer, Leonard Squirrell, Algernon Talmage and Clifford Webb. Nine of the visitors were or would become Royal Academicians.

paintings by Constable and Marie Laurencin and a bust of Euphemia Lamb by Sir Jacob Epstein. And, even in retirement, she begged, bought and commissioned further treasures for her girls. Her prized finds included a Renaissance altar panel by Ranieri di Leonardo da Pisa, whose proposed removal from the school chapel in 1998 prompted a hymn-singing protest by 155 pupils. Although a subsequent sale for £84,000 to pop star Rod Stewart helped to fund a new sports hall and theatre, Miss Silcox would have seethed. Fury would have followed the recent sale of Christopher Wood's *The White Farm*, given to the school in her memory. And the disposal of the Ivan Mestrovic statue secured as a Great War memorial – after the school returned from evacuation to Dumfriesshire, Derbyshire and North Wales – would have caused an explosion.

*Miss Silcox*, Hilda Carline, oil on canvas, 1925.

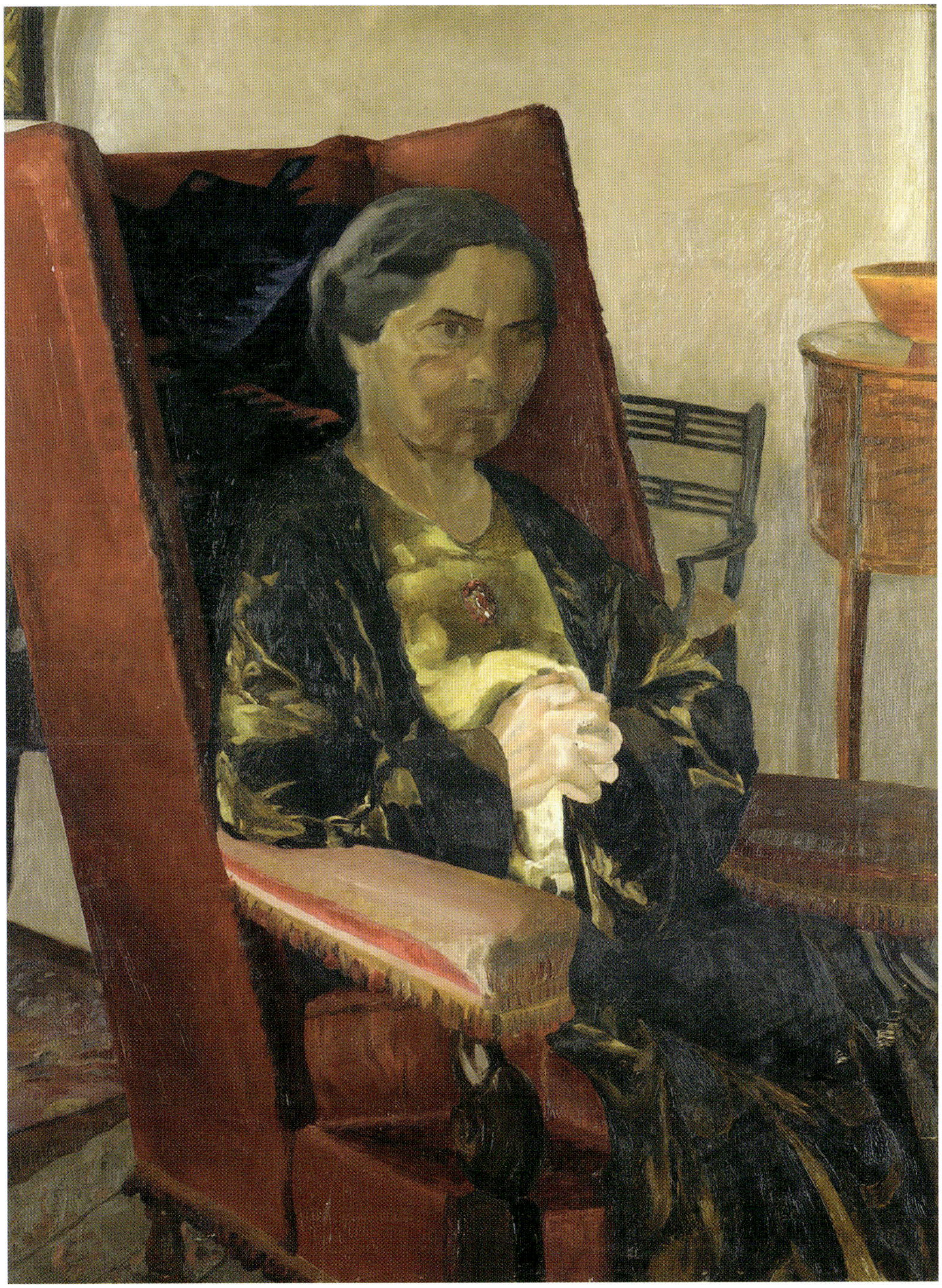

Miss Silcox was as idiosyncratic a character as the authors she admired – from the Polish mariner who jumped ship at Lowestoft to become Joseph Conrad, to the poets Walter de la Mare and Edward Thomas. She sat for several portraits, but the 1925 sessions with a honeymooning Stanley Spencer – plus his bride Hilda and brother Gilbert – went famously awry. Sitting for Stanley could be a disconcerting experience at the best of times, with several models reporting that he began the process by depicting a single, perfectly-formed eye. On this occasion the patience of the subject, worn by protracted sittings and possibly by the presence of two other painters, finally snapped when Stanley wiped his canvas almost clean. But she continued to admire him from a distance. More happily, there was a completed likeness by Harry Becker, from whom the headmistress also bought a study of Blythburgh church. The hard-up artist had given an unsuccessful lecture at the school when his wife Georgina was employed as the art teacher – with pupils' unwanted pictures taken home to Hinton so that he could work on the backs.

On the eve of her retirement Miss Silcox appointed Marjorie Lilly (1891-1980) to preside over the art department in a brand new studio which was her pride and joy. This accomplished painter and printmaker had studied at the Slade under 'Tonks the Terrible' and fallen under the spell of Camden School artists Harold Gilman, Charles Ginner, Robert Bevan and, most especially, Walter Sickert. Her 1973 account *Sickert: The Painter and his Circle* included her own special contribution to the saga – a hilarious misadventure at St Felix School.

The studio was to be hung with modern pictures, and Miss Lilly was entrusted with the task of securing for the school a suitable work from the Sickert studio and a lecture from the eminent artist. Both were duly promised and, one afternoon in 1926, the art teacher was thrilled to greet her mentor at Southwold station. They were served blackened tea and over-boiled eggs in her lodgings, but the visitor was so delighted with the prospect of his talk and the aspect of a landlady of 'mountainous proportions' that he happily 'ate two bricks and drank several cups of ink'. Then, from his battered Gladstone bag, he produced a picture. His devotee had imagined a procession of magnificent paintings – Dieppe cathedrals, Old Bedford music-halls, Venetian bridges, Georgian squares in Islington, garrets in Camden Town, dawn in Mornington Crescent. But what he unwrapped was a 'tiny, very slight, very dark oil sketch' of Thérèse Lessore, the painter he had lately married and who now appeared from her likeness to be deeply depressed. Miss Lilly felt doom descending at the thought of a sombre postage stamp affixed to a vast white wall.

'After tea, we took a turn by the sea; shaking off my worries for the time being, I gave myself up to the charm of his company,' she wrote. 'He was enchanted to renew his acquaintance with the old town of Southwold, which he had visited once before with Whistler, in the nineties. To his great satisfaction, it had hardly changed since then and he diverted me with stories about the Butterfly, how he insisted on wearing his pumps when walking, or rather limping along the beach, how discomfited he was generally with life out-of-doors. I did not gather that much work had been done by either on this occasion; Whistler destroyed most of what he did do and the place, much as Sickert enjoyed it, was too cosy, picturesque and prosperous, to stir him into action.'

Sickert was to dine with Miss Silcox, whose large ideas did not extend to food and dining rooms. Four people were crammed into the equivalent of a nun's cell to await monastic rations and a conversation that never came. For the fourth member of the party was Mademoiselle, with whom Sickert gabbled merrily in her native tongue. The headmistress, speaking barely a word of French, was reduced to sullen silence. Afterwards, they proceeded to the assembled school for the lecture, where Sickert surveyed a sea of white dresses and shawls and declared: 'Charming! Like a flock of little white doves!'

He then launched into an erudite talk on artists of whom no little bird had heard, and galleries none had seen – the unmagical mystery tour larded with arch jokes in boulevardier French. Sickert, concluding that those dumbfounded doves might be bird-brained, barked: 'But you do learn French

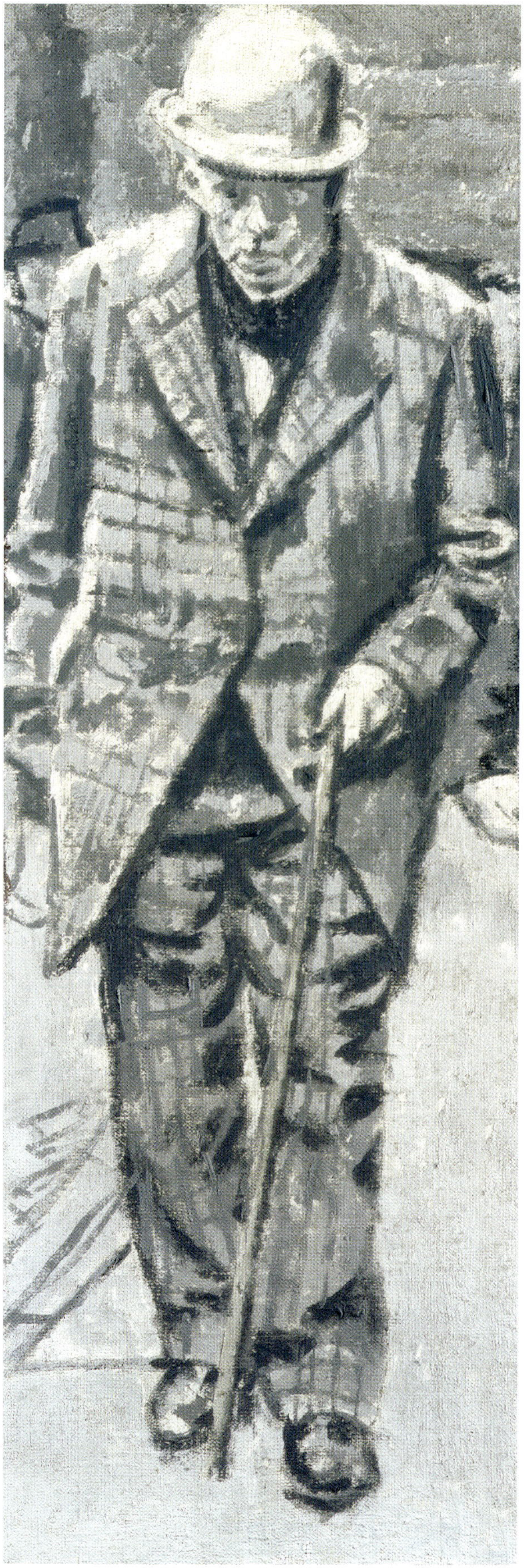

*Self-portrait,* Walter Richard Sickert, oil on canvas, 1930.

here, don't you? I thought this was a school!' How tickled Miss Silcox must have been by that.

Next morning the indomitable Sickert strode through rain to view the pupils' paintings, and here he waxed lyrical at last...before spying the nine-subject timetable on the studio wall. 'Three subjects are enough – Latin, English and mathematics,' he announced. 'Then the pupils may leave school knowing a little about something which would give them the confidence that is so necessary for their future studies, instead of nothing about anything at all. Nine subjects indeed!'

Miss Silcox sighed deeply before attempting a final appeal. 'Mr Sickert, what aesthetic influences do you suggest for the girls?'

But – as Miss Lilly recorded – the painter had dismissed the subject of education for that day; it was getting too near lunch-time. 'Pretty creatures!' he exclaimed.

The Lessore sketch was returned to the artist by a mortified Miss Lilly, who also confessed that Miss Silcox had selected a more suitable portrait from the Goupil Gallery (later erroneously likened to Virginia Woolf and eventually sold by St Felix's governors). 'Ah well, I am pleased that the good lady is pleased,' said Sickert. 'Probably it is another of those forgeries and not by me at all.'

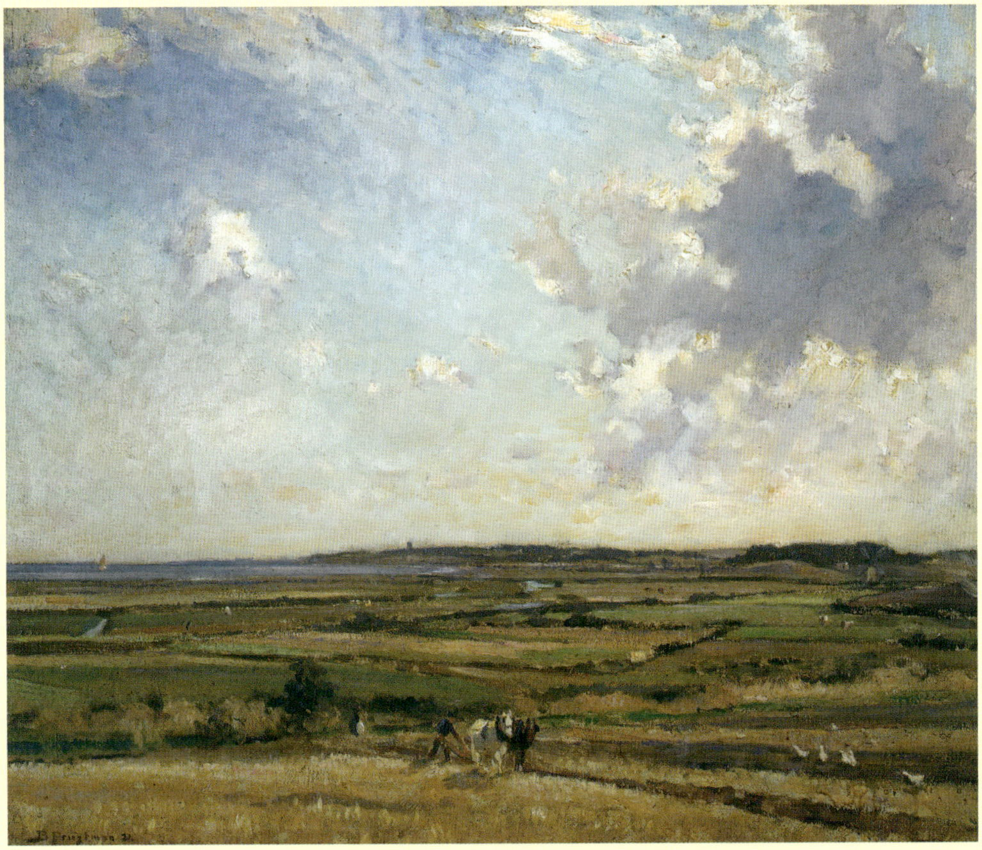

BERTRAM PRIESTMAN (1868-1951) was dubbed 'a modern Constable' on being elected a Royal Academician soon after completing this 1921 view of Walberswick Marshes. In 1914 the much-travelled Priestman had bought Windy Haugh, a house designed by Frank Jennings, and added a garden studio where he would tutor students including Edward Seago.

For a time the Priestman daughters went to St Felix School along with Margaret and Catharine Alexander - the latter recalling in 1989: 'We had a very happy childhood and not many lessons! We had to invent our own amusements. There were no children living in Walberswick except ourselves and the artist Bertram Priestman's family of five. Erica was my age and also drew and painted and became my great friend...'

She added: 'I only went to St Felix for one year. We used to bicycle the three miles daily in all weathers, even in snow, first crossing by the ferry then picking up our cycles from the fisherman's shed on the further side of the river. After a year Margaret and I both left school and our father endeavoured to teach us (as he had been a headmaster in Hampstead). My sister learned quite a lot, but I thought of nothing except illustrating and writing books, drawing and painting.' But it was Margaret who would become the eminent calligrapher.

*Southwold,* Stanley Spencer,
oil on canvas, 1937.

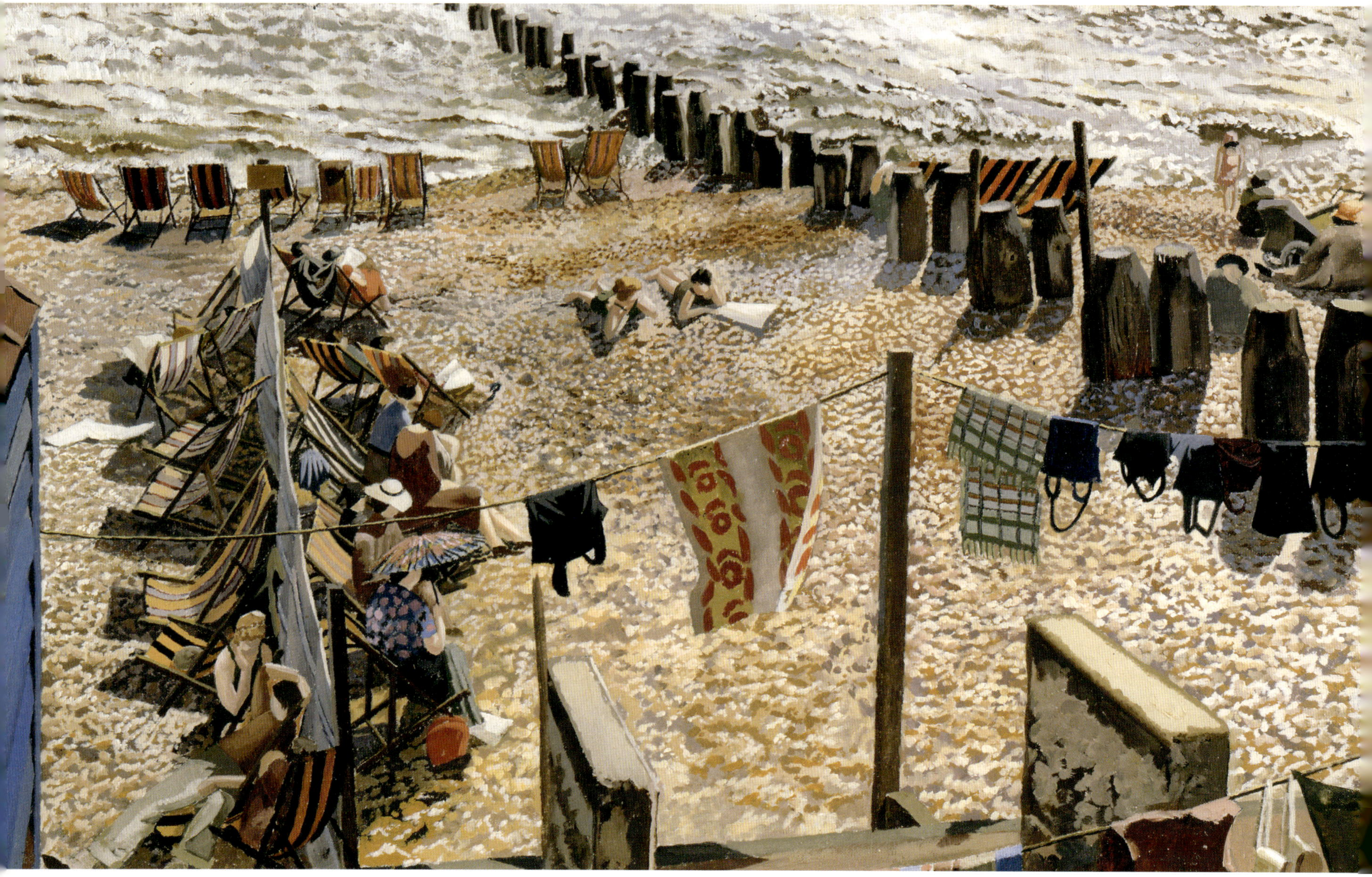

Chapter Fourteen

# Wangford Wedding

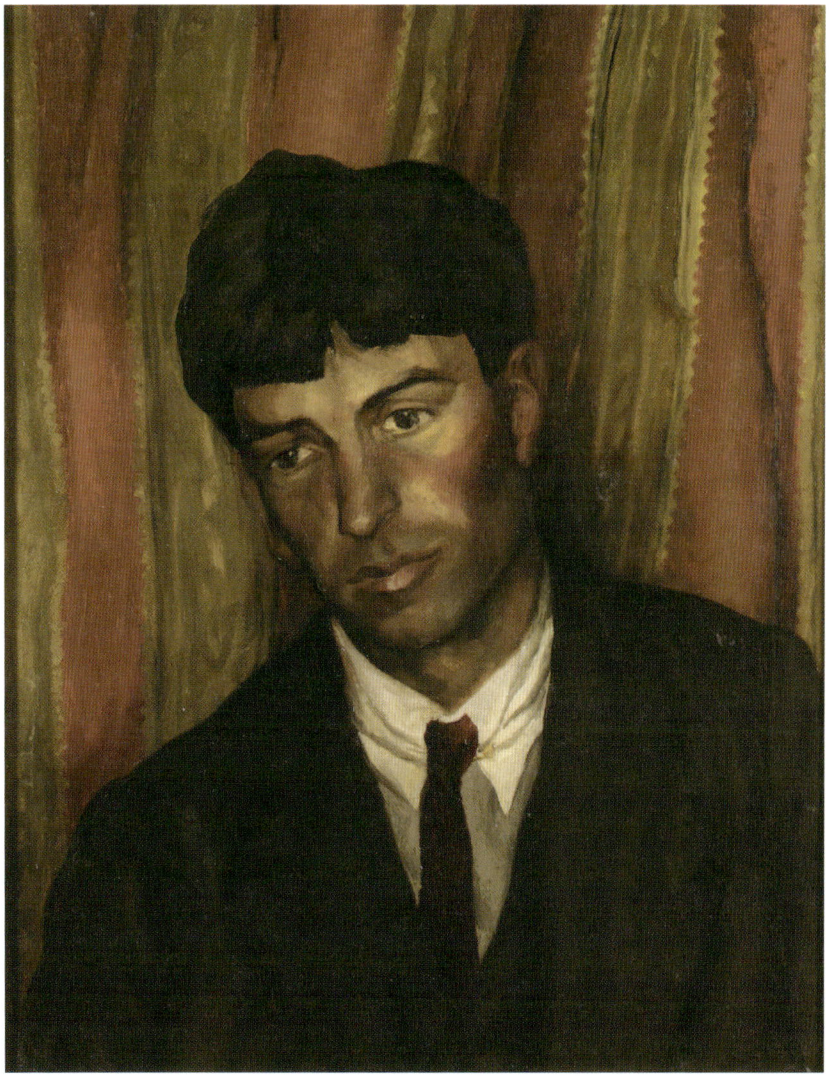

*Stanley Spencer*, Hilda Carline, oil on canvas, 1923.

**STANLEY SPENCER** (1891-1959) was an English visionary with a childhood steeped in Berkshire, Bach and the Bible. The artist's father was an organist and music teacher, who, at least to his nine surviving children, looked and sounded like Cookham's answer to an Old Testament prophet. Stan was the youngest disciple save for brother Gilbert, who also became a noted painter. Both would be drawn to Suffolk. And in and around Southwold Stanley Spencer would glimpse the promised land.

In his native village in the years before the First World War Stanley saw images of paradise everywhere. Attending London's Slade School at its most impressive period – when fellow students included David Bomberg, Carrington, Mark Gertler, Paul Nash, Christopher Nevinson, Gwen Raverat, William Roberts, Isaac Rosenberg and Edward Wadsworth – he rushed from classes to catch the homeward train. His nick-name was Cookham. Here he nurtured his lasting sense of the extraordinary nature of everyday things: flower-beds recalled the Garden of Eden; regatta crowds paused to hear Christ preaching, while their forebears rose from tombs in the churchyard which the artist likened to a 'holy suburb of heaven'.

But the world of innocence was shattered by war, in which Stanley served first as a medical orderly and then as an infantryman in the Macedonian campaign. After all the suffering he witnessed, plus the loss of an elder brother killed in action, heaven henceforward was to be shadowed by hell – and this acutely-sensitive artist would live for much of his later life in a state of limbo. As he told Tate director John Rothenstein: 'When I left the Slade and went back to Cookham I entered a kind of earthly paradise. Everything seemed fresh and to belong to the morning. My ideas were beginning to unfold in fine order and along comes the war and smashes everything. When I came home the divine sequence had gone. I just opened a shutter in my side and out rushed my pictures anyhow. Nothing was ever the same again.'

The art of love might be the means of redemption. Through Gilbert, Stanley met the prize-winning Slade student (Annie) **HILDA CARLINE** (1889-1950), and soon he had replaced his sibling as her suitor. Hilda's father, George Francis (1855-1920), sustained a large family by portrait painting; her mother, Annie, produced naïve pictures which, shown in André Lhote's Paris studio in 1939, were admired by Soutine. Hilda and her four brothers were encouraged to paint and draw – with three of the five training as artists. The Carlines also held

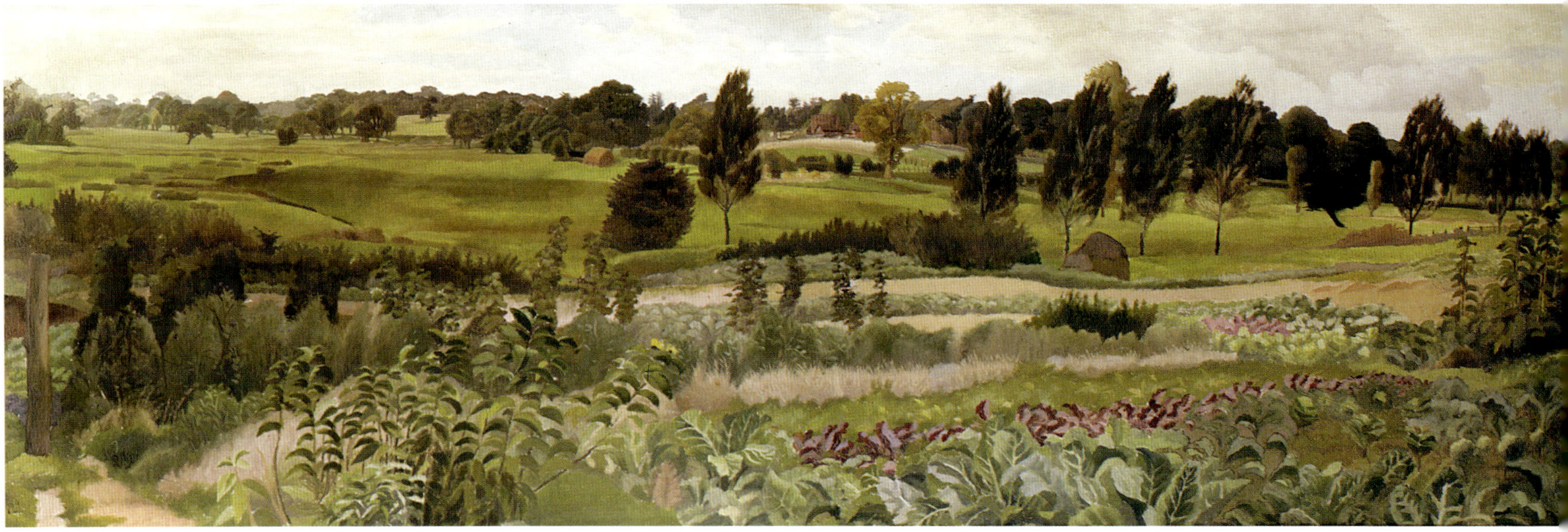

*Near Southwold*, Stanley Spencer, oil on canvas, 1924.

open-house sessions in Hampstead at which Stanley was reunited with many of his Slade contemporaries. He accompanied the family on a painting holiday to Yugoslavia in the summer of 1922, and on their return Hilda and Stanley became engaged.

The courtship was tortuous and, at times, tortured. Now based in Hampstead, Stanley was toiling on the vast *Resurrection* painting which would be bought for the Tate at his first solo show, in 1927. He was also sketching the cycle of war murals later to adorn the Sandham Memorial Chapel, while dreaming of the contrasting decorations for a church dedicated to love. His approach to work and to life was obsessive. He may have drawn out a fateful instability in Hilda

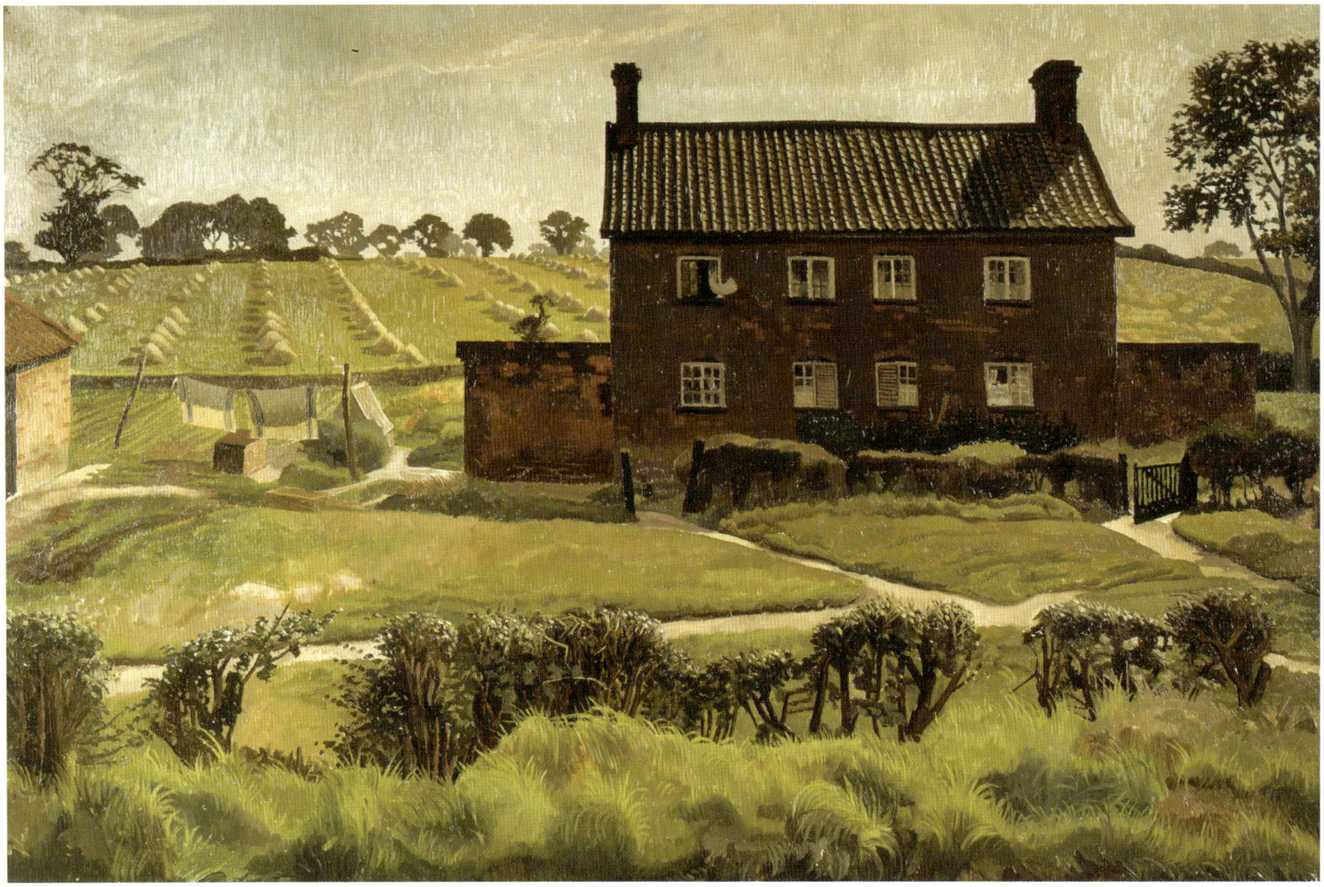

*The Red House, Wangford,* Stanley Spencer, oil on canvas, 1926.

from the start – even in her 1923 self-portrait she looks ominously guarded.

Hilda's art training had been interrupted by a war-time stint with the Women's Land Army, and a posting to a farm near Wangford. With free hours spent painting, her spell in deepest Suffolk had been a time of unexpected joy. In one of her Wangford pictures she was shown with her friend Cora Stoop returning on horseback from a day in the fields; Stanley had thought a study of sheep 'heavenly'. By the summer of 1924 she was desperate to revisit the village – and by the autumn Stanley had followed her there.

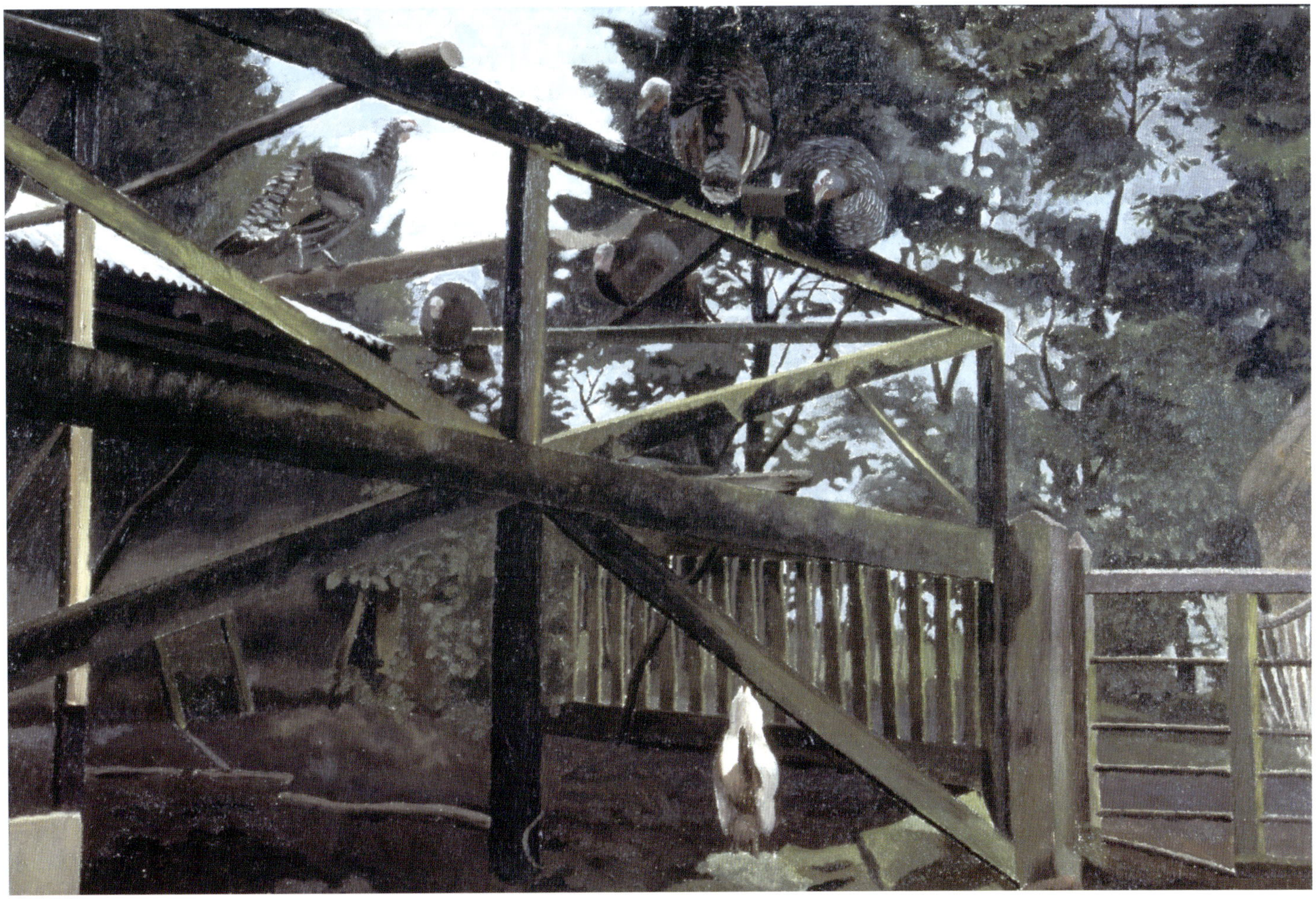

*Turkeys in Holland's Garden*, Stanley Spencer, oil on canvas, 1925.

At Wangford, both artists worked with gusto. Stanley painted a panorama of the marsh beyond the village. It was his largest and most sophisticated landscape painting to that date, and the unusual elongated shape set the pattern for several future studies. In a notebook entry written amid the traumatic upheavals of 1937, he looked back on the effort as 'the first landscape I ever enjoyed painting. I very much liked the place. It was a wandering marsh land but full of character.' He also remembered that the vegetation, painted with typically painstaking detail, had hidden a 'lot of snipe making their funny noises with their wings'.

Despite further problems in their relationship, the couple returned to Wangford to be married, on February 23 1925, in a place where Hilda had been happy. They were joined by Hilda's mother, and by brothers George and Sydney who acted as witnesses (the latter was already an artist of proven gifts, especially in views of aerial warfare destined for the Imperial War Museum). Stanley sketched the parson, the Rev T. H. Edwards, shortly before he vacated the living of Wangford-cum-Henham-cum-Reydon (a photo of this drawing can be seen in Reydon Church). At Hilda's request, Gilbert arrived for the honeymoon, recording in his memoir that the trio lodged in a cowman's cottage at Hill Farm in Wangford and painted out of doors – the new Mrs Spencer working on a 'long landscape'. Both

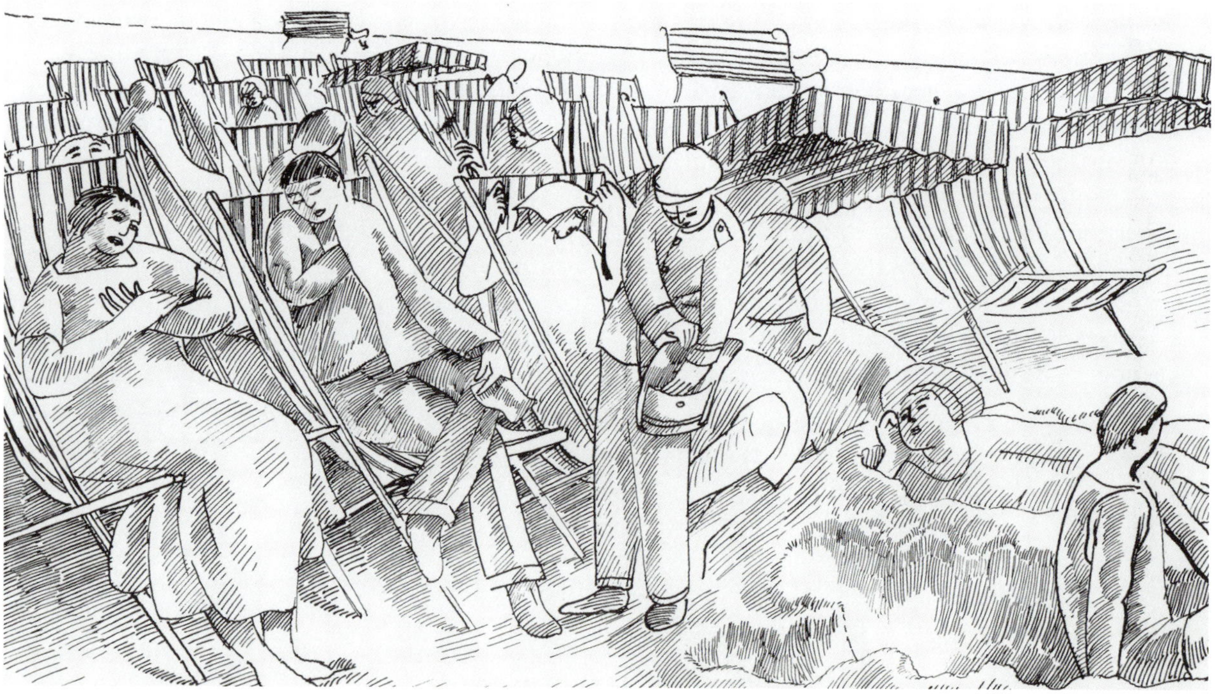

*The Month of August: On the Beach*, Stanley Spencer, ink drawing, c1927.

brothers tackled views showing the local windmill (now gone). Stanley, who loved the clutter of pig pens and chicken coops, probably produced the picture he called *Turkeys in Holland's Garden*, now in the Tate. He also tackled a small grey painting called *Sky at Wangford* and a larger work entitled *The Red House, Wangford* which gave him particular pleasure. 'I enjoyed doing this,' he recalled in 1937. 'The garden in front of the cottage was below the level of the road and well worn with little paths and the poor children were playing football there most days. I was a little puzzled at hearing the word "anguish" now and then uttered by one or other of them but it referred to the old oil merchant who came every Saturday afternoon and sold sweets as well as oil, hence his popularity.'

The following summer Hilda and Stanley – by now the parents of a baby girl, Shirin – journeyed to Wangford once more. They lodged with the Lambert family in an end-of-terrace cottage boasting a fine view over the village from the Southwold Road. Among several pictures completed during this trip, Stanley painted a landscape dominated by a patch of nettles, with the tower of the church where he had been married barely visible behind a tree. As on their previous visits, the artists enjoyed outings to Southwold. Here Stanley conceived the idea for a pen and ink study reproduced as *The Month of August: On the Beach* in the Chatto and Windus Almanac of 1927. The two figures in the deckchairs on the left of the picture are surely Hilda and Stanley. The background benches suggest the now-celebrated array of seats lining the cliff-top promenade from Gun Hill to North Parade.

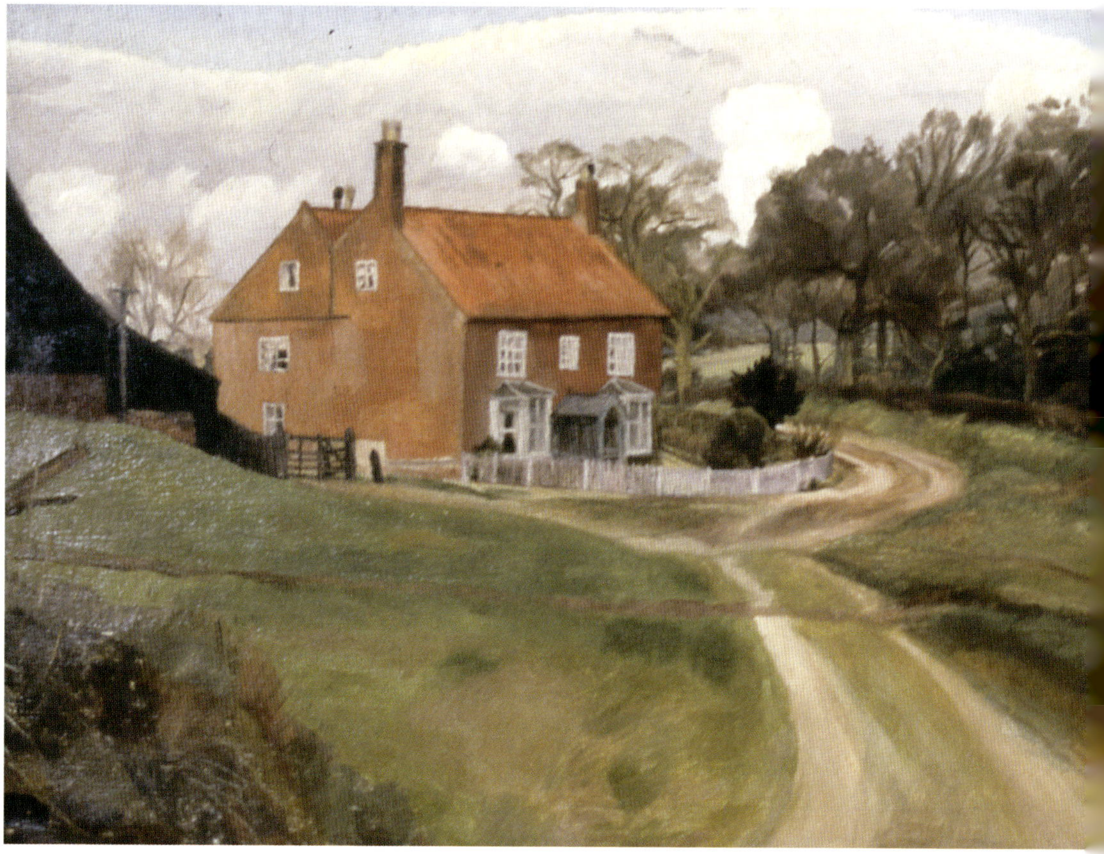

The subsequent collapse of the Spencer marriage, and the ongoing crisis for both parties, forms one of the most poignant stories in the history of 20th century British art. The sad truth was that, despite the great depths of their love, the characters of Hilda and Stanley were incompatible. She was a Christian Scientist, he was a pantheist who saw God everywhere, and especially in himself. His self-absorption, poured into incessant work, or endless talk, burst into irritability with the pain from kidney stones. Save for Suffolk, Hilda preferred to be in London; never caring for Cookham, she was horrified when Stanley's memorial chapel commission forced a move to Burghclere – dismissing the Hampshire countryside as the most 'meaningless' in England. In 1929, in an age without antibiotics, Sydney Carline died from pneumonia following a visit to the artist John Nash one frosty night (George, an anthropologist, would follow three years later, leaving only one of Hilda's beloved brothers, Richard, surviving). For all these reasons, she spent more and more time with her widowed mother in Hampstead – especially after the birth of a second daughter, Unity, in 1930.

But also in 1929, on a visit to Cookham, Stanley had met Patricia Preece, a chameleon figure who passed off paintings by her lover, Dorothy Hepworth, as her own. He was sexually infatuated, she was seriously in need of cash. Once the Spencers had moved to a substantial house in Cookham, in 1932, Patricia began to model for Stanley – receiving masses of jewellery, dresses and lingerie in return for sitting for some of the most naked portraits ever painted. Spying related pictures from this period in a London gallery window in 1950, Sir Alfred Munnings pressed a prosecution for obscenity. With the *Daily Express* reporting that the owner had put his foot through the offending images, Stanley hid *The Leg of Mutton Nude* under his bed. Seen publicly only after his death, its brutal honesty would ultimately have a big impact on Lucian Freud.

In the summer of 1935 Hilda moved with the children to Hampstead, while Stanley plunged further into debt and delusion – imagining that he could somehow find a way of living with both his muses. He reluctantly agreed to a divorce from Hilda in May 1937, and married Patricia a week later. Their union was effectively ended on a disastrous honeymoon in Cornwall. Patricia, her financial claim on Stanley now secure, lived with Dorothy Hepworth for the rest of her life. Stanley headed for Hampstead – there to paint a portrait of *Hilda, Unity and Dolls* in which betrayal exudes from blanked expressions.

Stanley then battled to win Hilda back. In fact, he had never been reconciled to losing her. Days before their divorce he had written: 'I think that even while now we are in the middle of this legal fight that away in our real selves we continue to be utterly at one, rejoicing in our oneness.' Afterwards he was convinced that if only they could get back to Suffolk, to the very bedroom of their honeymoon, to the beach at Southwold where they had searched for cornelians, all would be well again. Hilda regarded his pleadings as adulterous. Stanley left for Wangford alone.

Settled with the Lamberts once more, he revisited old haunts. 'I walked to the spots from whence 11 years before I had painted landscapes,' he wrote in 1938. 'I got through the fence and walked over the marshland to where there used to be a clump of stinging nettles which in 1926 I had painted…and they were still there. I felt like a ghost.' He was relieved to find that the

*Smoke from the Southwold Train , Wangford,* Hilda Carline, oil on canvas, 1925.

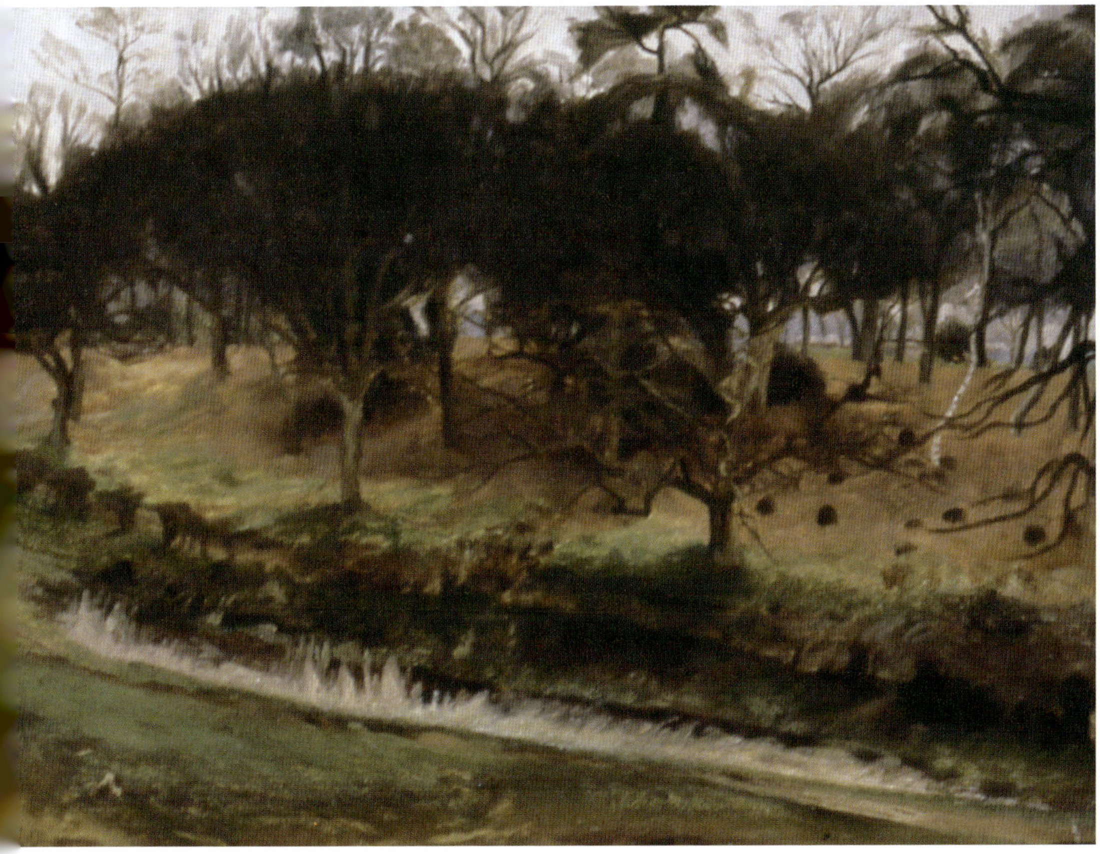

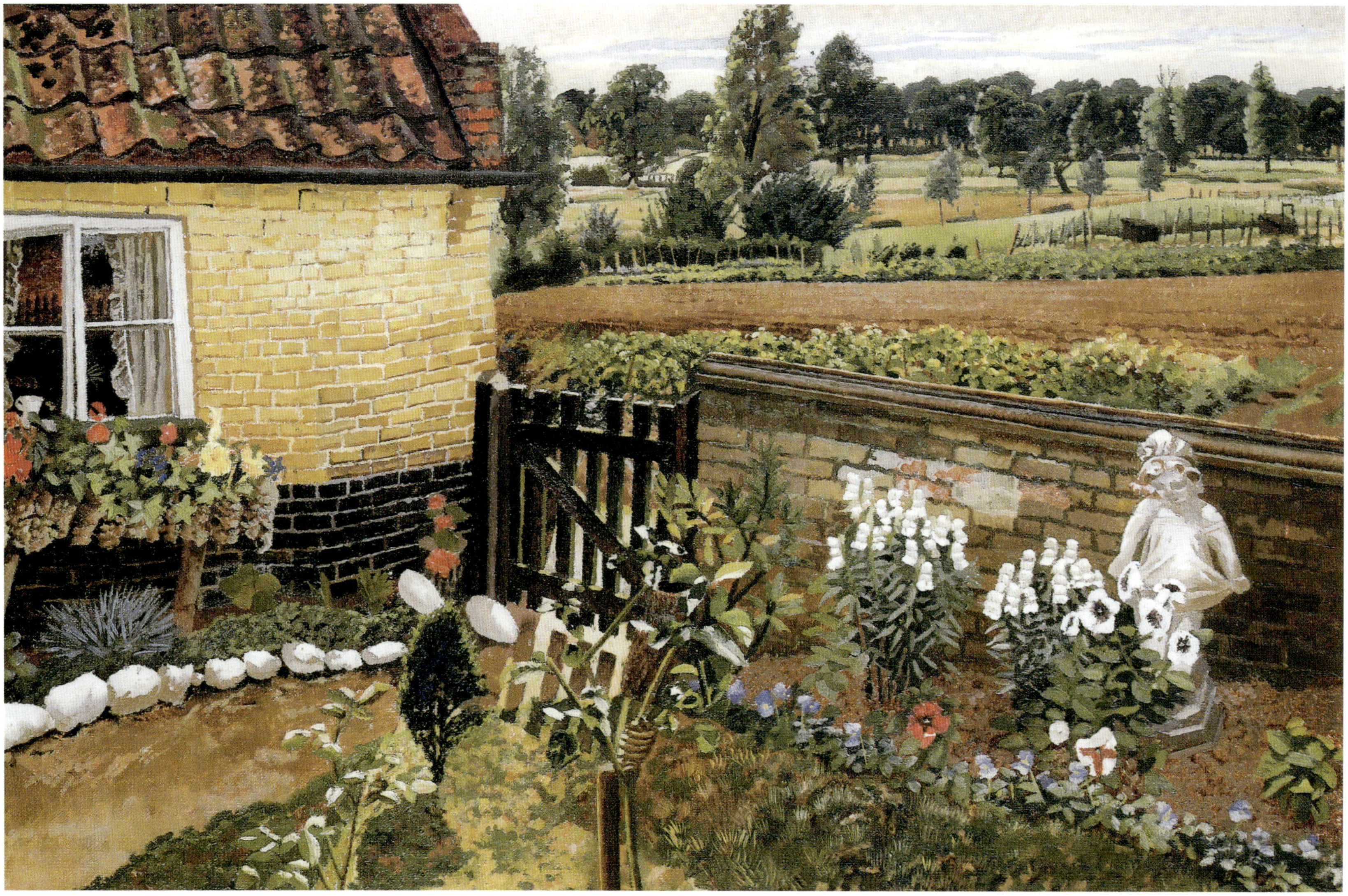

*The Cottage at Wangford,*
Stanley Spencer,
oil on canvas,1937.

surrounding scenes displayed the 'mystery' and 'special effects' he had captured in his pictures.

It was possibly the next day that the widow of artist Harry Becker, taking the bus from her home in Wangford to Southwold, recognised a small and dishevelled figure sitting in front of her. Even from that angle Stanley Spencer was unmistakable. He alighted in the market square and made for the beach, where he would work on a major painting. He confided in his notebook that the 'dirty washing water colour' sea was 'splashed by homely aunties' legs and the air was full of suburban seaside abandonment'. Each day he regained his vantage point between two beach huts by remembering the distance between piles of dog dirt. He observed the holidaymakers – sunbathers, a girl composing a letter, a group of young people 'swaying about and singing badly' – as if from a great distance. 'I felt a kindred feeling with the bathing suits on the line in front of me,' he wrote, 'in the sense that they seemed to be taking no part as I was not with the activities on the beach.'

Using only small brushes, the artist crawled across each canvas painting every detail separately – as if making a mosaic. A single layer of pigment gave an enamel-like quality of illuminated intensity which in this case brilliantly captured the feeling of summer holidays by the sea. Despite the scene's air of spontaneity, the lines of deckchairs harked back to the pen and ink drawing from the 1920s. Stanley wrote: 'There are about fifty repetitions of the same view. Another view which would have been interesting was standing on a fallen pile on the beach and looking along the beach at the succession of partitioned worlds of seaside and seasiders divided by loose hanging awning which I presume is a wind screen. One is seen in this landscape edge on.'

Private catastrophe left the artist with permanently perilous finances. He was forced to rely on kindly patrons such as the Martineau family, with whom Gilbert Spencer would spend his final years at Walsham-le-Willows, near Bury St Edmunds. As late as 1958 Jack Martineau commissioned Stanley to paint a searing Crucifixion for the chapel of Aldenham School in Hertfordshire, for which, in the year before his death, he received £1000. In 1990 it sold at Sotheby's for £1.3 million.

Plum commissions for mystical pictures aside, Stanley hated the speed with which he had to work to earn his living, and often scorned the saleable scenes he was compelled to produce. 'My landscapes compared with my other work are carried out with a hard relentless persistence and dogged determination to go through with it, which gives them a competent and finished but lifeless and hard look,' he complained. During the 1937 escape to Suffolk he also painted a landscape called *The Cottage at Wangford*. After working from the same spot for 11 successive afternoons, his easel balanced on a well, he felt that he had been rooted there for a lifetime.

To the end Suffolk would remain deeply rooted in his memory. He and Hilda had always written copiously to one another – in the early days even writing side by side, then reading their missives aloud. Letters stretching to hundreds of pages at a time filled their years of separation. They ran through Hilda's mental breakdown in 1942 and did not wholly cease with her death, from cancer, in 1950. Having painted a *Love Letters* tribute to his first wife and last love, Stanley carried on writing.

In 1948 he wrote that he couldn't remember whether they had first made love in Wangford or in Hampstead, but he recalled the walk from the church after their wedding with absolute clarity: 'At last, we were alone. I can feel the gravel & tarmac under my feet now...We did not hurry but listened to ourselves loving. We stood singly about like things set adrift. How lovely it was...It was like in my (Tate) *Resurrection*; no one was in any hurry to go anywhere, everywhere was this new place of our love, it was air around our face...

'We wanted to get to where there was, on the right, a great plain. Our longing to marry seemed like a longing to see that place & our approach now was as if we were on the way to be married. There was an opening to the right, at the corner of a road crossing our lane, & there we could see it going away to left & ahead & to the right; in some part of it maize was growing. It was the vast Gobi desert of you that I longed to wander into & about in & to put here & there the me things...Wangford was you...Wangford is the native land of our you & me self...'

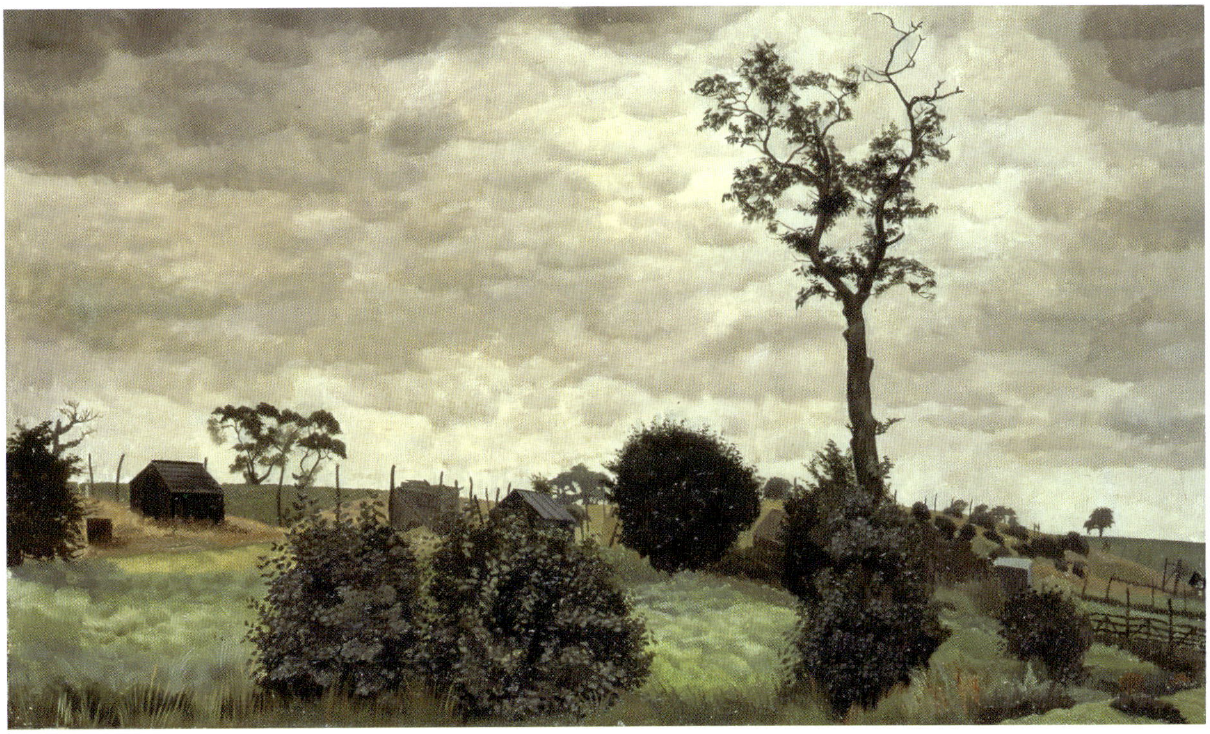

*Tree and Chicken Coops, Wangford,* Stanley Spencer, oil on canvas, 1926.

*Trinity Fair at Gun Hill, Southwold,*
Allan Gwynne-Jones, etching, 1927.

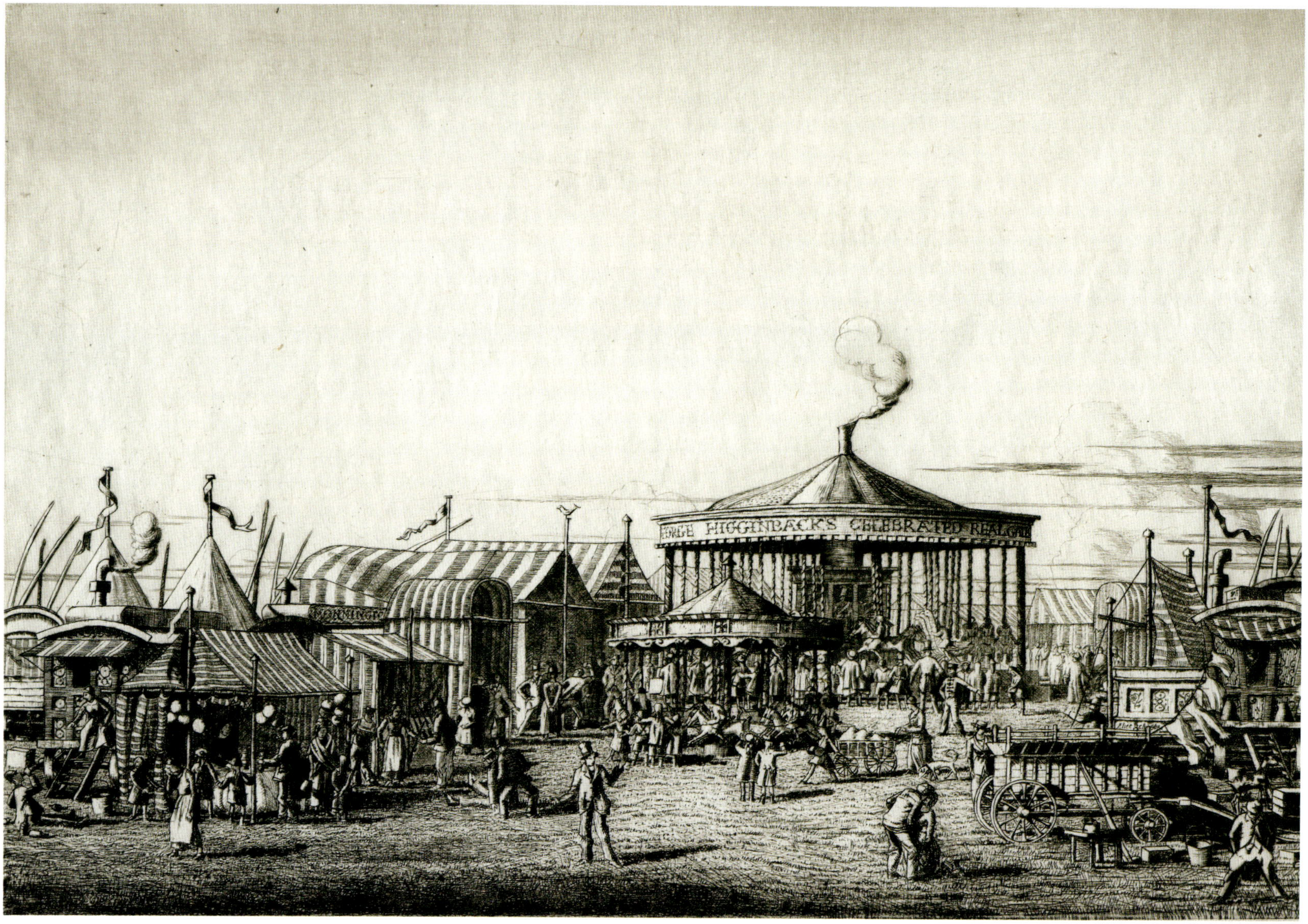

Chapter Fifteen

# Fairs and Circuses

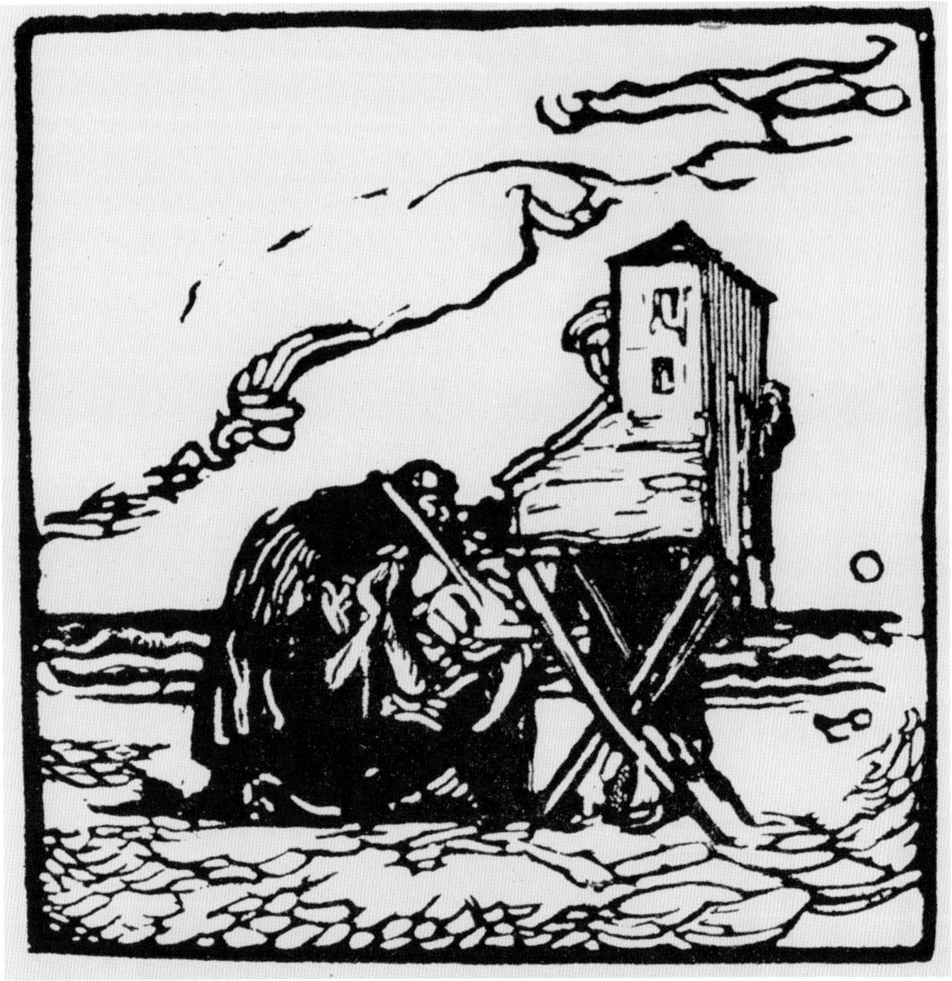

*Seaside Entertainer*, Edward Gordon Craig, wood engraving.

Composer Martin Shaw (1875-1958), whose *God's Grandeur* was premiered at the first Aldeburgh Festival, grew up in Southwold. In 1897 he met Ellen Terry's actor son EDWARD GORDON CRAIG (1872-1966) here, prompting a 60-year friendship. Learning the art of wood-engraving from William Nicholson, Craig was fascinated by the way that light could be made to emerge from a dark background. With related drawings and models at this time he was evolving the avant-garde stage designs for which he would be famous. His holiday was shared with Scottish painter JAMES PRYDE (1866-1941) – whose sister Mabel had married Nicholson and, in 1894, given birth to another budding artist: Ben.

In Southwold Pryde drew and wooed the postman's daughter, while Craig sketched performers on the beach – notably pierrots, whose hooded forms would feature prominently in later designs. The pair also devised an entertainment in the Crown to fund train fares for a stranded company of players. Pryde and Craig acted out scenes based on the life of cut-throat poet Francois Villon, with Shaw providing stirring music on the bar piano.

Happy memories of Southwold led Craig on a solitary sketching tour of the area the following summer, until, lonely in Dunwich, he urged his girlfriend to join him. She was followed by a detective hired by his deserted wife, May. After that, the appeal of Suffolk palled.

Based latterly in Blythburgh, Shaw became a celebrated hymn-writer. At an 80th birthday thanksgiving service in St Edmund's church Ralph Vaughan Williams departed from his script to roar: 'Cursed be all who do not listen to Martin Shaw!'

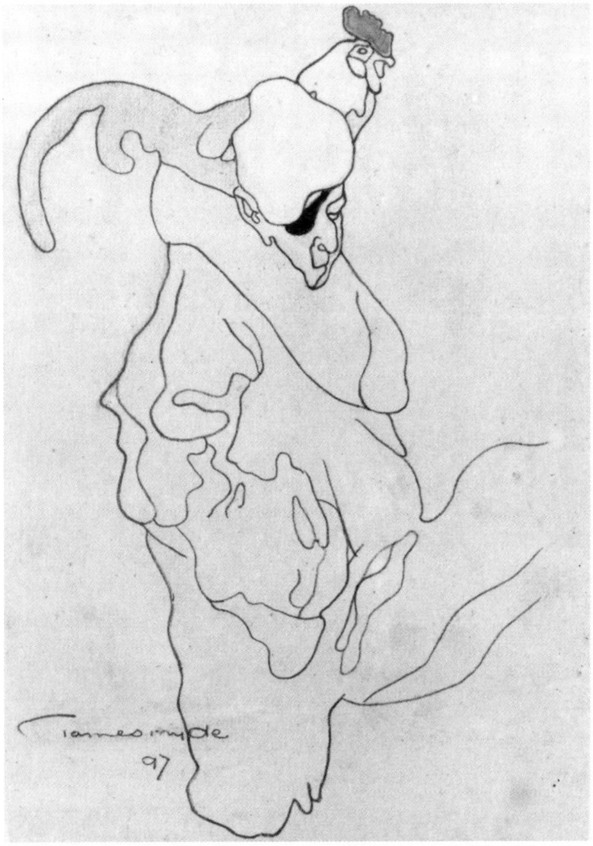

*Pierrot*, James Pryde, pencil, watercolour and chalk, 1897 (right).

For all its tranquil reputation, Southwold has been a place of wild revelry – with fairs and circuses, parades and pageants, firework displays and sporting clashes, and a great deal of singing and dancing. In 1844, when fighting cocks and prancing bears were still popular amusements, the town played host to Hylton's Royal Menagerie, with its 'group of real Caffrarian Forest Lions…the Noble Male performing Elephant…and the Ostrich landed at Dundee by Capt Hutchinson and purchased at great cost'. The beastly assembly also included an 'ursine sloth, tigers, panthers and hunting leopards…all enlivened by a splendid brass band led by the celebrated Mr Mackintosh'. More than a century later Fanny Foster, thrice mayor of Southwold, recalled seeing an elephant being transported on the Blyth Ferry.

Further entertainment was provided by likenesses of the famous and infamous. In 1845 James Ewing's Entirely New Collection of Royal Wax Figures – a rival to Madame Tussaud, whose gory relics had crossed the Channel after the French Revolution – arrived in Southwold, with '100 Public characters, as large as life' in five fire-warmed and gas-lit caravans. Besides patriotic exhibits such as Queen Victoria's marriage to Prince Albert, or proud Mr Darling alongside heroic daughter Grace, there was the titillating figure of 'Lord Byron in Greek Costume' plus models of seven murderers as they appeared at crowd-pulling public executions.

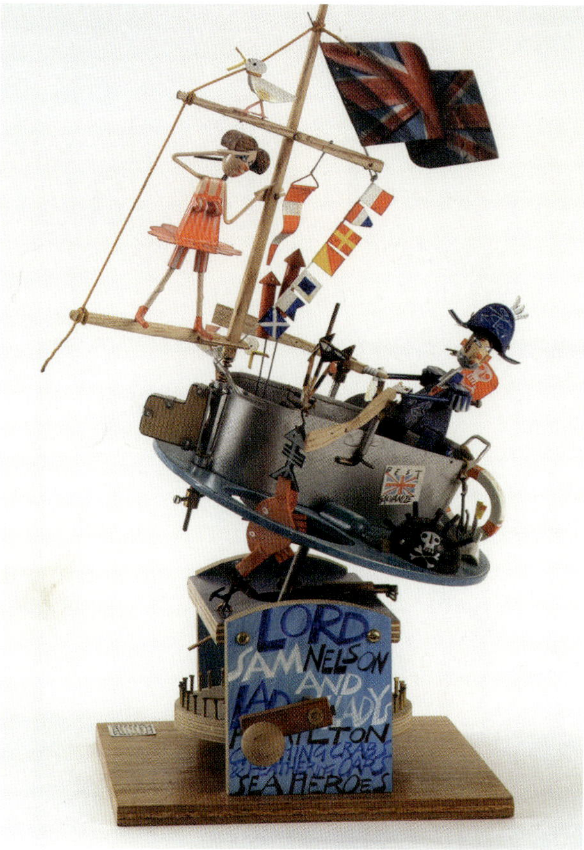


*Lord Sam Nelson and Lady Gladys Hamilton catching crabs & feathering oars - Sea Heros,* Ron Fuller, wood and metal automata, 1999.

Cruelty-free circuses continue to be staged on the Common each summer – though during the 2004 season the Big Top was laid low by a lightning strike – while fêtes, bazaars and bizarre fund-raising events flourish more widely. In 2005 **RON FULLER** (b1936), maker of amusing animated models and toys, provided a donations

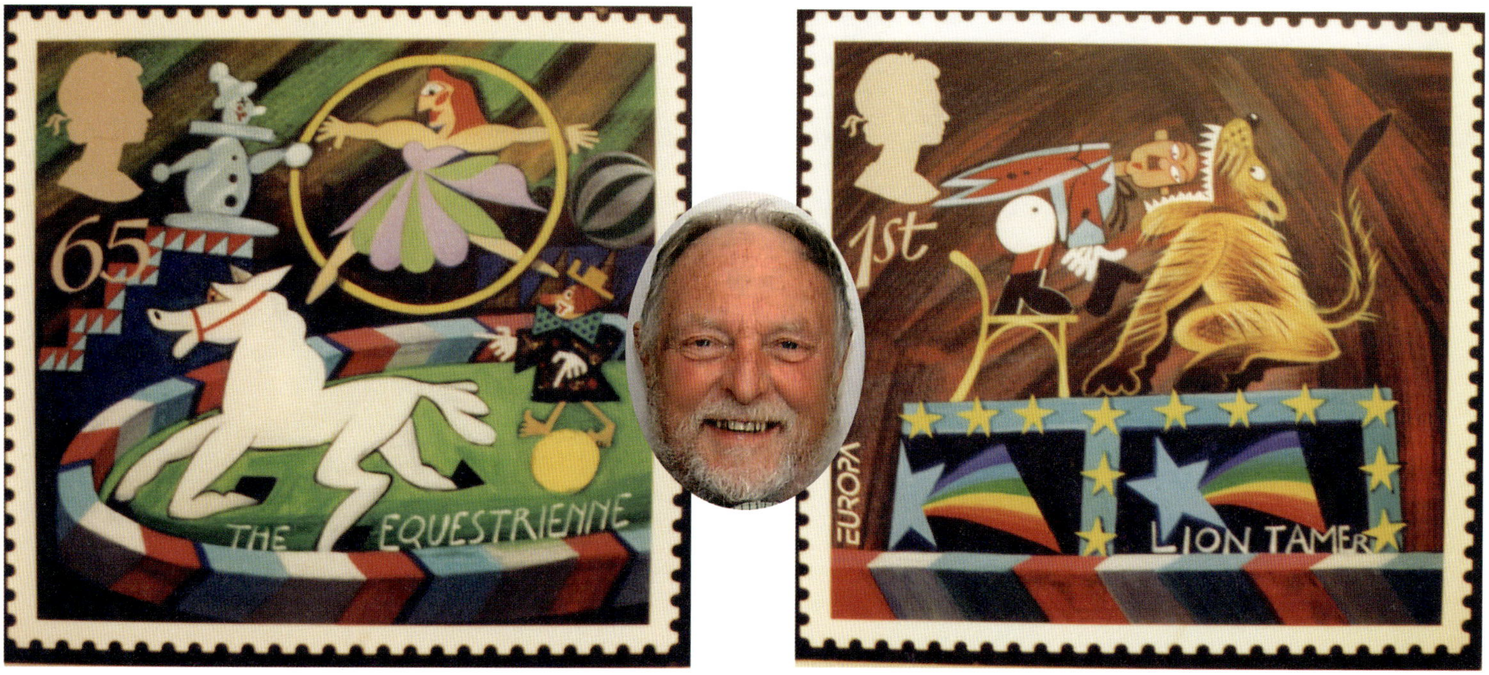


Ron Fuller & designs for two of a set of commemorative stamps.

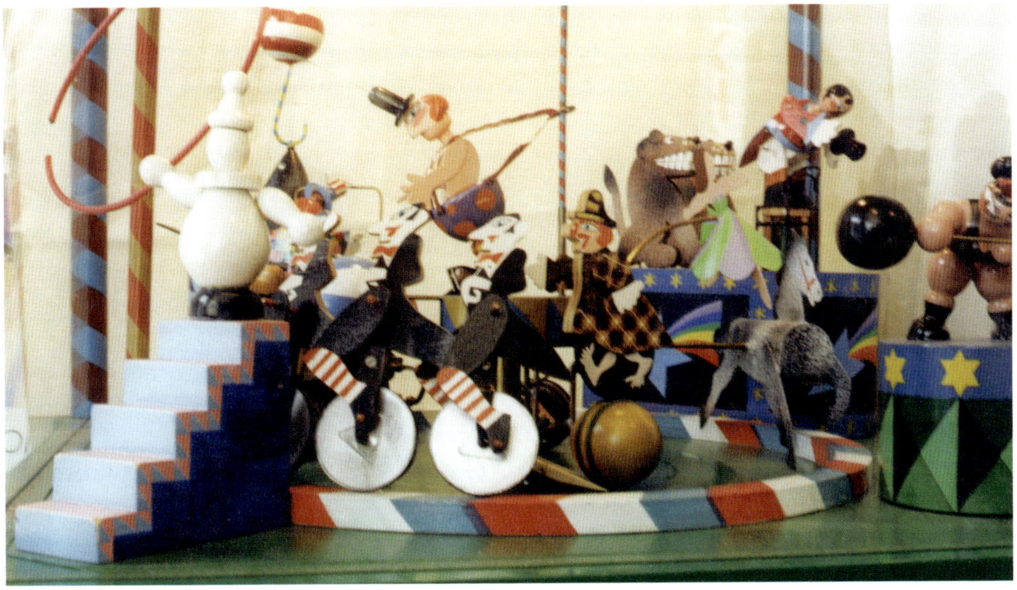

Animated circus toy for Craftco, Ron Fuller.

box for Southwold Museum based very loosely on the romantic legend of the Battle of Sole Bay's Earl of Sandwich and a Sutherland House serving wench. At the drop of a coin a shipwrecked mariner and a bathing belle adrift in a tin bath are shown 'having a good row'. Born in Cornwall, and training initially in Plymouth and Falmouth, he coincided at the Royal College of Art with Pop Art stars Peter Blake, Tom Phillips and a pre-blond David Hockney, and also with print-maker Moss Steed from Great Bealings in Suffolk, whom he later married. He gave up teaching in 1972 and moved to Laxfield, near Halesworth, to work as an artist-craftsman. Fusing folk art traditions and a wily line in mechanics he has made scores of moving models in painted wood and sheet metal. He contributed to an immense fairground-style project called *The Ride of Life*, commissioned for a Sheffield shopping centre but never installed, and his work has been a mainstay of the Craftco crafts co-operative in Southwold since 1987. Here a model of the circus big top for which he remains best-known – original drawings prompting a set of commemorative postage stamps – can be activated with a 20p coin. Then the band strikes up and lion-tamers, acrobats, muscle men and clowns in barrels or on bicycles all perform for our delight and delectation.

Southwold's biggest annual party remains the Charter Fair, originally granted to the borough by Henry VII and long known as Trinity Fair. What began as a hiring fair later sprawled into a general three-day jamboree, with stalls starting at South Green and for many years spilling down the High Street as far as the junction with Victoria Street. Despite periodic attempts by South Green-residing civic dignitaries to move it on to the Common, or to the base of Constitution Hill, it still fills Southwold's premier green in the first week of June.

One fan of such fairs was **ALLAN GWYNNE-JONES** (1892-1982), who determined to be a painter after early holidays in Southwold – when, encouraged by Scottish artists E.A. Walton and Francis Newbery, he had started to paint watercolours of north Suffolk landscapes. In 1912, when his parents' marriage ended, he made drawings of Trinity Fair. Discord was obviously in the air that year, for Southwold folk were in a fury over the most concerted civic attempt yet to shift their fair to the Common. The young visitor sketched the surviving festivities and produced a beautiful watercolour on silk, *Southwold Fair*.

Family pressure forced the would-be artist to train initially as a lawyer and so he had barely enrolled at the Slade School in London when the First World War began. He enlisted almost immediately, and was then away on military service for nearly five years – winning a Distinguished Service Order during the 1916 Battle of the Somme. He returned to the Slade on being demobbed, and William Rothenstein's admiration for his pictures in a 1922 student exhibition led to his being offered the post of

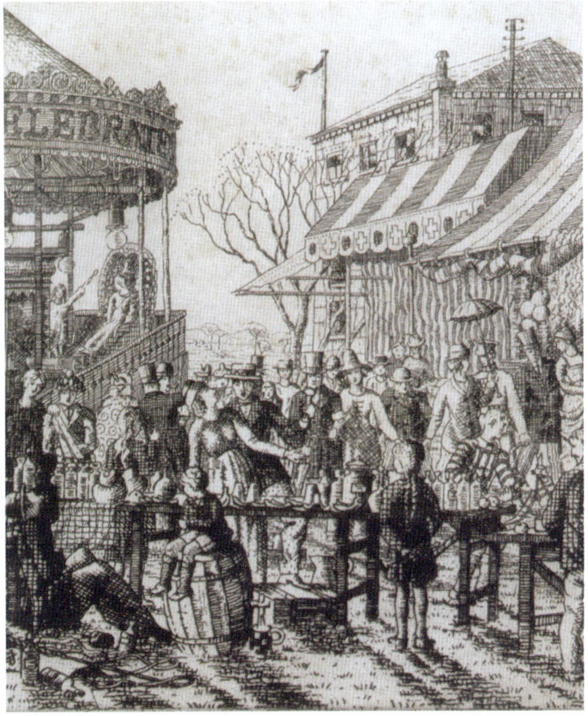

*Southwold Fair*, Allan Gwynne-Jones, etching, 1927 (right).

Professor of Painting at the Royal College of Art. Decades of teaching followed, in which his skills as a painter of portraits, landscapes and still-life studies were not always utilised. When able, he escaped to the countryside, producing gentle scenes in and around Wenhaston in the inter-war period showing the influence of Walton.

But while tutoring at the Royal College he also studied etching under his colleague Malcolm Osborne – producing 11 plates in 1926 and 1927, then abandoning the medium he had so clearly mastered. Two of his subjects were based on Southwold fair drawings from 1912. Interviewed for his 90th birthday exhibition at the National Museum of Wales, he said: 'All those figures started from what I call a mathematical shape. Everything is story-telling but to make it concrete it has to be translated into human beings and things. The moods are there.' He wasn't telling the whole story. The legend MONNINGTON on a trailer in the etching on page 114 refers to fellow Slade student, and future Royal Academy president, Tom Monnington. The name Alice Schwabe, in tiny letters behind the line of washing lower-right, hints at the artist's youthful affair with the wife of Slade professor Randolph Schwabe - another great ally. Schwabe is said to have challenged Gwynne-Jones to a duel over the illicit liaison, and fellow artists Monnington and William Rothenstein were to be seconds. When the rivals met at the appointed hour they fell into each other's arms, and the whole party then went off for breakfast. Allan Gwynne-Jones married former Slade student Rosemary Allan in 1937. Their daughter Emily Gwynne-Jones (b1948) and son-in-law Frank Beanland (b1936) continue to paint in and around Southwold along representational and abstract lines respectively – the latter known from the 1960s for work akin to images of bright pebbles on a beach.

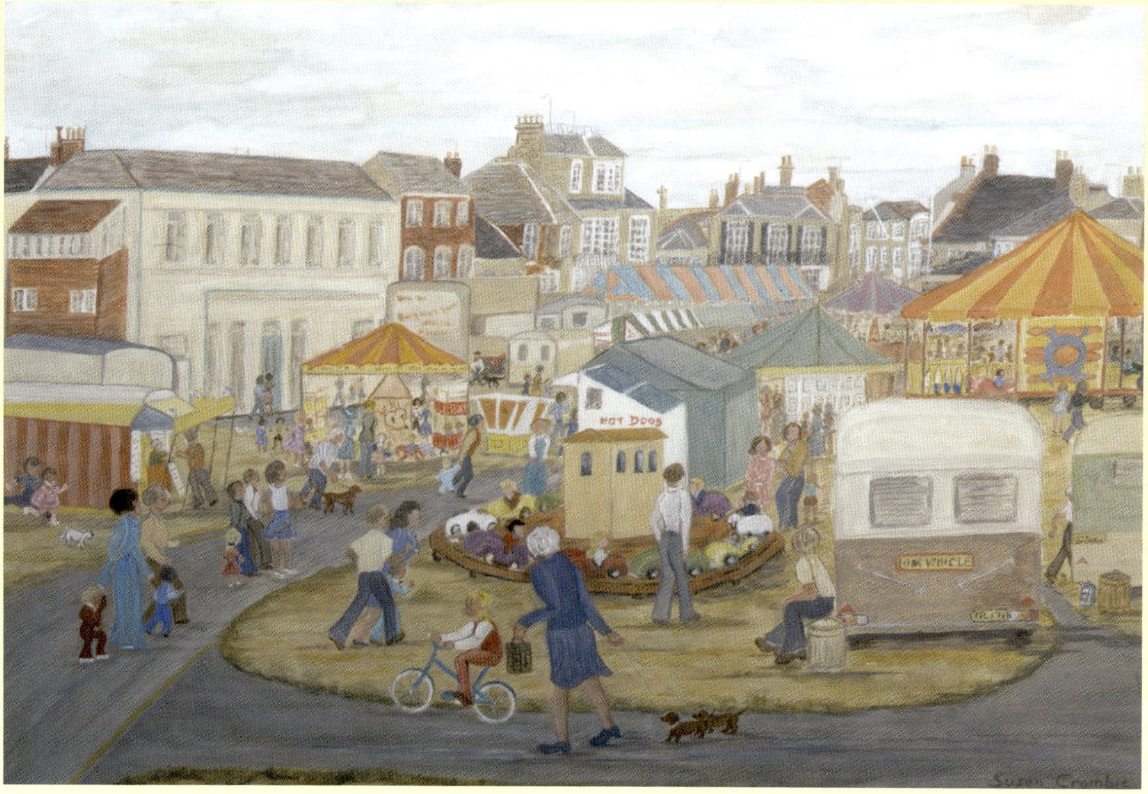


Self-taught artist SUSAN CROMBIE (1921-1986), who exhibited with the Southwold Art Circle from 1973, loved to paint Trinity Fair arrayed below her South Green cottage window. Fair families bought several of her pictures.

This 1976 oil shows the artist's cousin, Nancy Fox, with attendant dachshunds. Her brother Anthony made a fortune on the stock market which ultimately funded the provision of more than 20 dwellings for local people at nominal rents. The Fox Trust continues to play a key role in Southwold life.

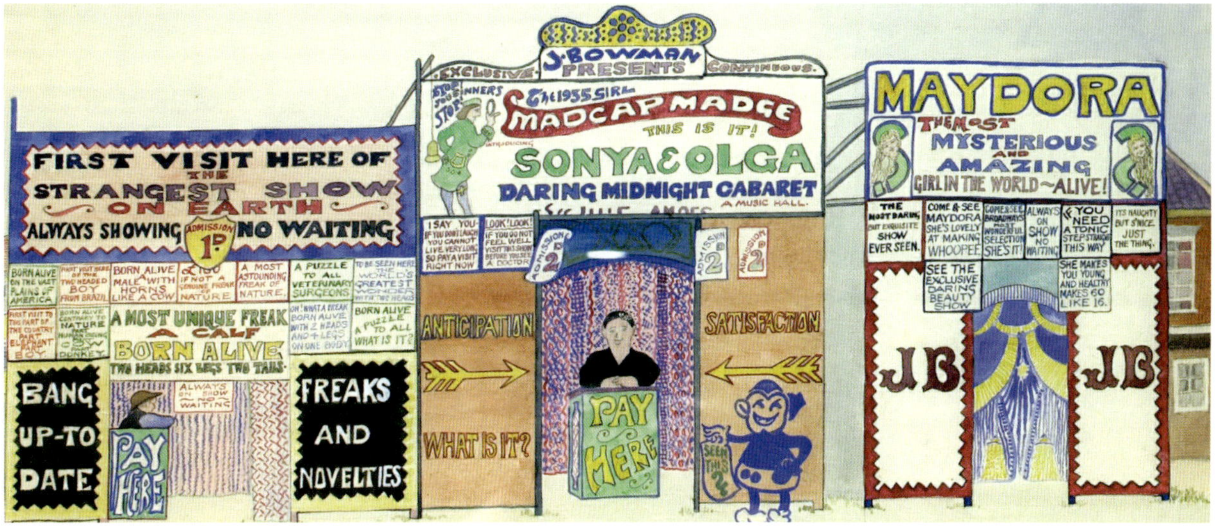


Roll up! Roll up! John Doman Turner sets the scene for his scroll record of Southwold's 1933 Trinity Fair. Eight watercolour extracts are reproduced on the next three pages.

In 1933 a profoundly deaf London stockbroker's clerk named **JOHN DOMAN TURNER** (1873-1938), who had received painting lessons from Walter Sickert and Spencer Gore, but who had apparently failed to build on early promise, put aside his private and professional troubles to embark on a panoramic view of that summer's Trinity Fair. He was to roll up yards and yards of painting after working for two years and following the travelling showmen and women – to Laxfield, Stradroke, Aldeburgh – on their seasonal tour across East Anglia in order to complete an out-sized scene. Acquired by Adnams in a sorry state, the paper scroll has now been painstakingly restored and divided into wraparound wall hangings in an annexe of the Swan Hotel's dining room. It is a revelation and a riot.

Mr Showman Turner sets the scene for this 'World's Fair and Fun Carnival' with a list of attractions (writ large with his own idiosyncratic spelling). There are 'cocoanuts, dart and shooting saloons, round-uns, panams, freaks, houp la, beauty shows, swings, motor and scenic roundabouts, galloping horses and cockerels. With all the latest amusements and most popular tunes played by steam with 500 horsepower on a new orchestraphone and a wonderful amplifier.' And then there are 'dodgem auto scooters, wheel 'em ins, post office, cake walk, skittles, wiggle-wooggel, tip the lady out of bed, crystal gazing, palmistry, phrenology, Noah's Ark menagerie, Touch 'ems and Emmas – all beautifully lit with electric light.' 'Can be heard five miles on land and in Holland when the wind is favourable,'adds our painter-scribe. 'First class side shows including the Spotted Lady and also the rarest show on earth – Phoebe the world famous one-eyed beauty of Epping, once seen, never forgotten, so hurry up before the grave has you.'

Hurrying-up are lots of ladies in silky 1930s fashions, some possibly produced at Southwold's HomeKnit factory which flourished from 1909 to 1940. Elaborately permed coiffures can be glimpsed beneath cloche hats and parasols. There are also children, dogs, horses and carts. One Joseph Alexander Martin is shown painting a roll-a-penny board and, scattered throughout, is the Stock family of travelling showmen. Against a backdrop of barely-altered houses and pubs, all set in a sea of Southwold green, innocents walk among a crew of illusionists (possibly the polite word for con artists). Alongside a billing for 'London, Paris, Vienna, New York – the Great and Gifted Professor Leo: Palmistry and Clairvoyance, Crystal Gazing, Phrenology and Medical Adviser' there is the rather more modest 'Madame Amiee, the Great East Anglian Palmist, late of South Beach Felixstowe'. And close to a hoarding

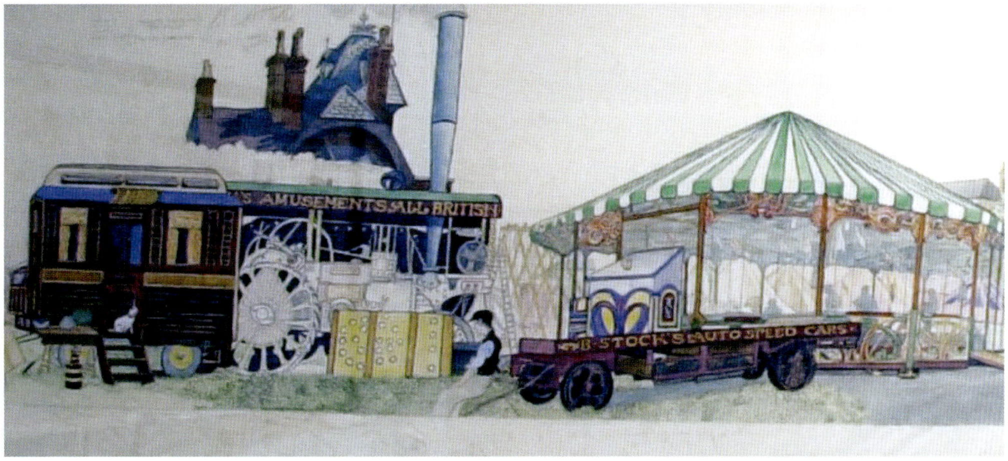

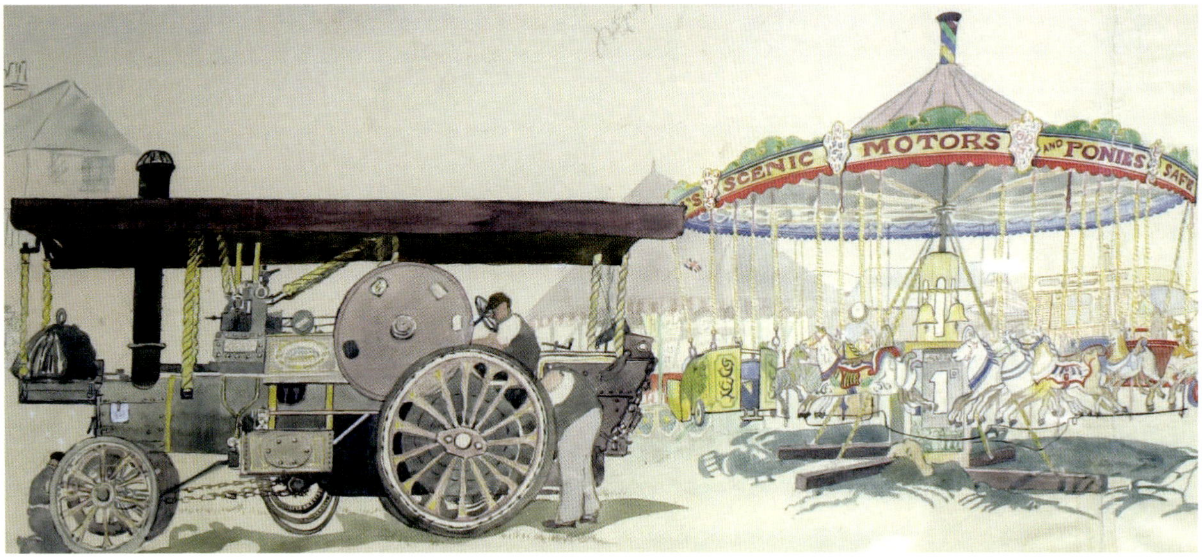


boasting 'Stock's Amusements All British' there's a demonstration of the Spanish Tango and a solo artiste who – for a fee of 2d – promises you a Peruvian gold ring if he fails to guess your weight to within four pounds. Beside the advertised charms of Maydora – 'The most daring but exquisite show ever seen. She makes you young and healthy, makes 60 like 16' – there's Sonia and Olga's Daring Midnight Cabaret. The entrance door is labelled Anticipation, the exit Satisfaction. The Superior Cokernut Saloon Patronised By His Majesty seems to contain two errors in one sentence. And, overall, you can't help feeling as you survey the merry scene that soon the laughter will turn to loud shouts of disappointed punters demanding their money back and, even in sedate Southwold, to fisticuffs.

History hangs heavily even over this slice of supposedly unchanging England. The Centre Cliff Private Hotel – a grand residence and a school at different points in its history - has now been split into a row of splendid flats and houses. And amid many pencilled descriptions in the margins, this note may be the most poignant: 'Southwold Suffolk Hospital Bazaar from doorway of Constitutional Club South Green, Wed Aug 9 1933.' It's a relic of that pre-NHS era when the funding of public hospitals was left to the hopelessly inadequate efforts of valiant volunteers. The Constitutional (or Conservative) Club was soon to be blitzed by a 1000lb bomb – during a war in which more than 2800 incendiaries and other missiles rained down on Southwold. Although 13 civilians died in the partly-evacuated town, club steward Mr Maltby was pulled alive from the rubble – earning the British Empire Medal for two of his rescuers.

Simon Loftus, Adnams chairman, says: 'The scroll needed exceptionally careful conservation because of the fragility of the lining paper on which it was painted. That fragility, however, also meant that the work was seldom displayed (there are a few signatures from when it was last on view, in the 1950s) and the colours are still as fresh as when originally applied. Now mounted on special conservation board and protected from

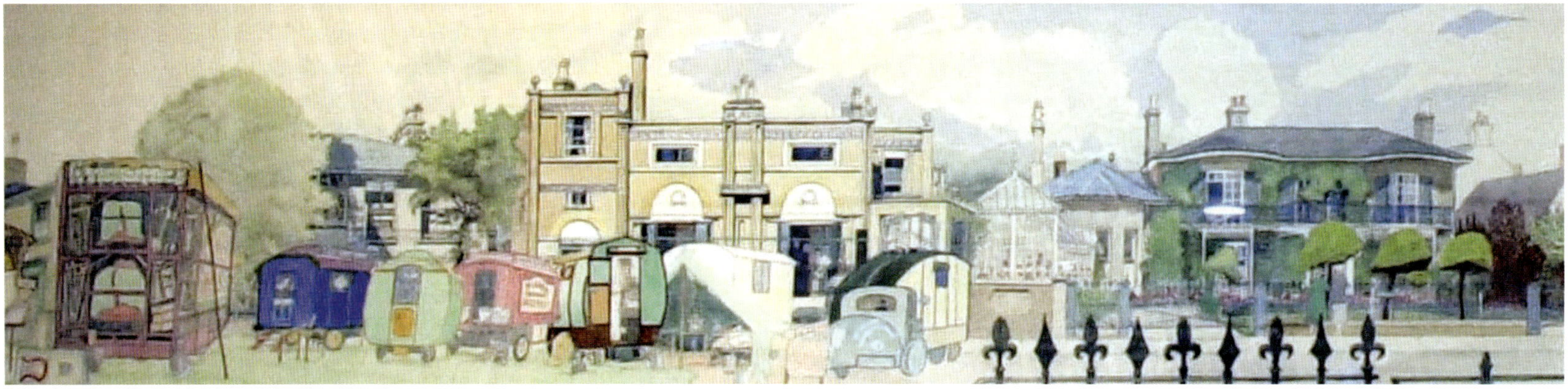

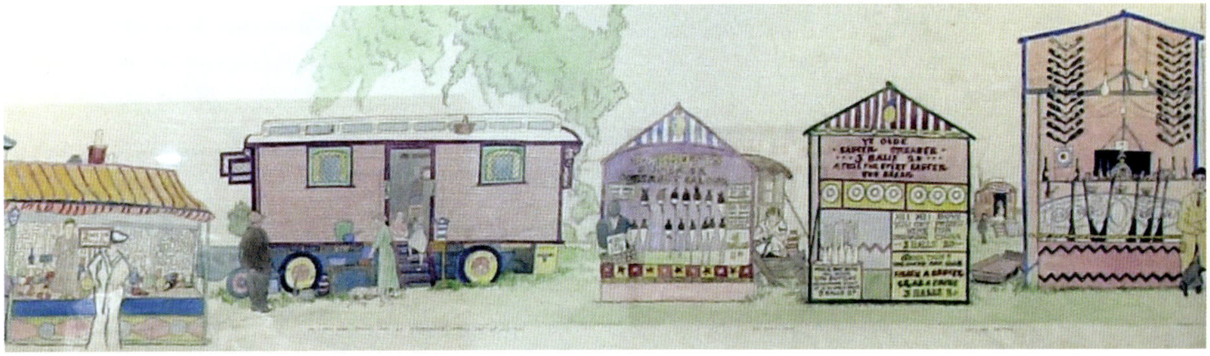

ultraviolet light, it should continue to delight future generations – as a unique record of Southwold life in 1933.'

But what of the little-known artist who compiled such a lengthy and loving portrait of his favourite resort? The scroll shows flashes of artistic flair alongside clumsy touches and apparent losses of confidence. But in his book *Artists at Walberswick: East Anglian Interludes 1880-2000*, author-painter Richard Scott devotes more space to John Doman Turner than to any other figure. Although among the 16 members of the pioneering Camden Town Group formed in 1911 by Walter Sickert, Spencer Gore and Harold Gilman, he soon vanished from public view. Long after his death heaps of his smaller-scale watercolours were discovered in a Lowestoft junk shop, and the Norfolk and London art dealer Michael Parkin used them as the basis for a tribute show to *The Forgotten Camden Towner* in Belgravia in 1977.

But he also completed at least four panoramic scrolls of the Suffolk coast. The first, of 1930, depicted the houses along Southwold's Ferry Road. Many were to be swept away in the 1953 floods, along with the artist's summer residence – a caravan named Jane after a lady friend. Next came a 123-foot (37.5 metre) whopper called *A Dioramic Pictorial Record of a Suffolk Village* which detailed every dwelling in Walberswick. Presented to the local community, it was later installed in the casing of an old pub football game and can now be viewed on video or (by appointment) at the turn of a handle. And, after the Trinity Fair epic, he also produced a gigantic portrait of the travelling circus which still visits Southwold each summer. This charming review is now in the London Theatre Museum.

If there is a sad suggestion of a limited artist hanging over even the liveliest Doman Turner scene, there is also the underpinning of a wholly winning wit. For stuck below an image of the Spotted Lady attraction at the 1933 fair in Southwold is a *News Chronicle* cutting from 1934. Beneath the headline LEOPARD WOMAN FRAUD – HER SPOTS SUPPLIED BY TATTOOIST the story reads:

'A "leopard woman" found at a fair was the subject of a prosecution at Doncaster yesterday when James Ainscow, amusement caterer, and Walter Asquith…were sent to prison for a month for obtaining money by false pretences.

'It was stated that the men were showing the "leopard woman" whom Asquith described as "a living freak, part animal, part fish, part woman – the 'it' woman newly introduced from America".

'The leopard woman, said the police, was merely Asquith's wife. She was perfectly normal except that she had tattoo marks on her chest. She was submerged in a tank of water but the police discovered she was able to breathe through a glass dome invisible to the public.

'When her husband was arrested Mrs Asquith said: "I must do something to get my money back. The tattooing cost me £50."'

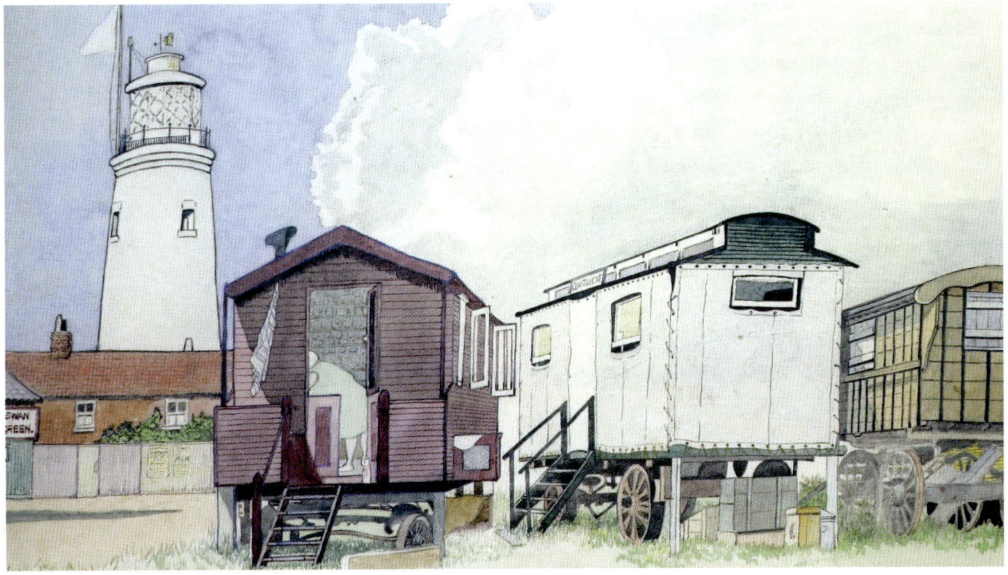

*View of Southwold from the Lighthouse*,
Frederick Baldwin, watercolour, 1934.

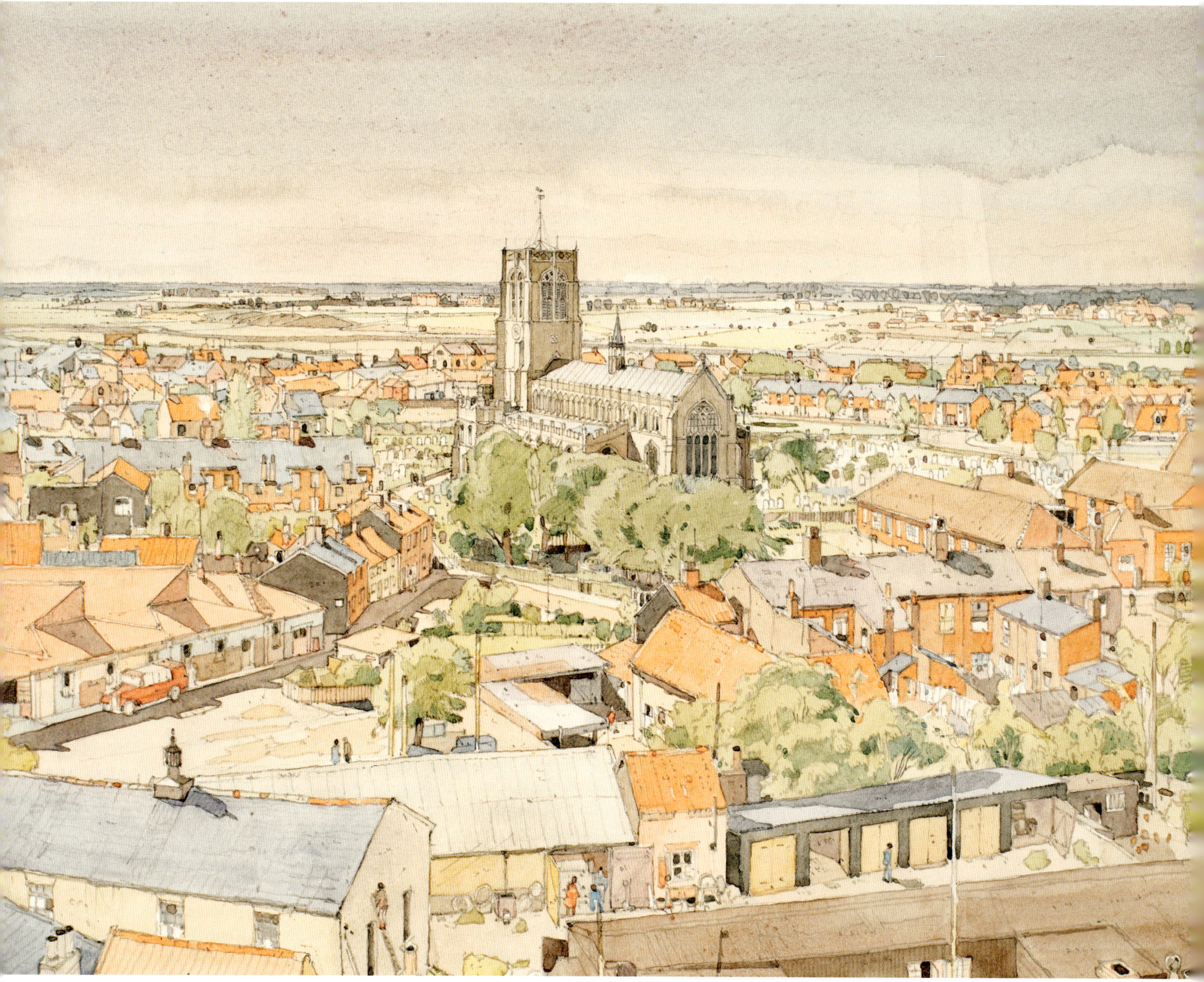

Chapter Sixteen

# Flame and Flood

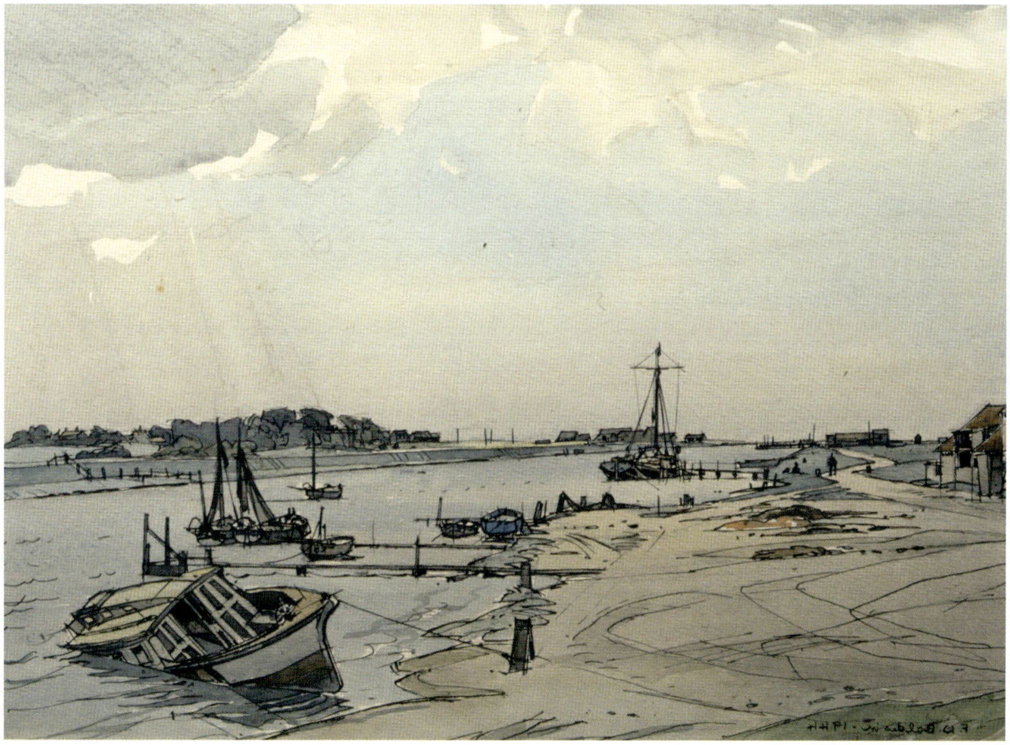

*War-time Harbour,* Frederick Baldwin, watercolour.

They say that Southwold never changes, and on the day in 1934 when **FREDERICK WILLIAM BALDWIN** (1899-1984) climbed to the observation platform of the lighthouse, to paint the town arrayed below him, he may well have thought that he was paying tribute to solidity and permanence. But within the next decade so much of the surrounding scene would be damaged or destroyed.

Fred Baldwin was an expert recorder, having turned early design and architectural drawings into works of art – first for his builder father and then when employed by shipbuilder Brooke Marine in his native Lowestoft. In 1923 he had met watercolourist Leonard Squirrell who was to prove a key influence and life-long friend. They went on many working tours together, Squirrell making notes and sketches and his companion injecting greater vigour and vitality into a self-taught art by producing intricate watercolours on the spot. Baldwin had married in 1928 and, when the economic slump forced the closure of Brooke Marine, he and his wife moved to an ancient cottage near the church at Westhall. From this rural base he delighted in depicting the interiors of old barns as agricultural cathedrals.

But that panoramic 1934 image of Southwold had shown a townscape apparently unclouded by any kind of troubles. The heart of the community was dominated by the majestic church and, amid the close-knit terrace cottages, by the sprawl of brewery outbuildings. Northwards from this compact settlement lay undeveloped fields and marshes in the scattered parish of Reydon. The somewhat sleepy scene was soon to awaken with a bang. Between August 1940 and the end of the war in 1945 bombs and incendiaries would kill 13 civilians in Southwold and injure a further 49. Some 2,299 properties would be damaged and 77 destroyed – the latter tally including Hollyhock Square to the left of the church (in an attack which also levelled churchyard trees and blew in most of the church windows) and St Edmund's Hall on the rightward edge of Baldwin's picture. Further afield the Marlborough and Dunwich hotels were demolished along with most of the houses on Marlborough Road and the bungalows on Ferry Road. Stripped of iron railings, and with many windows boarded up due to lack of glass, Southwold had never appeared in such a sorry state since the great fire of 1659.

In addition, a lot of damage had been self-inflicted as part of the exhaustive defence effort on an exposed coast. Although the town had taken in evacuees from London in the first chaotic days of the conflict, later its own children were sent away, some of them never to return. All save essential workers (more than two-thirds of the peacetime population) were pressed into leaving, and the Grand Hotel and Centre Cliff schools were among buildings requisitioned by the War Office for use by an incoming garrison of soldiers. Here and there were gun emplacements, pillboxes, and air-raid shelters, while piles of

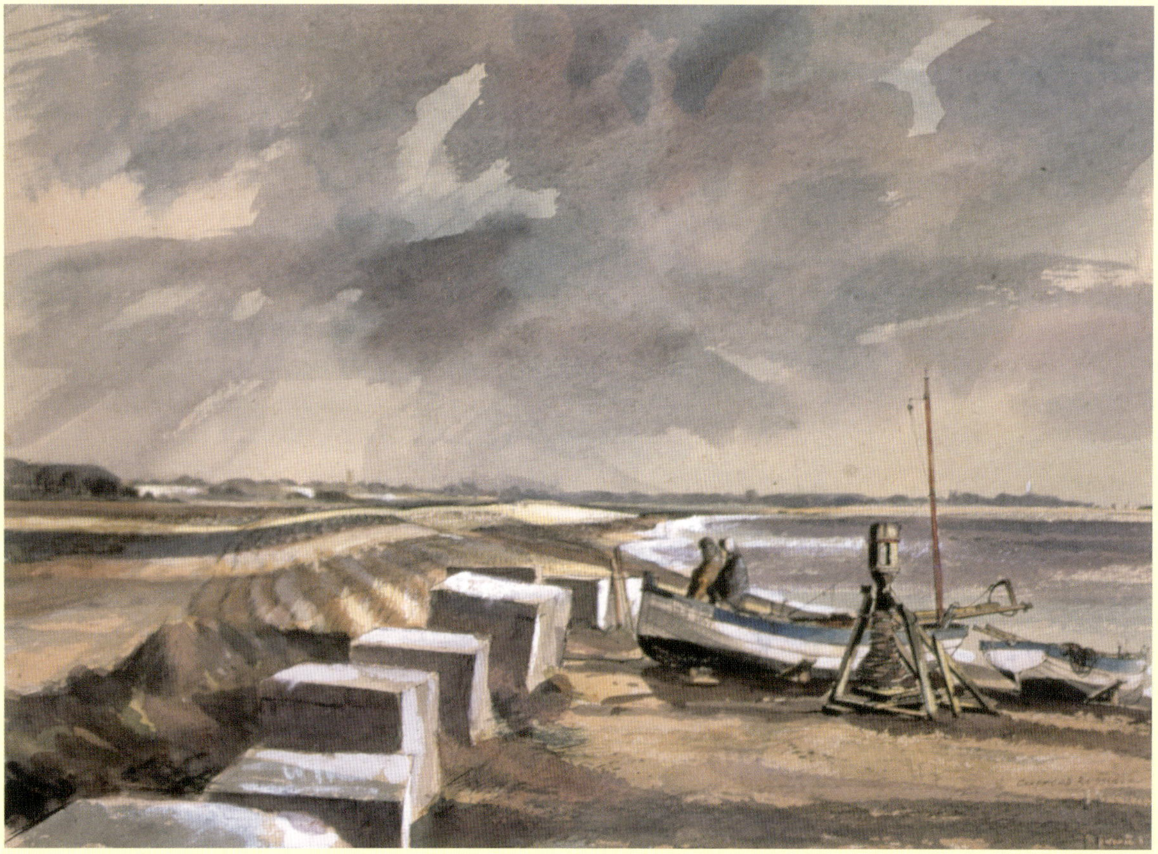

In the 1950s and 1960s friends Frank Forward, Eric Scott and CLIFFORD ALLAN RUSSELL (1919-2003) often exhibited at the Homestead – the former Debney's department store on South Green, now divided into flats. The latter artist, Scottish born and London raised, had been introduced to the Suffolk scenery when posted to the Orford Armoured Training Range during the preparations for D-Day. A veteran of the Norway campaign, he was part of the allied advance through France, Belgium and Holland – painting and drawing from the gun turret of his tank in quiet moments. But he was blown up after the crossing into Germany and confined to a wheelchair thereafter. One of the first patients at Stoke Mandeville spinal injuries unit, he was given five years to live without tobacco or alcohol. He ignored the advice on alcohol and died at 83. Sent to Southwold to convalesce – and living in Hotson Road – he later moved to Walberswick and then Frostenden. Father of the artist Tassie Russell, he sketched and painted to the end. In the 1950s he undertook graphic commissions for Adnams, including the painting of inn signs and in 1955 set up the Southwold Art Circle with Nicholas Loftus. Although war-time defensive blocks dominate the foreground of this stirring Sole Bay watercolour view from Dunwich, Clifford Russell was a sensitive recorder of peaceful Suffolk scenes. His love of buildings led to a late career as an architect.

sandbags were everywhere. Beach huts were strewn across the common to prevent planes from landing and the seafront became a tangled mass of barbed wire, steel scaffolding spikes and concrete interspersed with buried land mines to prevent troops from coming ashore. The pier was sectioned and the old railway bridge over the Blyth blown up. A boom of spikes and cable was stretched across the harbour mouth, with further homespun fortifications on either side. Boats were sunk in the fairway – a sadly surreal scene caught in a watercolour by Fred Baldwin, who created most of his best work in and around the war years. But visitor Winston Churchill had no time to indulge his passion for painting. Touring the town's defences, and being put up in the Swan Hotel (which remained opened for much of the war as a morale-boosting measure), Britain's leader declared himself well-satisfied with what he had seen.

Londoner **PRUNELLA CLOUGH** (1919-1999) had known and loved Suffolk from

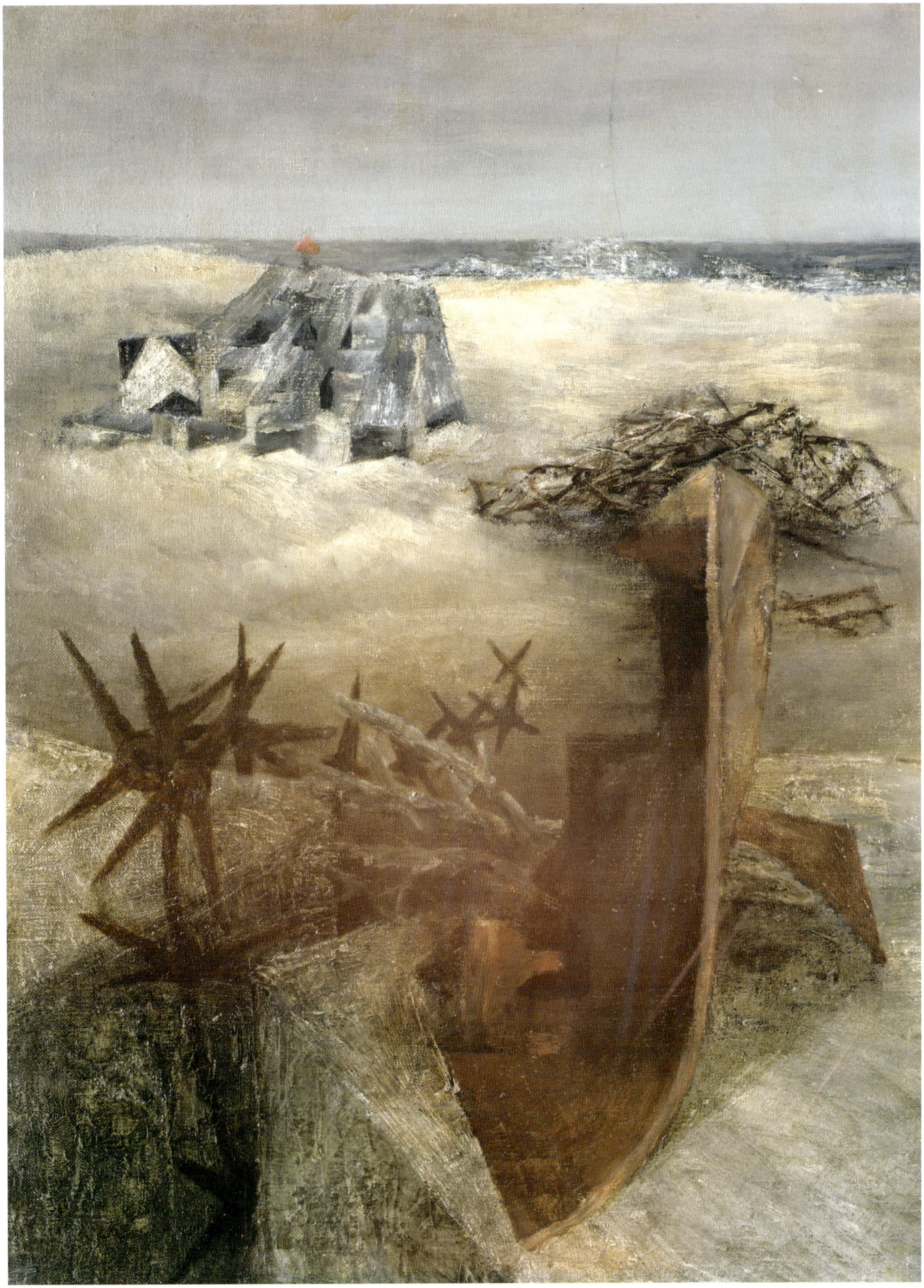

*Closed Beach*, Prunella Clough, oil on canvas, 1945.

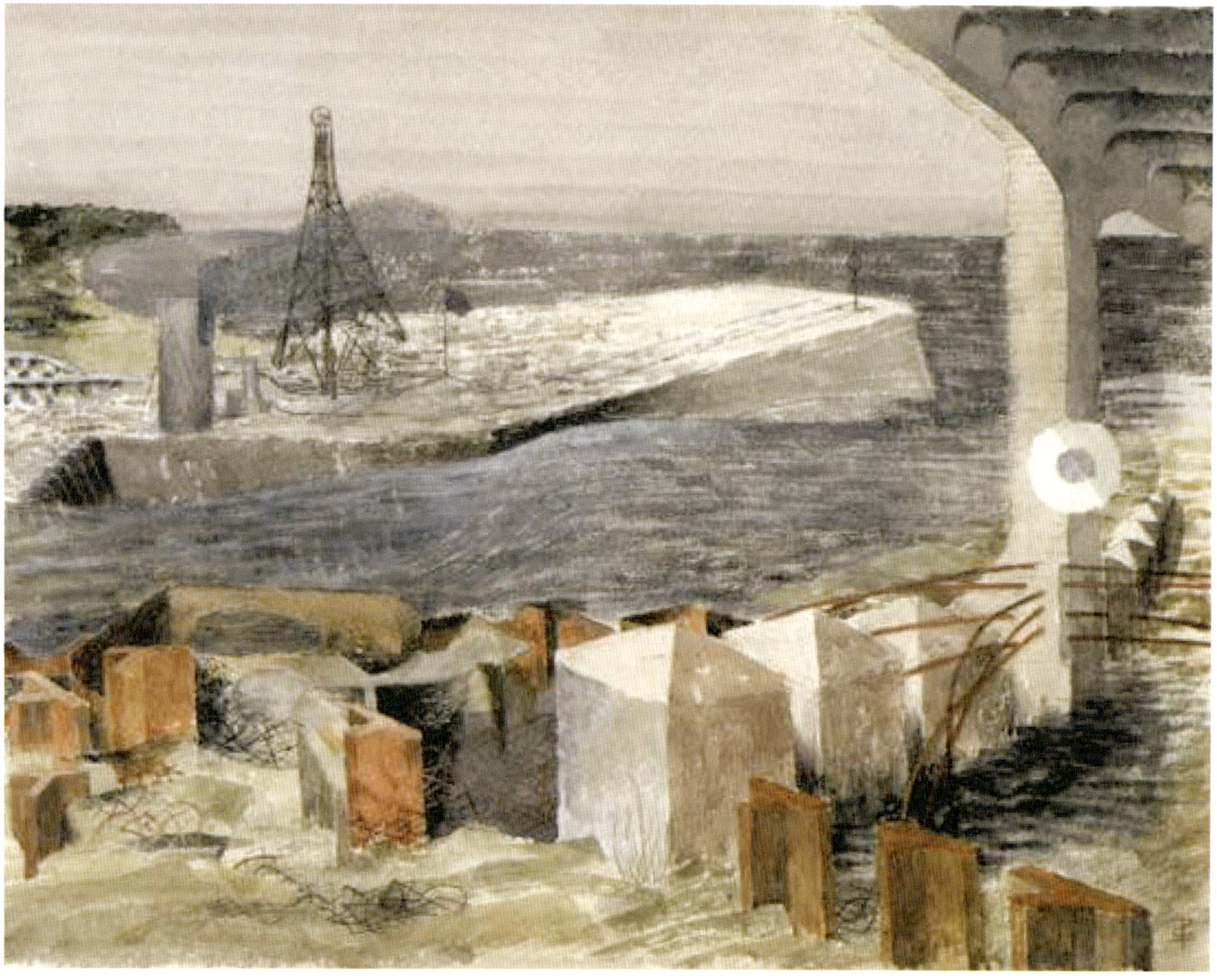

*Harbour Works*, Prunella Clough, watercolour, pencil and gouache, 1942.

childhood stays with family friends and latterly lodging in Woldside, on Constitution Hill – a tall house carved from a corner of grand Hill House and boasting sweeping views to Blythburgh and across Gun Hill to the sea. As an only child raised in Chelsea, she had valued the cliff-top town and surrounding coast and countryside as a haven, not least from the snobbish and fashionable concerns of her widowed mother. Here she recharged her batteries and honed her skills as an artist. Graduating from Chelsea School of Art as Britain plunged into war, she often escaped to Southwold in breaks from the Blitz. During these visits she created dramatic drawings and watercolours of war defences along the beach and harbour – the gaunt, jagged and geometric shapes of metal and concrete prefiguring her later drift through industrial imagery towards pure abstraction.

Inventing her life as well as her art, Clough remained guarded even in her diaries. But in one densely-written journal, given to a friend shortly before her death and now in the Tate archive, she expresses an ardent love of Southwold. The narrative covers a three-year period from November 1944, opening in the late war-time era when the artist was bicycling to the basement of Selfridges to produce maps, graphs and charts for the Office of War Information (USA) amid a blizzard of V1 and V2 bombs. In mid-April 1945

Prunella Clough in the garden at Woldside, 1930s.

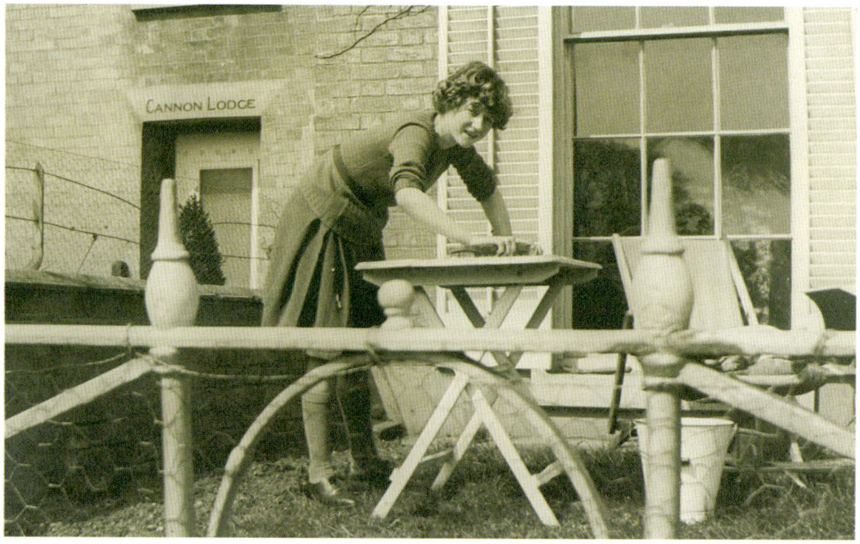

she was savouring a respite at Woldside amid uncannily sunny weather, drawing boats pulled up by the pier and harbour, buying wood from the Henham Estate for carving (her Chelsea tutor Henry Moore and her friend Gertrude Hermes had urged a move into sculpture), and savouring a letter from her designer aunt Eileen Gray who had weathered the war in France. Listening on the radio she heard that the Russians were 15 miles from Berlin and the Buchenwald concentration camp was overrun.

Back in Southwold on May 6, having completed a map of the Pacific, she wrote: 'It is all headlines (and wandering populations and chaos)...Southwold, after and in these cold weeks, is like a piece of time isolated and a photograph – its only trace my ability to start a painting…'

*Shoreline and War Defences*, Prunella Clough, watercolour and gouache, c1941-42.

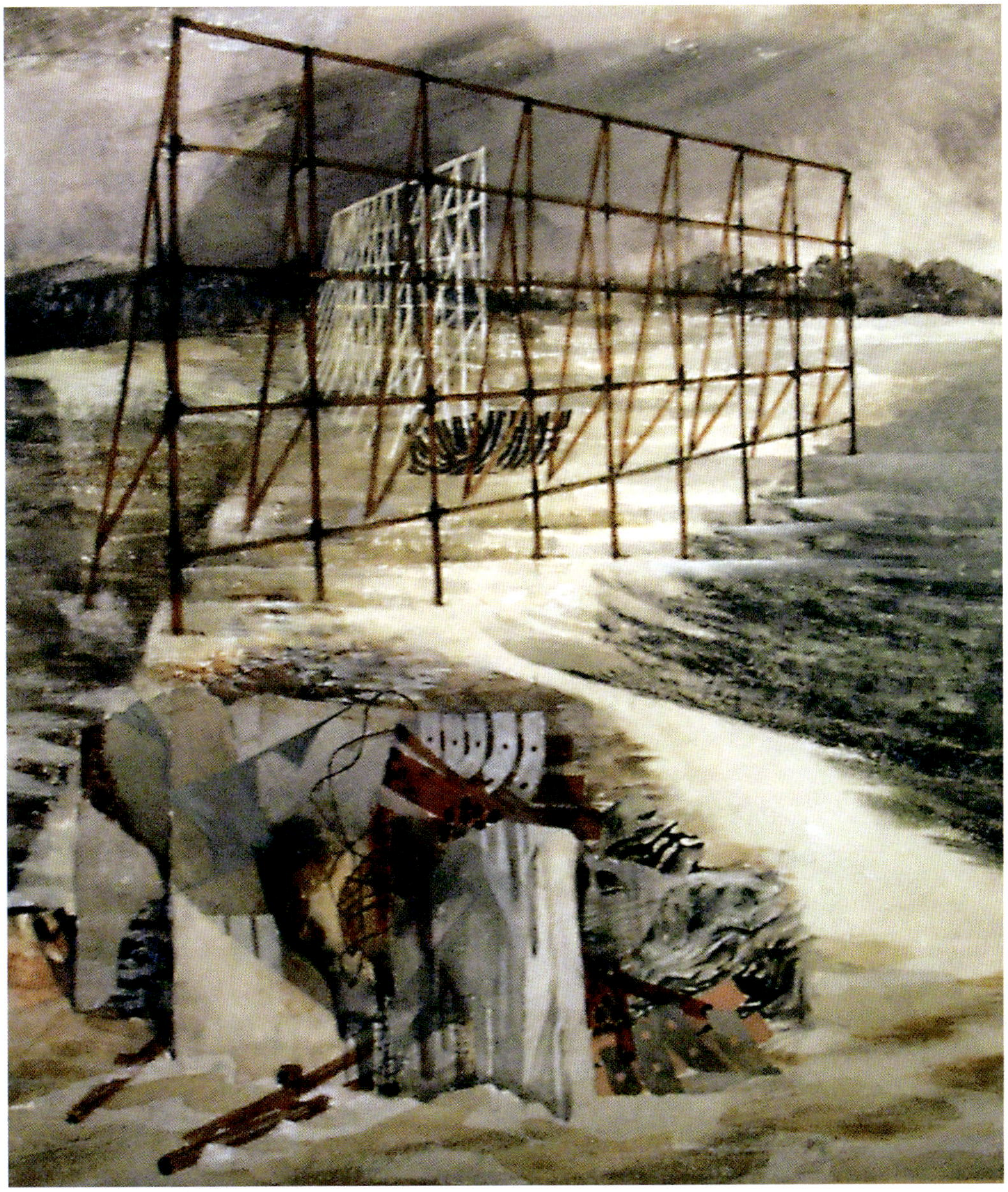

And this on May 7: 'The German army has surrendered – but is still fighting near Breslau & at Prague. Announcement at 3 followed hourly by various statements, mostly concerned with public holiday tomorrow: Hopeless situation trying to get work done. German radio still operating in Oslo but admitting capitulation. Littered with flags and bunting may be bought without coupons. US army found Ezra Pound in Genoa. One can say again & again – it is over, but just as one knew it had begun without changing times immediately, so now gradually, only thankful for less death and violence…'

Back in London she tried to paint and continue with OWI work in the midst of Victory in Europe celebrations, finally completing a Southwold-based seascape. The following month she finished an oil of a bleached bone in the sand and another of mines, barbs and ramps in *Closed Beach* (p.125) for display at the Redfern Gallery. Ever a severe critic of her own work, she wrote: 'I feel they are not misdirected at least.'

In Southwold again on July 3 Clough was horrified to find a For Sale notice in Woldside and pressed her mother for the funds to buy it. By way of distraction she began a painting based on wire and 'the brilliance of those yellow flowers in the sand at the harbour'. On August 6 the first atom bomb was dropped on Japan, with the artist writing two days later: 'It put out of my head the good news that M is buying Woldside for 1400£. This means so much. To be able to count on it, to plan to work there, is also an enormous relief.' And on August 10 she added: 'Japan will surrender if we let the emperor alone. Whatever negotiations go on it can't be long, in fact the ticker-tape is flying…Personally I have a feeling of freedom now since I deny the moral right of any ministry to compel me in peace-time. My methods of rebuilding the world are my own to choose.'

Rebuilding the Clough world meant spending a lot of time in Southwold. In September she was installed at Woldside and steering clear of other people ('S'wold is my child's paradise & I will not admit strangers'). In fact, what she wanted was a breathing space. Although Southwold produced pivotal pictures – bird skeletons and torn-out tree roots on the tide line adding an epitaph to the deadly dislocations of war – Clough's restless

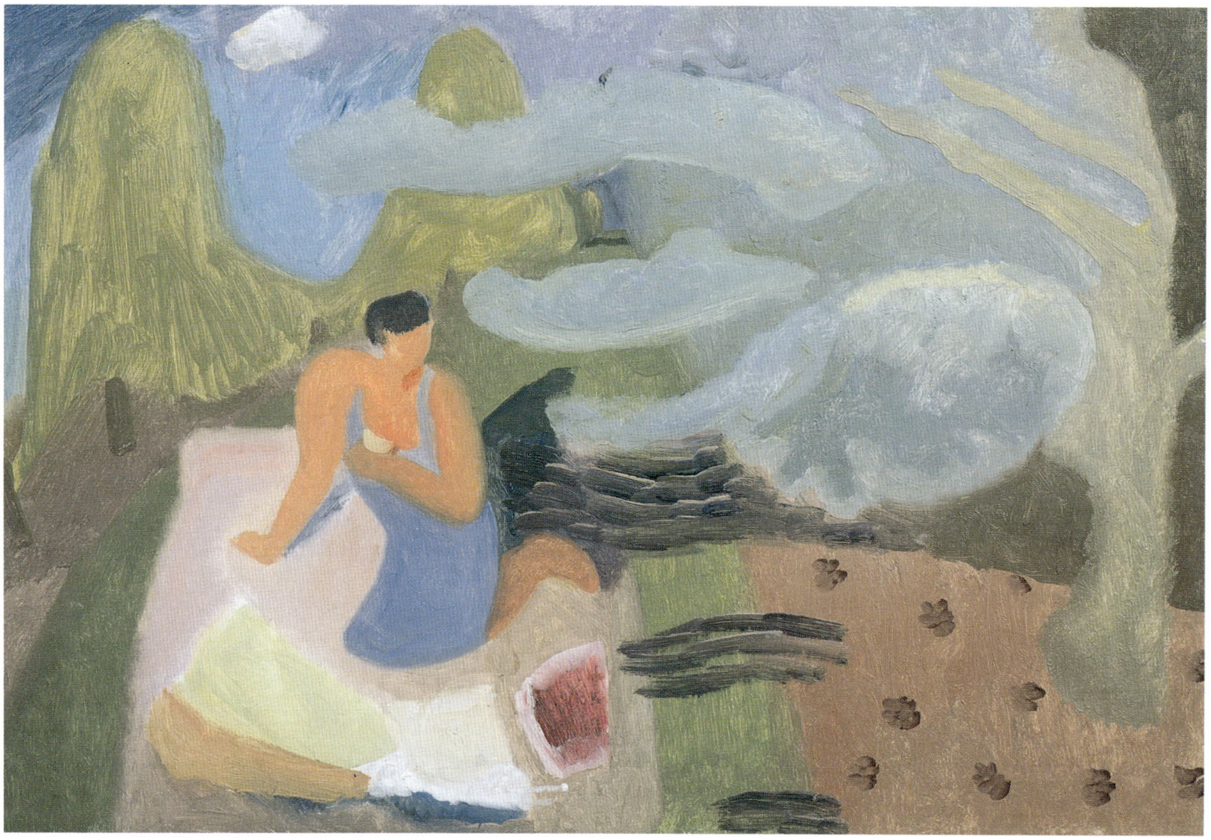

*Picnic, Sizewell*, Ivon Hitchens, oil on canvas, 1933.

vision soon moved elsewhere. In 1947 she rented a studio in Lowestoft, beside the harbour whose bustle was reproduced in semi-cubist prints and paintings. She was there for one of the coldest winters on record – writing on February 22 1948: 'Renewed blizzard snowed up most of N yesterday & people skated from Beccles to Lowestoft which has not been done since 1894; ships in ice on way to Sweden; N Sea 2 degrees below at all depths which may kill fish.'

But, although she owned Woldside until 1966, from the early 1950s Prunella Clough's creative focus turned to London. With much of her free time consumed by weekend trips to France, to care for the ageing Eileen Gray, she managed only brief sorties into the industrial hinterland from Gravesend to Grimsby where, increasingly, inspiration lay. Suffolk lost its youthful appeal. But in 1953, having produced prints of masts, floats, nets and breakwaters for an Aldeburgh Festival calendar

*Exercise Kruschen (Dunwich Common): Tank Fascines; the 'Snake' Ronson flame throwers*, Edward Bawden, ink and watercolour, 1943.

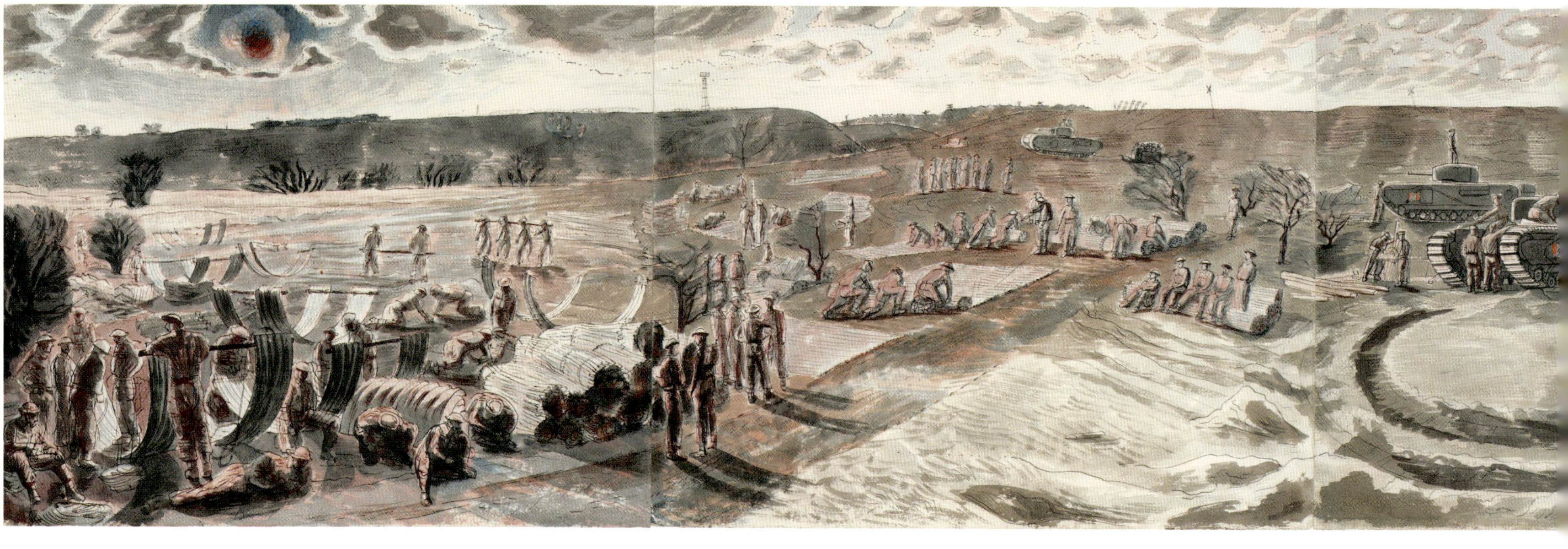

(Mary Potter and John Piper adding four prints apiece) she wrote to her painter friend David Carr at Starston Hall near Harleston: 'Do you know that lovely beach at Sizewell has been smothered in shingle by the flood? – Not only that, but the most appalling iron monsters have appeared. One is better than any Lynn Chadwick. It has its base in concrete with a long curving body, sickle jaws and hideous eye…(Spread of machine consciousness – of a kind…)'

In lovely Sizewell, where the artist **IVON HITCHENS** (1893-1979) had a cottage in the early 1930s, and where John Piper met his second wife, Myfanwy Evans, in the summer of 1934, far more monstrous figures would appear in subsequent decades. Huge pylons, stalking across the countryside two by two, would connect the successive nuclear power stations of Sizewell A and B to the national grid – the latter plant constructed shortly before a moratorium on atomic energy on cost grounds. Machine consciousness had spread to the heart of the Suffolk heritage coast.

The Great Flood of 1953 came almost without warning on the last night of January, on a surge tide and fierce north-easterly wind, inundating much of

East Anglia's EDWARD BAWDEN (1903-1989) created exquisitely evocative images as a watercolourist, illustrator, designer and print-maker – rejecting the medium of oil which he likened to painting with toothpaste.

He spent most of his life in North Essex, being born in Braintree, presiding over an art and craft colony at Great Bardfield from the early 1930s and living latterly in Saffron Walden. But he also had roving adventures as an Official War Artist from France to the Middle East, with a spell in a lifeboat after his ship was torpedoed off the West African coast. Shortly before his death, when interviewed by the author, he recounted the saga of being cast adrift with a distraught French child who believed her mother had drowned. But, on being rescued, Bawden was able to witness the reunion of daughter and parent. After a pause, he ended his narrative with a note of typically mordant wit. 'I never heard of her again,' he said. 'Perhaps she was eaten. The French will eat anything – and possibly anyone too.'

There was no humour to be had, however, when, in April 1943, catastrophe seemed to have struck close to home. Bawden was busy sketching Dunwich heath ablaze in an apparent battle. He had been summoned to record Exercise Kruschen, part of the preparations for D-Day. The artist produced matter-of-fact ink and watercolour representations with prosaic titles: *Projector Infantry Anti-Tank Gun, Two and Three Inch Mortar Smoke Bombs, Man-Pack Flame Thrower, Ronson Flame Throwers, Churchill Tanks, Tank Fascines.* And then he placed these pieces in a five-sheet battlefield panorama. Ranged across the heath and through the pine trees are a dozen tanks, scores of soldiers and a solitary dog. A red sun top left is reflected far away in an explosive encounter top right. Close to the engagement, men wander through a smoking field as if burning stubble. All these related images are now in the Imperial War Museum.

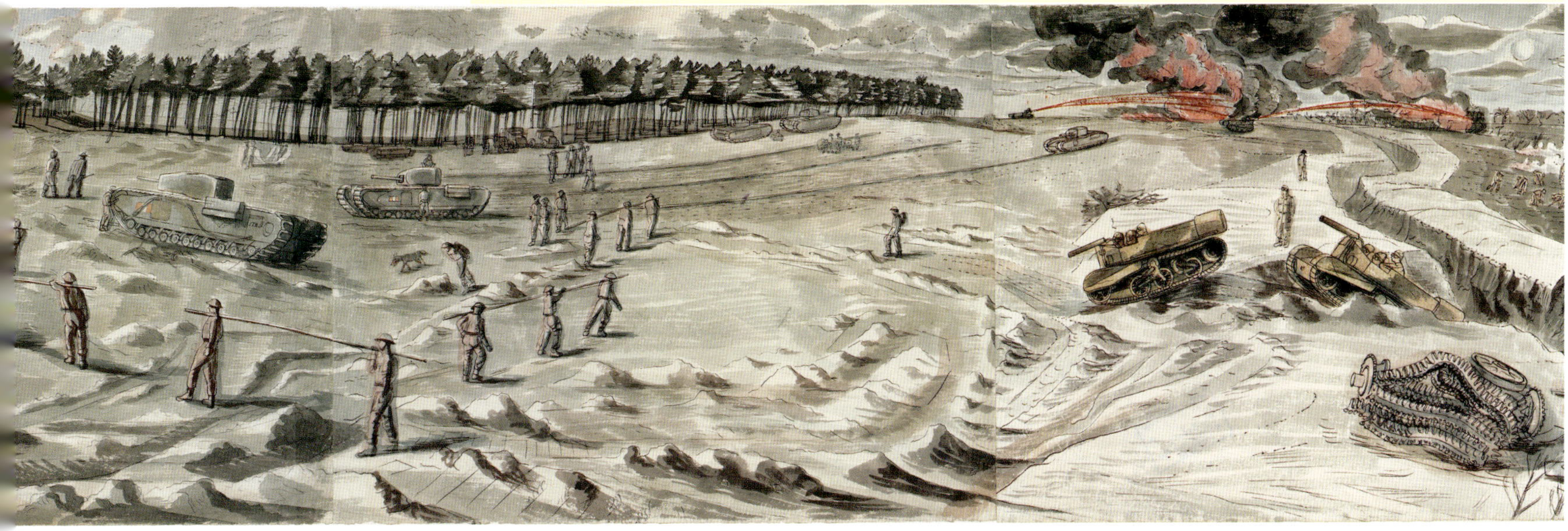

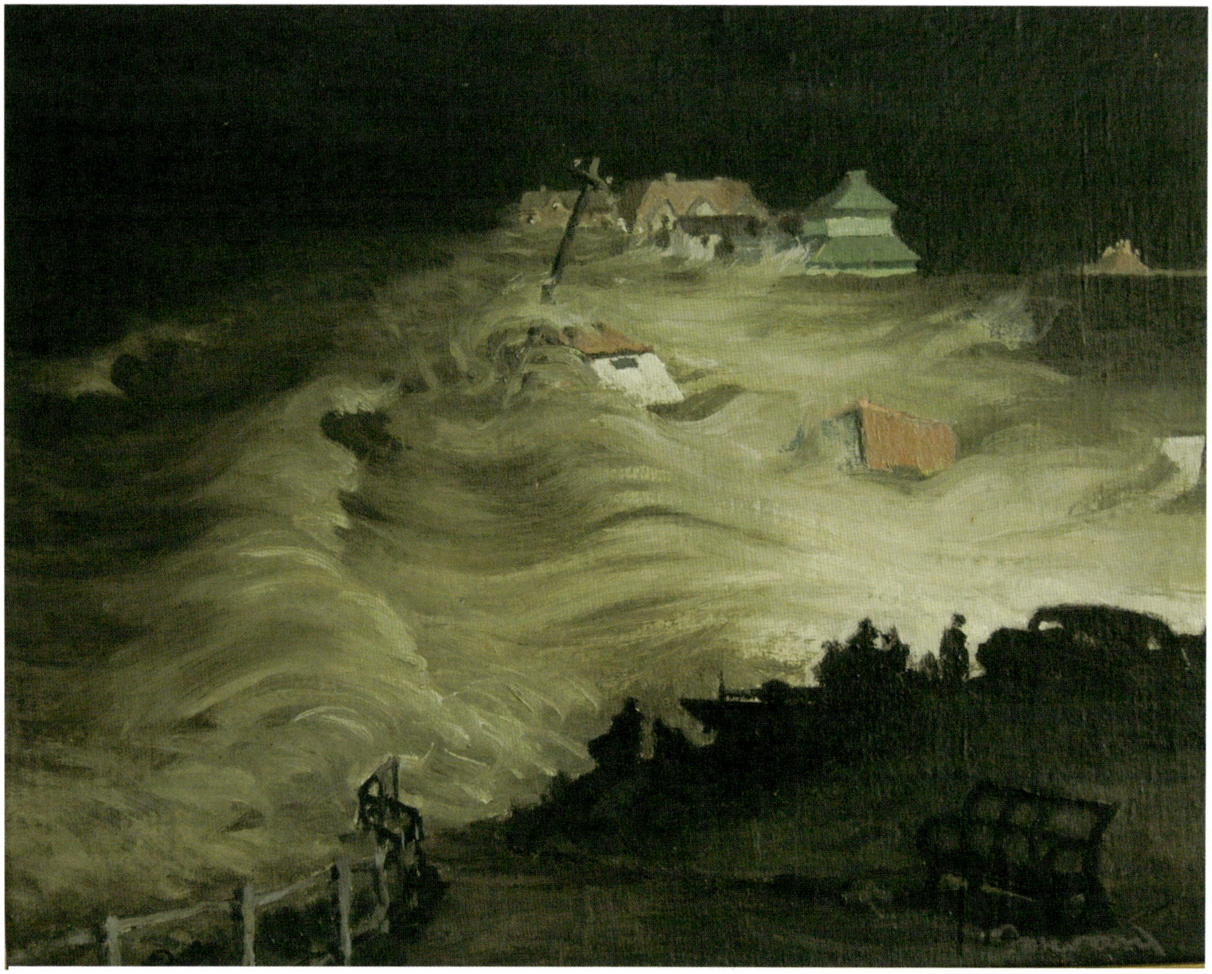

In this Frank Forward oil picture, now hanging in Southwold Town Hall, the rescue operation in flooded Ferry Road is illuminated by car headlamps from Gun Hill.

*Flooded Pier*, Frank Forward (below).

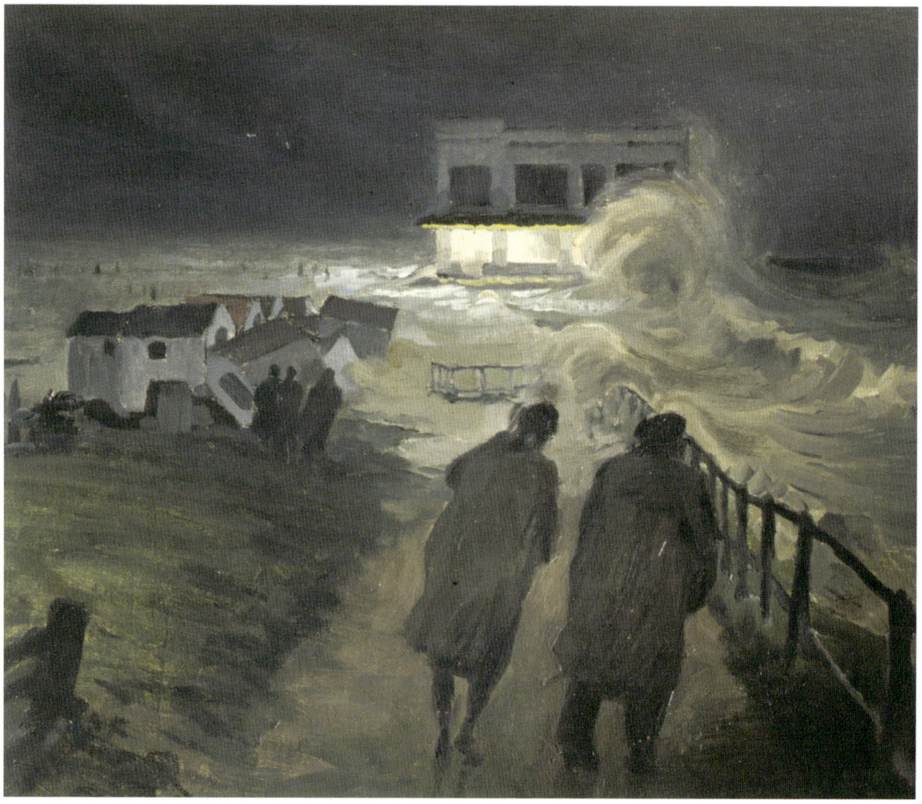

the east coast and bringing mayhem to Southwold. Five people were drowned along Ferry Road when the sea crashed through, covering the marshes in up to 16 feet of water and wholly surrounding the town. Those harbour-side artists' studios at Walberswick not broken up for war-time firewood were now crushed into matchwood. Donald and Irene Horwood, friends of painters and poets and only lately relocating from Bloomsbury to Blackshore, were marooned in upstairs rooms with two small children and a stranded fisherman. In the moonlight they saw Walberswick's Wave Crest tearoom float past, with dainty lace curtains and window boxes still in place, before the wooden structure smashed against the bailey bridge and vanished forever. Fishermen ferried dozens of people to safety – cars on Gun Hill training headlights on the submerged marshes to aid the rescue of folk clinging to an all-but-engulfed roof. The *Illustrated London News* of February 21 carried two oil studies of the calamity by **FRANK FORWARD** (1901-1974), painted with a frantic frenzy. Both are reproduced here. His family ran a grocery store in Reydon and he had returned to Suffolk after training at the Slade, working as a perspective artist for a London architect and doing war service.

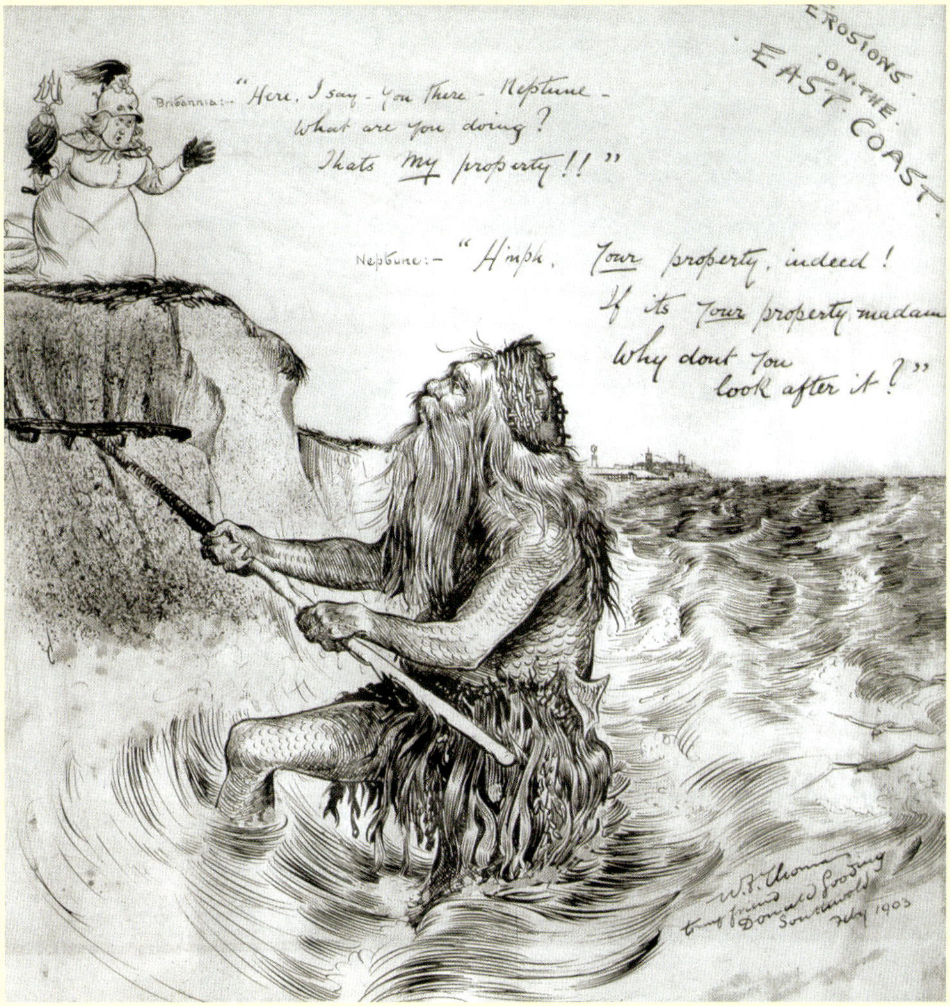


This William Fletcher Thomas ink cartoon, entitled *Erosions on the East Coast* and inscribed 'to my friend Donald Gooding, Southwold February 1903' was drawn in the wake of terrible winter storms, with the town appearing to dither amid a threat of imminent inundation. Hence the exchange between Britannia and Neptune. Britannia: 'Here, I say – you there – Neptune – What are you doing? That's MY property.' Neptune: 'Hmph, YOUR property, indeed! If it's YOUR property madam, why don't you look after it?'

The fury of the Forward oils contrasts with the quiet voices of six Southwold flood witnesses, recorded by Radio Suffolk as an Oral History Project in the late 1990s, a copy of which is now in the town museum. But they paint the same picture. 'The sea was mountains high,' says Beatrice King. We hear how an ambulance overturned in raging waves on Ferry Road. Frank Hurr was swept away as he clambered out but, grabbing a passing door, surfed clear over the marsh to land safely on the Common. 'I looked at the marshes themselves and saw Southwold as an island which I had fondly dreamed about as a boy but do not want to see ever again,' says John Winter. And Harold Fisk relates the rescue of aged Mrs Pickering – whom he had saved from a similar plight a few years earlier. This time, breaking a kitchen window and wading through waist-high water, he found her numbed and dumbfounded and afloat on a dining table. The surreal scene was lit by a standard lamp plugged in way below the water line. Unable to rouse the trauma victim he signalled with a light until attracting the attention of a police sergeant who 'shouted in the old dear's ear that he was ordering her to leave her bungalow NOW because she was being a damn nuisance to other people'. As that still failed to do the trick Mr Fisk handed the officer a bottle bobbing in the briny drink and he 'tipped the old girl's head back and poured quite a quantity of whisky in'. Taking large swigs themselves and feeling 'quite a lot better', the two rescuers then carried the paralytic pensioner to a waiting boat.

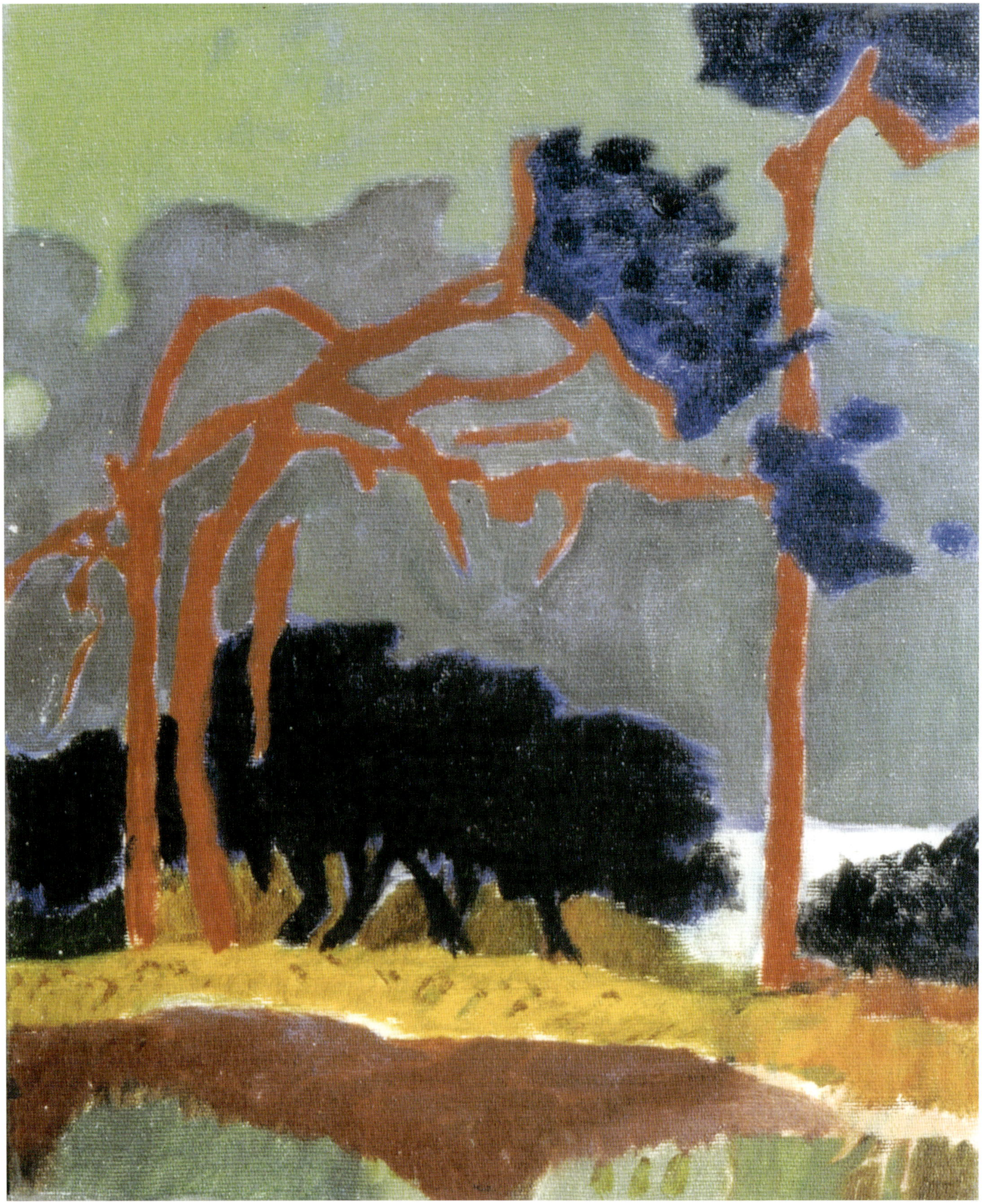

*The Heronry*, Joanna Carrington, oil on canvas, 1993.

Chapter Seventeen

# The Hidden Painter

Walberswick has been closely associated with the Freud family since the 1930s – when Sigmund's youngest son, Ernst, having lately fled Berlin, was amazed to find a similar atmosphere to that recalled from childhood holidays on the Baltic island of Hiddensee. The émigré architect designed the Hidden House for his wife Lucie, and their sons Stephen, Lucian and Clement. In 1954 his psychoanalyst sister Anna bought Far End, following the death of the Freuds' Arts and Crafts metal-worker friend Philip Frederick Alexander, and would see patients in a consulting room built in the garden – also welcoming visitors such as the writer Arthur Koestler. Former Fenland MP Sir Clement Freud has retained links with the village, and his wife Jill founded the Southwold Theatre which has performed each summer since 1983. Their daughter Emma and her scriptwriter husband Richard Curtis (*Blackadder, Four Weddings and a Funeral, Notting Hill*) are now part-time residents. The novelist Esther Freud – who herself has a Walberswick base together with her actor husband David Morrissey, and whose 2003 saga *The Sea House* was rooted locally and peopled with familiar ghosts embattled in exile, war and flood – says of Lucian's absence: 'My father is just about the only member of my family who doesn't love Walberswick. He said he could never paint there because he would be put off by all the amateur lady artists wearing amber necklaces.'

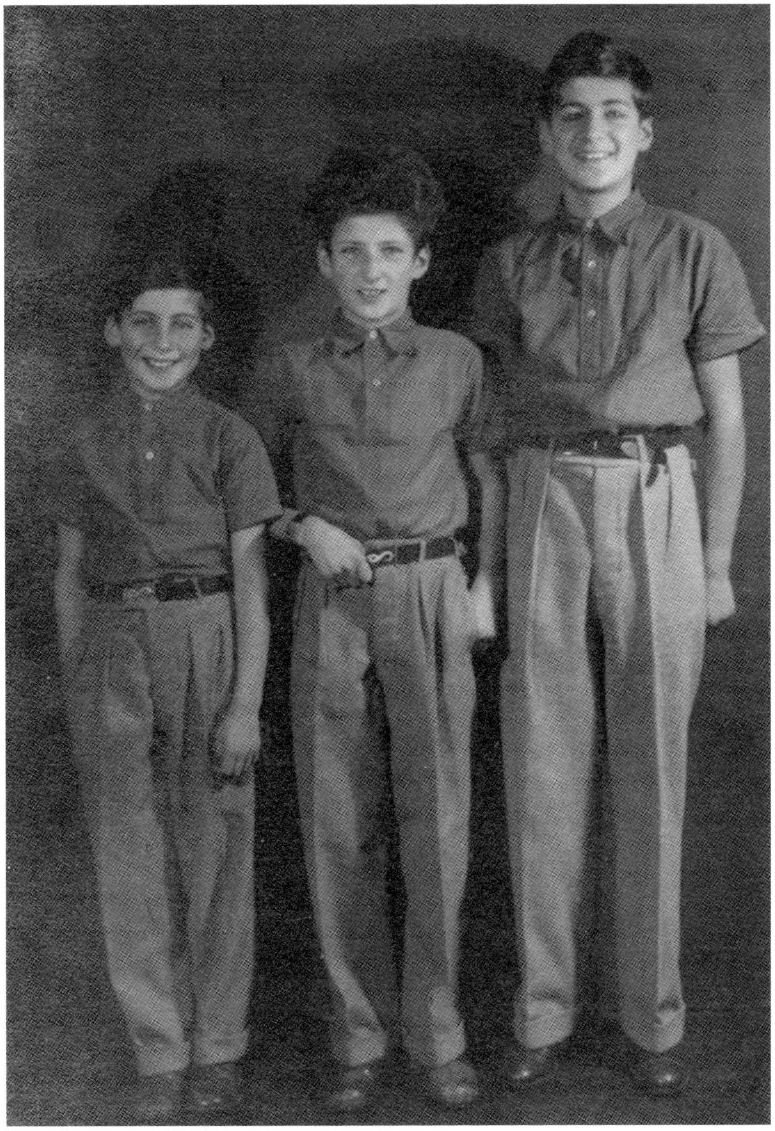

The Freud brothers: left to right, Clement, Lucian and Stephen. From the Alexander family's photograph album for 1936.

But **LUCIAN FREUD** (b1922) ran wild here during schoolboy and student holidays, exploring the beach and the harbour, the woods and the heath. With a railway station simply abandoned in the gorse and bracken in 1929, leaving a well-stocked ticket office as a den for children, this was a fertile place for the growth of creative imagination. The future grand old man of British painting took to sketching hereabouts, especially during breaks from studies at the East Anglian School of Painting and Drawing run by Cedric Morris and Lett Haines on the Suffolk-Essex border. At least one drawing of his mother – later to number among his most poignant and persistent subjects – was completed here. He also came with friends and fellow students David Carr and **JOAN WARBURTON** (1920-1996), the latter born in Edinburgh but spending much of her life in the Stour Valley. Her diary for August 23 1939 contains the following entry: 'Went with

David and Lucian to Walberswick, another boiling day. We had lunch with Lucian's family, his mother, his grandmother and two brothers. His father was in London looking after his old father who has been ill now for a long time.' Sigmund Freud, the father of psychoanalysis, only recently rescued from Vienna (from where his aged sisters would go to the gas chambers), died a month later.

In the summer of 1942 Lucian Freud met the painter and femme fatale Lorna Wishart in Southwold, and they began a passionate affair. Lorna, married to the Marxist publisher Ernest Wishart, took another year to end a lengthy liaison with the poet Laurie Lee. She was the youngest of the brilliantly talented, beguiling and occasionally batty Garman sisters, one of whom wed sculptor Jacob Epstein and another the poet Roy Campbell. A brother, Douglas, had a stormy affair with the American heiress and future art patron Peggy Guggenheim, the couple clashing on a Norfolk Broads sailing holiday in 1936 after which Peggy fled to Woodbridge for some recuperative shopping. With Lorna much in mind, the critic John Russell has noted: 'It was in 1945 that Lucian Freud began to handle oil-paint in a specifically adult way. This was due to a new density of involvement with individual human beings.' But when the key muse broke with the unfaithful Freud soon afterwards – saying 'I thought I'd given you up for Lent, but I'm giving you up for good' – he told his friend John Craxton that he would never again love a woman more than she loved him. Both Freud and Laurie Lee went on to marry Lorna's nieces.

That chance meeting in Southwold had come about because the Wisharts were in the habit of holidaying with their family in a wooden beach house – both their children, Michael and Sylvia, would become artists after formative experiences on the Suffolk coast. In his 1977 memoir *High Diver* Michael Wishart (1928-1996) recalled an 11-year-old's novel artistic apprenticeship in Southwold on the eve of war: 'When tired of painting sand and dilapidated boathouses I found a new theme. At the time it was my ambition to be a beautician. I cut the faces of women out of newspapers and magazines and improved them with gouache. As I worked I spoke to my clients in the soothing voice I knew that ladies in beauty parlours used. "Now I suggest Modom requires a rather fuller mouth" – adding carmine to the mean mouth of some lady who had made the front page – or "Shall we try the effect of a fringe on Modom?"– obliterating the lines of stress from the forehead of perhaps a widow, snapped leaving her husband's funeral, with a meticulously applied coating of brunette, and so forth. I am still deeply interested in tribal warpaint, and the nearer home the better. When the mirror disappoints, who can be blamed for altering the image?'

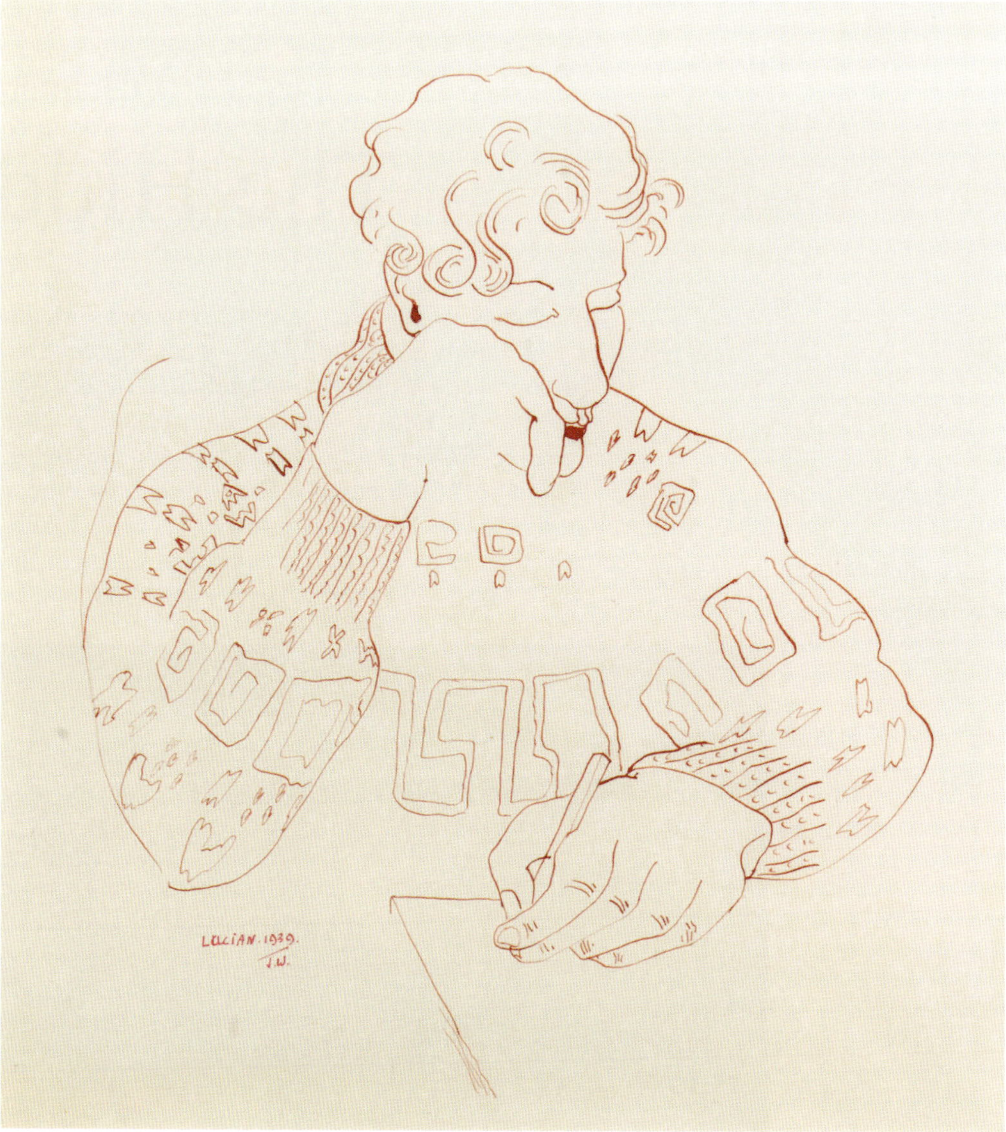


*Lucian, 1939*, portrait drawing of Lucian Freud by Joan Warburton.

Michael Wishart, who would follow Freud and David Carr (another of his mother's former boyfriends) with a stint at the East Anglian School of Painting and Drawing, had a fatefully successful show in London when aged 16. Pitched into the heady world of his friends Freud and Francis Bacon, he lacked the ruthless application of their sustained visions. After a failed marriage to the painter Anne Dunn he travelled widely, prey to self-destructive addictions and obsessions. But a come-back exhibition with the Norfolk and London art dealer Michael Parkin in 1985 showed him again meditating lyrically on the English coast, albeit from his home in Hove.

Meanwhile, the influence of Ernst Freud was to linger beside the Blyth in the decades after his death. His refugee circle included friends from Vienna – the painter and sculptor Hansi Bohm (1907-1996), who settled in Walberswick soon after the war, and potter Lucie Rie (1902-1995), a frequent visitor. The architect also built a cottage for the astonishing Countess Elisabeth von der Schulenburg (1903-2001) and her then husband Fritz Hess. Tisa Schulenberg had rebelled against her aristocratic Prussian background, marrying a divorced Jewish businessman and studying sculpture in Berlin. The couple fled to England in 1933 and, until their divorce in 1938, divided their time between Highgate, Walberswick and Durham – Tisa teaching wood-carving to unemployed miners. This friend of Henry Moore and member of the anti-fascist Artists' International Association then returned to Germany for her father's funeral (also attended by Hitler), after which she was barred from re-entering Britain. Although four of her five brothers were pro-Nazi – and all would be dead by the end of the war – the fifth, Fritz-Dietlof, was hanged for his part in the July Plot against Hitler in 1944. Following another divorce Tisa converted to Roman Catholicism and, in 1950, entered a convent in the Ruhr. Her harrowing sculptures and drawings moved from mining to Holocaust themes, and she often revisited England.

*Beach Huts, Walberswick*, Joanna Carrington, oil on canvas 1969.

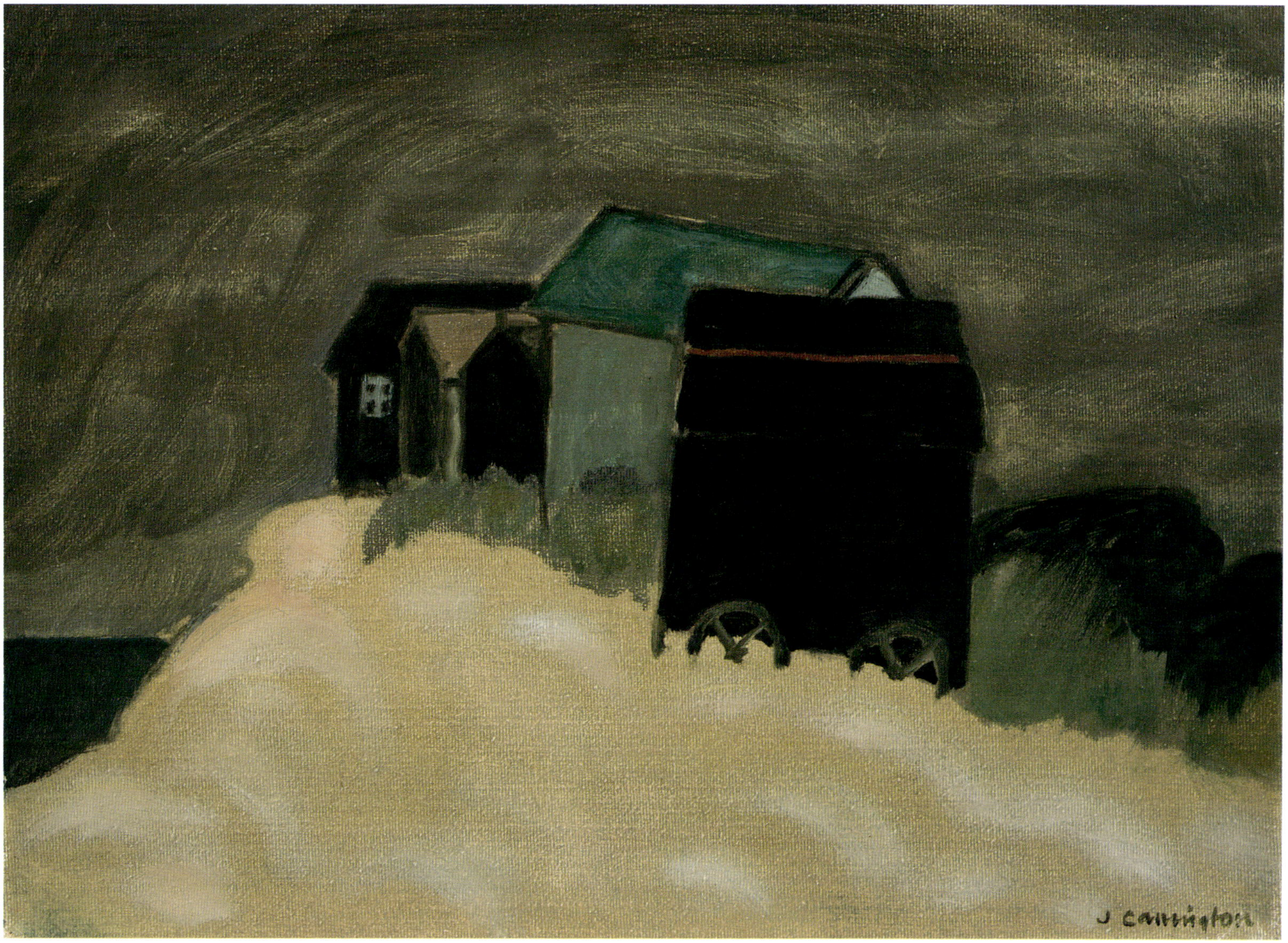

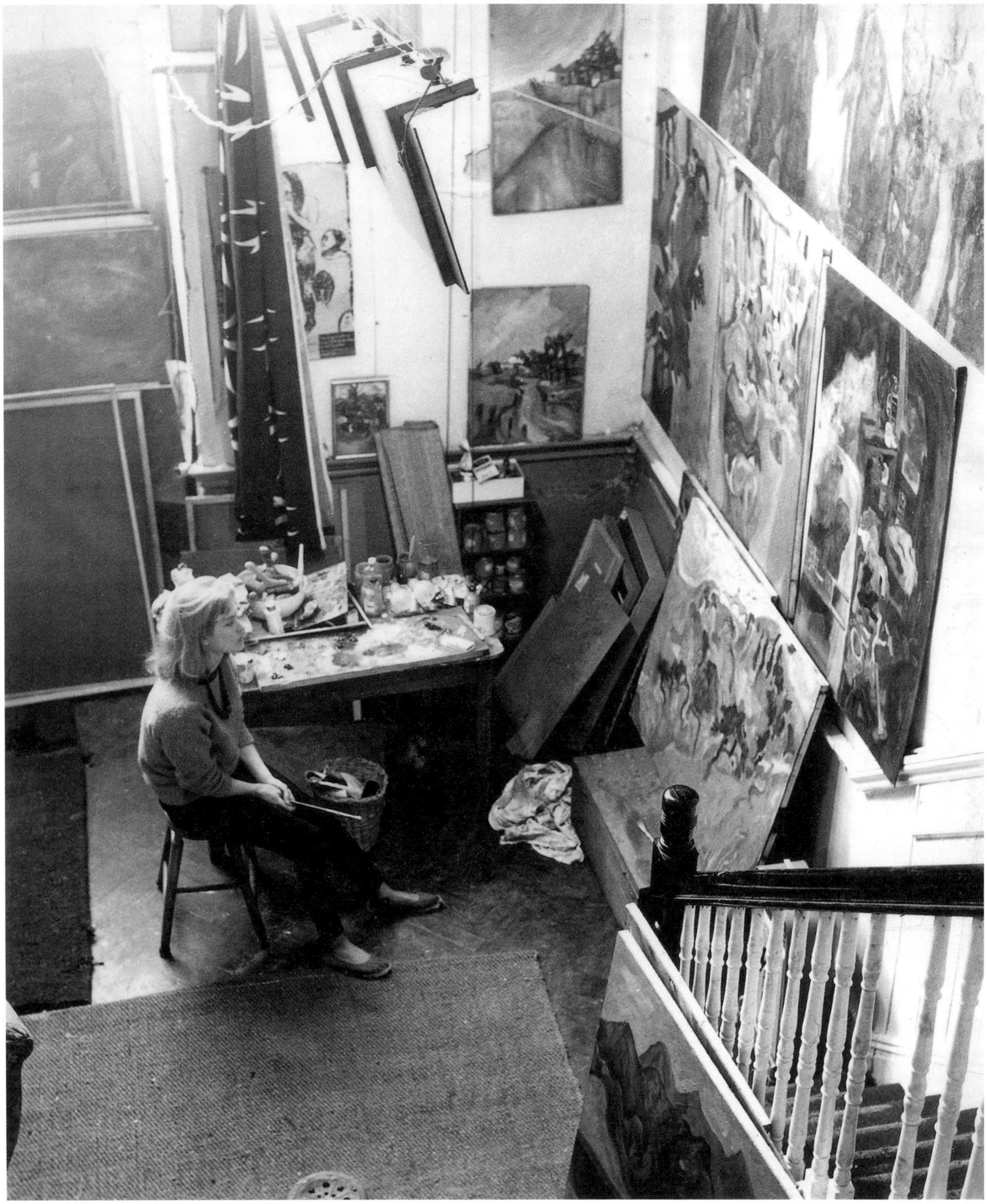

Joanna Carrington in her London studio, 1960.

**JOANNA CARRINGTON** (1931-2003) was only a few months old when her aunt, the Bloomsbury artist (Dora) Carrington, committed suicide after the death of companion Lytton Strachey. Joanna's outlook was to be altogether sunnier. Her parents – Noel, who created Puffin books, and Catharine – gave her an idyllic childhood, with blissful family holidays in Walberswick. In a 2005 memorial book, widower Christopher Mason wrote: 'Clearly she was a happy, extrovert child, and never happier than in the holidays spent in Walberswick…where her Alexander grandparents had a house overlooking the marshes. All through her life she would return. She would take a sketchbook and walk for hours along the shingle beach, or inland among the pine trees, or past the moored fishing boats in the River Blyth. She particularly loved a little group of huts

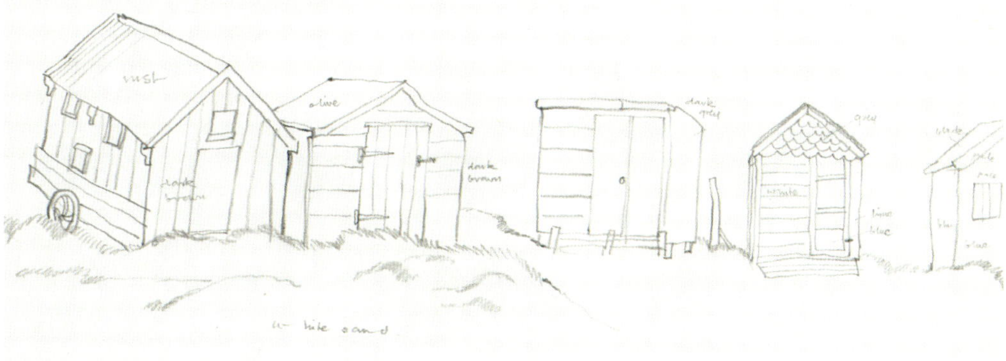

*Walberswick beach huts*, Joanna Carrington, drawing and notes for painting.

on the dune and often painted them.' Joanna stayed with her Alexander grandparents until 1954, by which time her distinctive art was emerging after studies at the East Anglian School of Painting and Drawing, where Cedric Morris had 'never had a student that showed so much promise', and with Fernand Léger in Paris. From 1966, with painter/film-maker Christopher Mason (who produced screen profiles of Alfred Wallis and Duncan Grant), she lived largely in France – but often borrowed writer Anthony Sampson's cottage to keep her links with the Suffolk coast alive. Here she found the inspiration for richly-coloured landscapes and seascapes shown in London's New Grafton and Thackeray galleries. Her husband penned this sonnet in her memory:

*Did we (I wish I could remember*
*But I am old and it was years ago)*
*Find a cornelian when the tide was low*
*And yellow plastic that I swore was amber?*
*I know I waited while you sketched a bridge*
*And saw above you in the golden sky*
*Black-headed gulls begin to wheel and cry*
*As fishing boats chugged in to anchorage.*
*These days I go to Walberswick alone,*
*Walk through the marshes like we did before,*
*Watch little children playing on the shore,*
*Then cut inland across the dunes and pick*
*Sea campion and a spray of feather'd grass*
*To put beside your portrait in a glass.*

Valley Farm, on the seaward side of The Bell inn, Walberswick, was the farm at which Philip Wilson Steer often lodged during his visits from 1884. From the 1960s when it was owned by Anthony Sampson, visiting artists ranged from Kitchen Sink School founder Derrick Greaves to Christopher Mason and Joanna Carrington.

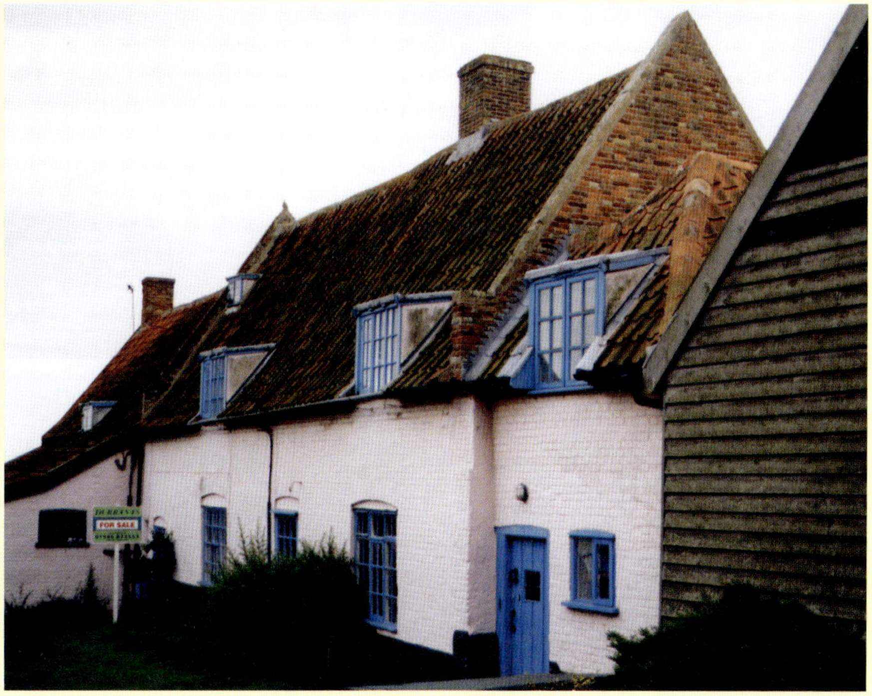

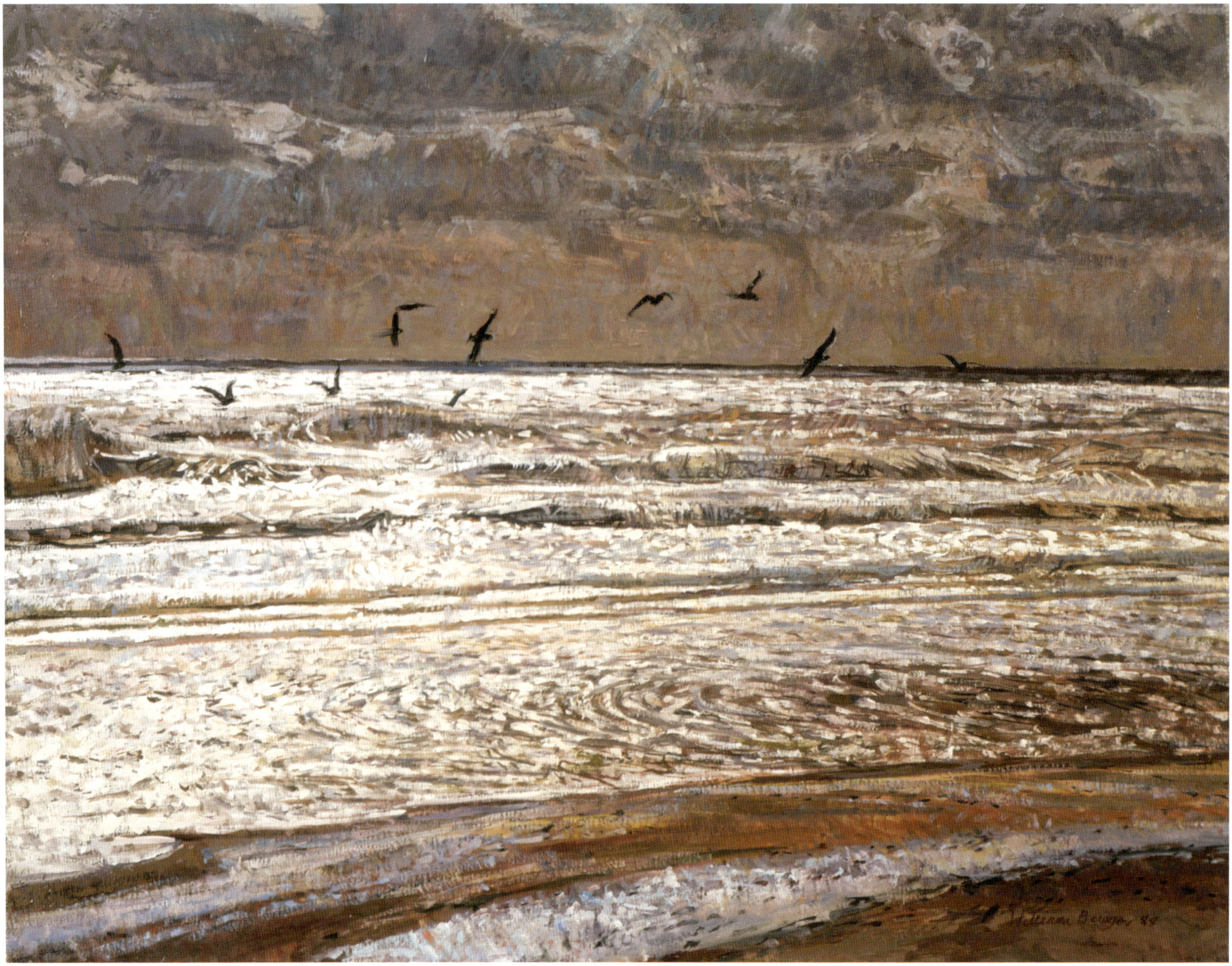

*Silver Sea, Walberswick*, William Bowyer, oil on canvas, 1988.

Chapter Eighteen

# First Resort

When Donald and Irene Horwood moved from Bloomsbury to Number One Blackshore in 1951 the couple had barely had time to fill their house with books and pictures when they, plus a passing fisherman, were marooned upstairs by the Great Flood. Once the sea retreated, a steady flow of creative visitors advanced.

Donald, a schoolmaster, was a close friend of the latterly Norfolk-based George Barker – and would eventually act as best man at his Sheringham wedding to Elspeth Langlands. The wild and wonderful man of poetry, who could be almost as lyrical in paint as in words but who would at times be banned from his local pub, often came to wander beside the Blyth. One of his best poems, *On a Friend's Escape from Drowning off the Norfolk Coast*, was inspired by a Horwood family trauma at Walberswick. Donald, in dire difficulties during a swim, had been rescued by Irene while their three small children played obliviously on the beach ('…*she drove through his drowning like Orpheus and tore/Back by the hair/Her escaping bridegroom. And on the sand their son/Stood laughing where/He was almost an orphan…*'). By a strange coincidence, one of Irene's best friends married **KIT BARKER** (1916-1988), brother of George, who became a painter of meditative seascapes despite an early accident in which the future poet blinded him in one eye while fencing. That, too, prompted heart-rending verses.

*Walberswick Strand*, Kit Barker, oil on canvas, 1967.

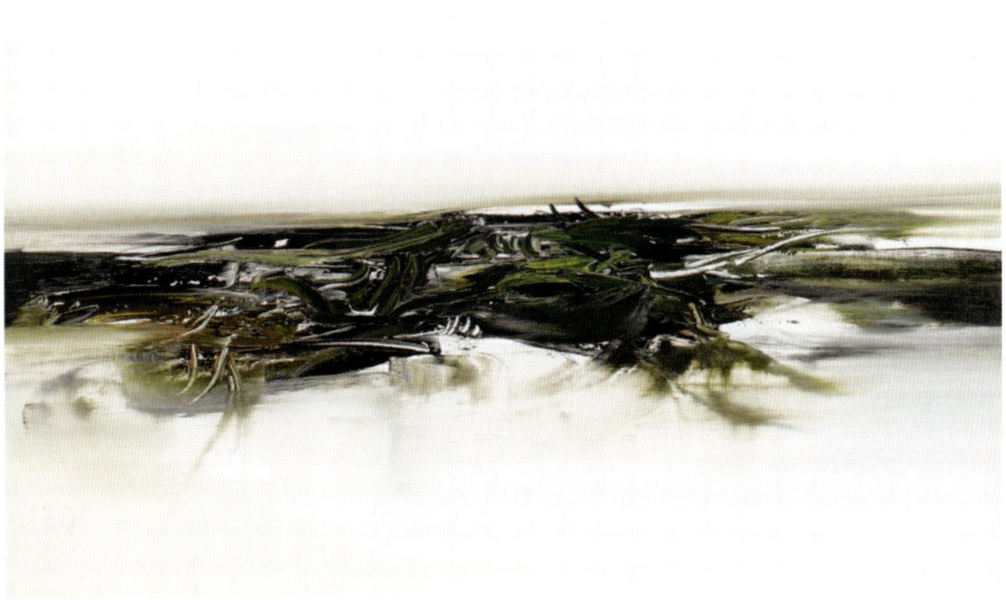

After their marriage, in 1954, two other great friends of the Horwoods – **OLIVE COOK** (1912-2002) and **EDWIN SMITH** (1912-1971) – spent a month or two each summer in the adjoining house on Blackshore. Both partners saw themselves primarily as artists, though London-raised Smith was 'an architect by training and a photographer by profession' and Cook a Cambridge born and educated academic who turned from typography to writing – also aiding the war-time evacuation of National Gallery treasures to Wales and contributing several watercolours to the Pilgrim Trust's Recording Britain scheme. They had met in Hampstead, where their circle had included Stanley Spencer and Hilda Carline.

Edwin Smith is best known for 40 volumes illustrated with only a small fraction of 60,0000 photographs in his career-long album, the best now bequeathed to the Royal Institute of British Architects. His majestic pictures – of ancient buildings, landscapes, gardens and decorative details across the British Isles, France and Italy, plus portraits of working people – were made all the more monumental for being rendered in stark black and white via a Victorian plate camera on a tripod (with the lensman's head covered in a cloth). His widow, whose books included studies of Suffolk, Cambridgeshire and Breckland, tirelessly promoted his talent. Between 1942 and the early 1970s both contributed to the *Saturday Book* – the annual for adults, an eccentric miscellany of people, places and things, proving an ideal vehicle for their eclectic interests.

In the *Saturday Book* of 1952 Cook and Smith collaborated on a *Beside the Seaside* celebration – the idiosyncratic illustrations including a ship's

This bronze sculpture – inscribed on the base 'Inspired by Margaret and Elizabeth swimming at Southwold' – was bought at a car boot sale. It's a far cry from the bust of General William Booth in Westminster Abbey, tiny copies of which were sold to the Salvation Army faithful in 1907 at a penny a time. But the artist in both cases was MARY BOOTH (1885-1969), grand-daughter of the founding Salvationist. She herself converted to the cause when aged five and standing beside her grandmother's coffin.

Mary was the second of the seven children of Bramwell Booth, who followed his father as head of the Christian charity in 1912. The Booths first visited Southwold in 1909 in the vain hope that fresh air might help their ailing daughter Miriam – her early death was to contrast with the longevity of Mary's remaining siblings whose spans ranged from 90 to 104.

In 1913 General Booth purchased a house called Crapstone (later The Turrets) in North Road, where he lived incognito under his wife's maiden name of Soper. It was rumoured that he feared assassination; he certainly prized privacy, walking on the beach and Common and avoiding the town centre. And in 1929 the local telephone switchboard was jammed, and Salvationists and journalists came flocking, as the now fatally-ill leader refused all pleas to retire from office.

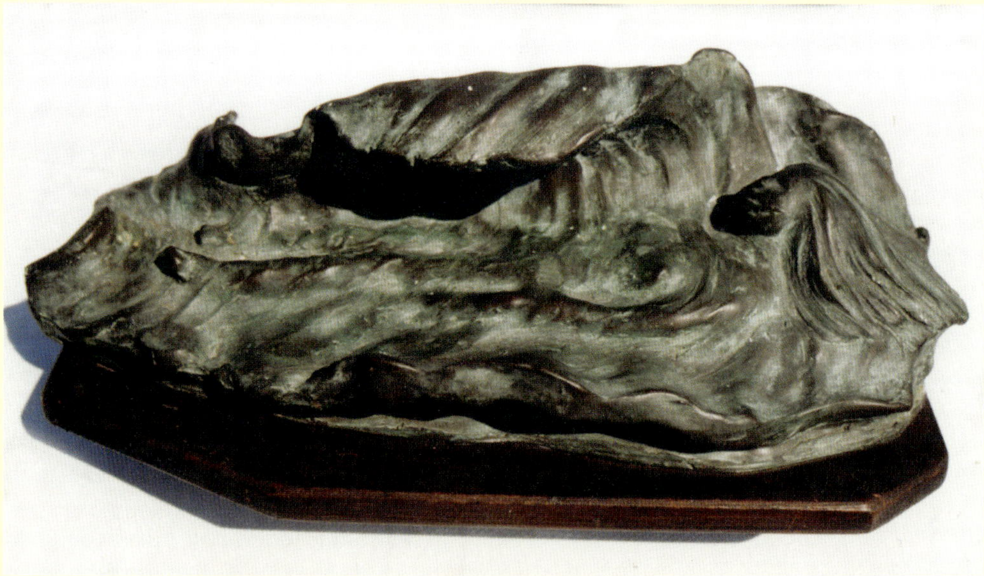

After working in France during the First World War, then in Germany, the West Indies and Denmark, Colonel Mary Booth continued to help refugees in Brussels when Belgium fell to the Nazis in 1940. Arrested as a spy, she expected to share the 1915 fate of Norfolk nurse Edith Cavell in front of a firing squad. But after 30 months in cells and camps she was released in a prisoner exchange. During her detention she made rag dolls for displaced infants.

figurehead and a bicycle in a Southwold yard. They credited Dr Richard Russell, a fashionable physician in Georgian London, with the creation of bracing resorts. 'He recommended a concoction of crabs' eyes, burnt sponge, vipers' flesh, cuttle-fish bones, snails, tar and a tincture of woodlice to be swallowed with a pint of seawater,' wrote Cook. 'But to complete the cure a dip in the sea itself was necessary.

'There was no joy in the dip,' she continued. 'Winter was considered to be the most beneficial time for the ceremony, for the pores of the skin had to be closed; and the bather could neither dodge nor postpone the horrid moment of immersion, for he was at the mercy of the dipper. That extraordinary and, happily, defunct official, usually fierce and female…stood fully clothed, up to her thighs in the sea, by the door of the bathing machine, from which the victim was thrust into her embrace and plunged into the waves.' Swigs of brine were prescribed, the author also noted, by a more hedonistic follower of Dr Russell who insisted they would 'enliven, invigorate and actuate the whole mass of the blood to a sweet, balsemick, spirituous and sanguinous temperament, which naturally incites men and women to amorous emotions and titillations'.

Summer bathing – if not amorous emotions and titillations – was being encouraged in Southwold by the early Victorian era when town chronicler Robert Wake issued his 1839 'hints' to sea-bathers in a commanding tone. Having described three bathing machines 'attended by strong and careful persons' and each consisting of a 'commodious wooden chamber', steps and canvas awning, he added: 'Best of all is a single act of immersion. This requires to be to all parts of the body at once, and made in deep water as safety and convenience may admit. Moreover the descent into the refreshing surface should be much more gentle than the generality of bold and ambitious bathers are wont to exercise. Meanwhile, the posture of the descending body should be much more horizontal than the rapidity and eagerness of the aquatic enterprizer will condescend to adopt.'

The guide continued: 'The time which is to be occupied is also of great importance. Bathers should know that such healthful action will not be promoted by a continuance in the bath one instant beyond the point where the thrill and glow of animal exhilaration should have begun to be experienced. And the process of drying and dressing should be dispatched as quickly as

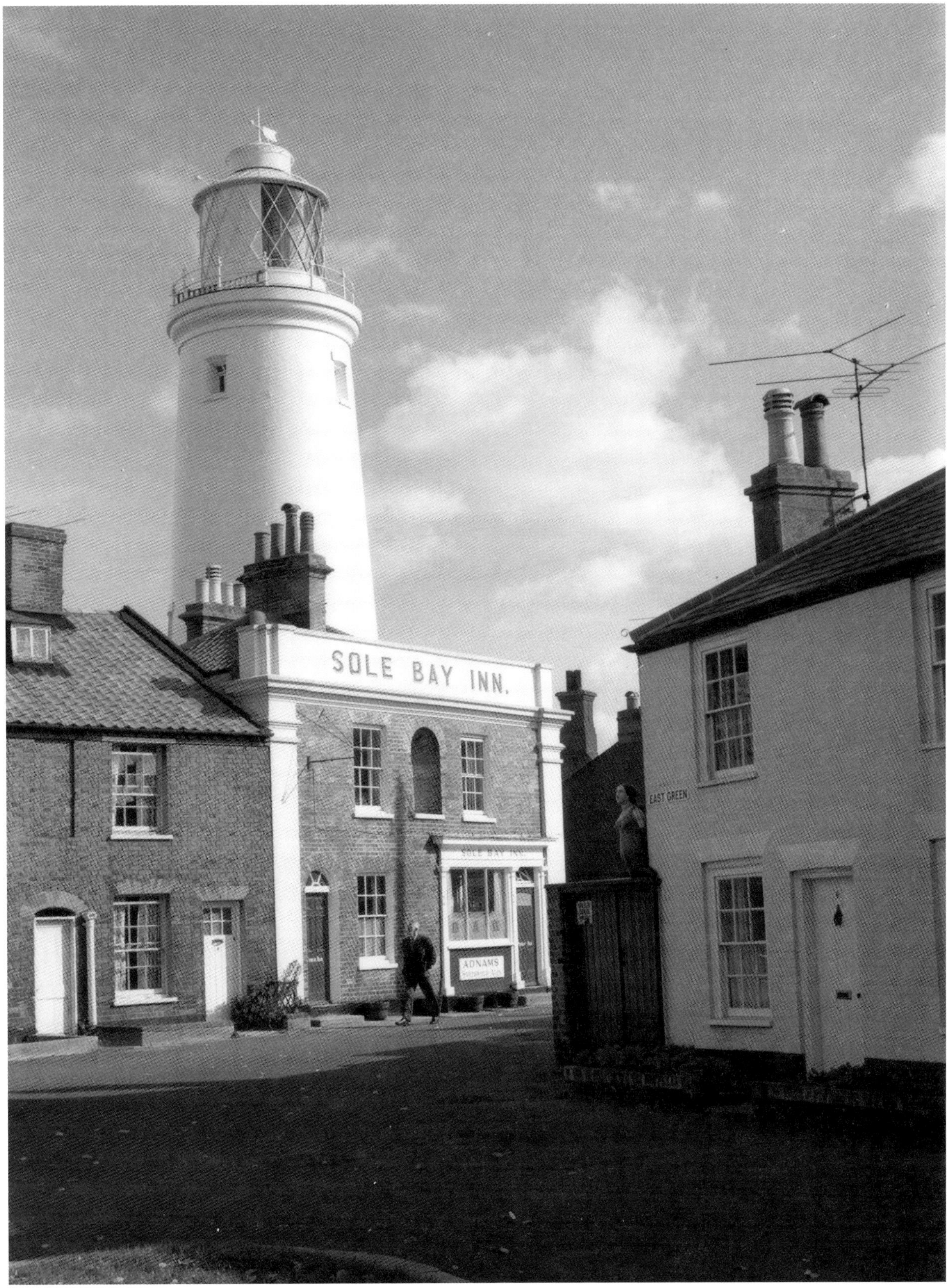


East Green, Edwin Smith, from Angus Wilson's *England*, 1971.

possible. If health is to be improved by the bath, let the bath be used simply with a view to health. Conducive to this, sea bathing may indeed become – if it is used in moderation. Too frequent use of it may be injurious to the health of the subject, as indiscreet intimacy is to friendship.' Puritanism died hard on the Suffolk coast.

By Edwardian times lines of wheeled bathing machines – licensed to local families such as the Mays, Smiths and Herringtons – punctuated the fleet of berthed boats on the beach and were drawn and painted by many visiting artists. Allan Gwynne-Jones would always remember being held in the water by a burly dipper during childhood holidays, after which he was given glasses of milk to drink which were two-thirds cream. Even now some bathing machines survive as converted beach huts – original names like Klondike and Yukon lingering amid a more recent row of cosy, witty and romantic titles (Watershed, Chatterbox, The Dog House). The salty medicine came to be sweetened with all manner of seaside amusements and entertainments – the promenade in 1900s Southwold hosting Punch and Judy shows, the beach a camera obscura hut (a prism in the roof reflecting a panoramic view of the coastline on to a table in the darkened interior) and rides in goat-drawn wicker chaises being offered on the edge of the Common. But prudery remained a bulwark against rudery. When, in 1906, a Mr Crabbe was seen leaving the Centre Cliff Hotel in a bathing costume – and in the company of a lady – the price of the ensuing swim was a ten-shilling (50p) fine for infringing a local bylaw. On being apprehended by an Inspector Ruffles, he said: 'Give my compliments to the

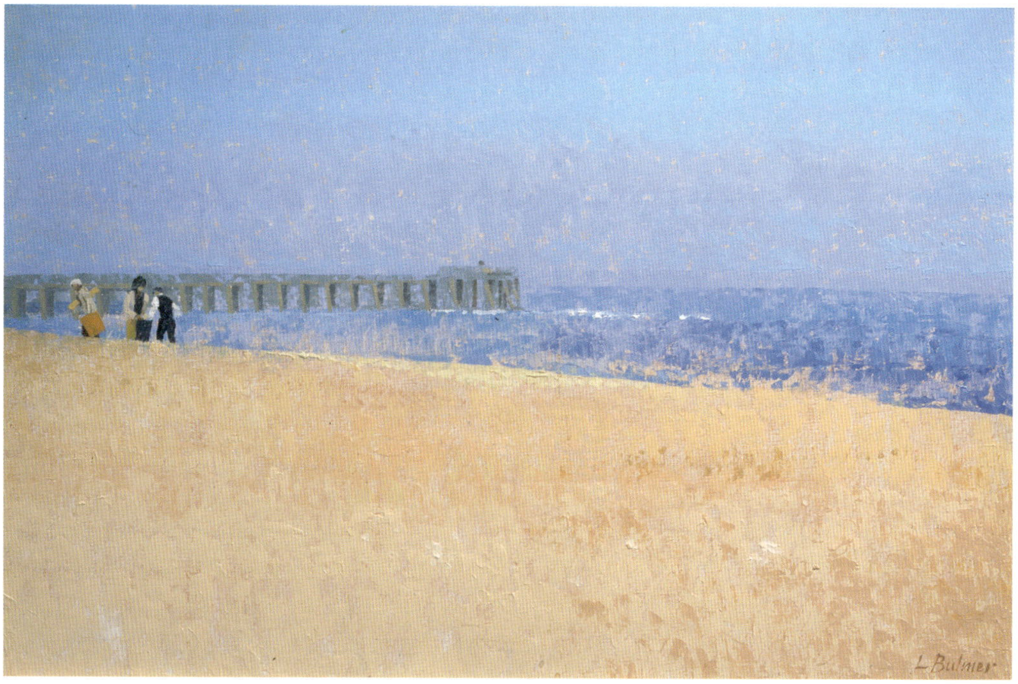

*Figures on the Beach, Southwold,* Lionel Bulmer, oil on board.

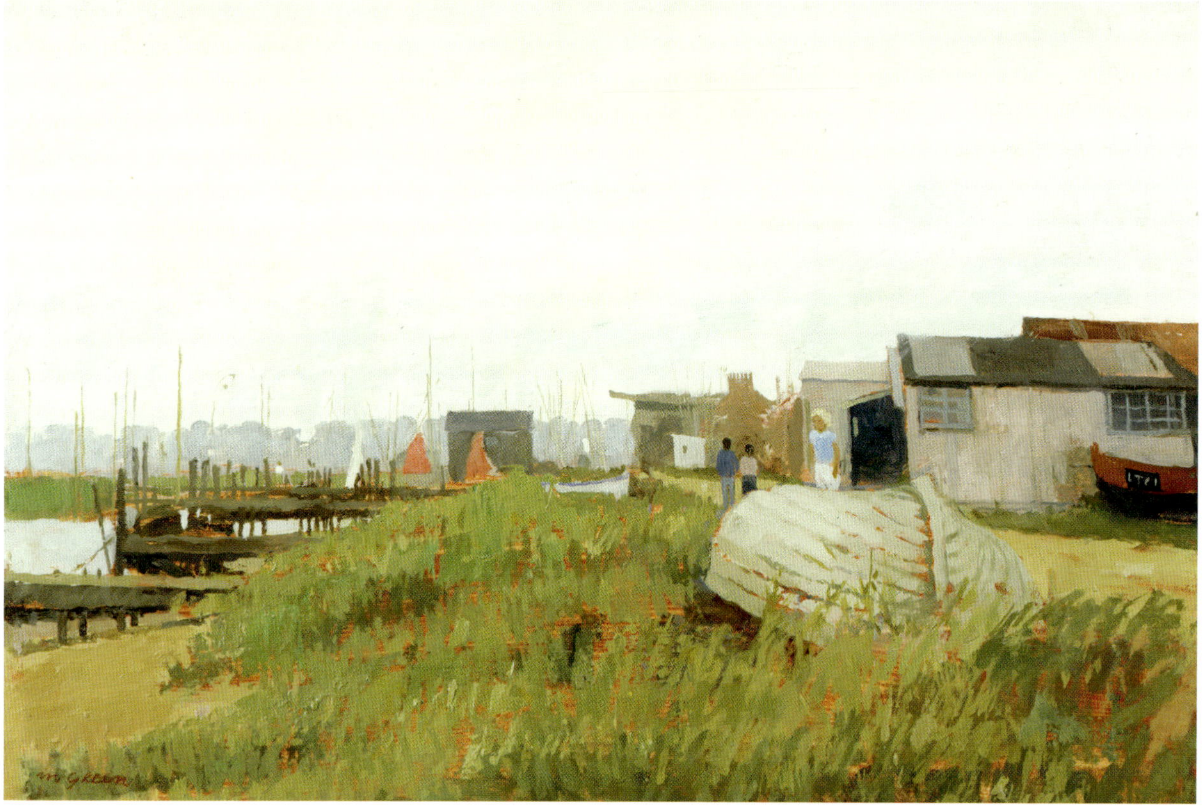

*Southwold Harbour,* Margaret Green, oil.

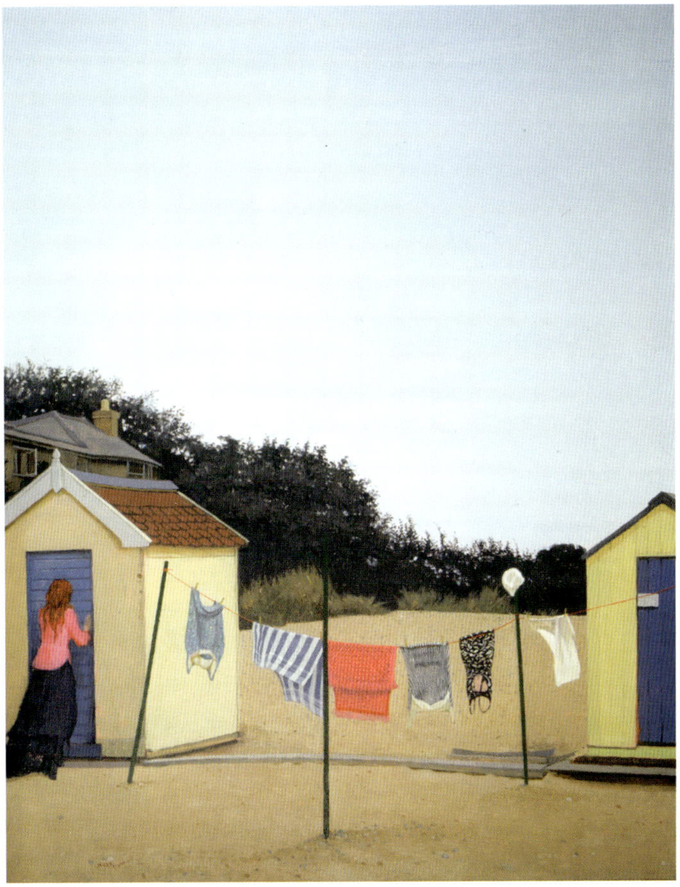

*Beach Huts below Gun Hill*, Margaret Green, oil.

Mayor and tell him to go to Hell and to take his Corporation and bylaws with him.' Another shocking crime wave in Southwold.

Olive Cook and Edwin Smith – who had stayed latterly in Iona on Constitution Hill and Little White Lodge on Gun Hill – loved all this hilarious history, and after Smith's untimely death his widow seriously considered moving to Southwold. In the end she remained in their home in Saffron Walden, while still paying visits to the place that had been loved so dearly in two dove-tailed lives.

Yet more friends of the Horwoods were **LIONEL BULMER** (1919-1992) and **MARGARET GREEN** (1925-2003) whose paintings of Southwold over 35 years from the 1950s defined the dazzling pleasures of modern summers in what many came to regard as one of England's first resorts. Bulmer and Green – son of a London architect and daughter of a stock-taker in a West Hartlepool steel plant who was also a keen amateur artist – had learned to look from an early age. Their paths coincided at the Royal College of Art during its war-time relocation to the Lake District, and in the landscape of Wordsworth a scholarship student and a former

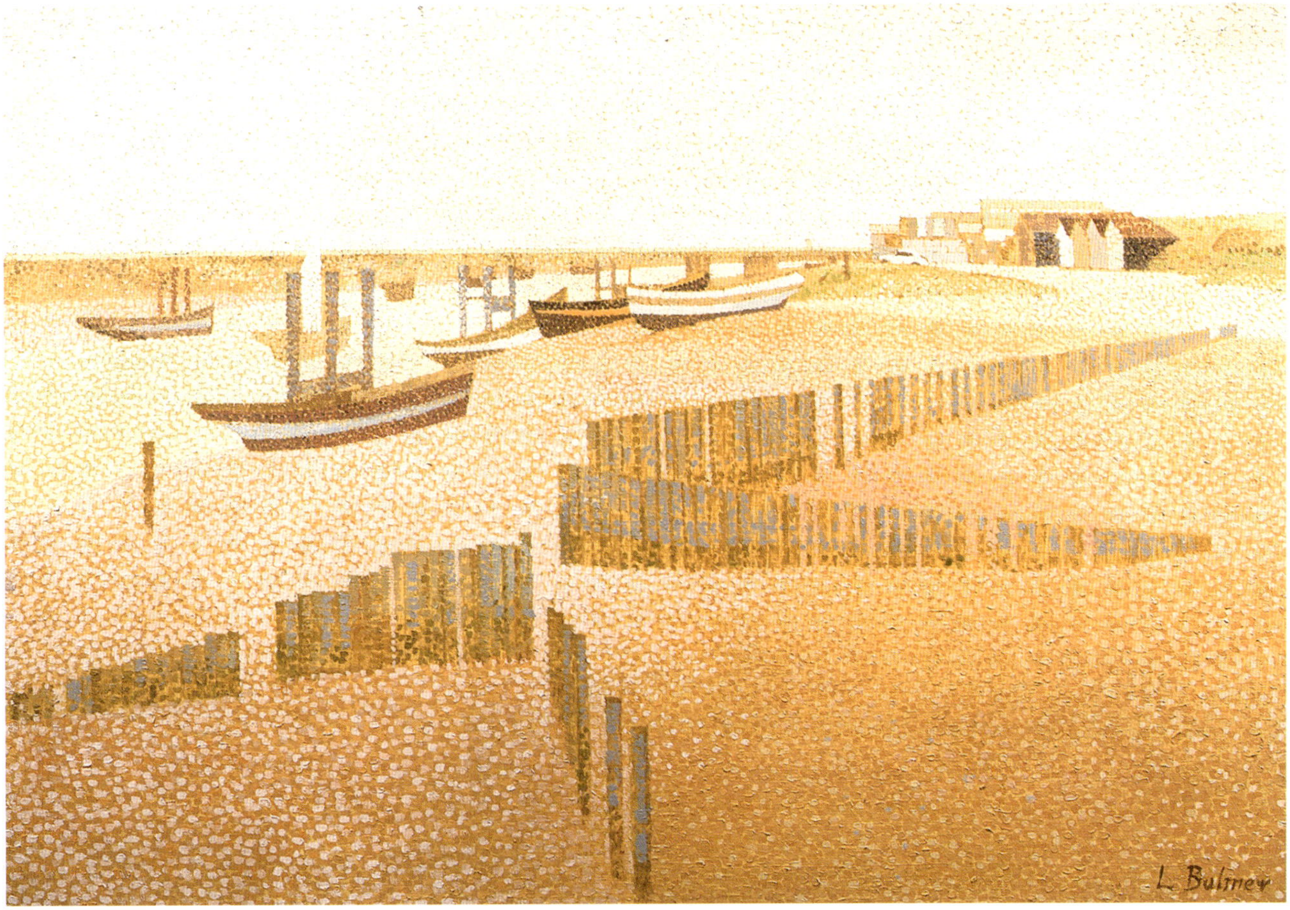


*Low-tide at Southwold Harbour*, Lionel Bulmer, oil.

soldier found they were soulmates. They shared a Chelsea studio while teaching at various art colleges, but yearned for a rural base close the sea. At first they paid prolonged visits to the South Coast – but settled on Southwold and Walberswick as a sketching ground after buying a dilapidated medieval hall house in its own wilderness near Stowmarket. Adding a light-filled studio to the restored dwellings, and creating a magical garden, they worked here on beach and harbour images plotted in notes and sketches over successive summers beside the Blyth.

A visitor in those years could scarcely have failed to spot them. Margaret liked a vantage point with her back against a breakwater or harbour wall, so that no onlooker could peer over her shoulder; Lionel preferred to build himself a barricade of windbreaks and deckchairs like a castle in the sand. Often, however, they were driven to risk public exposure by their desire to work side by side as they would at home, hunching their shoulders and closing ranks against the world around them. When their pictures were becoming indistinguishable, even to themselves, the partners agreed that Bulmer should break away and explore the pointillism of Seurat in a palette progressing from warm to hot. A combination of searing pinks, blues, emerald and lilac came to catch the essence of high summer at the seaside. Green's edgier pictures continued to suggest the brevity of August holidays in which brilliant sunshine could also mean a short interval between showers.

It was all the more appropriate that Bulmer and Green should have focused on Southwold and

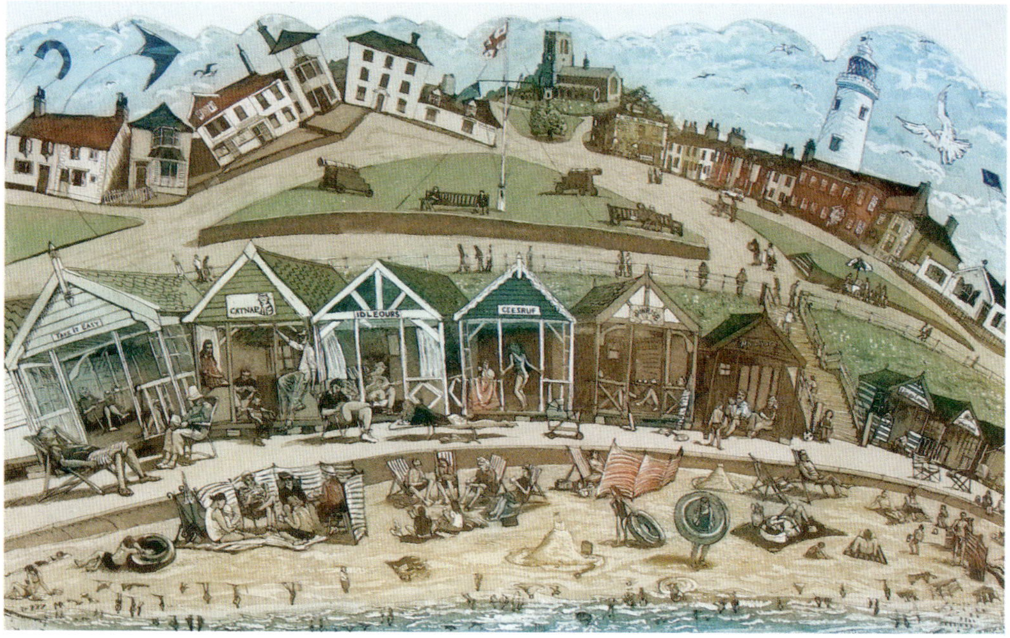

Cambridge-based print-maker GLYNN THOMAS (b1946) often trawls the Suffolk coast for inspiration – creating a series of distorted depictions which amiably caricature the essence of Southwold's holiday atmosphere.

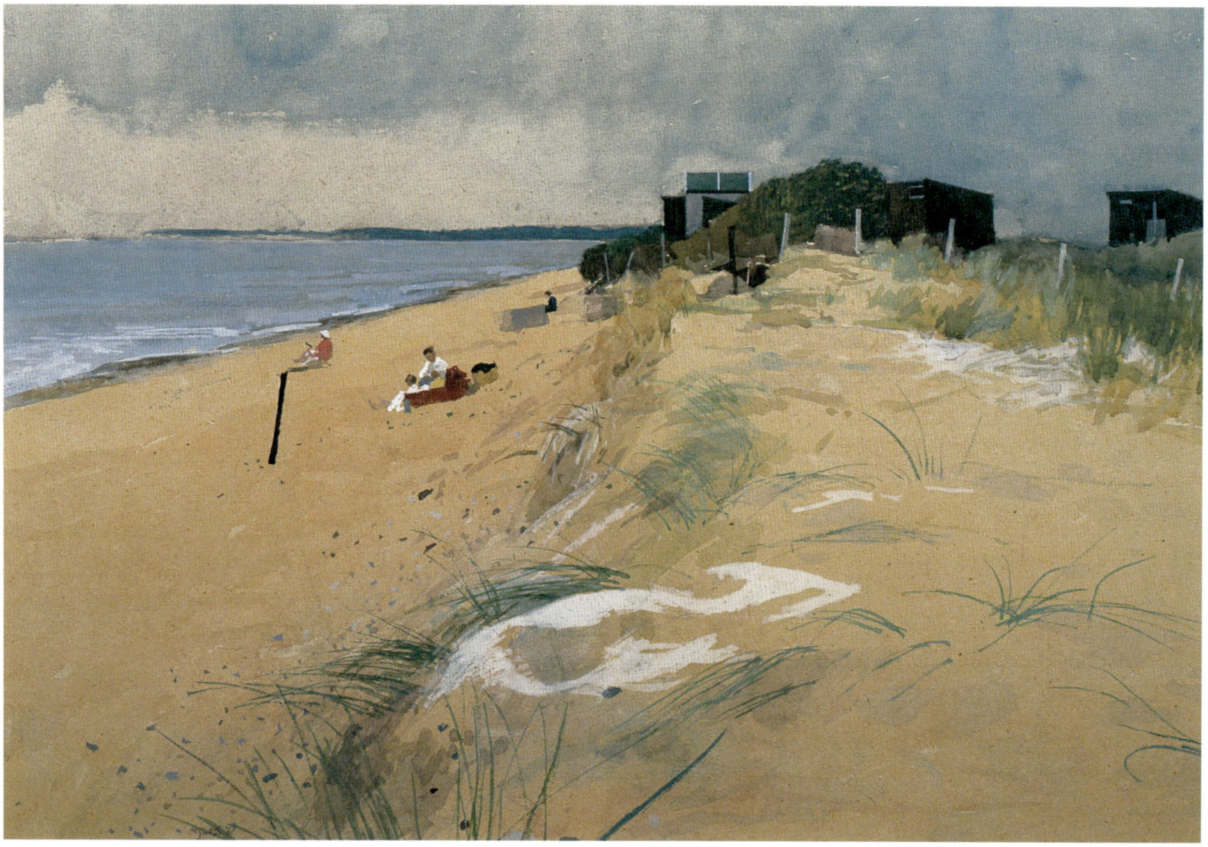

*Approaching Rain, Walberswick,* Alfred Heyworth, watercolour.

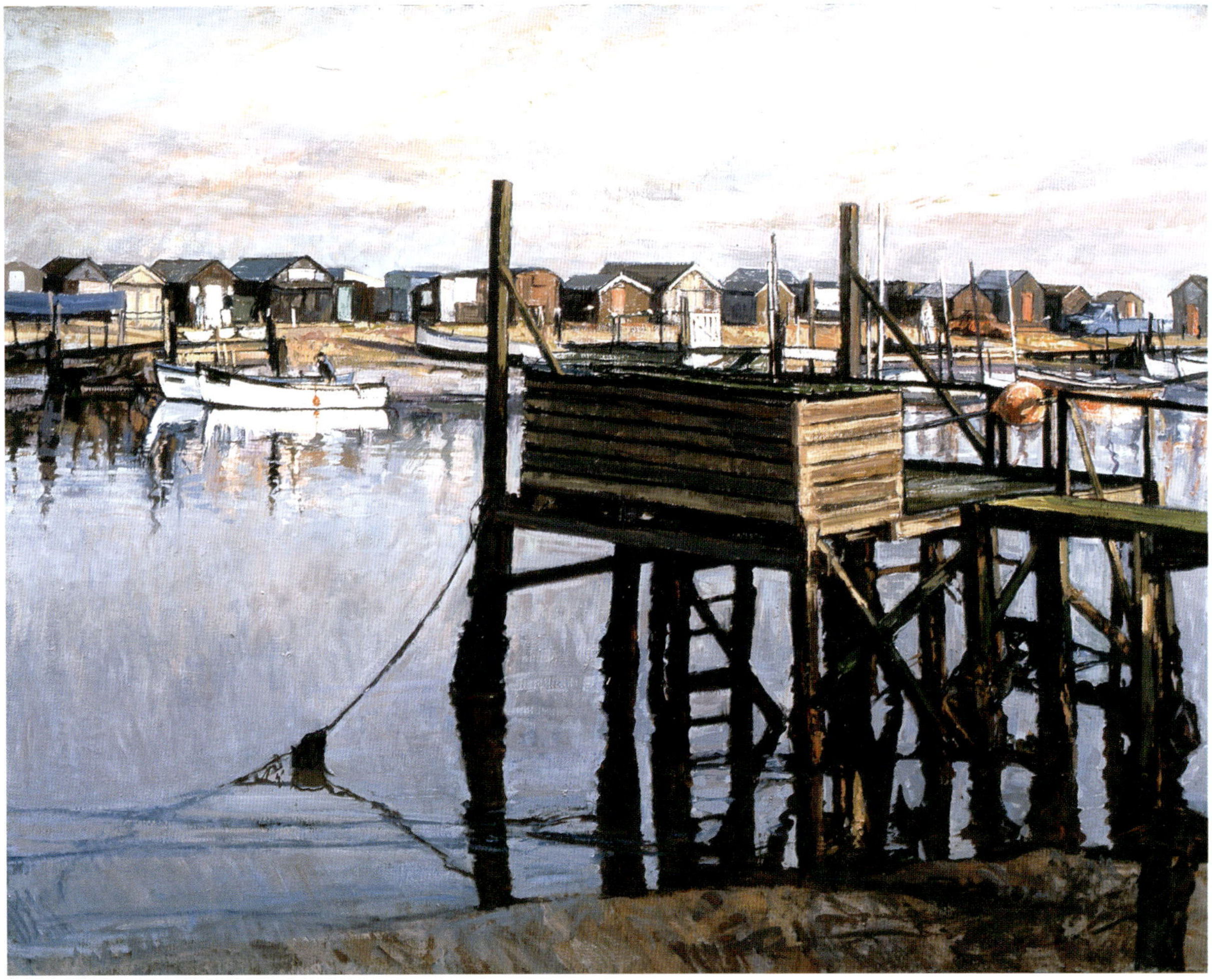

*Across the Harbour to Southwold*, William Bowyer, oil on canvas.

*Southwold Sports*, graphic design by Clifford Russell, c1950.

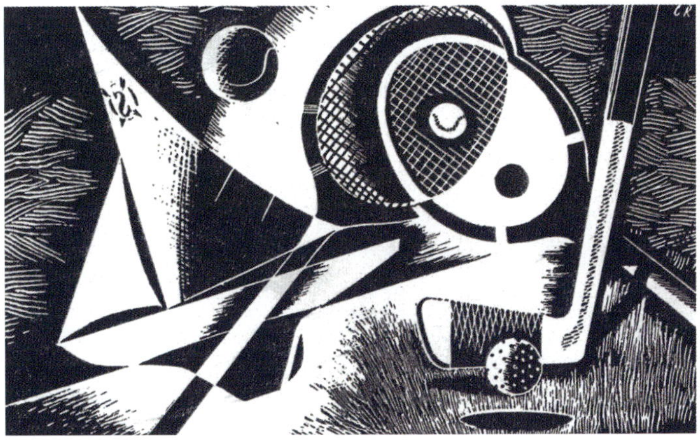

Walberswick because they were leading lights in the New English Art Club whose founding spirit had been established here by Philip Wilson Steer and his associates. (Indeed, Steer's painting *Knucklebones* which is on display in Christchurch Mansion, Ipswich, may have spurred the Bulmer shift to pointillism.) They also found themselves in kindred company, with the East Anglian chapter of the NEAC including their friends Margaret Thomas, Fred Dubery and – most significantly of all for this study – William Bowyer.

Long a recorder of Thames-side West London, **WILLIAM BOWYER** (b1926) arrived in Walberswick almost by accident when, in 1958, an artist friend called **ALFRED HEYWORTH** (1926-1976) said he knew a marvellous place to paint and promptly drove him there. Pitching two bivouac tents behind the dunes, they found so many subjects to depict each day that they were too tired to throw a pub dart in the evening. After that Bill and Vera Bowyer and their three children spent part of each summer on the Suffolk coast, painting, fishing and playing cricket, camping or staying in a caravan. In 1993 the artist bought a house in Walberswick and had a studio built in the garden, henceforward spending half the year beside the North Sea and the remainder in Chiswick.

Staffordshire-born Bill Bowyer attended evening classes at Burslem School of Art while a Bevin Boy conscript in a nearby coalmine, before escaping to London's Royal College of Art. Tutors Carel Weight and Ruskin Spear became his close friends and mentors, and he in turn taught Peter

Blake at Gravesend School of Art (both would be elected Royal Academicians on the same day). A noted portraitist – with likenesses of miners' leader Arthur Scargill and cricketer Viv Richards in the National Portrait Gallery – his warm affinity with other people helped him to lead the New English Art Club for 30 years and to paint blithely amid crowds of spectators on Southwold beach. In one amusing picture he even painted a trio of gawping onlookers on Centre Cliff. In other ways he had the scene to himself, for Fred Heyworth died prematurely and Bowyer never once met his friends Lionel Bulmer and Margaret Green in their shared coastal haunts. Despite claims from other chums that he has depicted all of Walberswick and much of Southwold down the decades, his sons Francis (b1952) and Jason (b1957) – both now leading lights in the New English Art Club – have found fresh angles in recent years.

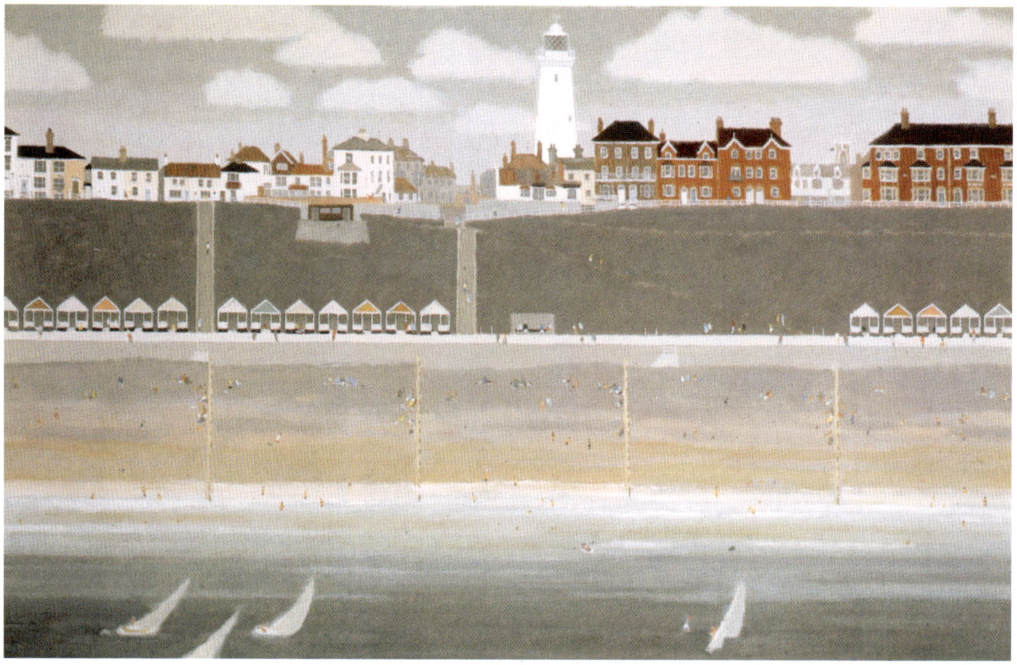

*Southwold*, Ronald Rutherford, watercolour (above).

*Lighthouse II*, Brian Lewis, polymer on gesso (below).

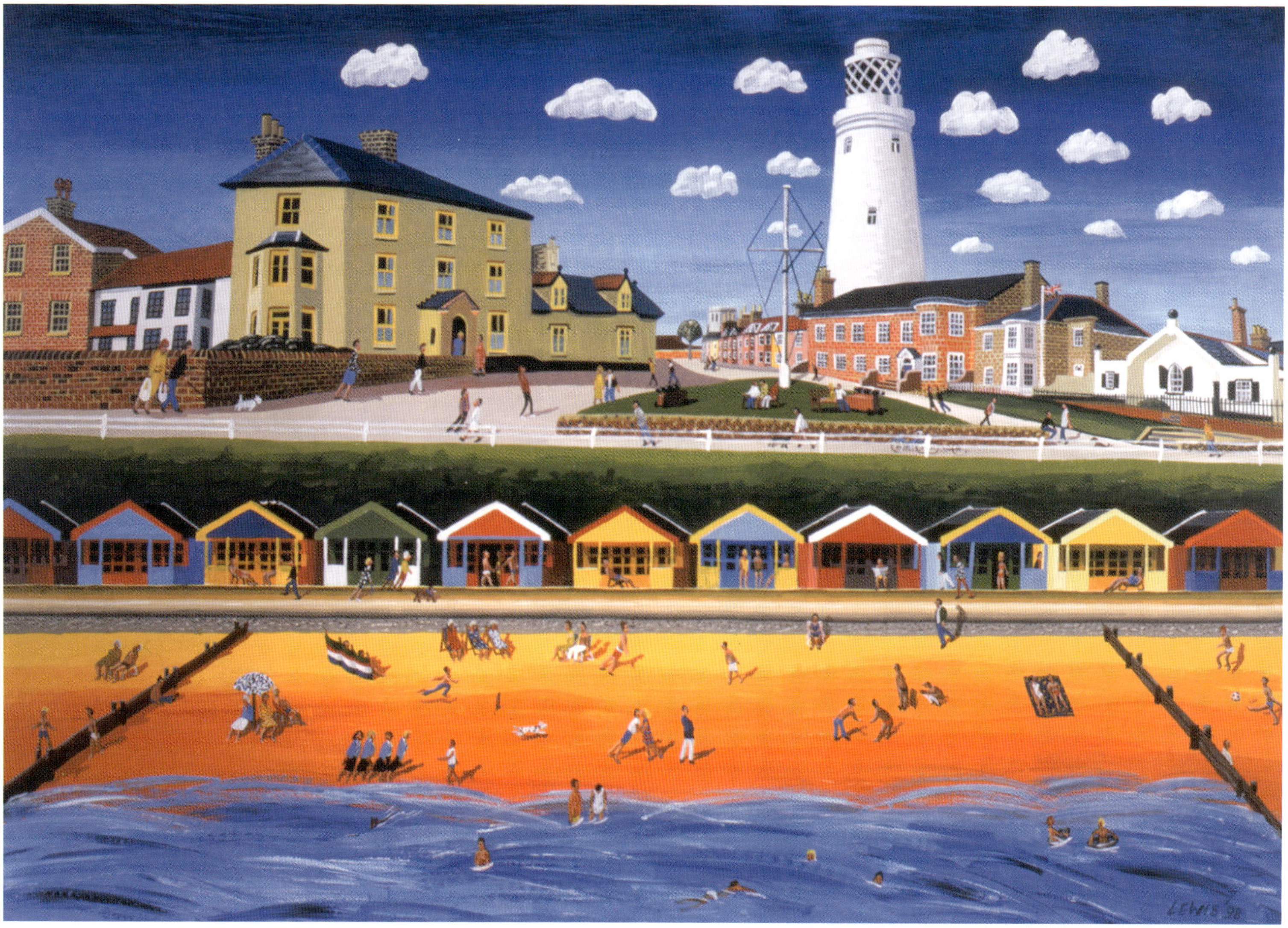

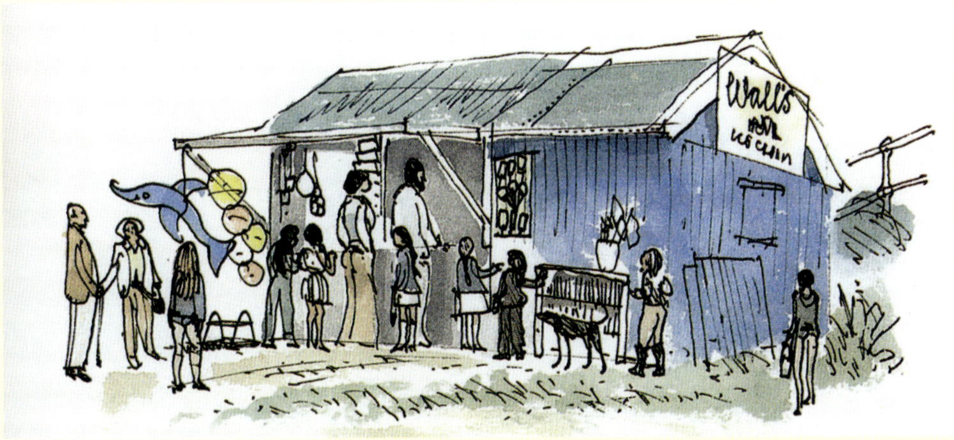


DAVID GENTLEMAN (b1930), *Gun Hill Tea Hut*, watercolour drawing from *David Gentleman's Britain*, 1982. This much-travelled painter, print-maker, and postage stamp designer whose many illustrated works include George Ewart Evans's oral history books on Suffolk, has long had a base at Huntingfield near Halesworth.

At the age of 18 **RONALD RUTHERFORD** (b1913) went to Estonia, where he spent time in the studio of a Russian artist and studied icon painting. Later he trained at the Architectural Association in London and practised as an architect in England and Rhodesia. Retiring in 1973 to concentrate on art, for the next 15 years he lived in Southwold. His study of the town from the sea was conceived in the imagination and executed with the help of individual drawings of each of the featured houses on North Parade.

Around the year 2000 **BRIAN LEWIS** (b1947) chose a similar vantage point for working visits to Southwold in search of typically quirky images. The Surrey-raised painter had been lucky enough to attend one of only two secondary schools in the country to run an arts stream (another pupil was future rock star Eric Clapton). He then trained at Epsom, Guildford, Croydon and the Royal Academy art schools in a marathon apprenticeship which only really ended with a chance discovery of the North Norfolk coast in 1980. The artist has been based there ever since, focusing fully on deceptively innocent paintings which take a wry and sly look at humanity at play – with an ironic (comic, sardonic) sheen exuding from the medium of polymer on gesso board, frequently translated into glossy prints. While Brian Lewis has long looked like an East Anglian painter, his adopted patch is now starting to look like a Brian Lewis. As with Beryl Cook's Plymouth and L.S. Lowry's Salford, coastal outposts such as Cley, Blakeney and Wells-next-the-Sea, and seaside resorts as far south as Lowestoft and Southwold, can be viewed in the sharp new light of idiosyncratic paint.

Possibly the only professional artist to graduate from the Coldstream Guards, HUGO GRENVILLE (b1958) is the second painter of note to be based in the Waveney Valley village of Mendham, birthplace of Sir Alfred Munnings. Descended on his mother's side from Samuel Morton Peto, developer of Victorian Lowestoft, Grenville often paints on the Suffolk coast in a career drawing inspiration from Cuba to Venice. His work is concerned with the fall of light and the feel of colour – and frequently focuses on Southwold. Running art courses from his home, he sometimes brings students to paint on the beach or beside the harbour. This 1999 oil on canvas is called *Gun Hill Tea Hut*.

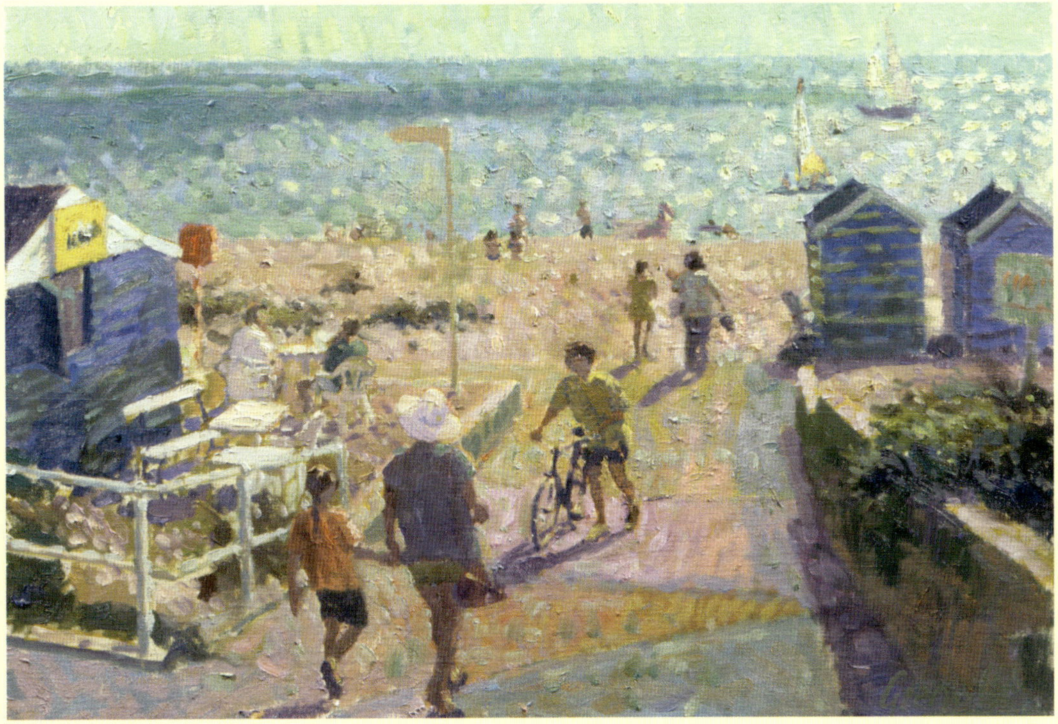

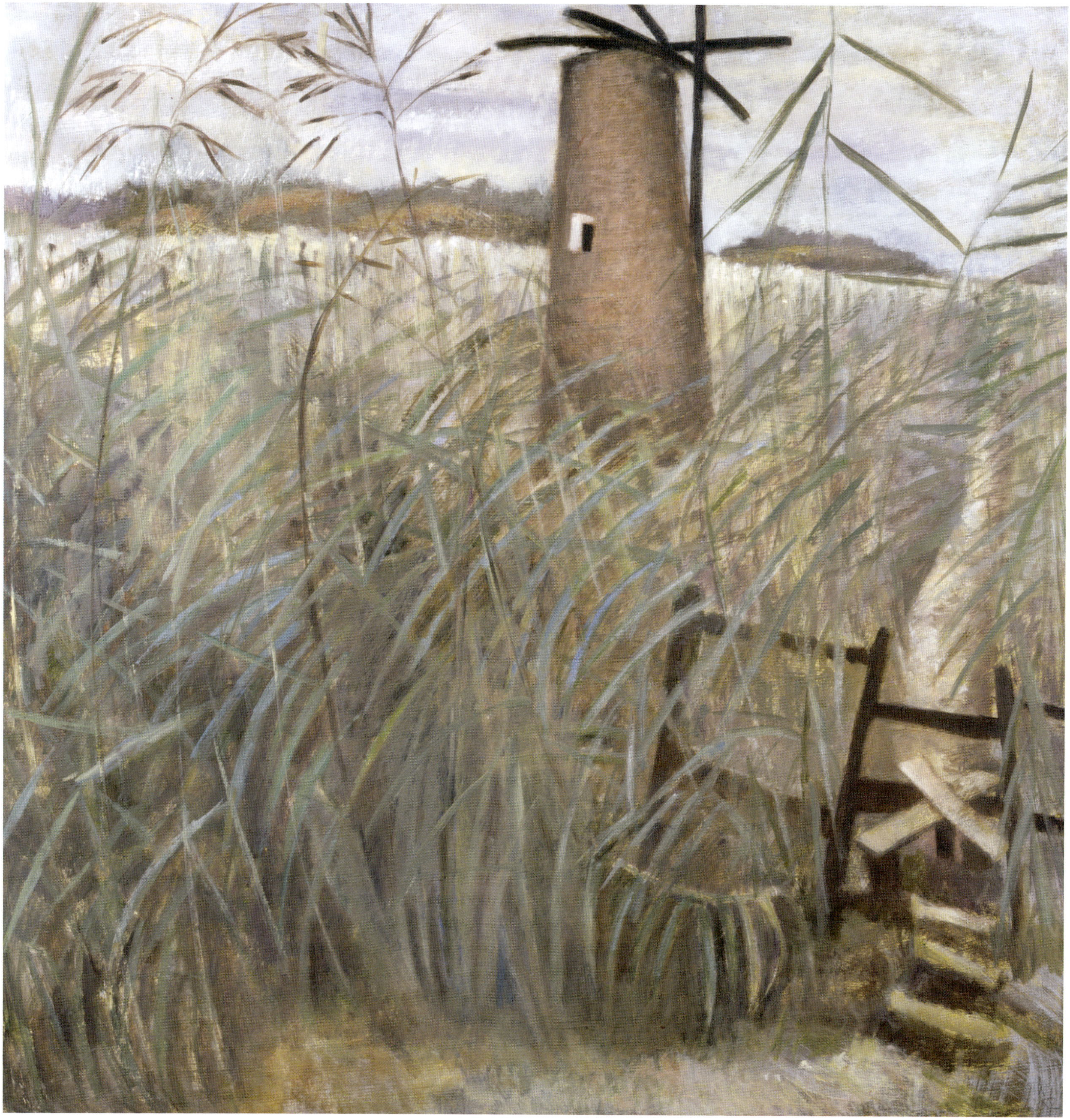

*The Walk at Dingle,* Tessa Newcomb, oil on board, 2002.

Chapter Nineteen

# Wildlife Refuge

Southwold is an island edged by the North Sea, the River Blyth and Buss Creek and tied to Suffolk, as writer and former mayor John Miller puts it, only by a bridge. Within this miniature world the Common has been protected since a 1509 bequest from William Godell and the entire town is now a conservation area. Cross the bridge and you soon enter a patchwork of nature reserves carefully managed by English Nature, the National Trust, Suffolk Wildlife Trust and the Royal Society for the Protection of Birds and extending for miles in all directions. Part of the Suffolk Heritage Coast, the territory of this book, from Kessingland to Dunwich, includes some of the most varied scenery in Britain – sandy beach and shingle bank, dune and cliff, river and estuary, lake and lagoon, mudflat, reedbed, marsh, grassland, heath, field, wood and forest. Wildlife abounds and so do wildlife artists.

In this elemental domain, the boundary between land and sea is constantly shifting and the sea would have made greater gains had it not been for writer, public servant and agricultural reformer Sir Henry Rider Haggard. The Norfolk-born author of some 60 novels, including *She* and *King Solomon's Mines*, latterly settled on his wife's family estate at Ditchingham near Bungay but in 1895 he bought two rows of linked coastguards' cottages on the edge of the cliff at Kessingland as a seaside retreat. In a fleet of bedrooms named after British admirals his extended family could be easily accommodated –

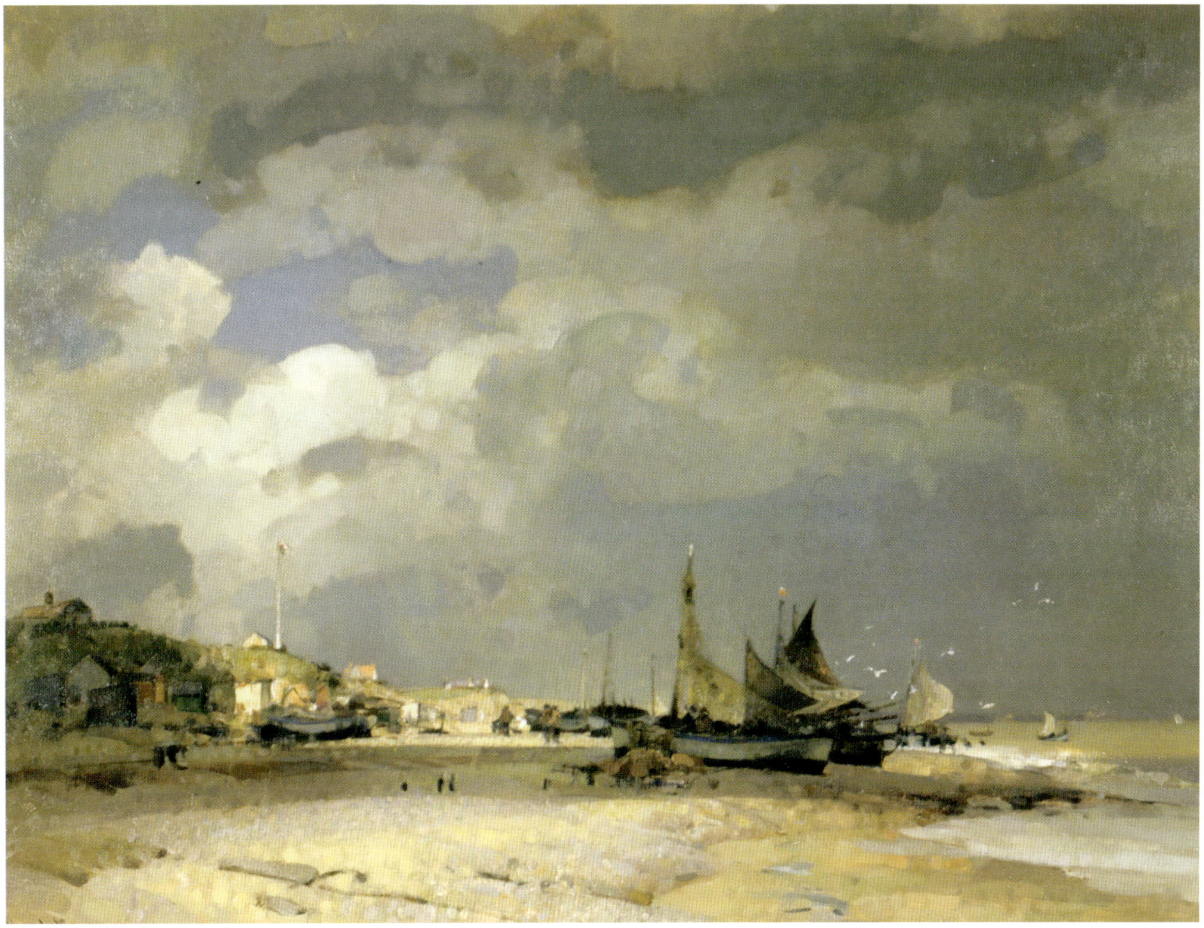

*Kessingland Beach*, Sir John Alfred Arnesby Brown, oil on canvas.

as could visiting friends such as Rudyard Kipling and artist Maurice Greiffenhagen (1862-1931), whose stirring illustrations to Rider Haggard's stories decorated the walls alonside Landseer paintings, sacred pictures and samplers, Kings of England prints, Zulu assegais and other African trophies. This noted portrait painter would also capture the swashbuckling author's care-worn likeness in 1920, which the subject felt should be properly titled 'Wrinkles'. Perhaps, five years before his death, he was exhausted by travels for the Royal Commission on Coastal Erosion, to

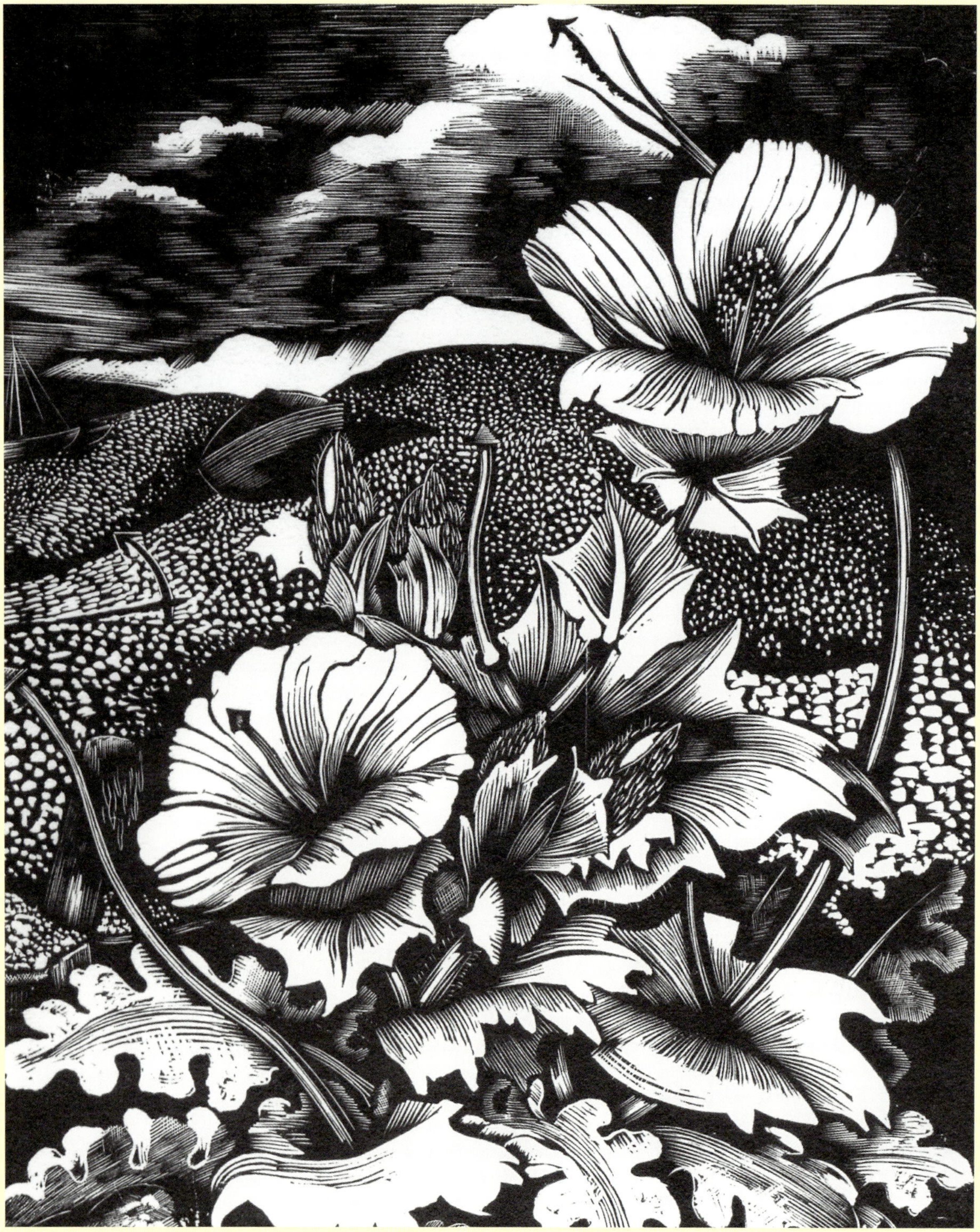

Painter-plantsman JOHN NASH (1896-1977), raised in Buckinghamshire and based for his latter decades on the Suffolk-Essex border, knew the East Anglian coast from early visits to the artist Claughton Pellew in north Norfolk. Soon after the war he spent a working holiday in Dunwich with Edward Bawden, and was often to be found sketching plants and places hereabouts. An emblematic *Sea Pea* pen drawing appeared on the cover of the 1956 Aldeburgh Festival Programme Book. This rich wood engraving *Horned Poppy*, with its hint of Suffolk coastline, featured in the celebrated 1927 volume *Poisonous Plants: Deadly, Dangerous and Suspect.*

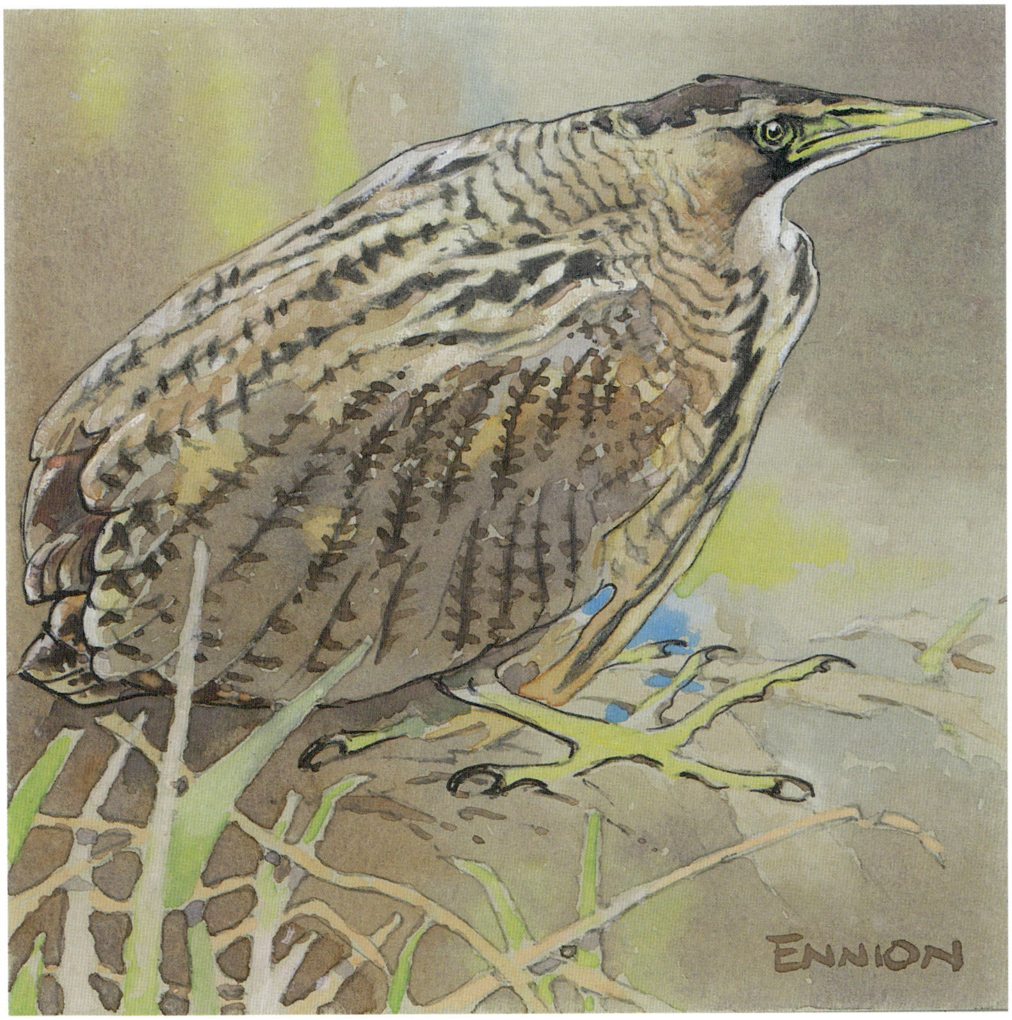


*Bittern* (above) and *Bearded Tits* (right), Eric Ennion, watercolours.

which he had been co-opted by Lloyd George after relating the succcess of experimental marram grass plantings at Kessingland. Rider Haggard's cliff-top eyrie, wrecked after requisitioning by the army during the First World War, was swept away by a tide of development after his death. Bought by a speculative builder, it was levelled for a holiday camp.

Now that the antlion has been saved from extinction on Dunwich heath, and ospreys have been seen hooking fish in their talons in the Hen Reedbeds before wintering in Africa, the Southwold area is reaffirmed as a place of wild adventure. True, the weight of bird numbers noted by Daniel Defoe during his *Tour Through the Eastern Counties* in 1724 has vanished into history. He saw 'near a million' swallows covering the roof of Southwold church and surrounding houses before migration to a mystery destination. Writing 115 years later, town historian Robert Wake said that local people had previously believed swallows to over-winter in hollow trees, or else immersed in lakes and ponds, but that modern ornithologists now deemed this impossible. Lost, too, are local dialect names for many animals which lingered into the 20th century – among them Southwold crow (gull), draw-water (kingfisher), ranny (shrew), pot-ladle (tadpole), jacob (toad), lobster (polecat), mouse-hunt (weasel), shuffle-wing (hedgesparrow) and harnsey (heron). But the Walberswick reedbeds are now the largest in England. And the cast of exotic and balletic birds to be glimpsed close to the shoreline is no longer composed entirely of small companies of avocets, whose nests are anyway almost commonplace these days. For the coastline north and south of Southwold now also plays host to visiting spoonbills, egrets and cranes.

**ERIC ENNION** (1900-1981) followed his father as a doctor in the Cambridgeshire fens until deciding to making a profession of twin passions for nature and art. He went on to produce deft watercolour drawings to illustrate ten of his own books and a similar number by other authors – many of them Shell titles. For five years from 1945 he and his wife Dorothy led courses in wildlife art and natural history at the Flatford Mill Field Study Centre on the Suffolk-Essex border. Then they set up a similar centre on the Northumberland coast before 'retiring' with their books and binoculars to Wiltshire. To the end the artist most loved birds of 'the reeds, the rocks and mud' which he followed from winter quarters on the Suffolk coast to breeding grounds around Icelandic lakes and Texel polders and in the bogs

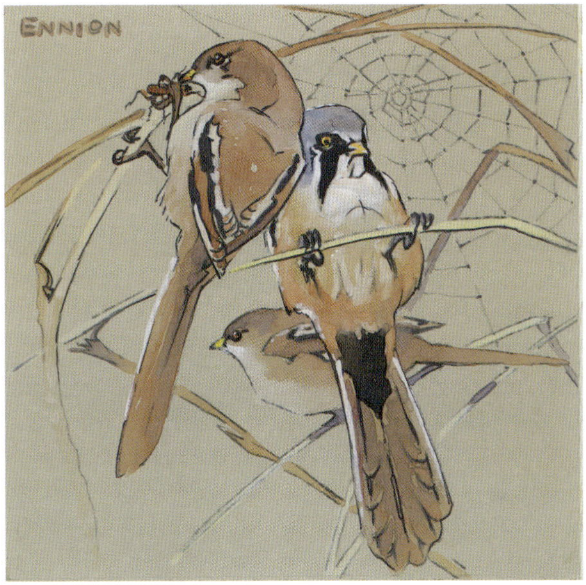

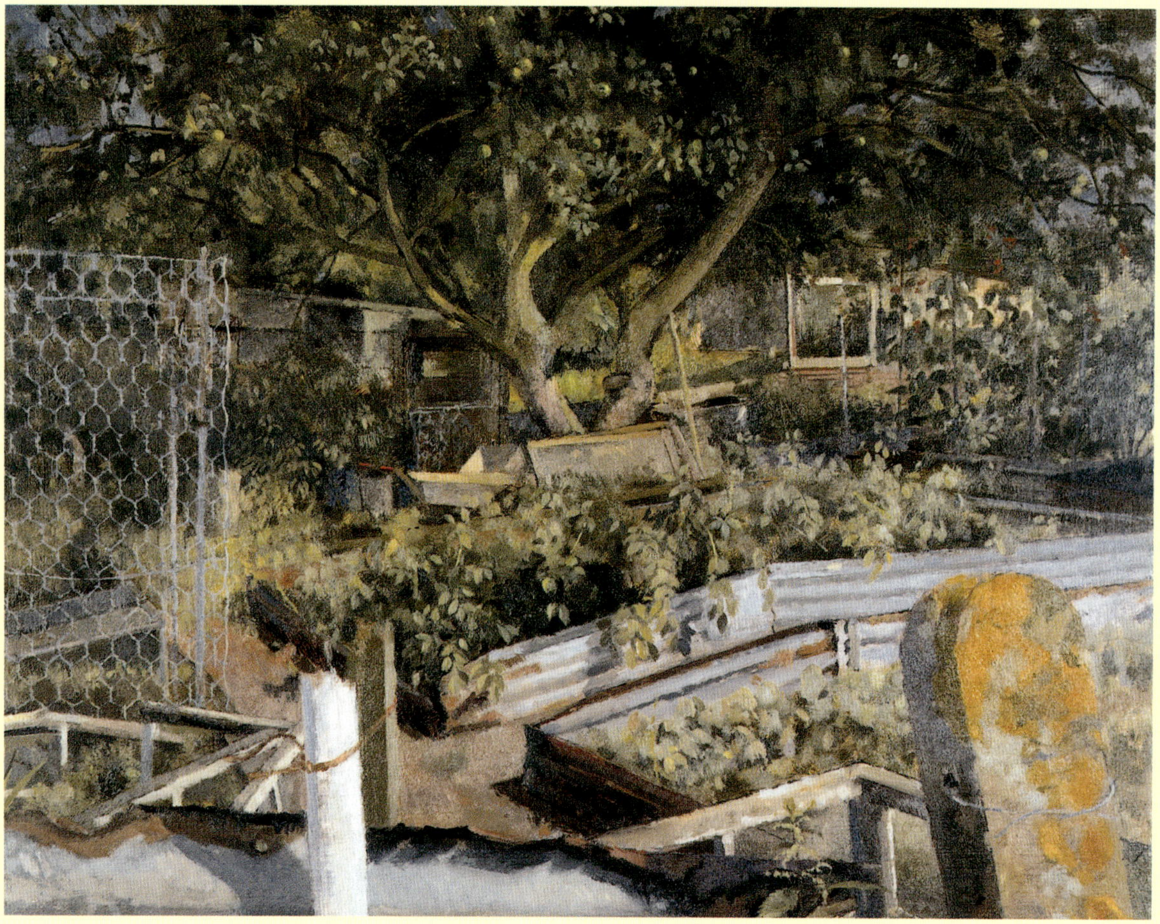

JOHN MORLEY (b1942) was raised partly on an estate in Kent, where his grandfather was a gardener, and he himself has created a noted snowdrop nursery within a garden of rare plants near Beccles. A love of order and structure pervades both his plantings and his paintings of still-life studies, domestic landscapes and flower pieces seen annually at Royal Academy summer shows from 1964. But the Southwold-visiting artist clearly relished a change of scene in the jumble of tin, wire and concrete dividing the allotments beside the Common. He has also depicted the wide sea views from the Gun Hill beach hut used by Lionel Bulmer and Margaret Green.

and forests of Arctic Lapland. Cley-based Robert Gillmor – with whom Dr Ennion founded the Society of Wildlife Artists in 1964 – said: 'He imbued his birds with life and vitality, the product of intense, intelligent observation...His work seemed odd to those more concerned with identification than in the sheer joy of watching birds and wondering at their uniqueness.'

Perhaps Dr Ennion's greatest claim to fame was as mentor to **MARY NEWCOMB** (b1922). The then Mary Slatford attended a week-long course at Flatford Mill in 1946, returning as a student helper in successive holidays. She stayed in Willy Lott's Cottage in a room with a view over the millpool – a scene straight from a Constable painting. 'Eric was a major influence for me,' she said, 'because although his courses were very informal they taught me the importance of acute observation, with lots of note-taking and sketching on the spot. Also, no one could ever be bothered to look at my drawings before, but he was very encouraging. He got me into the way of working as an artist.' An intended career as a science teacher was gradually abandoned.

Mary Newcomb, who had been born at Harrow-on-the-Hill but raised in rural Wiltshire, paid a visit to Minsmere with a party of leading ornithologists, including Eric Ennion and possibly Peter Scott, to consider the siting of a new scrape to attract avocets to the fledgling nature reserve. 'It was still sealed-off due to war-time restrictions, and we had to get a permit to go there,' she remembered. 'On another occasion someone called to say that an avocet had been spotted on a beach north of Southwold and we all rushed off to see it. We also used to camp at Walberswick and Eric would show us how to make clearings in the reedbeds for avocets. We'd often see bearded tits, and bitterns could be heard booming.' That sound of the courting male, from a species lost as a British breeding bird for 44 years from 1868, and whose extinction was again averted in the 1990s by a high birthrate in Walberswick, can carry for upwards of three miles.

Here Mary edged her way along the bank of a dyke until within six feet of a bittern – its body

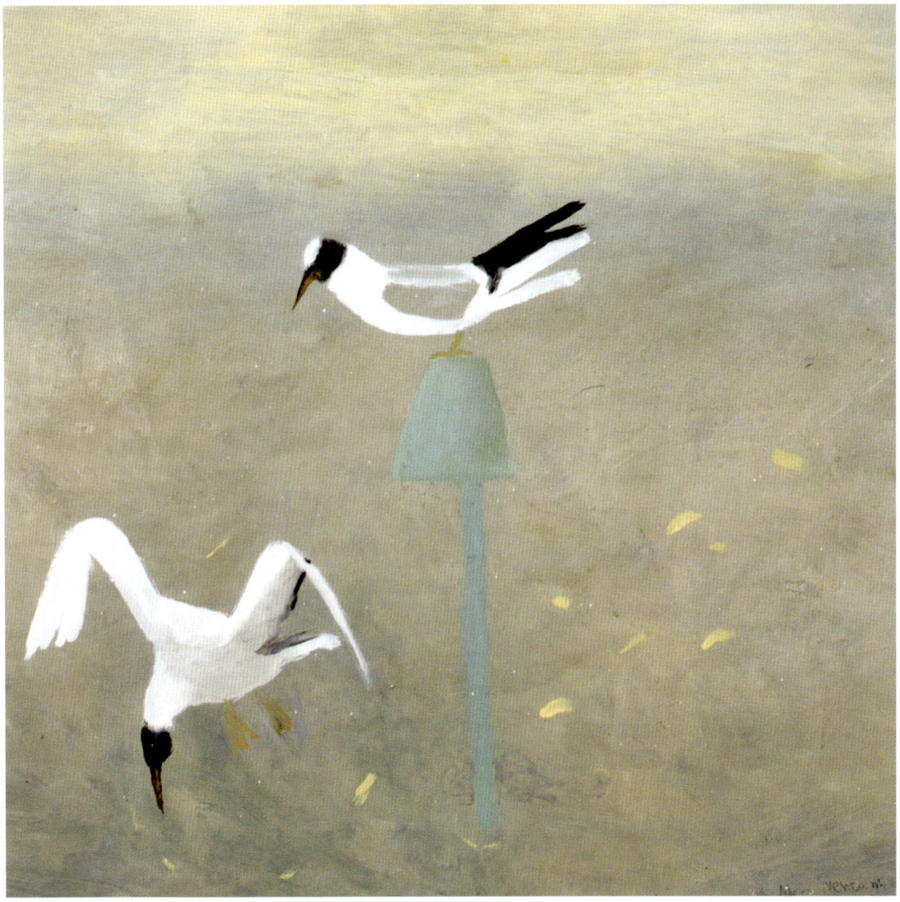

Mary Newcomb painted this pair of oils in 1983 after watching a tern feeding its young on a harbour post. The artist wrote that the mother dived several times into the still centre of a whirlpool then 'hovered over the young tern, manoeuvring herself until she could lower the vertical fish, awkwardly, as from a crane, into the horizontal mouth of the bird below her. The task completed, she went back diligently to catch another. People came and went along the bank. A postman pushed his bicycle across the iron bridge behind. The sun came out and went in again. The tide continued to flow and fill up the river. An hour had gone by.'

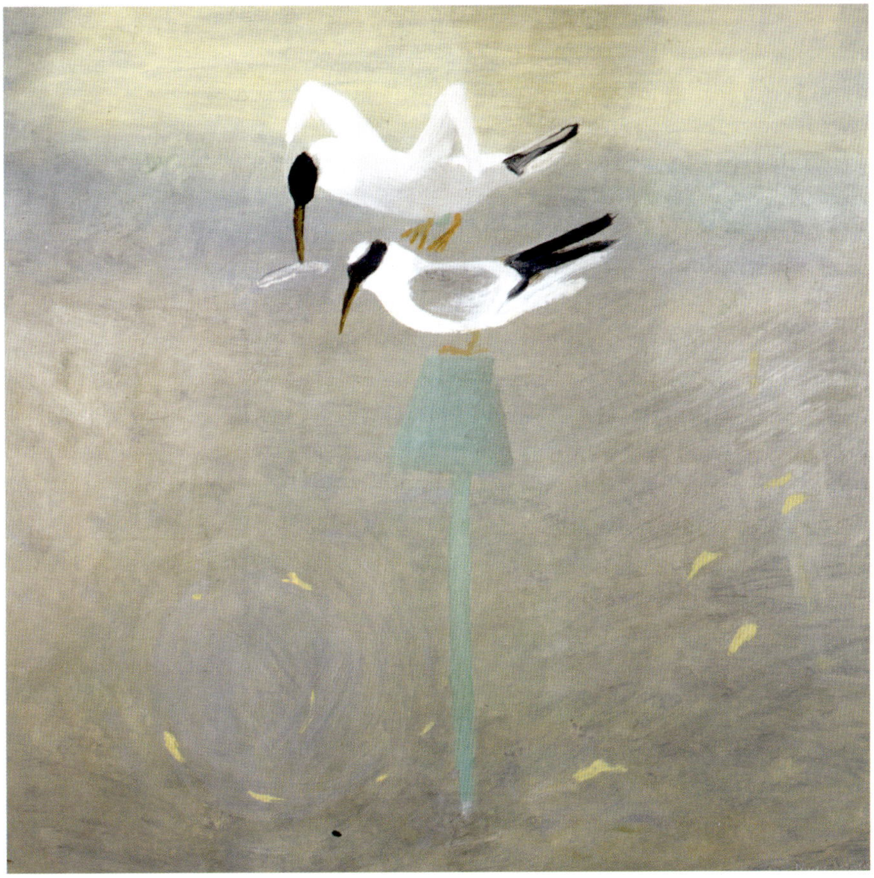

pointing upwards like a speckled-brown trumpet and its slimmed outline perfectly camouflaged as it swayed in the breeze with surrounding reeds. Here, too, while camping at Westwood Lodge, she met her future husband – Godfrey Newcomb, then an agricultural student, later a farmer and potter in the Waveney Valley.

Touring the countryside on foot, bicycle and bus Mary Newcomb was to visit Southwold and the surrounding area regularly for almost 60 years. Admired by artists as diverse as Ben and Winifred Nicholson, William Scott and Mary Fedden, her pictures of the rural scene were evocations of a poetic interior vision, but sparked by observed incidents which were acutely recalled and recorded in the truthful way that Dr Ennion had taught her. She claimed to have no theory about art and no knowledge of artistic techniques, merely responding naturally in pencil and paint to all that she saw and felt. And so time and again identifiable local details appeared as if by magic in her abstracted art – lighthouse, pier and ferry, walkers on the golf course (a work now in Tate Britain), a horse-rider on the beach, a tern feeding its young on a post. In lyrical late pictures

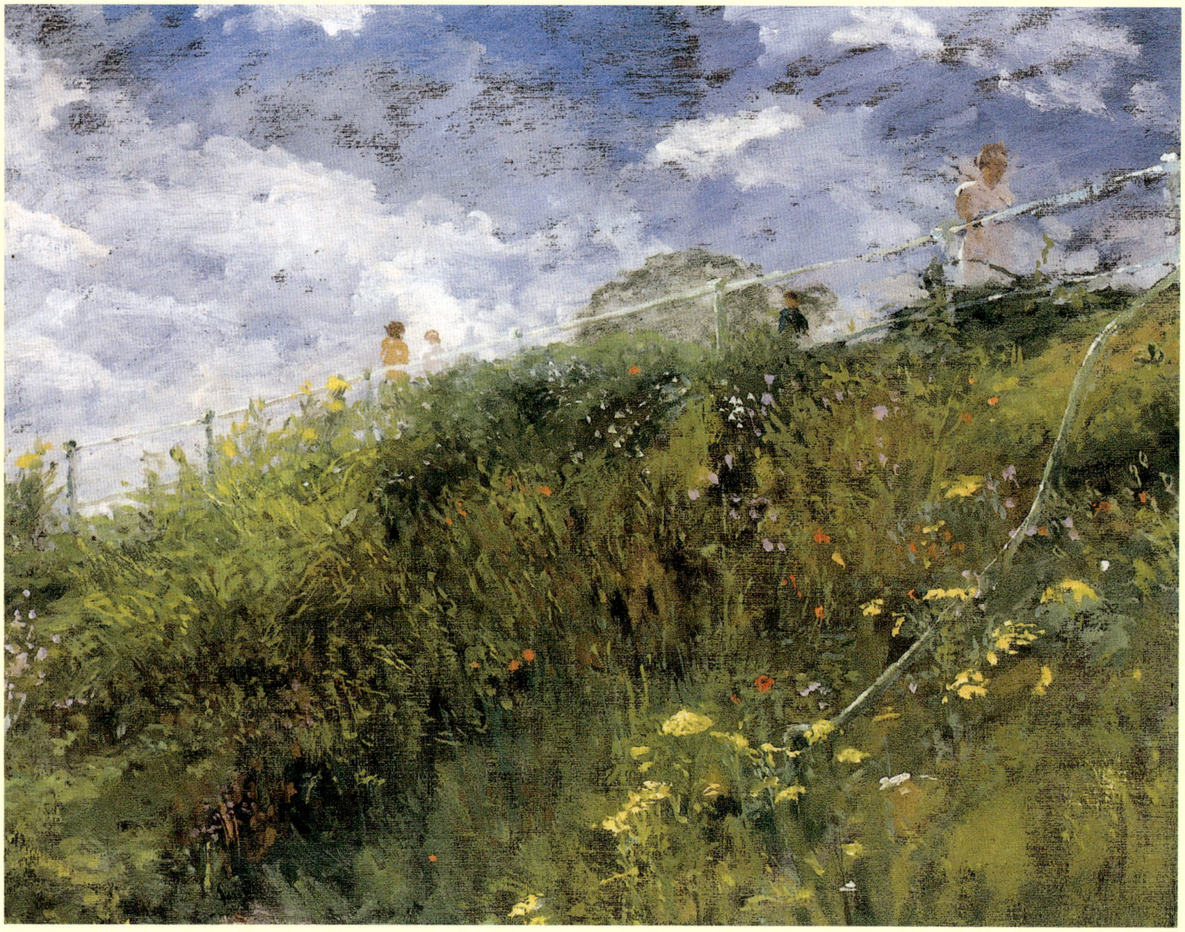

*Gun Hill Flora*, FRED DUBERY (b1926) – one of several meditations in oil paint on the wild cliff between well-tended greens and beach huts by this New English Art Club stalwart. Showing at the RA from 1950, teaching at the Royal Academy Schools from 1964 and writing books on drawing and perspective, an East Anglian talent has displayed a life-long love of France in exhilarating images which revel in colour and patterning and pay homage to Vuillard and Bonnard. Latterly based near Stowmarket, he often painted with close friends and neighbours Lionel Bulmer and Margaret Green whose pictures have a similar sparkle.

the features of the real world appear to be dissolving into light.

But although wildness and wilderness may seem the defining characteristics of scenery around Southwold, there have been stoical attempts in this wind-blown and salt-blasted location to propagate exotic plants and cultivate gardens. The Dunwich rose, for instance, was traditionally thought to have been introduced in medieval times from northern England by the friars of Greyfriars, one outer wall of whose ruins now teeters on the cliff edge. Still appearing in Suffolk plots, this small white rose with black hips used to run rampant in the Dunwich area in a reminder of all the gardens lost to the sea. John Tradescant and his namesake son, with family roots in Wenhaston, scoured the known world of the early 17th century as plant collectors for noble and royal gardens – bringing back the first lilac, acacia and tulip tree, and introducing the plane trees of London squares and the tradescantia of countless grand and humble flower beds. Many of their precious plants were sent to cousins in Walberswick, where their double daffodil continues to bloom each spring.

Artist-gardener **ARTHUR DACRES RENDALL** (1861-1936), who had trained in Paris with Philip Wilson Steer in the early 1880s, was to build on the Tradescant legacy after purchasing Eastwood Cottage (previously Coral Cottage) in 1891. He oversaw successive horticultural overhauls, with an early phase of this ongoing project described by Gertrude Jekyll in her book *Gardens for Small Country Houses*. His tombstone in Walberswick churchyard – denoting his interests and achievements in symbols (spade, sword, scales, doves, artist's materials and clasped hands of friendship) and bearing the legend 'His work for art endures' – is a fine sculpture by **ERIC KENNINGTON** (1888-1960). The painter and draughtsman John Craxton, who was at school with Kennington's son Christopher, recalls staying with the family in 1937 when they were lent the Walberswick cottage in exchange for

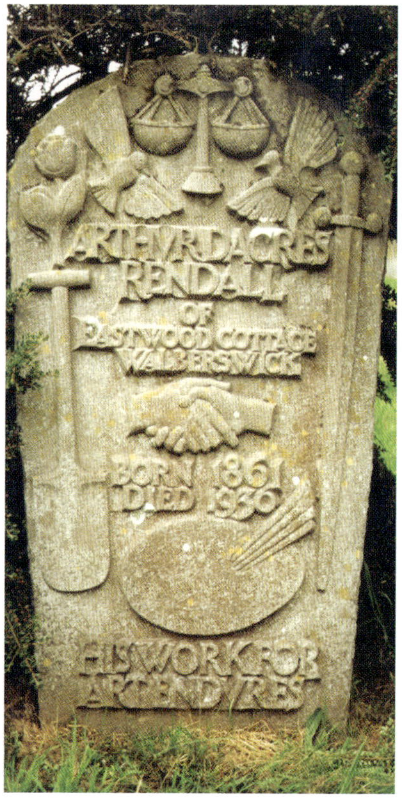

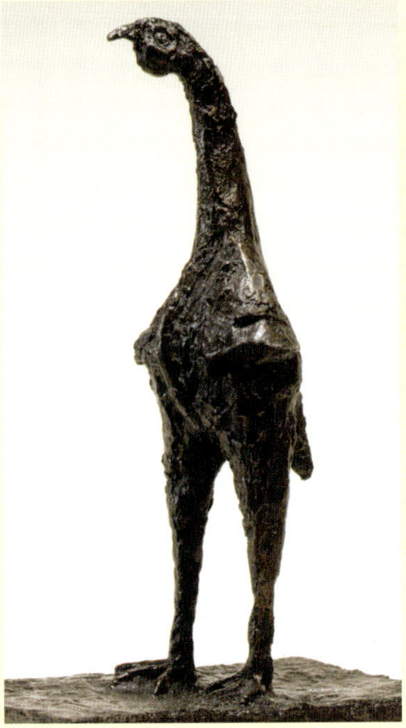

Sculptor ROSALIND STRACEY (b1907) was born in London but raised at the family seat in Norfolk – Rackheath Hall set in 3000 acres near Norwich – where she spent much of her time riding and shooting. Her love of birds extended to bagging pheasants, partridges, snipe, duck and woodcock for the pot. The great great great grand-daughter of Richard Brinsley Sheridan, and kinswoman of composer Dame Ethel Smythe, took creative talent in her stride, but travelled widely before enrolling in the sculpture class of Chelsea Art School in 1947. There she was soon joined by Elisabeth Frink, who had a similar upbringing in East Anglia. In 1955 she built her first studio at Walberswick – 'a wonderful place; the birds were out of this world' – and was to work here for more than 40 years on human and animal figures modelled in resin or plaster and then cast in bronze. The sculpture illustrated here is *Chicken*.

the gravestone. There were sketching trips and walks to Southwold and the sculptor, resting from his labours on the portrait head of Lawrence of Arabia for St Paul's Cathedral, had warm words of encouragement for Craxton's already-fluent drawings.

Adrian Bell, visiting Southwold in November 1956, was impressed and amused by the fortitude of local gardeners – writing in the *Eastern Daily Press*: 'roses bloom brilliantly behind low walls, and petunias, even in November. The wind, the salt air, desiccated soil – nothing can stop Dames of the British Empire making gardens where the sea roars, I saw an old lady in sea-boots. How far they went up under her skirt there was no knowing. They clanked at every step. She had a great hat turned up in front like a sou'wester, and a face of destiny, like Wellington's. She was standing breast-high in dahlias where only rushes should grow.'

Born in Surrey, and concluding prize-winning studies at the Royal Academy Schools under Peter Greenham, DIANA HOWARD (b1947) became an associate of Peter Blake's Brotherhood of Ruralists. While most of the Samuel Palmer and William Blake-influenced ruralists looked westwards, Diana Howard turned ever further eastwards – settling near Beccles with husband John Morley as her artistic influences moved from Celtic mythology to eastern mysticism. Her spiritual pictures have also shown an increasing reverence for elemental landscape, as in this oil on canvas image *Cloudy Summer, Blythburgh Marshes*, 2001.

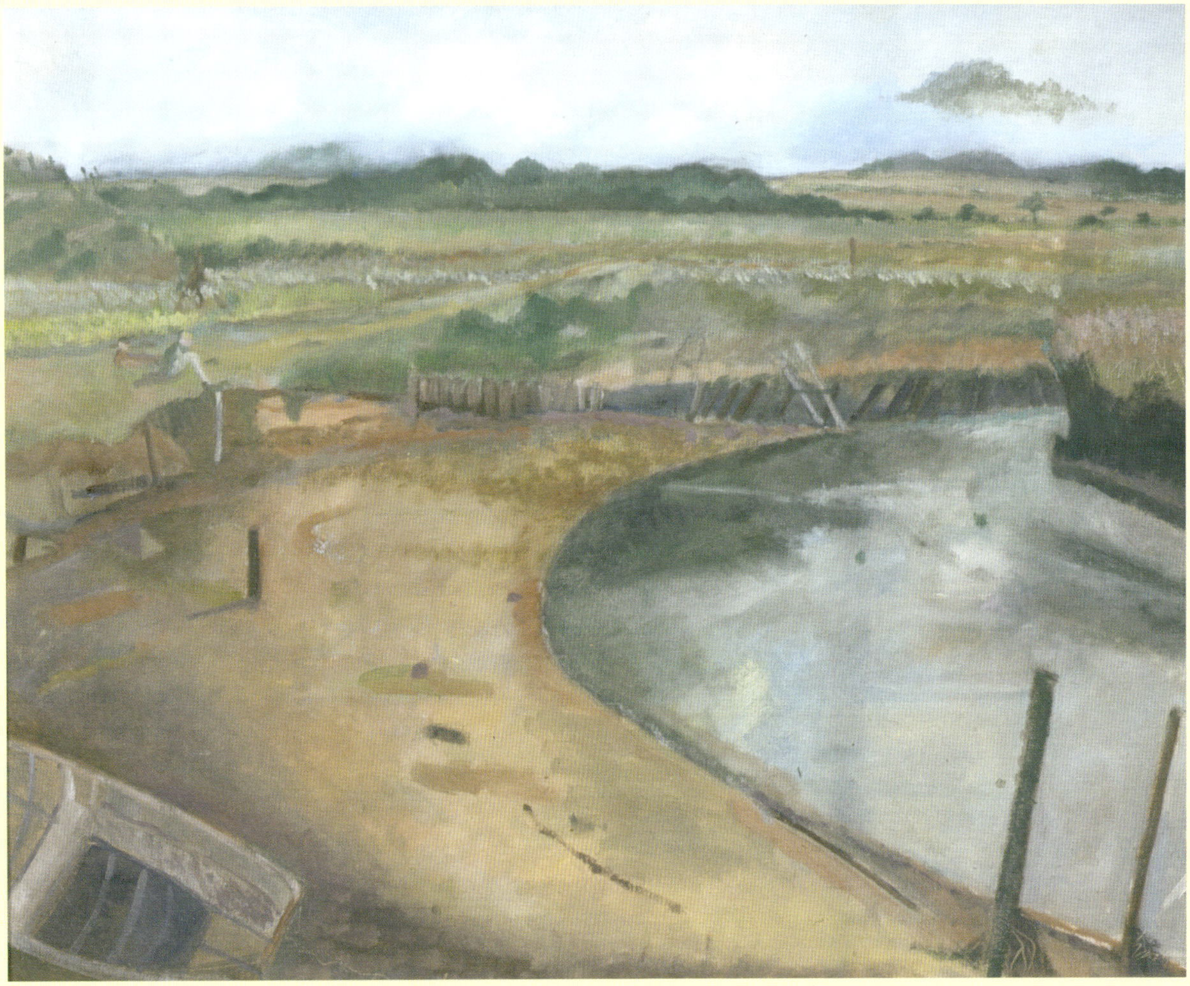

*Southwold, Summer*,
Katherine Hamilton, oil on canvas.

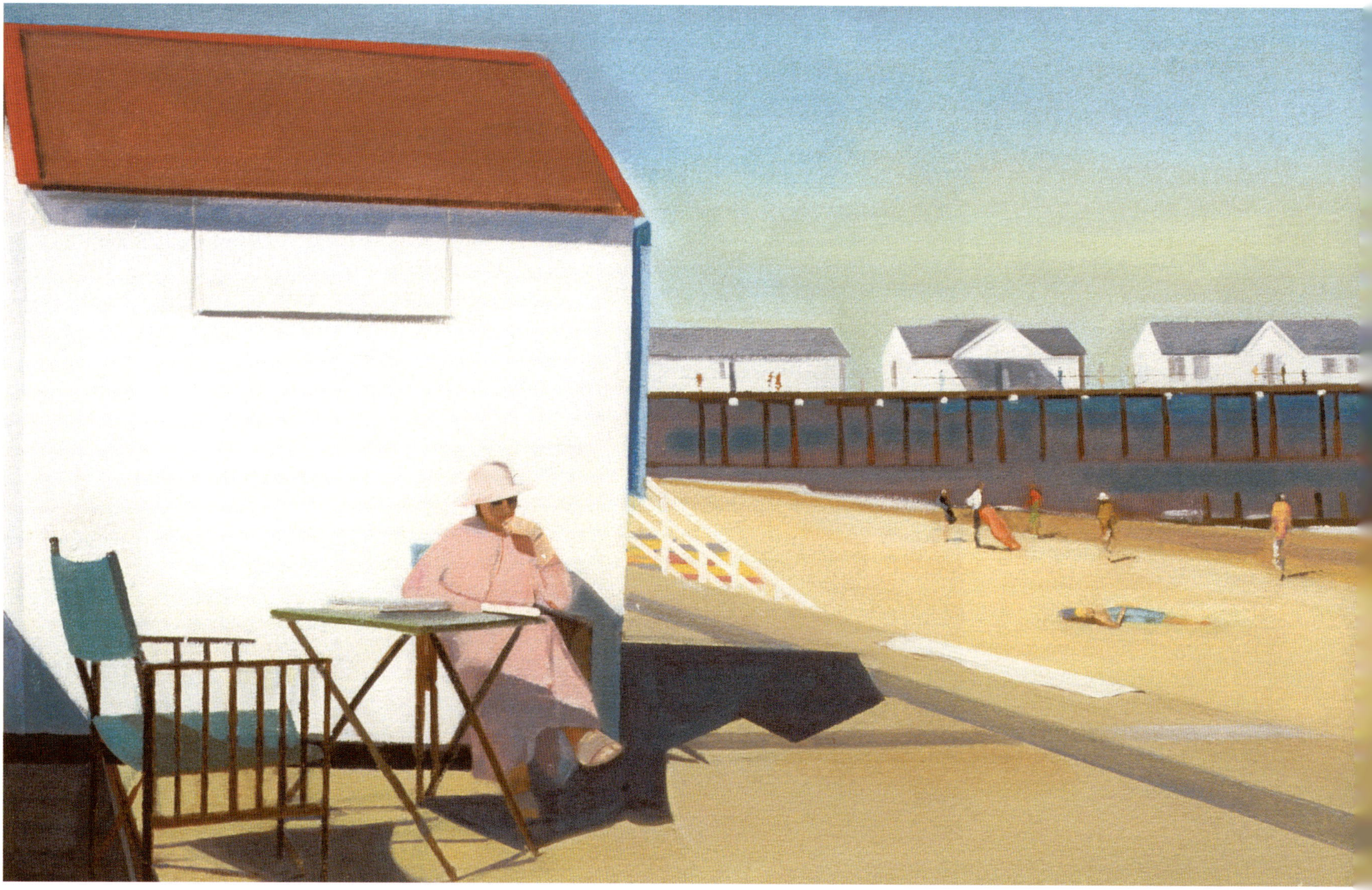

Chapter Twenty

# Peerless Pier

On August 15 2001 a front-page article in the *Los Angeles Times* found water-tight proof of British weirdness. The first pier to be built from a UK beach in 50 years had lately been opened at Southwold – to provide, as Sir John Betjeman had once put it, 'a walk on the sea without the disadvantage of being seasick'.

But to reporter Marjorie Miller it was an elemental error. Readers near a balmy Pacific shore were informed that piers ignited something barmy in the British spirit which drove them to the beach 'even when it is cold and gray – which it nearly always is'. Hard to square such a woeful picture with the warm festivities on July 3 when the new pier had been launched by the Duke of Gloucester, flanked by civic dignitaries and town crier, morris dancers, musicians and Punch and Judy puppeteers, plus a crowd of thousands. Some 620ft out to sea a crane was still in place at the end of the T-shaped structure, immobile amid a celebratory flotilla of bobbing boats.

**KATHERINE HAMILTON** (b1954), who

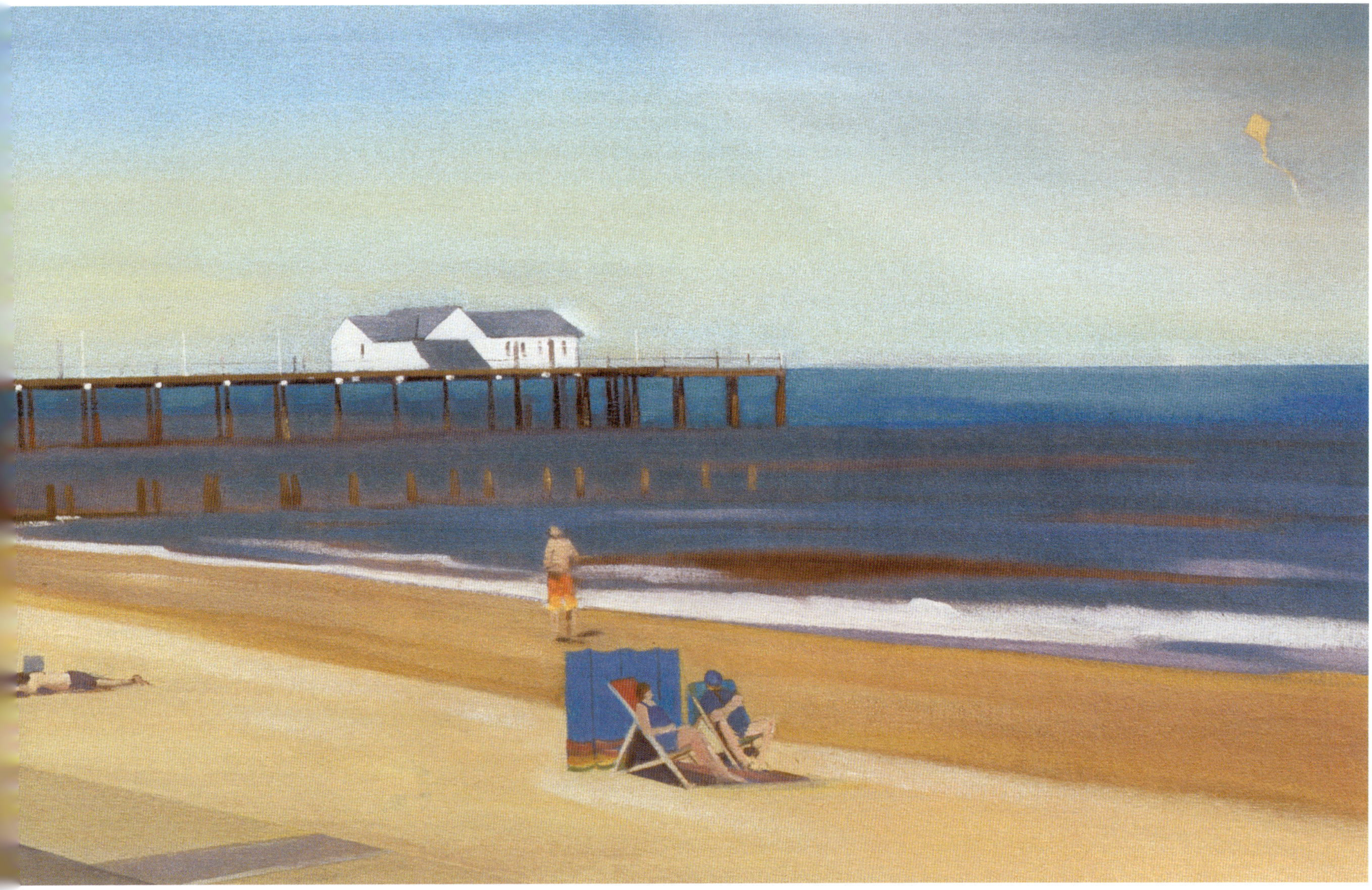

had previously worked as a dancer and choreographer from New York to Addis Ababa, and lived as a painter in Italy, France and Spain, was by now relocated to Reydon. In between trips to Africa, Asia or the Americas, she found inspirational imagery along the Suffolk coast in which a life-long love of movement was balanced or even eclipsed by an eerie stillness. She worked on a suitably elongated canvas in which the depleted crowds of a summer afternoon seem strangely frozen in time, like characters in an Edward Hopper painting. The most prominent presence is the pier, which also appears to have been in place for an eternity. But the absence of a copper lantern on the roof of the last pavilion – a finishing touch by architect Brian Haward – pegs this picture to a brief period in 2001.

Months earlier the construction process had been captured in a gull's-eye view by Brightlingsea-based **JAMES DODDS** (b1957) as part of his series of panoramic linocuts of East Coast ports. This shipwright turned painter and printer of maritime scenes, the son of artist and illustrator Andrew Dodds (see p.27), likes to depict a sense of passing hours and decades in these compacted and characterful presentations. Here he evokes the overlap of two millennia by dint of the silhouetted crane laying the planks of the new pier.

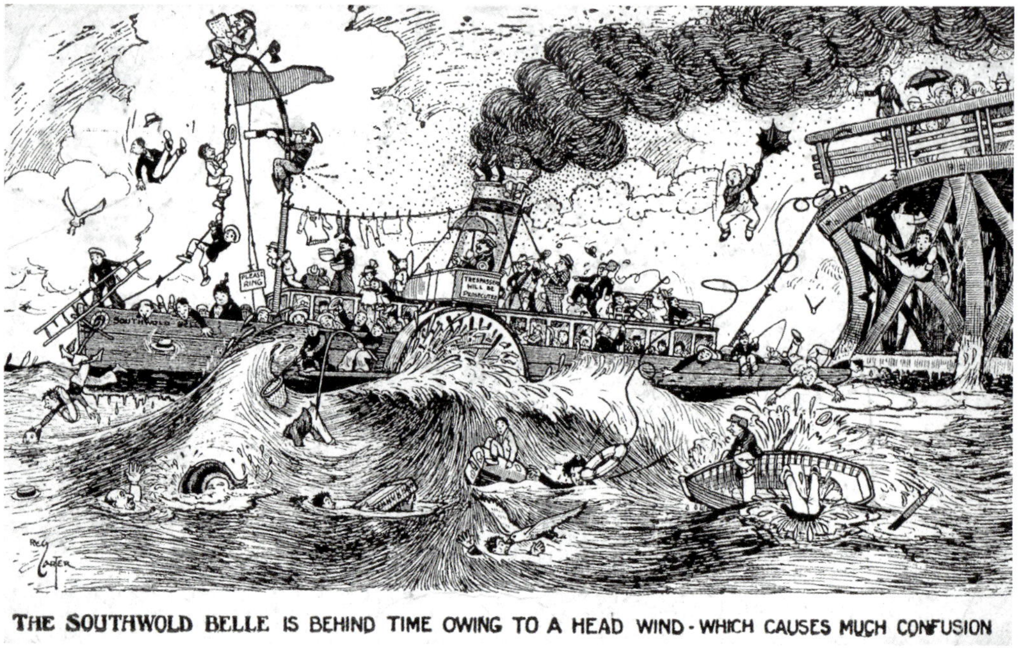


Reg Carter, scourge of the Southwold Railway, turns his attention to the Southwold Belle steamer, picturing a collision with the pier.

Back in 1987 entrepreneur Chris Iredale had bought the stump of an older structure, sweeping aside alarming builders' and accountants' estimates in his passion to recreate the greatest lost glory of Southwold. With planning permission finally secured, he set to work with a tiny European Union grant, a bank loan rising to £1.5 million and the blithe confidence that remaining costs could be met along the way. And a brilliant

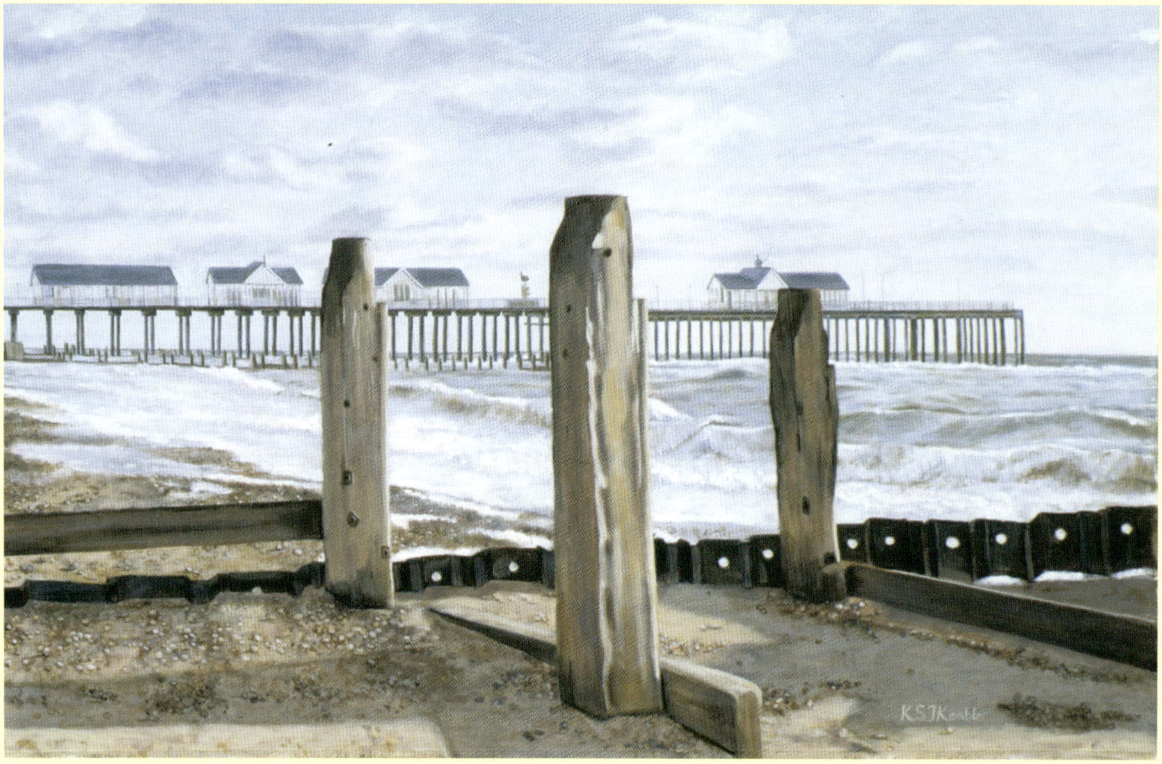

Great Yarmouth-born KAREN S.J. KEABLE (b1966) toured the globe from Norway to Singapore and Australia thanks to her husband's work for the oil and gas industry, and during a stint in Aberdeen brushed-up her skills as a painter. Running a guesthouse on Southwold's North Parade from 1998, she decorated the walls with acrylic scenes from her travels and watched the rebuilding of the pier from her studio while producing new, beach-centred pictures. After her work was spotted by Mary Gundry during a drinks party, and then hung in the Garden Gallery, sales flowed. Favourite Keable subjects show forests and spinneys of break-water posts, laced with rusted metal groynes and lapped by foaming waves over which the pier now confidently strides. This is the world below her window.

fund-raising scheme to sell inscribed plaques was duly devised, so that the pier handrail became studded for its entire length with jolly or poignant messages – minor works of art recording births, marriages and deaths and many memorable high days and holidays in between. Along with the commemorative legends on scores of benches, and a solitary memorial plaque on a breakwater post, more lovers of Southwold are now recorded on the seafront than in the churchyard.

With its deliberately plain profile, and its tasteful amusements and attractions, the 21st century pier embodies Southwold's understated traditions and echoes the wood-and-iron structure whose first pile was driven on October 2 1899 by Mrs E.M.U. Adnams, wife of the deputy mayor. This venture had been devised by the Coast Development Company – co-founded by London solicitor Clive Pritchard, who would soon have a holiday home in Pier Avenue (one son, Fleetwood, set up the Southwold Trust charity in 1962; another, Jack, features on p.165). In June 1900 a pier 810ft in length received a gala launch, to be followed early in the next year by the opening of the associated Grand Hotel.

Southwold was thus set fair to prosper in the Edwardian era when nearly 100 piers served as landing platforms and promenades in what became the golden age of British resorts. As well as its miniature connection to the national rail network, the Suffolk resort had a major transport link by sea thanks to the Belle steamers ferrying passengers between London Bridge and piers en route to Great Yarmouth (Southend, Clacton, Walton-on-the-Naze, Felixstowe, Southwold and Lowestoft). Those with the means to holiday in style would be met at the new pierhead by Grand Hotel porters and led to a haven which, as the *Southwold and Neighbourhood Guide* put it, had a handsome dining room brilliantly lighted by electricity, radiator heating in winter, and an Otis Safety Elevator to all floors. 'Needless to say the sanitary arrangements have received especial attention and are as perfect as modern science can make them,' the rave review added.

The pier now became a focal point for topographical artists, who had previously concentrated on Southwold's more naturalistic charms. Both Sylvester and Lilian Stannard

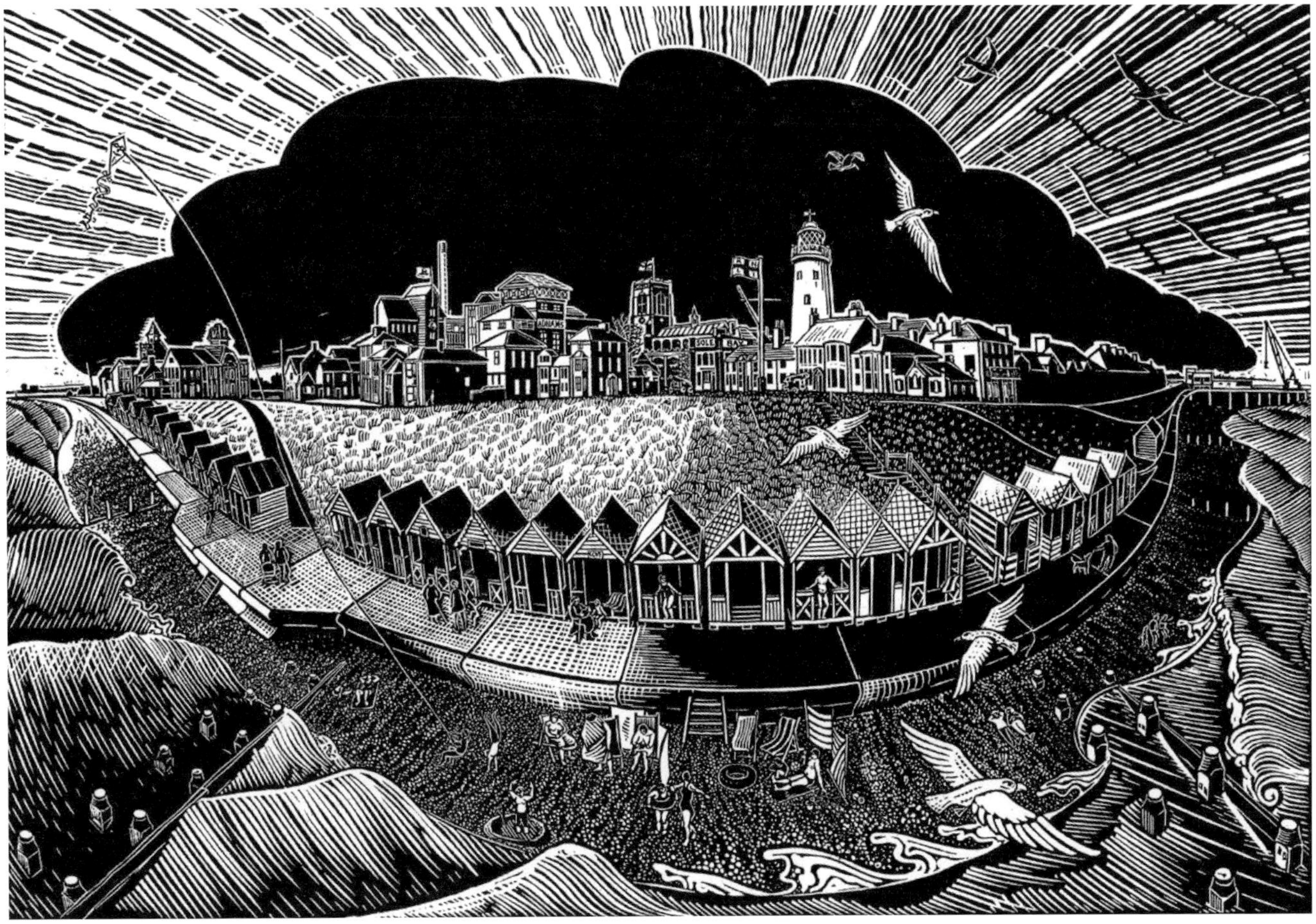

*Southwold*, James Dodds, linocut, 2000.

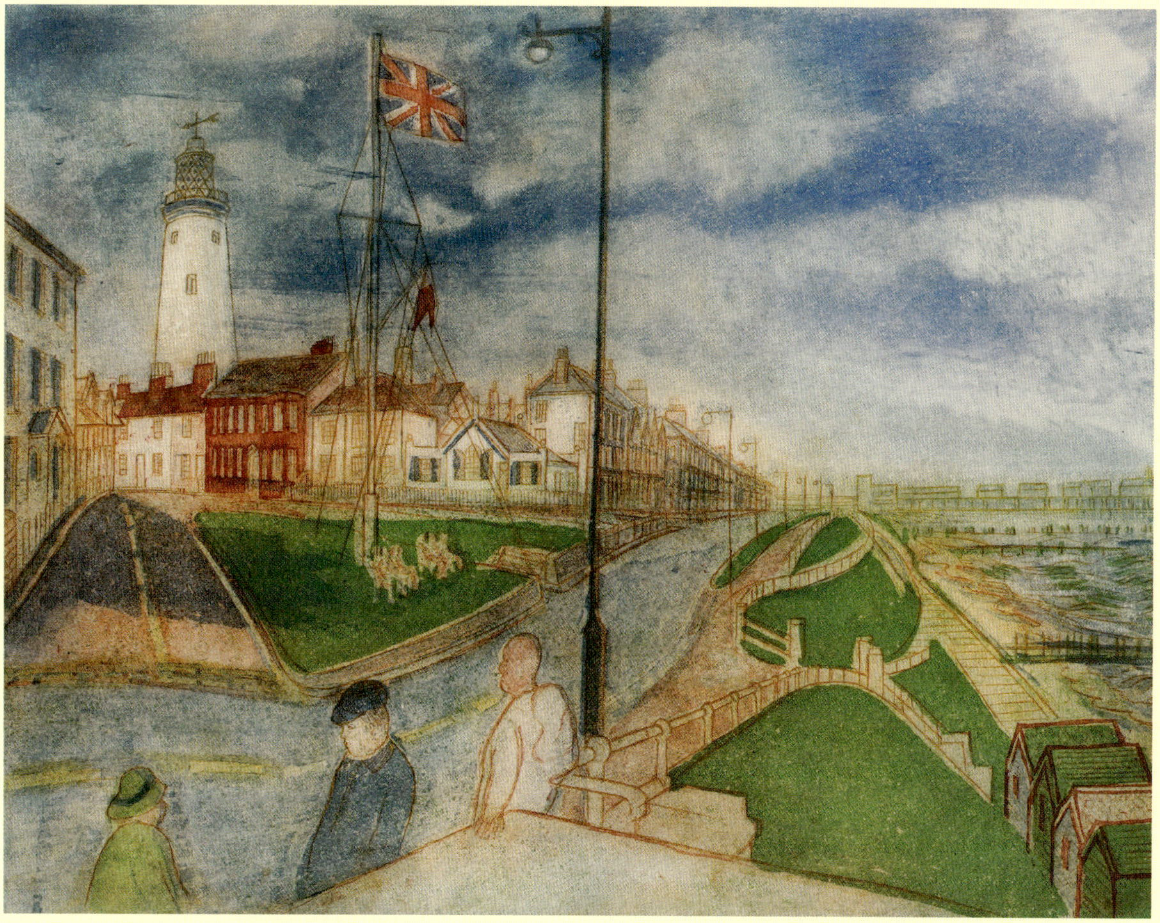

Over May and June of 2005, RICHARD BAWDEN completed a watercolour sketch of the northward view from the roof of Southwold's seafront lavatory block. Between the twin anchors of lighthouse and pier, his sweeping composition takes in the old coastguard station and guesthouses of North Parade, the promenade and hut-fringed beach. The image (above) has been commissioned as an aquatint print to mark the publication of this book.

HENRY HOLZER (b1907), who had depicted war-time defences around Walberswick in 1940s lithographs, returned to East Anglia after serving as head of print-making at Hornsey Art School in London. In the borderlands of Norfolk and Suffolk, until his eyesight faded, he painted intricate and deeply-felt landscapes and seascapes. This 1971 oil, looking northward from the beach below Gun Hill to what was left of the old pier, became a best-selling greetings card.

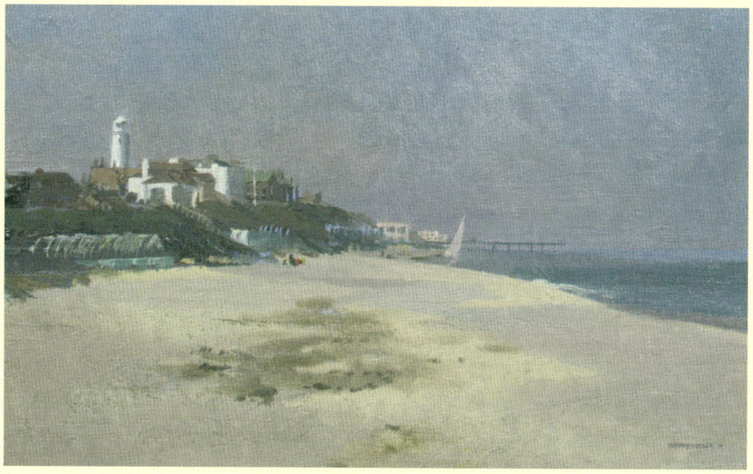

produced watercolours featuring the new structure which were then turned into popular Edwardian postcards. Joseph Southall depicted a particularly golden afternoon on the beach below the pier in the inter-war period. Pier-based attractions which had begun with a sea angling competition every Wednesday afternoon were extended to confetti battles above the waves and to musical entertainments, plays, revues and dances in the pier pavilion added in 1936. Elsie and Doris Waters began their stage career here appearing, in those days of innocence and ignorance, with Harry Pepper's White Coons concert party.

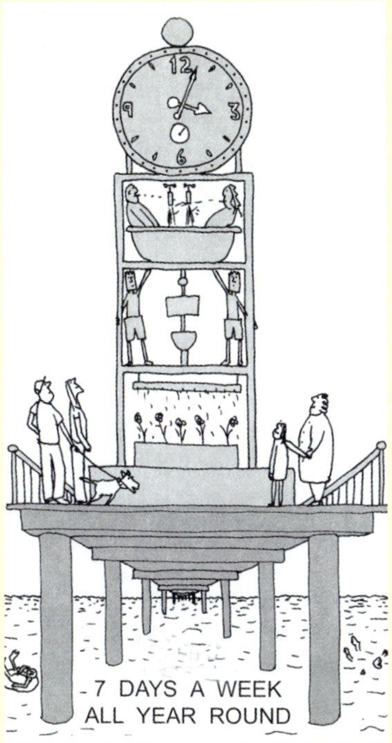


Cartoon by Tim Hunkin.

Operating at that magical point where science, technology, engineering, art and seaside entertainment all meet, TIM HUNKIN (b 1950) is a madcap genius. Based at Bulcamp since 1976, he has created pyrotechnical flying sheep and cows for Pink Floyd, cartoons for the *Observer* magazine, *The Secret Life of Machines* series for Channel 4 and a related basement display in the Science Museum.

Most of Hunkin's recent work is on Southwold pier 'waiting to get vandalised, sued or flooded by the next high tide'. His novelty automated amusements in the Under The Pier Show feature wild guard-dogs and chiropodists, and witty invitations to view a solar eclipse, dive into the deepest secrets of the North Sea and take a virtual walk around Southwold guided by the ghostly voice of the maestro's puppeteer wife, Meg Amsden.

Most striking of all is the bawdy water clock from which, regular as clockwork, two boys pass water every half-hour. Sculpted in galvanised steel and copper, and with long-time collaborator Will Jackson making the escapement mechanism, it was originally designed for a Thames Water display on recycling.

'I thought that recycling was a rather worthy subject which needed lighting up with some laughs,' its creator recalls. 'The clock was unveiled at a very formal reception full of county folk. There was a lot of polite applause until the boys dropped their shorts and started peeing. Then there was silence.'

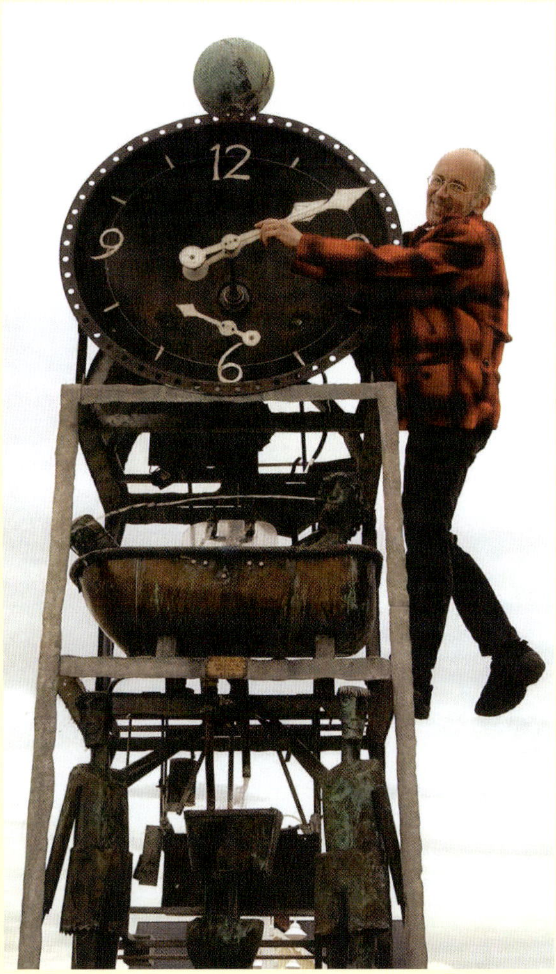

But Belle vessels barely outlasted the Southwold railway when battle was waged with cars and coaches, and the sea was to prove an even more implacable foe. In the early days cartoonist Reg Carter had imagined a steamer crashing into the pier and Frank Forward would set down in swirling paint the waves he witnessed smashing over the truncated structure in the Great Flood of 1953 (p.132). The first body blow had been recorded in December 1933, when huge seas claimed the end of the T-head and the shelter on it. More was gnawed away the following November. And although the damage of war-time sectioning in two places was made good in 1948, the sea struck again in 1955 – tearing out the middle and leaving half of the remaining pier as an island, to be blown up when a national restoration appeal failed. The 240ft remnant on the shoreward end was later to be blitzed by a drifting tanker, and bashed by yet more storms, so that what Chris Iredale finally purchased was a stub barely reaching the water's edge and posing a monumental challenge. Stephen and Antonia Bournes, who bought the revamped pier in 2005, also have a major task of conservation and consolidation ahead.

Although built on massive reinforced steel piles – far stronger than corroded Victorian iron – Southwold's peerless pier needs constant maintenance. Paintwork must be kept spruce, and the wooden decking rock solid. As wood shrinks in saltwater, at the end of each summer season every nut on the entire pier has to be tightened. But the structure looms large in the imaginations of all Southwold devotees – one of whom is the poet Sarah Wardle. Her volume *Fields Away* (Bloodaxe, 2003) features a poem entitled *On Southwold Pier* from which these lines are taken:

*Waves breathed in and out, like a child sleeping.*
*Geese flew in formation, low above the water.*
*The pier on stilts was a flock of herons wading.*

*Estuary Trees*, Margaret Mellis,
oil on canvas, 1950s.

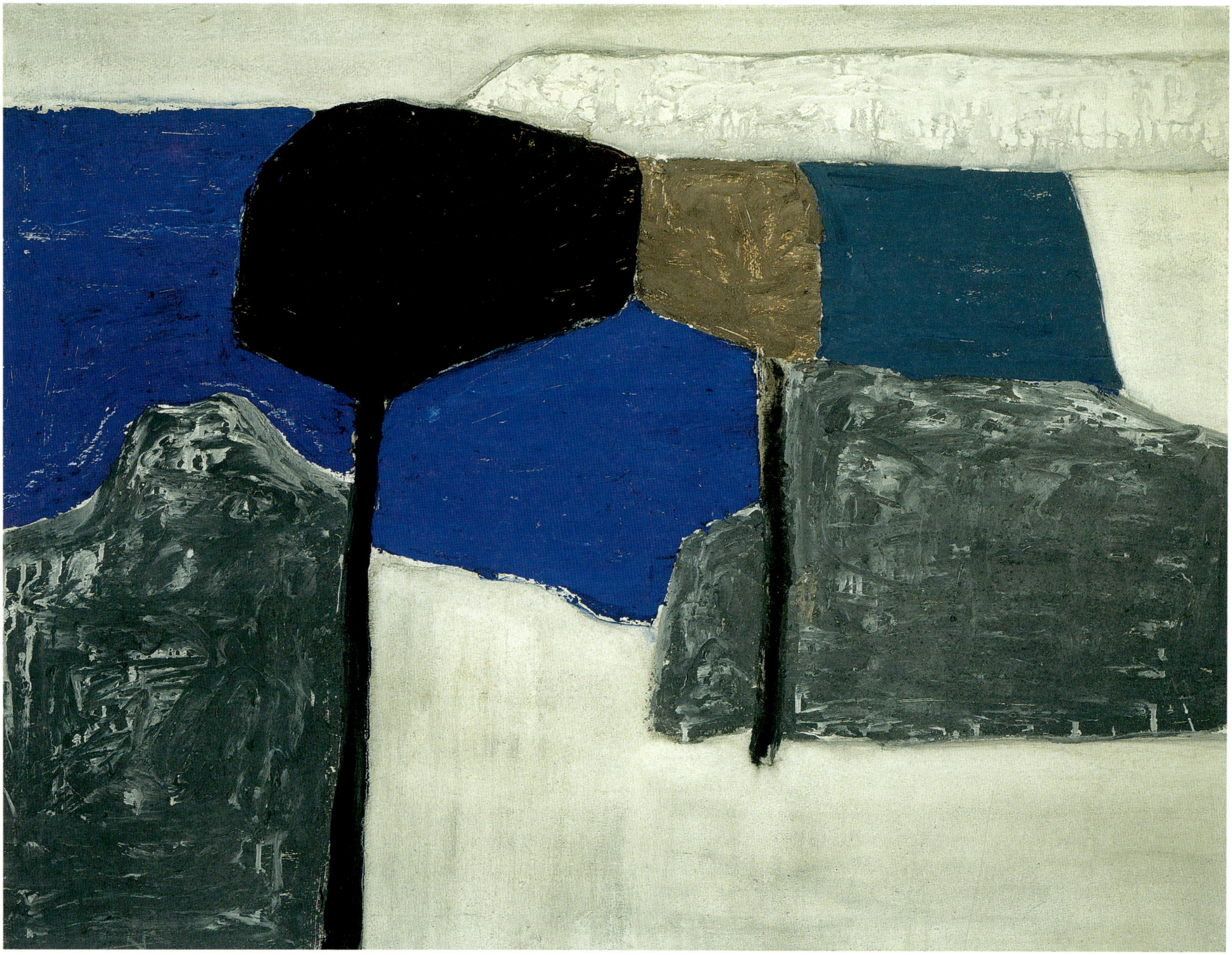

Chapter Twenty One

# March of Modernism

London's Hayward Gallery in 1983 hosted a comprehensive survey of a century of British landscape painting in which the coastal counties of Suffolk and Cornwall inevitably loomed large – and background details, pinning painters to particular places, loomed larger still in the catalogue. Visitors who ventured upstairs found a contrasting exhibition of torn paper collages by someone called **FRANCIS DAVISON** (1919-1984), an artist who revealed no other personal details and gave no map to his abstracted world in which landmark motifs were vaguely visible. Here a teenage **DAMIEN HIRST** (b1965), on a visit from Yorkshire, saw things 'that blew me away'.

A couple of years later, while working on London building sites as he got a portfolio together to win a place at Goldsmiths' College, Hirst spied more of the mysterious collages in Cork Street's Redfern Gallery. He learned that Davison had recently died and that his widow, **MARGARET MELLIS** (b1914), continued to live in Southwold. She, too, was set for a Redfern exhibition which left the would-be art student 'equally blown away'. A fan letter was

*Cottage*, Francis Davison, oil and gloss paint on card, 1950-51.

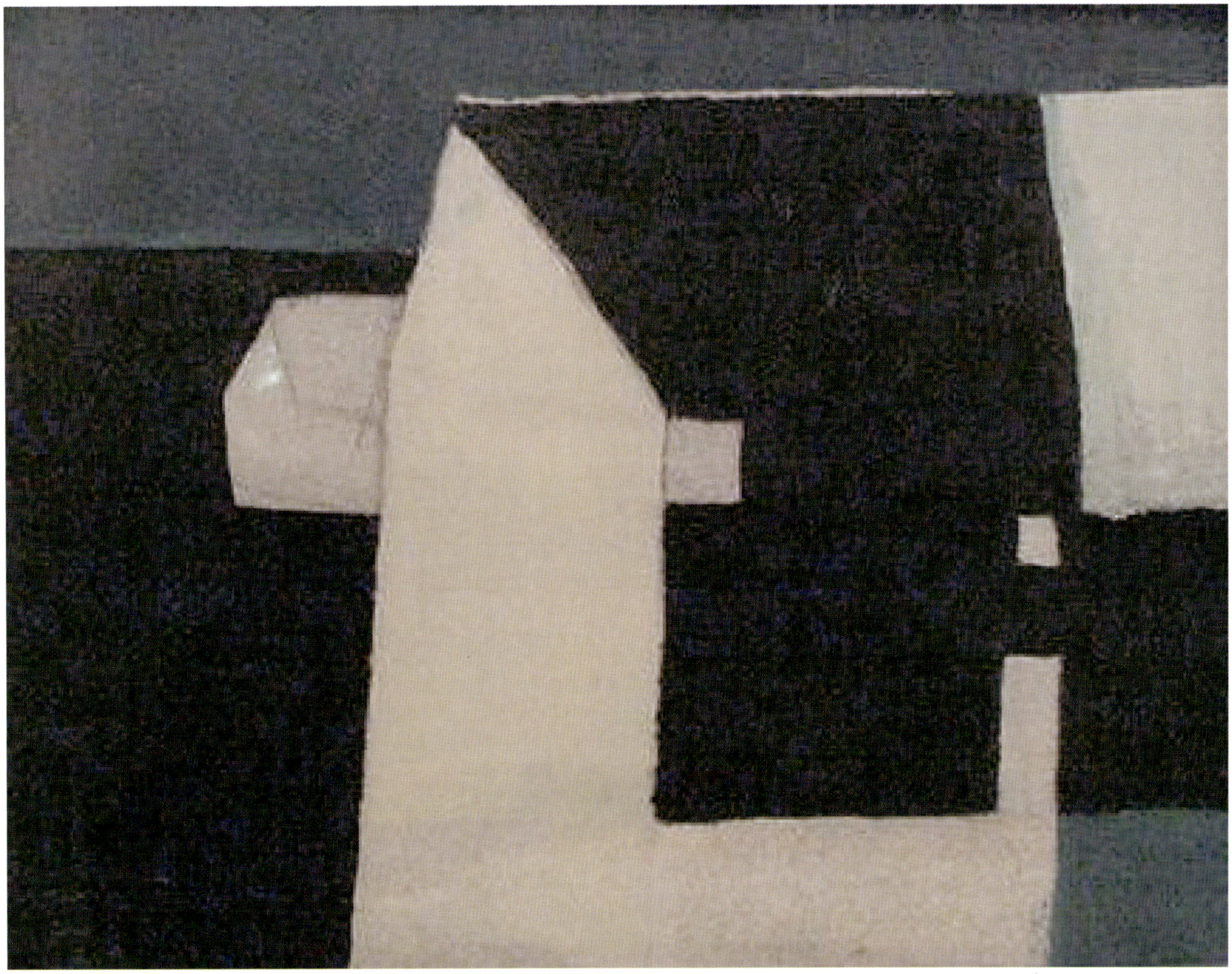

despatched and back went the information that there were lots of unseen Davison collages and Mellis constructions in Southwold – along with an invitation to view them over a weekend. Damien Hirst promptly hopped on a train to Darsham.

In a foreword to Margaret's 2001 exhibition in Newlyn and at Austin/Desmond Fine Art in London, Hirst recalled: 'At the time I was working on collages and constructions in the vein of Kurt Schwitters.' His Southwold trip was to be a seminal experience. He savoured the singular Mellis approach to housekeeping and cooking – a plaice from the harbour would be pressed skin-down in a pan until sizzling in its own oil, then steamed briefly and served; road-kill birds were casseroled; soured milk was made into cream cheese; a perfect salad was grated turnip, orange and garlic. Margaret's personality combined purity, resourcefulness and vibrant physicality. Her visitor remembered that she 'forced me to swim in the sea every day, as she had always done (a savage wake-up). So I was rudely fresh and invigorated when I looked at her studio and felt

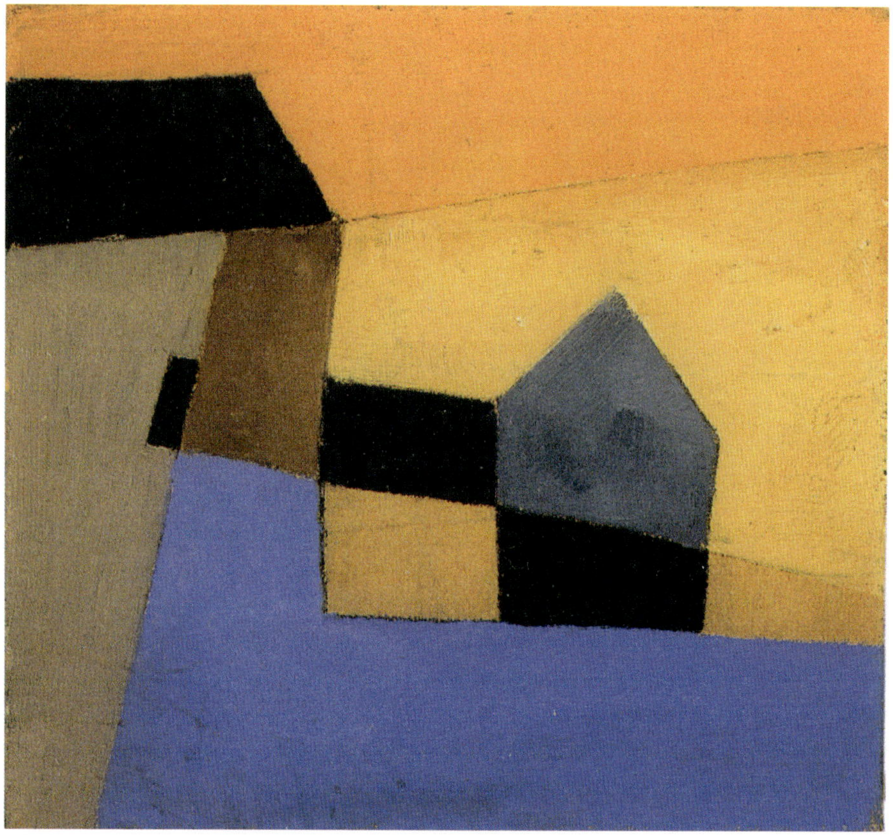

*Orange, Brown, Purple, Grey House,* Francis Davison, oil on board, 1950-51.

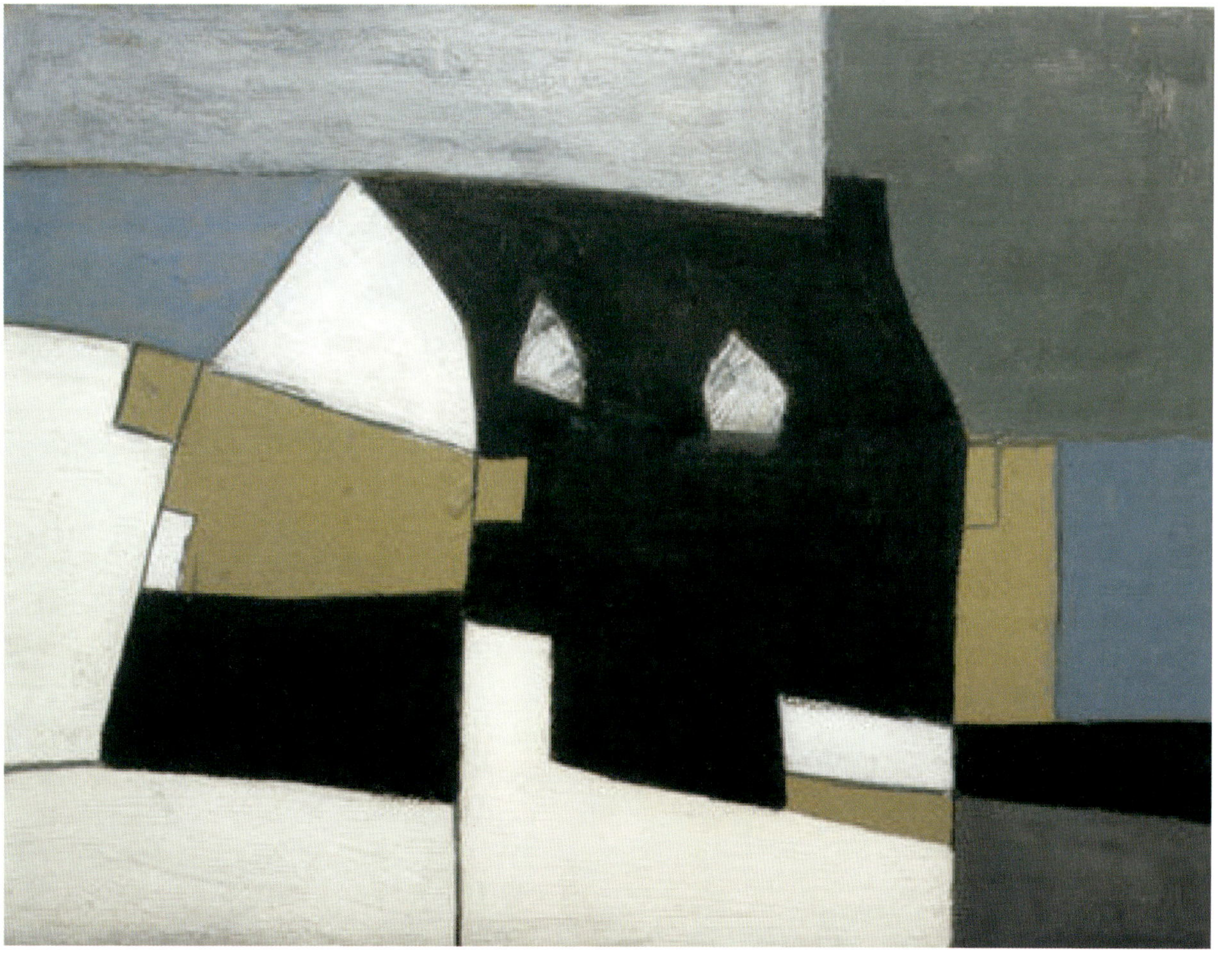

*Black House,* Francis Davison, oil and pencil on board, 1950-51.

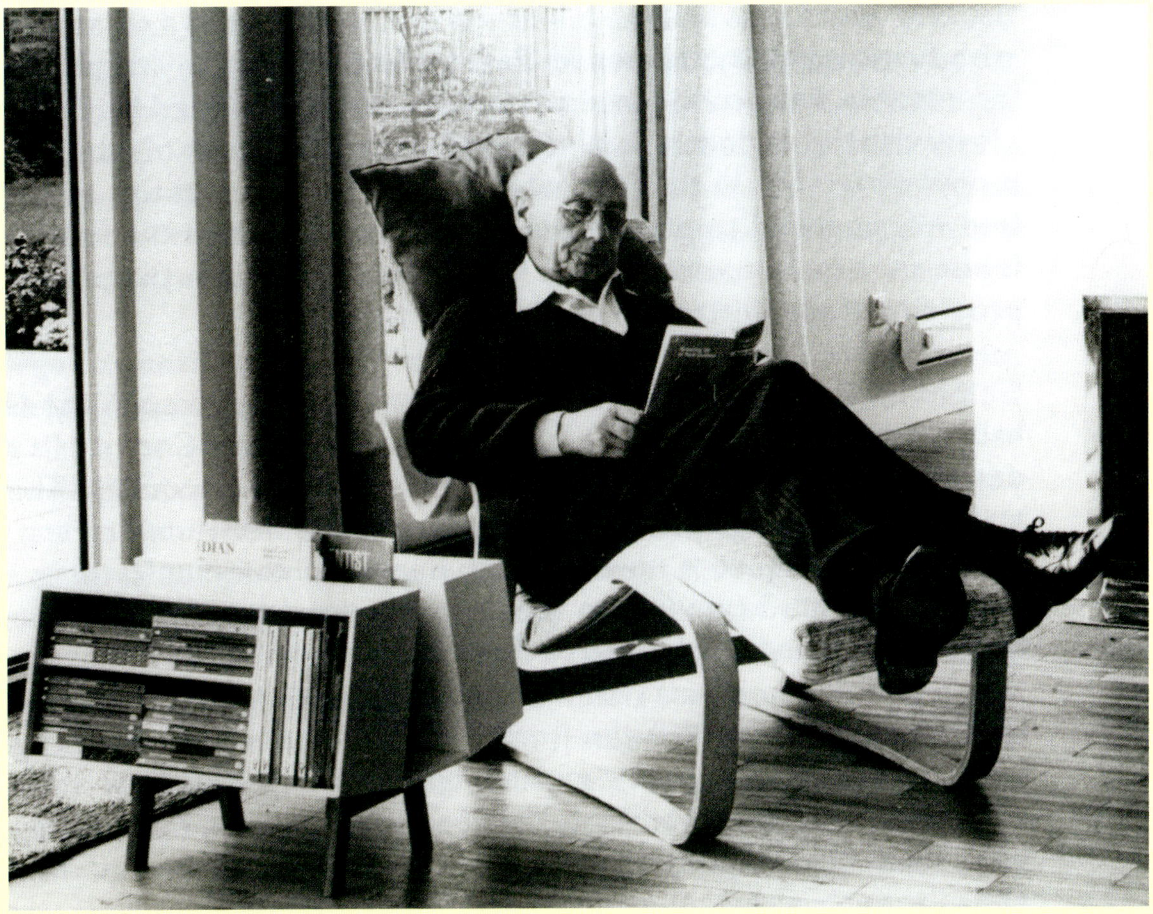

Jack Pritchard at Blythburgh with two modern design classics (the Isokon long chair and Penguin donkey).

In 1934 Wells Coates designed the Lawn Road Flats in Hampstead along strikingly modernist lines likened by Agatha Christie, a war-time tenant, to an ocean liner. One of the first residents, alongside commissioners J. Craven Pritchard and his wife Molly, was Adrian Stokes. Jack 'Plywood' Pritchard (1899-1992) was a modernist entrepreneur who had lately founded the Isokon ('Isometric Unit Construction') company allying cutting-edge design with mass production. After Hitler's rise to power Pritchard rescued the Bauhaus pioneer Walter Gropius, and his wife Ise, with the promise of work and a Lawn Road flat. Other Bauhaus refugees, including Laszlo Maholy-Nagy and Marcel Breuer (who was to design Isokon's classic long chair), also made use of the Hampstead haven whose Isobar club drew locally-based artists and intellectuals, including sculptors Henry Moore, Barbara Hepworth and Naum Gabo. Pritchard then introduced Gropius to Henry Morris, the forward-looking chief education officer of Cambridgeshire, and the result was Impington Village College which set the pattern for post-war school building in Britain.

Although born in Hampstead Pritchard had known Southwold from early childhood for, in 1907, his barrister and developer father had commissioned the fine Arts and Crafts Craven Cottage in Pier Avenue as a holiday home from architect Allan Ovenden Collard. The house, with a tennis court and croquet lawn and an upturned boat in which Jack's American sister-in-law, Miriam, often painted, remained with the family until 1972.

But in 1961 Jack and Molly had bought land in Blythburgh, on which they built Isokon – a single-storey modernist dwelling of glass and wood designed by Jennifer (Jack's daughter) and Colin Jones. The sunken swimming pool and attached sauna became a focal point for friends including Margaret Mellis and Francis Davison.

With his beliefs in planning, child-centred education, modern design, sunbathing and free love, Jack Pritchard was a controversialist readily lampooned by Osbert Lancaster. But many of the designs he fostered are now classics. And at the party for Gropius's 85th birthday in his adopted America the great man accepted the greetings of the assembly and added: 'Now fill your glasses and drink to Molly and Jack for saving our lives.'

an enormous affinity with her constructions and the way she worked'. They also went on long walks together, beachcombing for driftwood and other raw materials for their related art.

Looking back to a time before he had pickled his first shark or sheep or produced a single spin, spot or butterfly painting, or made films and music, or opened a restaurant, the hero of Brit Art continued: 'We lost touch. I don't really know why. Maybe it was the age difference, maybe it was because I got into art school. I think it was also because I felt such an affinity with her – there you go – it was all three and a sprinkling of selfishness.' Nevertheless the 1995 Turner Prize winner delivered a ringing complaint that Margaret had been neglected by critics and curators and deserved to be 'up there – large on the map with her contemporaries' and her work in 'the museums where it belongs'.

Margaret Mellis was born in China to a missionary father and spent her first birthday on the boat returning the family to their native Scotland at the outbreak of World War One. Her earliest memory was of 'being bathed in a blue and white china basin with dragons on it and lying on an orange sofa – at that moment I thought I'd just been born'. An absorption in brilliant colour would be the key to her life. She was to have been a pianist until switching with typically complete commitment to painting and entering Edinburgh's College of Art at 15. Here her teachers included the Scottish Colourist Samuel John Peploe; William Gear and Wilhelmina Barns-Graham were fellow students. She won a scholarship to train with André Lhote in Paris, before returning to a student fellowship in Edinburgh. Revisiting the French capital for the Cézanne exhibition of 1936 she met Adrian Stokes, an established art theorist and emergent painter with magnetic looks and charm. They married two years later, visiting Ezra Pound during their Italian honeymoon.

Amid the false hopes of Munich, the Hampstead-based Stokes was convinced that London would soon be blitzed, so he and Margaret scoured the coast of Norfolk and Suffolk for a possible place of escape. They failed

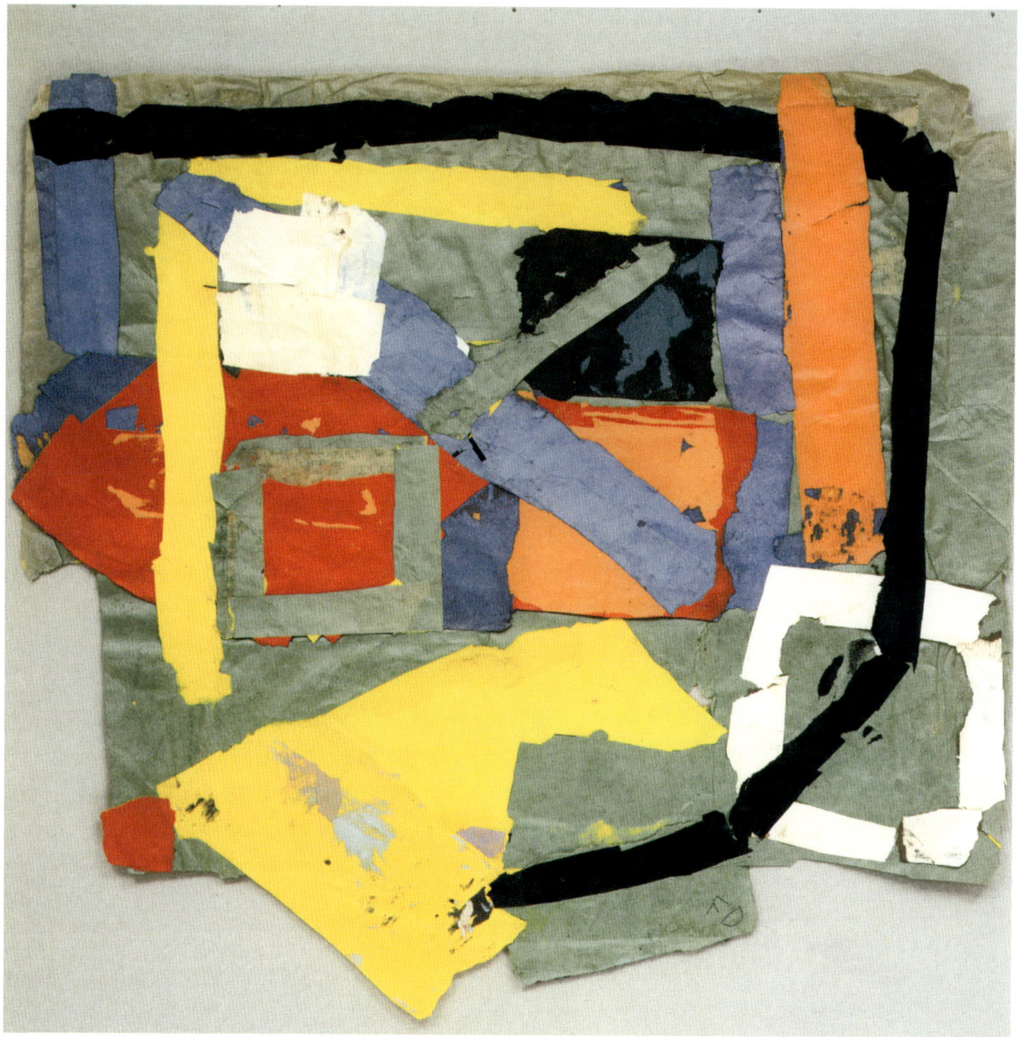

Francis Davison, *Bright Colours Bound with Black*, collage on Essex board, c1978-82.

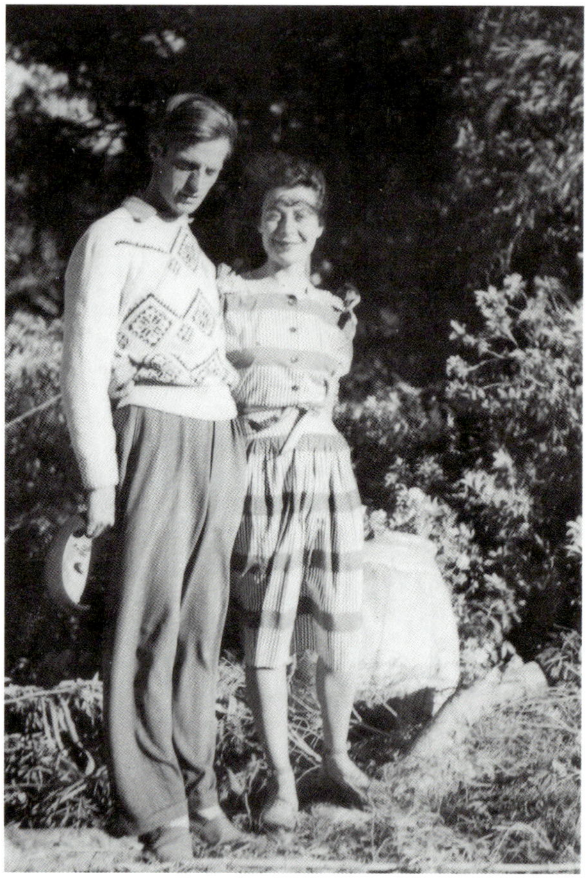

Margaret Mellis and Francis Davison (left) at Cap D'Antibes, c1948.

to secure the property they wanted in Walberswick and almost settled for the Martello tower at Slaughden, on the shingle spit below Aldeburgh – but felt threatened by the tide rather than by Hitler's advancing armies. The long search then turned to Cornwall, where the discovery of the ideal house, just outside St Ives, was to change the course of modern British art.

For it had been agreed in advance that Ben Nicholson and Barbara Hepworth would join the couple in their rural bolt-hole, wherever it might be. And so in August 1939 Ben and Barbara – plus triplets, nursemaid and cook – travelled to the far west of Cornwall rather than to the most easterly district of Britain. The constructivist Naum Gabo and his wife Miriam followed shortly afterwards. Other visitors included Victor Pasmore, Graham Sutherland, William Coldstream, Julian Trevelyan and Peter Lanyon. Nicholson went on to incorporate aspects of local landscapes into his seemingly abstract paintings, to teach Lanyon and to influence the next wave of artists drawn to the St Ives area – notably Roger Hilton, Patrick Heron, Terry Frost and Bryan Wynter. Hepworth remained in Cornwall for the rest of her life. How much of that creative concentration might have come instead to Southwold if a certain house had been available

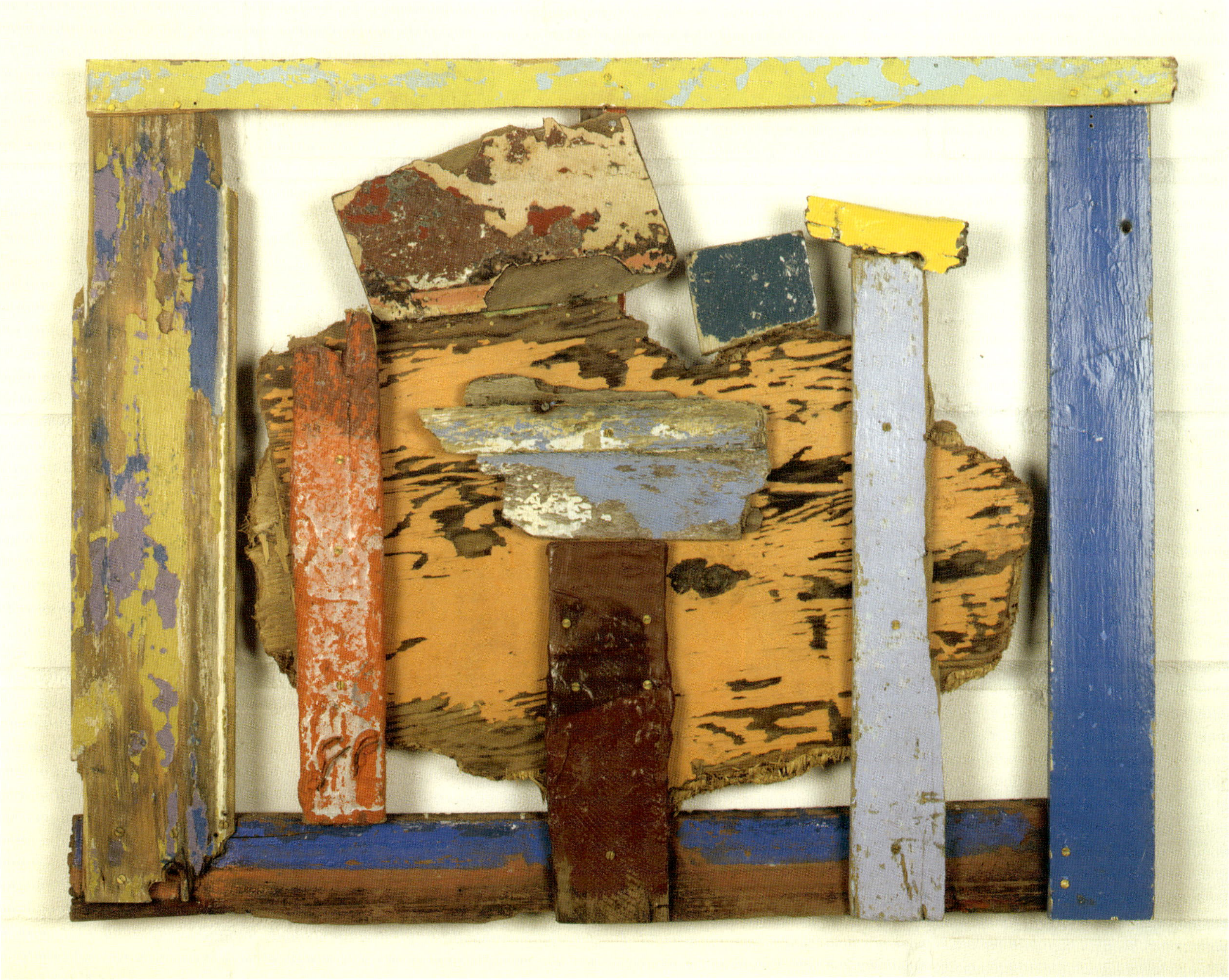

*Cloud Cuckoo Land*, Margaret Mellis, driftwood, 1991.

in Walberswick back in 1938?

Far away from war – and the social realism of London's Euston Road School to which Stokes had unwisely steered her – Margaret was encouraged by Nicholson and Gabo to produce small abstract compositions. These were to be the springboards to all her daring works of the future. But first came crippling conflict. Jealousies abounded – someone said the St Ives artists 'fought like ferrets in a sack' – and Adrian was the most jealous of all. Margaret was meant to be the submissive housekeeper, even before her husband's attentions and affections shifted to her sister, Ann. In 1946 the marriage ended. Adrian left and Margaret would have killed herself, but for the need to care for their young son, Telfer. Patrick and Delia Heron then went to keep her company and invited along a lately-divorced schoolfriend of Patrick's – Francis Davison. In similarly wounded states, Margaret and Francis struck up an immediate rapport. They married in 1948 and were rarely parted thereafter.

Francis Davison was born in London and adopted as a baby – his later self-effacement possibly rooted in the fact that he never discovered his real parents. He was given the name of his adoptive father, George Davison, a Lowestoft shipyard carpenter's son who made a fortune managing the Eastman Kodak photographic empire from 1900. Davison appointed George Walton, a Glasgow contemporary of Charles Rennie Mackintosh, to design shops for his company and modernist houses for himself. Then this restless and anarchic figure bought an unfinished Cap d'Antibes mansion begun for the King of Belgium. Naming the new base the Chateau des Enfants after his five children – four of them adopted - he also played host there to Scottish Colourist John Duncan Fergusson and painter Margaret Morris, who also threatened to bring along her experimental dance troupe. No wonder Francis came to love order and privacy.

After their marriage Margaret and Francis, together with Telfer, camped out in the spartan chateau as their spirits slowly revived. They returned to England in 1950, on being loaned a fisherman's shack beside the harbour at Walberswick. Here the lasting pattern of their lives together really began, as self-sufficiency entwined with mutually-supportive creativity. Margaret embarked upon a series of still-life paintings featuring fish, the mainstay of their diet, some of which now hang in the dining-room of Southwold's Crown Hotel. Now and again she would add a glimpse of level landscape through a window. Francis proceeded to pare down his paintings into simple flat forms, in which the starting point might be a tarred shed, boat, cottage door or window, or else a grid suggesting the lines of estuary, river, field and hedge. As both artists journeyed into abstraction along highly personalised routes there was a parallel with the painterly explorations of William Scott, whose son Robert went to school for a time with Telfer.

After a few months they were able to abandon the harsh conditions of life on the harbour's edge when a small legacy allowed the purchase of a

*Caught*, Damien Hirst, Mixed Media, 1983-5.

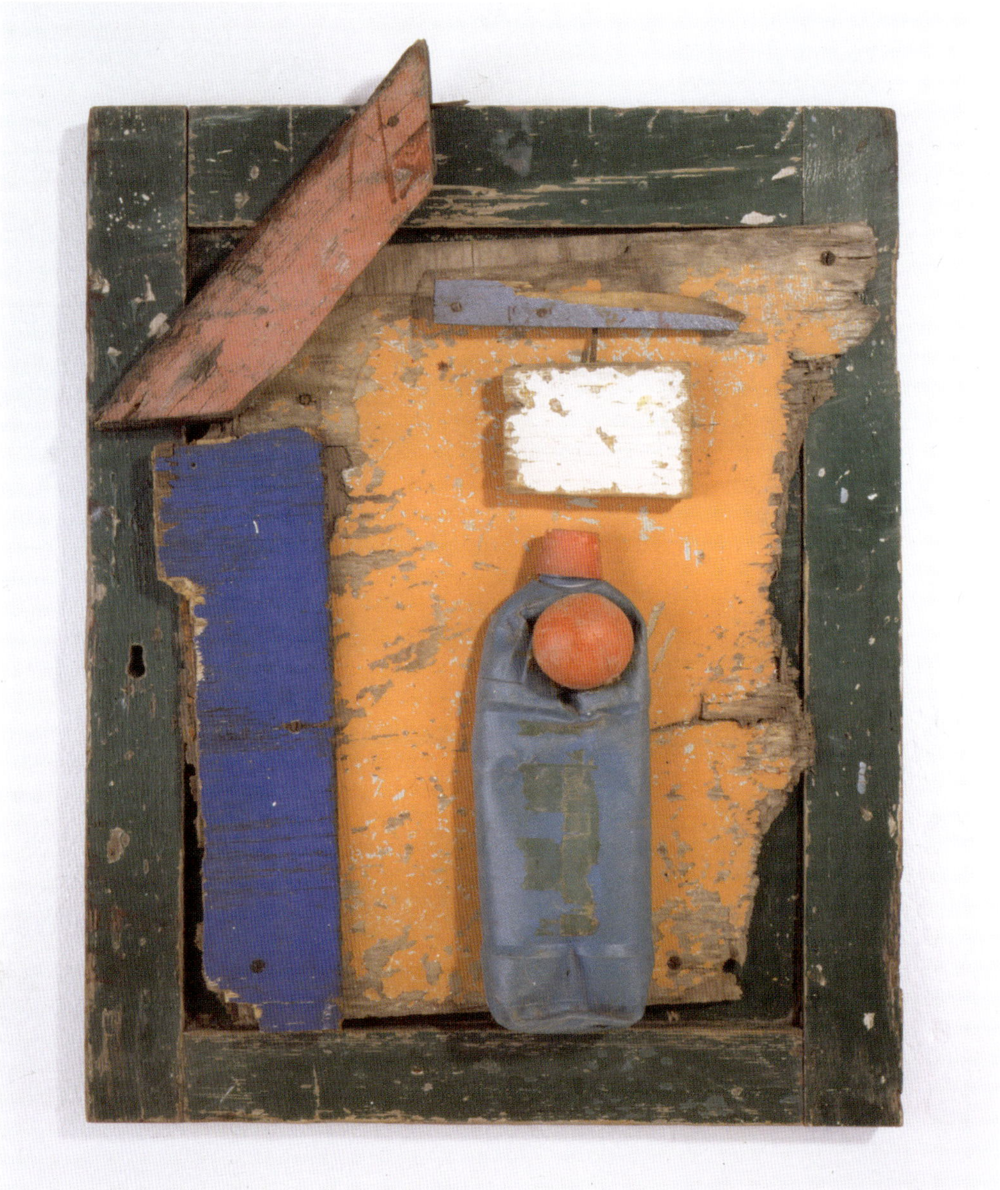

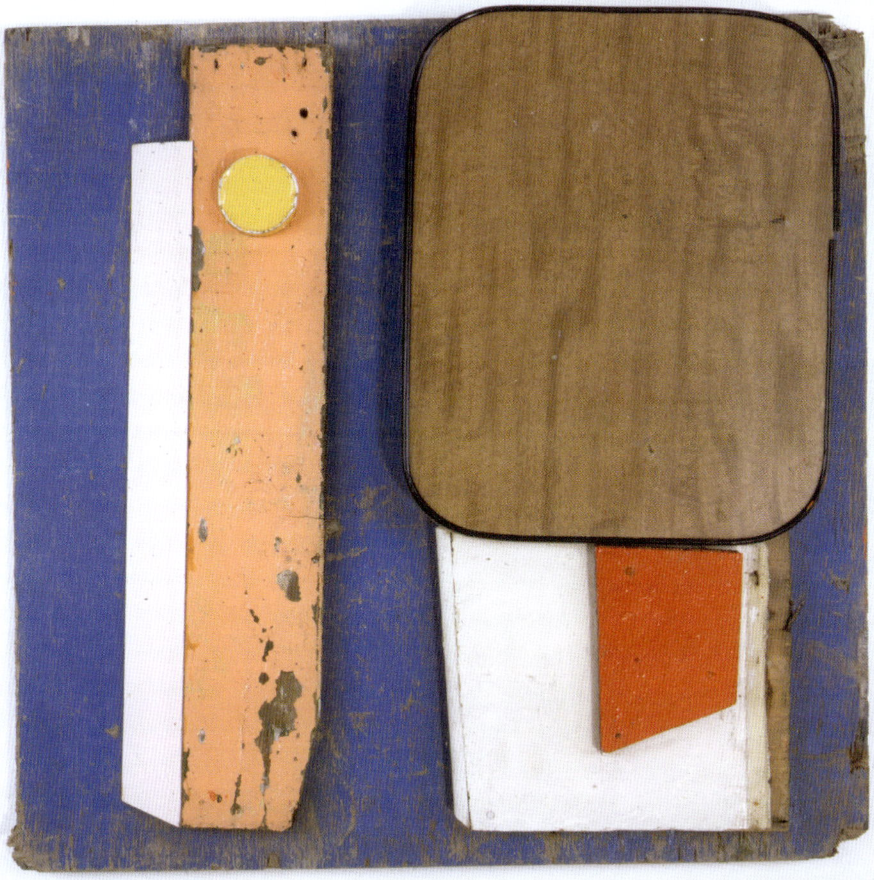

*Two Figures*, Damien Hirst, Mixed Media, 1983-5.

cottage and four-acre smallholding at Syleham, near Diss. Here, for the next 25 years, they thrived in splendid isolation – eking out a living by selling eggs and chickens, and by growing barley and the herbs, fruit and vegetables of a French-style kitchen garden. A few artists were allowed to visit, among them Patrick Heron, Roger Hilton, Mary Potter, Mary Newcomb and Cedric Morris's former pupils, David and Barbara Carr. Otherwise they were perfectly content in their own company, giving each other the key freedom to work as they wished.

In 1952 Francis abandoned painting when the Gimpel Fils gallery reneged on the promise of an exhibition, turning to the medium of collage which his oil pictures had anyway suggested. Paper was also cheaper than paint – and all the more so because he insisted on used plain papers and preferred torn to scissored edges. He had no choice but to launch into muted colours because, in that era of post-war rationing and restriction, bright hues were not yet available. Such a limitation, fitting with the artist's fastidious nature and the austerity of the East Anglian landscape, only confirmed his mastery of tone. The artists had produced a mass of mostly-unseen work when the ravages of fowlpest and Margaret's sudden bout of rheumatoid arthritis made life at Syleham untenable. With help from Ann – by now Adrian's widow – they moved to Southwold in 1976, to a house with a tiny garden but with sweeping views over South Green and Gun Hill to the sea. The move had an amazing effect on both of them. Margaret, with rigorous exercise and rigid diet, regained her lithe form and boundless energy. By 1978 she had given up painting in favour of driftwood constructions – combining beachcombed finds of vividly-coloured bits of boats and beach-huts with everything from boards used in the kippering process to discarded timbers from Blythburgh church which deathwatch beetles had gouged into honeycomb. Working solely on colour, as affirmed and amended by form and structure, she produced relief sculptures with great wit and verve, in which semi-representational images unintended at the outset – soaring angels, dipping boats, surging seas – came to be imprinted as if by magic.

Francis, driven frantic by Southwold's summer crowds, and also exhilarated by the coastal light

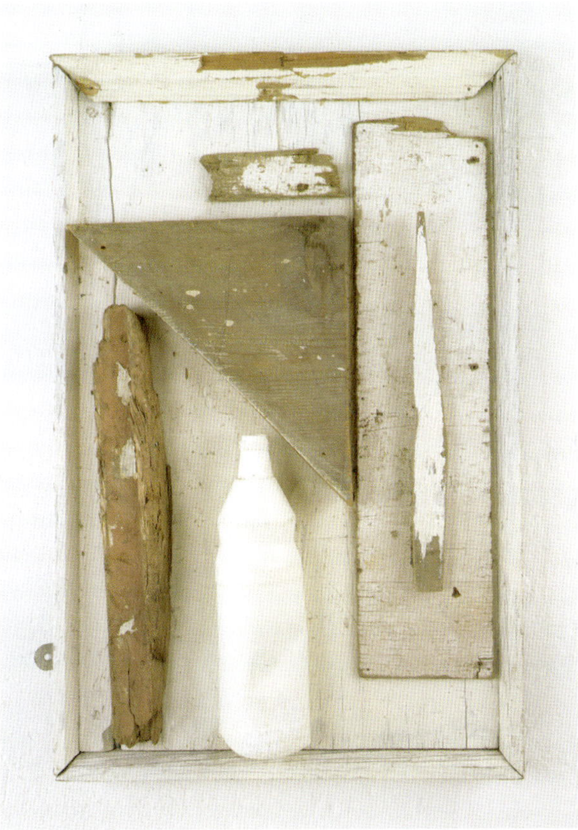

*With Whites*, Damien Hirst, Mixed Media, 1983-5 (right).

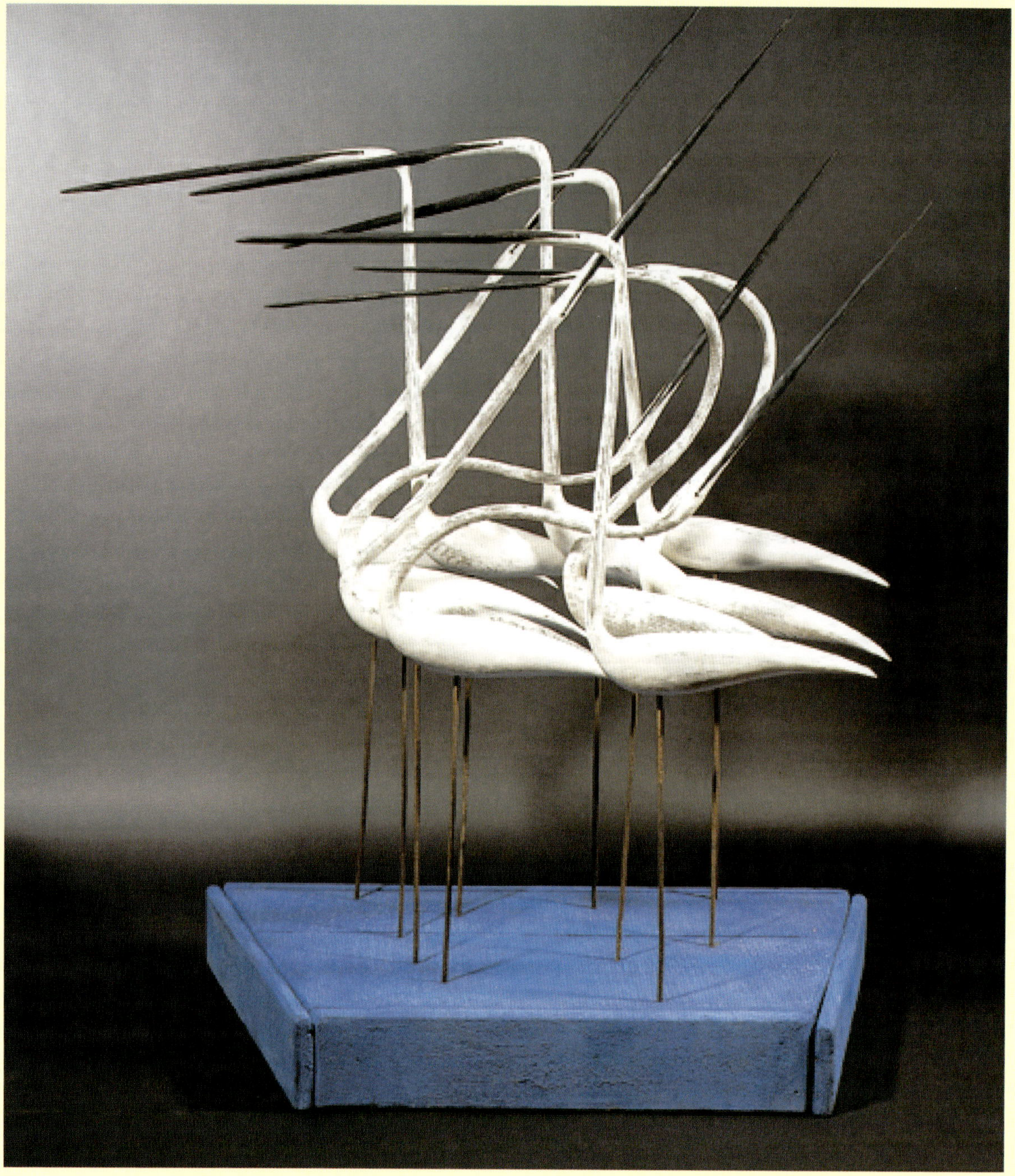

Egrets are now a common sight along the coast from Covehithe to Minsmere, a bird-rife strand appealing to Wivenhoe's GUY TAPLIN (b1939) – as this 2004 assembly in painted wood suggests. The East End-raised artist, who taught himself to whittle avian images in wood while caring for the ornamental waterfowl in Regent's Park, developed a late friendship with Margaret Mellis. In 1998 she said: 'Whether Guy Taplin draws on paper or carves in driftwood he makes the most beautiful shapes which transform the medium and embody the spirit of the bird he is depicting. The satisfaction is in the beauty of the shape.

'When I make a construction in driftwood I don't carve it and only occasionally paint it. If the transformation takes place it is because of the way the pieces of wood react against each other when joined. Just as colours alter each other, so do shapes. Something different appears which I didn't know about before it happened. My own satisfaction is in this discovery – which can suggest something else or stay abstract (it doesn't matter which).

'The different ways in which driftwood can be used fascinate me. Guy Taplin and I are poles apart in some ways, but we enjoy and admire each other's work.'

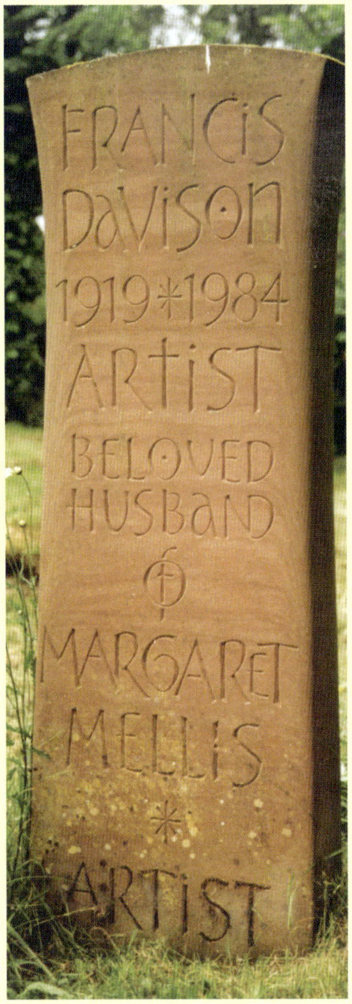


Standing in Walberswick churchyard, this tombstone was designed and carved by JAMIE SARGEANT (b1954) of The Carving Workshop in Cambridge, who later emigrated to Australia. The red sandstone sculpture was commissioned via Snape-based Memorials by Artists.

and vast views, worked in a frenzy on brighter and brighter collages in ever more complex compositions. They became akin to aerial photography from a fast-spinning plane. Then, just when Margaret began to get better, Francis started to get ill with the brain tumour that would eventually kill him. 'When Francis was half-paralysed, and I had to hold his papers so that he could tear them, I found out how absolutely precisely he worked,' his widow recalled. 'There was enormous control, and every tiny little bit of paper was torn and nitched to exactly the shape he wanted.'

Margaret worked on in Southwold, filling her attic studio with a mountain of driftwood – material which also came to be piled high in the front garden and all but to obliterate the backyard. Surrounding herself with friends, she saw fresh possibilities from the letters cascading from her kitchen mantelpiece – opening out the envelopes and producing pastel drawings of flowers on the coloured or patterned insides. Exploring these irregular shapes, she paid unconscious tribute to the marine painter Alfred Wallis whose house she had helped to clear, and whose funeral she had helped to fund and organise, in St Ives in 1942. She had left a heap of his oddly-shaped pictures of boats and lighthouses – later hailed as highlights of modern British art – for anyone who wanted them; but no one did.

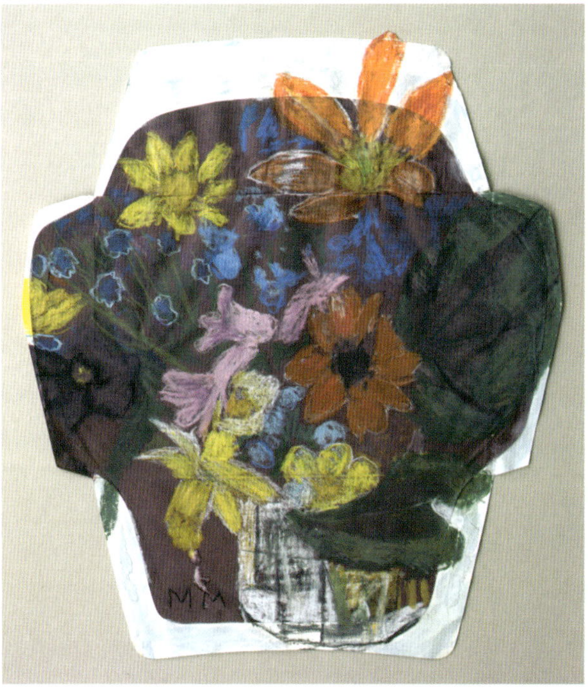

*Flower drawing*, Margaret Mellis, pastel on opened-out envelope, c1995.

Filmed in Suffolk and Cornwall in 1992, for a profile screened on Anglia TV, Margaret Mellis swam, danced, bicycled and created a construction on camera which she titled *Marsh Music*. Her first and last loves came together at the end. 'If I were on my death bed and I heard a good tune, I'd get up and dance,' she said. 'It would be a good way to go, actually.'

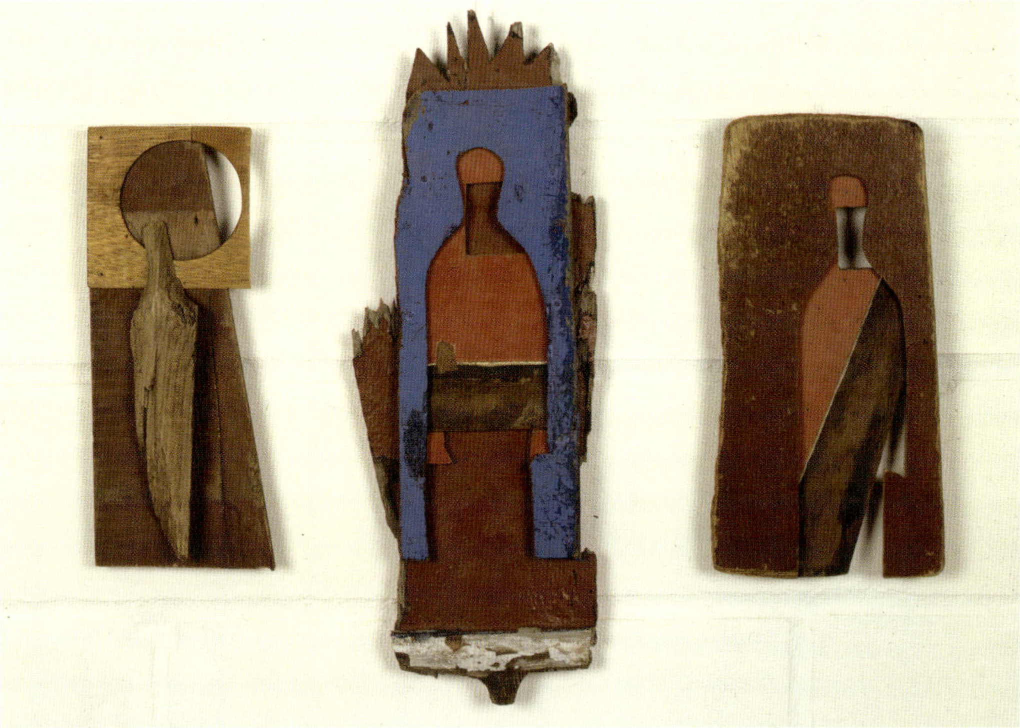

*Triptych*, Margaret Mellis, driftwood, 1985.

# Index of Artists



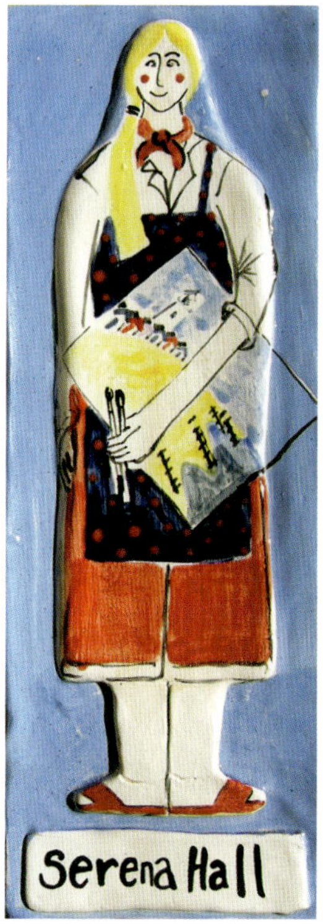


From Serena Hall's mural of tiled portraits for the Stella Peskett Millennium Hall. *All The Town's People* is a fund-raising project and an exercise in folk art.

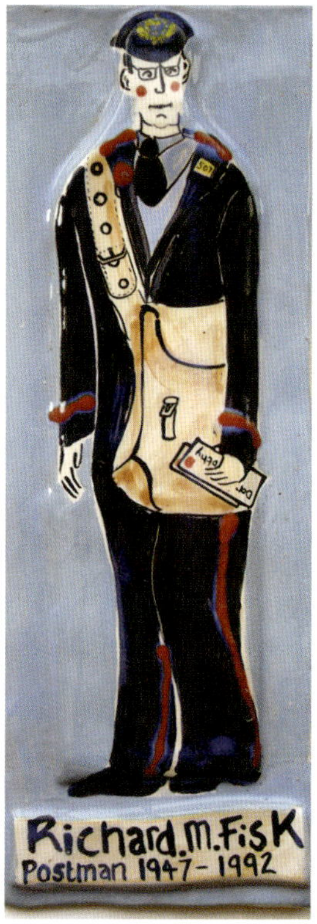

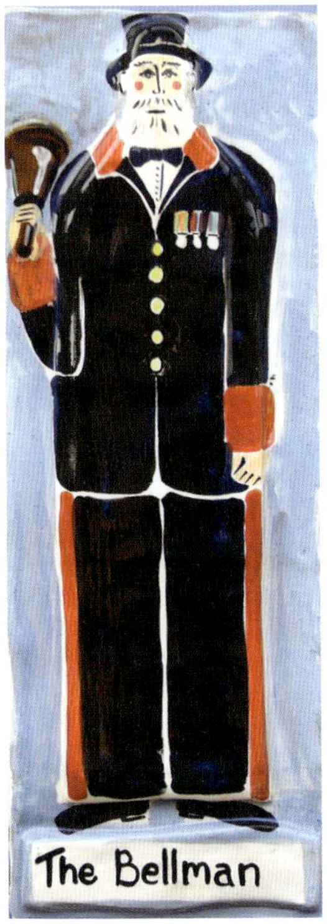
The Bellman

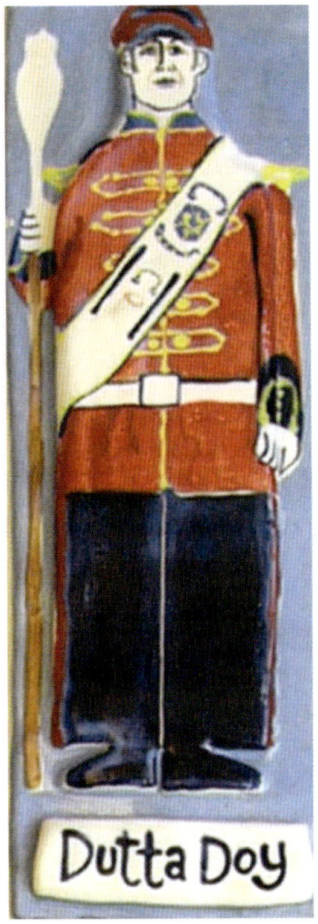
Dutta Doy

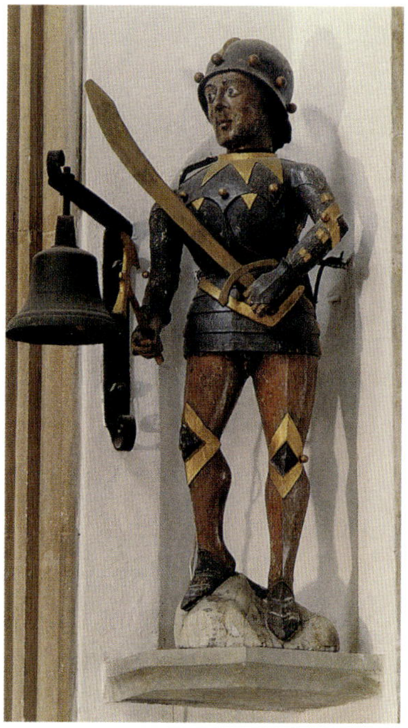

Southwold Jack, bell-striking War of the Roses soldier in St Edmund's church. A carved Jack of 1682 also survives at Blythburgh.

Prunella Clough, c1925.

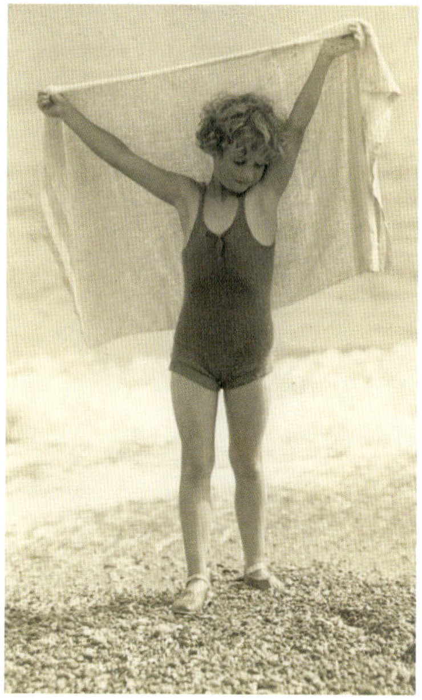

# Acknowledgements

Pictures on the following pages reproduced with permission of: i Emily Whalley. ii, v, vi (lower), vii, 1, 14 (lower), 34, 63, 138, 142 (top and lower), 143 (lower), 144 (lower), 145 (top), 147 (lower), 149, 155 (lower), 156-157, 170 and back cover reproduced courtesy of Messum's - pictures on pp v, 142-143 on behalf of the Peggy Somerville, Lionel Bulmer and Margaret Green estates. iv, 5 (top), 12 (mid and lower), 14 (top), 38 (lower), 39 (top), 56, 59 (lower), 60 (right), 62, 86 (left), 93 (top), 119-121, 130 (top) Southwold Museum. vi (top), 33, 148, 153 Crane Kalman Gallery. viii, 2 (top) National Maritime Museum. All postcards - pp 2, 35, 45, 54-55, 59-60, 67, 78-82, 158: private collections. 3 Historic Royal Palaces. 4, 11 (lower left) Private Collection. 6, 10 (top), 11 (top left), 12 (top) Sailors' Reading Room, Southwold. 7, 8-9 (top), 10 (lower) private collections. 8 (lower), 16-18 (top), 21, 70, 86 (right), 143 (top), 146 (top) Orwell Press. 9 (lower) Manchester City Art Gallery. 10 (lower) Sally and David Kibble. 11 (top right), 27 (top), 61, 119-121 Swan Hotel, Southwold. 13 Private Collection. 15 (top) Fine Art Society. 18 (lower) British Museum. 19 Private Collection. 20, 22 (top) Private Collection. 22 (lower), 46 (lower), 124, 145 (lower) Tassie Russell. 23 Courtesy of the artists. 24 Prudential Art Collection/John Piper Estate. 25 Redfern Gallery. 26 (lower) John Piper Estate. 27 (lower) Private Collection. 28 (top) Tate London/John Piper Estate. 28 (lower) Grapevine Gallery, Norwich. 29 Courtesy of the artists. 30 (top), 160 (top) Richard Bawden. 30 (lower) Fry Art Gallery, Saffron Walden/Edward Bawden Estate. 31 Private Collection. 32 National Portrait Gallery. 35 (lower) National Portrait Gallery, Smithsonian Institution. 36 Private Collection. 37 Lord Nelson inn, Southwold. 38 (top) Private Collection. 39 (lower) 40 (top and lower), 117 (lower) Jeff Horwood. 41 Peter Tolhurst. 42-44, 48 (mid), 49 Adnams Brewery. 45 (top) Private Collection/Bonham's. 46 (top) Private Collection. 47, 146 (lower) Brian Lewis. 48 (top) Mary Gundry. 50 National Gallery London. 51 Joachim Jacobs. 52 National Gallery of Victoria. 53 Norwich Castle Museum. 57 Private Collection. 64 Private Collection USA/Orwell Press, 65 Browse & Darby, 67 (top) Tate London, 68 Fitzwilliam Museum, Cambridge, 69 Musée d'Orsay, Paris: All works by Philip Wilson Steer courtesy of the Steer Estate. 66 Private Collection. 71 Private Collection/Richard Green Gallery. 72 Guildhall Art Gallery, City of London/ Bridgeman Art Library. 73 (top) Ulster Museum. 73 (lower), 75, 105 Christchurch Mansion, Ipswich. 74 (top) National Portrait Gallery. 74 (lower) Private Collection/Sickert Estate. 76-77 Norfolk and Norwich Millennium Library. 83, 172-173 Serena Hall. 84 Oldham Art Gallery, 85 National Portrait Gallery, 87-91 Fine Art Society: all works by Joseph Southall, the Barrow family. 92 Private Collection USA/Richard Green Gallery. 93 (lower), 94 private collections. 95 Peter Nahum at the Leicester Galleries. 96, 98 (mid and lower) Hunterian Art Gallery, Glasgow. 97 British Museum. 98 (top) Sotheby's. 99, 100, 102 private collections. 103, 107 Christie's. 104 National Portrait Gallery. 106 Aberdeen Art Gallery, 108 (top) Bradford Art Gallery, (lower) Ferens Art Gallery, Hull, 109 and 113 Tate London, 110 (top) Piccadilly Gallery, 110 (lower)-112 private collections: all works by Stanley Spencer and Hilda Carline, DACS. 114, 115 (top) private collections. 115 (lower) Fine Art Society. 116-117 (top) Ron Fuller. 118 Private Collection. 122 Birmingham Art Gallery. 123 Private Collection. 125 Jonathan Clark Fine Art, 126 (top) James Hyman Fine Art, 127 Annely Juda Fine Art: all Clough images Prunella Clough Estate. 128 Jonathan Clark Fine Art for Ivon Hitchens Estate. 128-129 Imperial War Museum. 130 (lower), 131 Southwold Town Council. 132-133, 135-137 Christopher Mason. 134 Private Collection/Joan Warburton Estate. 139 Canon Gallery, Petworth. 140 Private Collection. 141 RIBA Library. 144 Glynn Thomas. 147 (top) David Gentleman. 150 Ronald Blythe/John Nash Estate. 151 Wildlife Art Gallery, Lavenham. 152, 154, 158 (lower), 159 courtesy of the artists. 155 (top) Piano Nobile Gallery. 160 (lower) Private Collection. 161 (left) courtesy of the artist, 162-164 Austin/Desmond Fine Art. 165 Jonathan Pritchard. 166-167, 172 (right) and (lower) Telfer Stokes. 168-169 Damien Hirst.

Every effort has been made to trace copyright holders of pictures illustrated. The publisher will be pleased to hear from any omitted party for redress and for amendment to any future edition.

This book would have lost without emotional and financial support from a dear friend who wishes not to be named. And all thanks to my publisher, Peter Tolhurst of Black Dog Books, lover of new books and old buildings, who laid out both this volume and Southwold's conservation area.

I am particularly indebted to Messum's – the premier London gallery for East Anglian art, to Geoffrey Munn, Richard Scott, my editor and proof reader Paddy Kitchen and to the Eastern Daily Press and the East Anglian Daily Times. I also thank Diana Steel and the Antique Collectors Club, Ronald Blythe for a most generous foreword and Lesley Kershaw for technical wizardry.

Robert Cotton has been a perfect principal photographer, but I have also been greatly aided by Richard Webster of the Orwell Press, Douglas Atfield, David Kibble, Peter Tolhurst, Robert Temple, Prof Keith Roberts, Peter Jordan, Mary Scott, Bill Darnell of the EDP and all museums and galleries listed in the picture credits.

This study has benefited hugely from original researches shared by James Hartley (F.W. Baldwin), Hilary Huckstep (Reg Carter), Helen Pitcher (Edwin Edwards) and Roger Preston (P.H. Emerson). I'm also grateful to Christopher Mason for Catharine Carrington's unpublished memoir.

Praise to expert staff of the Tate, British Museum, British Library, London Library, Witt Library, National Portrait Gallery, Victoria & Albert Museum, Imperial War Museum, Royal Academy of Arts, Hampton Court Palace, Ipswich Christchurch Mansion, Dunwich Museum, Suffolk Records Office, Norfolk and Norwich Millennium Library, Norwich Castle Museum, Aldeburgh Foundation, Bonhams, Christie's and Sotheby's. Special thanks to David Lee and David de Kretser at Southwold Museum (whose archives, particularly the Ida Critten papers, were invaluable), Douglas Pope and John Winter at the Sailors' Reading Room and Simon Loftus , chairman of Adnams.

Further thanks to Abbott & Holder, Peter Adam, George Amore, Ann Baer, Arthur and Avery Bailey, Robin Banks, George Barrow, Gill Booth, Paul Botright, Vera Bowyer, Pen Bray, George Breeze, David Buckman, the late Nancy Carline, Dani Church, Michael Cook, John Craxton, John Day (Eastbourne Fine Art), Caroline Denham, Michael Dickens, John and Thelma Durrant, East Anglian Traditional Music Trust, Harriet Frazer (Memorials by Artists), Esther Freud, Charlotte Gere, Lady Penelope Gilbey, the late Henry Hallam, Jeff Horwood, Irene Horwood, Mrs Lawrence Hughes, W.J. Hurr, John Illston of the Lord Nelson inn, Bob and Annie Jellicoe, Miss A.M. Jenkins, Peter Kennedy Scott, Lyn Knights, Dot Little, Patrick Mackie, Kenneth McConkey, Pam, Ben and Anthea Marriner, Jane Martineau, John Miller, Susan Morris (Richard Green Gallery), Mary and Ivan Moseley, Robin Ollington, Twig O'Malley, Sylvia Park (Science Ltd), Michael Parkin, Kenneth Pople, Nancie Pelling, Jonathan Pritchard, Nicole Roberts, Patrick Roberts (Print Wright) Tassie Russell, the Salvation Army, the late Anthony Sampson, John Sansom, Norman Scarfe, James Scott, Judith Smyth, Peyton Skipwith (Fine Art Society), Frances Spalding, Unity Spencer, Telfer Stokes, D.J. Taylor, John Tooke, Frank Upcraft, Chloe Veale, Iris and Nigel Weaver, Michael Wickins (Peasenhall Art & Antiques Gallery), Jane Wight, Stephen Wildman, Julie Winyard.

I applaud the scores of people who responded to press appeals for information, and all those I pestered. Most of all I am grateful to 250 artists past and present who made this book possible. Any errors are my own.

Ian Collins

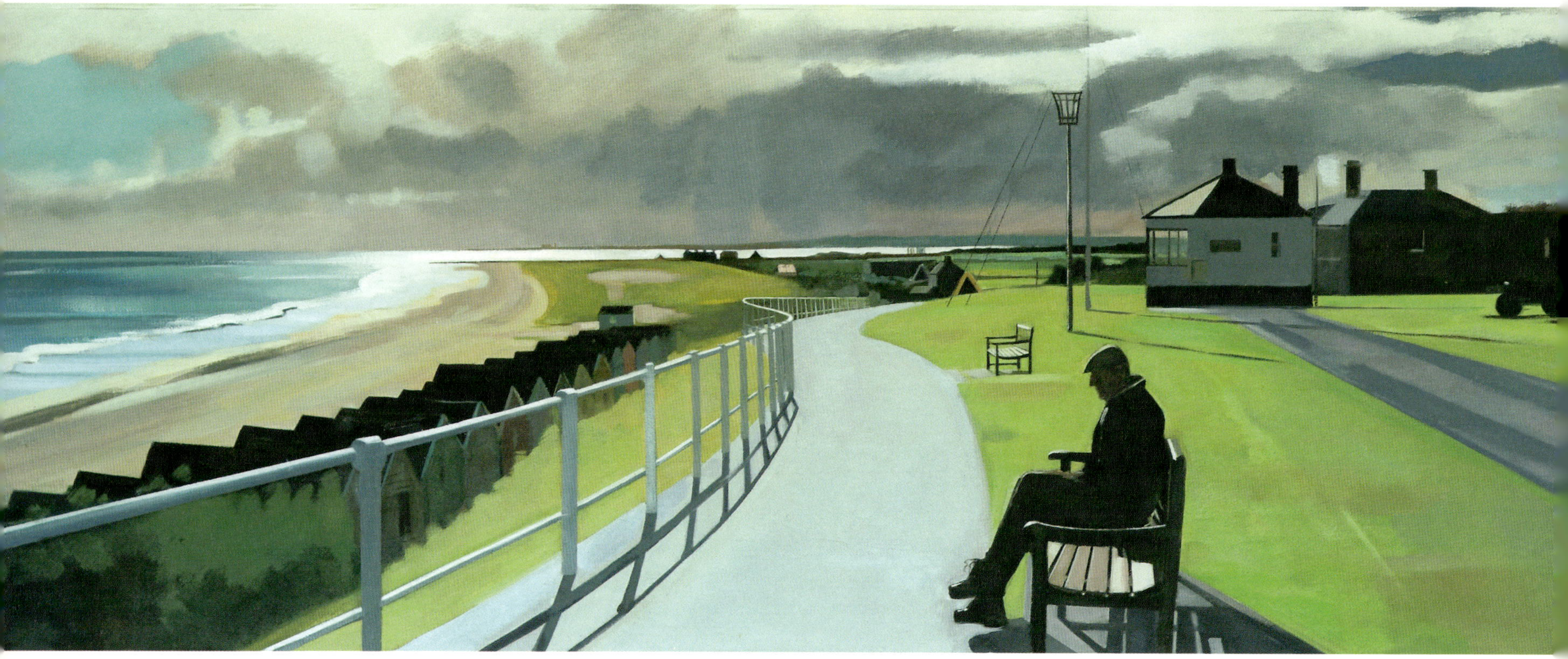

*Gun Hill,* Katherine Hamilton, oil on canvas, 2004.